STO

ALLEN COUNTY PUBLIC LIBRARY
3 1833 00137 7438

Y0-AAB-661

Macroeconomic

PRENTICE-HALL, INC.,

Theory

Gordon Brunhild
and
Robert H. Burton

University of South Florida

ENGLEWOOD CLIFFS, NEW JERSEY

Library of Congress Cataloging in Publication Data

Burton, Robert H.
Macroeconomic theory.

Includes bibliographies.
1. Macroeconomics. I. Brunhild, Gordon
joint author. II. Title.
HB171.5.B975 339 73-4692
ISBN 0-13-542639-1

MACROECONOMIC THEORY

Gordon Brunhild
and
Robert H. Burton

Printed in the United States of America

10 9 8 7 6 5 4 3 2 1

Prentice-Hall International, Inc., *London*
Prentice-Hall of Australia, Pty. Ltd., *Sydney*
Prentice-Hall of Canada, Ltd., *Toronto*
Prentice-Hall of India Private Limited, *New Delhi*
Prentice-Hall of Japan, Inc., *Tokyo*

Contents

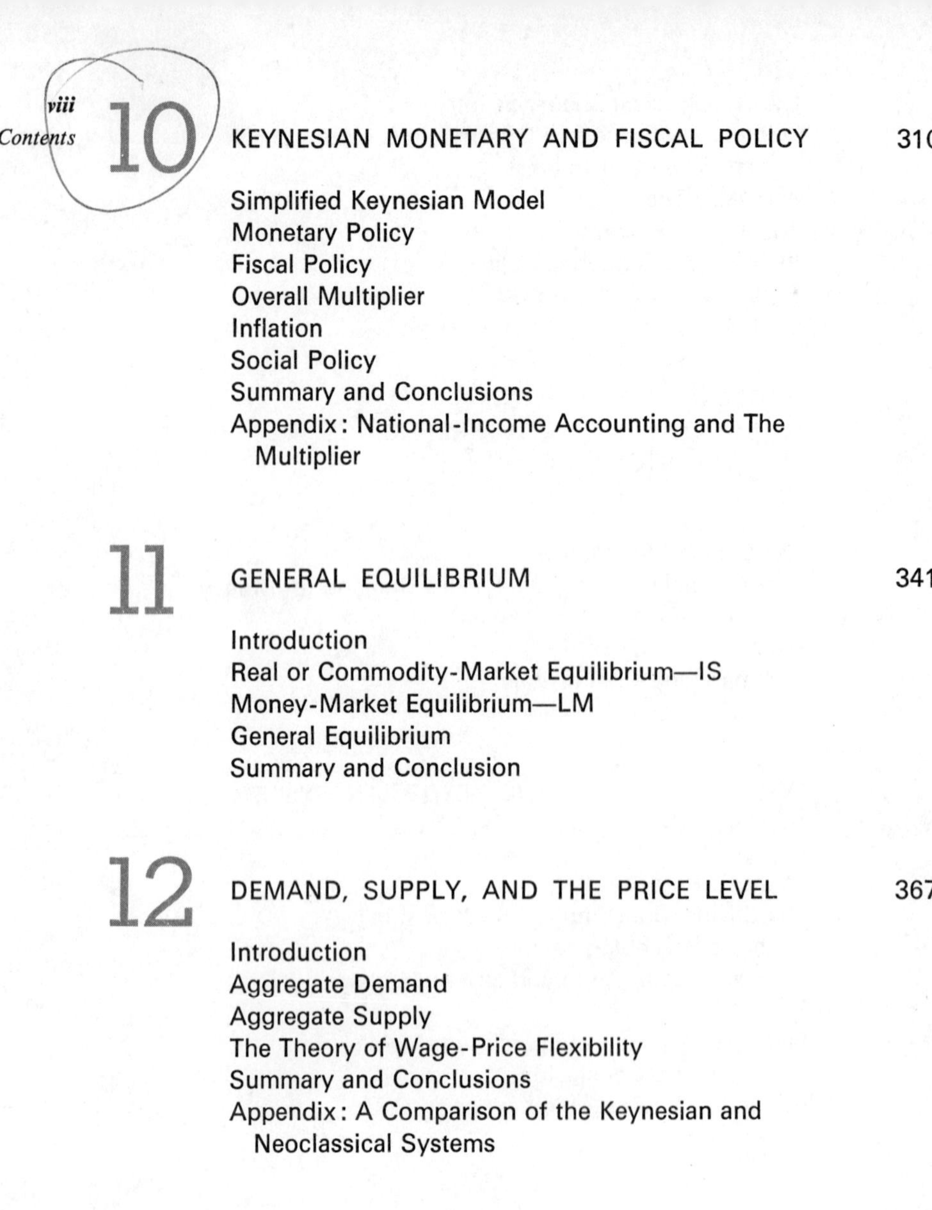

Preface

This book is designed as a text for an upper-level undergraduate course in macroeconomics. The subject has been developed from a foundation of microeconomics because macroeconomics developed from the neoclassical approach, which was essentially microeconomic.

Because the proposed approach is to build a theory of macroeconomics from a microeconomic foundation, the student may find an intermediate course in microeconomics helpful. However, the microeconomic foundations will be explicated in sufficient detail in Chapters 2 and 3 so that the micro course should not be required as a prerequisite. For those who have had an intermediate micro course, Chapters 2 and 3 may be skipped, except perhaps for the few points sometimes omitted in a standard micro course, such as Slutsky's technique for separating the income effect from the substitution effect or Edward's theory of oligopoly behavior.

Following the review of microeconomics, Chapters 4 and 5 present a thorough discussion of national income accounting including input-output techniques and a detailed evaluation of our entire national income accounting system.

Pre-Keynesian, Keynesian, and post-Keynesian theories are developed in order, beginning in Chapter 6, with a discussion of the policy implications of each, a section of a chapter on the pre-Keynesian, and a chapter each on the Keynesian and post-Keynesian policies. However, in certain cases, we have departed from the strict historical order of development, where such a departure helps to clarify the presentation of the theory, because this is a book on macro theory and not one on the history of economic thought. For example, the Keynesian sections include certain of the post-Keynesian developments but only those that add reality to the Keynesian system without making any fundamental changes in the theory. Modifications and clarifications included are those that we feel Keynes himself would have accepted in his theory. One might cite especially the three major modern theories of the consumption function that are generally offered as post-Keynesian developments, but that we have included in the Keynesian section because they are clearly anticipated although not rigorously formulated in the *General Theory*.

At the same time, because our interest is to present the basic Keynesian model in the Keynesian section, some of his ideas (specifically some of those extensions mostly introduced after his Chapter 18 in *The General Theory*, "The General Theory Restated") have been used in our presentation in the post-Keynesian, modern section. The reason for this is that these ideas were offered as extensions of his basic theory by Keynes. But as they have been rigorously worked out by post-Keynesian economists, they have led to fundamental changes in the Keynesian theory. So in summary, where post-Keynesian developments fit neatly into the Keynesian framework, they have been presented in that framework. And where Keynes's own ideas subsequently have resulted in the development of the modern, post-Keynesian theories, those ideas have been used to introduce the post-Keynesian section.

The last five chapters concern contemporary problems and theories. One of the most persistent sources of concern recently has been inflation, and our discussion of inflation theories includes some of the more recent and more interesting theories as well as the traditional topics.

In addition to discussing the work of the modern monetary theorists as perhaps the most important post-Keynesian development, we have also included in our chapter on the money market topics such as credit availability and financial intermediaries.

A lagging growth rate and adverse cyclical developments while inflation was in progress were pressing problems while this book was being written. Consequently, our coverage of economic growth and business fluctuations includes the theories that are most interesting and most useful in explaining our recent experience.

The final policy chapter covers policies designed to foster growth and stability. The purpose of this chapter is to help the student achieve a sense of the directions in which the more recent developments in economics are tending. Also, the use of modern macroeconomics in developing economic policy is a logical culmination for the book.

The book was designed for a semester course. Schools having shorter terms can restructure the material to suit their needs and their students' background.

Chapter 1 Chapter 2 Chapter 3	May be omitted where an adequate background in methodology and micro-theory is present (Sections E-H of Chapter 1 may be desirable.)
Chapter 4 Chapter 5	May be omitted where pure theory is stressed to the exclusion of national income accounting

Chapter 6	Neoclassical		standard topics covered in macro courses
Chapter 7, Chapter 8, Chapter 9, Chapter 10	Keynesian theory		standard topics covered in macro courses
Chapter 11, Chapter 12	Post-Keynesian topics based on Keynesian theories		
Chapter 13	Theories of inflation		Post-Keynesian theories covered in whole or in part in a "standard" (i.e., Keynesian) course.
Chapter 14	Monetarist theory		
Chapter 15	Theories of growth		
Chapter 16	Theories of business fluctuations		
Chapter 17	Policy		

In writing this book we received assistance from many sources. We are especially indebted to Mr. Alan Odendahl of the Small Business Administration for doing most of the research and writing on Chapters 4 and 5. His expertise on national income accounting is profound, and profoundly appreciated.

We are also indebted to Mr. Charles Briqueleur and Mr. Michael Melody of Prentice-Hall for outstanding help in getting this project organized and for arranging for reviews of the material.

We are grateful for the comments and criticism of the manuscript that were offered by the following: Prof. William I. Abraham of Harvard University, Prof. John Anderson of the University of South Florida, Prof. Arthur Benavie of the University of North Carolina, Prof. David J. Cantor of Nasson College, Springvale, Maine, Prof. Milton Friedman of the University of Chicago, Prof. Michael A. Goldberg of the University of British Columbia, Prof. W. James Herman of the University of South Florida, Prof. Richard Hoffman of Arthur Young and Company and the American University, Prof. James Holmes of the State University of New York at Buffalo, Prof. John Hotson of the University of Waterloo, Prof. Axel Leijonhufvud of the University of California at Los Angeles, Prof. Emil Kauder of the University of South Florida, Prof. Sylvia Lane of the University of California at Davis, Dr. J.R. Longstreet of the University of South Florida, Prof. Stanley H. Masters of the University of Notre Dame, Prof. Robert Murphy of the University of South Florida, Mrs. Sarah Pardo of the University of South Florida, Prof. Howard Ross of City University of New York, Prof. Lawrence Southwick, Jr. of the State University of New York at Buffalo, Prof. Ernest Swanson of the University of West Florida, Prof. Douglas Vickers of the University of Western Australia, and Prof. Ruth Walsh of the University of South Florida. The comments of a number of students at the University of South Florida were also helpful. Mrs. Kathy Schoonmaker and Mrs. Helen Bazin did most of the typing, and we thank them sincerely.

The Nature of Economics

1

THE BASIC ECONOMIC PROBLEM

Economics is the social science with the longest history, and consequently with the most carefully developed methodology and scope. However, the scope of the subcategories, microeconomics and macroeconomics, is not so clearly delineated—and for good reason: The two are simply different ways of looking at the same phenomena, and the main distinction between micro- and macroeconomics is that macroeconomics consistently employs a greater degree of aggregation. Therefore, our purpose in Chapter 1 is to develop the scope and methodology of economics as a whole, rather than to concentrate only on the scope and methodology of macroeconomics. For those students already familiar with methodology and microeconomics, it might be advisable to skip directly to the section beginning on page 14 and to skip Chapters 2 and 3 entirely.

Economics has been variously defined, but currently the most common definition is this: Economics is the study or science of the *efficient* use of *scarce* productive resources to satisfy *unlimited* human wants. The questions then asked are, What are human wants? What are productive resources?

Human Wants (Demand)

First, "human wants" are much broader than necessities; they include all human desires. "Necessities" connotes the physiological requirements of life—air, water, food, clothing, and shelter. "Human" activity, by contrast, includes painting, dancing, playing cards—and a myriad of other physiologically unnecessary activities.

Consider the necessities of life. Air is virtually free to the breather. Water, next to air the most vital necessity, is supplied to the drinker at a very low cost. Furthermore, suppliers of physiological necessities go generally unrecognized in our society. Unless one has a relative who works for the water department, he is not likely to know the names of the suppliers of water. Farmers, who supply the third most necessary commodity, do not generally achieve renown. And the best-known suppliers of clothing—the fourth necessity—are those whose products enhance the wearer without providing much protection from the elements.

So, in general, the suppliers of the true necessities of life go unrecognized in our culture. In contrast, those who provide physiologically unnecessary goods—for example, painters, architects, dancers, and football players—are often well known. Members of advanced economies think in terms of a "standard of living" that is far above a "subsistence level of living"; consequently, "necessity" (in the sense of air, water, food, clothing, and shelter) often has little meaning in our society's economy, and the indication is that our society is sufficiently productive so that necessities are taken for granted.

The standard of living is socially determined by what people picture as a satisfactory level of income and consumption. At the same time, the level of living—that is to say, the style of life actually achieved—is determined by levels of production and distribution. Briefly, the standard of living is what one wants, and the level of living is what one has achieved. In our culture, the standard of living for the mass of our society is largely determined by the level of living achieved by the social pacesetters—those of the higher income levels; thus there is a constant gap existing between the standard of living and the level of living in most of society. Economists speak of this gap by referring to "unlimited" human wants. These may seem unlimited, but they are not infinite in any time period. Over time, the standard of living will continually increase and remain ahead of the level of living for the mass of society. Only a few pacesetters, possibly at the top of each income group, will bring their level up to their standard in any time period, and even their standard may grow away from their level of living over time.

Since our wants are a function of society, many of them are created by social forces, such as advertising, which change the natural hierarchy of our individual wants. The process of want creation is a variable that is economically significant, since it changes our preference patterns and may even change our standard of living. As we shall see in Chapter 2, demand for goods and services is based on human wants.

Productive Resources (Supply)

Economics considers only scarce resources—that is, those resources that are scarce in quantity relative to the demand for them and that therefore command a price. Thus air, the most important resource of all, is eliminated from consideration, since the supply is still large enough relative to demand that air commands no price. Air, or any resource so liberally supplied by nature that no one need pay for it, is known as a free good. (Of course, air is no longer free to the firm or crowded city that must pay for air-pollution control devices; so even air is no longer a free good under all circumstances.) The economic resources with which we deal include any natural, created, or human agent used in the production of goods and services. Traditionally, economists classify resources under these three categories: land, capital, and labor. In recent years a fourth resource, entrepreneurship, has been added.

Land, or natural resources, comprises those factors of production that appear in their present form without the intervention of man. Examples are unprocessed materials such as iron ore or crude oil, and natural harbors, rivers, or prairie land. These examples imply that land is rarely immediately productive unless it has been transformed by applications of labor and capital. As a result of this transformation, land assumes many of the aspects of capital.

Capital is the accumulated stock of produced goods available for use in further production. Examples of capital are buildings, communications equipment, roads, inventories, and machines used in the further production of consumer or capital goods. Other disciplines may consider money a form of capital; however, in economics, "capital" generally refers to directly productive goods. Money does not enter directly into production, although it may be used to measure the value of capital and other productive resources.[1]

Labor, the human resource used in the production of goods, includes both physical and mental effort. Labor comes in various qualities as well as quantities, so census figures may not accurately reflect the availability of labor to an economy. For example, large populations weakened by chronic disease or malnutrition may be unproductive. The quality of labor may also be limited by the availability of education. A large population of illiterates is not the most productive labor force in the computer age.

Turning to the fourth resource, *entrepreneurship*, the return to the entrepreneur—that is, the owner-manager—is a noncontractual cost. The owner cannot validly promise to pay himself a particular return. The classical economists included the return-to-entrepreneurship profits with interest as a return for furnishing capital to the firm. Modern theory divides profits into three distinct categories: the income of managers for running the enterprise, a reasonable return on the owner's investment, and a residual usually referred to as "pure profit." This residual in a highly competitive industry is generally considered to be a reward for innovation and for bearing the market risk inherent in running the enterprise. In an imperfectly competitive

---

[1] This point should be qualified: A certain part of a firm's assets may have to take the form of money for the firm to operate. That necessary amount of money is identified as part of capital by some economists.

industry, the residue is, in part at least, due to the monopoly advantage of the respective firms in the industry.

Obviously, distinguishing resources as land, labor, capital, and entrepreneurship is arbitrary and artificial. For example, a trained worker embodies human capital, and an energetic worker embodies proper nutrition—the product of land. However, the traditional classification of resources is retained in this book, because the analysis is used to solve such problems as the unemployment of labor, and because our national income-accounting system uses the traditional approach for classifying resources.

In the final analysis, perhaps the only real resource is within the mind of man. Of two men lost in the same woods, one may starve while the other lives comfortably. As Professor Erich Zimmermann put it, "Knowledge is truly the mother of all other resources. . . . The difference between neolithic man, who roamed the earth in misery and fear, and man today, who lives in relative comfort and security, is knowledge—knowledge of petroleum and natural gas, of sulphur and helium, of chemistry and physics; the countless wonders of modern science."[2]

The state of our knowledge and the availability of physical resources together result in our producing less than the members of our society would demand. To say that resources are scarce is simply to say that the amount society would like to consume is more than it is able to produce. Therefore, unsatisfied wants will always exist, and society will always have to allocate its available output among competing demands for that output.

FUNCTIONS OF ANY ECONOMIC SYSTEM

Society has adopted various systems for organizing the employment of resources in satisfying human wants. There are at least three relatively "pure" types of economic organizations or systems:

1. Custom-directed—economies that are organized by tradition or custom, such as the economies of Yap or of the Yaghin Indians
2. Centrally directed—economies in which major decisions are made by a small, centralized group; for example, the economies of Hungary or Russia
3. Market-directed—economies in which decisions are made by the individual producers and consumers; for example, the United States in the 1850's

In practice, all economies tend to become somewhat mixed versions of these three pure types, although some one element generally predominates. The economy of the United States is basically a market-directed system, containing elements of tradition and central direction. A number of factors, such as industrialization, the population explosion, urbanization, changes in the family structure, pollution, and increasing personal mobility, have all

---

[2]Erich Zimmermann, *World Resources and Industries*, rev. ed. (New York: Harper & Row, 1951), p. 10.

combined recently to expand the role of central direction in the economy of the United States. However, none of these important developments has changed the basic fact that in order to function, all economies must face reality and answer certain questions, which follow.

What Is to Be Produced?

The first question facing any economy, regardless of its ideology or organization, is what to produce. Should the available resources be devoted to the production of automobiles, or roads? Or if both, in what proportions? Should most of the effort devoted to construction of buildings be to build homes, or hospitals, or factories, or schools? It is the classic choice between guns and butter. As long as human wants run ahead of productive capacity, any economy must set up a system of priorities to decide which goods, from the infinite number of potential choices, will actually be provided.

How to Use Resources?

Once the decision has been made regarding what to produce, society must then decide how to combine resources in the production of those goods. In most cases, our goal is the effective use of resources—normally, the greatest output of goods for the smallest input of resources in order to satisfy as many human wants as possible. In a modified market system such as that in the United States, we rely on market values to answer this question of how to use resources. But tradition can intervene, prohibiting some techniques of production considered dangerous, unlawful, or reprehensible. Furthermore, central direction can intervene—for example, by encouraging the employment of "hard-core" unemployed or by prohibiting the use of child labor.

Who Gets the Output?

A third basic function required of all economic systems is to ration available output among ultimate consumers, since they cannot acquire enough goods and services to satisfy all their wants. In the United States, the solution to this economic question is largely left to the operations of the price system. That is to say, one's share of the nation's income is directly related either to one's own production and bargaining power or to the prices paid for, and the productivity of, whatever factors of production one owns. But here, too, clear cases can be found of central direction changing the market's solution to the distribution of our nation's income—for example, through Social Security, welfare, or subsidy payments.

Level of Resource Use

In one way or another, any economy must determine the level of resource use. How much of the nation's potential will be used up now, and how much will be reserved for the future? At times this question of conservation seems to be disregarded; but apparent disregard is in reality simply another answer, an answer that says future generations will have to fend for themselves.

Conservation is more than simply not using resources, since resources often deteriorate through disuse. Machines may rust whether or not they are used; land may become unproductive through human disuse as well as through use, as may be seen in the once-productive Cradle of Civilization in Iraq. After a sufficient period of disuse, human labor also becomes ineffective, through deterioration of skills or of the will to work. In addition, there is the more traditional argument that once a day's labor is lost through unemployment, it is lost forever. Losing labor through involuntary unemployment is a complete waste of resources, as long as workers are capable of producing anything of value or even maintaining their own skills. As long as goods and services are scarce relative to human wants, then unemployed resources lead to less want satisfaction than is possible with full employment.

Economic Expansion

Finally, any economy must decide how fast a rate of economic expansion it is willing to accommodate. In order that economic expansion occur, a greater quantity of output must be produced from available resources.

Often, in economics, we act as though the solution to the question of how much economic expansion society should encourage is answered simply by the statement that more is better than less. Therefore we act as though economic expansion should be as rapid as possible. This is a reasonable conclusion, as long as the level of living is systematically behind society's standard of living. However, economic expansion can cause social instability, so there may be some optimum rate of expansion at which society's best interests are served.

If a society decides economic expansion is worth the cost and effort, the problem of how best to achieve it still remains. Some economists infer that maximum expansion over any given time is achieved by optimum resource allocation. Yet optimum resource allocation can lead to more consumption and less investment, if society has a preference for present goods over future goods. Such a preference pattern may retard growth, since the rate of economic expansion depends on, among other factors, the rate of investment.

All five of the questions above must be answered by any economy if it is to function at all in achieving the basic economic goal of satisfying unlimited human wants through employing scarce resources. Wisdom and flexibility are required if the society is to answer these five questions successfully.

METHODOLOGY

Economists have developed a methodology that parallels that of other fields. One useful distinction in economic methodology made by John Neville Keynes, the father of John Maynard Keynes, is between positive and normative economics.[3] Positive economics is "a body of systematized knowledge concerning what is," and normative economics is a "normative or regulative science . . . relating to criteria of what ought to be, and concerned therefore with the ideal as distinguished from the actual; an art as a system of rules for the attainment of a given end. The object of a positive science is the establishment of uniformities, of a normative science the determination of ideals, of an art the formulation of precepts."[4]

Positive Economics

Positive economics is an objective approach to economics as it is. It proposes theories in which a change in one variable may lead in some regular and predictable way to a change in a second variable. Regularity and predictability in scientific theories are relative things. Where formerly the economist proposed "laws," the modern economist speaks of "tendencies" and "propensities," often implying that a relationship between variables is merely a statement of probability.

There are three different approaches to positive economics: apriorism, pragmatism, and empiricism. The apriorists believe that economic science is a product of pure reason—a system of *a priori* truths. The theoretical pragmatists place primary emphasis upon the predictive powers of a theory or model. The empiricists, on the other hand, start with a body of facts, rather than a system of axioms.

From economic hypotheses based on particular sets of assumptions, apriorists proceed by the use of logic to conclusions, in an effort to describe how the economic system operates. Each functional (or behavioral) proposition takes the form, if *A* is true, then *B* follows; or it is expressed as a functional equation with dependent and independent variables. A series of propositions or equations is generally combined to form an economic model or theory.[5] Often some definitional equation or proposition will be included for clarifica-

---

[3]J. S. Mill and Nassau Senior had earlier sought to distinguish the art of economics from the science. For example, see J. S. Mill, *A System of Logic*, 8th ed. (London: Longmans, 1874), Book VI, Chap. 12; and Marian Bowley, *Nassau Senior and Classical Economics* (London: Unwin, 1937), pp. 54–55, reprinted in 1949 by A. M. Kelly, New York.

[4]John Neville Keynes, *The Scope and Method of Political Economy*, 4th ed. (1917) (New York: A. M. Kelly, 1963), pp. 34–35.

[5]Supply and demand of a commodity in the short run may serve as a simple example. We may say, regarding commodity X:

$Q_d = f_1(P_x, P_y, Y_c, T_c)$ (demand function holding P_y, Y_c, and T_c constant)
$Q_s = f_2(P_x, Z)$ (supply function holding Z constant)
$Q_d = Q_s$ (market equilibrium condition)

where:

Q_d = quantity demanded
P_x = price of commodity X
P_y = prices of all other goods
Y_c = consumer's income per time period
T_c = consumer's taste
Q_s = quantity supplied
Z = factors other than price involved in costs of production

tion along with the functional or behavioral propositions. These definitional propositions often take the form of truisms or *a priori* statements. For example, as we shall see, a useful truism defines gross national product (GNP) as both the sum of expenditures or the sum of received income (a relationship to be considered in detail in Chapter 4).

Through the use of abstract theory, less-relevant data can be eliminated. Some contact with reality is thereby lost, but by the reduction of the number of facts to manageable proportions, the relevant factors can be considered individually. Without a theory, we would be lost in a mass of detail in most real-world situations. Theory suggests some relevant questions to ask, some fruitful places to look for answers, and some tentative conclusions to be investigated.

From the *a priori* standpoint, logical consistency is the only valid test of theory, and no theory is bad unless its internal logic is flawed. However, if economic theories are to be used in the real world, they must be tested in other ways as well. One such test of theoretical usefulness is to check the assumptions to see if they correspond to reality. According to this test, a logically correct theory based on realistic assumptions would be acceptable. On the other hand, to the pragmatists, the reality of the assumptions is not a meaningful test. According to this view, economic theory is valid only if it is useful in solving problems.

To the theoretical pragmatists, it is important that an economic theory have the possibility of being verified through the successful prediction of quantitative data; for without the possibility of quantitative verification, one can never be safe from falling into the trap of circular reasoning, or of irrelevance. The position of the economic pragmatists is represented by Professor Friedman:

> . . . a theory cannot be tested by comparing its "assumptions" directly with "reality." Indeed, there is no meaningful way in which this can be done. Complete "realism" is clearly unattainable, and the question whether a theory is realistic "enough" can be settled only by seeing whether it yields predictions that are good enough for the purpose in hand or that are better than predictions from alternative theories.[6]

Testing hypotheses is relatively straightforward in the case of economic predictions when historical data are available; one simply sees if the prediction is fulfilled over time. In other situations, where data are not available or where variables cannot be isolated, testing a theory becomes more complicated. Even where the relevant data are available, accurate tests of theories may be difficult or impossible if the values of too many variables change simultaneously. Generally, economists cannot conduct controlled experiments in which the investigator holds constant all variables but one. The economic investigator uses statistical techniques in an attempt to isolate phenomena in order to test for some regular pattern.

---

[6]Milton Friedman, "The Methodology of Positive Economics," in *Essays in Positive Economics* (Chicago: The University of Chicago Press, 1953), p. 41.

However, there is no certain verification of the general applicability of a theory through the use of statistical techniques. History enables us only to accept or reject a theory in a particular situation. Due to the multiplicity of factors operating in an economic system over time, the attempt to hold variables constant through statistical techniques can never be entirely successful.

Even though no theory can be based on completely realistic assumptions, an extremely pragmatic approach should not cause the economist to disregard the reality of his assumptions. Although it is conceivable that a useful theory may be based on unrealistic assumptions and sometimes may yield correct conclusions, it is quite possible that a theory in which the predictions seem to correspond to reality (where the assumptions are obviously false) is a case of what statisticians call "spurious correlation."

The extreme pragmatists overlook the fact that in a real sense all theory is tautology, since the conclusions may be logically inferred from the assumptions. A completely logical thinker would not need theory, but only assumptions, in order to reach a logically valid conclusion. For example, in *The Dialogues of Alfred North Whitehead*, Lucian Price reports a conversation between Whitehead and Professor P. A. Samuelson in which the philosopher asked, "What do people mean by talking about the future being obliged to pay for the wars of the present?" Apparently through logic rather than through a formal economic model, Whitehead concluded that "all you are saying when you refer to the future as paying for wars of the present is that you are bequeathing to posterity a changed form of society."[7] He relegated the monetary cost of war—the main concern of the man in the street—to an unimportant position compared with the real costs in terms of lost alternatives.

In contrast, the average man would probably need a theoretical model as an aid to logic in arriving at the same conclusion. Theoretical models offer a step-by-step process to aid the student in arriving at logical conclusions. But can unrealistic assumptions lead to realistic conclusions except through chance?

Most economic empiricists believe that the inductive rather than the deductive method should be used in developing a complete model. That is, they generally start by gathering all the facts they can on the subject, and from these facts they derive hypotheses. Then they test each of these propositions to see how well it predicts real-world phenomena in situations other than those in which the facts were gathered. Unlike the pragmatists, however, most empiricists are not so interested in formulating generalized models that apply to a wide range of problems, but rather in developing models that are extremely accurate in their predictions. One problem that arises from this approach is that the empirically valid models that are developed may have little generality. A model that accurately predicts the price that General

---

[7] Lucien Price, *The Dialogues of Alfred North Whitehead* (New York: New American Library, 1954), pp. 122–23.

Electric will charge for its toasters may not be applicable to any other firm or product. Since the real world is so complex, it is often necessary to abstract from it, at least in the initial stages of successful model building.

In developing generalized models, the empiricist brings in all the possible variables that have any measurable effect, in order to achieve the highest possible degree of accuracy. In their attempt to make theories realistic, empiricists have often introduced so many variables that in some cases the individual can no longer comprehend all the factors involved in the theory. For example, the Federal Reserve-MIT model, which can handle some two hundred endogenous variables may give satisfactory predictive results. But since one cannot grasp all these interrelationships, the unwieldy computer model may not allow men determining public policy to understand the relevant variables under their control. A successful economic theory must strike a trade-off between the cost of realism through bringing in large numbers of variables and the benefit of the manageability of the theory.

Finally in this imprecise world there are very few data whose validity and reliability cannot be challenged. The truth of any hypothesis empirically derived can be no better than the data on which it is based. The problem of imprecise data also applies to the pragmatists with regard to the reliability and validity of their predictions.

A vast majority of economists use a combination of all three approaches to positive economics, because each approach by itself is subject to severe criticism. The scientific method seems to require a constant reappraisal of one's position as new facts are discovered, as new generalized models are initiated, and as all models are tested with regard to their predictability.

Normative Economics

In contrast with positive economics, which attempts to abstract theories that describe and predict successfully in the real world, normative economics is concerned with two different things: (1) setting up values or goals for the economy, and (2) evaluating the theory in practice.

Determining Values Values are an expression of feelings, preferences, or beliefs of an individual or a society. In economics, as elsewhere, there is no way to determine the validity of a system of values. Students of normative economics must set up their own values or use those given them by society. Within any society, certain values tend to become generally accepted as worthwhile economic ends. At the individual level in the tradition of Western economics, the greatest utility or satisfaction for the individual has been accepted as the single most worthwhile end (as long as one individual does not unjustly deprive another.) In addition, Western society has generally selected economic growth, stability, justice, and freedom as worthwhile goals.

Because of the emphasis on individual well-being, *economic growth* has come to mean increases in economic output or the quantity and quality of goods and services, per capita. Since "economic output" has been considered the equivalent of gross national product (GNP), economic growth would seem to be an unambiguous concept. Yet it leads to a bias against nonmarket activities that are not included in GNP. Simply considering economic growth in terms of GNP is a substitution of market values for social values. Thus billboards, offensive to many, are included in GNP at construction cost just as are hospitals, which offend few. Similarly, equating economic growth with GNP excludes *social costs*, such as depleting natural resources or polluting the air. A GNP analysis that considered both the positive and negative aspects of economic growth might be revealing, but since determining which goods are good is a value judgment, agreement would be hard to reach. Furthermore, selection of a proper measure of these social costs would be difficult in such a study. Conversion to dollars of such values as the offensiveness of a billboard would be practically impossible.

In addition, the greater objective of maximizing utility or satisfaction may be in conflict with economic growth. Increased output of economic goods may be accomplished at the expense of leisure and could result in decreased utility if the leisure is more highly valued than the goods.

Stability is a goal of the economy that can take on many different meanings from time to time and from person to person. In general, what the economist has in mind is a period of relatively stable prices with consistently high employment. However, as in the case of growth, any particular formulation of what these generalizations mean is subject to criticism. Stability may also imply a dependable level of individual income, which involves the whole concept of Social Security and social welfare.

In economics, *justice* usually concerns income distribution. For some, justice means distribution according to need; for others, distribution according to productivity. Under the latter definition, unearned monopoly profits would be unjust; under the former, justice would require increased welfare payments to the underpriviledged—although *underpriviledged* is a relative concept and must be defined by society. A third interpretation defines *justice* as the income distribution that optimizes the sum of total individual utility or satisfaction. This test would require some measure of utility; income would be redistributed as long as the transfer resulted in an increase in utility for the recipient that is greater than the loss of utility to the transferor. Still others would say that because there is no scientifically meaningful way to compare the utility levels of people, a change in income distribution is not just unless the change does not hurt anyone else.[8] Whichever definition of *justice* one accepts, there seems to be a growing inclination to also include under the idea of economic justice some sort of social insurance against calamity, misfortune, or old age. Finally justice has come to entail preventing

[8]Note that this interpretation of justice does not necessarily maximize total satisfaction because the rule just proposed does not allow transfers from one who would get less satisfaction to one who would get more. For example, if Smith has a candy bar and Jones has none, we would not give Smith's candy to Jones just because Jones would enjoy it more than Smith. However, if Smith gets no enjoyment at all from the candy, then it should be transferred to Jones in order to optimize the distribution of goods in this instance.

deception in economic practices, on the theory that a buyer has the right to know what he is buying. Some attempts to involve justice in the economy are antitrust legislation, labor legislation such as workman's compensation and Social Security, consumer protection legislation such as pure food and drug laws, and programs such as disaster relief.

A fourth value—economic freedom—is generally interpreted in our society to mean production in accordance with consumer demands in a competitive market in which there are no restrictions by either the government or custom. This implies freedom to do what we want with our resources, to produce what we want for sale at unregulated prices, with a minimum of government or social coercion. In contrast, from a socialistic point of view, freedom in a capitalistic system means sufficient income to avoid coercion or exploitation by owners and managers of the means of production.

Efficiency is an overriding value in economics. To whatever goals society adopts, the economist will add the criterion of efficiency, regarding it much as the physician regards good health or as the policeman regards law and order: Its maintenance is his chief concern. Some economists have even confused efficient resource allocation with economic growth. But they are two different concepts, even though they are related in that both imply increased output. Efficient use of resources involves obtaining the maximum output for a given cost level of inputs, and economic growth means increasing levels of output over time.

Values are set up in terms of both things that should be done and things that must not be done. For example, in India one of the goals is to increase economic growth, especially the output and consumption of high-grade protein. However, the use of cattle as an efficient means to achieve protein consumption is forbidden for religious reasons.

On another level, the economist, too, brings values into his analysis. In selecting problems to be studied, the economist will be guided by his own values; he will select only problems that he finds worthy of study. In addition, his values will determine what methods are permissible to solve the chosen problem. Once the economist has been presented by society with a set of goals, then his own values will determine the suitability of available means. Therefore, value-free economic policy is impossible, and the same may be true of pure theory, because the assumptions an economist starts with are usually determined by his own values. In dealing with policy, the economist should state his values so that others can better interpret his position and be forewarned regarding his underlying assumptions.

Much of the current criticism of standard economics is based on normative grounds. The group of "third-world" economists led by Raul Prebisch has maintained that new theories are required because adherence to existing theories keeps less-developed economies at a disadvantage.[9] The economists of the New Left similarly criticize existing economics on normative grounds.

---

[9] Raul Prebisch, *Towards a New Trade Policy for Development* (New York: United Nations, 1964). [United Nations document E/CONF. 46/3.]

Underdeveloped enclaves exist within developed economies, which, according to the New Left, will persist for as long as we continue to follow the prevailing theories of economics. The changes they recommend specifically involve, among others, (1) changing from markets (chaotic and unfair) to some more direct means of registering preferences; (2) decentralizing economic power and decision making; and (3) collective ownership of capital. Virtually all the changes recommended by the New Left are based on the normative idea that the entire population would be better served by a new system, because the present one serves well only a small number at the expense of the majority.

In effect, the New Left critics of traditional economics want to reorder the goals, giving greater weight to justice and freedom, and proportionately much less weight to economic growth. The fourth goal, stability, evidently would take care of itself in a decentralized economy, in their view.

The Nixon attempt at price and wage controls is another example of reordering goals, in this case by the government. The trade-off in this instance was between stability and freedom. The Nixon administration felt that the gain from wage and price stability would outweigh the loss of economic freedom.

Evaluation of Theory to Achieve Goals Part of normative economics is a study of the application of theory to achieve goals. In this process, a cost–benefit approach should be used in order to choose the most efficient of the alternative policies available and to appraise the performance of the policy chosen. In the latter case, an economist acts as a quality-control expert, trying to measure whether the desired goals have been achieved and at what costs by the program. For example, the process of evaluating a theory works as follows: if our goal is to reduce unemployment, first a program would be selected, based either on the past performance of similar programs or, if no historical precedent is available, on a theoretical model that seems to fit the particular case. After a trial period, the performance of the program can be evaluated by comparing the pattern of unemployment rates before and after its implementation with the total cost that was expended to achieve the results. But limitations of measurement are such that in many cases, neither costs nor benefits can be directly quantified. For some types of analysis, an inability to quantify may be a serious impediment. Nevertheless, even where one cannot directly measure costs or benefits, it may be possible to determine the direction of change resulting from a given policy. For example, it is impossible to measure units of defense, but it is possible to determine whether a given policy will increase or reduce military power. Even where quantifiable measures exist, they may not provide sufficient or relevant enough data to determine the best alternative policy to achieve a given goal. In evaluation of road-building programs, the number of miles of highway constructed is significant, but it reveals neither the quantity of new transportation made available nor its value to society. Or to illustrate further, the Small Business Administration can count the number of publications distributed to its clients, but there is no way to measure the contribution to good management made by those publications.

Appropriate tools of measurement must be invented in order for us to know whether goals are being achieved. Thermometers were required before our Fahrenheit heat-measurement systems could be used. Before the invention of thermometers, heat could be ranked relatively—"June is hotter than February" was a reasonable pre-thermometer remark—but a *degree* measure of heat, such as, "June is ten degrees hotter than February," would have been meaningless. Even with thermometers, any measure of the temperature depends on the accuracy of the instrument and the skill of the observer, both of which are inevitably imperfect.

At present imprecise data plagues economics because theories are often tested by, and policies often based on, data that is less accurate than most thermometers. In Leontief's words, "the weak and all too slowly growing empirical foundation clearly cannot support the proliferating superstructure of pure, or should I say, speculative economic theory."[10]

Finally, it is necessary to distinguish between the effectiveness of programs and the efficiency of their execution. To take an ancient example that has certain modern counterparts, the effectiveness of the Egyptian pyramid program as a source of long-lasting tombs is unquestioned, but the efficiency of the pyramid program itself (extensive use of slave labor and little capital equipment) is a different matter. On the other hand, the Polish army cavalry drills were performed with great efficiency during the early days of World War II; but their performance against German tank attacks indicated that the program was ineffective. Thus, the normative economic ideal is *the achievement of relevant goals through efficient and effective programs.*

STATICS AND DYNAMICS

Subtle distinctions have been made between static and dynamic analysis in economics. However, for our purposes the distinction can be drawn fairly simply. A static model does not involve a time dimension—statics treats the economy as though time were standing still—and static analysis is not concerned with the path of the economy to equilibrium. Comparative static analysis can be used to show economic equilibrium before and after a change in one or more variables without regard to the time required. Dynamic analysis involves the study of an economic system over time, and of the path through which an economy moves in the process of economic change. In dynamic analysis, which requires all variables to be dated, the functional relationships between variables, whether or not they lead to equilibrium, will commonly involve time leads or lags. The study of the time dimension in the functional relationships is a key to dynamic analysis.

---

[10]Wassily Leontief, "Theoretical Assumptions and Nonobserved Facts," *The American Economic Review*, 61 (March 1971), 1.

Some important macroeconomic concepts fall into a gray area between static and dynamic analysis. For example, the Keynesian multiplier discussed in Chapter 8 requires an infinite number of time periods to develop completely, since its value depends on the complete working out of an infinite convergent geometric series. However, the multiplier is generally presented through comparative statics, by showing equilibrium before and after some change in an independent variable (that is, an exogeneous change). Even though the resulting equilibrium position will never be completely achieved, it will be approximated closely enough to make it a very useful concept.

MICROECONOMICS AND MACROECONOMICS

Microeconomics is concerned with individual producers and consumers. It deals with the flow of production from firms to consumers and with the flow of resources from consumers to firms, and also with the determination of prices—the ratio between the real flows of goods and services and the counterbalancing monetary flows. In contrast, macroeconomics deals with the whole economic system rather than the component parts. Macroeconomic analysis tends to ignore the individual firm, the individual consumer, and the individual resource owner. In general, macroeconomics deals with the aggregate flows of productive resources and commodities and considers overall price levels instead of prices of individual resources or commodities.

However, the line between micro- and macroeconomics is not entirely clear. Although macroeconomics focuses on behavior in the aggregate, the aggregate behavior of populations results from individual decisions. (Yet, microeconomics has always included certain aggregates, such as aggregating firms to form an industry or aggregating the demands of individual consumers to form a market-demand curve.) So our description of economic phenomena starts from the basis of individual decisions and proceeds to the aggregate.

The *fallacy of composition* is one of the key distinctions between micro- and macroeconomics. The fallacy of composition concerns the assumption that what is true of the parts of the system must necessarily be true for the whole. An example often used is that of a spectator at a ball game. The individual spectator can improve his view by standing, but it would be a fallacy to conclude that each spectator in the stadium can improve his view if all stand.

The same holds for some economic analysis. Certain policies might be advantageous pursued alone by an individual firm, but could be injurious if all firms followed the same policy. To take an economic example, if, during a period of full employment, one firm arranges a large loan in order to purchase a new machine, it will probably improve the firm's position in the industry. However, if all firms try to arrange large loans, the result will almost certainly be higher interest rates, higher prices throughout the aggregate economy, and possibly leaving each firm no better off than if it had not tried to borrow.

However, some things that are true for the individual also hold true for the aggregate. For example, if our one spectator stands up and starts to jump up and down, his pulse rate will rise; and if all the spectators do likewise, all their pulse rates will rise (unless the stands collapse and they are all killed). Whether or not the fallacy of composition applies, it may be useful to proceed from the individual parts to the aggregate to gain a better understanding of those individual parts, and to isolate the points where the fallacy of composition occurs. In economics, where the fallacy of composition does affect the analysis, the cause is often external to the firm and due to the actions of other firms.

THEORIES AND GOALS IN MACROECONOMICS

After we present the current theory of macroeconomics, we will consider how the theory can be used to achieve the goals set by society. J. M. Keynes, the father of modern macroeconomics, developed his approach to macroeconomics from the opposite direction: The pressing social needs for more employment and output during the depression of the 1930's provided the goal that stimulated his theoretical writing. Today, in addition to the goal of maintaining high levels of employment and output, we add the goal of price stability. Keynes also recognized the need to fight inflation during normal times, but he pointed out that there was little need to fight inflation during a severe depression. (However, the early 1970's showed that the right mixture of economic abuse could result in combined inflation and unemployment, a combination unknown before the 1950's.)

The two goals of macroeconomics—a high employment level and stable prices—can be merged and described as part of the single goal of economic stability. In addition, economic stability may also involve other ingredients suggested earlier, such as stable real income over an individual's lifetime.

The foregoing is not intended to imply that pre-Keynesian classical and neoclassical economists were uninterested in stability. They merely felt that the workings of a free market would restore full employment and price stability very quickly after any major disruption in the economic system had occurred.

CONCLUDING COMMENT

Aside from the conventional approach to economic methodology, definitions, and classifications discussed in this chapter, others have been suggested. Part of the intellectual game requires that when one proposes a new approach, any conflicting ideas of predecessors must be discredited and discarded. However, although it is often satisfying to justify one's own methods and definitions, it will usually be unnecessarily inhibiting if at the same time one denigrates the methodology and classifications of others. A given investigator may find a certain method best suited for a purpose, but economic problems are so complex and varied that any insightful method deserves a hearing. Out of the number of available methodological approaches, selecting the right one is the crucial problem in the practice of all disciplines, including economics.

The science of economics lies in the body of available valid theory, whereas the art of economics lies in the selection of the correct theory to apply to a given problem. The economic practitioner must be especially careful to see that the assumptions (and predictions based on history) inherent in the theory correspond reasonably well to the facts.

Defining the scope of a science or classifying its concepts is arbitrary. The practitioners within each field, by their definitions, carve out a piece of the intellectual world through a process of squatter sovereignty. According to accepted definitions in standard texts, there is little discernible definitional difference between economics and engineering. Similarly, the accepted classification systems within a discipline are generally arbitrary but useful. Thus the distinction between micro- and macroeconomics enables us to classify difficult problems for analysis. But the separation of economists into micro and macro experts could lead to certain blind spots and to the neglect of certain fields. For example, regional analysis has been too largely neglected because it does not fit neatly into either the micro- or the macroeconomic mold.

A final word of warning: Watch out for the three-shell game that is often played by economists. When they set up their scope, classification, methodology, and assumptions, they often force the conclusions. As John Ciardi described the felonious entry of a man named Finchley into the home of Mr. Billy Jo Trant, the homeowner reversed the usual order; he shot three times, and then said, "Hands up!" Ciardi's moral: "Commit yourself to another man's premises and you may, in logic, have to accept his conclusions."[11]

QUESTIONS AND PROBLEMS

1. Why are human wants unlimited relative to resources?
2. What are the basic questions facing any economy?
3. Differentiate positive economics from normative economics.
4. How does static analysis differ from dynamic analysis?
5. What are the goals of aggregate economics?
6. How are economic goals determined?
7. Discuss which economic goals you consider to be most important and why.
8. Differentiate between apriorism, pragmatism, and empiricism. Which approach do you believe is best?
9. Distinguish between microeconomics and macroeconomics.

---

[11] John Ciardi, "A Missouri Fable," in *In Fact* (New Brunswick, N.J.: Rutgers University Press, 1962), p. 31.

ADDITIONAL SELECTED REFERENCES

THE SCOPE AND METHOD OF ECONOMICS

BOULDING, KENNETH E., *The Skills of the Economist*. Toronto: Clark, Irwin, 1958.

HARROD, ROY, "Scope and Method of Economics," *Economic Journal*, 48 (September 1938), 383–412.

HIGGINS, BENJAMIN, *What Do Economists Know?* Carlton, Australia: Melbourne University Press, 1951.

KNIGHT, FRANK H., "Methodology in Economics—Parts I and II," *Southern Economic Journal*, 27 (January and April 1961), 185–93, 273–82.

KRUPP, SHERMAN ROY, ed., *The Structure of Economic Science: Essays on Methodology*. Englewood Cliffs, N.J.: Prentice-Hall, 1966.

LANGE, OSCAR, "The Scope and Method of Economics," *Review of Economic Studies*, 13, No. 1 (1945), 19–32.

MARSHALL, ALFRED, *Principles of Economics*, 8th ed., pp. 1–48; Appendices C & D, pp. 770–84. New York: Macmillan, 1920.

NAGEL, ERNEST, "Assumptions in Economic Theory," *American Economic Review*, 53 (May 1963), 211–19; with discussion by Paul A. Samuelson, 231–36.

ROBBINS, LIONEL, *An Essay on the Nature and Significance of Economic Science*, 2nd ed. London: Macmillan, 1952.

RUGGLES, NANCY D., ed., *Economics*. Englewood Cliffs, N.J.: Prentice-Hall, 1970, 182 pp.

RUGGLES, RICHARD, "Methodological Developments," with comments by Evsey D. Domar and Milton Friedman, in *A Survey of Contemporary Economics*, ed. B. F. Haley, Vol. II, pp. 408–57. Homewood, Ill.: Richard D. Irwin, 1952.

VON MISES, LUDWIG, *Epistemological Problems of Economics*. Princeton, N.J.: Van Nostrand Reinhold, 1960.

CRITIQUE OF ECONOMIC METHODOLOGY

MACHLUP, FRITZ, "Are the Social Sciences Really Inferior?" *Southern Economic Journal*, 27 (January 1961), 173–84.

SCHOEFFLER, SIDNEY, *The Failures of Economics: A Diagnostic Study*. Cambridge, Mass.: Harvard University Press, 1955.

THE PLACE OF GENERAL THEORIES

FORES, M. J., "No More General Theories?" *Economic Journal*, 79 (March 1969), 11–22.

EVALUATION OF THEORY TO ACHIEVE GOALS

NOVICK, DAVID, ed., *Program Budgeting* (Rand Corporation Sponsored Research Study). Washington, D.C.: U.S. Government Printing Office, 1965.

PROST, A. R., and RALPH TURVEY, "Cost-Benefit Analysis: A Survey," *Economic Journal*, 75 (December 1965), 683–735.

The Microeconomic Foundations of Macroeconomics—Demand

2

The essence of microeconomics is supply and demand of firms, industries, and households. Supply and demand functions take price to be the independent variable and the quantity of a particular good to be the dependent variable. We begin our consideration of the microeconomic basis of macroeconomics with the concept of demand, because in our Western social framework, it is generally accepted that the satisfaction of consumer wants is the end purpose of economic activity. Unlimited human wants are central to the definition of economics, as we saw in Chapter 1, and the satisfaction of those wants to the greatest degree possible is considered to be the basic purpose of the economy.

The fallacy of composition, which so often distinguishes micro- from macroeconomics, does not apply to the theories that underlie demand analysis, because demand theory applies both to the individual and to the aggregate, as long as the constraints facing individuals are not changed by the process of aggregation. The theory of consumer demand appears valid even though it may be that no individual consumer ever planned his purchases in the way that will be described in this chapter. The theory of consumer demand is analogous to the thought processes that a rational consumer would employ in making his decisions.

Our purpose in this chapter is to build a theory of consumer demand on the assumption that consumers behave rationally in the aggregate, even though knowledgeable individual consumers on occasion behave irrationally by failing to maximize their satisfaction from their given income. For example, a consumer might give way to an impulse and pay too high a price or buy a product he doesn't really want or need. Demand theory in microeconomics generally assumes that individual incomes are given and that the price for a particular good is the independent variable. In contrast, macroeconomics is generally concerned more with consumer aggregate income than with the aggregate price level as the independent variable. Therefore, although demand theory in microeconomics serves as the basis for a macro theory of consumer behavior, the application is somewhat limited. The purpose of including a theory of consumer behavior in macroeconomics is to assist in making both price and income endogenous variables—that is, variables determined within the system.

UTILITY THEORY

The Concept of Utility

Economists define *utility* as the satisfaction derived from the consumption of a commodity. "Satisfaction" must be interpreted more broadly than as pleasure; in fact, it need not involve actual pleasure. For example, the services of a doctor in the setting of a broken arm are a source of great satisfaction to an accident victim but do not provide pleasure—merely relief from pain. Furthermore, "consumption" in this definition could imply the broadest interpretation of "goods and services," even including savings, which also provide utility (and savings decisions are a most important part of macro theory). Although utility may be inherent in almost any conceivable activity, and any activity could therefore be considered a form of consumption, consumption usually has a more restricted definition, referring specifically to the utilization of economic goods that command a price.

The most basic utility concept, total utility, refers generally to the total amount of satisfaction derived from consuming one particular commodity (although it could refer to the total satisfaction derived from the consumption of all goods and services). More consumption is assumed to give greater total utility than does less consumption, so that as the consumption of any commodity is increased, total utility also increases. Consumption or utilization of certain commodities implies physically using them up: For example, when food or gasoline have been utilized, they have been literally consumed; they have ended their useful life. But other commodities—for example, books—may be fully utilized by one user but not consumed, and then passed on to another, who may derive further satisfaction from them and still not wear them out or consume them in a physical sense.

Commodities may be classified as durable and nondurable goods on the basis of whether or not utilization implies physical consumption. However, durability is a matter of degree; any accounting system that distinguishes durables from nondurables must have an arbitrary cutoff period, usually one year. The national-income accounting system described in Chapters 4 and 5 defines goods expected to last more than a year as consumer durables and goods expected to last less than a year as nondurables.

By assumption, consumers maximize total utility by consuming from the available range of all goods and services that particular combination of goods and services providing the most total utility.

Diminishing Marginal Utility

Marginal utility is defined as the change in the total utility resulting from a one-unit change in the consumption of a commodity per unit of time. In other words, marginal utility could be defined as the rate of change in the total-utility function. If we plotted the total- and marginal-utility functions on a graph, marginal utility would equal the slope of the total-utility curve at any point.

The *law of diminishing marginal utility* proposes that beyond some point as additional units of any commodity are consumed, marginal utility, the additions to total utility, will become increasingly smaller; that is, the additional satisfaction to be derived from consuming an additional unit of the product will decrease. Eventually the consumer will become satiated with the product. Beyond the point of satiation, further consumption will actually reduce total utility, so that the increments to total utility, marginal utility, become negative. For example, a popular form of torture in ancient China was to force victims to eat beyond their capacity, beyond the point where total utility begins to decrease and marginal utility becomes negative.

In a free-market situation, no consumer will knowingly approach the point where he becomes completely satiated with any commodity, because there will always be some alternative use for his income that will produce positive satisfaction at the margin. However, it has been suggested that perhaps the "super-rich" approach saturation in all their recognized wants for consumer goods. In general, rational consumers in free markets will operate where total utility is increasing and marginal utility is decreasing but still positive.

Even though there is not now any objective measure of utility, the law of diminishing marginal utility seems to hold in any conceivable situation. For example, the average family with two drivers would get increased satisfaction from owning a second car, but probably the increase would not be as great as that experienced from purchasing the first. Almost certainly, a third car would add less additional satisfaction than the second, since only two cars could be in use at any time. Ownership of a fourth and fifth car could conceivably provide negative marginal utility, since the consumer's residence would begin to look like a used-car lot. A similar pattern can be noted in the consumption of additional units of virtually any good.

Utility theory by itself considers only the satisfaction derived from consumption—not how much consumption the individual can undertake with his restricted income. Since there are no measures of the actual satisfaction derived from the consumption of a good, we will use indifference curves, an approach to utility theory that requires that consumers need only rank their preferences. This they are able to do even though there is no numerical measure of utility.

Nature and Characteristics of Indifference Curves

The only assumption required for indifference-curve theory is that if a consumer is offered two different bundles of goods, he will choose one in preference to the other or else he will be indifferent as to which bundle he gets; in other words, that he will be able to decide that one bundle gives greater satisfaction than the other or that the satisfaction derived from the two would be equal.

An indifference curve is a function connecting all the combinations of commodities that would provide the consumer with equal utility; therefore, it is a matter of indifference to him which combination he gets, as long as he remains on the same indifference curve. For example, in Figure 2-1, any point on curve I_1 would provide a consumer with a combination of food and bonds yielding an equal amount of satisfaction.[1] For simplicity, we restrict our consumer's choice to only two items—food and bonds—where the quantity of food is plotted along the x-axis (horizontal axis) and the quantity of bonds along the y-axis (vertical axis). We also assume that the consumer can buy fractional units of each item, so that the indifference curves are continuous. If the consumer were offered the bundle of goods represented by point a, containing 1 bond and 3 units of food, he would feel just as well off as at point b, with 3 bonds and .8 units of food. Therefore, he derives the same utility at either point a or point b, or at any other point on curve I_1.

In order to show higher levels of satisfaction, we must move to higher

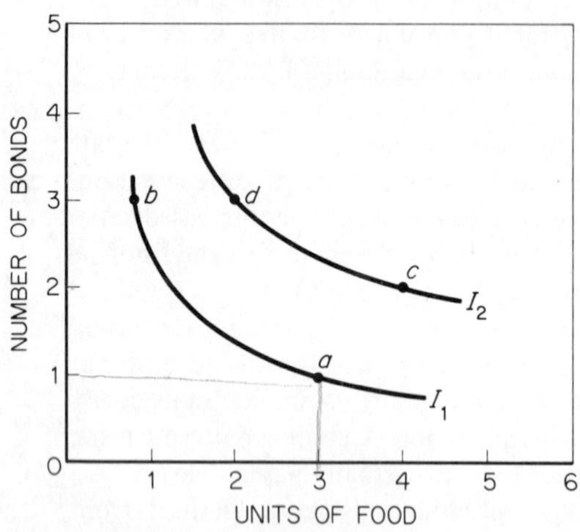

FIG. 2-1 Indifference Curves

[1] In this illustration, we have used one consumption good, food, and one form of savings, bonds, to anticipate the consumption–savings relationship to be developed later as one of the key ingredients of macroeconomic theory. The bonds in this illustration stand in for the eventual purchase of all goods other than food.

indifference curves. For example, at point *c* on curve I_2, 2 bonds and 4 units of food would provide greater utility than any point on I_1, as would point *d*, which includes 3 bonds and 2 units of food. By definition, any higher indifference curve provides more utility than any lower indifference curve, although how much more is not generally specified. Under indifference-curve analysis, there is no need to assume that the amount of utility derived can be quantified. The consumer need only know that all points on I_1 would give him the same satisfaction and that any point on I_2 would give him more satisfaction than I_1, although, since utility cannot be measured numerically, the consumer would not know how much more satisfaction he was getting on the higher indifference curve.

Certain general characteristics of indifference curves can be inferred from our example:

1. All combinations of goods on any one indifference curve give the consumer the same total satisfaction.
2. Any higher indifference curve yields more satisfaction than any lower curve.
3. Therefore, indifference curves cannot intersect, because it would be impossible for one curve that defines points of equal satisfaction to provide both more and less utility than another curve that also defines points of equal satisfaction.
4. Indifference curves generally slope downward and to the right, because in order to maintain a constant level of satisfaction, whenever a consumer gives up units of one item, he must obtain additional units of the other.
5. Indifference curves are generally convex to the origin because of diminishing marginal utility. The more a consumer has of one item, the more important the other becomes. Therefore, a consumer will generally be willing to exchange a greater quantity of the item he has in large amounts in order to obtain a smaller additional quantity of the other. For example, in Figure 2-1, a consumer operating at point *a* on curve I_1 would be willing to give up only .2 of a bond in order to obtain 1 additional unit of food. However, the same consumer operating at point *b*, where he has more bonds and less food than at point *a*, would be willing to give up about 1.4 bonds in exchange for 1 additional unit of food.
6. Indifference curves need not be equidistant. Some goods are subject to a greater degree of diminishing marginal utility than are others, and the rate may vary at different levels of consumption. For example, necessities such as food may provide high levels of utility at first and then decline very sharply at the margin, while the additional utility derived from other items such as bonds will probably tend to decrease more slowly as their quantity is increased.

Because a consumer derives the same total satisfaction from any point on an indifference curve, the slope of the curve itself defines the rate at which the consumer would be willing to exchange one item for the other—his marginal rate of substitution (MRS). Notice that the slope of the curve shows only the consumer's willingness to trade off one item for the other, not necessarily his ability to do so. Since the marginal rate of substitution of one commodity for another can be defined as the amount of one commodity the consumer would be willing to give up in order to obtain one unit of the other, the average slope of the indifference curve between any two units of one commodity shows the marginal rate of substitution of the one commodity for the other; in formula form, the MRS of good y for good x may be stated

$$MRS_{yx} = -\frac{\Delta Q_y}{\Delta Q_x}$$

where ΔQ_y and ΔQ_x equal the change in the quantity consumed of good y and good x respectively. The minus sign designates that the curve is negatively sloped. For example, at point b in Figure 2-1, the consumer would be willing to trade off about 1.4 bonds to obtain 1 unit of food. Or, ignoring signs, the marginal rate of substitution of bonds for food at that point is 1.4 to 1, or

$$MRS_{bf} = 1.4{:}\ 1$$

However, at point a, the consumer is willing to give up only .2 bonds in order to obtain 1 additional unit of food; therefore, at point a

$$MRS_{bf} = .2{:}\ 1$$

A normal indifference curve that is convex to the origin implies that the goods are neither perfect substitutes nor perfect complements and that the consumer enjoys having a variety of items. At the same time, because the goods are subject to diminishing marginal utility, the proportion of each good in the consumer market basket is a matter of some significance. However, the proportion of ownership becomes unimportant where goods are perfect substitutes for each other; that is, the consumer would be willing to substitute at some constant ratio with no change in his utility. Indifference curves relating perfect substitutes would be straight lines running from the y- to the x-axis. Since straight lines have a constant slope, the linear, negatively-sloped indifference curve illustrates that the consumer is indifferent to which combination of the commodities he holds. For example, if Tom Smith gets exactly the same utility from Wheaties as from corn flakes at breakfast, his straight-line indifference curves relating Wheaties and corn flakes would indicate that his total utility would remain constant as long as the number of servings remained constant, regardless of the proportion of the two goods consumed in any given time period.

In contrast to the case of perfect substitutes, indifference curves relating two perfectly complementary goods would be right-angle functions, with the rays parallel to the axes. Perfect complements are goods that must be used in some fixed proportion. For example, an indifference curve relating corn flakes and cream would be a right angle, because the consumer would derive no additional utility from more corn flakes unless they were accompanied by additional units of cream (assuming that no utility could be derived from bowls of dry corn flakes or from bowls of pure cream).

In summary, perfect substitutes are in effect the same good to a consumer, so the proportions can change without changing the consumer's utility as long as the total quantity is unchanged. And perfect complements that must be consumed together in some fixed proportion are in effect only one good, so more of one without more of the other provides no additional utility.

Maximizing Satisfaction from a Given Budget

The objective of rational consumer behavior is to maximize satisfaction from a given money outlay. Virtually all consumers are constrained by a limited budget, and are therefore restricted in the choices they can make in the market place. This budget constraint facing consumers can be shown graphically quite simply. Suppose, for example, the consumer discussed previously devotes all his available budget to the purchase of food. If his budget were \$60 a week and the price of food remained constant at \$18.75 per unit, then the consumer would be able to buy 3.2 units of food (assuming that fractional units can be bought). On the other hand, if he devoted his entire budget to the purchase of bonds (assuming he buys Savings Bonds, which cost \$18.75 and return \$25 each) then he would be able to buy 3.2 bonds instead. His budget restraint would then be equal to the line labeled B_{60} in Figure 2-2, a function that defines a constant outlay of \$60 distributed between the two items, bonds and food, measured on the y-axis and x-axis respectively. The slope of this budget line can be derived as follows, ignoring the negative sign:

$$\frac{Y_c/P_y}{Y_c/P_x} = \frac{Y_c}{P_y} \times \frac{P_x}{Y_c} = \frac{P_x}{P_y}$$

Therefore, the slope of the budget line is P_x/P_y, where Y_c represents the con-

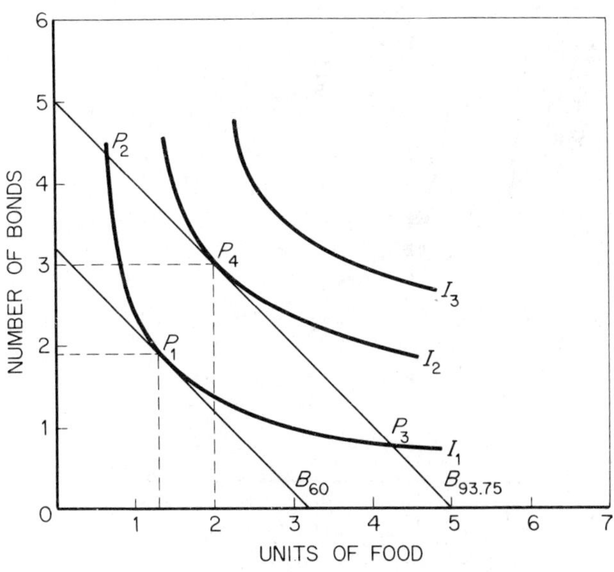

FIG. 2-2 Consumer Equilibrium

sumer's budget of \$60, P_x the price of food, and P_y the price of bonds. Since the price of both food and bonds is \$18.75 in this illustration, the slope of the budget line must equal negative 1.

With his given budget of \$60 a week, the consumer could operate at any point on line B_{60} or any point to the left of and below that line. In equilibrium, he will operate at point P_1, the point of tangency with indifference curve I_1, where he will buy 1.9 bonds and 1.3 units of food, because that is the highest indifference curve he can achieve with his income.

Now suppose that his budget increases from \$60 to \$93.75. The consumer could then operate at any point on line $B_{93.75}$. For example, he could purchase the quantities of bonds or food designated at point P_2 or P_3. However, points P_2 and P_3 will provide him a smaller amount of satisfaction than P_4, the point of tangency with the highest achievable indifference curve, I_2. He would prefer the combination of bonds and food represented by the I_3 indifference curve; however, his budget-restraint line, $B_{93.75}$, will not allow him to operate on this higher indifference curve. Therefore, the utility-maximizing consumer will operate at point P_4, where he will buy 3 bonds and 2 units of food, a combination of purchases that exhausts his budget of \$93.75 and provides him the maximum possible utility.

Suppose that while the consumer's budget is still \$93.75 a week, inflation sharply increases the price of groceries, but the price of bonds is held constant. If the price of a unit of groceries jumps from \$18.75 to \$52.08, the maximum amount of groceries the consumer could buy, if he devoted all his budget to groceries, would be reduced from 5 units to 1.8 units, and his budget line would shift to the left, from B_1 to B_2, as is shown in Figure 2-3. With this

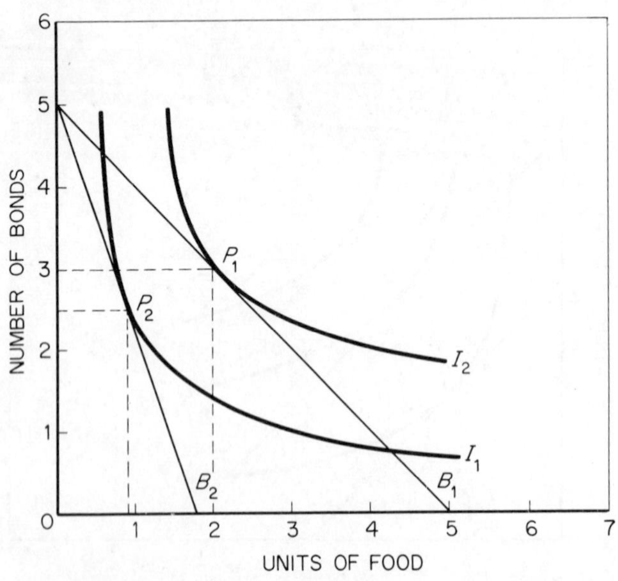

FIG. 2-3 Consumer Equilibrium Before and After A Price Change

consumer's given indifference map, his consumption of groceries would drop from 2 units to .9 units as a result of the shift in his budget line owing to the price change. In addition, because of the reduction in his budget-constraint line, he will also reduce his purchase of bonds from 3 to 2.5. Because his purchase of food has declined less proportionately than the increase in price, this consumer has less income to spend on bonds.

If this consumer's indifference map had been different, he might have reduced his purchases of food more than was the case in this illustration and, therefore, had more rather than less of his income available to buy bonds. However, because food is a necessity while bonds are a luxury, most consumers would probably behave like the one in our example and reduce their purchase of food less than proportionately when the price of food increased.

Constructing the Demand Curve

A demand curve for a product relates the various quantities of a commodity that will be bought at various prices. A shift in a demand curve, referred to as a "change in demand," therefore requires a change in some other factor; that is, in one of the variables, such as the price of other commodities; consumer income, taste, or habit; discovery of a new substitute; assumed constant in demand analysis. Such a shift must be distinguished from a movement along the demand curve, the latter usually referred to as a "change in quantity demanded," which is caused by a price change.

Indifference-curve analysis can be used to build the demand curve for any commodity whose price changes. We have already learned from Figure 2-3 that the quantity of food consumed at point P_1, 2 units, corresponds to a price for food of \$18.75 per unit, and that the quantity of food consumed at point P_2, .9 units, corresponds to a price of \$52.08 per unit. Assuming a linear demand curve, the two points derived from Figure 2-3 are sufficient to determine the demand curve for food, plotting price on the y-axis and quantity along the x-axis. The demand curve for units of food derived from the data in Figure 2-3 is presented in Figure 2-4, where P_1 and P_2 represent the two price-quantity points mentioned above.

The demand for bonds could have been developed in the same way—by holding the price of food constant and changing the price of bonds—to discover the consumer's equilibrium position at both prices; that is, the quantity of bonds he would buy at each price under equilibrium conditions.

Income and Substitution Effects

The *law of demand* suggests that when the price of a commodity increases, the quantity demanded normally decreases. Part of the reason for the change in quantity demanded is that the consumer's real income is reduced by higher prices. The reduction in real income is demonstrated by a leftward shift in the budget-restraint line (for example, from B_1 to B_2 in Figure 2-3). The income effect is measured by the loss of utility the consumer derives from his fixed

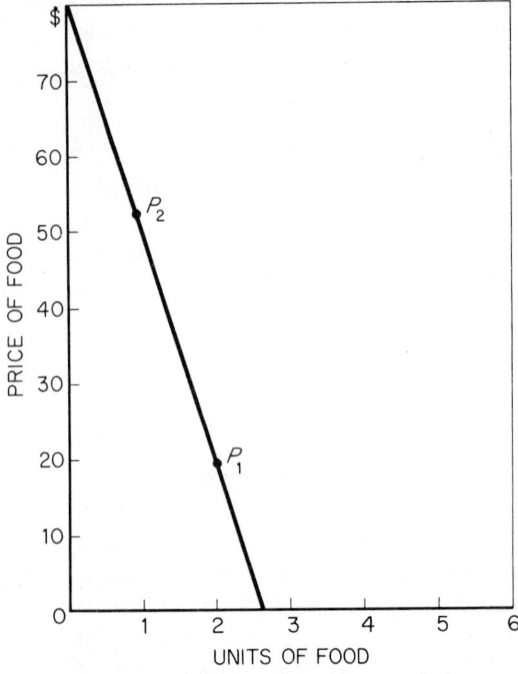

FIG. 2-4 Demand Curve for Food Derived from FIG. 2-3

money income. Higher prices shift the budget restraint to the left and move the point of tangency to a lower indifference curve. On the other hand, when the price of one good falls relative to another, the consumer will generally prefer the relatively cheaper good, and this preference is called the substitution effect.[2]

Generally, demand curves are constructed to include both substitution and income effects. However, if we desire to draw a demand curve that shows constant real income rather than constant money income, then the demand curve would include only the substitution effect without the income effect. How can we neutralize the income effect and show only the substitution effect? One method for eliminating the income effect is shown in Figure 2-5, where the consumer is assumed to spend his money on two commodities—food and clothes. The consumer starts in equilibrium at point *a*, the point of tangency between the B_1 budget-restraint line and the I_1 indifference curve. Now,

[2]This section on the income and substitution effects was suggested by M. Friedman, "The Marshallian Demand Curve," *Journal of Political Economy*, 57 (December 1949), 463–95. For the original idea, see Eugene Slutsky, "Sulla teoria del bilancio del consumatore," *Giornale degli economisti*, 51 (1915), 1–26, reprinted in G. J. Stigler and K. E. Boulding, eds., *Readings in Price Theory*, American Economic Association, Vol. VI (Homewood, Ill.: Richard D. Irwin, 1952), pp. 27–56.

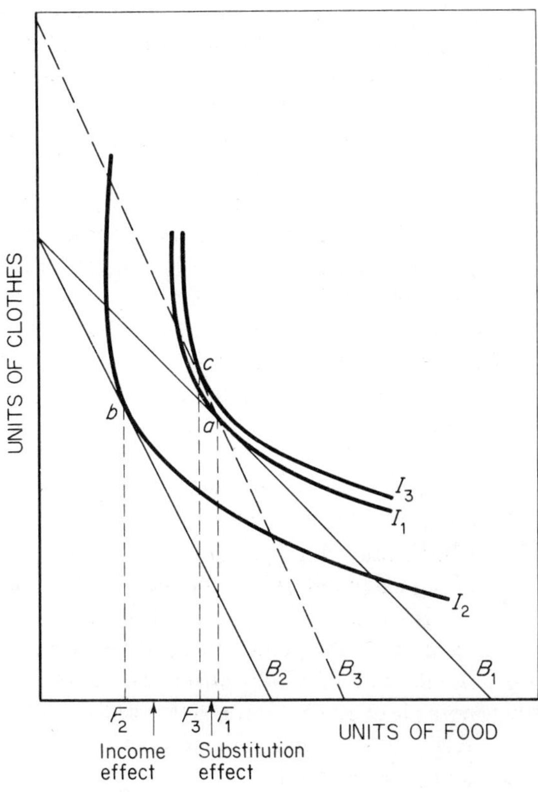

FIG. 2-5 Separating the Income and Substitution Effects by Means of a Compensating Income Change

assume the price of food increases so that his budget-restraint line shifts down to B_2. His new equilibrium occurs at point *b*, the point of tangency of the new B_2 budget-restraint line and the I_2 indifference curve. His consumption of food will shift from F_1 to F_2.

One practical method proposed to hold his apparent real income constant while retaining the new price relationship between food and clothes is to construct a new budget-restraint line, B_3, which passes through point *a* but is parallel to B_2. Drawing the lines parallel maintains the constant price ratio between the two goods, and drawing B_3 through point *a* restores a level of income with which the consumer could purchase the original bundle of goods, if he so desired. The new B_3 budget-restraint line is tangent to the I_3 indifference curve at point *c*, indicating that food consumption with the compensating income change will fall from F_1 to F_3, rather than from F_1 to F_2, as a result of the price increase. The restoration of the consumer's ability to buy the original bundle of goods after the price of food has increased actually permits him to attain a slightly higher indifference curve,

I_3 tangent to B_3 at point *c*, because the new B_3 budget-restraint line cuts through the old I_1 indifference curve at point *a*.[3]

For the individual consumer, it is clear that the distance between F_2 and F_3 in Figure 2-5 represents the income effect, and the distance between F_3 and F_1 represents the substitution effect. The substitution effect causes him to buy more clothes and less food at point *c* than at *a*, because clothes are now relatively cheaper. Separating the income and substitution effects is particularly significant from a macroeconomic point of view, because in the process of aggregation, the income effect tends to be neutralized. The income effect of the shift from B_1 to B_2 in our illustration because of higher food prices could in the aggregate be offset by a diversion of part of the consumer's income to the merchants he buys from. The substitution effect, which is entirely due to relative prices, would still hold in the aggregate, as consumers in general would prefer the now relatively cheaper clothes to the more expensive food. Consequently, resources will be diverted from food to clothes, and a mere change in the relative prices of two commodities does not affect the availability of productive resources in the aggregate, as long as they all remain fully employed. (The above disregards the partially offsetting effect of higher prices due to the increased demand for clothes.)

Because the quantity of productive resources remains constant, an increase in the demand for one commodity relative to other commodities should not generally affect the aggregate level of output, except for the possible effect that is due to the redistribution of income from buyers to sellers. A greater demand for one commodity does nothing to increase aggregate output, even if it leads to more production of the one good, since output of other goods must fall. Suppose, for example, that the price of medical services increases; the quantity of medical services demanded may remain about the same—if you fall off a horse and break an arm, the quantity of medical services demanded is fixed and you're not likely to dicker over the price with your orthopedist. The result of the higher price will be a transfer of real income from the patient to the doctor—in other words, after the price increase, the doctor can demand more real goods and services and the patient less.

On the other hand, a price increase in an industry in which buyers have the option to drop out may result in the sellers' receiving less income. For example, if the price of automobiles increases, most drivers have the option to drive their old cars longer and not buy a new car. The result may be that new-car sales will fall because of the price increase and that car sellers will

---

[3]Alternatively, J. R. Hicks, in *Value and Capital* (Oxford: Clarendon Press, 1939), Chaps. 1 and 2, proposes constructing the compensated budget restraint, B_3, tangent to I_1, so point *c* would fall on I_1. However, as a practical matter, the sum of money that would make it possible for the consumer to return to point *a* can be discovered, whereas the shape of indifference curve I_1 can only be roughly determined in a real-world situation, because the curve exists only inside the consumer's mind, and to derive the curve empirically would require an infinite number of observations. Therefore, it seems more practical to follow Slutsky's technique and keep the consumer's apparent real income constant by going through point *a* rather than attempting to hold real income constant by returning to I_1.

receive less income. The question of who receives income (as distinct from how much aggregate income is generated) can have a significant impact on the aggregate economy since the indifference curves of each individual will be distinct. Therefore the aggregate substitution effect might be different depending on who gains or loses from the price change.

In conclusion, indifference curves are a technique for presenting a theory of consumer behavior. Both the neoclassical and the Keynesian systems of macroeconomics are based on a world of consumers who order their choices, and who therefore may be described through indifference curves in terms of the representative consumer in this chapter. A major distinction between the neoclassical and Keynesian systems lies in the assumed order of preferences for present consumption relative to future consumption. The preference pattern of the typical neoclassical consumer is presented in Chapter 6 and that of the typical Keynesian consumer in Chapter 8. Now, however, we must consider other aspects of consumer demand, especially the responsiveness of quantity demanded by a consumer to changes in either price or income.

PRICE ELASTICITY OF DEMAND

The Concept of Elasticity

A demand curve, such as the one constructed in Figure 2-4 from the information derived from Figure 2-3, relates the various quantities of a commodity that consumers are willing and able to purchase at all possible prices. As we have seen, a typical demand curve is negatively sloped, indicating that at lower prices, consumers will buy larger quantities of the commodity.[4]

Although it can be generally concluded that as the price is decreased, the quantity demanded will increase, the question remains: How responsive is the quantity demanded to a given change in price? The slope of the demand curve indicates only the absolute change in quantity. More significant is the proportionate change in quantity associated with a given change in price, and that requires a different measure. The absolute change in quantity resulting from a given price change is uninformative because (1) it does not indicate whether total receipts will increase or decrease as a result of the price change; and (2) it does not permit a comparison of the relative response of demand of two commodities measured in different units (such as bales and bushels) or (3) it does not permit a comparison where there is a significant difference in price (a $5-per-unit change in the price of toasters would probably have a large effect on the quantity demanded, while a $5-per-unit change in the price of automobiles would have little effect on the quantity of automobiles de-

[4]If the demand curve at first makes you somewhat uncomfortable, it may be because economic theory has traditionally reversed the usual mathematical presentation in this case, by putting the independent variable on the vertical axis and the dependent variable on the horizontal axis.

manded). Measuring the slope of a demand curve does not even permit comparison between two different versions of the demand for the same commodity stated in different units. For example, the demand for raw cotton could be stated either in bales or in pounds, and if demand is stated in pounds, it would seem much more responsive to any given price change than would the same demand drawn up in bales.

Alfred Marshall proposed a scheme for measuring elasticity that eliminates difficulties due to differences in scale or measurement such as those just discussed.[5] Marshall proposed that a proper measure of elasticity would be the ratio between the percentage change in quantity and the related small percentage change in price. Each percentage change in quantity and price is itself the ratio between a given absolute change and some base, so the elasticity formula can be stated in either of the following two ways:

$$\epsilon = -\frac{\%Q}{\%P}$$

or

$$\epsilon = -\left(\frac{\Delta Q}{Q} \div \frac{\Delta P}{P}\right)$$

where Q equals the quantity demanded and P equals the price of the commodity. Since the normal demand curve has a negative slope, price elasticity of demand will normally be negative. (To avoid using negative signs, the absolute value, $|\epsilon|$, is used throughout the rest of this section.)

Point Elasticity

The shorter the length of the arc over which it is measured, the more precise is the concept of elasticity; therefore, it follows that the most precise measure of elasticity occurs when the ends of the arc approach each other and the length of the arc approaches zero. The concept of elasticity computed for such an arc is known as *point elasticity*, since the size of the arc approaches the size of a single point. In the previous section, we determined that the basic formula for measuring elasticity without regard to signs (+ or —) is

$$|\epsilon| = \left(\frac{\Delta Q}{Q} \div \frac{\Delta P}{P}\right)$$

That formula can be rewritten

$$|\epsilon| = \frac{\Delta Q}{Q} \times \frac{P}{\Delta P} = \frac{\Delta Q}{\Delta P} \times \frac{P}{Q}$$

In Figure 2-6, if we compute the elasticity of demand at point P_1, we will note first that triangle $P'OQ_2$ is similar to any included right triangle—for

[5] Alfred Marshall, *Principles of Economics*, 8th ed. (New York: Macmillan, 1920), pp. 102–04.

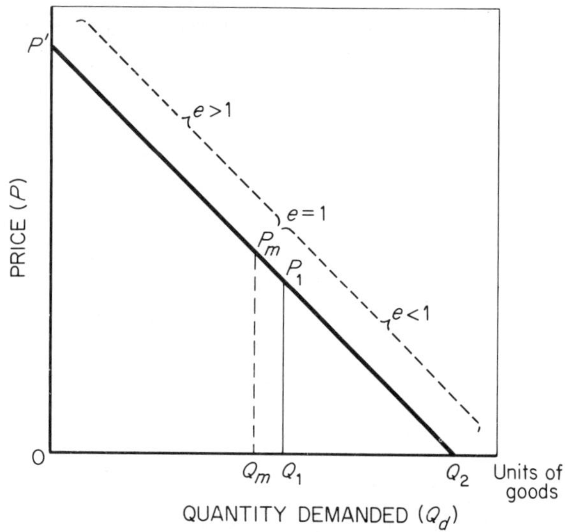

FIG. 2-6 Demand Curve Showing the Elastic and Inelastic Portions

example triangle $P_1Q_1Q_2$—because the ratios of the sides of similar triangles are equal. If price drops from P_1 to zero, quantity demanded would increase from Q_1 to Q_2. In computing the elasticity of demand at point P_1, we can represent the change in quantity by the line segment $\overline{Q_1Q_2}$ and the change in price by the line segment $\overline{P_1Q_1}$. If we use the line segment $\overline{P_1Q_1}$ for the base price and the line segment $\overline{OQ_1}$ for the base quantity, we may rewrite the elasticity formula

$$|\epsilon| = \frac{\Delta Q}{\Delta P} \times \frac{P}{Q} = \frac{\overline{Q_1Q_2}}{\overline{P_1Q_1}} \times \frac{\overline{P_1Q_1}}{\overline{OQ_1}} = \frac{\overline{Q_1Q_2}}{\overline{OQ_1}}$$

We may conclude that the coefficient of point elasticity can be determined by dropping a perpendicular from any point on a linear demand curve and reckoning the distance between the x-axis intercept of the perpendicular and the x-axis intercept of the demand curve (or of a tangent to the point on a nonlinear curve). The result is then divided by the distance between the origin and the x-axis intercept of the perpendicular to determine the elasticity coefficient.

It is obvious that the coefficient of elasticity at point P_m, the midpoint of a linear demand, must be unitary, since line segment $\overline{Q_mQ_2}$ equals $\overline{OQ_m}$. Therefore, the elasticity coefficient figured for any point to the right of the midpoint of the demand curve will be less than 1, and the elasticity coefficient figured for any point to the left of the midpoint on a linear demand must be greater than 1. The closer the point gets to the y-axis intercept of the demand curve, the larger the coefficient of elasticity will be, and the closer it gets to the x-axis intercept, the smaller it will be.

The significance of the measure of elasticity is that it enables us to determine whether a point on the demand curve is relatively elastic, inelastic, or of unitary elasticity. Whenever the coefficient of elasticity is greater than 1, the demand curve is elastic; whenever it is less than 1, the demand curve is inelastic; and when the coefficient of elasticity equals 1, the demand is unitarily elastic.

The elasticity coefficient indicates what effect, if any, a given price change will have on an individual's total expenditures on any commodity. When price is decreased and demand is elastic, total expenditures by the individual increase; if the price is decreased and demand is inelastic, the total expenditures decrease. In other words, price and total expenditures are inversely related where the demand is elastic and are directly related where the demand is inelastic. Where the coefficient of elasticity equals 1, a price change does not change total expenditures. Knowledge of the value of the coefficient of elasticity allows firms to determine beforehand what effect any given price change will have on their total receipts, since total expenditures by individuals for a given product sold by a particular firm are equal to the total receipts of the business firm.

Demand elasticity permits full knowledge of the effect on total revenue of any given change in price, including the price of resources. For example, controversy has centered about the effect of wage increases on the aggregate income of workers. However, this controversy often disregards the all-important question of whether the economy is operating in an elastic or inelastic segment of the demand curve for labor. If the demand for labor is elastic, a wage increase causes a reduction in the total wage bill; if the demand for labor is inelastic, as most unions seem to assume, the total wage bill will increase when wages rise. Since wages make up some two thirds of our total aggregate income, it is clear that the elasticity of demand for labor has far-reaching implications for the distribution of aggregate income. In fact, the size of the total wage bill is a question of central importance in macro theories, once price and wage changes are introduced into the model.

Other factors besides the position of the demand curve help determine the degree of elasticity of demand for a product or resource. The more uses there are for a commodity or resource and the more good substitutes there are, the more elastic will be the demand. For example, the demand for aluminum is likely to be more elastic than the demand for molybdinum, partly because aluminum has more uses and more useful substitutes in most of its applications.

ENGEL CURVES

The Concept of the Engel Curve

Change in consumer income is a particularly important cause of changes in consumer demand. In fact, a function has been designed to relate the consumption of a commodity to consumer income. That function is known as the

Engel curve, named after Ernst Engel (1821–1896), head of the Prussian Bureau of Statistics, who first described the relationship between the level of income and the consumption of certain commodities.[6] Engel discovered that the proportion of income spent on food tends on the average to decrease as income increases, other things remaining equal, a relationship now known as *Engel's Law*.

Engel curves may be derived very similarly to demand curves, by using an indifference-curve model. The consumer's income is first changed without changing the price of commodities. Then the points of tangency between the indifference curves and parallel budget-restraint lines are found. Finally, the quantities of consumption of one commodity are plotted against the corresponding income levels. Figure 2-7, which essentially reproduces Figure 2-2, can be used to illustrate the construction of an Engel curve from indifference curves and budget-restraint lines. The figure shows the consumer's indifference curves for products, bonds and food, and two budget restraint lines. In the first instance, with a budget of $60, the consumer buys 1.3 units of food. Then, with his budget increased to $93.75, he consumes two units of food. Since the prices of the commodities are unchanged, the two budget lines are parallel.

The Engel curve for food is plotted from the information above in Figure 2-8, measuring money income along the vertical axis and units of food consumed along the horizontal axis. Point P_1 corresponds to a budget of $60

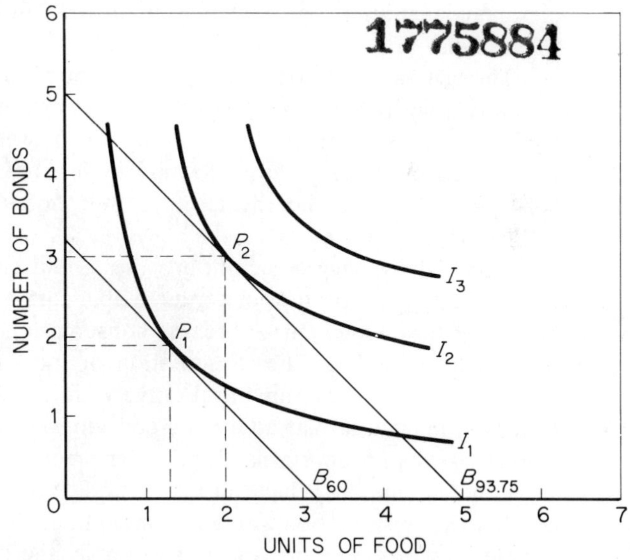

FIG. 2-7 Consumer Equilibrium Before and After an Income Change

[6] J. A. Schumpeter, *History of Economic Analysis* (New York: Oxford University Press, 1954), p. 961.

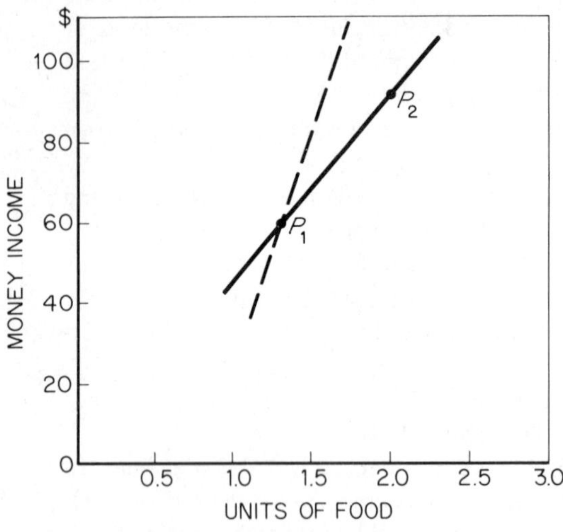

FIG. 2-8 Engel Curve for Food

and consumption of 1.3 units, and point P_2 corresponds to an income level of \$93.75 and consumption of 2 units. Therefore, the consumer discussed in our illustration is atypical, since he spends about the same proportion of his higher income on food as he did of his lower income. A more typical consumer would have an Engel curve for food more like the dotted line in Figure 2-8.

The general characteristic of an Engel curve plotted for a normal good is that it is positively sloped, showing that as income increases, consumption tends to increase. This positive relationship between income and consumption, noted empirically since the mid-1800's, has become one of the key concepts in the Keynesian theory of macroeconomics, which will be described in Chapter 8.[7]

Engel curves suggest significant clues about consumption patterns. For example, the consumption of certain stable commodities, such as salt, may have a vertical Engel curve, because consumption remains constant almost regardless of income. The consumption of most necessities, such as food and clothing, will have an Engel curve with an increasing slope as income increases, indicating that additional consumption of these commodities increases less than proportionately as income increases.

Other commodities have an Engel curve with a decreasing slope, indicating that the consumption of those commodities increases more than proportionately as income increases. For example, the consumption of vacation-travel services, education, and landscape architecture all tend to increase

[7]When the Engel-curve concept is introduced in macroeconomic theory in Chapter 8, the axes are reversed, with income plotted on the x-axis and consumption plotted on the y-axis, to follow the traditional presentation.

more than proportionately at higher income levels. (The increasing consumption of education, in turn, generally leads to further increases in income levels.)

In certain rare cases, the consumption of some commodities may even decrease as incomes increase. Such commodities, called inferior goods, have backward-bending Engel curves. For example, the consumption of bread may be reduced at higher incomes, as families substitute other food items in their diet.

Income Elasticity of Demand

The formula for deriving the elasticity of Engel curves is similar to the formula for deriving the elasticity of demand, except that the Engel curve is normally positively sloped whereas the demand curve is negatively sloped. The income-elasticity formula (ϵ_e) is

$$\epsilon_e = \frac{\Delta Q}{Q} \div \frac{\Delta Y}{Y}$$

where Q equals the quantity demanded and Y equals income.

The determination of a consumer's income elasticity can be determined very simply by extending the Engel curve to the x-axis, as has been done in Figure 2-9. If the extension passes through the y-axis as line E does, the Engel curve is elastic, because the intersection with the y-axis before reaching the x-axis indicates that a greater proportionate change occurs in quantity consumed than in money income. On the other hand, if the Engel curve intercepts the x-axis at a positive value (to the right of the y-axis), as line E' does, then we would say that the curve is inelastic, because a proportionately greater change occurs in money income than in quantity consumed. Finally, if the extension of the curve passes through the origin, the coefficient of elasticity equals 1, because the change in quantity consumed would always be proportionate to the change in money income. By using the point-elasticity

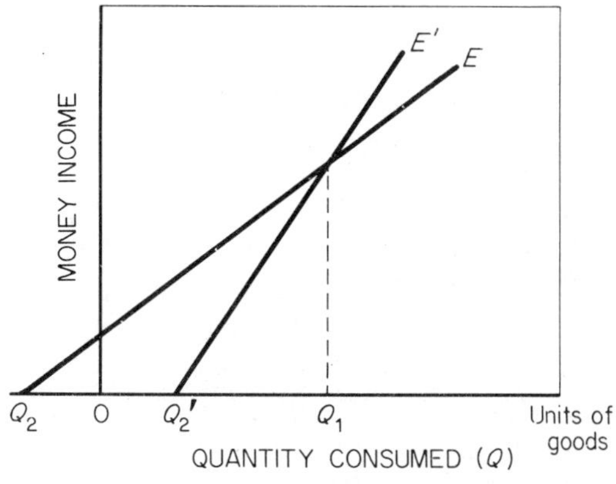

FIG. 2-9 Engel Curve to Demonstrate Elasticity

concept, we can demonstrate that the above relationships will hold concerning the elasticity of Engel curves. The point-elasticity formula as applied to income elasticity is as follows:

$$\epsilon_e = \frac{\overline{Q_1Q_2}}{\overline{OQ_1}}$$

It is clear that for curve E in Figure 2-9, the income-elasticity coefficient would be greater than 1, since the x-axis intercept of curve E occurs to the left of the origin, indicating that line segment $\overline{Q_1Q_2} > \overline{OQ_1}$. The x-axis intercept of curve E', on the other hand, occurs to the right of the origin, showing that line segment $\overline{Q_1Q_2'} < \overline{OQ_1}$, so the elasticity of E' is less than 1. It is also clear that for any curve that passes through the origin, the coefficient of elasticity would always equal 1, since Q_1 would occur at the origin, forcing line segment $\overline{Q_1Q_2}$ to equal $\overline{OQ_1}$.

AGGREGATING CONSUMER MARKET BEHAVIOR

The demand functions of individual consumers can be aggregated through a process of horizontal summation to form the market demand for a particular commodity. The process of horizontal summation is illustrated in Figure 2-10. Assume that the market is made up of two consumers, A and B, each of whom has a straight-line demand curve for commodity X. The aggregate-market demand is derived by simply summing horizontally the two individual demand curves, D_a and D_b. For example, at a price of \$1.50, consumer A would buy 5 units of X and consumer B would buy 4 units of X; therefore, the aggregate quantity demanded at a price of \$1.50 equals 9 units of good X. At a price of \$.60 per unit, consumer A would buy 14 and consumer B would buy 11 units of X; therefore, the aggregate quantity demanded at a price of \$.60 would be 25 units. By calculating the amount of goods both consumer A and consumer B will purchase at various prices, our aggregate-market demand curve can be constructed. Such a curve, labeled ΣD, is plotted in Figure 2-10. Because D_a and D_b are linear, the aggregate-market demand, ΣD, is also a linear function. In general, the market demand for any commodity is equal to a horizontal summation of the individual demand curves of the consumers who constitute the market for that commodity. In our illustration, for simplicity, we have assumed only two consumers; however, any number could be accommodated. The aggregate-market demand, like the individual demand, relates the various quantities that consumers would be willing and able to buy at all possible prices.

The responsiveness of market demand to a change in market price depends on the marginal purchases caused by the price change. Marginal change in quantity demanded may be due either to incremental purchases by consumers already in the market or to incremental consumers attracted to the market (or repelled from it) by the price change.

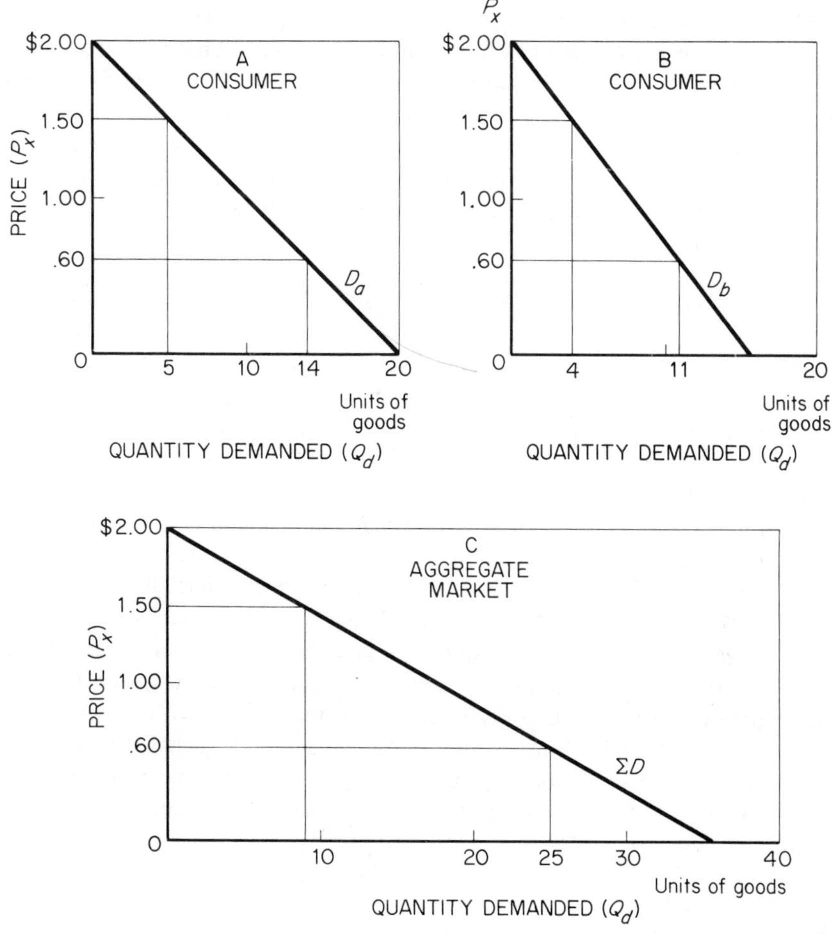

FIG. 2-10 Individual and Market Demand Curves

Likewise, all the individual Engel curves for any commodity can also be summed horizontally to derive an aggregate-market Engel curve relating consumption of a particular commodity to all possible levels of income. Then in turn each market curve for a given commodity can be summed horizontally to construct an aggregate Engel curve for a particular commodity. If Engel curves for each commodity could be summed, an aggregate Engel curve for the whole economy could be constructed.

The Engel curve is the concept underlying the consumption function, a major theoretical construct in Keynesian macroeconomics. The consumption function is, in effect, an aggregate Engel curve used to describe the relationship between the consumption of *all* commodities in general to various levels of aggregate income. The relationship of aggregate consumption to aggregate income, which is designated as the consumption function in Chapter 8, becomes one cornerstone of the Keynesian theory of macroeconomics.

The response of all individual consumers determines the responsiveness of aggregate consumption to changes in income. That responsiveness, or the elasticity of the Engel curve or consumption function, depends on the income elasticity of demand for all goods relative to the elasticity of demand for savings as aggregate income changes. In fact, the level and elasticity of the consumption function is a major determinant of how the economy reacts to a change in many exogenous variables, such as government spending and taxes.

SUMMARY AND CONCLUSIONS

In this chapter we have developed the theory of consumer behavior, using indifference curves and budget-restraint lines. The theory of consumer behavior is based on the decision-making processes of rational consumers. Diminishing marginal utility is a sufficient condition for inferring that a normal demand curve would be negatively sloped. However, the constraint imposed by a limited budget indicates that even in the absence of diminishing marginal utility, the demand curve for any normal good would still have to be negatively sloped, because the limited budget that all consumers have at any point in time will have to be divided among several commodities.

The advantage of indifference-curve theory over utility theory is that the indifference-curve approach does not require the assumption that utility be directly measurable. Maximum consumer satisfaction occurs when the consumer is spending his total budget in such a way that the marginal rate of substitution of good Y for good X equals the price ratio of the two goods. In formula form, ignoring the minus signs, this is expressed

$$\frac{\Delta Q_y}{\Delta Q_x} = \frac{P_x}{P_y}$$

This equality of the marginal rate of substitution and the price ratio occurs at the point of tangency between an indifference curve and a budget-restraint line, since the slope of the indifference curve is the marginal rate of substitution, and the slope of the budget-restraint line is the price ratio of the two goods.

The techniques employed in this chapter can be used to derive demand curves that relate the consumption of commodities to the price charged, or to derive Engel curves that relate the consumption of commodities to the various levels of consumer income.

The degree of response by the dependent variable, quantity, to a given change in the independent variable, either price or income, is known as elasticity. The greater the percentage change in quantity in relation to a given percentage change in price or income, the more elastic is the demand curve or Engel curve. In computing elasticity, we employ the point-elasticity method, which defines the elasticity at a given point on a demand or Engel curve.

We also found that when the price level changes, there is both an income effect and a substitution effect, and that the income effect may balance out in the aggregate but the substitution effect would not.

In the last section, we found that consumer demand curves or individual Engel curves can be aggregated to form market curves and that an aggregate Engel curve for the whole economy is basic for understanding Keynesian macroeconomics.

The theory of consumer behavior described in this chapter is only half the theory of microeconomics, because in addition to the willingness and ability of consumers to buy goods, we must also consider the production of those goods that makes them available in the marketplace. The theory of production is the topic of our next chapter.

QUESTIONS AND PROBLEMS

1. Why might the substitution effect be more significant than the income effect in aggregate economic analysis?
2. Why might a simple horizontal summation of individual demand curves give misleading results in constructing a market demand?
3. What is the consumer's goal assumed to be? Does it seem realistic?
4. What determines the slope of the budget line? What determines its level?
5. List the factors that underlie a consumer's indifference curves.
6. Describe how a rational consumer reaches his equilibrium.
7. Why are indifference curves normally negatively sloped and concave from above?
8. Under what conditions of demand elasticity might a business firm be better off lowering its price?
9. "The demand curve for a monopolist is always inelastic." Comment.
10. What can an aggregate Engel curve reveal about:
    a. A particular product
    b. Consumption in general
11. Why is the elasticity coefficient positive for an Engel curve and negative for a demand curve?
12. Suppose $P_y = \$2$ and $P_x = \$3$. Given the following indifference curves, plot the consumer's Engel curve for X on top of page 42, assuming that the consumer's income changed from \$60 to \$72. (Assume a straight-line function.)

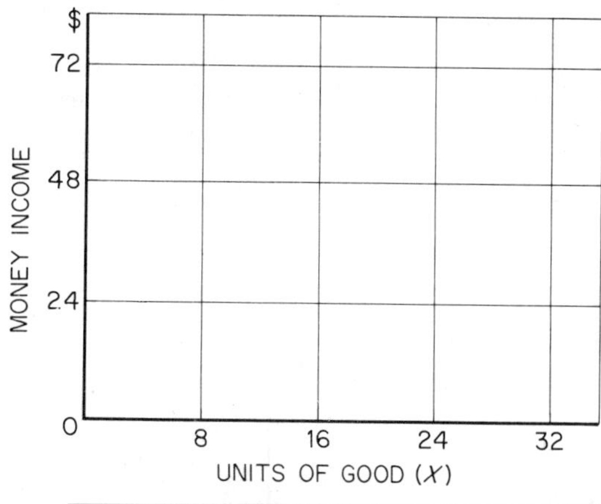

Problem 12

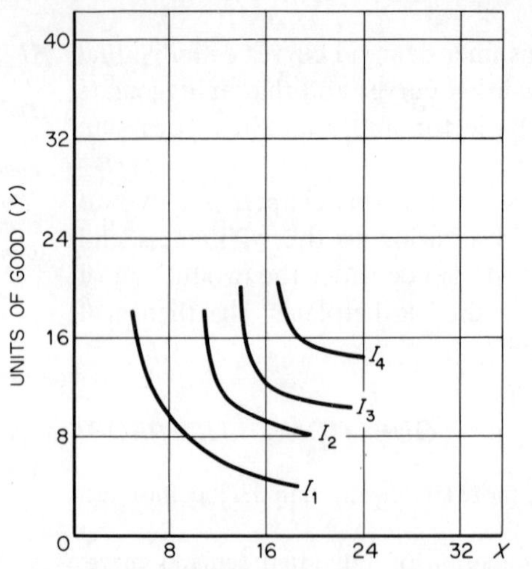

Problem 12 (continued)

13. Plot this consumer's demand for X, assuming that $P_y = \$2$, his budget = \$60, and P_x changes from \$3 to \$2. Include both the income and substitution effects.

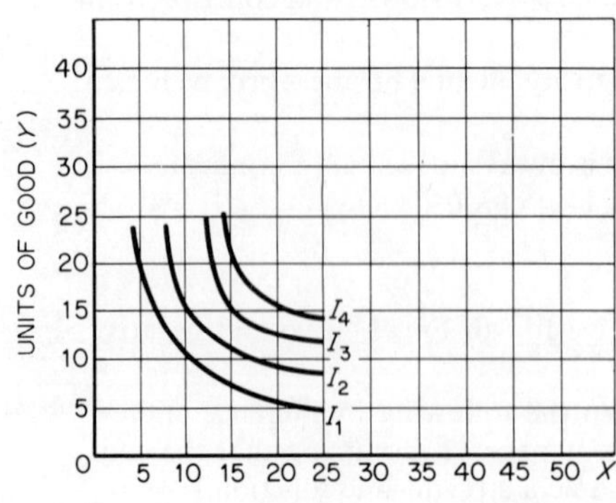

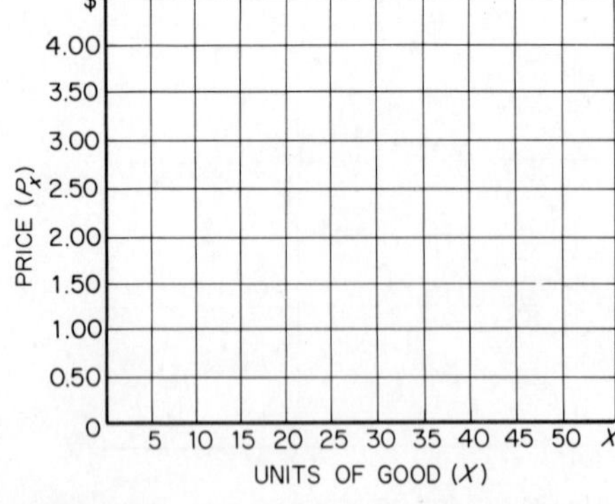

Problem 13

ADDITIONAL SELECTED REFERENCES

THEORY OF DEMAND

ALCHIAN, ARMEN A., "The Meaning of Utility Measurement," *American Economic Review*, 43 (March 1953), 26–50.

CLARKSON, GEOFFREY P. E., *The Theory of Consumer Demand.* Englewood Cliffs, N.J.: Prentice-Hall, 1963.

COCHRANE, W. W., and C. S. BELL, *The Economics of Consumption.* New York: McGraw-Hill, 1956.

HICKS, J. R., *A Revision of Demand Theory*. London: Oxford Univeristy Press, 1956.

SELECTED ARTICLES FOR ADVANCED STUDENTS

ALLEN, R. G. D., "The Nature of Indifference Curves," *Review of Economic Studies*, 1 (February 1934), 110–21.

———, "A Comparison Between Different Definitions of Complementary and Competitive Goods," *Econometrica*, 2 (April 1934), 168–75.

———, "Professor Slustsky's Theory of Consumers' Choice," *Review of Economic Studies*, 3 (February 1936), 120–29.

CLARK, J. M., "Realism and Relevance in the Theory of Demand," *Journal of Political Economy*, 54 (August 1946), 347–53.

HOLT, C. C., and P. A. SAMUELSON, "The Graphic Depiction of Elasticity of Demand," *Journal of Political Economy*, 54 (August 1946), 354–57.

HOUTHAKKER, H. S., "An International Comparison of Household Expenditure Patterns, Commemorating the Century of Engel's Law," *Econometrica*, 25 (October 1957), 532–51.

LERNER, A. P., "The Diagrammatical Representation of Elasticity of Demand," *Review of Economic Studies*, 1 (October 1933), 39–44.

RICCI, UMBERTO, "Pareto and Pure Economics," *Review of Economic Studies*, 1 (October 1933), 3–21.

WEINTRAUB, SIDNEY, "The Foundations of the Demand Curve," *American Economic Review*, 32 (September 1942), 538–52.

The Microeconomic Foundations of Macroeconomics—Supply

3

In the previous chapter, we considered the theory of consumer demand as the basis for economic activity. However, the consumption of commodities is impossible without their production. Therefore, in this chapter we consider the other half of microeconomic theory—the production of goods and services—that is, the supply side of the market in contrast with the demand side.

THE PRODUCTION FUNCTION

The production function, whether for an individual firm or for an aggregate economy, is a statement that relates output of a finished product to inputs of resources; it relates the amount of resource inputs to the specific amount of output those resources produce. The production function may be stated

$$TP = f_3(N, R, K, T)$$

where TP equals total product, N is the employment of labor, R is the quantity of natural resources, K is the amount of capital, and T is the level of technology—that is, the current state of knowledge as applied to the productive process.

Although individual units of given resources may in reality differ in productivity, the assumption is generally made for analytical purposes that each individual unit of a given resource is the same. Unless otherwise noted, this assumption of homogeneous resources will be maintained throughout this book.

Since the firm's output is a function of the inputs of the various resources, the level of output can be increased or decreased only by increasing or decreasing the quantity or quality of resource inputs. Furthermore, since resources can to some extent substitute for one another in the productive process, various combinations of resources may be used to produce the same level of output. For example, 4 units of labor and 1 of capital may be employed together to produce 10 units of output, while the same output may also be produced with 3 units of capital and 1 of labor. Or, to consider the phenomenon of resource substitution from another angle, the level of output may be varied by varying the inputs of one resource while holding all the others constant.

The ability of a firm or of an economy to vary resource inputs depends partly on how much time is allowed to make the change. A time period too short to vary inputs and outputs at all is known as the "very short run." The actual calendar time will vary depending on the business. For instance, the very short run for a hamburger stand may be half an hour—a time period too short even to buy more buns and rolls; while the very short run for a coffee fazenda may be six or seven years—the time required to bring new trees into production.

When sufficient time is allowed to vary some inputs but not all, economists describe the situation as the "short run." For example, a firm producing toasters may be able to change its output by hiring more workers and buying more steel, plastic, and wire, but still not be able to change its plant and equipment inputs, which generally require more time to change than do labor and raw materials. In such a situation, capital (plant and equipment) is the fixed factor, and the others are variable. In macroeconomics, when we refer to "short-run analysis," we mean that firms in the economy have enough time to vary their employment of labor but not enough time to change their plant and equipment or the level of technology they incorporate.

The "long run" means that enough time is allowed to vary all resource inputs except technological change, which is usually assumed constant. The long run will vary from one industry to another. A hamburger stand may be able to vary its plant and equipment in a week, while a manufacturing plant might require eighteen months. Therefore, the market-supply curve is a function of time, with all resources being held constant in the very short run, some of them being held constant in the short run, and all of them variable in the long run.

Macroeconomic analysis generally disregards the very short run and pays only passing attention to the long run (except in the matter of economic growth). Instead, it concentrates on the short run, in the sense that natural resources, capital, and the level of technology are held fixed and only labor resources are variable. Problems of unemployed workers and rising prices are usually restricted to short-run analysis. And any questions of unemployed or overemployed plant capacity are short run by definition, since the total amount of capital remains unchanged when capital is unemployed or overemployed.

The Firm's Production Function

As the inputs of one resource are increased, holding all other resources constant, the rate of increase in total output of the finished product may at first increase; but beyond some point, according to the law of diminishing returns, the rate of increase in total product will decrease. Eventually, total product will decrease absolutely when the employment of the variable resource becomes excessive.

Suppose, for example, we consider labor to be the variable resource used with a fixed amount of capital on a 20-acre cotton farm. The response of total product to the input of labor will be fairly dependable. Table 3-1 illustrates

TABLE 3-1 Production Schedules for a Cotton Farm

Fixed Resources		Variable Resource	Total Product *TP*	Marginal Product of Labor MP_L	Average Product of Labor AP_L
(1) *Quantity of Land R*	(2) *Quantity of Capital K*	(3) *Quantity of Labor N*	(4) *Bales of Cotton*	(5)	(6)
20 Acres	1 tractor	1	1.5	1.5	1.5
20 Acres	1 tractor	2	5	3.5	2.50
20 Acres	1 tractor	3	10	5	3.33
20 Acres	1 tractor	4	16	6	4
20 Acres	1 tractor	5	20	4	4
20 Acres	1 tractor	6	23	3	3.83
20 Acres	1 tractor	7	25	2	3.57
20 Acres	1 tractor	8	26	1	3.25
20 Acres	1 tractor	9	26	0	2.89
20 Acres	1 tractor	10	25	−1	2.50

the principle of diminishing returns, in this case to the labor factor. Typically, land and capital are assumed to be fixed in the short run, and the employment of labor is assumed to be variable. In our illustration in Table 3-1, the first two columns show the inputs of the fixed factors, land (R) plus capital (K). The third column gives the input of the variable resource, labor (N). The fourth column shows the total product (TP), and the fifth column the rate of change in total product—that is, marginal product of labor (MP_L). (Marginal product, MP, is defined as the change in the total product that results from employing one additional unit of a resource.) The sixth column lists the average product of labor (AP_L), which is computed by taking column 4 and dividing it by column 3. The farm in this illustration is assumed to have 20 acres of land, and its capital equipment consists of one tractor. The first worker hired is able, working alone, to produce 1.5 bales of cotton. Since output equals zero in the absence of any workers, the marginal product or incremental output attributable to the first worker is 1.5 bales. The average product of the first worker is also 1.5 bales, since average product, *AP*, equals the total product divided by the number of units of the variable resource, in this case labor.

When the second worker is employed, the total product increases from 1.5 bales to 5 bales. Therefore, the second worker is responsible for adding 3.5 bales to the total product, and the average product of each of the first two workers employed equals 5 bales divided by 2, or 2.5 bales. In Table 3-1, diminishing returns set in after the fourth worker is hired, because the marginal product added by the fourth worker is 6 bales, which is the highest value in the marginal-product schedule.

The data from Table 3-1 are plotted in Figure 3-1, with the total-product curve, *TP*, plotted in the upper panel. The average product of labor, AP_L,

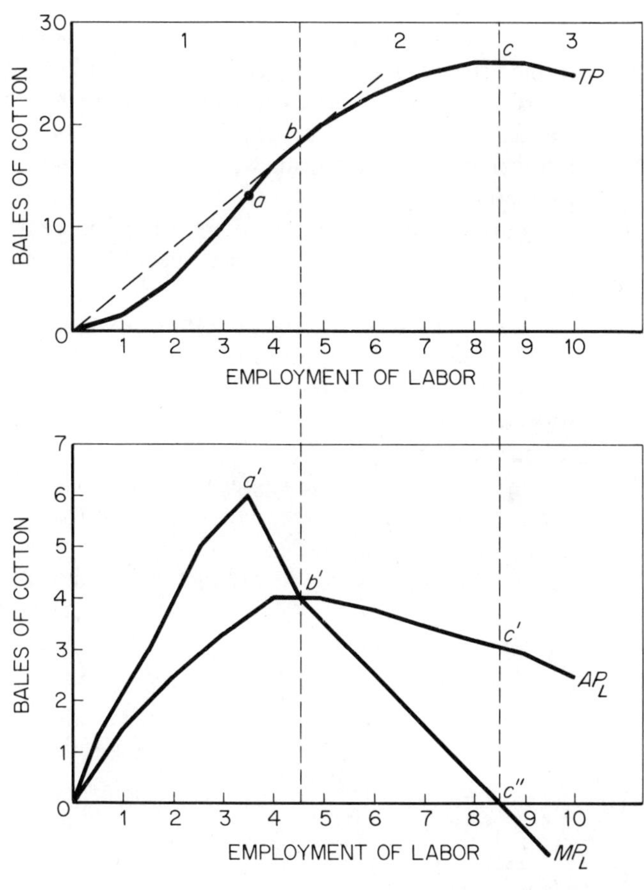

FIG. 3-1 Stages of Production

and the marginal product of labor, MP_L, are plotted in the lower panel.[1] The point of inflection in the TP curve, point a, is the point where the rate of change in output per unit of labor hits a peak and begins to decrease thereafter. Up to point a, TP increases at an increasing rate, and from point a to point c it increases at a decreasing rate. The MP_L in the lower panel measures the rate of change in TP. Therefore, MP_L, the slope of the TP curve at each point, reaches a peak with the employment of the fourth worker at point a', directly below point a on the TP curve. The AP_L curve increases up to point b' directly below point b on the TP curve. MP_L exceeds AP_L to the left of point b' and falls below AP_L to the right of b'. The relevant segment of the MP_L curve is the part that is positive and below the AP_L curve, since to the left of b' each new worker raises the AP_L of all workers and so makes all workers more efficient. To the right of c'' each new worker reduces TP, which hits a peak at point c.

The Aggregate Production Function

A short-run aggregate production function based on and similar in shape to the firm's production function will be used in Chapters 6 and 12 to represent the aggregate-production function for the economy, both in the neoclassical and Keynesian models. We will also assume that as employment of a resource increases, aggregate output will increase at a decreasing rate owing to diminishing returns.

Furthermore, in both chapters, labor will be used as the variable input, since labor is generally conceded to be the variable resource in short-run aggregate models.

Ideally, both labor inputs and the output of finished goods would refer to homogeneous units of labor and goods. Unfortunately, such uniformity is unrealistic in the aggregate. Therefore, in practice we must settle for a weighted index of man-hours to represent labor input and a production index to represent output.

In applying a simple aggregation of firms' production functions to the aggregate economy, we proceed on the implicit assumption that both the input and the output indexes contain virtually the same types of workers and goods as we move along the production function. We can only hope that the assumptions above do not distort reality so much that the results of aggregate analysis are meaningless.

---

[1] Marginal values are often plotted at the midpoint between two adjacent levels of output to indicate that the change occurs as one moves from one level of output to the next, as we have done in Figure 3-1 and the other figures in this chapter that use marginal values.

THE LEAST-COST COMBINATION OF RESOURCES UNDER PERFECT COMPETITION

Assumptions of Perfect Competition

Much of the following analysis, including the assumptions of a constant product price and a constant resource price, is based on the assumption that the firm buys its resources and sells its output in perfectly competitive markets. A perfectly competitive market is one in which the following conditions exist: (1) A very large number of purchasers buy from a very large number of sellers. The number must be so large that no individual buyer or seller can appreciably influence the price or the quantity sold. This applies to both the resource and the product market. (2) All the sellers of resources and commodities are offering for sale a completely homogeneous product; each unit of each resource or product is identical to all other units of that resource or product, so buyers have no preference for one supplier over another. (3) The firms and all the resources the firms use to produce their output are freely mobile within the country. There is the possibility of free, unhampered entry and exit of firms and of resource suppliers to any market, so markets offering the highest return will be able to attract firms and resources away from markets offering lower returns. (4) Good market knowledge exists, so users and suppliers of products and resources are aware of the general market condition regarding the availability and prices of the products and resources they want to buy. (5) The behavioral assumptions of perfect competition are that business firms are trying to maximize profits and that consumers are trying to maximize utility. (6) There are no market restrictions or imperfections, such as legislative restrictions on the entry of new firms into industries, government price supports, collusion on the part of firms or resource suppliers to limit prices or output (monopolistic labor unions would be included in this injunction), or artificial restrictions, such as industry codes that prohibit the use of prefabricated buildings or particular materials in construction. (7) Since we assume the existence of a very large number of sellers, we implicitly assume that sellers who are very small relative to the size of the market can be efficient. And finally, (8) under perfect competition, it is necessary to assume that prices are freely flexible and that they are not set by custom or convention or through any rule-of-thumb process, such as a standard markup over cost, because the effect of such a customary method of price determination might not lead to profit maximization. (Some would argue that a businessman's desire for profits will lead him to employ profit-maximizing behavior even when he thinks he is using a rule of thumb, just as a good billiards player does not consciously employ the rules of physics.)

The Firm's Demand and Supply for Resources

How does the perfectly competitive firm determine from all the possibilities available which particular combination of resources to employ? Table

3-2 presents the relevant production data abstracted from Table 3-1 (columns 1, 2, and 3), combined with additional information on the selling price of the finished product (column 4) and the resource price (column 7). We still

TABLE 3-2 Employment and Output of Labor Under Pure Competition

(1) Quantity of Labor N	(2) Marginal Product of Labor MP_L	(3) Total Product TP	(4) Product Price P_x	(5) Total Revenue TR	(6) Marginal-Revenue Product MRP_L = (2) × (4)	(7) Resource Price Per Unit of Labor (P_L) or Marginal-Resource Cost (MRC_L)
5	4	20	$100	$2,000	$400	$200
6	3	23	100	2,300	300	200
7	2	25	100	2,500	200	200
8	1	26	100	2,600	100	200
9	0	26	100	2,600	–0–	200

assume the land input to be fixed at 20 acres and the capital input to be fixed at one tractor. We assume further that the selling price of the finished product (P_X), cotton, is \$100 per bale (column 4). Column 5 lists the total revenue of the cotton farm, which is column 3 times column 4. The change in total revenue (TR) that occurs because of the 1-unit change in the employment of the variable factor is known as the marginal revenue product (MRP) of that factor, shown in column 6. It can be seen from Table 3-2 that marginal-revenue product of labor (MRP_L) would be equal to the marginal product of labor (MP_L) multiplied by the price per bale (P_x). Column 2 times column 4 equals column 6, or

$$MRP_L = MP_L \times P_x$$

The wage, or price of labor (P_l in column 7), is the marginal cost of labor to the firm or marginal resource cost (MRC_L), assumed to be \$200.

How many workers will the firm employ in this illustration? The fifth worker is responsible for adding 4 bales of cotton to total output; therefore his contribution to total revenue (MRP_L) is \$400, but his wage cost to the firm is only \$200. Therefore, the fifth worker will be hired. The sixth worker is responsible for adding 3 bales to total output, so his marginal-revenue product of \$300 is also greater than his additional cost to the firm. The seventh worker is responsible for adding 2 bales of cotton to the total output, and therefore he adds \$200 to the firm's income, which is just equal to his wage of \$200. This firm will hire up to seven workers but will not hire the eighth worker, who only brings \$100 into the firm while costing \$200. Therefore, when the firm is maximizing its profits, the marginal-revenue product of labor (MRP_L) equals the price of labor (P_L). In summary, the firm maximizes profits where

$$MRP_L = P_L$$

or

$$MRP_L = MRC_L$$

The constant wage level defines the supply curve of labor when the firm employs labor under competitive conditions, since each firm employs a small enough number of workers that it can hire all it wishes without affecting the wage rate, and the same would be true of any resource employed under perfect competition.

The marginal-revenue product function of any resource is the firm's demand for that resource, because the marginal-revenue product for any level of employment indicates the highest price the firm would be willing to pay for each given amount of the resource.

Resource Supply-and-Demand Equilibrium for the Competitive Market

The market demand for any resource could be calculated by a horizontal summation of all the individual firms' demand curves for that resource (MRP) if we disregard external effects. However, external effects, or externalities, may be significant and occur even in perfect competition, because changes in employment of a resource change the level of output for the entire industry, which in turn can change the product price and rebound to affect the resource demand function. For example, if the price of labor decreases, the actual quantity of labor demanded will not be as great as the apparent requirement for labor before the change, since the decrease in price necessary to sell the added output reduces the MRP_L, the firm's demand curve for the resource.

Figure 3-2 demonstrates how to derive the market-demand curve for labor under these assumptions. The MRP_{L_1} curve for the firm in panel A is plotted from Table 3-2. If the initial price of farm labor is \$200, then the firm would hire 7 workers. If we assume there are 1,000 firms (cotton producers) in the market, then 7,000 workers would be hired in the industry at a wage of \$200; thus point a in panel B is one point on the market-demand curve D_m for labor.

Suppose that the price of labor falls to \$100. Assuming that enough workers are available, each firm will increase its employment of labor and therefore its output of cotton. The consequence is that the market price of the product will fall from \$100, say, to \$67, and the individual firm's demand curve for labor will shift downward to MRP_{L_2} in panel A of Figure 3-2. When all adjustments have been made, each firm will hire 7.5 workers at the reduced wage of \$100. Multiplying 7.5 workers by 1,000 firms, we get 7,500 workers, the total number employed at \$100. Thus, point b in panel B of Figure 3-2

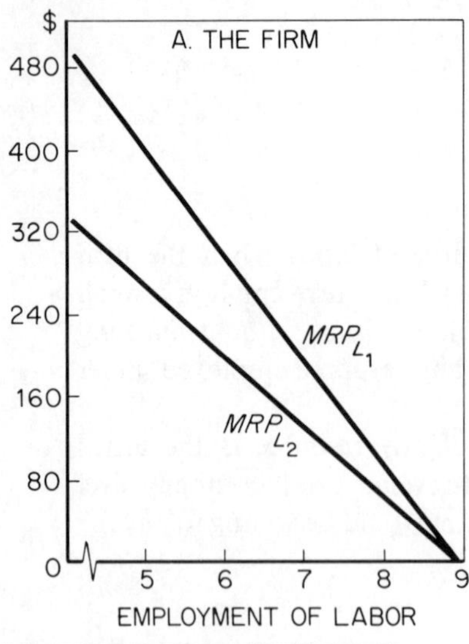

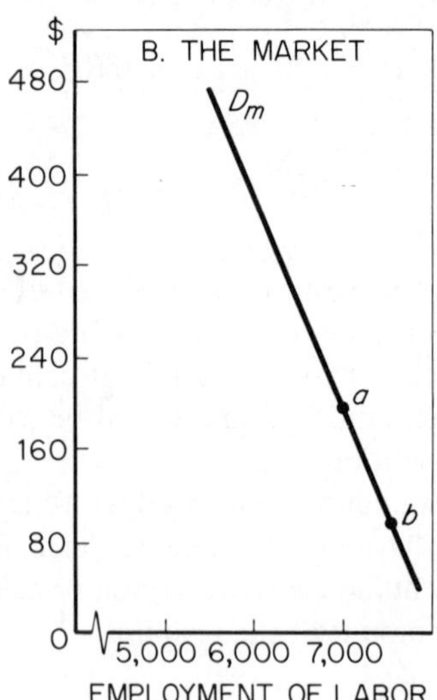

FIG. 3-2 The Demand for Labor

represents a second point on the market-demand curve for farm labor. Obtaining other points in similar fashion enables us to construct the entire market-demand curve for farm labor (the demand curve, D_m, in panel B of Figure 3-2). This procedure is a good illustration of the fallacy of composition when moving from the individual firm to the market, since less aggregate labor is required than one would suppose by just looking at the demand-for-labor curves formed by the individual firms.

The market supply of a resource represents the various quantities of that resource that a resource supplier will offer for sale at different prices. Usually a resource-supply curve is positively sloped, because higher prices induce suppliers to offer for sale more of their resources. For example, offering higher wages should attract more workers to an industry by bidding them away from other industries. (Note the distinction between the horizontal supply facing the firm and the upsloping market supply.)

Combining the market demand and supply curves for a resource determines the equilibrium price and quantity that will clear the market. If the resource price is above the equilibrium level, resource suppliers will desire to sell more than buyers will be willing to employ at that price. Therefore, unemployment would occur, and those who possess unemployed resources will lower their price in order to sell their resource. The price will continue to decline until equilibrium is reached, at which point the market is cleared. At a price below equilibrium, demand will exceed the quantity that resource owners are willing to supply, and buyers will bid up the price for the resource in short supply, until equilibrium is again established.

Aggregate Demand and Supply for Labor Under Competition

If we assume that the market demand and supply curves can be aggregated to form an aggregate labor demand and supply, then the concept of downsloping aggregate labor demand and upsloping aggregate labor supply can be applied to help us understand how the aggregate economy operates. For example, unemployment was a difficult problem to solve in the early 1970's, possibly because the marginal-revenue product of the last unemployed worker was low relative to the going wage. Consequently, with the given wage and price level, the unemployed could be reemployed only (1) if their marginal product increased—a long-run process involving investment in plant, equipment, and technology—or (2) if wages fell and equilibrium occurred at a lower wage level, allowing a movement to the right along an existing labor-demand curve. In this simple, neoclassical supply-and-demand theory, unemployment can occur only if wages are above equilibrium. As we will see later in this and subsequent chapters, unemployment equilibrium is possible given different assumptions about the nature of the supply of labor.

THE LEAST-COST COMBINATION OF RESOURCES UNDER MONOPOLY IN THE PRODUCT MARKET

By definition, monopoly is the opposite extreme from perfect competition: It is a situation in which there is only one firm in the industry. In this sense, an industry must be defined to include all products that are very close substitutes for each other. Therefore, a monopolist is the only producer of a product for which there are no very close substitutes.

The Monopolist's Demand and Supply for Resources

Suppose that a firm facing a perfectly competitive market in the purchase of its resources has a monopoly in the market for its finished product.[2] Because the monopolist is the only firm producing in the industry, the monopolist faces the entire market demand and not just an infinitesimally small portion of it, as was true of the competitor.

Since the demand curve faced by a monopolist is usually negatively sloped, an increase in output requires that the firm must cut its price to sell the greater output. Because the monopolist's price is not constant as output varies, marginal revenue (*MR*), the additional income from the sale of one more unit of output, no longer equals price in the case of monopoly, as was true in perfect competition.

---

[2]Monopoly may occur on either the buyer's side or the seller's side of the resource market, as well as on the seller's side of the product market (or conceivably on the buyer's side in the product market). We have considered only the most likely cases.

The distinction between the *MR* curve of the monopolist and that of the perfectly competitive firm is the basis for the differences between their demands for resources. As additional units of the resource are employed by the monopolist, not only will the marginal productivity of the resource decline, as in the case of the firm selling its output in perfect competition, but also the marginal revenue earned from the sale of the additional units of output produced by the resource will fall, because additional sales can occur only if the product price is reduced. Therefore, the additional revenue that a monopolistic seller earns from the employment of additional units of a resource will decline for two reasons: (1) diminishing marginal productivity, and (2) diminishing marginal revenue. The incremental revenue earned by a resource—for example, labor—employed by a perfectly competitive firm was previously stated as follows:

$$MRP_L = MP_L \times P_x$$

However, in the case of the monopolistic seller, the incremental revenue attributable to the employment of more units of labor can only be stated

$$MRP_L = MP_L \times MR_x$$

because, in the case of a monopolist, the marginal revenue and the price of his finished product are no longer equal.

How a profit-maximizing monopolist determines the quantity of labor he should hire is shown in Table 3-3, which concerns the operations of the cotton

TABLE 3-3 Employment and Output of Labor Under Monopoly

(1) Quantity of Labor N	(2) Marginal Physical Product of Labor MP_L	(3) Total Product TP	(4) Product Price P_x	(5) Total Revenue TR	(6) Marginal Revenue Product MRP_L	(7) Resource Price Per Unit of Labor (P_L) or Marginal-Resource Cost (MRC_L)
4	6	16	$118.75	$1,900		
5	4	20	107.50	2,150	$250	$200
6	3	23	102.17	2,350	200	200
7	2	25	100.00	2,500	150	200
8	1	26	99.00	2,574	74	200
9	0	26	99.00	2,574	0	200

producer previously described (assuming he has now become a monopolist). Columns 1, 2, and 3 are the same as those presented in Table 3-2 for the competitive firm.[3] The product price (P_X) in column 4 does not remain constant as the pure competitor's price did, but decreases every time more output is sold. Total revenue (*TR*) in column 5 is computed by multiplying column 3

[3]Unlike Table 3-2, Table 3-3 shows the MP_L and the *TP* when the fourth unit of labor is added, in order to derive the MRP_L when the fifth unit of labor is added.

by column 4. Column 6, the marginal revenue product (MRP_L), shows the change in total revenue (TR) due to the employment of one more unit of labor (N).

In Table 3-3, MRP_L must be computed as the difference in TR from one worker to the next, even though MRP_L is defined as MP_L times MR_x, because MR_x is not available in this illustration, since Table 3-3 does not show 1-unit changes in output, but rather 1-unit changes in inputs of labor.

Column 7, the resource price (P_L) or marginal-resource cost (MRC_L), is assumed to be constant because perfect competition is assumed in the labor market. That is, the monopolist does not hire enough workers to influence the price of labor. Therefore, the wage is $200, as in Table 3-2. The monopolist, like the competitor, will maximize profits by hiring labor up to the point where the marginal-revenue product of labor equals the price of labor (P_L), which is the same thing as the marginal-resource cost of labor:

$$MRP_L = P_L$$

or

$$MRP_L \times MRC_L$$

In Table 3-3, equilibrium occurs when the sixth worker is hired, whereas in Table 3-2, equilibrium required hiring 7 workers, even though in both cases MRP_L and the wage are equal at $200. Comparing perfect competition and monopoly (Table 3-2 with Table 3-3) reveals that if the firms are equal in size, the employment of resources will be lower under monopoly than under competition. Therefore, even though resource suppliers receive their marginal-revenue product under either type of market, workers are worse off under monopoly because employment is lower at the same wage, or wages must be cut to achieve the same level of employment.

A comparison of the demand for labor under monopoly and under perfect competition is shown in Figure 3-3. The two demand curves are simply the MRP_L curves taken from Tables 3-2 and 3-3, where the MRP_{Lc} is the demand for labor by the perfectly competitive firm and the MRP_{Lm} is the demand for labor by the monopolist. The figure indicates that the monopolist hires fewer workers than the competitor at the same wage. In each case, the supply of labor is the horizontal straight line labeled S_L.

Resource Supply-and-Demand Equilibrium for the Monopolistic Market

If each firm in the market for a particular input, labor in this case, were a monopolist in their product markets, then a horizontal summation of all firms' demand for labor would give us a labor-demand curve. In the case of monopoly, external factors need not be taken into account, since the MRP_L curve faced by the monopolists incorporates the fact that increased output of the product can be sold only at a reduced product price.

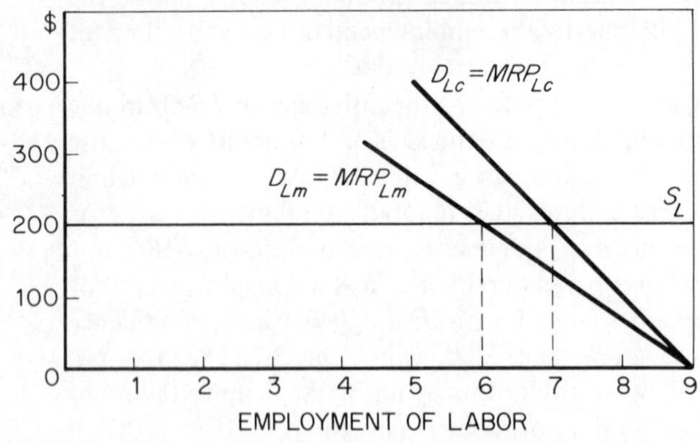

FIG. 3-3 The Demand and Supply of Labor Facing a Firm under Perfect Competition and Monopoly

The fact that all the firms in the market are monopolies need not affect the labor-supply curve. Therefore, the market-supply curve for labor may be the same whether the firms hiring resources in the market are monopolists or perfect competitors with regard to the demand for their products. Consequently, the supply curve for labor will be positively sloped if higher wages induce more workers to sell their services in any particular market.

The negatively sloped demand curve for the resource, labor, can then be combined with a positively sloped labor-supply curve in order to determine an equilibrium market price for the resource.

Monopoly in the product market does not necessarily imply monopoly in the resource market, because the same resource may be suitable for many different employments. In fact, monopolistic firms and competitive firms may be competing for the same resource. In such a case, if external effects could be ignored, the demand curve of each firm desiring the given type of labor can be summed horizontally. However, taking external effects into account means that the market-demand curve for the resource can be determined only by finding at each resource price the amount of the resource that will maximize the profits of each firm in the market, and then summing the quantities of the resource used by each firm.

Aggregate Demand and Supply for Labor under Monopoly

The existence of monopoly in the product market does not affect the aggregate-supply curve for labor. However, the aggregate-demand curve would be reduced compared to the competitive case. Therefore, both the wage level and the level of employment would be lower under monopoly than under perfect competition when the economy is in equilibrium.

In the real world, faced with a range of labor markets varying from highly competitive to monopolistic, one would expect the equilibrium labor market to lie somewhere between the monopolistic and competitive solutions. We will return to a comparison between a monopolistic and a perfectly competitive labor market in Chapter 12.

MONOPOLY IN THE SUPPLY OF RESOURCES—Example: Labor Unions

The supplier of resources can also establish a monopoly.[4] The most obvious case is that of labor unions, which become the bargaining agents for the entire supply of some particular kind of labor in a given market. Since the union can control the quantity of labor supplied, it may be able to determine levels of employment and unemployment for its members. However, in the long run, a union cannot force employers to hire workers above and to the right of their *MRP* function. Therefore, as is true in the case of any monopoly, monopolistic resource suppliers are limited by the demand for their product and are free to operate wherever they want along their demand function.

Where on the demand curve they will choose to operate is difficult to tell, because the goals of a monopolistic resource supplier are not as clear-cut as simple profit-maximizing; for one reason, the union does not bear the cost of supplying labor. If, for example, the union's goal were to maximize the total earnings of its members, then that union would set its wage at a level coinciding with the midpoint of the aggregate demand for its type of labor, because at that point the elasticity of demand equals one and total wage receipts are maximized. (Total wage receipts of workers are the union's total revenue for its product, labor.) Alternatively, unions may have a goal of larger employment and attempt to move to the right along the *MRP* curve by being willing to accept lower wages. Wage reductions to increase employment are limited either by the minimum wage workers will accept or by the availability of workers, whichever restriction is encountered first. In other words, the union cannot operate below and to the right of the labor-supply curve. Unions may have the goal of higher wages for a more restricted membership; this case is probable where unions are controlled by older members with more seniority and little fear of layoffs. Union membership in such cases may be artificially restricted, to reduce the effective supply of labor and to disguise the existence of unemployment. Some unions' unrealistically long apprenticeship requirements may be an example of such restrictive practices.

A "Keynesian" Labor Supply

Whatever goals unions might pursue, one constraint they all seem to share is a steadfast refusal to accept lower wages. Such a refusal, whatever the reason, can lead to a labor-supply curve in a particular market that is hori-

[4]Obviously, other types of monopoly could occur, such as monopoly in the hiring of resources, but they are unimportant for our purposes.

zontal or perfectly elastic up to the point of full employment. At full employment, the curve would turn vertical if no more workers were available, or would become positively sloped if more workers would make themselves available at higher wage levels.

Unemployed workers usually cannot afford the high cost of simultaneously searching in all possible labor markets. Consequently, the information available to each worker, employed or unemployed, regarding alternative employment and wage opportunities is incomplete. A worker who is fired or laid off would probably be disinclined to accept work for a lower wage, because he knows that competitive forces in the labor market determined his original salary, and he feels that if he was worth a certain salary before the layoff, he will be worth the same salary after. So he will prefer to shop for a job at the old wage, rather than accept whatever lower wage is available, as long as the anticipated search cost does not exceed the loss of potential income that would result from immediately accepting a lower-paying job. In fact, the worker may consider temporary unemployment to be a worthwhile investment, because he may be able to search for a new job more easily while unemployed.

As a result, at any time, but especially during recessions, there may be a number of unemployed workers who are willing to work for the going wage but not for less. Search costs and imperfect information can combine realistically to cause a horizontal segment of the labor-supply curve such as Keynes envisioned.[5]

However, search costs cannot be the whole story. Many employed workers do keep informed about the labor market, and many active job searchers are currently employed. Furthermore, mass layoffs can hardly be evidence that workers, as a group, refuse to work for lower wages, choosing to seek jobs with equal pay elsewhere. And it hardly seems rational for employers to decide to shut down in preference to offering lower wages for fear that workers might quit. Another possible explanation of workers' refusal to accept lower wages involves the fallacy of composition. In the aggregate, the market would function efficiently if wages fell to the equilibrium level. However, each worker who accepted a wage cut would find himself relatively worse off compared with other workers.[6] There is a general disinclination to be the first (and possibly the only one) to suffer from a wage cut.[7]

Keynes himself suggested a third possible explanation early in Chapter 1 of *The General Theory*, that workers work for money wages (not real wages—money wages divided by the price level) and that they will resist money-wage

---

[5]Armen A. Alchian, "Information Costs, Pricing, and Resource Unemployment," *Western Economic Journal*, 7 (June 1969), 109–28.

[6]James Tobin, "Inflation and Unemployment," *American Economic Review*, 62 (March 1972), 2–5.

[7]Example: In 1971, George Romney cut his own salary, hoping to lead a counter-inflationary revolution. When it did not develop, he restored his salary in 1972. Romney felt he could afford the gesture, at least temporarily; the typical worker probably does not, and certainly does not have the option to restore his own salary at a later date.

cuts by withdrawing their services from the labor market either by strikes or otherwise.[8] This fixation on money wages has been called "money illusion"; we will return to this concept in Chapter 12. In contrast, the neoclassicists assumed that workers would think only of their real wage.

The Keynesian labor-supply curve is illustrated in Figure 3-4. (To facilitate a comparison of the Keynesian and neoclassical systems, we might assume

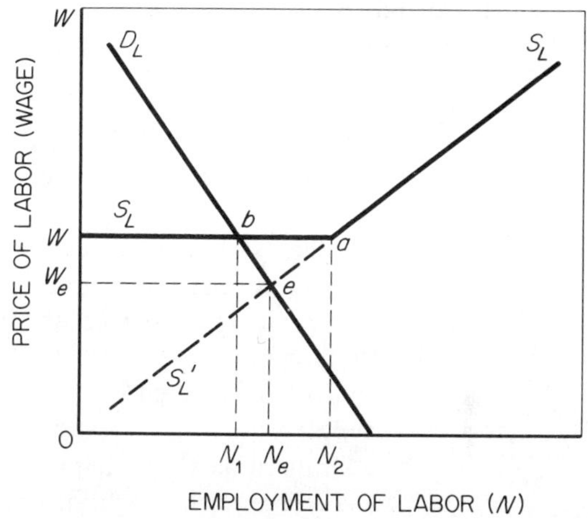

FIG. 3-4 The Labor Market with a Horizontal Segment in the Supply Curve

constant prices.) The supply of labor that would exist in a perfect market is labeled $S_L'aS_L$. The dotted $S_L'a$ segment is unattainable, because market imperfections have effectively imposed a money-wage floor of W.[9] The effective supply of labor is S_LaS_L, with a horizontal segment and a kink occurring at point a where full employment occurs.

If the demand for labor is D_L, then the level of employment, N_1, is determined by the intersection of supply and demand at point b. In contrast, if the labor market had been perfect as the neoclassicists assumed, the wage would have fallen to W_e and employment would have increased to N_e. An employment level of N_e would be a full-employment level, since all workers who were willing and able to work for a wage of W_e would be employed. But with a wage of W, N_2 workers would like to work while only N_1 can find jobs. So

[8]J. M. Keynes, *The General Theory of Employment Interest and Money* (New York: Harcourt Brace Jovanovich, 1936), pp. 8–13.

[9]Until now, we have used P to represent the price of resources generally, with subscripts to denote particular resources. Here we use W to denote the wage, to emphasize that the price of labor is distinct from the price of other resources. The uniqueness of the wage rate lies in the fact that wages are a price for human services, as distinct from the prices of other, nonhuman resources.

$N_1 - N_2$ workers are unemployed when the demand for labor equals D_L and when money wages are rigidly held up to an arbitrary level.

Keynes saw that in the 1930's millions of unemployed workers wanted nothing more than to work for the going money wage, and in fact, many were willing to work for a lower money wage. But market imperfections held the wage at a level above the full-employment equilibrium level. As a consequence, Keynes proposed a perfectly elastic labor-supply curve up to full employment, a concept underlying implicitly or explicitly much of the theory in Chapters 8, 10, 12, and 13.

The Labor Market and the Economy

The labor market is crucial in macroeconomic analysis. Nearly all macroeconomists are concerned about problems of unemployment and questions involving wage levels.

In the classical system presented in Chapter 6, we specifically introduce normal (positively sloped) labor-supply and (negatively sloped) labor-demand curves, which represent perfectly competitive markets. The Keynesian system, especially the material in Chapters 8, 10, 12, and 13, is based (implicitly in Chapters 8 and 10 and explicitly in Chapters 12 and 13) on a perfectly elastic, horizontal supply of labor, rather than on the traditional, positively sloped curve. In addition, in parts of Chapters 12 and 13, the assumption of perfect competition is relaxed, allowing a degree of monopoly power on the part of firms and labor in order to modify the simpler, competitive theory and demonstrate the employment-reducing effects of monopoly.

For the most part, throughout the rest of this book we implicitly assume a simple horizontal summation of the markets' labor-demand and the workers' supply curves. Therefore, the analysis of the section above generally applies without modification to the aggregate economy.

ISOQUANTS AND ISOCOSTS

Isoquants

The output of the firm can be described by a function that is very similar to the indifference curves presented in the last chapter. Such curves, known as isoquants, indicate all the different combinations of resources that would produce some given level of output. For example, the isoquant labeled q_{20} in Figure 3-5 indicates that 20 units of good X could be produced by combining 3 units of labor with 3 units of capital (point a), by combining 5 units of labor with $2\frac{1}{2}$ units of capital (point b), or by combining the services of 1 worker with $5\frac{1}{2}$ units of capital (point c). Similarly, 20 units of output could be produced by any combination of inputs anywhere along isoquant q_{20}.

Isoquants are also similar to indifference curves in that the combinations of inputs described by higher isoquants are capable of producing more output than those combinations described by lower isoquants. Any point on curve

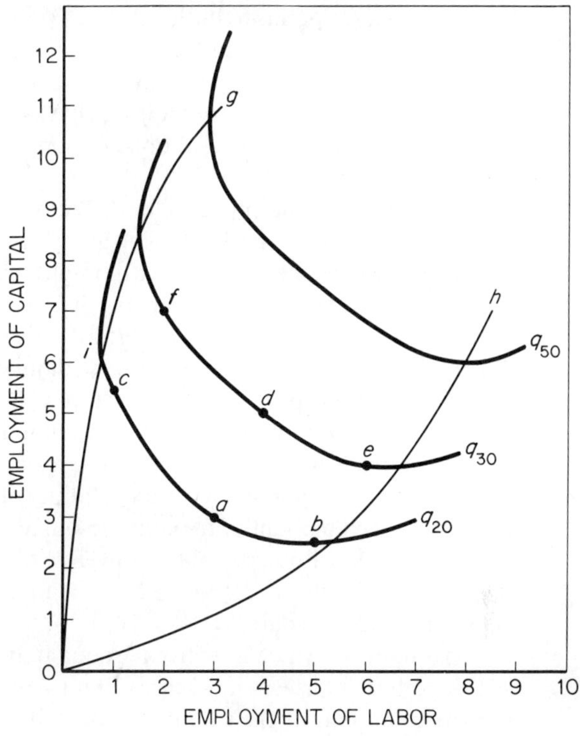

FIG. 3-5 Isoquants and Ridge Lines

q_{30} is capable of producing 10 more units of output than any combination along isoquant q_{20}. For example, 30 units of output could be produced by combination *d*, which employs 4 units of labor and 5 units of capital; or 30 units could be produced by combination *f*, using 2 units of labor and 7 units of capital; or by *e*, which requires 6 units of labor and 4 units of capital.

The characteristics of isoquants are generally similar to those for indifference curves. First, isoquants cannot intersect, because they are drawn on the assumption of efficient use of resources, and intersecting isoquants would indicate that two different levels of output were being produced with the same combination of resources. Second, isoquants slope downward and to the right because if resources are substitutes in the productive process, the use of less of one must be compensated by the use of more of another if output is to remain at the same level. Third, isoquants are convex to the origin because of diminishing returns; beyond some point, continuously larger amounts of the one resource must be added to make up for constant reduction in the inputs of the other. For example, if the firm operates on isoquant q_{20} in Figure 3-5, when capital inputs are reduced from 5 units to 4, the addition of only six-tenths of one worker would compensate for the lost capital. However, if capital inputs are reduced from 4 units to 3, then 1.2 workers are required to compensate.

Ridge lines *Og* and *Oh* connect the points at which the isoquants begin to turn back. All the points to the left of line *Og* represent combinations of inputs in which capital is used so intensively relative to labor that the employment of additional capital will reduce output rather than increase it. Similarly, all points to the right of line *Oh* indicate that labor is being used so intensively relative to capital that the addition of more workers in the production mix will reduce output.

By permitting the input of both factors to vary while output is held constant—which is to say, by moving along some one given isoquant—we can determine the degree of resource complementarity or substitutability. If resources were perfect complements, the isoquant for any level of output would be a right angle with one vertical and one horizontal ray, indicating that additional inputs of one resource without corresponding increases in the other would result in no additional output. On the other hand, if resources were perfect substitutes for one another, diminishing returns would not exist, and the isoquant would be a straight line with a negative slope running from axis to axis, indicating that a certain quantity of one resource could be substituted for a fixed amount of the other resource continuously without changing total output. Any isoquant that is convex to the origin, such as those drawn in Figure 3-5, includes a degree of both complementarity and substitutability between the two resources.

The point at which any given isoquant becomes vertical (wherever the left ridge line intersects it, such as point i on isoquant q_{20}) determines the minimum amount of the resource measured on the horizontal axis that can be employed in order to obtain some given quantity of output. For example, in Figure 3-5, if 20 units of output are desired, no fewer than .8 units of labor could be employed. Likewise, the point at which the isoquant becomes horizontal defines the minimum amount of the input measured on the vertical axis that could be employed to produce any given level of output. To produce 20 units of output, the minimum possible employment of capital would be $2\frac{3}{8}$ units. Isoquants demonstrate that resources are both complements and substitutes for each other and show directly the minimum inputs of each resource required to produce any level of output. Isoquants also show directly the most efficient combination of resources when combined with an isocost curve.

Isocosts

Isocosts connect all the various combinations of inputs that could be purchased for some given money outlay. For example, if capital can be purchased for \$10 a unit and labor can be hired for \$5 a unit, then line C_{30} in Figure 3-6 connects all the possible combinations of capital and labor that the firm could hire for an outlay of \$30.

The end points of an isocost are determined by dividing the price of each resource into the total outlay. If capital costs \$10 a unit and the firm's total outlay is \$30, then the maximum amount of capital the firm could employ would be 3 units; the maximum amount of labor the firm could hire at \$5 a

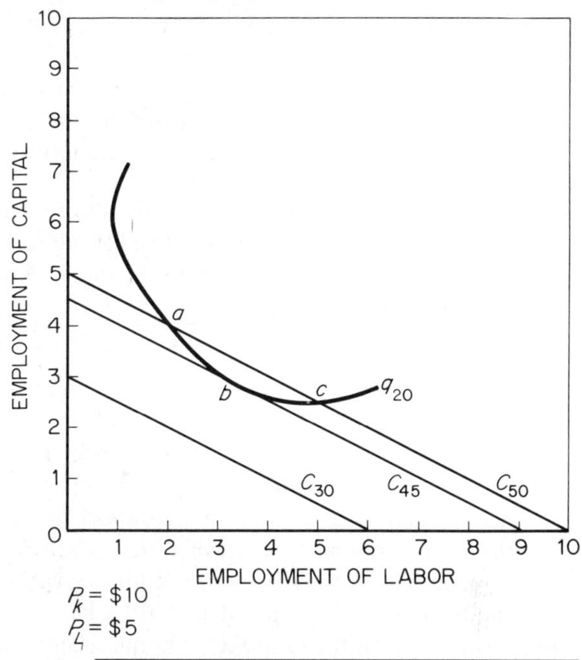

FIG. 3-6 Cost Minimization for a Given Output

unit would be 6 units. If these two points are connected by a straight line, that line will pass through all the combinations of capital and labor that will exhaust the $30 expenditure. For example, 2 units of capital and 2 units of labor together cost $30, as do $1\frac{1}{2}$ units of capital and 3 units of labor, so line C_{30} passes through those points as well as all others that would require an outlay of $30.

Every time the total outlay is increased, the isocost curve shifts upward parallel to the previous function, as long as the prices of the two inputs remain unchanged. For example, if the expenditure is increased to $45, the isocost shifts out to line C_{45}, where a maximum of $4\frac{1}{2}$ units of capital or 9 units of labor could be hired; if the outlay is increased to $50, the isocost shifts out to line C_{50}.

Cost Minimizing

Suppose the firm represented in Figure 3-6 decides to produce 20 units of output. How can it determine the least-cost combination of resources that would produce that level of output?

To produce 20 units, the firm must operate somewhere on isoquant q_{20}. It could operate at point *a*, for example, employing 4 units of capital and 2 units of labor to produce its 20 units of output, or at point *c*, employing $2\frac{1}{2}$ units of capital and 5 units of labor. The total outlay at either of those points would be $50. However, the firm could also operate at point *b* to produce 20 units of output, employing 3 units of capital and 3 units of labor. At point *b*, the total cost would be $45. Point *b* represents the minimum achievable cost on isoquant q_{20}, because at that point the isoquant is tangent to an isocost. Any isocost curve lower than that tangent to a particular isoquant will not come in contact with it, and therefore an isocost curve that just touches a particular isoquant represents the minimum cost for a given level of production.[10]

In Chapter 9, isoquants and isocosts are used to demonstrate the behavior of business firms when capital as well as labor is a variable resource. Isoquants can also be used to demonstrate economies and diseconomies of scale, as we will see in the next section.

ECONOMIES OF SCALE

Early in this chapter, we mentioned that macroeconomic theory is generally assumed to operate in the short run. However, that generalization must be qualified: The macroeconomic short run does not precisely coincide with the microeconomic short run of the firm. For example, investment theory, presented in Chapter 9, treats capital as a variable resource, but, as you know, capital is usually assumed to be the slowest resource to change and so is assumed to be the fixed factor in microeconomic analysis. Therefore, certain aspects of long-run micro theory are significant in short-run macroeconomics. Furthermore, dynamic and long-run macroeconomic theories such as those presented in Chapters 15 and 16 specifically assume that all resources are variable and that technological change can occur.

Most of the significant long-run considerations can be grouped under the general heading, "economies of scale." The main issue is, What happens to output when all inputs are varied? There are three possibilities.

1. Output may increase proportionally more than inputs. (For example, a 10 percent increase in inputs may cause a 15 percent increase in output.) Such a case is called "increasing returns to scale" and is evidence of the existence of economies of scale.

2. Output may increase proportionately less than the increase in inputs. (For example, a 10 percent increase in inputs may cause a 5 percent increase in output.) This case is known as "decreasing returns to scale" and is evidence that diseconomies of scale exist.

3. Output may increase in the same proportion as inputs. (For example, a 10 percent increase in inputs may cause a 10 percent increase in output.) Such a case is called "constant returns to scale."

---

[10]We may describe the slope of the isoquant as $-\Delta K/\Delta N$ and the slope of the isocost as $-P_L/P_k$. Therefore, in equilibrium, where the two curves are tangent, and multiplying both sides of the equation by minus 1

$$\frac{\Delta K}{\Delta N} = \frac{P_L}{P_k}$$

and the absolute level of the total outlay (*TO*) on both capital and labor is determined by the quantity of inputs and by their prices, or

$$(P_L \times N) + (P_k \times K) = TO$$

What could cause returns to scale to vary? Why should they not always be constant? Let us consider first the case of increasing returns to scale. Adam Smith proposed that as a firm grew from a one-man operation, the addition of more workers would allow specialization, resulting in the development of better skills and the loss of less time moving from task to task. In addition, some resources, particularly capital, are available in lumpy increments, and some productive techniques require that resource inputs be employed in large units. A small laboratory cannot buy half an electron microscope. Still another reason why economies of scale might exist is that a large firm may be able to take advantage of the law of large numbers in minimizing risk. A large merchant may be able to maintain a proportionately smaller inventory, or a large bank may not need to maintain as much money in the till proportionately, compared to a small merchant or a small bank.

However, growth does not always lead to increasing returns to scale. Sometimes larger size leads to inefficiency and decreasing returns. One reason often proposed for decreasing returns is the difficulty of managing large-scale enterprises. Communication channels may become clogged in large firms, sometimes by bureaucrats passing papers to other bureaucrats in an endless chain that may only garble the original communication. Often such bureaucratic communicators, who seem to flourish mainly in large firms, create empires that could be entirely eliminated without reducing the firm's output. One of the positive functions of a recession is that it provides a motive for eliminating such corporate fat.

Constant returns to scale simply implies the absence of any factors that would cause increasing or decreasing returns; or if any such factors exist, they cancel each other out.

Increasing, decreasing, and constant returns to scale are shown graphically in Figure 3-7, assuming two variable resources, capital and labor. Panel A depicts increasing returns to scale. The three isoquants are drawn to show equal increases in output resulting from smaller proportionate increases in inputs of labor and capital. Increasing returns are implied by the fact that, as the firm expands along ray 0*r*, 0*a* is greater than *ab*, and *ab* is greater than *bc*.

In contrast, panel B illustrates decreasing returns to scale. The isoquants that show equal increases in output become more widely spaced as inputs are increased, indicating that successively greater amounts of capital and labor are required to obtain equal increases in output as output grows.

Finally, panel C of Figure 3-7 demonstrates constant returns to scale, as implied by the equality of 0*a*, *ab*, and *bc*.

An industry may be subject to a phenomenon generally called "externalities" or "external effects." For example, when atomic energy was in its infancy, labor was supplied by only the most high-powered scientists, but now that the industry has developed, competent workers and technicians are available in fairly large numbers. Or to consider another example, specialized facilities for communications, transportation, and storage may develop and permit the industry to become more productive as it grows. Such external improvements will shift the firm's isoquants down and closer together.

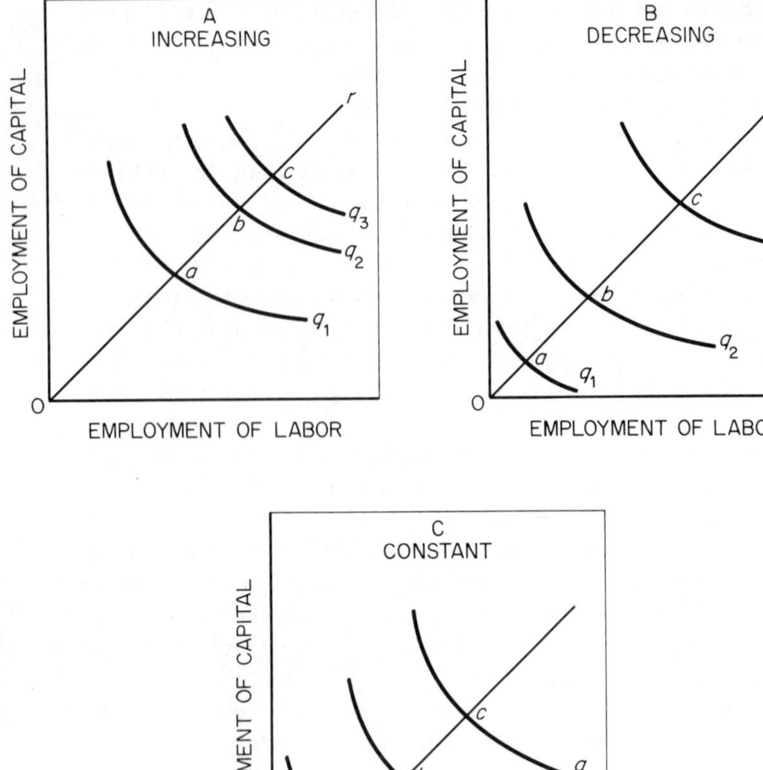

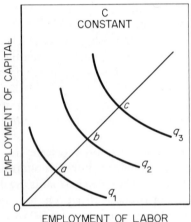

FIG. 3-7 Returns to Scale

The reverse effect can also occur. Industry growth can lead to overloading communications, transportation, and storage facilities. The result of such unfavorable externalities would be to shift isoquants up and separate them.

Furthermore, over a long period of time, new productive techniques may be developed and implemented that would shift the isoquants down, indicating that the same output can be produced with less inputs, or more output with the same level of inputs.

In addition, the new isoquants after a technology change may become more nearly horizontal or vertical, depending on whether the new techniques are more capital- or more labor-intensive. For example, the development of a computer-directed manufacturing process would tend to replace labor with capital and would not only shift the isoquants down but would also make them more vertical.

As we will see in Chapter 5, the first approach to studying the aggregate economy, input–output analysis, assumes constant returns to scale. Knowledge of the underlying theory of economies of scale is helpful for an understanding of the implications of that assumption.

MARKET BEHAVIOR OF THE FIRM

An earlier section presented the theory of isoquants and isocosts and demonstrated how to determine the least-cost combination of resources for any level of output. However, isocosts and isoquants by themselves do not determine the firm's equilibrium level of output, because equilibrium requires that we consider not only costs but also revenue.

Up to now, we have assumed that firms limit their employment of resources and therefore limit their output to the level that maximizes profits. In other words, firms will employ each resource until the marginal-revenue product equals the marginal-resource cost (generally equal to the resource price):

$$\frac{MRP_L}{MRC_L} = \frac{MRP_k}{MRC_k} = 1$$

or

$$\frac{MRP_L}{P_L} = \frac{MRP_k}{P_k} = 1$$

However, only highly competitive firms are forced to maximize profits to survive. Imperfectly competitive firms may choose to operate at a less-than-maximum profit level and simultaneously pursue other, nonprofit goals. Unregulated monopolists may choose to operate at any point on the industry demand curve, without having to take rivals' reactions into consideration.

However, unregulated monopoly is rare in the United States. Most American industry, particularly the most visible industries characterized by large firms, is oligopolistic. Oligopolies are typically industries dominated by a few firms that are large relative to the size of their market. The characteristic that distinguishes oligopoly from other industry structures is *interdependence*. The policies of one firm influence the decisions of other firms.

The number of possible forms that interdependence might impose on an industry are enormous. There is no generally accepted model of oligopoly behavior. However, price leadership is considered to prevail in a large number of oligopolies; one or two firms set prices, and the other firms follow their lead. The follower firms are price takers, much like perfectly competitive firms; the main distinction is that the market may impose a limit on the quantity an oligopolist can produce and sell, whereas the perfect competitor can theoretically sell an unlimited quantity without affecting the price.

In such cases, the dominant firm determines the strategy for the industry. It may set a price that maximizes the firm's profits or one that seeks to achieve other goals as well. The pursuit of multiple goals other than only profits by the dominant firms can be illustrated through the use of indifference curves. One representative theory, proposed by Edgar O. Edwards, assumes that firms seek both profits and size.[11] The firm will be interested in output and sales as well as profits in the short run, because size provides the firm with more power and prestige and may contribute to its leadership position. Furthermore, increasing size is the firm's way of achieving economic growth, which is still considered to be a positive good by a majority of our society, especially when it can be accomplished without ecological damage or other social costs.

In order to describe Edwards' theory we start with the obvious observation that total profits to the firm are the excess of total revenue over total cost. The costs of producing a unit of output are relatively high when the firm is operating inefficiently. Therefore, costs per unit are relatively high when output is either too small or too large for efficiency, and costs are relatively low when the firm is operating at an efficient level. Therefore the average cost curve faced by a typical firm is shaped like a U when output is plotted along the x-axis and average cost is plotted along the y-axis. A total cost curve is positively sloped, at first increasing at a decreasing rate and eventually increasing at an increasing rate.

If the firm has a negatively sloped, straight-line demand curve, total revenue is parabolic, increasing while demand is elastic, reaching a maximum where elasticity is unitary, and decreasing thereafter.

Combining total cost and total revenue for a profitable firm, we may suggest that typically, total cost will exceed total revenue when output is small, giving negative profits; that total revenue will exceed total cost when the firm operates at a more efficient level of output, and that total cost will again exceed total revenue as output is increased further, after total cost increases rapidly while total revenue increases at a decreasing rate. The area of profit opportunity faced by the firm could be plotted by determining the vertical distance between total cost and total revenue for each level of output. Such a profit opportunity curve, labeled π, is plotted in Figure 3-8, where total profit is measured along the y-axis and output along the x-axis.[12] Breakeven points occur where π crosses the x-axis. Losses (negative profits) are represented by the dotted segments and profits by the solid part of the curve. The profit-maximizing firm would operate at point a, the peak of the profit opportunity curve.

Curves labeled U_1, U_2, U_3, U_4, and U_5 are indifference curves for the firm. In this case, the firm is assumed to derive utility both from profits, measured along the y-axis, and from increasing levels of output, measured along the x-axis. Each indifference curve shows that the firm would be equally well

---

[11] Edgar O. Edwards, "An Indifference Approach to the Theory of the Firm," *Southern Economic Journal*, 28 (October 1961), 123–29. Other works on multiple goals include W. J. Baumol, *Business Behavior, Value and Growth* (New York: Macmillan, 1959), pp. 45–82; and H. A. Simon, "Theories of Decision-Making in Economics and Behavioral Science," *American Economic Review*, 49 (June 1959), 252–83.

[12] Figure 3-8 was adapted from Edwards, *ibid.*, pp. 123–29. For a theory that proposes that profits should be traded off against leisure, see Tibor Scitovsky, *Welfare and Competition* (Homewood, Ill.: Richard D. Irwin, 1951), pp. 142–47.

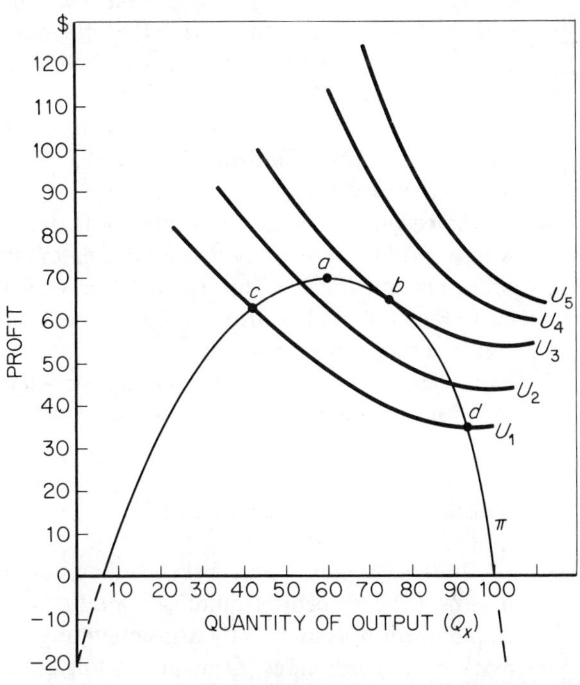

FIG. 3-8 Utility Maximizing by the Firm

satisfied operating at any point on one given curve. For example, the firm would be equally well satisfied either at point *c* or at point *d* on curve U_1. However, as in the case of all indifference curves, the higher curves represent greater utility, and curve U_1 is not the highest curve the firm can achieve with its particular set of profit and output opportunities. The firm in equilibrium will operate at point *b*, where curve U_3 is tangent to the profit opportunity curve, π, because U_3 is the highest indifference curve the firm can achieve. The firm is not able to operate on curves U_4 and U_5, which would provide more satisfaction, because its profit-opportunity curve does not come in contact with those two utility curves. The higher utility functions are assumed to become steeper because each higher curve represents a higher profit potential, and as the firm's profits increase in the short run, profits become subject to diminishing marginal utility and size becomes relatively more important. Lanzillotti[13] found that many large companies' price policies are set with a target return on investment. If a firm's goal is consistent with the theory above, then profits are more important when they get below a certain level and less important when they are above the target level.

The significance of multiple goals on the part of a dominant firm in an

[13]Robert F. Lanzillotti, "Pricing Objectives in Large Companies," *American Economic Review*, 48 (December 1958), 921–40.

oligopoly is that when profits are satisfactorily high, output may be greater and price less than is the case if the firm were maximizing profits. Thus, in Figure 3-8, the dominant firm would produce and sell 75 units of output as a utility maximizer, whereas the same firm would produce and sell 60 units as a profit maximizer. In addition, the firm would employ more resources than would the profit-maximizing firm, so that the marginal-revenue product will be less than the marginal-resource cost.

Since the utility curves become less steep as utility is decreased, a firm whose profit-opportunity curve decreases sharply may approximate the profit-maximizing position. In such a case, it is possible that if the demand curve faced by such a firm is reduced, the firm might find it attractive to increase rather than reduce prices. This analysis may help explain why some industries raised prices when the industry-demand curves decreased during the recent recession.

SUMMARY AND CONCLUSION

In this chapter, we have sketched an outline of the theory of production, based on the concept of diminishing returns. We considered the pricing and employment of resources by firms operating in competitive and monopolistic markets. In both cases, firms are willing to employ resources according to their marginal contribution to production. However, in the case of perfect competition, that contribution equals the marginal product of the resource times the price of the product; in the case of monopoly, the payment to each resource equals its marginal product times the marginal revenue. The significance of this distinction is that perfect competitors are generally willing to pay a higher price for their resources and to employ more of each resource than are monopolists.

Where a monopolistic resource seller such as a union faces a competitive group of firms, that seller can offer for sale a quantity of the resource that may fall anywhere along the aggregate-demand function for that resource. The monopolistic seller's decision regarding the particular quantity to offer will depend on his particular goals.

The Keynesian labor-supply curve, with its perfectly elastic segment, was considered and some possible explanations of its shape were discussed, including search costs, relative wages, and money illusion.

Where more than one resource is variable, the isoquant–isocost approach is a practical means for determining the minimum cost of production for any level of output. In addition, the isocost–isoquant technique is useful to demonstrate that resources are both complements and substitutes for each other in production. Isoquants are also useful in illustrating increasing, decreasing, and constant returns to scale.

Finally, we developed a technique using utility functions or indifference curves to determine equilibrium for firms with multiple goals. In our illustration, employing the case of a firm that desired profits and output, we discovered that equilibrium in such a situation occurred where neither profits nor output were being maximized but where an optimum combination of the two was achieved.

The theory of production covered in this chapter involves firms combining the inputs of various productive resources in order to produce goods and services for sale. The production function of the individual firm is useful in evaluating the assumptions of input–output analysis in Chapter 5, where we will expand this input–output concept and aggregate the input-output relationships of all industries to form an aggregate input–output model of the whole economy. In addition, the theory of production developed in this chapter is an important foundation of the aggregate neoclassical supply theory developed in Chapter 6 and of the Keynesian model presented in Chapter 12. But first we must describe the fundamentals of the national–income accounting system.

QUESTIONS AND PROBLEMS

1. Describe a typical short-run production function.
2. Distinguish the least-cost combination of resources under perfect competition and under monopoly.
3. What social welfare implications are implicit in your answer to question 2?
4. What are the characteristics of isocosts and isoquants?
5. Discuss the welfare implications of monopoly in the supply of resources.
6. How does the Keynesian labor-supply curve differ from the standard? How can the two concepts be reconciled?
7. What goals might a firm have besides simply maximum profits?
8. What are the welfare implications of utility maximizing rather than profit maximizing?
9. How are economies of scale significant?
10. Given the following TP curve, plot the marginal product and average product of labor, and show stages I, II, and III on the blank graph on the top of page 72.

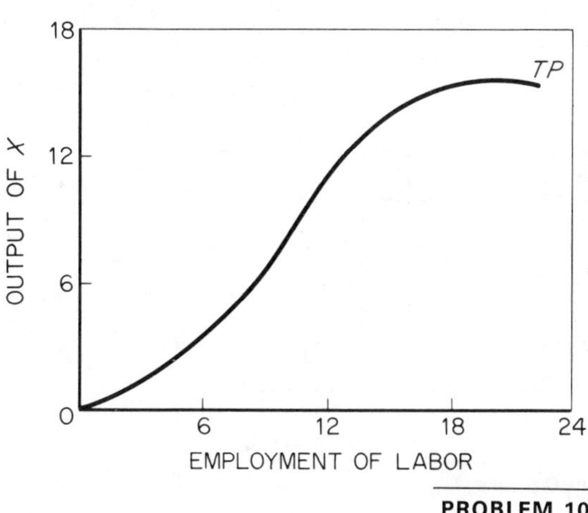

PROBLEM 10

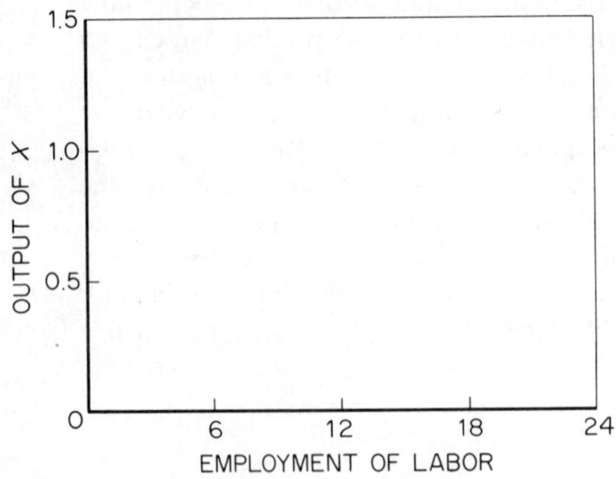

PROBLEM 10 Continued

11. Suppose the following combinations of a and b can each produce 100 X:

$2a$, $9b$
$3a$, $5b$
$5a$, $3b$
$10a$, $1b$

a. Sketch, on the graph below, the $100X$ isoquant.
b. If $P_b = 2P_a$ which combination will be employed?
c. Sketch one isoquant below and one above the $100X$ isoquant to show increasing returns to scale (decreasing costs).

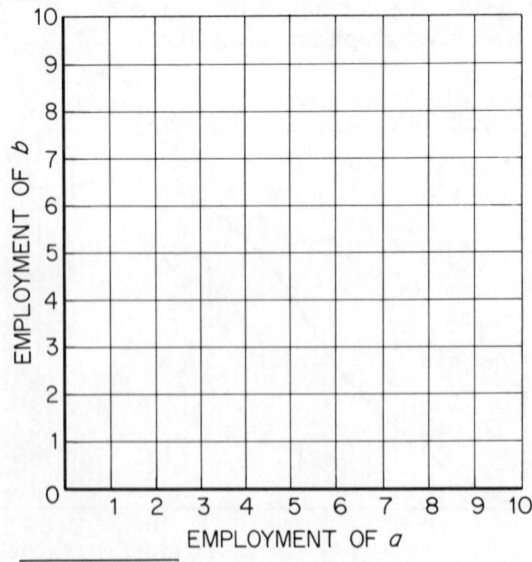

PROBLEM 11

ADDITIONAL SELECTED REFERENCES

PRODUCTION FUNCTION

Conference on Research in Income and Wealth, M. Brown, ed., *The Theory and Empirical Analysis of Production.* New York: National Bureau of Economic Research, 1967.

Frisch, R., *Theory of Production.* Skokie, Ill.: Rand McNally, 1965.

RESOURCE PRICING

Alchian, Armen A., "Information Costs, Pricing and Resource Unemployment," in *Micro-economic Foundations of Employment and Inflation Theory*, ed. E. S. Phelps, pp. 27–52. New York: Norton, 1970.

Chamberlin, Edward H., *The Theory of Monopolistic Competition* (6th ed.), pp. 177–90. Cambridge: Harvard University Press, 1948.

Rees, Albert, "The Effects of Unions on Resource Allocation," *Journal of Law and Economics*, 6 (October 1963), 69–78.

Robinson, Joan, *The Economics of Imperfect Competition*, pp. 235–91. London: Macmillan, 1933.

SELECTED CLASSICAL ARTICLES FOR ADVANCED STUDENTS

Cassels, John M., "On the Law of Variable Proportions," in *Explorations in Economics*, pp. 223–36. New York; McGraw-Hill, 1936. Reprinted in American Economic Association, ed. W. Fellner and B. F. Halley, *Readings in the Theory of Income Distribution*, Vol. III, Chap. 5. Philadelphia: Blackstone, 1946.

Coase, R. H., "The Nature of the Firm," *Economica*, 4 (November 1937), 386–405.

Knight, Frank H., "Diminishing Returns from Investment," *Journal of Political Economy*, 52 (March 1944), 26–47.

Lindbloom, Charles E., "The Union as a Monopoly," *Quarterly Journal of Economics*, 62 (November 1948), 671–97.

Mosak, J., "Interrelations of Production, Price and Derived Demand," *Journal of Political Economy*, 46 (December 1938), 761–87.

Reynolds, Lloyd G., "The Supply of Labor to the Firm," *Quarterly Journal of Economics*, 60 (May 1946), 390–411.

Robinson, Joan, "What is Perfect Competition?" *Quarterly Journal of Economics*, 49 (November 1934), 104–20.

Sraffa, Piero, "The Laws of Returns under Competitive Conditions," *The Economic Journal*, 36 (December 1926), 535–50. Reprinted in American Economic Association, *Readings in Price Theory*, ed. G. J. Stigler and K. E. Boulding, Vol. VI, Chap. 9. Homewood, Ill.: Richard D. Irwin, 1952.

Weintraub, Sidney, "Monopoly Pricing and Unemployment," *Quarterly Journal of Economics*, 61 (November 1946), 108–24.

CONTROVERSY WITH REGARD TO FIRM'S BEHAVIOR

Lester, R. A., "Shortcomings of Marginal Analyses for Wage-Employment Problems," *American Economic Review*, 36 (March 1946), 63–82.

———, "Communications," *American Economic Review*, 37 (March 1947), 135–48.

MACHLUP, FRITZ, "Marginal Analyses and Empirical Research," *American Economic Review*, 36 (September 1946), 519–54.

———, "Rejoinder to Lester," *American Economic Review*, 37 (March 1947), 148–54.

———, "Theories of the Firm: Marginalist, Behavioral, Managerial," *American Economic Review*, 57 (March 1967), 1–33.

Committee on Price Determination, E. S. MASON, Chmn., *Cost Behavior and Price Policy*. New York: National Bureau of Economic Research, 1943.

PAPANDREOU, ANDREAS G., "Some Basic Problems in the Theory of the Firm," with comments by Richard B. Heflebower and Edward S. Mason, in *A Survey of Contemporary Economics*, ed. B. F. Haley, Vol. II, pp. 183–222. Homewood, Ill.: Richard D. Irwin, 1952.

MICROECONOMICS TEXTS FOR CHAPTERS 2 AND 3

FERGUSON, CHARLES E., *Microeconomic Theory*, 3rd. ed. Homewood, Ill.: Richard D. Irwin, 1972.

FRIEDMAN, MILTON, *Price Theory*. Chicago: Aldine, 1962.

LEFTWICH, RICHARD H., *The Price System and Resource Allocation*, 4th ed. Hinsdale, Ill.: Dryden Press, 1970.

MANSFIELD, EDWIN, *Microeconomics*. New York: Norton, 1970.

SHOWS, W. E., and ROBERT H. BURTON, *Microeconomics*. Lexington, Mass: D. C. Heath, 1972.

National-Income Accounting

4

You may recall from Chapter 1 that the whole subject of economics can be divided in a general way into macroeconomics and microeconomics. Chapters 2 and 3 explored the behavior of the individual micro-units that comprise the aggregate system. We concentrated on those elements of micro-unit behavior that help explain the workings of the aggregate macroeconomic system. At this point, we begin to look at the whole economy (for example, of the United States) as a unit that is the sum of a limited number of components (for example, consumers and investors; or the steel, chemical, and other industries). Each such component is itself the sum of many of the smaller units, households and firms, dealt with by microeconomics.

Some subdivisions are clearly recognizable and easily defined, like the chemical industry mentioned above. Other macro subdivisions, such as investment or imputed rent, are really mental constructs, useful when they help us understand the real economic world or predict its behavior. Even the mental constructs, to be really useful, should be definable in terms of things existing in the real world, even though the definition may not be immediately obvious.

The whole field of *national-income accounting* can be thought of as a way to describe and measure a total economy *in the real world* by breaking it down into a fairly small number of components that can be measured and whose interaction helps to explain and perhaps to predict the behavior of that real-world economy. Both obvious groupings and not-so-obvious theoretical constructs appear in national-income accounts, but the constructs of theory must be adapted to definable and numerically measurable segments of the real world. In a fundamental sense, the accounts are the real-world application of theoretical macroeconomics. In fact, the successful casting of economic reality into terms of macro theory by means of the national-income accounts stands as one of the main justifications for the theory itself.

As the name implies, the national-income accounts quantify and explain the national income by means of a system of accounts. Actually, they are more correctly called the "National Income and Product Accounts of the United States." The words "and product" are very important (even though they are usually deleted, to shorten the phrase), because without production, there can be no national income.[1] This statement stems from the nature of the productive process in any economic system, but especially in a specialized, industrial, monetary economy like ours. In every society, human beings have wants and needs to be satisfied. In all countries above the "subsistence-economy" stage, in which each family produces for its own wants, goods and services are produced by people for sale to others.

CIRCULAR FLOW OF ECONOMIC ACTIVITY

Normally, the producers of goods and services are business firms that have to hire others to provide the factors of production: land, labor, capital, and entrepreneurship. Suppliers of land or space in buildings receive compensation in the form of rent. Employees, from laborer to corporation president, receive wages and salaries in payment for their services. Interest is received by those who supply money to business firms to buy capital equipment and buildings. (Interest is also an unstated part of dividends paid by corporations and of profits of unincorporated firms.) Entrepreneurship is provided by the owner in a sole proprietorship, while in a corporation the return to entrepreneurship is split among hired managers' salaries, dividends, and undistributed profits.

In any case, the production of goods and services to satisfy human wants in a market economy causes a double *circular flow of economic activity*. One of the most basic macro concepts, the circular flow of economic activity consists of a circular flow of money payments matched by an equal but reverse circular flow of goods and services. Figure 4-1 illustrates the two circular flows, which are constantly going on in every market economy. On the right are business firms of all kinds, which produce goods and services. To produce their output, firms have to hire resources (mostly labor) and pay the entrepreneurs a return for labor, investment, and risk taking. These payments eventually all go to individuals, shown at the left, who must supply productive resources as their part of the bargain. The upper half of the *inner* ring shows the movement of productive services from people to businesses; while the upper half of the *outer* ring shows the payments made to individuals for their productive services.

[1]There could be *personal income*, however, even in the aggregate, because of transfer payments. We will cover that paradox later in this chapter.

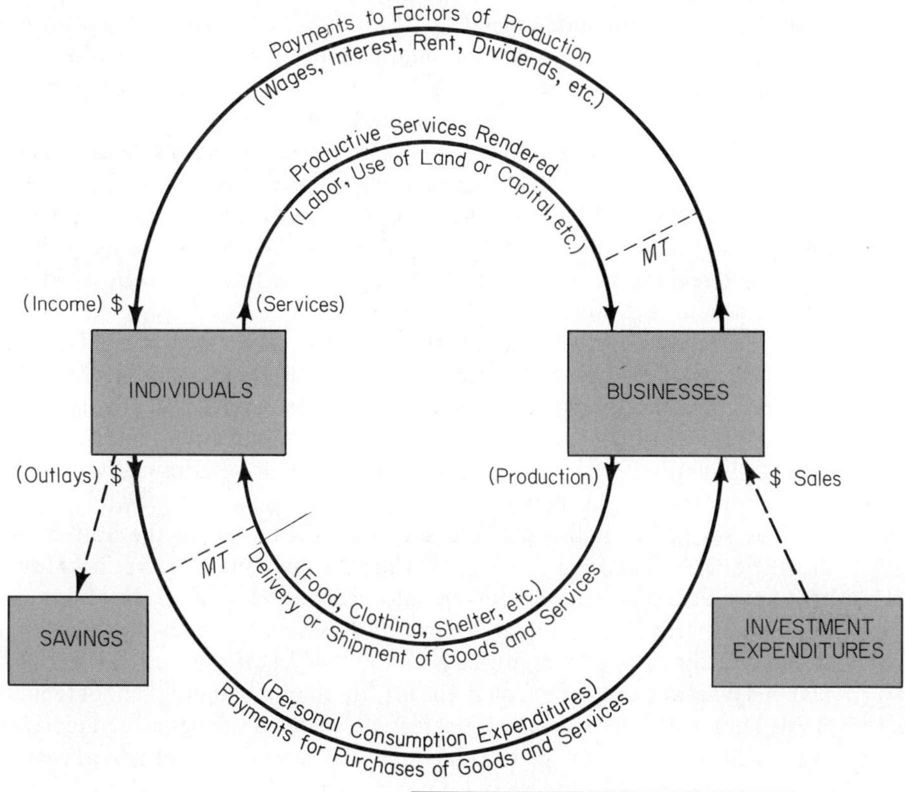

FIG. 4-1 The Circular Flow of Economic Activity

Individuals who earn income can spend it to satisfy their wants for goods and services of all kinds. The outlays or payments individuals make appear in the lower part of the *outer* ring in Figure 4-1 and represent sales or receipts by businesses. To keep their part of the bargain, firms must deliver goods and services to consumers. The delivery of the actual goods or services is shown by the lower half of the *inner* circular flow in Figure 4-1. The complete inner ring represents the real circular flow of resources, services, and tangible goods between people and business firms. The flow in the outer ring represents the payments of money in the economy—income payments to individuals in the upper half, and payments for purchases of goods and some services, which are called *personal-consumption expenditures*, in the lower half.

The outer and inner rings of Figure 4-1 are connected on the diagram by bands marked "MT." The lower halves of both rings represent a market transaction—the familiar one in which money is exchanged for goods and services. The upper halves of both rings are also connected by a market transaction—the one in which labor or other resources are exchanged for money income. In both the upper and lower transactions, the value of the actual services and commodities moving in the inner ring can reasonably be assumed to equal the money paid for them in the outer ring. This principle is important in national-income accounting, and helps to explain why there must be a national product to generate national income, and why (conceptually) national income must equal national product.

Circular flows also go on between individuals (as we buy each other's used cars, for example) and among businesses (as between retailer and wholesaler, or between refrigerator manufacturer and electric-motor suppliers, for example). These internal flows within each of the two sectors are omitted from the circular-flow diagram and, as we shall see later, from the national-income accounts as well.

Although the dual circular flow goes on constantly, it must not be assumed that it always goes on at the same level, that the same quantity of goods, resources, and money changes hands in each time period. Individuals sometimes save rather than spend, and firms also save in the form of undistributed profits. (Note that profits distributed in dividends or withdrawn by proprietors stay in the circular flow.)

The savings of individuals are shown in Figure 4-1 as the dotted line flowing out of "individuals' outlays," while the investments of business firms are shown as the dotted line flowing into "businesses."[2] If all the savings of individuals were used to finance business investments, the result would be a stable circular flow continuing at a constant level. If planned savings and planned investments are not equal, the level of the circular flow cannot remain stable but must either increase or decrease. If planned savings exceed planned investments, the size of the circular flow will diminish eventually, because savings represent income received but not spent. Clearly, the savings taken out of the circular flow will not be fully replenished by the investment flowing back in, and the flow must decrease.

On the other hand, if planned investment exceeds planned savings, the size of the circular flow will increase over time, because investment in excess of savings causes spending to exceed income received.

Both businesses and individuals can spend more than they receive, but they are limited by the size of their previous savings or by how much they can borrow. The volume of the circular flow varies constantly, and the explanation of these variations is the central concern of macroeconomics.

The measurement of national income and national output is done through a system of accounts, just as the income of a business firm is measured through a set of accounts. In a small firm, it is possible to measure sales, for example, by merely adding up cash-register receipts, but such an unsophisticated measure usually leaves so many unanswered questions as to be unsatisfactory. (What was sold? Are we making a profit, and if so, on which items?) Therefore, more sophisticated accounting records are implemented by most firms. Similarly on the national level, early attempts to measure the national income directly by adding up the incomes of the various units in the economy gave

[2]For simplicity, business savings are not shown in Figure 4-1.

way to the creation of an integrated system of *national-income accounts*, which bear a close relationship to and are based on the accounting records of business firms. So let us start by examining the accounts of a typical small business.

ACCOUNTING STATEMENTS OF A FIRM

All transactions of a business firm using standard accounting procedures are presented in an interlocking system of accounts. Each account has both a left-hand, "debit," and a right-hand, "credit," side. An entry on the left side of one account has to be balanced by an equal entry or entries on the right side of some other account. This "double-entry bookkeeping" system can become quite complex in a substantial enterprise.

Balance Sheet and Income Statement of a Firm

Each individual account relates to either the *balance sheet* or the *income statement*. Together, these two primary statements are called the *financial statement* of a firm and appear in corporate annual reports to stockholders. The balance sheet pictures the firm's financial condition at a single point in time, usually the close of business on December 31. A balance sheet shows the stock of assets on the left side, the total of which must equal the total of the firm's liabilities plus net worth or owners' equity shown on the right. Hence, the balance sheet always balances.

Table 4-1 shows a balance sheet for a mythical firm. A quick look at it does not tell us much about the progress of this antifreeze manufacturer. This small corporation is solvent, certainly, since it has retained earnings of $50,000 accumulated from profitable operations in 1972 or in previous years. It seems to owe a lot of money in bonds, taxes, notes, and so on; but it also appears to have some valuable assets—machinery, buildings, inventory, plus a trademark that may be worth much or nothing, depending on customer acceptance of the brand (the arbitrary figure of $10,000 is probably meaningless). In short, one balance sheet is not helpful in assessing the current profitability of a business, because the balance sheet presents the level of stocks of assets, liabilities, and net worth at an instant of time, whereas profits are a flow—so many dollars per month or per year, just as the flow of water through a pipe is stated in gallons per minute or per hour. If we compared one balance sheet, as in Table 4-1, with another for the same date one year earlier—in this case, December 31, 1971—we could see how assets, notes payable, retained earnings, and the other items had increased or decreased during 1972. Indirectly, some conclusions about profitability can be inferred, but such vital information as the flows of sales and expenses would remain unstated.

In contrast, Table 4-2 shows the income statement, which is tailored to measuring the current operations of a business—the flows of income, ex-

TABLE 4-1 Balance Sheet of Polar Icecap Antifreeze Company, Inc. as of December 31, 1972

Assets			Liabilities and equity		
Current assets:			Current liabilities:		
Cash (including $6,000 in savings account)		$ 20,000	Accounts payable		$ 15,000
Inventory:			Notes payable		28,000
Finished antifreeze	$ 15,000		Taxes payable		17,000
Chemicals and other raw materials	45,000	60,000			
Fixed assets:			Long-term liabilities:		
Machinery and equipment	$200,000		Bonds payable		140,000
Buildings	120,000		Total liabilities		$200,000
	$320,000				
Less:			Stockholders' equity (Net worth)		
Depreciation reserve	60,000	260,000	Capital stock (10,000 shares @ $10 each)	$ 100,000	
Other assets:			Retained earnings (Surplus):	50,000	
Trademark		10,000	Total stockholders' equity		150,000
Total assets		$350,000	Total liabilities and equity		$350,000

TABLE 4-2 Income Statement of Polar Icecap Antifreeze Company, Inc. for the Year Ending December 31, 1972

Expenses			*Income or Receipts*	
Purchases from other firms:			Sales to:	
Raw materials (chemicals)	$ 22,000		Prairie Dog Bus Lines	$ 11,600
Containers	10,500		Subzero Motor Freight Transportation Co.	26,000
Office and plant supplies	1,800		Glacier Air Force Base	22,300
		$ 34,300	Northland Drug Stores	33,000
Wages and salaries		35,500	Direct-mail sales to consumers	9,100
Social Security contributions		1,000	Interest received on savings account	300
Change in inventory:				
Beginning inventory, 1-1-72	$ 63,000			
Less: Ending inventory, 12-31-72	60,000			
Net change in inventory		3,000		
Depreciation charges		6,000		
Cost of goods sold		$ 79,800		
Interest payments		8,300		
Indirect taxes (sales and property)		2,200		
Cost of sales and general expenses		$ 90,300		
Gross profits before taxes		12,000		
Corporation income taxes	$ 3,500			
Dividends paid (30c per share)	3,000			
Undistributed profits	5,500			
Total current expenses		$102,300	Total current receipts	$102,300

penditures, and profits. In the income statement, we find much more information on current operations than the balance sheet provides.

Beginning first with the income or receipts side on the right, we see in Table 4-2 that our small manufacturer sold $102,300 worth of antifreeze during 1972. Less than 10 percent, or $9,100, was sold directly to customers, and nearly one third went to a drugstore chain for resale to the public. The remaining sales, almost 60 percent of the total, was sold for use in trucks and buses under contracts with two transportation firms and a government agency. Nonoperating income was received only from interest on a savings-bank account, but many firms also receive income from dividends and rent.

More interesting is the allocation of income, shown on the left side of the statement. First, the firm purchased $34,300 of materials and supplies from other firms. These purchases are *not* direct payments to the factors of production. Instead, they indicate only that this company did not produce packaged antifreeze from the most fundamental raw materials, such as coal, water, and iron ore, but purchased chemicals and steel containers from other firms that had already completed the earlier stages of processing. In terms of the circular-flow diagram of Figure 4-1, these purchases of *intermediate products* cancel out within the entire business sector, because one firm's purchases are another firm's sales, where such sales between firms are not final sales.[3] (This concept will be covered in some detail in the next chapter, in our discussion of input–output analysis.)

Polar Icecap Antifreeze Company did, however, make direct factor payments. The firm paid $35,500 for wages and salaries to the factor labor, plus $1,000 for Social Security contributions, a fringe benefit to labor. It also paid $8,300 in interest to the holders of bonds and notes, who supplied $168,000 in money capital (see the liabilities on the balance sheet in Table 4-1).

Nonfactor payments included $6,000 as the current year's allowance for *depreciation*, the capital consumption allowance for the wearing out and obsolescence of machinery and buildings. Those particular businesses that are subject to indirect business taxes, such as excise or sales taxes, view these taxes as a cost of doing business that is related to sales or to ownership of assets rather than to profits. Thus, in Table 4-2, $2,200 of indirect business taxes are included as an expense.

One other cost item requires explanation: "Net change in inventory." Between January 1 and December 31 of 1972, this firm's inventory went down $3,000. If we assume that this decline represented entirely finished goods rather than raw materials, the firm must have sold $3,000 more than it produced in 1972 by selling part of its inventory of finished goods produced in 1971 and earlier years. Treating this inventory reduction as an explicit expense enables all the remainder of the expense items to refer to production in the

[3]Accountants are faced with a similar problem when preparing consolidated financial statements for related firms. For example, if Polar Icecap and Northland Drug Stores were to merge, intercompany sales and purchases of $33,000 (see Table 4-2) would be eliminated on the consolidated income statement.

given year.[4] If inventories had increased during 1972, some production would have been for 1973 and later years, and net change in inventory would have been negative. Then actual 1972 production outlays would have been reduced by this "minus" item, so that cost of 1972 sales would correspond with 1972 sales receipts on the right-hand side of the income statement.

After adding interest payments and indirect taxes to cost of goods sold, the total cost of 1972 sales and general expenses comes to $90,300. But the two sides of the income statement must balance. Total current receipts must equal their allocation among all expenses plus profit, the residual or balancing item, which could come out positive, negative, or zero. Not only is profit important in itself to company owners, but it also tells the health and efficiency of the firm in gaining sales and reducing costs, relative to each other. In this example, receipts of $102,300 minus total costs of $90,300 left gross profits before taxes of $12,000. As a corporation, the company had to pay $3,500 income tax, and it voted dividends of 30 cents per share, or $3,000, leaving $5,500 as undistributed profits. (Undistributed profits are included in the $50,000 "surplus" item in the balance sheet of Table 4-1; presumably, the company began the year with a surplus of $44,500.)

The income statement forms the primary building block that aggregates into the flow of national income and product totals. The sums of individual balance sheets, in contrast, are useful in estimating the stock of *national wealth*, the national stock of assets minus liabilities. National income is a flow item, and so must be measured over some arbitrary time period, usually a year.

Stock, Flow, and Ratio Variables

The distinction between stock (such as wealth) and flow (such as income) variables is significant throughout macroeconomics. A stock variable is always measured at a point in time, whereas a flow variable must be measured over time. Stocks change only through flows. Therefore, balance-sheet (stock) variables can change only as a result of flow variables. For example, the stock of retained earnings could change only as the result of the inflow of earnings less the outflow of dividends. (Conceptually, a stock is similar to the volume of water in a bathtub, into which water is flowing from a faucet at the same time it is running out through the drain.) An aggregate summation of stock variables is possible to determine aggregate stocks such as national wealth. Or an aggregate flow variable such as aggregate consumption could be determined by summing the flow of consumption expenditures of each of the individual persons between the same two points in time. In addition, we might add a third type: ratio variables, which can relate two stocks,

[4]In the traditional accounting income statement, the change in inventory, as well as wages, purchases of raw materials, etc., is usually included in a separate determination of "Cost of goods sold," rather than being listed explicitly on the income statement itself, as in Table 4-2.

two flows, or a stock and a flow. Price is an example of a ratio variable—the ratio of a flow of dollars spent to buy a certain amount of output.

Production Statement

Because current output or production, rather than current sales, is the basic measure of national income, it is necessary to convert an income statement into a production statement. The production statement shows the disposition of all the goods produced during the year, whether to sales or inventory, as well as the allocation of the expenses and profit incurred or earned in producing that bundle of goods. In other words, the focus of a production statement (and of the national accounts) is on goods produced, rather than on goods sold, as is true of an income statement.

The major change necessary to convert an income statement to a production statement is to transfer "Net change in inventory" from the left- to the right-hand side of the statement, but with an opposite sign. Therefore, net change in inventory in Table 4-2 becomes −$3,000 on the right side of Table 4-3, showing that $3,000 of the listed sales came out of previously manufactured inventory, and that production of antifreeze during 1972 was actually only $99,000, instead of $102,000, the sum of sales, or total receipts excluding interest, on the income statement. (Perhaps this entry would be easier to understand if inventories had increased by $3,000 during the year. Then −$3,000 on the left of the income statement becomes +$3,000 on the right of the production statement, showing that $105,000 of current production was distributed, $102,000 to sales and $3,000 to the firm's own inventory.) The only other change is a minor one—the $300 interest received is netted against the $8,300 of interest payments on the left side to yield $8,000 net interest. Now, the right side shows only production of antifreeze. With these changes, the production statement appears as in Table 4-3.

Given a production statement like this for every enterprise in the country, the economic statistician can begin to estimate the national income and product totals, the aggregate production of the economy.

GNP—THE PRODUCT SIDE OF THE NATIONAL ACCOUNT

The three letters GNP have become part of the household lore of millions of Americans during the last twenty years—a familiar part of the alphabet soup, like PTA, TVA, HUD, or IBM. Most newspaper readers or television watchers have some idea that the higher the GNP, the better off the country.

GNP is a simple concept; the gross national product, or GNP, is the market value of all goods and services produced in the nation during a given year. It is the total output of the country, including durable goods such as washing machines, nondurable goods such as cigarettes, and services such as those of doctors or barbers, all valued at market prices.

TABLE 4-3 Production Statement of Polar Icecap Antifreeze Company, Inc. for the Year Ending December 31, 1972

Cost or Expenses			*Production and Sales*		
Purchases from other firms:			Sales to business firms:		
Raw materials (chemicals)	$ 22,000		Prairie Dog Bus Lines	$ 11,600	
Containers	10,500		Subzero Motor Freight Transportation		
Office and plant supplies	1,800		Company	26,000	
		$ 34,300	Northland Drug Stores	33,000	
Wages and salaries		35,500			$ 70,600
Social Security contributions		1,000	Sales to government (Glacier Air Force Base)		22,300
Depreciation charges		6,000	Sales to consumers (direct mail)		9,100
Cost of goods produced		$ 76,800	Net change in inventory		−3,000
Net interest (payment)		8,000			
Indirect taxes (sales and property taxes)		2,200			
Cost of production and general expenses		$ 87,000			
Profits before income taxes		12,000			
Corporation income taxes	$ 3,500				
Dividends paid	3,000				
Undistributed profits	5,500				
Total costs and expenses		$ 99,000	Total production		$ 99,000

Immediately, we must make one qualification: GNP is the market value of the *final* goods and services produced in a given year. A great many transactions are not counted in GNP, such as sales of intermediate products—for instance, wool that is sold to cloth manufacturers, and cloth sold to dress and suit makers. Those intermediate products must not be counted in the GNP, because their value is already included in the value of the ultimate product. We would be guilty of double (or triple or quadruple) counting if we included them.

For example: A man's suit retailing for $80 may have been sold to the retail store by the clothing factory for $45. The suit may have been made from cloth costing $15 that was made from $3 worth of wool and $2 of synthetic fiber. If we added up all these transactions at their sales prices, we would show an output of $145, but society would still have only one suit, worth $80. And if the suit manufacturer had first sold it to a wholesaler, who then sold it to the retailer for $55, the national output from the suit would zoom up to $200. But there would still be only one suit.

In the antifreeze illustration, the amount purchased by consumers is final output, and the part bought by other firms is not, even though all bought the same antifreeze and did not reprocess it. Table 4-2 shows that most of Polar Icecap's sales represented intermediate products. The $9,100 in direct-mail sales to consumers is clearly final. The sales of $33,000 to the chain drugstores are not final, because the drug chain added a markup and resold it. The sales to the bus line and the trucking company are intermediate, because these firms used the antifreeze in producing transportation services. Oddly enough, the $22,300 of antifreeze sold to the air base is counted as final product, even though it could similarly be said to be consumed in producing national defense. But by a convention of the national-income accounts, all purchases of goods and services by the government are considered final and become part of GNP.

There is one exception to the final-vs.-intermediate-product rule. All additions to inventories *may* become part of the gross national product, whether they are final or otherwise. All unsold cloth, steel, antifreeze, and so on are, for the moment, part of the national output. But since some unsold or unprocessed goods are always on hand, only the increase, if any, in such inventories held by businesses is part of the GNP in any given year.

There are three ways to estimate the gross national product:

1. By adding the final products bought by consumers, by business on capital account, by government (all goods and services), and by the rest of the world. This method yields GNP viewed from the "product side" of the national income and product account.

2. By adding the payments (wages, interest, rent, and profits) to factors of production for their services that were used in producing GNP. Technically, this method of summing the incomes (including profits) created in making the national output yields "charges against gross national product." Sometimes this mirror image of GNP is called "gross national income." Since the latter must exactly equal GNP, it is probably better to consider it as GNP viewed from the income side of the national income and product account. (This ignores certain adjustments to be

explained later that are required to make national income equal gross national product.)

3. By summing the *value added* by each firm (or each industry) in the national economy. The value added by any business equals the sales value of its production (whether final or intermediate product) minus the sum of all purchased materials, goods and services. In the men's suit example above, the textile mill sold cloth for $15 that it produced from $5 worth of raw wool and man-made fiber. Its operations added $10 to the value of the fabric; therefore, $10 is the mill's value added. Similarly, the clothing factory has a value added of $30 ($45 factory price of the suit less $15 of purchased cloth), and the retail store's value added equals its markup of $35 ($80 − $45). Even the raw materials represented the sum of small amounts of value added by someone (e.g., sheep ranchers, transportation, carding mills; or coal mines and chemical fiber makers). Adding the $5 of raw materials to the rest of value added ($10 + $30 + $35) gives $80, the final sales value of the suit. The sum of value added throughout the economy therefore equals the total production of all final goods and services, or GNP computed by method 1 above. Since in any firm the value added must consist of all factor payments, including profits, the value-added method also gives results identical to method 2, the flow-of-income method.

Even though the value-added method avoids decisions between final and intermediate products, it has not been used by the Department of Commerce in estimating the official U.S. GNP, purely for reasons of data availability.[5] Both the other two methods are used, however, as checks on each other, and represent the product and the income sides respectively of the national income and product account, the most important of the system of five interlocking accounts employed by the Office of Business Economics (OBE) of the U.S. Department of Commerce.[6]

Table 4-4 shows the national income and product account of the United States for 1972. Looking first at the right-hand or product side of the account, we see that GNP represents the sum of four major kinds of products or expenditures:

1. Personal-consumption expenditures
2. Gross private domestic investment
3. Net exports of goods and services
4. Government purchases of goods and services

These four categories represent the distribution of final sales, or more accurately, production, to different classes of users: individuals, business firms, foreigners, and government. At the same time, these four categories also represent the opposite side of the coin—the expenditures on goods and

[5]The Commerce Department does make periodic auxiliary studies of GNP by major industry (of origin), from which one summary table is now published annually. As explained in Chapter 5, these studies estimate value added by industry, but use a flow-of-income method. The best discussion of the value-added method as such is probably that in Richard and Nancy D. Ruggles, *National Income Accounts and Income Analysis* (New York: McGraw-Hill, 1956), pp. 49–60.

[6]This agency has very recently been renamed the Bureau of Economic Analysis. It is far better known to economists under its old name, or simply as the OBE; and we will continue to refer to it as such.

TABLE 4-4 National Income and Product Account of the United States for 1971 (all values in billions of dollars)

Income Side

Line	*Income Side*				
1	Compensation of employees				$644.1
2	Wages and salaries			$573.5	
3	Disbursements		$572.9		
4	Wage accruals less disbursements		.6		
5	Supplements to wages and salaries			70.7	
6	Employer contributions for social insurance		$34.1		
7	Other labor income		36.5		
8	Proprietors' income				70.0
9	Rental income of persons				24.5
10	Corporate profits and inventory valuation adjustment				78.6
11	Profits before tax			$83.3	
12	Corporate profits tax (income) liability		$37.3		
13	Profits after tax		45.9		
14	Dividends	$25.4			
15	Undistributed profits	20.5			
16	Inventory valuation adjustment			−4.7	
17	Net interest				38.5
18	NATIONAL INCOME				$855.7
19	Business transfer payments				4.6
20	Indirect business taxes				101.9
21	Minus: Subsidies less current surplus of government enterprises				.9
22	Capital consumption allowances				93.8
23	Statistical discrepancy				−4.8
	CHARGES AGAINST GROSS NATIONAL PRODUCT				$1,050.4

Product or Expenditure Side

Line	*Product or Expenditure Side*				
24	Personal consumption expenditures				$664.9
25	Durable goods			$103.5	
26	Nondurable goods			278.1	
27	Services			283.3	
28	Gross private domestic investment				152.0
29	Fixed investment			$148.3	
30	Nonresidential		$105.8		
31	Structures	$38.4			
32	Producers' durable equipment	67.4			
33	Residential structures		42.6		
34	Change in business inventories			3.6	
35	Net exports of goods and services				.7
36	Exports			$66.1	
37	Imports			65.4	
38	Government purchases of goods and services				232.8
39	Federal			$97.8	
40	National defense		$71.4		
41	Other		26.3		
42	State and local			135.0	
	GROSS NATIONAL PRODUCT				$1,050.4

Source: Office of Business Economics, U.S. Department of Commerce, "U. S. National Income and Product Accounts," 51 (July, 1972), 14. Discrepancies due to rounding.

services out of the income received by each group. Personal-consumption expenditures on the product side of the national account thus represents both production by business destined for individuals and sales receipts by business from the public (the two lower loops in Figure 4-1). In an even more general way, we can think of the product side of the national account as representing the activities of the business block on the right of the circular-flow diagram (Figure 4-1) in producing output and as recording the transactions represented by the two lower loops. Conversely, the income side of the national income and product account represents the "individuals" block and the transactions in the upper loops.

Personal-Consumption Expenditures

Personal-consumption expenditures (PCE) account for by far the largest part of GNP, about 63 percent, or $665 billion out of $1,050 billion in 1971. The figure comprises all purchases of goods and services by individuals and nonprofit institutions, which are classified into the personal sector, plus the market value of products such as food and clothing received as income in kind. Traditionally, PCE is divided into durables, nondurables, and services, a classification that is often useful in analysis.

Durable goods, mainly automobiles, furniture, and appliances, in 1971 accounted for about 15.6 percent of total PCE, a share that has tended to stay roughly the same since 1950, although it is higher in prosperous years like 1955, 1965, and 1968 than in recession years like 1958, 1961, or 1970. In 1971, the remaining 84.4 percent of PCE was split almost equally between nondurable goods—such as food, clothing, gasoline and oil, drugs, and tobacco—and services—including housing, household operation, auto repair, purchased transportation, cleaning and laundering, and medical care, among others. Back in 1947, nondurable goods amounted to $90 billion, while expenditures on services were less than $50 billion; services have been increasing relative to nondurables ever since.[7] Part of the relative increase in services is usually attributed to general affluence, but much of it comes simply from the much greater rise in prices of services than of nondurables between 1947 and 1971.

Gross Private Domestic Investment

Gross private domestic investment (GPDI) is essentially the gross increase in the privately owned stock of productive capital during the year. GPDI includes buildings (both residential and nonresidential); producers' durable equipment (including machinery, office furniture, instruments, trucks, aircraft); and change in business inventories. Expenditures on nonresidential

[7]Office of Business Economics, U.S. Department of Commerce, *The National Income and Product Accounts of the United States, 1929–1965: Statistical Tables: A Supplement to the Survey of Current Business* (Washington, D.C.: U.S. Government Printing Office, 1966), p. 41. Hereafter cited as *Statistical Tables.*

structures or buildings tend to move steadily with the growth of the economy, so that business analysts find the volatile movements of producers' durable equipment (or PDE) more significant and particularly important for short-range forecasts of business activity. Residential construction (or structures) also may fluctuate sharply, because it is affected by mortgage interest rates and availability of credit as well as by general economic activity. Construction of a new house, incidentally, is included in investment even if the owner is a private citizen who lives in it himself; for this purpose, he is considered to be in business, renting his own home from himself.

All these items listed under "fixed investment" (line 29 of Table 4-4) represent business purchases on capital account during a year. However, the purchase of capital goods is *not* shown on the income statement of the individual firm, even though capital purchases change the balance sheet.

From a long-term standpoint, capital goods *are* intermediate products, for plant and equipment are used in making other goods. However, only a relatively small portion of any newly produced capital goods is used up in producing consumer goods during any one year. Therefore, it is convenient to think of capital goods as final products, so that increases in investment over the previous year represent increases in economic activity. The depreciation allowance permits a correction, albeit a rough one, for the small portion of new capital goods produced in a year that is consumed the same year.

Change in business inventories is classified under investment partly for arbitrary reasons. As discussed above, all production during an accounting period must be included, even if it only went into inventory (recall the conversion of an income statement into a production statement for Polar Icecap Antifreeze), and even if it consists of increases in inventories of intermediate products. This portion of GNP has to be entered somewhere. After all, a stock of merchandise for resale may be the retailer's major investment. Including the increase or decrease in inventories under investment is, however, of the greatest importance for macroeconomics, because as a result of unintended inventory accumulation or depletion, total gross private domestic investment may not come out to the figure intended by businessmen.

Net Exports of Goods and Services

Net exports of goods and services can be quickly summarized. Production going to foreign countries as exports is still part of current U.S. production and must be included in GNP. At the same time, individuals and firms in this country import merchandise and services from the rest of the world. Conceptually, it might be better to deduct imported automobiles, wines, and trips on foreign airlines from personal-consumption expenditures, and imported turbines from investment. However, import figures *en masse* are readily available from the Bureau of Customs, and retail markups on imported products are value added, properly included in GNP. Netting imports against exports avoids complicated calculations, corresponds more closely to balance-of-payments figures, and allows PCE to more nearly resemble family-budget patterns. (Do any families budget specifically for purchases of domestic products?)

Government Purchases of Goods and Services

All government purchases of goods and services are included in GNP. This decision, adhered to consistently by the OBE, has become one of the most controversial in national-income accounting. The OBE assumes that all government activity creates a product desired by society.

Services provided by government are not normally sold to the public in individual transactions, so the government can neither show a profit nor sustain a loss. The obvious measure of the value of government services then is their cost, consisting of supplies and equipment, salaries of government employees and military personnel, weapons systems and other military hardware, and construction of buildings and roads (excluding the cost of land).

Although the convention of valuing government services at cost has the appealing virtue of simplicity, it has come under attack. Some argue that many government services such as defense, education, and law and order are priceless—infinitely valuable because no organized society and hence no productive activity could exist without them. In contrast, others maintain that government and military personnel have a much lower productivity per hour than corresponding employees in the private sector and that the OBE method overvalues government output. Practicable techniques for estimating the necessary correction in either direction, however, have not been forthcoming from the critics.

Government expenditures or "production" should be divided into capital goods (such as highways and buildings) and current expenditures (such as wages paid congressmen), and the two categories shown separately and explicitly as "Government investment" and "Government consumption."[8] However, such a breakdown presents the problem of defining what constitutes government investment. For example, is the expenditure for an army jeep an investment expenditure producing a service, defense, or is it a consumer good? If army jeeps, what about a submarine?

A persistent criticism has been that much government activity produces only intermediate products. The most obvious examples are government services directly aiding business, such as weather forecasting, nontoll roads and bridges, agricultural research and county agriculture agents, and compilation of national income and business statistics. Although such services are often helpful to the general public, they primarily benefit business firms. To farmers and trucking firms, for example, weather forecasts and roads are inputs into their products as surely as are seed and trucks.

---

[8]Solomon Fabricant, "Capital Consumption and Net Capital Formation," in *A Critique of the United States Income and Product Accounts, Studies in Income and Wealth*, National Bureau of Economic Research, Vol. 22 (Princeton, N.J.: Princeton University Press, 1958), p. 441. Hereafter cited as *Critique*.

Another class of government services creates an "infrastructure" or a framework within which economic activity can take place. National defense, the maintenance of law and order, education, and sanitation, among others, fall into this category. In some fashion, the cost of these activities is a part of the cost of producing every product and service on the market.[9] Actually, the attainment of a safe social atmosphere is a precondition for all aspects of civilized life and benefits the ultimate consumer as well as the producer of goods. Therefore, part of the "infrastructure" is in reality a consumer good.

Those who desire to separate government expenditures into intermediate and final products would eliminate the intermediate products supplied by government from the national product entirely, as is done with privately produced intermediate products. The costs of highways, for example, would have to be divided among consumers and business users, with only the consumers' share entering GNP.[10] However, the statistical problems of making such a split, especially for "infrastructure" items, may be insurmountable.

In addition, defenders of the present method point out that government services to business, if furnished by other businesses, would raise the prices of final products and would get into GNP through the consumption, investment, or export components. It is further pointed out that some items of consumer expenditures now included in gross national product—like watchdogs, burglar alarms, and shipping charges on mail-ordered items—are in reality "intermediate products" in the same welfare sense that is applied to government services.[11] They should also be eliminated from GNP if intermediate government expenditures are excluded.

In any case, under the present system, the cost of government production, or the sum of all government purchases of goods and services, enters GNP as its second largest component, amounting to nearly $233 billion in 1971, with well over half being spent by state and local governments.

NATIONAL INCOME AND GNP—THE INCOME SIDE OF THE NATIONAL ACCOUNT

Now we consider the second way to estimate the total output of an economy: by adding up the payments to the factors of production that created the national product. The total of these factor payments plus adjustments yields "Charges against gross national product," a figure exactly equal to GNP. Some textbooks unofficially call GNP "gross national income"

---

[9]Raymond T. Bowman and Richard A. Easterlin, "The Income Side: Some Theoretical Aspects," in *Critique*, pp. 177–79. There are many other references to the "government" or "duplication" controversy throughout *Critique*.

[10]Everett E. Hagen and Edward C. Budd, "The Product Side: Some Theoretical Aspects," in *Critique*, q.v., p. 241.

[11]George Jaszi, "The Conceptual Basis of the Accounts," in *Critique*, q.v., pp. 70–75.

when defined this way, as a sum of income flows. Regardless of the term used, the listing of the various income items constitutes the left or income side of the national income and product account. It corresponds to the left or "expenses" side of the income statement of a single firm, as in Table 4-2, and of the production statement, Table 4-3, because the expenses of a firm represent income to those supplying inputs to it.

Referring to Table 4-4, the first group of five major income items adds up to *national income*, as the term is used by OBE in official U.S. accounts. The Commerce Department defines national income (NI) as "the aggregate earnings of labor and property which arise from the current production of goods and services by the Nation's economy. Thus, it measures the total factor costs of the goods and services produced by the economy."[12] NI is sometimes called "national income at factor cost."

Although we have discussed payments to factors of production, or factor cost, as representing all of GNP, this is not strictly the case. GNP is the sum of *market prices* of a collection of goods, and market prices include nonfactor items such as sales taxes and other indirect business taxes, as well as depreciation. These two nonfactor payments plus three smaller items discussed below constitute the group of five items—shown in Table 4-4, as lines 19–23—that make up the difference between national income, or income earned by means of production, and gross national income, or charges against GNP.

The income side of Table 4-4 shows that the major divisions of national income are these:

1. Compensation of employees
2. Proprietors' income
3. Rental income of persons
4. Corporate profits and inventory-valuation adjustment
5. Net interest

Compensation of Employees

As might be expected, wages and salaries are the major item under "Compensation of employees." (In Table 4-4, lines 3 and 4 simply convert actual disbursements of wages and salaries to an accrual basis to correspond with calendar-year production; the adjustment was small in 1971.) However, supplements to wages and salaries, or "fringe benefits," as they are popularly known, amounted to over 10 percent of employee compensation. Contributions by employers for Social Security and unemployment compensation represented almost half of total supplements, and the other part consists of other labor income, mainly employer contributions to private pension and welfare funds, group insurance, and compensation for injuries.

---

[12]Office of Business Economics, U.S. Department of Commerce, *National Income*, 1954 edition, a supplement to the *Survey of Current Business* (Washington, D.C.: U.S. Government Printing Office, 1954), p. 58. Hereafter cited as the 1954 *National Income* supplement.

Proprietors' Income

Proprietors' income was called "income of unincorporated enterprises" until 1958. Neither title is wholly descriptive, for the series includes partnerships and cooperatives as well as single proprietorships. "Unincorporated enterprises" is perhaps more general, but hardly embraces all three of the following areas of economic activity covered by this OBE concept (two of which may scarcely seem to be "enterprises" in the popular usage of the term):

1. Farms—all except incorporated farms, which are of relatively minor importance
2. Independent professional practitioners—mostly doctors, dentists, lawyers, engineers, and accountants
3. Unincorporated business enterprises—perhaps 5 million small business firms, plus own-account nonprofessional workers operating from their homes, such as carpenters and painters[13]

"Proprietors' income" only roughly represents a return for entrepreneurship, even disregarding the kinds of enterprises or activities covered. Proprietors' income is an amalgam of wages and salaries for personal work by the proprietor, interest on invested capital, rent on his property, and pure profit, which may be negative in many cases. The statistical problems of separating these elements are too formidable, however, for the task to be attempted. It is difficult enough to calculate income of unincorporated firms and farms from income tax data or by subtracting current outlays from receipts.

Rental Income of Persons

Rental income of persons consists of two components: (1) land rentals from land, dwellings and business and farm property, paid to landlords not primarily in the real estate business, plus mineral and patent royalties; and (2) imputed rents on owner-occupied homes. The latter element comes from one of the most important fictions or "imputations" in national-income accounting—that all homeowners are little business firms that pay themselves rent on their own houses. As businessmen, homeowners receive payments for the "space-rental value" their houses would rent for on the open market. These imputed rent payments are classified under "Personal-consumption expenditures" on the product side of the accounts. After paying depreciation, interest, maintenance, insurance and taxes, the homeowner-businessman is assumed (imputed) to pay the remaining net rent back to himself as owner of a factor of production.[14]

There is one important reason for this seemingly senseless charade, which raises GNP on both product and income sides by the estimated rental value of all the owner-occupied houses in the nation. The GNP and national-income totals should not change simply because of shifts between rental and

---

[13]Ibid., pp. 76–78 and footnote 3, p. 80.

[14]Ibid., p. 46.

owner-occupied housing.[15] In the first decade after World War II, millions of people became homeowners for the first time. Without the imputation, their housing costs would have disappeared from the GNP. Similarly, when apartment rentals became relatively more popular in the late 1960's, partially because of high interest rates, the national-income aggregates did not take a spurious upward jump.

In place of using imputed rent, personal-consumption expenditures could have been increased to include homeowners' actual expenditures for mortgage interest and principal repayments, taxes, insurance, and maintenance. Although that technique would make PCE correspond more closely to actual family budgets, other items would be unnecessarily complicated by so doing. Many mortgage payments go to purchase *used* houses, and by definition must be excluded from GNP as not representing current income. Furthermore, repayments of mortgage principal are purely financial flows or transfers, which cannot be counted in the national output. Netting the interest insurance and maintenance expenditures within the business sectors also has advantages of simplicity and convenience.

Estimates of both actual and imputed rents are not very precise, involving multiplication of numbers of dwelling units by national-average rents. For imputed rent of owner-occupied homes, scanty data on rental houses must be used. The whole series of *rental income of persons* is among the weakest of national income statistics;[16] fortunately, the item is a relatively small one, even though it amounted to $24.5 billion in 1971! (It is this small mainly because the bulk of apartment rents are paid to business firms, incorporated or unincorporated, rather than to persons.)

Corporate Profits and Inventory-Valuation Adjustment

Corporate profits comprise all accounting profits before taxes (as shown on line 11 of Table 4-4), just as wages and salaries are shown before withholding deductions for income tax. Lines 12–15 of Table 4-4 show the disposition of before-tax profits: $37 billion out of $83 billion goes to corporation income taxes (federal and state, on the accrual basis). The remaining $46 billion is split as follows: $25 billion to dividends and $21 billion retained as undistributed profits. (Only 30 percent of total corporate profits before taxes was distributed to stockholders in 1971!)

Corporate profits do not cover the entire return for corporate entrepreneurship, since salaries for the work of owners and managers are usually included as part of business expense on the part of corporations and therefore are not included as part of corporate profits.

The inventory-valuation adjustment is more complex. Business firms have to place a value on their stock of inventories at the end of each account-

---

[15] W. Lewis Bassie, "Suitability of the Accounts for Short-Term Analysis," in *Critique*, q.v., p. 386.

[16] 1954 *National Income* supplement, q.v., pp. 86–91.

ing period, for both balance-sheet and income-statement purposes. Each inventory valuation is achieved by multiplying price by quantity, with the result that an increase in the value of inventory may be due to an increase in price, or in quantity, or both. However, most business firms use the first-in, first-out accounting method (FIFO), which calculates the dollar value of any change in inventories by multiplying the number of units consumed by the cost per unit of the earliest units purchased. If prices have changed since the period when the cost of the earliest units in inventory was incurred, the value of inventory on the firm's books will be different from the value of the inventory on a current replacement-cost basis.

From the national-income standpoint, however, increases in inventory represent an increase in the stock of goods produced in the current year, and should be valued at their average replacement cost over the year and not by the FIFO method. The national income and product accounts should reflect real physical changes in inventory, coupled with the average price change during the current year; they should not include a spurious extra element of value simply because prices increased since the time the earliest units entered some firm's inventory. Therefore, an inventory-valuation adjustment is needed to exactly neutralize the effect of FIFO, by reducing the value of inventories when prices rise and increasing it when prices fall.[17] The inventory-valuation adjustment also carries this correction over to corporate profits, through its effect on cost of goods sold.[18]

If we refer to the income statement for a single firm in Table 4-2, we see that if ending inventory is misleadingly high, perhaps owing to a FIFO inventory-valuation method, the net change in inventory is too low, cost of goods sold is too low, and profits are too high. Because many corporations had a misleadingly high inventory valuation in 1971, the adjustment is made to reduce corporate profits to a more accurate level that does not include inflation-induced gains in inventory values.

A sufficient number of firms were on a FIFO basis in 1971, a year of sharply rising prices, that in the aggregate the inventory change recorded by firms was overvalued by \$4.7 billion. Therefore, an inventory-valuation adjustment of −\$4.7 billion (on line 16 of Table 4-4) was necessary.

An inventory-valuation adjustment is also applied to noncorporate profits, or proprietors' income, and is included in the figure for proprietors' income on line 8 of Table 4-4.

Net Interest

Net interest conceptually and primarily represents interest paid by business firms to all sectors of the economy (individuals, government, other business firms) *minus* interest received by business from all economic sectors.

---

[17]Even with a LIFO (last-in, first-out) accounting system, an inventory-valuation adjustment is required, but only when the physical volume of inventories is decreasing (not generally the case in recent years).

[18]1954 *National Income* supplement, pp. 44–45.

Essentially, it includes interest on corporate bonds, plus interest payments to depositors by banks and savings and loan associations, minus interest received on loans by banks and savings and loan associations. Net interest also includes interest received from the rest of the world, minus interest paid abroad.

The total of monetary net interest is quite small and for many years was negative, but it is augmented by two imputed items: services received by persons from banks and other financial institutions without payment, and property income of life insurance companies and pension funds not passed on to policyholders in dividends or declared as profits.[19] Both these items are really disguised interest payments. Service charges collected by banks on demand deposits do not cover the costs of handling checking accounts. Banks make up the difference by lending out at interest most of the money on deposit. A sum equal to the interest income earned by banks, less profits of the banks, less the interest actually paid on deposits, is "imputed" (that is, assumed to have been paid) to depositors as interest income. This imputed-income item for persons is balanced on the product side of the national-income account by an equal item of personal-consumption expenditures entitled, "Services furnished without payment by financial intermediaries." In the case of life insurance, premiums charged on policies are a little smaller because the companies lend the premium receipts at interest. This interest too is treated as if it were passed on to policyholders, and forms the final component of imputed net interest. In 1971, the imputed-interest items accounted for $27.7 billion out of total net-interest income of $38.5 billion.[20]

The five major items described above, taken together, constitute *national income*, or the sum of income payments to the factors of production.

Nonfactor Payments

As previously pointed out, certain nonfactor payments must be added before the income side can add up to GNP, or total production at market prices. The five nonfactor payments are these:

1. *Business transfer payments* are payments by business for which no current productive services were rendered. In this way, they are analogous to government transfer payments. Business transfers consist mostly of corporate gifts to nonprofit (usually charitable) institutions and of bad debts of consumers written off by business.

2. *Indirect business taxes*, the most important nonfactor payment, basically consist of all payments by business to government, except for employer contributions to social insurance and corporation income taxes. The most important items are sales, excise, and property taxes. Also included are such nontax payments as inspection fees, fines and penalties, rents, and donations.[21] As part of the market

---

[19] *Statistical Tables*, pp. x and 151.

[20] Office of Business Economics, U.S. Department of Commerce, "U.S. National Income and Product Accounts," *Survey of Current Business*, 51 (July 1972), p. 45, Table 7.2; lines 1, 4, and 6. Hereafter cited as July 1972 *Survey*.

[21] *Statistical Tables*, p. xi.

prices of products, indirect business taxes are part of GNP, even though they do not create income for any factor of production.

3. The item *Subsidies less current surplus of government enterprises* is subtracted from the other items, apparently to avoid the negative numbers that would result if item 21 in Table 4-4 were expressed as "Surplus less subsidies." Government subsidies to agriculture or the merchant marine create factor payments without correspondingly raising the market price of the product. Government enterprises include such diverse activities as the Postal Service and municipal bus systems; the surplus of those enterprises is conceptually similar to private corporate profits.

Government subsidies are not included in GNP, yet as part of the cost of production they must be included in NI. Surplus of government enterprises is a reverse subsidy and is already included in the market price of government services. However, there is no provision for government profit as a part of NI. Therefore, subtracting "Subsidies less surpluses" from NI brings it closer to market prices before adding the other four items to arrive at GNP.

4. *Capital consumption allowances* consist almost entirely of depreciation charges shown by corporate and noncorporate business and nonprofit institutions. Perhaps 3 percent of the total represents an estimate of accidental damages to fixed capital occurring from fire, business motor-vehicle accidents, or other casualty losses. Since a 1965 revision of some national-income definitions by the Office of Business Economics, virtually all the remainder is depreciation taken from federal income tax returns for corporations and unincorporated businesses. The only alterations made by the OBE are upward adjustments to cover nonreporting firms and owner-occupied homes.[22] The income tax laws permit depreciation to be computed by any of several different methods, under certain "guidelines" specifying useful lives for various classes of buildings and equipment. (However, the method chosen by a firm must be followed consistently year after year.)

Depreciation declared for tax purposes need not be the same as that used by a business in its own cost accounting or in controlling its operations (for example as shown on its financial statement). Generally, a firm will try to write off its capital purchases as fast as the Internal Revenue Service permits. A fast write-off concentrates capital consumption allowances in years of high investment expenditures. Furthermore, tax laws and regulations on depreciation change periodically, causing abrupt shifts in depreciation declared on tax returns and entering the national-income accounts.

The point of all this is that the estimate for capital consumption allowances is quite rough. Subject as it is to the vagaries of depreciation accounting, it is one of the least reliable national-income components. Nevertheless, it does give some idea of the amount of capital goods used up in producing the output of the current period. Incidentally, only depreciation of buildings and equipment is part of capital consumption allowances; depletion of mineral or oil deposits or of timber resources is never included.

5. *Statistical discrepancy*, shown on line 23 of Table 4-4, is simply the difference between GNP calculated from the product side of the national income and product account and GNP added up independently as the sum of the income-side items.

Recently, statistical discrepancy has consistently been negative, indicating that the sum of estimates of income exceeds the sum of estimates of expenditures on production. It might normally be assumed that information on sales or production would be easier to obtain than information on income derived from sources such as

---

[22] *Ibid.*, pp. x–xi. 1954 *National Income* supplement, q.v., pp. 150–51. Office of Business Economics, U.S. Department of Commerce, "The National Income and Product Accounts of the United States: Revised Estimates 1929–64," *Survey of Current Business*, 45 (August 1965), 13. Hereafter cited as August 1965 *Survey*.

income tax returns. People are notably reluctant to reveal their income, often because they want to reduce their tax payments. However, the reverse is true. Reported income is larger than reported production and sales, and no one is sure why. One possible explanation is that some people may be "honestly" reporting illegal income.

We must be careful to avoid one trap: A negative statistical discrepancy is not caused by saving or by increases in saving. Some income received by persons does not go into personal-consumption expenditures and is thereby saved, but this saving is exactly offset on the product side by an equal amount of investment. Any income that the consumer does not spend piles up in the form of unbought goods or additions to inventory, which by definition are a kind of investment. Therefore the national income and product account always balances, because its investment (I) always equals saving (S), when viewed in an *ex post* sense. We will learn in Chapter 8 that S can differ from I *ex ante*, but that total income or GNP adjusts so that they always come out equal *ex post*. In this context, *ex ante* means "planned" and *ex post* means "realized."

FIVE MEASURES OF NATIONAL OUTPUT OR INCOME

The various income-side items, both factor incomes and nonfactor payments, add up to gross national product, or GNP. However, there are four other measures of U.S. national output or income that are commonly used and are regularly published by the Department of Commerce. In descending order of size below GNP, the other four national-output aggregates are these:

Net national product
National income
Personal income
Disposable personal income

Net National Product

Net national product, or NNP, is simply GNP minus capital consumption allowances—the *net* final output produced by the economy during the accounting period. As such, it includes the purchases of goods and services by consumers and government (which, as final products, are net by definition), net exports of goods and services, and net investment. Net investment is the increase in the stock of capital goods in the economy during the year; it is the production of new capital goods less the wearing out or using up of old capital goods (which occurred in producing the year's output). The part of old capital goods that was used up can be regarded as part of the production of previous periods that gets transformed into, and included in, current output. It is really a form of intermediate product, similar to the cloth going into a suit or tires into automobiles. Gross investment, then, is all the new capital goods produced in the current period. The difference between gross and net investment is exactly the same as the difference between GNP and NNP; namely, capital consumption allowances, or depreciation.

Of the five U.S. national-income or output aggregates, NNP most closely corresponds to the elusive Keynesian "aggregate income," or *Y*, used later in this book to represent income as used in theoretical models of income determination.

And yet, NNP is not the most-used national-income aggregate, and some economists consider it misleading or of doubtful value.[23] The disadvantages of net national product, entirely practical in nature, consist of the near impossibility of calculating reliable estimates of *net* domestic investment, because there are no independent measures of depreciation other than figures reported in tax returns or financial statements.[24] Depreciation obtained by the OBE from tax returns is geared to the current provisions of the tax laws much more closely than it is to the actual wearing out of plant and equipment. Also, under any recognized accounting method, much of the depreciation allowance represents estimates of obsolescence rather than wear, and the judgment on obsolescence is affected by competitive factors such as the newness of a competitor's equipment. Conservative accounting procedure requires that estimates of both obsolescence and wear be maximized rather than minimized; hence, in some industries, machines that were fully "written off" many years ago continue to operate.

Such overstatement of depreciation and consequent understatement of net national product would be less serious if they were consistent over time—that is, if the year-to-year change were reliable even if the level of NNP is not. Unfortunately, the clustering of depreciation in periods of heavy investment by firms desiring a fast write-off, plus sudden changes in the tax laws and regulations, tend to make NNP a less reliable measure of changes in national output over short periods than is GNP. One authority considers these short periods to encompass as much as ten years.[25]

Of course, it is true that over very long periods, a trend line through NNP does clearly give a better indication of long-run economic growth than does GNP, which progressively overstates the most recent period, particularly as an economy becomes more capital-intensive. Nonetheless, it is interesting that it is only the more theoretically oriented economists who speak of NNP, whereas national-income specialists, business analysts, and economists who are oriented to practical matters of quality of data deal almost exclusively with GNP.

National Income

National income has been defined previously; it is the sum of all payments to factors of production that come out of current production. On the income side of the national income and product account, we have shown that

---

[23]Sam Rosen, *National Income: Its Measurement, Determination, and Relation to Public Policy* (New York: Holt, Rinehart & Winston, 1963), p. 71.

[24]*Ibid.*

[25]*Ibid.*, p. 70.

national income is the sum of the five factor payments previously discussed. Since payments to the factors of production are the factor costs of production, national income in this sense, as it is defined by the Commerce Department, is sometimes called "national income at factor cost."

Both GNP and NNP are measured in terms of market prices, but national income, as well as personal income and disposable personal income, represents factor costs. The main difference between the market price and the factor cost of anything (after depreciation on capital equipment has been taken out of market price) is indirect business taxes, since the government cannot be considered a factor of production but the price of the product normally includes sales, property, and other indirect business taxes.

Three other items that are not payments to factors of production are also excluded from NNP in arriving at national income (NI); namely, business transfer payments, statistical discrepancy, and the current surplus of government enterprises. Subsidies, on the other hand, have to be added back into NI; they result in factor payments but are not a part of market prices paid for the commodity or service. The actual technique used is to add back "net subsidies"; that is, subsidies minus the surplus of government enterprises, which are in effect negative subsidies.

Note that direct taxes (meaning income and payroll taxes) *are* included in national income. About the only defense for the disparate treatment between direct and indirect taxes is that people often think in terms of pre-direct-tax income, whereas indirect taxes are generally not considered income by anyone.[26]

Although we have come close to saying that NI is merely whatever the Commerce Department says it is, actually it does have some valid uses. For determining the relative shares earned by and accruing to the various factors of production (labor, capital, land, and so on), national income is clearly the correct total to use.

Historically, national income was the first aggregate-output measure to be developed for the United States during the early 1930's. In fact, the term "national income" is now often used in a much broader sense than the narrow OBE factor-cost definition. "National income" frequently means the whole field of national income and product accounting and represents any of the *five* measures of national output or income—from GNP down to disposable personal income (DPI).

Personal Income (PI)

Personal income appears at first glance to be a simple concept: the total before-tax income received by individuals. One might conclude that personal income equals national income minus corporate profits, plus dividend

[26]George Jaszi, "The Conceptual Basis of the Accounts," in *Critique*, pp. 53, 118–19. 1954 *National Income* supplement, p. 31. The opposing view is presented by Kenneth D. Ross, "The Product Side: A Business User's Viewpoint," *Critique*, pp. 279–80.

payments to stockholders. That conclusion would be wrong, however, because of four complicating facts:

1. Personal income is not just the income of persons; it is the income of the personal sector of the economy, and the personal sector is defined to include nonprofit institutions and organizations.
2. Not all the income received by persons is earned—i.e., comes out of current production.
3. Personal income, unlike GNP, NNP, and NI, is computed on a cash rather than accrual basis.
4. An arbitrary decision has been made to exclude one tax directly paid by individuals, the Social Security tax, from personal income.

In calculating personal income, the following three items are subtracted from NI because they represent income earned but not actually received by individuals during the year:

1. Corporate profits are eliminated from personal income because three of the four components of profits—namely, undistributed profits, corporate income taxes, and inventory-valuation adjustment—are not paid out to individuals by corporations. Dividends, the fourth component, are paid out by the corporation to stockholders, and are received as income by individuals. Therefore, dividends must later be added back into personal income.

2. Any excess of accrued wages over wage disbursements is also subtracted from national income (line 4 of Table 4-4, the national income and product account) in order to get personal income on a cash basis, since GNP, NNP, and NI are computed on the accrual basis.

3. The third item subtracted from national income is contributions for social insurance, whether paid by employees or employers, since these taxes are deducted from a worker's earnings and therefore are not part of the paycheck workers receive. The decision to exclude Social Security taxes from personal income but to include similarly withheld income taxes is essentially an arbitrary one, taken for the convenience of the OBE.[27]

Next, four additions have to be made to national income after the subtractions above:

1. Government transfer payments
2. Business transfer payments
3. Corporate dividends
4. Interest paid by government and by consumers

Three of the four additions are income items actually received by the personal sector but not considered to have been earned in current production. The fourth addition, dividends paid to stockholders by corporations, is already included in national income but was subtracted above when we deducted all corporate profits from NI.

Government transfer payments are by far the most important numerically of these items, comprising some $89 billion in 1971. Transfer payments have been defined as "income received by persons, generally in monetary form,

[27] 1954 *National Income* supplement, p. 51.

for which no services are rendered currently."[28] Government transfer payments comprise mainly Social Security benefits, including Medicare; state and railroad unemployment insurance benefits; railroad retirement; military and civilian pensions; public assistance or welfare benefits; and veterans' benefits. For many of these transfer payments, services were obviously performed, but in some, often remote, past period rather than currently. Since transfer payments are money received (but not earned) during the current time period, they must be included in personal income.

Business transfer payments, in contrast to those paid by the government, consist of business contributions to nonprofit organizations, classified as part of the personal sector, and bad debts, which are treated as if they were gifts from business to individuals. Business transfers are unique in that they are specifically included in every U.S. national-income aggregate except national income.

Dividends are a genuine source of income to individuals, a portion of the payment to the factor of production entrepreneurship. Since all corporate profits were deducted previously, dividends have to be added back.

The final item is "Interest paid by government (net) and by consumers." Net interest paid by government—essentially interest on government bonds held by persons, minus interest received from sources such as overdue taxes—is part of personal income, as are dividends, since individuals' money income is increased in both cases. Government interest payments, however, unlike dividends, are not considered a payment for current productive activity. At least since World War II, most of the government debt and the interest paid on it have been incurred financing war expenditures and bear little relation to the cost of government capital goods or to current government activity. The whole postwar period would be overstated in comparison to the prewar if government interest were included in GNP.[29] Other portions of the government debt arose merely through annual deficits in the budget, reflecting periods when current expenditures, mostly for salaries and currently consumed supplies, simply outran tax revenue. Again, government capital goods were not correspondingly acquired.

At present, interest paid by consumers is treated like government interest for the same reasons. Consumer interest, a large item, amounting to $17.6 billion in 1971, represents neither the cost nor the value of consumer capital goods.[30] Since all homes, including owner-occupied homes, are classified in the business sector, and since autos, furniture, appliances, and other consumer durables are considered current consumption expenditures, there is really no concept of consumer capital goods remaining to be recognized by U.S. national-income accounting. Even if there were, much of consumer interest, especially on credit cards and charge accounts, goes to finance spending on clothing, gasoline, hotel and restaurant bills—all current expenditures

---

[28] *Statistical Tables*, p. x.

[29] Ruggles, *National Income Accounts*, pp. 53–54.

[30] August 1965 *Survey*, p. 10 (footnote 6).

by any standard. The present decision, that only interest spent by business predominantly reflects the services of capital goods and therefore only interest payments by business can enter the GNP, appears to be an eminently reasonable one.

In addition, the present practice brings the U.S. accounts into conformity with the United Nations system and with practice in most other countries. Before 1965, consumer interest was included in GNP; then in 1965 the OBE established its present system of accounting for consumer interest and revised its published figures for 1929–64 in such a way as to exclude consumer interest from GNP, NI, and PCE.[31] Yet consumer interest must still be included in personal income, because consumer interest payments are personal interest income that was not counted in net interest. Like the interest paid on government securities, consumer interest increases the money income of individuals.

After the three subtractions and four additions just discussed, the resulting figure is personal income, PI. However, PI is seldom used in analyzing consumer behavior, because disposable personal income, DPI, which subtracts out the personal income tax, is preferable for this purpose. Personal income is published monthly by the OBE, but the other income aggregates are published only quarterly; so personal income is often used as an interim proxy measure for the other measures of national output or income. Nevertheless, the use of PI as a proxy is likely to be misleading, as the number and size of the adjustments necessary to convert PI to any of the other aggregate-output or income measures would indicate.

Disposable Personal Income (DPI)

One adjustment converts PI to disposable personal income, DPI—often called disposable income, DI. Personal tax and nontax payments to government are subtracted. Federal and state personal income taxes comprise the largest part of this item, and estate and gift taxes, motor vehicle licenses, and personal (not real estate) property taxes make up nearly all the rest.

DPI is one of the most useful national-income aggregates, because it measures the amount of money consumers have at their disposal to spend. In fact, DPI *must*, by definition, be either spent or saved by consumers—there can be no other alternatives—and the percentage saved is remarkably constant. In most years, personal saving varies only between 6 and 7 percent of total disposable personal income. (It reached an unusually high 8.2 percent in 1971, indicating that unusual consumer uncertainty caused by recession may increase the desire to save.) Based on the past stability in the percentage of DPI saved, we know that total consumer spending will run between 92 and 94 percent of DPI—near perfect correlation in statistical terms. Therefore, to predict the demand for almost any major item of consumer expenditure, the analyst usually begins by predicting disposable personal income. Recently, our national-income accounting system has equated total consumer

---

[31] *Ibid.*, p. 10.

spending to personal outlays, not personal-consumption expenditures (PCE). Personal outlays equals PCE with consumer interest added back in, plus a small item, personal transfer payments to foreigners (which, like consumer interest, was previously part of PCE). A true measure of consumer spending (or nonsaving) has to include interest payments and remittances abroad (personal transfer payments to foreigners) actually expended by consumers. However, for simplicity, throughout most of this book, we will divide disposable personal income between consumption and savings only.

A Tabular and Graphical Presentation of National-Income Aggregates

Table 4-5 summarizes the magnitudes of the adjustments from GNP to disposable personal income for 1971. It also includes the allocation of disposable personal income between personal outlays and personal savings. The table merely incorporates the various adjustments already discussed, so that the student may obtain an idea of the relative and absolute size of the various components and adjustments to national income.

TABLE 4-5 Relation of Gross National Product, National Income, Personal Income, and Disposable Personal Income, 1971 (millions of dollars)

Gross national product			$1,050,356
Less:	Capital consumption allowances		93,758
Equals:	Net national product		956,598
Less:	Indirect business tax and nontax liability	$101,923	
	Business transfer payments	4,610	
	Statistical discrepancy	−4,817	
Plus:	Subsidies less current surplus of government enterprises	866	
Equals:	National income		855,748
Less:	Corporate profits and inventory valuation adjustment	$78,570	
	Contributions for social insurance	65,322	
	Wage accruals less disbursements	559	
Plus:	Government transfer payments to persons	88,973	
	Interest paid by government (net) and by consumers	31,077	
	Dividends	25,425	
	Business transfer payments	4,610	
Equals:	Personal income		861,382
Less:	Personal taxes and nontax payments		117,007
Equals:	Disposable personal income		744,375
Less:	Personal outlays		683,444
	Personal consumption expenditures	$664,901	
	Interest paid by consumers	17,555	
	Personal transfer payments to foreigners	988	
Equals:	Personal savings		60,931

Source: Office of Business Economics, U.S. Department of Commerce, *Survey of Current Business*, 52 (July 1972), 25.

A graph of the various national-income aggregates is shown in Figure 4-2. The larger rectangles in the center represent the five national-income measures, GNP, NNP, NI, PI, and DPI, with the flows indicating the major changes in going from one national-income measure to another. Figure 4-2 therefore recasts the simple circular-flow chart of Figure 4-1 into these na-

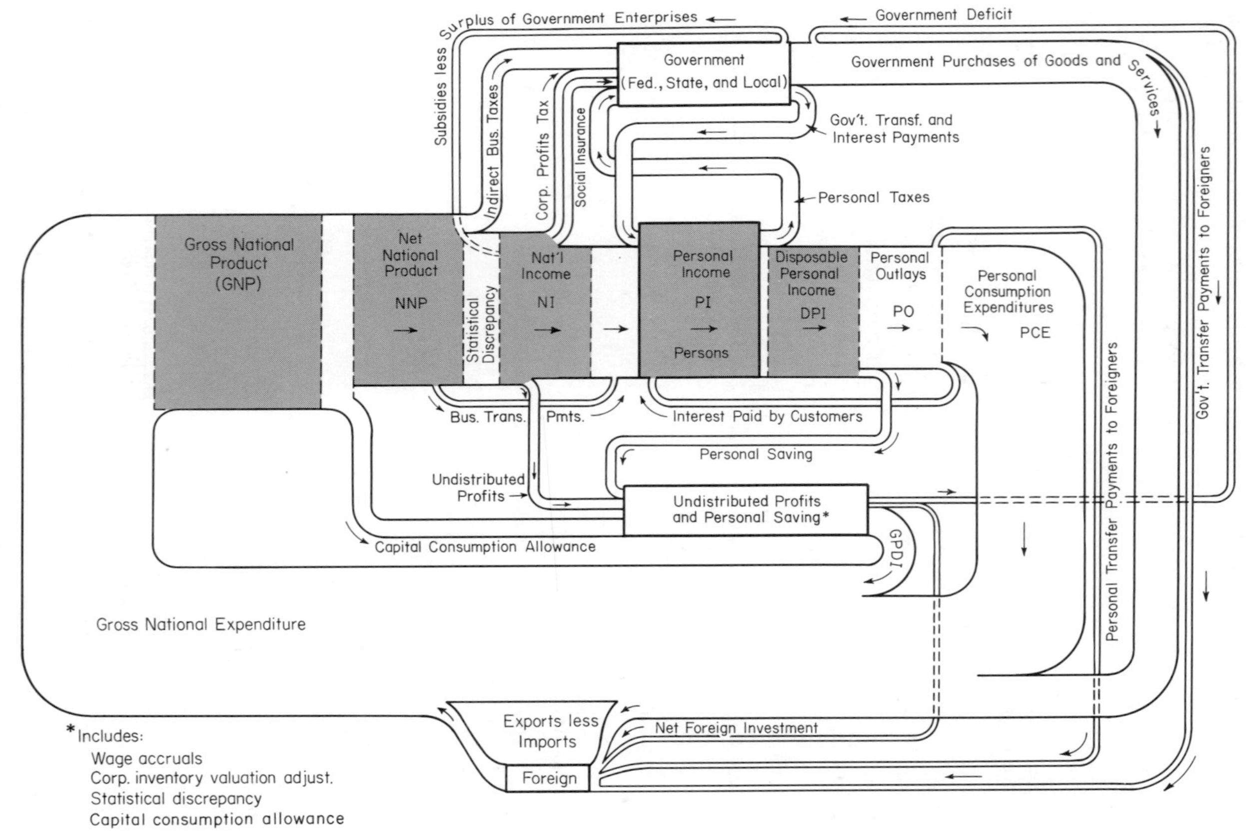

FIG. 4-2 The Flow of Income in a Given Time Period (Source: John P. Lewis and Robert C. Taylor, *Business Conditions Analysis* (New York: McGraw-Hill, 1967), inside covers.)

tional-accounting terms; the aggregates measure the major flow at various stages, and the components are subflows. The role of government is presented at the top of Figure 4-2, with the various revenue items going to the government coming out of the national-income aggregates and the various government expenditures flowing back into them.

The savings and investment flows are shown directly below the major national-income aggregates. In addition to undistributed profits, we have personal savings and capital consumption allowance flowing into the pool of savings available to finance investment. The savings pool also includes wage accruals and corporate inventory valuation adjustment.

Further subsidiary flows show interest paid by consumers flowing out of DPI back into PI, as the previous discussion implied. Business transfer payments are shown to flow directly from net national product into personal income, bypassing national income, since transfer payments are not paid for productive services provided in the current time period. The foreign sector is represented at the bottom of Figure 4-2. For simplicity, one minor item—capital grants received by the United States—is excluded. Statistical discrepancy is shown as a dotted line between NNP and NI to indicate where the balancing between the income and product sides is performed. The effect of statistical discrepancy can then be neutralized in savings in order to equate savings and investment. The following section takes up in detail sector analysis, introduced here by our discussion of the government sector, the foreign sector, and the investment and savings sector.

SUBSIDIARY SECTOR ACCOUNTS

So far, we have examined only one major account, the national income and product account shown in Table 4-4, and the five aggregate measures of national income derivable from it. Actually, the OBE records economic flows in an interrelated set of five accounts, consisting of the national income and product account plus four accounts for "sectors" or subclassifications of the economy and of economic transactions. As shown in Table 4-6. these subsidiary sector accounts are as follows:

Personal income and outlay account
Government receipts and expenditures account
Foreign transactions account
Gross saving and investment account

Taken together with the national income and product account of Table 4-4, which is repeated as panel 1 of Table 4-6, these four additional accounts in Table 4-6 constitute the complete National Income and Product Accounts of the United States.[32] Panels 2, 3, and 4 of Table 4-6 summarize personal, government, and foreign transactions sectors repectively. The last account,

---

[32]July 1972 *Survey*, pp. 14–15.

TABLE 4-6 The National Income and Product Account in Addition to the Sector Accounts of the United States for 1971 (Number of Sector Tables Includes as 1.—National Income and Product Account, which is the same as Table 4-4. The complete set of 5 tables constitutes the National Income and Product Accounts of the United States for 1971.) (All values in billions of dollars)

1. National Income and Product Account of the United States for 1971

Line	*Income Side (Payments)*					*Line*	*Product or Expenditure Side (Receipts)*				
1	Compensation of employees				$644.1	24	Personal consumption expenditures (2-3)				$664.9
2	Wages and salaries			$573.5		25	Durable goods			$103.5	
3	Disbursements (2-7)		$572.9			26	Nondurable goods			278.1	
4	Wage accruals less disbursements (3−7+5−4)		.6			27	Services			283.3	
5	Supplements to wages & salaries			70.7		28	Gross private domestic investment (5-1)				152.0
6	Employer contributions for social insurance (3-15)		$34.1			29	Fixed investment			$148.3	
						30	Nonresidential		$105.8		
7	Other labor income (2-8)		36.5			31	Structures	$38.4			
8	Proprietors' income (2-9)				70.0	32	Producers' durable equipment	67.4			
9	Rental income of persons (2-10)				24.5						
10	Corporate profits and inventory valuation adjustment				78.6	33	Residential structures		42.6		
11	Profits before tax			$83.3		34	Change in business inventories			3.6	
12	Corporate profits income tax liability (3-12)		$37.3			35	Net exports of goods and services				.7
13	Profits after tax		45.9			36	Exports (4-1)			$66.1	
14	Dividends (2-11)	$25.4				37	Imports (4-3)			65.4	
15	Undistributed profits (5-5)	20.5				38	Government purchases of goods and services (3-1)				232.8
16	Inventory valuation adjustment (5-6)			−4.7							
17	Net interest (2-13)				38.5	39	Federal			$97.8	
18	NATIONAL INCOME				$855.7	40	National defense	$71.4			
19	Business transfer payments (2-17)				4.6	41	Other	26.3			
20	Indirect business taxes (3-13)				101.9						
21	Minus: Subsidies less current surplus of government enterprises (3-6)				.9	42	State and local			135.0	
22	Capital consumption allowances (5-7)				93.8						
23	Statistical discrepancy (5-10)				−4.8						
	CHARGES AGAINST NATIONAL PRODUCT				$1,050.4		GROSS NATIONAL PRODUCT				$1,050.4

2. Personal Income and Outlay Account

Line	Expenditure			Line	Income		
1	Personal tax and nontax payments (3-11)		$117.0	7	Wage and salary disbursements (1-3)		$572.9
2	Personal outlays		683.4	8	Other labor income (1-7)		36.5
3	Personal consumption expenditures (1-24)	$664.9		9	Proprietors' income (1-8)		70.0
4	Interest paid by consumers (2-15)	17.6		10	Rental income of persons (1-9)		24.5
5	Personal transfer payments to foreigners (net) (4-5)	1.0		11	Dividends (1-14)		25.4
6	Personal saving (5-3)		60.9	12	Personal interest income		69.6
				13	Net interest (1-17)	$38.5	
				14	Net interest paid by government (3-5)	13.5	
				15	Interest paid by consumers (2-4)	17.6	
				16	Transfer payments to persons		93.6
				17	From business (1-19)	$4.6	
				18	From government (3-3)	89.0	
				19	Less: Personal contributions for social insurance (3-16)		31.2
	PERSONAL TAXES, OUTLAYS AND SAVING		$861.4		PERSONAL INCOME		$861.4

3. Government Receipts and Expenditures Account

Line	Expenditure			Line	Income		
1	Purchases of goods and services (1-38)		$232.8	11	Personal tax and nontax payments (2-1)		$117.0
2	Transfer payments		91.6	12	Corporate profits income tax liability (1-12)		37.3
3	To persons (2-18)	$89.0		13	Indirect business tax and nontax liability (1-20)		101.9
4	To foreigners (net) (4-4)	2.6		14	Contributions for social insurance		65.3
5	Net interest paid (2-14)		13.5	15	Employer (1-6)	$34.1	
6	Subsidies less current surplus of government enterprises (1-21)		.9	16	Personal (2-19)	31.2	
7	Less: wage accruals less disbursements (1-4)		.2				
8	Surplus or deficit (-), national income and product accounts (5-8)		−16.9				
9	Federal	$−21.7					
10	State and local	4.8					
	GOVERNMENT EXPENDITURES AND SURPLUS		$321.6		GOVERNMENT RECEIPTS		$321.6

TABLE 4-6 Continued

Line	Receipt from Foreigners		Line	Payments to Foreigners	
	4. Foreign Transactions Account				
1	Exports of goods and services (1-36)	$66.1	3	Imports of goods and services (1-37)	$65.4
2	Capital grants received by the United States (5-9)	.7	4	Transfer payments from U.S. Government to foreigners (net) (3-4)	2.6
			5	Personal transfer payments to foreigners (net) (2-5)	1.0
			6	Net foreign investment (5-2)	−2.1
	RECEIPTS FROM FOREIGNERS	$66.9		PAYMENTS TO FOREIGNERS	$66.9
	5. Gross Saving and Investment Account				
Line	*Investment*		*Line*	*Savings*	
1	Gross private domestic investment (1-28)	$152.0	3	Personal saving (2-6)	$60.9
2	Net foreign investment (4-6)	−2.1	4	Wage accruals less disbursements (1-4)	.4
			5	Undistributed corporate profits (1-15)	20.5
			6	Corporate inventory valuation adjustment (1-16)	−4.7
			7	Capital consumption allowances (1-22)	93.8
			8	Government surplus or deficit (-) national income and product accounts (3-8)	−16.9
			9	Capital grants received by the U.S. (4-2)	.7
			10	Statistical discrepancy (1-23)	−4.8
	GROSS INVESTMENT	$149.8		GROSS SAVING AND STATISTICAL DISCREPANCY	$149.8

Numbers in parentheses indicate accounts and items of counterentry in the accounts.

Source: Office of Business Economics, U.S. Department of Commerce, *Survey of Current Business,* 52 (July 1972), 14–15. Discrepancies due to rounding.

Gross saving and investment, covers all transactions on capital account and the saving by all sectors ultimately required to finance capital investments.

The term "sectors" has to be used with care; it does not refer to individuals or organizations as much as it does to kinds of transactions. The same person will appear in more than one sector: as a consumer, as a wage earner, as a taxpayer, and as a saver. If he imports goods directly or sends money to relatives overseas, he also gets into the foreign transactions account. Thus, "sectoring" divides people or organizations according to the *roles* they play at the time of certain transactions.

Furthermore, each transaction is shown twice, once as a payment and again as a receipt by some other sector or transactor. The receipt entry appears on the right-hand (or credit) side of one account and must be balanced by an equal expenditure entry on the left-hand (or debit) side of another account. This method corresponds to the interlocking system of double-entry bookkeeping commonly used in business. Within each sector, income received, as shown on the credit side, is exactly balanced by the expenditures made by that sector on the debit side. Thus, all personal income is shown on the credit side of the personal income and outlay account, while expenditures and the residual savings are shown on the debit side.

A very simple example should clarify the interlocking nature of the system. Assume a rather primitive economy, with no saving or investment, no government, and no foreign transactions. Only food and clothes are produced, and the only expenses are for wages (perhaps including shelter as a fringe benefit). Then the complete system of national income and product accounts would be as follows:

1. National Income and Product Account (or Production Account) $ millions

Payments		*Receipts*	
Wages	$300	Personal-consumption expenditures (Sales of nondurable goods)	$300

2. Personal Account

Payments		*Receipts*	
Personal-consumption expenditures	$300	Wages	$300

Here, $300 million in wages and salaries has been debited as a payment by the production account (which in the official U.S. system is the "National income and product" account) and credited as an equal receipt by the personal account ("Personal income and outlay" account). Similarly, payments of $300 million for food and clothing have been debited to the personal account as payments for personal-consumption expenditures and credited to the production account as receipts for sales of an equal amount.[33]

---

[33]William I. Abraham, *National Income and Economic Accounting* (Englewood Cliffs, N.J.: Prentice-Hall, 1969), pp. 60–61.

These items can be found on the official sector accounts at their 1971 U.S. magnitudes. The wage-payment transaction appears on Table 4-6 as item number 1-3 on the left side of the national income and product account and as item 2-7 on the credit side of the personal income and outlay account. Consumption expenditures are simultaneously item 2-3 on the left of the personal account and item 1-24 on the right of the national income and product account. Similar treatment is given all other items in Table 4-6 when this simple example is extended to include our actual economy. The numbers in parentheses help to explain the interrelations of the national-income components.

We have used the term "production account" in our example as synonymous with the national income and product account. This usage is correct, but only because the present U.S. framework of sector accounts provides for no "production sector." Production, which is overwhelmingly carried on by private business, is consolidated in Table 4-4, or panel 1 of Table 4-6, into the national income and product account, the summary account in the present five-account scheme.

Before 1958, the OBE used a six-account sector framework; the extra account, now eliminated, was the "Consolidated business income and product account." The present five-account system is admittedly easier to use, because it simplified some of the previous mass of detail, but in the process, useful information was sacrificed.[34] The previous method did make much clearer the role of the private business sector, which included unincorporated proprietors, landlords, homeowners, and government enterprises, as well as corporations.[35]

A few comments are required on each of the subsidiary sector accounts in Table 4-6. In the present system, the personal sector includes nonprofit organizations and institutions, as indicated previously. Personal income, the sum of the receipts side of the personal sector account, also includes earnings of unincorporated enterprises *retained in the business*. This item is included in personal saving and muddies that concept, too.

The government sector represents a consolidation of all governmental units, federal, state, and local. Therefore, the deficit is not merely the well-publicized federal deficit but also includes any surplus or deficit incurred at any other level of government. Furthermore, the tax receipts and expenditures are the actual figures, not the projected or budgeted figures that receive such wide press coverage. These actual figures, rather than the often politically motivated budget figures, have the real economic impact.

---

[34]Office of Business Economics, U.S. Department of Commerce, *U.S. Income and Output, A Supplement to the Survey of Current Business* (Washington, D.C.: U.S. Government Printing Office, 1958), pp. 50–51.

[35]In fact, any student who has difficulty understanding how production statements of individual firms aggregate to the national income and product account (in our discussion above) would be well advised to consult and study the old six-account system. See 1954 *National Income* supplement, pp. 31–37 and 160–61.

The foreign transactions account actually represents the viewpoint of foreigners with regard to the debiting and crediting of payments: Receipts by foreigners (like any other receipts) go on the right-hand side as a credit, and inflows of funds from abroad for our exports, or capital grants, appear on the left side as a debit. Apparently to relate to the terms "imports" and "exports" of the United States, the sums of the foreign transactions account are labeled "payments to foreigners" and "receipts from foreigners," on the opposite sides from which receipts and payments appear in every other account. This converts the focus to Americans who deal with foreigners. Here, "Net foreign investment" means U.S. investment in foreign countries. Long term investment, for the most part, is real investment as the term is used in this book, whereas short term foreign investment is mostly unpaid commercial balances by foreigners used as a balancing item.

The gross saving and investment account is probably the most important of the sector accounts from the standpoint of macroeconomic theory, because it spells out the important identity that *ex post* saving equals investment in the abstract model we build in Chapters 7, 8, and 9. Statistical discrepancy must be included as savings to make the system balance. Panel 5 of Table 4-6 also shows the sources of saving to finance investment in capital goods. In addition to personal saving, these are wage accruals, undistributed profits, inventory-valuation adjustment, and capital consumption allowances along with a government surplus, if any, and capital grants received by the U. S. (in other words, government and business can save, as well as persons).

However, as we have already stressed, only business and foreigners are allowed to invest. By definition, all purchases by consumers and government are considered current expenditure (land purchases by government are eliminated, and home buying is classified into the business sector).

Notice that the National Income and Product account regards the economy from the standpoint of the business firm. The receipts of business firms, shown on the right, are the expenditures of all the customers listed on the left in panels 2, 3, 4, and 5—allowing for the transposition to the foreign viewpoint in panel 4. The expenditures of business firms, shown on the left of panel 1, are income of the firms' customers and resource suppliers, considering taxes a receipt for services rendered and savings a balancing item.

Items not included in the overall national income accounts listed in panel 1, but which involve an expenditure or income in a specific sector, are included in the applicable subsidiary account with an offsetting debit or credit somewhere in the system.

The system of sector accounts is not used by analysts as much as might be supposed. They generally prefer to work with the supplementary tables appearing in every July issue of the *Survey of Current Business*, because those tables are somewhat geared to specific analytical and research uses. However, in going from one to another of the approximately 80 supplementary tables, the analyst loses the relationships among the various items, and refers to the sector accounts for guidance. The sector accounts are valuable then as a road map to the accounting system, as well as for a pedagogical device.

IMPUTATIONS: NONMARKET TRANSACTIONS INCLUDED IN THE NATIONAL ACCOUNTS

Imputations, nonmonetary income and product transactions, are one complication in the national-income accounting system that we have already encountered. The OBE has chosen, from a wide range of possible imputations, those whose omission would create disturbing anomalies and those hallowed by tradition.

In 1971, the net imputations, or nonmarket transactions, included in GNP comprised $78.9 billion out of a total GNP of $1050.4 billion, or about 7.5 percent of the total. Imputations rose steadily as a proportion of GNP from only 5.1 percent in 1947 to their peak of 7.6 percent in 1970. And during the depressed 1930's, the proportion was even greater—a full 10 percent of 1933's low GNP.[36]

The main reason for the postwar rise in the relative importance of imputations is that the lion's share of imputations consists of the space-rental value of owner-occupied homes. Adding together both nonfarm dwellings and farmhouses, imputed rent on owner-occupied homes amounted to about $59 billion in 1971, or 75 percent of all imputations included in GNP.[37] Not all this imputed rent winds up in "Rental income of persons" on the income side; over $44 billion is deducted for capital consumption allowances, taxes, and interest. We have already discussed imputed rent, but it should be reiterated that the entire imputed space-rental values entering GNP as part of personal-consumption expenditures are statistically quite weak, being based on fragmentary data on rents charged on dwellings similar to owner-occupied homes in some cities.

The second largest nonmarket transaction included in GNP is services furnished without payment by financial intermediaries (it amounted to $14.4 billion in 1971). This item was discussed above as one of the two imputed components of net interest, on the income side of the GNP account. There it appears, you may recall, as "Imputed interest"—interest income of banks and savings and loan associations, less profits and interest paid on deposits, that is assumed to have been passed on to depositors even though no such transaction actually occurred. On the product side, it appears as an imputed expenditure for service charges that should have been, but were not, collected from depositors, to cover the full cost of handling checking and savings accounts.

Another nonmarket transaction, or imputed output, is food and fuel produced and consumed on farms. Many farmers produce some food for themselves; they may also cut firewood from their wood lots for their own use as fuel. As farmers shift away from this kind of "subsistence-economy" activity and into the "market economy" of sales and purchases, total output

---

[36]Calculated from *Statistical Tables*, pp. 152–53, and from July 1972 *Survey*, p. 45.

[37]*Ibid.*

as measured only by market transactions would show an increase unwarranted by the actual work performed or the actual output produced on farms. Food and fuel produced and consumed on farms is perhaps the clearest example of the need for imputations. In the United States, the magnitude of this production was only $0.7 billion in 1971; it is of far greater relative importance in underdeveloped countries, where subsistence farming continues to a greater extent.

Another imputation entering into the national-income aggregates is wages and salaries paid "in kind." Some employers furnish meals and sometimes lodging to employees, and the government issues uniforms to military personnel. In 1971, these three items together amounted to $2.8 billion. Presumably, the employee paid in kind receives lower money wages than he would if meals and lodging were not included in his employment contract; his payment is partially in cash, as a market transaction, and partially in barter, outside the market economy. In this case, the goods or services supplied "free" are final products. They *are* part of the costs of some enterprise, private or government, and would be shown on its income statement as expenses, but in the form of supplements to wages and salaries. As part of the factor costs of production, they must be shown on the income side of the national income and product account. As final products not resold, they must appear on the product side, as part of personal-consumption expenditures.

It would be possible to extend, much farther than is presently done, the inclusion of nonmarket transactions in the national income and product totals by means of imputations.[38] The major omission at present is production carried on within the household by unpaid family members, especially housewives. Nearly every activity that a housewife engages in also commands a price in some sector of the market—whether cooking, cleaning, laundry, child care, or whatever. In other words, a housewife performs, on a "subsistence-economy" basis, services also commonly bought in the "market economy." Yet her work is eliminated from GNP.

Furthermore, as housewives cease to make soap, bake bread, sew clothes, and grow tomatoes, GNP, measured by market transactions, rises more than does the true physical volume of output produced and consumed. The current popularity of preprocessed and precooked foods only accentuates the trend. In fact, an unknown but substantial part of the economic growth registered in the history of the United States (especially since about 1880) consists of the same kinds of final products previously produced at home but now made and sold commercially.

On the other hand, the recent increased importance of "do-it-yourself" activities by householders, and of such presumably productive hobbies as woodworking, operates in the opposite direction: GNP fails to increase as much as it should when the relative importance of such nonmarket output

---

[38] Still another kind of imputation, too complex to be discussed adequately here, is the OBE treatment of life insurance.

increases. On balance, the lessening of GNP from this source is surely swamped by the declining importance of subsistence manufacturing in the household.

Clearly, these distortions and anomalies could be eliminated by an imputation similar to the one for food and fuel produced and consumed on farms. However, the size of the imputation would be enormous. According to estimates, the market value of housewives' services may equal 25 percent of the present national income! The estimate would necessarily be a very rough one, superimposed on more precise estimates for production flowing through and priced by markets. To do the job properly, imputations would also have to be extended to lawn mowing, car washing, shoe shining, tax-return preparation, and similar home activities. The net effect would probably be to *reduce* the usefulness of the national-income aggregates for policy decisions and forecasting.

Nevertheless, it is probably household production that vitiates international comparisons between developed and underdeveloped countries. Some less-developed countries are reported to have per capita incomes of less than $100 per year, whereas U.S. disposable personal income per capita was $3,595 in 1971 (personal income per person was almost $4,200). Of course, the statistics indicating very low per capita annual incomes are based largely on market production, whereas much production in less-developed countries occurs within the household or village. It has been observed that if these very low figures were correct, "the inhabitants of the poorest countries would all have starved a long time ago."[39] Furthermore, the costs of industrialization, such as pollution, that plague developed countries—but are not deducted from GNP—do not afflict less-developed economies and therefore increase relatively the real but unmeasured part of income.

CONCLUSION

At this point, we can summarize the meaning and usefulness of the five measures of national income and output.

Gross national product, or GNP, is the primary measure of the total national output produced and available for use in the short run. Because it makes no adjustment for capital goods used up, it overstates national product available over long periods. In wartime, when capital goods are usually allowed to run down, GNP is the most relevant measure of the economy's capacity to produce. Statistically, it is probably the most reliable of the five measures, because the whole accounting system statistically and definitionally is oriented toward producing correct GNP estimates.

Net national product, or NNP, measures national output after allowing for consumption of capital goods, whether by depreciation or accidental damage. As such, it is the conceptually appropriate measure of total income,

---

[39]Simon Kuznets, as quoted by Oskar Morgenstern, *On the Accuracy of Economic Observations*, 2nd ed. (Princeton, N.J.: Princeton University Press, 1963), p. 278 (footnote).

Y, and for the most part, when we use the aggregate-income concept throughout the book, we will mean NNP. The practical usefulness of NNP is greatly reduced by the difficulty of estimating a true allowance for capital consumption from business depreciation charges, and its statistical reliability is accordingly relatively low.

National income, or NI, measures the sum of payments to the factors that produced the net output; that is, it measures net output at factor cost. Its practical usefulness is limited, but its historical importance is considerable. The statistical reliability of NI is reasonably good, and probably slightly better than that of NNP.

Personal income (PI) and disposable personal income (DPI) measure incomes received by individuals, the first before and the second after personal taxes. Neither is more than distantly related to national output. DPI particularly is valuable as a base for estimating and predicting personal consumption and savings. The statistical reliability of either personal-income measure is probably second only to GNP.

An attempt has been made to give full coverage to our national-income accounts, where necessary by using imputations for some nonmarket transactions. However, a great many money transactions in the market economy never enter the national-income accounts or the major aggregates. Virtually all intrasector transactions are excluded. Fortunately, these intrasector transactions usually represent either items not produced during the current time period or intermediate products used in the production of final goods and services. For example, purchases and sales of used furniture, used cars, or any used item between one person and another are eliminated, since both individuals are in the personal sector and secondhand goods were counted as production when originally sold.

Most payments from one firm to another within the business sector are excluded, since such payments for current purchases are both sales and expenses within the business sector, involving only the flow of intermediate products.

Purchases on capital account are also made by one firm from another firm, but these are included in GNP because capital is considered to be final output. The presence of the gross saving and investment sector guarantees that capital investments become transactions across sectors instead of within a sector, and accordingly are counted in GNP. As previously mentioned, capital is really an intermediate good in the long run.

Two other kinds of intermediate products, as well as capital goods, do enter the GNP as exceptions to the general rule that intermediate products are excluded. Any intermediate product that goes into business inventories and represents an increase over the level at the end of the previous period becomes part of GNP through change in business inventories. In addition, certain government goods and services (such as county agricultural agents and roads strong enough for commercial trucks) are intermediate products supplied free to business, but nevertheless are included in government purchases of goods and services.

Purely financial transactions are not covered by the national-income accounts. Sales and purchases of financial assets or claims (such as stocks and bonds), capital gains, lendings, and borrowings are excluded, even if they occur between sectors (for instance, newly issued stock sold to the public, or a government loan to a business firm). Yet the stockbroker's margin or commission *is* a part of GNP.[40] Another kind of social accounting system, *flow-of-funds* or money-flows accounts, now compiled by the Board of Governors of the Federal Reserve System, focuses primarily upon these various financial flows, adding them up to gross-saving and gross-investment totals, which unfortunately differ because of definitional differences from the corresponding national-income accounts.

One more type of market transaction is firmly and virtuously excluded by the OBE: illegal activities. Expenditures on gambling, prostitution, or narcotics appear nowhere in the accounts. It is presumed that earnings from illegal sources will go equally unreported on the income side of the national income and product account. However, if a gambler or prostitute should honestly report earnings (or some part of them) on a tax return, possibly under another occupational title, the whole income side will exceed the product side, yielding a negative statistical discrepancy. (The OBE describes the exclusion of illegal transactions as a "tradition-based convention" and as a "Victorian embellishment of the national income structure.")[41]

Incidentally, when Prohibition ended in 1933, the GNP went up (or actually, did not fall as much as it would have), because PCE now included expenditures on alcoholic beverages. In fact, $2.0 billion of the recorded increase in GNP of $7.0 billion between 1932 and 1934 represented only the legalization of alcohol! Should marijuana become legal in the future, the GNP will experience a similar increase.

QUESTIONS AND PROBLEMS

1. How do imputations affect GNP?
2. How are the five aggregate-income concepts related?
3. By what means is double counting avoided in national-income accounting?
4. Should government purchases be counted as consumption or investment? Discuss.
5. Why are corporate profits and proprietors' income treated differently in national-income accounting?
6. Of what use is sector analysis?
7. If we compute GNP by class of expenditure what four major categories are included?

---

[40]The gross profit margin of used-car dealers and secondhand furniture stores is also considered to be value added, and is included in GNP.

[41]1954 National Income supplement, p. 30. George Jaszi, "The Conceptual Basis of the Accounts," *Critique*, p. 143.

8. What other two approaches have been used to compute GNP?
9. Which one of the three techniques is not much used in practice?

ADDITIONAL SELECTED REFERENCES

BOOKS ON NATIONAL-INCOME ACCOUNTING

EDEY, H. C., and A. T. PEACOCK, *National Income and Social Accounting*. London: Hutchinson's University Library, 1959.

HICKS, J. R., A. G. HART, and J. W. FORD, *The Social Framework of the American Economy*, 2nd ed., pp. 117–97, 241–57. Oxford: Oxford University Press, 1955.

JASZI, GEORGE, "Taking Care of Soft Figures: Reflections on Improving the Accuracy of the GNP," in *The Economic Outlook for 1972*. Ann Arbor: University of Michigan, Department of Economics, 1972.

National Accounts Review Committee, *The National Economic Accounts of the United States*. New York: National Bureau of Economic Research, 1958.

Office of Business Economics, U.S. Department of Commerce, "The Economic Accounts of the United States: Retrospect and Prospect." 50th Anniversary Issue of the *Survey of Current Business*, July 1971. Washington, D.C.: U.S. Government Printing Office, 1971.

POWELSON, JOHN P., National Income Analysis, pp. 3–116. New York: McGraw-Hill, 1960.

RUGGLES, N., and R. RUGGLES, *The Design of Economic Accounts*. National Bureau of Economic Research, No. 89 general series. New York: Columbia University Press, 1970.

SCHULTZE, C. L., *National Income Analysis*, Chaps. 1 and 2. Englewood Cliffs, N.J.: Prentice-Hall, 1967.

Studies in Income and Wealth, Vol. X, Parts I–III. New York: National Bureau of Economic Research, 1944.

VAN ARKADIE, BRIAN, and CHARLES R. FRANK, JR., *Economic Accounting and Development Planning*. Nairobi: Oxford University Press, 1966.

YANOVSKY, M., *Social Accounting Systems*, pp. 1–128. Chicago: Aldine, 1965.

An Alternative View of National-Income Accounting and an Evaluation of the System

5

The preceding chapter introduced the standard theory and methodology of national-income accounting to enable the student to interpret published data and to apply the U.S. accounts to macroeconomic models. Similarly, this chapter introduces an alternative approach, input–output analysis, which fills a gap in national-income data by describing the flows of intermediate products from industry to industry in the process of producing the final products included in GNP. We must have some appreciation of those *inter-industry flows* or transactions to understand fully the structure of economic activity and production, rather than simply to measure it in the aggregate.

In the previous chapter, we considered national-income accounting in current, inflated dollars. But such data are often more useful when presented in constant, deflated dollars. In this chapter, we study the techniques for removing the effects of price changes from the data. Also in this chapter, we evaluate our social accounting system, defined to consist of both the national-income accounts and, closely related and integrated with them, input–output tables.

First, however, it is desirable to review and expand upon one of the three major ways to compute GNP discussed in Chapter 4—the sum of value added by industry of origin.

THE VALUE-ADDED APPROACH TO COMPUTING GNP

In Chapter 4, you will recall, we learned that there are three ways to calculate GNP: (1) as the sum of final products, (2) as the sum of the income payments incurred in producing final products, and (3) as the sum of *value added* by each productive unit in the economy. Value added was defined as the value of output minus the value of materials, supplies, and services purchased from other firms. For example, if a power lawn mower selling for $50 f.o.b. factory is manufactured from a gasoline engine costing $20, and steel and other materials costing $10, value added by the mower manufacturer is $20.

Note that value added does not mean simply the value of outputs minus that of all inputs. Value added is defined as output minus certain *particular* inputs—raw materials and finished or semifinished goods to be incorporated into the given stage of production, plus all supplies and business services purchased from other firms (in short, all intermediate products). Some important inputs such as wages and salaries, interest, rental space, and the use of buildings and capital equipment are *not* deducted; they are part of value added. In fact, the only other major items needed to arrive at value added by this income-payments route are profits and the nonfactor-payment item, indirect business taxes.

In Chapter 4 we stated that the Office of Business Economics (OBE) does not use the value-added approach in actually estimating GNP. That statement is generally correct, but like most blanket statements, it has to be qualified. The national income and product accounts calculate GNP only by the flow of final product and flow of income plus nonfactor payments, but the OBE has also published auxiliary studies on several occasions since 1962 that estimate GNP by major industry of origin, and use a value-added approach.[1] In fact, the final-products approach is useless for estimating GNP by industry, because so many industries produce intermediate products, wholly or in part, so the value-added approach is used for this purpose.

Although the illustrative income statement of Table 4-2 and the production statement of Table 4-3 explicitly show purchases from other firms grouped in one place, total purchases of intermediate products are not so easy to obtain from many kinds of real-life income statements. Raw materials and factory supplies may be subsumed under "Cost of sales," office supplies often are included under "General expenses," and infrequently purchased business services (like window washing or computer time) will be hidden away under "Miscellaneous expenses." A correct total for intermediate pur-

---

[1]Jack J. Gottsegen, "Revised Estimates of GNP by Major Industries," *Survey of Current Business*, Vol. 47, No. 4 (April 1967), 18–24; Martin L. Marimont, "GNP by Major Industries, Comparative Patterns of Postwar Growth," *Survey of Current Business*, 42 (October 1962), 6–20; "GNP by Major Industries, 1958–62, Revised and Updated," *Survey of Current Business*, 43 (September 1963), 9–10; "GNP by Major Industries, 1963," *Survey of Current Business*, 44 (September 1964), 19–20.

chases may be impossible to obtain from published financial statements. In practice, then, the conceptually simple method of obtaining value added as output minus intermediate products turns out to give only rough estimates.

We have already seen that the sum of all factor and nonfactor costs, other than intermediate products, equals value added, which is identical to output minus intermediate products. Since data on wage and salary payments, indirect business taxes, corporate profits, and proprietors' income are available from various sources by major industry groups, the OBE can compute GNP by value added by industry, even though certain other figures, such as rental income and net interest, are difficult to classify by industry.[2]

In the past, the OBE has published GNP by major industries (which could also be called value added by industry) on several occasions between 1962 and 1967 (annual figures covering 1947–65). In addition, annual figures of GNP by industry group are now published every year.[3] These figures are of great value in assessing the relative importance of the various industries in production and for showing trends in their relative positions.

A SIMPLIFIED INPUT–OUTPUT MODEL WITH NINE BASIC INDUSTRIES

Interindustry relationships are explicitly elucidated by input–output analysis, developed by Wassily Leontief.[4] Input–output follows in the historical tradition of the French physiocratic school of economic thought,[5] and in our time, follows logically from the relationships of the inputs of factors to outputs of commodities by individual firms. In this section we extend our previous analysis of the firm's inputs and output to include the industry and ultimately the economy. We will use input–output analysis to build from the industrial sectors to the aggregate output for the entire economy.

The national–income accounting system and input–output analysis represent two different ways of approaching the aggregate output of the economy. The two systems have been developed independently; therefore, there have been discrepancies between their published results. However, analytically the results should be identical, and now that the OBE is responsible for both national-income accounting and input–output, the two systems are more effectively coordinated than in the past.

---

[2]Gottsegen, *op. cit.*, p. 18.

[3]Office of Business Economics, U.S. Department of Commerce, "U.S. National Income and Product Accounts," *Survey of Current Business*, 52 (July 1972), 24. Hereafter cited as July 1972 *Survey*.

[4]Wassily Leontief, *Input-Output Economics* (New York: Oxford University Press, 1966).

[5]The physiocrats prepared a *Tableau Economique* to illustrate the interactions of the parts of the economy. The *Tableau*, prepared in 1758 by Quesney, physician to Louis XV, traced the flow of goods and money through the economy. François Quesney, "Explanation of the Economic Table," in Arthur Eli Monroe, ed., *Early Economic Thought* (Cambridge: Harvard University Press, 1948), pp. 341–48.

Historically, input–output tables were developed and published irregularly by different departments of the government. They were published for 1939 and 1947 by the Bureau of Labor Statistics and for 1958 and 1963 by the OBE. The OBE has apparently adopted the UN suggestion that input–output tables be published every five years. This is a reasonable goal. However, it would be more helpful if the tables were constructed and published as quickly as other important statistical series. So far, we have experienced about a five-year delay before the input–output tables for a particular year have been released. Despite this serious delay in publishing the data, input–output analysis remains a useful approach to analyzing the operations of the aggregate economy and will undoubtedly become even more useful in the future.

Tables of GNP by industry are valuable for showing the magnitude of the contribution of each industry to the total national output. They therefore represent an advance over the consolidated aggregates of the national-income accounts. However, a much more comprehensive picture of the structure of U.S. production is revealed by input–output or interindustry tables. These tables clearly delineate interindustry flows from producing industry to consuming industry—or industry of origin to industry of destination.[6] Unless the industry of destination is a so-called final demand or final market—that is, one of the familiar product-side components of GNP—an input–output table deals *only* in intermediate products. In a nutshell, that is the contribution of input–output analysis: It specifies the interindustry flows of intermediate products.

Input–Output for an Industry

A simple input–output statement for one industrial sector of the economy, the construction industry, is shown in Table 5-1, the figures for which are taken from the 1963 input–output study made by the OBE. (Input–output analysis could start with an individual firm by taking the inputs of all resources, labeling each one according to its source, and relating those inputs to the firm's output. Such an input–output statement for a firm would be a mere modification of the firm's income and expense statement, where each of the expenses is shown according to its industry of origin.)

In Table 5-1, the "Purchases from other industries" entry under "Inputs" shows the value of payments to other industries by the construction industry for the purchase of intermediate goods and services. We classify the industrial system into nine categories. These particular components were chosen to correspond to the nine major industry groups employed by OBE. The statement also lists payments to factors, including employees' compensation, profit-type income, and net interest. The final entry in the left-hand column is "Adjustments," which includes everything required to go from the contribution of the construction industry to national income to the contribution of the construction industry to GNP. Those adjustments include business

[6]In contrast, the simple tables of GNP by industry show only industry of origin.

TABLE 5-1 Input–Output Statement for the Construction Industry ($ in millions)

Inputs		*Outputs*	
Purchases from other industries:		Sales to other industries:	
1. Agriculture, forestry, and fisheries	$ 326	1. Agriculture, forestry, and fisheries	$ 567
2. Mining	737	2. Mining	415
3. Construction	24	3. Construction	24
4. Manufacturing	31,564	4. Manufacturing	1,404
5. Trade	7,155	5. Trade	397
6. Transportation, communications, and utilities	3,187	6. Transportation, communications, and utilities	2,434
7. Finance, insurance, and real estate	1,003	7. Finance, insurance, and real estate	7,327
8. Services	3,657	8. Services	954
9. Other	639	9. Other	1,349
Total purchases from other industries	$48,292	Total sales to other industries	$14,871
Payments to factors:		Sales to final demand:	
1. Employees' compensation	$19,466	1. Sales to households	—
2. Profit-type income, including inventory-valuation adjustments	4,552	2. Gross private investment	$46,151
3. Net interest	180	3. Sales to government	24,290
4. Contribution of construction industry to national income	$24,198	4. Net sales to foreigners	2
5. Adjustments	12,824		
Total value added to GNP by construction industry	$37,022	Total Final Demand	$70,443
Total inputs	$85,314	Total outputs	$85,314

Sources of computation: Office of Business Economics, U.S. Department of Commerce, "Input–Output Structure of the U.S. Economy: 1963," *Survey of Current Business*, 49 (November 1969), 30–35.

transfer payments, indirect business taxes, and capital consumption allowances less net subsidies. In order to make the left-hand side balance with the right-hand side, the adjustments may also include statistical discrepancy.

If purchases from other industries were included in GNP, the result would be double counting. Therefore, in Table 5-1 the sum of all the inputs that are not purchased from other industries equals the contribution (or value added) by the construction industry to GNP. Total inputs include both value added and purchases from other industries.

The outputs of any industry can be classified just as the inputs are, by listing the sales of the one industry to all industries. In addition, the output column of Table 5-1 also shows sales to final demand, which includes sales to households, gross private investment, sales to government, and net sales to foreigners (the excess of exports over imports). Since "Net sales to foreigners" is a net figure, it need be listed on only one side of the table. Residential construction is counted as investment, so in Table 5-2 there are no sales to households by the construction industry, because those sales are included in gross private domestic investment. "Households" referred to in "Sales to households" is in most industrial sectors a larger category than "employees" in the corresponding "Employees' compensation" entry in the left-hand column, since households spend not only wages but income received from all sources, including rents, interest, profits, and transfer payments. "Gross private investment," the largest category in Table 5-1, includes residential buildings, plant and equipment, and net change in inventory. "Sales to government" refers to the government purchases of goods and services from the construction industry.

In summary, Table 5-1 shows in the left-hand column the inputs for the construction industry for the year 1963, including purchases from all industries and the value added by the construction industry to GNP. Outputs of the construction industry, listed in the right-hand column, include the sales to all industries, including the sales of construction firms to other construction firms plus sales to final demand.

Input–Output for the Economy

The data for all industries, such as that presented in Table 5-1 for the construction industry, can be combined to form an input–output table for the aggregate economy.[7] All the interindustry transactions of the nine major sectors, including construction, are presented in Table 5-2.[8] The inputs of

---

[7]Office of Business Economics, U.S. Department of Commerce, "Input-Output Structure of the U.S. Economy: 1963," *Survey of Current Business*, 49 (November 1969), 16–47. Hereafter cited as November 1969 *Survey*.

[8]The data in Tables 5-2, 5-4, and 5-5 are derived from previously mentioned input–output statistics published in the *Survey of Current Business* for November 1969. The *Survey* employs an 87-industry breakdown, which is condensed from the nearly 500-industry breakdown of the basic data. However, since even 87 industries is far too large a number for convenient presentation and understanding, we have further condensed the

TABLE 5-2 Input–Output Table for the U.S. Economy for 1963 (Interindustry Transactions) ($ in millions)

	Inputs									
Producers[a] (Outputs)	*Agri-culture*	*Mining*	*Construc-tion*	*Manufac-turing*	*Trade*	*Transporta-tion, Communi-cation, & Public Utilities*	*Finance, Insurance, & Real Estate*	*Services*	*Other*[b]	*Total Intermediate Sales*
Agriculture	$17,818	—	$ 326	$ 26,754	$ 169	$ 90	$ 2,560	$ 60	$ 789	$ 48,566
Mining	128	$1,135	737	14,638	14	2,619	122	15	189	19,597
Construction	567	415	24	1,404	397	2,434	7,327	954	1,349	14,871
Manufacturing	7,644	1,667	31,564	185,754	6,621	3,973	2,371	15,416	6,318	261,328
Trade	1,811	320	7,155	13,931	2,159	1,361	1,645	3,124	558	32,064
Transportation, communication, and public utilities	1,420	948	3,187	16,965	4,245	10,368	2,154	5,928	5,437	50,652
Finance, insurance, and real estate	2,830	2,717	1,003	6,760	8,313	2,368	13,068	6,861	305	44,225
Services	1,415	295	3,657	12,442	7,124	2,963	5,187	6,220	1,621	40,924
Other[b]	1,139	2,022	639	16,796	3,123	8,034	3,017	3,501	1,856	40,127
Total intermediate purchases	$34,772	$9,519	$48,292	$295,444	$32,165	$34,210	$37,451	$42,079	$18,422	$552,354

[a] *Columns show inputs, rows show outputs.*

[b] *"Other" includes government enterprises; foreign transactions; household industries; business travel, entertainment, and gifts; office supplies; and scrap.*

Source for computation: Office of Business Economics, U.S. Department of Commerce, "Input–Output Structure of the U.S. Econcmy: 1963," *Survey of Current Business*, 49 (November 1969), 30–35.

each major industry are found by reading down the appropriate columns, and the outputs by reading across the rows.

Table 5-2 covers the total interindustry transactions, without including the value added by each industry. The "Total intermediate sales" and "purchases" for the construction industry in the table are the same as the "Total sales to other industries" and "Total purchases from other industries" for the construction industry in Table 5-1. The other rows and columns in Table 5-2 could be used to construct a table similar to Table 5-1 for each major industry. In conclusion, Table 5-2 specifically covers the interindustry transactions that must be excluded from GNP in order to avoid double counting. The data are presented at producers' prices; these exclude distribution costs, which are included in trade or transportation.

Now that we have presented an input–output table of the nine major industries, we can relate the table to national income accounting. National-income data can be converted to an input–output format, and must be so converted if the input–output data are to be related to our national-income accounts. Table 5-3 shows GNP in the left-hand column as the total of the

TABLE 5-3 The Gross National Product—National Income and Product Accounts of the United States for 1963 ($ in millions)

Income Side		*Product or Expenditure Side*	
Earned income (national income at factor cost):		Personal-consumption expenditures	$375,540
Compensation of employees	$341,004	Gross private domestic investment	85,840
Profit-type income and inventory-valuation adjustment	109,946	Net exports of goods and services	5,812
Net interest	13,838	Government purchases of goods and services	123,197
Rental income of persons	17,139		
National income	$481,927		
Adjustments	108,462		
	$590,389		$590,389

Sources for computations: Office of Business Economics, U.S. Department of Commerce, "U.S. National Income and Product Accounts," *Survey of Current Business,* 47 (July 1967), 13, 15–16, 20.

Office of Business Economics, U.S. Department of Commerce, "Input-Output Structure of the U.S. Economy: 1963," *Survey of Current Business,* 49 (November 1969), 30–35.

---

figures to the nine-industry format of our own tables. This breakdown was chosen to correspond to the nine major industry groups employed by the OBE in many of their publications.

The *Survey* table did not break down the value added by each industry according to the contribution of each factor, such as employees' compensation, interest, and profits. Our allocation of value added among the factors of production is based on other 1963 national-accounts data, which were not incorporated by the OBE into their input–output study. Therefore, this allocation of value added might not coincide with the allocation the OBE would have made.

Our Table 5-5 was derived from the condensed data in Table 5-4, and therefore may not agree in all respects with the percentage, direct-requirements table published by the OBE in the *Survey of Current Business.*

various income components, and in the right-hand column as the total of the various expenditures.

On the income side, we show all the components of national income, which include all earned income generated in the production of our national output. The "Profit-type income" listed here includes both corporate profits and the "proprietors' income" or net receipts of unincorporated enterprises; and combining it with the inventory-valuation adjustment enables us to determine a realistic level of aggregate profits. The addition of "Adjustments," previously listed, converts national income to GNP.

The product or expenditure side of Table 5-3 enumerates the various major sources of expenditures: personal consumption, gross private domestic investment, net exports, and government purchases of goods and services. For input–output analysis to explicate the interactions of all the sectors of the economy, as well as to show GNP as the value added by each industry group, it is necessary to add to the nine-row and nine-column matrix presented in Table 5-2 the income and product accounts of Table 5-3 broken down by industry. The combination appears in Table 5-4.

The upper left-hand portion of Table 5-4 simply reproduces Table 5-2. The final values shown in the lower left- and the upper right-hand part of Table 5-4 are the final values by major sector industries in the GNP accounts. GNP is equal to the sum of the four "Final Demand" columns, which show expenditures on final demand in each industry by persons, investors, foreigners, and government. That final demand must equal total value added by all industries, which includes value added by employees (employees' compensation), owners of business (profit-type income), capital (net interest and rental income of persons)[9] and adjustments. As previously stated, adjustments include business transfer payments, capital consumption allowances, and indirect business taxes less net subsidies. The value added is equal to the net input of each industry and is shown in the second-to-last row of the table.

The total value of all inputs ($1,142,743 million) and the total output of all industries (total intermediate sales plus total value added) are equal. In the economy, just as in the firm, the value of sales equals expenditures plus profits, and profits are considered a payment to an input, entrepreneurship. Likewise, the total inputs, intermediate and value added, and total outputs, intermediate and final demand, are equal for each industry. Because total inputs equal total outputs for each industry, the latter are not shown in Table 5-4. However, there is no correspondence between "Total intermediate purchases" and "Total intermediate sales" for each industry. Similarly, there is no correspondence between "Total final demand" by industry on the one hand, and "GNP by industry" (value added) on the other. Nevertheless, the sum of the total final demand by each industry and the sum of the total value added by each industry must both equal GNP. The net

[9]By a convention of OBE, all rental income of persons (including royalties) is received from the finance, insurance, and real estate industry.

contribution of each industry in terms of value added to final output need not equal the final sales of that industry to persons, investors, foreigners, and government, because there is no necessary relationship between the industry's payments to its resources and its sales to final demand.

For example, agriculture's total intermediate sales to all industries, as shown in Table 5-4, are $48,566 million, while its total intermediate purchases from all industries are $34,772 million. On the other hand, the total final demand for agricultural products is $8,906 million, while the GNP by industry or value added (purchases of resources by agriculture) comes to $22,700 million. By either route, the grand total of all inputs or outputs in agriculture is $57,472 million.

Statistical Manipulation of Interindustry Transactions

Interindustry transactions are reported at the market price minus distribution costs and "trade" margins. These exclusions are made to avoid the appearance that each industry buys primarily from "trade" sources. Even though most interindustry transactions flow through wholesale and retail channels, they are recorded as moving directly from one industry to another, disregarding wholesale or retail transactions. The contribution of trade to the economy is measured as its operating expenses plus its profits, including the margin on interindustry transactions. Similarly, all interindustry transportation costs are presented as the output of the transportation industry.

Interindustry sales are those of a particular industry—for example, agriculture—to some other industry—say, manufacturing. In addition, interindustry transactions comprise not only purchases from other industries but also payments to labor, capital, entrepreneurship, and government (value added).

So far, we have presented input–output tables in terms of dollar value of inputs and outputs. Such tables can also be prepared in percentage terms, by showing the percentage of total inputs that the industry listed in a column obtained from each supplying industry named at the head of the row. A percentage version of the input–output table is presented in Table 5-5, derived from the data in Table 5-4, but eliminating final-demand data. To take the construction industry, for example, Table 5-5 demonstrates that construction buys about .38 of 1 percent of its raw materials from agriculture, approximately .86 of 1 percent of its raw materials from mining, and so on. If construction were to increase by $1 million, the additional output would require $3,800 from agriculture (.38 percent of $1,000,000) and $8,600 from mining. Thus, the table also indicates the output from each industry required to supply any other industry with its product. In our example above, agriculture and mining provided inputs for construction. Hence, for construction to increase its output by $1 million, agriculture and mining must increase their output by $3,800 and $8,600 respectively (or sell that much less to other customers).

TABLE 5-4 Input–Output Table for the U.S. Economy—1963 (including final demand and value added—$ in millions)

	Producers										Final Demand				
	Agriculture	*Mining*	*Construction*	*Manufacturing*	*Trade*	*Transportation, Communication, & Public Utilities*	*Finance, Insurance, & Real Estate*	*Services*	*Other*	*Total Intermediate Sales*	*Persons*	*Investors*	*Foreigners*	*Government*	*Total Final Demand*
Agriculture	$17,818		$ 326	$ 26,754	$ 169	$ 90	$ 2,560	$ 60	$ 789	$ 48,566	$ 5,065	$ 1,002	$ 3,012	$ −173	$ 8,906
Mining	128	$ 1,135	737	14,638	14	2,619	122	15	189	19,597	182	−42	536	298	974
Construction	567	415	24	1,404	397	2,434	7,327	954	1,349	14,871		46,151	2	24,290	70,443
Manufacturing	7,644	1,667	31,564	185,754	6,621	3,973	2,371	15,416	6,318	261,328	127,396	32,285	16,415	28,992	205,088
Trade	1,811	320	7,155	13,931	2,159	1,361	1,645	3,124	558	32,064	80,791	5,183	1,735	842	88,551
Transportation, communication, & public utilities	1,420	948	3,187	16,965	4,245	10,368	2,154	5,928	5,437	50,652	25,846	1,211	3,141	3,829	34,027
Finance, insurance, & real estate	2,830	2,717	1,003	6,760	8,313	2,368	13,068	6,861	305	44,225	70,757	1,225	434	945	73,361
Services	1,415	295	3,657	12,442	7,124	2,963	5,187	6,220	1,621	40,924	55,781	6	548	5,780	62,115
Other	1,139	2,022	639	16,796	3,123	8,034	3,017	3,501	1,856	40,127	9,722	−1,181	−20,011	58,394	46,924
Total intermediate purchases	$34,772	$ 9,519	$48,292	$295,444	$ 32,165	$34,210	$ 37,451	$ 42,079	$18,422	$552,354					
										Total Final Demand	$375,540	$85,840	$ 5,812	$123,197	$590,389
Employees' compensation	$ 3,534	$ 4,424	$19,466	$112,888	$ 54,960	$27,356	$ 16,610	$ 37,053	$64,713	$341,004					
Profit-type income	13,640	1,472	4,552	30,623	18,081	10,538	12,114	16,379	2,547	109,946					
Net interest	1,413	58	180	328	373	2,295	7,740	702	785	13,838					
Rental income of persons							17,139			17,139					
National income	$18,587	$ 5,954	$24,198	$143,839	$ 73,414	$40,189	$ 53,567	$ 54,134	$68,045	$481,927					
Added adjustments	4,113	5,098	12,824	27,133	15,036	10,280	26,568	6,826	584	108,462					
GNP (or value added) by industry	$22,700	$11,052	$37,022	$170,972	$ 88,450	$50,469	$ 80,135	$ 60,960	$68,629	$590,389					$ 590,389
Total input	$57,472	$20,571	$85,314	$466,416	$120,615	$84,679	$117,586	$103,039	$87,051						$1,142,743

Sources of computation: Office of Business Economics, U.S. Department of Commerce, "Input–Output Structure of the U.S. Economy–1963," *Survey of Current Business,* 49 (November 1969), 30–35.

Office of Business Economics, U.S. Department of Commerce, *The National Income and Product Accounts of the United States, 1929–1965: Statistical Tables,* a supplement to the *Survey of Current Business* (Washington, D.C.: U.S. Government Printing Office, 1966), pp. 90–145.

Office of Business Economics, U.S. Department of Commerce, "U.S. National Income and Product Account, 1963–1966," *Survey of Current Business,* 49 (July 1967), 16–17, 34–39.

TABLE 5-5 Technical Coefficients for Interindustry Transactions, 1963

	Users								
Suppliers	*Agri-culture*	*Mining*	*Construc-tion*	*Manufac-turing*	*Trade*	*Transporta-tion, Communi-cation, & Public Utilities*	*Finance, Insurance, & Real Estate*	*Services*	*Other*
Agriculture	31.00		0.38	5.74	0.14	0.11	2.18	0.06	0.91
Mining	0.22	5.53	0.86	3.14	0.01	3.09	0.10	0.01	0.22
Construction	0.99	2.02	0.03	0.30	0.33	2.87	6.23	0.93	1.55
Manufacturing	13.30	8.12	37.00	39.82	5.49	4.69	2.02	14.96	7.26
Trade	3.15	1.56	8.39	2.99	1.79	1.61	1.40	3.03	0.64
Transportation, communication, & public utilities	2.47	4.62	3.74	3.64	3.52	12.24	1.83	5.75	6.25
Finance, insurance, & real estate	4.92	13.23	1.18	1.45	6.89	2.80	11.11	6.66	0.35
Services	2.46	1.44	4.29	2.67	5.91	3.50	4.41	6.04	1.86
Other	1.98	9.85	0.75	3.60	2.59	9.49	2.57	3.40	2.13
Total intermediate purchases	60.49	46.37	56.62	63.35	26.67	40.40	31.85	40.84	21.17
Employees' compensation	6.15	21.54	22.82	24.20	45.57	32.31	14.13	35.96	74.34
Owners of business and capital (profit-type income)	23.73	7.17	5.34	6.57	14.99	12.44	10.30	15.90	2.93
Net interest	2.46	0.28	0.21	0.07	0.31	2.71	6.55	0.68	0.90
Rental income of persons							14.58		
National income	32.34	28.99	28.37	30.84	60.87	47.46	45.56	52.54	78.17
Added adjustments	7.17*	24.64*	15.01*	5.81*	12.46*	12.14	22.59	6.62	0.66*
Total	100.00	100.00	100.00	100.00	100.00	100.00	100.00	100.00	100.00

**Adjusted to 100%.*

Source for computation: Table 5-4.

The inputs required from each industry to produce one dollar of output by any one industry are known as "technical coefficients." Table 5-5 presents these technical coefficients; for the table to be useful, we have to assume that they remain constant as the level of output is changed.

Technical coefficients may be presented in either physical or money terms. A table constructed in physical terms would show the proportion of physical units of inputs required to produce one unit of output of a given industry. Table 5-5, however, is in money terms, showing the percentage of each dollar of output by one industry that goes to purchase inputs that are the outputs of other industries.

To allocate fully the dollar earned by any industry, we must include not only the industry's purchases of inputs from other industries but also its expenditures on resources, including other adjustments. These expenditures for inputs not purchased from other industries are included at the bottom of Table 5-5. In construction, for example, almost $.23 of each dollar goes to employee compensation, just over $.05 to profit, about $.002 for interest, and some $.15 for indirect taxes, depreciation, and other adjustments.

Direct and Indirect Effects

Table 5-5 includes only the direct or first-round effects of an interindustry transaction. For example, if the demand for the output of the construction industry increases, the industry will, as we have seen, purchase inputs from all other industries. Those purchases of additional inputs are known as the *direct effect*. However, the industries that supply the construction industry will themselves have to purchase more inputs from all the other industries, including construction, in order to supply those additional inputs to the construction industry. Those second-round requirements are known as *indirect effects*. A table supplying a simultaneous solution that includes both direct and indirect effects has been published by the OBE and is a considerable aid in tracing the effects of any given change in the demand of one industry. Such a table is known as a "total requirements table," and indicates the total effect of any given change in the demand for one industry on all the other industries of the economy. For example, such a table would enable us to determine the additional inputs required from the other industries in order to meet any increase in the demands for the products of the construction industry. In some cases, indirect effects may be greater than direct effects.

A simplified system for determining both direct and indirect effects is based on the information presented in Table 5-6, for simplicity including only three industries—manufacturing, trade, and public utilities (including transportation and communications)—and only one resource, labor. For example, Table 5-6 indicates that manufacturing buys 56 percent of its inputs from manufacturing, 4 percent from trade, and 6 percent from public utilities. Those inputs plus the 34 percent labor costs make up 100 percent of the inputs of manufacturing in our model.

Assume that final demand in manufacturing is forecast to be $250 billion,

TABLE 5-6 Simplified Input-Output Table (in percentages)

	Manufacturing	*Trade*	*Transportation, Communication, & Public Utilities*
Manufacturing	56	10	9
Trade	4	3	3
Transportation, communication, & public utilities	6	6	24
Employees' compensation	34	81	64
	100	100	100

trade is \$100 billion, and public utilities is \$50 billion. How much must each industry produce to achieve the forecast demand? The answer can be determined with the following set of equations, using M to represent manufacturing, T to represent trade, and P to represent public utilities.

$$M = .56M + .10T + .09P + 250$$
$$T = .04M + .03T + .03P + 100$$
$$P = .06M + .06T + .24P + 50$$

The equations are derived from Table 5-6 and from the forecast of final demand. To illustrate, the output in manufacturing, M, must equal $.56M$ in order to provide for its own internal demand; manufacturing must also produce an output equal to $.10T$ to meet the needs of trade. Likewise, it must produce $.09P$ to satisfy the demand for manufacturing by the public utilities industry. In addition, manufacturing must produce \$250 billion of output to meet its final demand.

It is a simple matter to solve the equations, and the solution provides us with the answer to the total output each industry must produce to satisfy both the interindustry demand and the final demand. In this case, M, the total output of manufacturing, including both intermediate and final demand, is \$624.02 billion; T, the total output of trade, is \$132.71 billion; and P, the total output of public utilities, including transportation and communications, is \$125.53 billion.

The labor input required to produce each industry's output can also be calculated by multiplying the percentage for employees' compensation given in Table 5-6 by the total dollar value of the output of each industry. We find that the total employment of labor by manufacturing amounts to \$212.17 billion at the going wage rate; total employment by trade comes to \$107.50 billion; and total employment by public utilities amounts to \$80.34 billion. The actual number of workers required can be determined by dividing the average wage into the total amount of wages paid. Assuming that the number of workers needed is actually available in the economy, the solutions are feasible.

The simplified example just discussed illustrates how direct and indirect effects can be combined to determine the final impact of any change on the economy. The table of direct and indirect effects that the OBE has prepared for 86 industries is, therefore, of great assistance to students of the aggregate U.S. economy.[10]

Assumptions of Input–Output Analysis

Input–output analysis assumes that all the inputs from supplying industries are continuously variable and, consequently, disregards the distinction between the short run and the long run. Furthermore, to assume constant technical coefficients means to assume no economies or diseconomies of scale. In other words, the proportions of the various inputs are assumed to remain constant regardless of the level of output. The presence of economies or diseconomies of scale would make that assumption untrue.

In terms of production functions, fixed technical coefficients imply right-angle isoquants, and further imply that those isoquants would move out from the origin in the exact proportion that output increases, revealing constant returns to scale. (Alternatively, parallel isoquants and constant input prices might be assumed, instead of right angles.)

In addition to the assumption of fixed technical coefficients, input–output analysis further assumes that the final output mix within each industry will remain unchanged. To take a concrete example, suppose the construction industry produces the same total value of output but changes its composition from mainly office buildings to mainly private dwellings. As a result, the technical coefficients will change because the production of private homes requires different inputs from the production of office buildings. More shingles and bricks will be required and less reinforcing rods and concrete. For macro-analytical purposes, one advantage of using a condensed table such as the nine-industry breakdown we have employed in Tables 5-4 and 5-5, compared with a more detailed breakdown that may use hundreds of industries, is that a change in the composition of output of one industry may be neglected because many changes may balance out in the larger aggregate. For example, the change in inputs from reinforcing rods to bricks would probably cause little change in the total purchased from the manufacturing industry. In contrast, a change would be required if brick- and steel-producing firms were presented as two separate industries. (However, for detailed analyses, narrower input categories, like those in the OBE's tables, would be essential. No one could construct a house with an input called "Manufacturing.")

Finally, to assume that the composition of final output remains unchanged is to assume implicitly that both prices and consumer demand remain unchanged. Otherwise, the values in Table 5-4 would have to change to reflect price changes or changes in demand.[11]

---

[10]November 1969 *Survey*, pp. 42–47.

[11]Hollis B. Chenery and Paul G. Clark, *Interindustry Economics* (New York: John Wiley, 1959), pp. 33–42.

Uses of Input–Output Data

Input-output analysis has a variety of uses. It can be used by business firms to project sales figures or to determine potential customers or suppliers. Government agencies have made extensive input–output studies on the economic impact of converting from a wartime to a peacetime economy or vice versa. (Mobilizing for World War II was one of the early uses of input–output analysis.) In addition, input–output analysis has been used in developing models to forecast GNP and other economic variables.

However, for our purposes, the most important use of input–output analysis is to predetermine the effect on various industries of some given change in aggregate demand. Such interindustry relationships often tend to be overlooked in most of the standard approaches to aggregate economic analysis, and in general, throughout the rest of this book such interindustry effects will be ignored, except for a few specific points such as the consideration of bottleneck effects in Chapter 12.

Suppose, for example, there is an increase in the demand for refrigerators. Initially, the effect would be shown as an increase in the output of manufacturers. But production of refrigerators calls for additional steel and other inputs, requiring an increase in the output of the mining and other manufacturing industries, which in turn will require additional inputs from still other industries. The operation of the new refrigerators, as well as their production, will require more power; their installation will require an increase in services; raising the money to produce refrigerators, as well as to finance their purchase, will require an increase in the output of the financial sector. Clearly, as more refrigerators are produced, indirect, secondary effects will spread throughout the economy. To determine the direct and indirect effects would necessitate either setting up a series of simultaneous equations including all affected industries or, more simply, the use of a table of direct and indirect effects such as that published by the OBE. Therefore, input–output analysis enables an observer to determine the interrelationships among the various sectors of the economy.

In this section, we have implied that input–output analysis has helped in aggregating from the individual parts of the economy to an aggregate level of economic activity. In a sense, therefore, input–output analysis is a convenient bridge from micro- to macroeconomic analyses.

Input–output analysis also illuminates a shadowy area between micro- and macroanalysis that was long disregarded by economists—namely, regional analysis. So far, this application has been mainly in terms of geographic regions, tabulating the inputs that one area receives from all regions, including itself, and indicating the flow of output to other regions. Larger tables can integrate all the industrial areas in several different regions and eventually build up to an input–output table for the entire aggregate economy, which would include the interrelationships of the various geographical regions.

In the area of international economic relations, input–output analysis has become quite important, particularly to indicate the degree of possible national self-sufficiency and the degree to which a country must rely on imports and exports to survive. This application is very similar to the interregional use of input–output analysis, since international trade is only interregional trade that happens to cross national boundaries. Input–output analysis has become politically popular throughout the world. For example, in 1967, a partial bibliography of input–output studies published by the United Nations required 259 pages and cited studies done in some 40 countries.[12]

Critique of Input–Output System

Perhaps the most important criticism leveled at input–output analysis concerns the necessity for assuming fixed technical coefficients. The requirement of rigid factor combinations in production is unrealistic and could be misleading:

1. Technical coefficients change over time, even with a given level of output and given resource inputs. Because technology changes constantly, input–output tables must be constantly revised if they are to be reliable. However, such revisions occur in the United States only infrequently; therefore, much of the analysis is carried on with out-of-date technical coefficients. In recognition of this difficulty there have been attempts made to develop techniques to bring the technical coefficients up to date without revising the complete table. It has been suggested that technological change is generally introduced through new capital equipment; so the technical coefficients could be amended according to how much new investment takes place in any given industry. Alternatively, it has been proposed that newer and better techniques of production will be introduced first by leading firms, and then spread through the rest of the industry; therefore, technical coefficients can be forecast for each industry by studying the productive techniques of the most advanced firms. However the best results would be achieved by more frequent construction of input–output tables. More frequent revision would require some technique for determining technical relationships not based on detailed Census of Manufactures data.
2. Technical coefficients may also change merely as the level of output changes if some of the inputs remain fixed, as they are likely to do in the short-run. As we saw in Chapter 3, economic theory generally assumes in the short run that the rate of change in output is not proportional to the rate of change in inputs. Thus,input–output analysis assumes away both increasing and diminishing returns, and assumes a linear total-product curve.
3. Even in the absence of technological change, the technical coefficients may change as output increases in the long run, when all inputs are variable. As we saw in Chapter 3, industries may be characterized by increasing and decreasing returns to scale as well as by constant returns, as input–output analysis assumes.
4. As we noted, resources are both complements and substitutes for each other. To the extent that they are substitutes, a change in relative resource prices will change the proportion of resources in the production mix. Input–output analysis does not allow for that sort of change.

However, in recent years it has been increasingly recognized that certain resources are complementary. In these cases, when output declines or

---

[12]United Nations, *Input-Output Bibliography*, 1963–66.

expands, all resources are laid off or reemployed simultaneously in the same proportion;[13] for example, the case in which machines are designed to be operated by a fixed crew. In addition, a superficial examination of the empirical evidence on the relationship of various inputs to each other in manufacturing shows that constant returns to scale are plausible.[14] But manufacturing represents not quite half of total intermediate sales, and there is little evidence that the other industries are also characterized by complementary resources or constant returns. Therefore, the assumption of fixed technical coefficients might be useful for solving problems involving manufacturing industries, especially when the changes to be analyzed are relatively small, but may be misleading as the pure theory of microeconomics might imply when applied to the whole economy.

NATIONAL-INCOME MEASURES IN REAL OR DEFLATED TERMS

So far, our national-income accounting system has been presented in terms of current market prices for each expenditure or production item. But we are all aware that because of inflation since World War II, $1 in 1973 buys a much smaller quantity of goods and services than it did in 1940 or 1945. Hence, comparisons over time of any of the aggregates or components in national-income accounting may in whole or in part merely reflect price changes.

For example, the subcategory, "Expenditures on new cars" (including a small item for dealers' margins on used cars) within PCE, affords a dramatic example of the effect of price changes. Dollar expenditures for new cars by consumers rose sevenfold, from $2,217 billion in 1940, to $17,748 billion in 1960. Yet an average automobile, selling for about $765 in 1940, would have cost about $2,000 in 1958 and $2,032 in 1960. Clearly, the real growth in auto sales between 1940 and 1960 was much less than seven times the beginning level. Much of the recorded increase in dollar sales figures simply represented higher car prices. After deflating for the effects of price increases, and when all figures are expressed in terms of constant 1958 dollars, automobile expenditures grew only from about $5.8 billion in 1940 to $17.5 billion in 1960.[15]

This example has introduced us to the procedure of deflating a current-dollar series into constant dollars to remove the influence of changing prices and to measure physical output. The economic statistician first picks a year

[13] George Stigler, "Production and Distribution in the Short Run," *Journal of Political Economy*, 47 (June 1939), 305–27.

[14] J. Johnston, *Statistical Cost Analysis* (New York: McGraw-Hill, 1960), pp. 136–94.

[15] Office of Business Economics, U.S. Department of Commerce, *The National Income and Product Accounts of the United States, 1929–1965: Statistical Tables;* a supplement to the *Survey of Current Business* (Washington, D.C.: U.S. Government Printing Office, 1966), pp. 46–49. Hereafter cited as *Statistical Tables.*

to serve as the "base" or reference year. (For the period from 1965 through 1971, 1958 has been used as the base year. However, starting in 1972, the base year has been changed to 1967.) Next, price indexes are constructed, if they are not already available, for each of the hundreds of items entering into GNP as measured by the product side of the national income and product account. Each price is expressed as a ratio to its base-year price. Multiplying each ratio by 100 then yields the corresponding series of index numbers. The base-year price has been set at 100.0 for all items, and prices for any other year are expressed as a ratio to 100.

Returning to our automobile illustration, to deflate the 1960 price of cars using 1958 as the base, we would divide the 1960 price, $2,032, by the 1958 price, $2,000, and multiply by 100. Thus the 1960 automobile price index is 101.6 when 1958 equals 100.

Given the price index for a product, it is easy to deflate the corresponding current-dollar expenditures by using the following formula:

$$E_{dg} = \frac{P_b}{P_g}(E_g) = \frac{100}{P_g}E_g = \frac{E_g}{P_g}(100)$$

where

E_{dg} = deflated total expenditures in a given year

P_b = price index in the base year = 100.0

P_g = price index in the given year

E_g = current-dollar total expenditures in the given year

Using (E_g/P_g) (100), simply divide the current-dollar total expenditures by its price index in the given year and multiply by 100 in order to compute the deflated total expenditure. For example, total expenditures on shoes and other footwear were $3,124 million in 1949, when their price index was 79.0 (with 1958 = 100.0).[16] Dividing 3,124 by 79.0 gives 39.54, which multiplied by 100 equals the deflated expenditure of $3,954 million. Similarly, 1971 consumer expenditures on shoes of $8,379 million were made at a price level of 154.9[17] which, when deflated, is $5,409 million (8,379 ÷ 154.9 × 100). Comparing the real value of 1971 purchases with the real value of 1949 purchases indicates that the *physical volume* of shoes bought by consumers increased by about 1.4 percent a year over 22 years.

Exactly the same process is used for deflating components of each major expenditure category, namely personal-consumption expenditures, investment expenditures, government purchases, and net exports. The deflated figures are then added to arrive at deflated *GNP in constant 1958 dollars*. If the constant-dollar GNP, obtained by aggregation as just described, is divided *into* the original current-dollar GNP, an implicit GNP deflator is

[16] *Ibid.*, pp. 45 and 163.

[17] July 1972 *Survey*, pp. 27, 49.

obtained. For many purposes, the implicit GNP deflator is the best single measure of price change in the whole economy, since it weights together price changes in all economic activities that yield final products.

When we deflate current-dollar expenditures, the values for the years before the base year will increase, and values for recent years after the base year will decrease, in a generally inflationary period. The constant-dollar estimates, indicating physical volumes produced or sold, will not increase as much as the corresponding current-dollar series, inflated as it is by price increases.

Taking the quality of the current-dollar estimates of GNP and its components as given, the deflated figures are only as reliable as the price indexes employed. Some of the component price indexes consist of a proxy measure of doubtful value, such as a cost index. These proxy indexes have to be used when no individual price index is available. In other cases, several price indexes have to be combined by a weighting procedure. Fortunately, major reliance in computing deflated prices is placed on the Bureau of Labor Statistics' consumer and wholesale price indexes, which are quite carefully constructed.

A separate price index could theoretically be constructed for each consumer, which would determine the effect of a price change on the individual's real purchasing power. Such an individual price index can be demonstrated through the use of indifference curves, and the effect of changing prices on the consumer's real purchasing power can be determined from his equilibrium position before and after the price change. For example, in Figure 5-1, assume that an individual consumer is in equilibrium at point *a* in 1967, the base year selected by the OBE, where his budget line B_1 is tangent to indifference curve I_1. The consumer's market basket of goods consists of Q_{y_0} units of Y and Q_{x_0} units of X for that year, while the price of Y is P_{y_0} and the price of X is P_{x_0}.

Now, assume that the price of commodity X increases from its 1967 level of P_{x_0} while the price of Y remains constant. What effect will this price change have on the consumer's consumption decisions? If his money income remained constant, his budget line would shift down to B_2, and his new equilibrium would occur at point *b*. Therefore, his real purchasing power has been reduced from I_1 to I_2 level of satisfaction. However, suppose that the individual's money income increases by enough to allow him to buy his 1967 market basket consisting of Q_{x_0} of good X and Q_{y_0} of good Y. Such an income change would be shown as a new budget line parallel to B_2 (indicating the new relative prices of X and Y) and passing through point *a*. Under these conditions, the consumer will choose to move to point *c* rather than point *a*, because good Y is now a better buy relative to X, and point *c* occurs on a higher indifference curve, I_3. Therefore, a price increase accompanied by a compensating income change leaves the individual slightly better off on the higher indifference curve.

The price index faced by the consumer has increased, because the price of X is higher and the price of Y is unchanged. A price index for the consumer

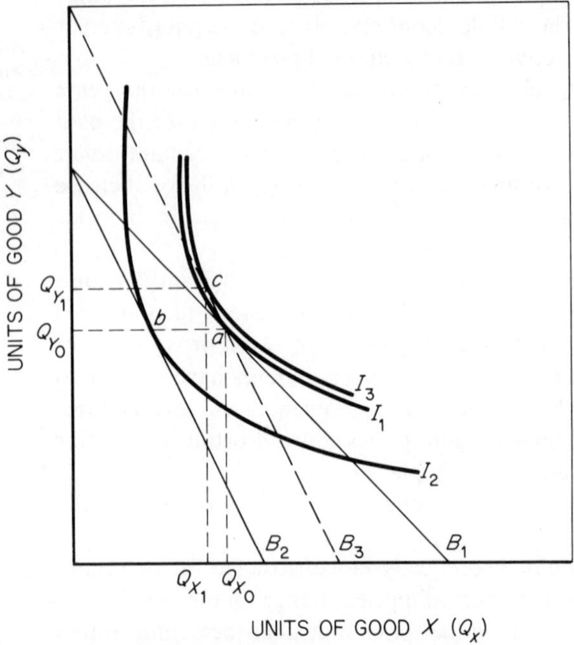

FIG. 5-1 Graphical Interpretation of Relationship between Consumer Welfare and Index Numbers

is calculated by measuring the changes from a base year in the cost of the market basket of goods purchased for a given year. The price index for the base year 1967 is arbitrarily set at 100, and the price index for 1968 would be determined as follows:

$$\text{Price index for 1968} = \frac{Q_{x_0}P_{x_1} + Q_{y_0}P_{y_1}}{Q_{x_0}P_{x_0} + Q_{y_0}P_{y_0}}$$

where Q_{x_0} and Q_{y_0} are the quantities of X and Y bought in the base year; P_{x_0} and P_{y_0} are the prices of X and Y in the base year; and P_{x_1} and P_{y_1} are the prices of X and Y in the given year.[18]

The consumer's money income, Y_c, would thus have to increase sufficiently to buy $Q_{x_0}P_{x_1} + Q_{y_0}P_{y_1}$ worth of goods. But as we have seen, because X is now relatively more expensive, the consumer would buy less X and more Y and thereby increase slightly his total satisfaction. Therefore, if the real income of the consumer (money income ÷ price index) in 1968 is equal to that in 1967, we can be sure that his welfare has increased slightly. In our example, the combination of Q_{x_1} and Q_{y_1} placed him on a higher indifference curve than Q_{x_0} and Q_{y_0}.

Turning from the individual to the aggregate, the major price index used

[18]In our simple illustration, the price of Y was held constant.

today is the Bureau of Labor Statistics' (BLS) consumer price index, which covers the market basket of moderate-income families living in large cities. The consumer price index can be contrasted to the implicit price deflator for personal-consumption expenditures, which is based on the proportion of each consumer item in GNP rather than on a typical big-city consumer's market basket. However, all price indexes present certain hazards. Consumer tastes change, changing the composition of the market basket, and making the weighting procedure outdated and erroneous. Quality improvements constantly occur in many products because of technological change. The BLS price indexes do make quality adjustments by reducing actual prices (perhaps too enthusiastically in the case of new automobiles!), but a myriad of small improvements, important in the aggregate, remain unaccounted for. (Likewise, quality deterioration is unmeasured in cases where "they don't make things like they used to.") Furthermore, there is no satisfactory way to "link" completely new products into a price index. (A television set is not just a substitute for a console radio.) Since incompletely accounted for quality improvements probably outweigh quality deterioration, the price-deflator index probably overstates inflation, but we cannot be sure.

An interesting problem arises in deflating GNP by major industries into real terms or constant dollars. Price indexes exist only for products; therefore, income payments and other income-side items (nonfactor costs) cannot be deflated directly. In fact, the real value of income has meaning only when the "market basket" of purchases is specified, and any two individuals may have radically different patterns. Incidentally, for these reasons, no aggregate other than GNP is published in real terms—not national income, disposable personal income, or even net national product!

EVALUATION OF THE SOCIAL ACCOUNTING SYSTEM

A certain amount of critical evaluation of the national-income and input–output accounting systems has been suggested throughout Chapters 4 and 5, as the various topics were discussed. The attempt has been to show the impressive logic and structure of our social accounting system and to indicate its usefulness for aggregate economic analysis. For example, the account for the gross saving and investment sector, a mental construct rather than a real-world group of people or firms, clearly shows the necessary equality of gross saving and gross investment as realized or measured over any accounting period. That equality of savings and investment is a fact of fundamental importance for macroeconomic analysis. Also, such decisions as the treatment of government interest and owner-occupied homes were made to avoid spurious shifts in the aggregates over time, decisions for which users of the data should certainly be grateful.

At the same time, we have tried to show how the definitions, the structure, and even the usefulness of the accounts are compromised in various instances by lack of reliable data. Some of these decisions have been controversial in that alternative treatments were possible, and in such cases we have tried to give the reasons for the existing treatment or methodology.

Nevertheless, some further general and specific remarks seem desirable, not only with regard to structure and definitions, but also regarding the reliability and accuracy of the numerical estimates themselves.

National Income Accounts: Definitions and Theoretical Structure

Most of the controversy over these matters has died down over the last decade (since the publication of *A Critique of the United States Income and Product Accounts* by the National Bureau of Economic Research in 1958, a publication that apparently represented the parting shot by most critics). The U.S. Commerce Department system has been almost universally accepted in this country and represents a standard to which many other nations' accounting systems aspire. In 1953, the United Nations issued a standardized system of national accounts and supporting tables, to which many nations now adhere. The UN system is more an elaboration of the U.S. national-income accounts than a contradiction.[19] In its 1965 definitional revisions, the OBE brought the United States accounts into conformity with the United Nations system with regard to the treatment of consumer interest and of some minor items like personal cash remittances abroad.

There is now little demand within the economics profession for changes in the inclusion of all government expenditures on goods and services in gross national product, even though this was a major controversy in the decade after World War II. Similarly, the inclusion of direct (income) taxes in national income but of indirect taxes only in GNP (or NNP) seems almost universally accepted.[20] Almost no one except professors and textbook writers seems to worry about the exclusion from national output of housewives' services or other household production.

About the only recent comments on national-income definitions are complaints that portions of GNP now counted should be excluded as intermediate products and that GNP should be adjusted for pollution and depletion of the nation's resources. Commuting costs are sometimes mentioned as a likely exclusion. It is argued that they should be tax-deductible and deducted from GNP. The problem in determining exclusions is, where do you stop? If commuting costs, why not educational expenses, or medical bills? Even sufficient recreation to maintain productive efficiency could logically be excluded.

Some authorities, including Arthur F. Burns (economist, presidential advisor, and chairman of the Board of Governors of the Federal Reserve

---

[19] United Nations, *A System of National Accounts and Supporting Tables* (New York: Statistical Office of the United Nations, 1953; and rev. ed., 1964).

[20] William I. Abraham, *National Income and Economic Accounting* (Englewood Cliffs, N.J.: Prentice-Hall, 1969), p. 30.

System as this is being written), maintain that pollution, or at least the cost of measures to control pollution, should be subtracted from GNP.[21] If one factory pollutes a stream so that other enterprises or municipalities must incur heavy expenditures to treat the water before use, it is double counting to include in GNP all the output of the polluting factory plus the pollution-control expenses.

By the same token, if automobiles cost more solely because of the installation of exhaust-pollution-control devices required by government, has the national output or the national welfare really gone up in any meaningful sense? Despite the claims of some that pollution-control measures are relatively inexpensive if properly applied, it seems likely that this issue will grow in importance in the near future and that the OBE may eventually find it desirable to attempt some estimates of pollution costs, or negative outputs (difficult though the process of estimation will certainly be). In addition, why don't we subtract depletion of the nation's natural resources from GNP in computing net national product? After all, once an oil well has been depleted, the resource is gone forever.

National Income Accounts: Sectoring

We should caution the prospective user of the national-income accounts on one point, before turning to the reliability of the numerical estimates. In using the national-income components, or even the aggregates other than GNP, keep clearly in mind the true meaning of the various *sectors* in national-income accounting (including input–output analysis).

The government sector includes all purchases by all levels of general government, plus capital expenditures of government enterprises (the Postal Service, municipal waterworks, and bus lines). However, *current* expenditures and receipts of government enterprises are in the business sector. (Since 1965, government sales of business-type products like timber and electricity—a small item, amounting to only $0.8 billion in 1964—have been subtracted from government purchases and from GNP as representing intermediate products.[22] Such commercial activity is no longer in the government sector.)

The business sector, which is splintered among the five-account sector system, includes at least two kinds of operations not normally considered private business: the current operations of government enterprises, and of homeowners who occupy their own residences. The *capital* expenditures of business (gross private domestic investment) include owner-occupied homes but not capital expenditures of government enterprises.

The personal sector is perhaps the most muddied of all. In addition to individuals, it includes all nonprofit organizations, private trust funds, private

---

[21] *Wall Street Journal*, June 27, 1969, p. 1.

[22] Office of Business Economics, U.S. Department of Commerce, "The National Income and Product Accounts of the United States: Revised Estimates 1929–64," *Survey of Current Business*, 45 (August 1965), 14. Hereafter cited as August 1965 *Survey*.

pension plans, and health and welfare funds, some of which are of considerable magnitude. Not included are expenditures by individuals in their capacity as homeowners. On the receipts side of the personal sector, income retained in unincorporated enterprises is included in personal income; on the expenditure side, such income drops into personal saving, adding an unexpected element to what people would normally consider saving. This hybrid definition of the personal sector makes personal-consumption expenditures (and especially the popular table of PCE by type of product, published each year in the *Survey of Current Business*) difficult to interpret in the usual household-budget sense.

Reliability and Accuracy of the Estimates

If we accept the structure and definitions of the national-income accounts, how good are the estimates? To answer that, we need some feel for the methods of construction of the estimates, without, however, engaging in excessive detail.

Reliability of Aggregates In general, the aggregates range from some highly satisfactory, relatively precise components to other, roughly estimated and thinly based items.[23] For example, the figure for wages and salaries, based on employers' reports to the Social Security Administration, is far more accurate and reliable than is either proprietors' income or rental income of persons. In fact, the whole "Compensation of employees" complex can be judged to be highly reliable in comparison with any other national-income component.

To use another illustration on the income side, corporate profits can be reliably estimated only after a lag of two to three years, when the Internal Revenue Service publishes its *Statistics of Income*. For more recent years, data on closely held nonpublic corporations are difficult to obtain, especially outside of manufacturing and fields like banking and transportation that are regulated by the federal government.

For an illustration of reliability on the product side, government purchases of goods and services, especially purchases by the federal government, are considered a very reliable item because each government agency prepares a reliable budget. In contrast, the level of inventories is highly volatile and not well reported by private business firms, especially small firms. In addition, the book values of each inventory level have to be revalued at average prices during the period in question, because firms use different methods of valuing inventories, a procedure that can introduce further error. Subtracting one inaccurate inventory level from another may result in a quite inaccurate "Change in business inventories."

---

[23]The following discussion is based on Office of Business Economics, U.S. Department of Commerce, "Reliability of the Estimates," *National Income*, 1954, a supplement to the *Survey of Current Business* (Washington, D.C.: U.S. Government Printing Office, 1954), pp. 62–67.

Estimates for producers' durable equipment and personal-consumption expenditures for goods are moderately reliable, but less so than government purchases. Structures and PCE for services are weaker yet, but still above the change in inventories.

Of course, it is important to note that not all errors on either the income or the product sides will be in the same direction. Many errors will offset or cancel each other. Therefore, the larger aggregates are more reliable than the components that went into them.

A Detailed Analysis of the Computation of Personal Consumption To give a feel for how data are compiled, let us briefly examine the procedure for estimating the largest national-income component: personal-consumption expenditures, PCE. In so-called bench-mark years, the "commodity-flow" method is used to estimate personal-consumption expenditures for most categories of goods. A bench-mark year for this purpose is any year in which a Census of Manufacturers is taken.[24] The commodity-flow procedure can be summarized as follows:

From the wealth of detail on manufacturers' shipments of processed goods valued at producers' prices, an allocation is first made of those goods eventually destined for consumers, as opposed to government, producers' durable equipment, or further processing (intermediate products within manufacturing). To the dollar values of each class of manufacturers' domestic shipments for eventual consumption are added producers' sales of nonmanufactured consumer goods, consisting entirely of agricultural products and fish. Next are added imported products, manufacturers' excise taxes, and transportation charges. Increases in wholesalers' inventories are subtracted, and wholesalers' markups are added to the commodity flow. Any exports by wholesalers are deducted at this point. Then the process is repeated for retailers—increases in retail inventories are subtracted and retail markups are added.

Finally, adding sales and retail excise taxes yields PCE by the commodity-flow method for the given class of commodity.[25]

For the last two comprehensive statistical revisions of the national-income accounts, made in 1965 and 1970, the input–output tables (also constructed by the OBE) for the bench-mark years 1958 and 1963 were employed. A by-product of the laborious and expensive construction of an internally consistent, large input–output table for the United States is better information on flows between manufacturer, wholesaler, and retailer, and on the crucial items of wholesale and retail markups. Thus, the commodity-flow method is more solidly based now than in pre-input–output years.

Certain other commodities are estimated directly for every year by the "retail-valuation" method. These are new automobiles (and gross margins on used cars); gasoline and oil; tobacco products; and flowers, seeds, and

---

[24]Postwar censuses of manufacturers were 1947, 1954, 1958, 1963, 1967, and 1972.

[25]Ibid., pp. 111–15.

potted plants. For these items, an average price is computed and is then multiplied by the number of physical units purchased. For new cars, sufficient information is available on sales by makes, models, and extra equipment to estimate an average retail *list* price rather closely. Deduction for discounts is based on actual prices paid for a limited number of models, as collected by the Bureau of Labor Statistics during the process of compiling the consumer price index. Multiplying the average price paid by dealers' sales of all new cars gives PCE for new automobiles. Similar methods are used for the other retail-valuation items.

Between bench-mark years, the commodity-flow items are extrapolated by retail sales of the most nearly applicable kind of store. Furniture-store sales would seem to be a reasonable proxy for sales of furniture and appliances, but what about furniture sales by department stores? And radio and TV sets are sold in many different types of stores. Surveying all retail sales is a virtual impossibility, since there are so many retailers compared to the number of manufacturers. For these reasons, the commodity-flow method was adopted for bench-mark years in preference to retail sales estimates. However, retail sales figures are used to interpolate between bench-mark years.

In the case of PCE for services, there are no bench-mark estimates as such, but individual items may be based on such infrequent sources as the Census of Population and Housing, taken every ten years. As a result, extrapolations have to be made from one census until data from the next census are available two or three years after completion. (In fact, the 1936 Census of Religious Bodies was not repeated until 1957!) Many other items of expenditure on services are available annually from a myriad of sources, and assuming careful extrapolation of the census items as well as liberal cancelling of errors, the annual figures may be tolerably accurate.

However, a distressingly large percentage of the quarterly estimates of PCE for services consists of items for which no extrapolator at all exists for periods shorter than a year. Then the OBE statistician has to resort to projection of the previous trend, which can be done on a linear basis (addition of equal dollar amounts each quarter) or by some approximation to a nonlinear function (such as equal percentage increases each quarter). Usually, at least two methods of trend projection can be supported with equal plausibility, and ingenuity can suggest methods for producing almost any reasonable desired result. The analyst *is* assisted here by the knowledge that expenditures for most services move regularly upward from year to year in a smoothly curvilinear fashion, and so they should within a given year, after proper seasonal adjustment. The foregoing example may represent the most clear-cut, but certainly not the only, example of judgment entering the estimating process. Within PCE for goods, similar but less serious data gaps exist; or there may be two equally unreliable extrapolators giving different results.

In addition to problems in extrapolating PCE, certain arbitrary changes have been imposed on the calculated figures from time to time. In the figures for the bench-mark year 1954 (published in 1958), a cut of $1\frac{1}{2}$ percent ($$3\frac{1}{2}$ billion) was made in total PCE and allocated proportionately among its components. The reduction was justified because the statistical discrepancy was large and positive, meaning that the income-side calculation of GNP was smaller than the product side, and much of the discrepancy was deemed to be in PCE.[26] Another example was an annual reduction of a few percent on expenditures for food, to take account of increasing nonfood sales in grocery stores between 1954 and 1958. The 1958 bench mark confirmed the reduction.

Morgenstern's Criticism of National-Income Accounting In a book entitled *On the Accuracy of Economic Observations,* Oskar Morgenstern takes to task national-income statistics and growth rates based on them.[27] Some of his more salient criticisms (in addition to the same kinds of comments on conceptual difficulties and data problems discussed above) are these:

1. Revisions in the aggregates for any given year or quarter are made again and again over a very long period, with the final figure not settled for many years.
2. The Commerce Department refuses to publish any measure of error associated with the estimates (as the Census Bureau, for example, publishes sampling errors for much of its data).
3. Even more deplorable, the actual percentage of error in such aggregates is of the order of plus or minus 10, or between ±5 and ±10 percent at best. When GNP is $1050 billion in current dollars (in 1971), these errors are enormous in absolute terms, amounting to $52.5 to $105 billion on either side of the estimated figure!
4. Even assuming more optimistic errors of only 1 to 3 percent, *growth rates* calculated from them can vary widely, because the difference in slope of a line between the lower limit of the earlier year and the upper limit of the later year, and that of another line running from upper limit to lower limit, is so large. ". . . The reliability of these figures is, for all practical purposes, zero."[28]

Evaluation of Morgenstern's Critique Probably the situation is not as grim as Morgenstern avers, even though the data obviously fall short of perfection.

1. Morgenstern cites the revisions of 1948 national income, where a figure of $224.4 billion, as first reported on the basis of quarterly data, was revised up to $226.2 billion, but later down to $223.5 billion, ten years after the fact, in 1958.[29] Morgenstern (whose book was published in 1963) must have been even more upset by the August 1965 general revision, which again revised national income for 1948 by +$0.7 billion to $224.2 billion! Furthermore, +$1.0 billion of this revision represented purely statistical revisions, 17 years after the date of occurrence, while definitional changes contributed an offsetting −$0.3 billion![30] (An overhaul of the imputed rental-income series was the major statistical change.)

[26]Office of Business Economics, U.S. Department of Commerce, *U.S. Income and Output*, a supplement to the *Survey of Current Business* (Washington, D.C.: U.S. Government Printing Office, 1958), pp. 74–76.

[27]Oskar Morgenstern, *On the Accuracy of Economic Observations*, 2nd ed. (Princeton, N.J.: Princeton University Press, 1963), pp. 242–301.

[28]Ibid., p. 136.

[29]Ibid., pp. 249–50.

[30]August 1965 *Survey*, p. 11.

Nevertheless, the number and size of revisions is probably healthy on balance. Revision of the components of GNP is a major function of the National Income Division. Some revisions stem from definitional changes, as in 1965, but most of them incorporate improved data or statistical methods. Those who complain about revisions are usually not aware of how thin and infrequently reported are the data upon which some of the components were originally based.

Also, publication of sizable revisions testifies to the OBE's independence and integrity, since the political and bureaucratic pressures are all in the other direction. Economic and political decisions are made on the basis of preliminary figures, and it is embarrassing to officials to have their decisions contradicted simply by statistical revisions in national-income data.

2. Regarding Morgenstern's second criticism, so much craftsmanship, judgment, and art goes into the major aggregates that measures of probable error would not be very meaningful. Also, the error limits would require as much "massaging" as the original data. It might be possible, however, to indicate sampling errors for some of the simpler components of GNP, such as wages and salaries, or corporate profits.

3. Morgenstern's estimate of a 10 percent error in national income (aggregates) was based on pre–World War II figures collected by the original developer of our national-income accounting system, Simon Kuznets. The error involved in modern GNP figures is probably much lower. Whole new data-collection programs, separate calculations for gross national income and product, and the services of an experienced and fairly large staff are advantages available to the OBE that Kuznets never dreamed of in 1942.

However, there is really no satisfactory way to measure the deviation of published national-income measures from their true-universe values, because no alternative estimates of the correct values exist. It is even possible that errors in GNP may actually be as high as those estimated by Morgenstern (10 or even 15 percent). If so, they are more likely to be systematic errors (elements of GNP consistently omitted or overestimated) than the random errors primarily discussed by Morgenstern. GNP or NI may be consistently reported too high or too low even though period-to-period changes are approximately correct. These changes from one period to the next are one of the major uses of national-income data, to indicate the direction and rate of economic growth and stability. Therefore, systematic errors may not seriously reduce the usefulness of the data. Also, it is the policy of the OBE to prefer a reliable estimate of period-to-period change over a reliable estimate of level, should a conflict occur.

Some evidence regarding errors in changes in aggregates can be adduced. In the vast majority of cases, changes in *goods output* (equal to GNP less services and structures) are in the same direction and of about the same magnitude as changes in the Federal Reserve Index of Industrial Production, a respected alternative measure of goods output.

Census-based data for either GNP or NI for bench-mark years such as 1958 vary from the interim estimates made by extrapolating the previous bench-mark years by margins of from less than 1 percent to about 2½ percent. (In 1965, GNP for 1958 was revised by 2.2 percent and 1958 national income by 1.2 percent, exclusive of definitional changes.)[31] In fact, the highest percentage revision Morgenstern found for *any* year between the first published figure for national income and the latest value as of July 1961 was 2.7 percent, for the year 1950.[32]

The percentage changes made in revisions may not measure the "true" error.

---

[31]Ibid., pp. 11 and 20.

[32]Morgenstern, *Accuracy*, p. 263.

Revised estimates could also be wrong and, even in bench-mark years, are based on some of the same methodology that originally caused the error. The revisions do, however, measure the cumulative error in extrapolation when compared with the somewhat independent new bench-mark figure.

Barring some improbable, large systematic error that may never become known, random errors in the national-income aggregates are, therefore, about ± 1 to $2\frac{1}{2}$ percent. But an error of only ± 1 percent means that the value for GNP in 1971 could be off by \$10½ billion on either side, and a 2½ percent error entails an absolute error of over \$26 billion on either side of the published figure. The whole quarter-to-quarter change, as reported even during inflationary periods such as 1968 to 1972, could easily be washed out by such an error. In 1963, GNP went up by \$5½ billion during the first quarter and by \$6½ billion during the second quarter, now revised to \$5.4 and \$6.8 billion respectively. Business writers at the time hailed the increase in the original figure as evidence that the economy was accelerating and "taking off." Yet an error of only 0.2 percent of the then prevailing GNP level of \$580 billion would have obliterated the \$1 billion completely! A similar but stronger observation can be made concerning small changes in deflated GNP, because the application of price indexes adds another element of possible error to the current-dollar figures.

Certainly no firm conclusions can be made about small changes of a billion or two in a trillion-dollar economy! At such high current-dollar levels a change has to equal \$10 billion or more to necessarily represent anything more than a 1 percent error in the GNP data. As Morgenstern has aptly stated:

It should be stressed that the present exaggerated practical applications must be avoided. It is not unusual, for example, to consider changes in the national income figures of plus or minus one-tenth of one percent (or even less!) as significant for either theory or policy. In the face of the facts such procedure is completely void of meaning.[33]

4. Morgenstern's point on growth rates is surely well taken: Assume reported GNP figures of \$550 billion and \$560 billion for two successive years indicating a growth rate of 1.8 percent. But suppose each figure is estimated with a conservative error of plus or minus 1 percent. Then the first GNP figure could be between \$544.5 billion and \$555.5 billion and the later GNP figure could be anywhere between \$554.4 billion and \$565.6 billion. If the true growth path went from the upper limit of \$555.5 billion in the first year to \$554.4 billion in the second year (here the lower limit). the growth rate could be as low as −0.2 percent. On the other hand, if GNP went from \$544.5 billion to \$565.6 billion (lower to upper limit) the growth rate could be as high as 3.9 percent. If nothing is changed, but the error in both GNP values is 3 percent, the rate of growth could vary anywhere from −4.1 to 8.1 percent![34] This little example should serve to show that if the current or deflated GNP figures are somewhat risky to use in themselves calculating growth rates from them is far more hazardous.

Statistical Discrepancy as a Gauge of Accuracy Sometimes the size of the statistical discrepancy is taken as a measure of the error in the GNP accounts. If this were true, errors would be reassuringly small: Statistical discrepancy in the annual figures has not exceeded 1 percent of GNP since 1951 (in 1971 it was about 0.5 percent and in 1967 only 0.1 percent of GNP).

---

[33]Ibid., p. 259.

[34]Ibid., pp. 287–89.

In the quarterly figures, statistical discrepancy has not exceeded 1 percent of GNP since 1954 and is usually under one half of 1 percent. In absolute terms, statistical discrepancy only once exceeded $5 billion (1969 for annual data) and before 1969 was generally below $3 billion.[35]

But a low statistical discrepancy (or even one of zero) does not imply accuracy of the reported GNP total. Both the income-side and the product-side estimates, while equal or virtually equal, could be substantially in error. What the statistical discrepancy does measure is the *residual* error remaining after all reasonable efforts are made to bring the two sides of the national income and product account into balance. The procedure is approximately as follows:

The initial estimates for GNP components submitted by individual OBE estimators are aggregated on both sides of the account. If the initial statistical discrepancy is high (meaning, for example, that product is running well below income) or has shifted abruptly, the individual estimators go back to rework their estimates in the desired direction (in the example above, up for product and down for income). Since, as the discussion on PCE estimation indicated, there are usually substantial areas where judgment determines the estimate because any one of two or more methods is equally valid, some adjustments of this kind are normally possible. After the adjusted figures for the two sides are re-added, any remaining discrepancy becomes the published statistical discrepancy.

It may be presumed that the procedure usually produces a more accurate GNP figure than if the initial estimates were unaltered. However, using the example of PCE, if the difficulty actually lay in an erroneous extrapolator, undetected by the analyst, or a faulty commodity-flow estimate in a benchmark year, the wrong item may be adjusted. This method could also cause a correct income-side GNP figure to be adjusted downward.

A large statistical discrepancy in any period compared with other years and quarters does indicate the presence of troublesome difficulties in the data, meaning errors that could not be resolved. Perhaps even more damaging are sudden shifts in the statistical discrepancy. For example, a discrepancy of +$2.1 billion in 1955 swung to −$1.1 billion in 1956 and then shifted back to 0 for 1957. Something is possibly wrong (or abnormally wrong) with the GNP estimate for one of those years.

Most of the statistical difficulties and problems of reliability that affect the national-income accounts also apply to real-life input–output tables. Only three large tables have been constructed in the United States for the postwar years (1947, 1958, and 1963).[36] Each is a Census of Manufactures year. As long as large input–output tables are constructed only for census

[35] *Statistical Tables*, pp. 12–13; Office of Business Economics, U.S. Department of Commerce, "U.S. National Income and Product Accounts," *Survey of Current Business*, 49 (July 1969), p. 14; July 1972 *Survey*, p. 18.

[36] November 1969 *Survey*, p. 16.

years, the need for extrapolation or estimation of any intercensal year will not arise in computing published statistics.

Conceptually, as we have discussed, the main problem with input–output models is that up to now, they all assume constant technical coefficients. Some chemical processes operate in this fashion, but in most productive operations, the proportions of inputs vary as the scale of production (and the quantity of output) increases.

The present models may yield good results when operated over small ranges of increased sector demand over the level prevailing in the census year. As the levels rise, however, errors become large. Nor do the present models have any way to incorporate technological changes in productive processes.

If an input–output table could be constructed for each year with little time lag, these problems would probably not be serious. Unfortunately, the OBE's resources are as yet too small to undertake annual production of interindustry tables. At present, a table is constructed every five years, with a time lag before publication of nearly six years, and it was quite an accomplishment for the small staff involved to publish the 1963 table by November 1969. Nevertheless, the use of input–output tables and demand for more frequent construction of them, despite the cost, seems sure to rise in the years ahead.

CONCLUDING COMMENT

The originator of input–output analysis, Wassily Leontief, has suggested that the bridge between theory and fact lies in the dependable relationships that persist over time among the various sectors of the economy.[37] The effects of any event are transmitted systematically, link by link, throughout the economy. Consequently, behavioral models derived from an input–output table, or the national-income accounting system, or any other representation of the aggregate economy, can give valid results only if (1) the assumed relationships are accurately described in the first place, and (2) the relationships do not change significantly after they have been defined.

The theories of the behavior of individual producers and consumers, described in Chapters 2 and 3, serve as a basis for macroeconomics only if the behavior of the individual components is unaffected by aggregation or if the effect is predictable and can be incorporated into the analysis.

Aggregate economic theories are made more dependable by the law of large numbers. Individual households' consumption patterns may vary markedly over a short time as income or age composition changes, or as any other significant changes occur. But the likelihood of such changes occurring simultaneously in a sufficient number of households to alter aggregate consumption patterns is slight over a short span of time. At the same time,

---

[37] Wassily Leontief, *Input-Output Economics*, p. 24.

individual consumers may naturally influence each other's behavior as they are aggregated.

In macroeconomics, the individual human actors do not behave with the certainty that can confidently be assumed for individual particles in the physical sciences. The predicted results of the 1968 tax surcharge, for example, were incorrect because enough people behaved contrary to expectations to throw off the results. In conclusion, the number of individuals in an economic system may not always be large enough to allow accurate prediction. Even if the population is made up of a dependable and an undependable segment, the undependable segment may throw off the results for the whole population. And even if the individuals behave as predicted, the results may not be as predicted if a change occurs in some assumed constant, such as the distribution of income. For example, suppose consumers relate their consumption expenditures to their income, and aggregate income increases. The increase in consumption would be less than anticipated if the distribution of income happened to change so that higher income was received mainly by individuals who save a greater-than-average proportion of their income.

There are two levels on which data may be misleading. First, the data may simply be incorrect, and their application to a theory may therefore give misleading results. Second, real-world data may be misleading when applied to theoretical constructs, because the theory usually proposes functional, continuous relationships among homogeneous, well-defined units, and observed data can normally provide only one point on such continuous relationships using units that are somewhat different than proposed in theory. For example, the consumption function proposes a set of relationships between PCE and income for all possible levels of income, but the national-income data can tell us only one realized value for PCE and one realized level of income for a given period of time. What is more, the purchase of a residence is not part of personal-consumption expenditures, whereas other consumer durables are, and nonprofit organizations are combined with households rather than with business firms.

Furthermore, significant relationships are often *marginal*, as we saw in Chapters 2 and 3, but observed data generally reveal *average* values of economic relationships. Therefore, even when observed data are accurate, they may not be capable of illuminating some of the most meaningful economic relationships. We never know, for example, whether an observed change in the proportion of income spent on consumption is due to a shift in the consumption function or to a movement along the curve. Even the statistical techniques developed to deal with this "identification problem" are, themselves, based on assumptions, and therefore are incapable of providing definitive solutions. The difficulties in applying observed data to economic theories are serious enough in microeconomics, but they may be magnified in macroeconomics, where small problems sometimes grow when they are aggregated.

Conceptually, the U.S. social accounting system is a generally splendid structure and a magnificent achievement. However, clear understanding of the definitions of some of the components and of the handling of certain transactions is essential in order to avoid misuse and misinterpretation of national income and output measures. Effective use of input–output tables as well as of the national-income accounts requires knowledge of the sectors as defined and of the interlocking relationship among the accounts.

One final word regarding accuracy and reliability: Our national-income system is an art as well as a science. On purely scientific grounds, the probable errors, although likely small in percentage terms, are large enough in absolute terms to make the popular emphasis on small changes a hazardous game at best. And much of the analysis of current business conditions does emphasize small changes in quarter-to-quarter movements, a point to keep in mind when headlines blare a change of 0.2 percent in the quarterly GNP increase.

Yet the vast majority of the OBE estimators are accomplished artists. A somewhat renewed measure of confidence in employing the published figures may be taken from their dedication and virtuosity. At the same time, the general weakness of much of the data underpinnings must always be kept mentally close at hand. Economic estimates do not have the accuracy of those in the physical sciences, such as the estimate of the speed of light.

QUESTIONS AND PROBLEMS

1. What uses can be made of input–output analysis?
2. What problems can occur in aggregating economic data?
3. In your opinion, what is the major shortcoming of our national-income accounting system? Justify your opinion. What would you do to overcome the problem?
4. Can you propose a technique for avoiding the assumption of fixed technical coefficients in input–output analysis?
5. How valid are our techniques for deflating current expenditures in national-income accounting?
6. Can statistical discrepancy be used as a gauge of accuracy?

ADDITIONAL SELECTED REFERENCES

AGGREGATION

GREEN, H. A. J., *Aggregation in Economic Analysis.* Princeton, N.J.: Princeton University Press, 1964.

LEONTIEF, W., "An Alternative to Aggregation in Input-Output Analysis and National Accounts," *Review of Economics and Statistics*, 49 (August 1967), 412–19.

NATIONAL INCOME IN REAL TERMS

HICKS, J. R., A. G. HART, and J. W. FORD, *The Social Framework of the American Economy*, 2nd American ed., pp. 198–218. New York: Oxford University Press, 1955.

AUKRUST, O., "An Axiomatic Approach to National Accounting," *Review of Income and Wealth*, 12 (September 1966), 179–90.

KUZNETS, S., "National Income: A New Version," *Review of Economics and Statistics*, 30 (August 1948), 151–79. Rejoinder: Milton Gilbert, George Jaszi, et al., "Objectives of National Income Measurement: A Reply to Professor Kuznets," *Review of Economics and Statistics*, 30 (August 1948), 179–95.

Office of Business Economics, U.S. Department of Commerce, "The Economic Accounts of the United States: Retrospect and Prospect." 50th Anniversary Issue of the *Survey of Current Business*, July 1971 (Washington, D.C.: U.S. Government Printing Office, 1971).

INPUT-OUTPUT ANALYSIS

CHIOU-SHUANG YAN, *Introduction to Input-Output Economics*. New York: Holt, Rinehart & Winston, 1969.

DORFMAN, R., "The Nature and Significance of Input-Output," *The Review of Economics and Statistics*, 36 (May 1954), 121–33.

———, P. A. SAMUELSON, and R. M. SOLOW, *Linear Programming and Economic Analysis*, Chaps. 9 and 10. New York: McGraw-Hill, 1958.

EVENS, W. D., and M. HOFFENBERG, "The Interindustry Relations Study for 1947," *The Review of Economics and Statistics*, 34 (May 1952), 97–142.

GHOSH, A., *Experiments with Input-output Models*. Cambridge: Cambridge University Press, 1964.

LEONTIEF, W., *Input-Output Economics*. New York: Oxford University Press, 1966.

———, *The Structure of the American Economy*, 1919–1939, 2nd ed. New York: Oxford University Press, 1951.

———, et al., *Studies in the Structure of the American Economy*. New York: Oxford University Press, 1953.

MIERNYK, W., *The Elements of Input-Output Analysis*. New York: Random House, 1965.

STONE, RICHARD, *Input-Output and National Accounts*. Paris: OECC, 1961.

VACCARA, B. N., "An Input-Output Model for Long-Range Economic Projections," *Survey of Current Business*, 51 (July 1971), 47–56.

The Neoclassical System

6

INTRODUCTION

Input–output analysis follows the preclassical French economic tradition commonly called physiocratic. However, neither the English classical nor neoclassical schools followed up the circular-flow "economic table" of the physiocrats; they struck off in a direction of their own.

Too often, the distinction is not made between the earlier, classical economic tradition of J.S. Mill or David Ricardo and the neoclassical tradition, represented in England by Alfred Marshall or A.C. Pigou, and in America by Irving Fisher or Henry C. Simons.[1] However, the distinction is significant, because modern macroeconomics grew out of the neoclassical and not out of the older, classical tradition. The classical theories can be sharply distinguished from the neoclassical on three lines: First, the whole field of marginal analysis, including indifference curves, is a postclassical development. Second, whereas the classical theorists emphasize supply, and the marginalists, demand, the neoclassicals divided their attention between supply and demand. Therefore, Keynesian emphasis on aggregate demand follows naturally from the postclassical theories. Third, the theoretical progress of the

[1]Perhaps Keynes himself is partly to blame for not distinguishing clearly enough the older classical tradition from that current at the time he was writing; although, in fairness to him, all classification systems are arbitrary. From our historical perspective, it is useful to distinguish the formulations of Ricardo and Mill, with their emphasis on the labor theory of value and cost of production, from those of Marshall and Pigou, with their balanced emphasis on both supply and demand.

neoclassicists was a case of two steps forward and one step back. Their refinement of microtheory was at least a two-step advance, but they lost ground by deemphasizing macroeconomics.

The formulation presented in this chapter is an abstraction of the neoclassical position. In a sense, to reconstruct a theory of macroeconomics from the neoclassical viewpoint, which largely disregarded macroeconomic questions, is unfair. The neoclassical theory was less well defined and more realistic than the abstract, oversimplified version presented here. Furthermore, it did not give macroeconomic problems much attention in its concern for price theory based on partial-equilibrium analysis.

The neoclassical microtheories described well-defined time periods—the very short run, the short run, and the long run. However, the macrotheories developed by neoclassical economists were not so clearly defined with reference to the relevant time periods. They seem to put their macrotheories into a sort of long-run macro time period that transcends the business cycle—a time sufficiently long to allow equilibrium to be established around a trend and to permit the underlying forces of change and continual flux to resolve themselves into an aggregate equilibrium, but not so long that it would permit institutional or structural change. The partial-equilibrium analysis of the neoclassicists, which focused on individual markets, disregarded the problems of general equilibrium. Consequently, the modern economists with neoclassical proclivities are forced to return to the general equilibrium of Léon Walras rather than the partial equilibrium of the English and American neoclassicists.

The Walrasian general equilibrium system represents the aggregate economy as a giant set of interrelated supply and demand functions in product and resource markets. A change in any one market can spread its effects throughout the whole system. For example, if a group of workers decides to drop out of the labor force, the supply of labor will decrease, reducing the output and raising the price of goods produced. Depending on the elasticity of demand for labor, the reduction in the labor force can cause either an increase or a decrease in total wages, which in turn can affect demand. So the change in the labor force can affect not only the supply function of various products but also their demand. The Walrasian system can be contrasted with a simple horizontal summation of supply and demand in two ways: (1) the Walrasian system with its multitude of individual supply and demand curves is able to portray the differing effects of any change in each market for each product and resource; (2) the simple horizontal summation of all products suffers from the defect of adding apples and oranges—a defect that must be weighed against the impossible complexity of the Walrasian system, which requires a separate supply and demand curve for each product and each resource in each market.

Different parts of the non-Walrasian aggregate demand model used in this chapter have different time spans from others. For example, equilibrium in the labor market is a short-run concept: Labor is variable and capital is fixed. Velocity, however, could only be considered constant over one or more business cycles; otherwise, the changes induced by the cycle would have to be taken into account. Additional random changes in velocity occur in the very short run for a variety of reasons. The modern synthetic versions of neoclassical theory combine incompatible time periods in a way no neoclassicist might have permitted—if he had ever put the parts of the theory together.

However, the policies suggested by the neoclassicists generally followed the theory as presented in this chapter. So as a practical matter, the neoclassical theory as synthesized here has considerable significance. And there are today still economists and commentators who recommend the neoclassical policies.

Throughout the classical and neoclassical periods, there existed a continuous *undercurrent* of theoretical as well as practical interest in what today would be called macroeconomics, including monetary matters, the business cycle, and underproduction. Lauderdale, Thornton, Malthus, Marx, Spiethoff, Aftalion, and Tugan-Baranowsky are a few of the better-known economists who concerned themselves with matters of aggregate economics during the period when most of the economic profession was mainly concerned with perfecting the value and distribution theory of microeconomics.[2] Our presentation of neoclassical macro theory follows the thinking of the main body of neoclassical economists, rather than of the economists who formed the undercurrents.

An understanding of the main body of neoclassical theory is important to an understanding of modern macroeconomics for several reasons. First, the development of price theory was a necessary step in developing our economic system. Second, neoclassical macro theory suggests monetary and fiscal policies still relied on by many, including some well-known commentators. Third, pre-Keynesian neoclassical formulations similar to that presented in this chapter are used by some contemporary critics of modern macroeconomics to attack the Keynesian system. Finally, many parts of the neoclassical theory have been carried over into modern macroeconomics.

---

[2]See, for example, Lord Lauderdale, *An Inquiry into the Nature and Origin of Public Wealth and into the Means and Causes of Its Increase*, 2nd ed. (Edinburgh: Archibald Constable, 1819); Henry Thornton, *An Inquiry into the Effects of the Paper Credit of Great Britain (1802)*, F. A. von Hayek, ed. (New York: Holt, Rinehart, and Winston, 1939); T. R. Malthus, *Principles of Political Economy* (London: John Murray, 1820), Chap. 7; Karl Marx, *Das Kapital*, Benedikt Kautsky, ed., (Stuttgart, Germany: Publisher Cotta Verlag, 1962), Vol. I, pp. 732–807; Arthur Spiethoff, "Vorbemerkungen zu einer Theorie der Überproduktion," *Jahrbuch für Gesetzgebung, Verwaltung und Volkswirtshaft*, 1902; Albert Aftalion, "La Réalité des Surproductions générales. Essai d'une Théorie des Crises générales et périodiques," *Revue d'économie politique*, 1909; ———, *Les Crises périodiques de surproduction*, Vols. I and II (Paris: Marcel Riviére et cie., 1913); Michel Tugan-Baranowsky, *Studien zur Theorie und Geschichte der Handelskrisen in England* (Jena, Germany: J. Fischer, 1901).

ASSUMPTIONS OF THE NEOCLASSICAL SYSTEM

The neoclassical theory was based on certain assumptions regarding human nature, society, competition, economic fluctuations, and institutional stability. Some of the assumptions were always made explicit while others were implied.

Human Nature

Man was assumed to be rational, intelligent, and knowledgeable. His assumed goal was to maximize pleasure and minimize pain. This concept of human nature underlies the utility analysis of Chapter 2. Veblen derided the neoclassical *homo economicus* as "a lightning calculator" of pleasure and pain. The neoclassicists probably wished they had said it first.

Society

In the neoclassical view, society was composed of a number of independent atoms—human beings—and was merely equal to the sum of its individual members. Such a view of society made the neoclassicists easy prey to the fallacy of composition, which plagued their macroeconomic models. In addition, it may be noted that the atoms comprising society were Victorians, tending to follow a highly developed Protestant ethical code. Disobedience carried its own penalties, as violators would suffer the effects of their own decadence and the retaliation of their peers. Accompanying this moral code was an optimistic feeling of progress. The world was pictured as moving on an upward plane on which economic growth would solve the major social problems, such as delinquency and crime. Victorians felt, as some people do today, that wealth and morality should go hand in hand; a good society will see that they do.

Alfred Marshall gave voice to the Victorian consensus:

> . . . now first we are learning the importance of insisting that the rich have duties as well as rights in their individual and in their collective capacity; now first is the economic problem of the new age showing itself to us as it really is. This is partly due to a wider knowledge and a growing earnestness. But however wise and virtuous our grandfathers had been, they could not have seen things as we do; for they were hurried along by urgent necessities and terrible disasters. We [Victorians] must judge ourselves by a severer standard . . . the nation has grown in wealth, in health, in education, and in morality; and we are no longer compelled to subordinate almost every other consideration to the need of increasing the total produce of industry.[3]

---

[3]Alfred Marshall, *Principles of Economics*, 8th ed. (New York: Macmillan, 1920), pp. 750–51.

Perfect Competition

The neoclassicists invariably made one assumption explicit: Perfect competition, as defined in Chapter 3, was the norm, some going as far as to maintain that it would develop inevitably, regardless of any efforts to thwart it.

Although their position was somewhat qualified, the neoclassical writers retained a view of business firms as having a limited life despite the growing dominance of large corporations, because successful firms eventually come under less adaptable or less highly motivated managers. A biological analogy was often used to imply this. For example, Marshall said

> here we may read a lesson from the young trees of the forest as they struggle upwards through the benumbing shade of their older rivals. Many succumb on the way, and a few only survive; those few become stronger with every year, they get a larger share of light and air with every increase of their height, and at last in their turn they tower above their neighbours, and seem as though they would grow on forever, and forever become stronger as they grow. But they do not. One tree will last longer in full vigour and attain greater size than another; but sooner or later age tells on them all. Though the taller ones have better access to light and air than their rivals, they gradually lose vitality; and one after another they give place to others, which, though of less material strength, have on their side the vigour of youth.[4]

Thus, not only might large firms become less efficient as they grew, but small firms could achieve efficient operations through vigorous management.

Economic Fluctuations

Many neoclassicists believed that business fluctuations were transient and temporary, and so they could be largely disregarded. At the same time, some neoclassicists, as we shall see in Chapter 16, were adopting the idea of a regular trade cycle, with each phase setting the conditions for the next. No matter which view they held, none felt that a depression equilibrium was a serious possibility.

Institutional Stability

The neoclassical writers believed in economic growth, but even so, they had a static view of the world's institutions. Although they felt that firms would eventually die, as would trees in a forest, the forest would endure forever. This assumption would have had considerable validity as a working hypothesis had it been made in some static culture, but the assumption that constant change would only continually renew the basic institutional framework is of doubtful value in Western civilization, where change itself has become institutionalized.

---

[4] *Ibid.*, pp. 315–16.

The Neoclassical System

The neoclassical system lends itself very readily to the supply-and-demand formulation. Production of goods and services was largely self-justifying because underlying the neoclassical system was *Say's Law*. The neoclassical writers, following J.B. Say and the later classical economists, held that, in the final analysis, supply would create its own demand:

> The only way of getting rid of money is in the purchase of some product or other. Thus, the mere circumstance of the creation of one product immediately opens a vent for other products.[5]

Goods exchange for goods in both a simple barter economy and a more sophisticated, monetary economy. As the flow diagram in Chapter 4 indicates, the income of households is derived from the sale of productive resources such as labor. The income received from the sale of productive resources must be either spent on consumer goods or saved for the purchase of investment goods.[6] The interest rate was expected to keep the amount that households saved equal to the amount that business invested. Thus, the cost of employing productive resources exactly equals the value of their output. A general glut could not occur, nor could a general scarcity of commodities. Furthermore, the economy would tend toward full employment of productive resources. We shall discuss Say's Law in greater detail shortly.

The Production Function

In Chapter 3, we developed the firm's production function and indicated that the production function facing the individual firm will at first increase at an increasing rate but will eventually increase at a decreasing rate when only one variable resource exists. Assuming that this pattern exists throughout the economy, we can construct an aggregate-production function through horizontal summation of the production functions of individual firms. Al-

---

[5] J. B. Say, *A Treatise on Political Economy*, 2nd American ed. (Boston: Wells and Lilly, 1824) Vol. I, p. 86.

Say's Law, as it exists in the tradition of English and American economists, is somewhat oversimplified. Say recognized at various places in his work that under certain conditions, overproduction, at least of particular products, is possible. For example, at one place he says, "Gentlemen, we will see that the products in general can be multiplied and can be sold against each other until a point is reached which I cannot assign positively and which depends on the local circumstances of each country. If this point is passed, certain products become too expensive for the utility they contain. That means the utility is not sufficient to indemnify the consumers for the sacrifice which they must make to buy the goods. Therefore these goods will no longer be produced and they will not be offered on the market for new products."

This representative quotation and others to the same effect may be found in J.S. Say, Cours Complet d'Économie Politique Pratique (Brussels: Société Typographique Belge, 1945), pp. 61–165. Reprinted, Rome, 1968. [Authors' translation.]

[6] This point was recognized as early as in Adam Smith's *Wealth of Nations*. Adam Smith, *The Wealth of Nations*, ed. Edwin Cannan (New York: Modern Library, 1937), pp. 639–41.

though such a production function could be constructed for any variable resource, we assume the variable resource to be labor, because in short-run neoclassical theory, capital, land, and technology were usually considered fixed factors and labor variable, since firms could usually hire additional workers more quickly than they could acquire more land or capital, or adopt new technology.

The functional relationship between real output and varying amounts of labor is shown in the upper right panel of Figure 6-1, where employment is

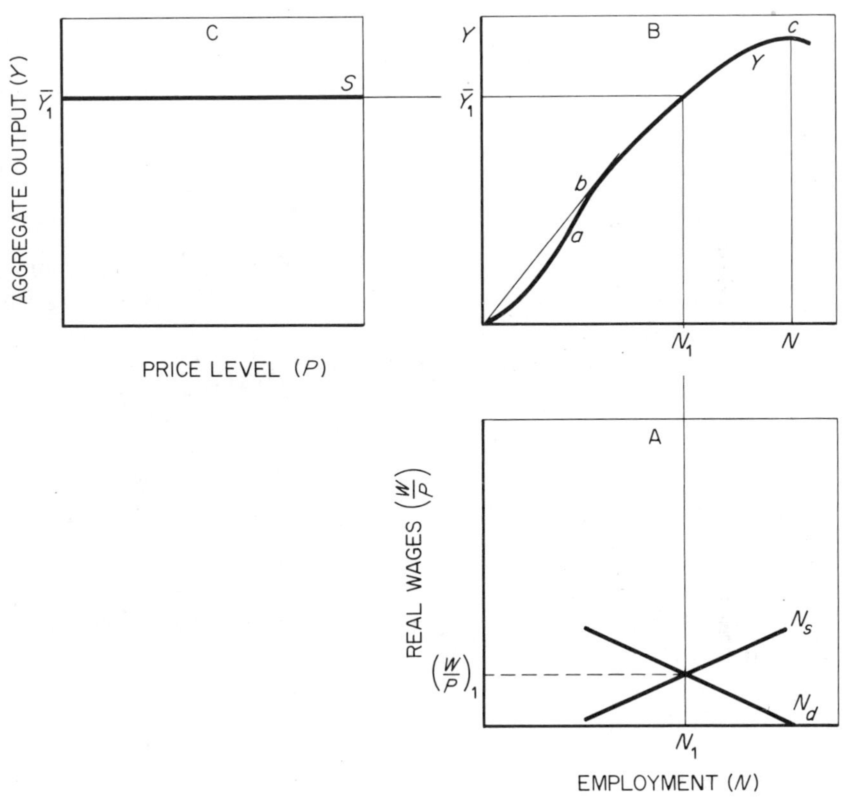

FIG. 6-1 Derivation of Aggregate Supply

plotted along the *x*-axis and aggregate output is plotted along the *y*-axis. Constant increases in labor (N) cause diminishing increments of aggregate output (Y) after point *a* is reached. Following standard practice, Y is used to represent aggregate output, real output at constant prices, the same thing as an aggregate-production function. In national-income accounting terms, Y may refer to any of the five aggregates described in Chapter 4, depending upon the context in which it is used. Generally it is assumed that Y refers to net national product, because it equals the total output of goods and services less production to replace worn-out equipment. The other symbols are the same as those used in Chapter 3. In equation form, the economy's aggregate-production function is

$$Y = f_4(N, R, K, T) \tag{6-1}$$

where

N = labor force

R = stock of natural resources

K = stock of capital

T = level of technology

Y = aggregate output, real output at constant prices for the economy

where R, K, and T remain constant in the short run.

The Labor Market

The firm's demand for labor under perfectly competitive conditions depends on the marginal-revenue product of labor (MRP_L). As you will recall from Chapter 3,

$$MRP_L = MP_L \times P_x \tag{6-2}$$

where

MRP_L = marginal-revenue product of labor

MP_L = marginal product of labor

P_x = price of the product produced by labor

Formula 6-2 can be reorganized to solve for the marginal product of labor, as follows:

$$MP_L = \frac{MRP_L}{P_x} \tag{6-3}$$

A competitive business will maximize profits by hiring workers up to the point where the money wage (P_L—marginal resource cost) equals the marginal-revenue product (MRP_L). If P_L or W equals the price of labor, then the firm maximizes profits where

$$MRP_L = P_L \text{ or } W \tag{6-4}$$

Since, under perfect competition when the firm is maximizing profits, each worker receives a money wage equal to the marginal-revenue product of labor, money wages (W) can be substituted for marginal-revenue product in formula 6-3:

$$MP_L = \frac{W}{P_x} \tag{6-5}$$

Using W/P_x instead of money wages converts a firm's demand curve for labor from money to real terms, the demand for labor becoming the MP_L curve instead of the MRP_L curve.

Remember, MP_L equals the slope of the total-product function, and will have a negative slope after diminishing returns set in. The demand curve for labor (MP_L) of the individual competitive firms can be summed horizontally to obtain the aggregate demand curve for labor, which is shown in the lower panel of Figure 6-1.[7] In algebraic form, this is expressed as

$$N_d = f_5\left(\frac{W}{P}\right) \tag{6-6}$$

or

$$MP_L = \frac{W}{P} \tag{6-7}$$

where N_d equals aggregate labor demand. When applied to the aggregate economy, W becomes the average money wage and P represents the economy's price level. Assuming that P equally represents the prices of goods produced by firms and the price of goods consumed by households, then W/P can be considered the average real-wage rate for labor throughout the economy.

The neoclassical economists considered the supply of labor offered by an individual worker to be a function of his willingness to offer his labor at all possible real-wage levels. Each individual's decision will be made on the basis of an indifference curve balancing the utility of leisure with the utility of real income. The resulting individual labor-supply curve has a positive slope, which implies that for each worker to offer his services, the marginal utility of the last bit of real income must be sufficient to overcome the disutility or tediousness of the last bit of work.[8] An aggregate supply curve for labor is

---

[7]A simple horizontal summation of individual firms' demand curves for labor ignores the aggregation problems involved, owing to the firms' interrelating to each other; an example of such a problem in connection with aggregating firms' marginal-revenue product curves in a particular perfectly competitive market was presented in Chapter 3.

[8]In some individual labor markets, it was recognized by the neoclassical economists that after a certain wage has been obtained, the supply-of-labor curve may bend backwards. The reason for this backward bend in the labor-supply curve is that increased real wages, after a satisfactory standard of living has been achieved, lead to a preference for leisure over additional work. However, in the aggregate, the neoclassical economists assumed that the labor-supply curve was positively sloped. If we plot hours of leisure along the horizontal axis and daily income (assuming an hourly wage, flexible working hours, and constant prices) on the vertical axis, we may determine the number of daily hours worked at various possible wage levels. That information can then be transferred to a labor supply curve.

Each indifference curve is drawn to show equal satisfaction from different possible combinations of income and leisure (both income and leisure are presented as positive goods). Lines *L-a*, *L-b*, and *L-c* represent the wage earner's opportunity curve given three different hourly wage rates, $2.00, $4.00 and $6.00. All three opportunity curves intersect the horizontal axis at 24 hours—the maximum amount of leisure per day and zero income regardless of the wage level. In our illustration, the utility-maximizing points of tangency between each opportunity curve and the highest indifference curve obtainable lead to a normal, positively sloped labor supply between the $2 and $4 wage levels—increasing derived by constructing a horizontal summation of all individual labor-supply curves. Such a labor-supply curve is a function of the real wage, or

$$N_s = f_6\left(\frac{W}{P}\right) \tag{6-8}$$

where N_s equals aggregate labor supply.

It would be theoretically possible to make labor a function of the money wage. However, the neoclassical theories were based on Say's Law, which held that goods exchanged for goods. If workers exchange a quantity of real labor for a quantity of real goods and services, they are not fooled by a reduction in real wages through price inflation.

The neoclassical theory provides us with a negatively sloped demand for labor and a positively sloped supply of labor that intersect at full employment, giving equilibrium where

$$N_s = N_d \tag{6-9}$$

If the real wage momentarily deviates from the full-employment equilibrium level, competition will bring the demand for labor and the supply of labor back into balance at full employment. *Full employment* in this sense means that all workers willing to work at a prevailing wage can find jobs; any worker holding out for higher wages would be voluntarily unemployed.[9]

The labor market is illustrated in panel A of Figure 6-1, where N_d is the labor-demand curve and N_s is the labor-supply curve. At equilibrium, the

---

his hours of work from 8 to 10—(reducing his hours of leisure from 16 to 14), and to a backward-bending labor supply as the wage increases from $4 to $6—decreasing his hours of work from 10 to 7 (increasing his hours of leisure from 14 to 17).

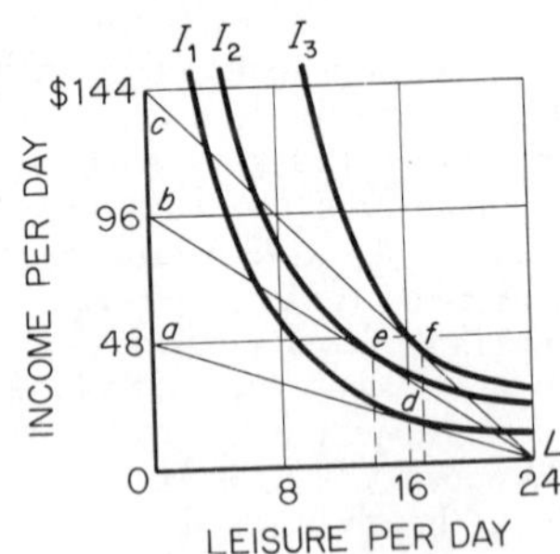

[9]"Full employment" is generally not defined as simply 100 percent employment. The concept usually excludes workers who are frictionally, seasonally, or technologically unemployed. Frictional unemployment refers to workers unemployed during the necessary delay when changing over from one job to another. Technological unemployment refers to workers who are unemployed because their skills are not demanded, even though other job openings exist. Full employment is most often used to mean that there is no "involuntary unemployment," a situation in which more workers with the required skills are willing and able to work for the going wage than there are jobs available.

level of employment is N_1 and the real wage is $(W/P)_1$. As we previously noted, in panel B aggregate output is plotted along the y-axis and employment along the x-axis to form the production function. With the level of employment set at N_1 in panel A, aggregate output is determined from the production function in panel B at $\bar{Y}_1$, which represents the full-employment level of output. Once the full-employment level of output is determined on the production function, that level of output will be maintained regardless of the price level, P. Therefore, the aggregate-supply function (S) presented in panel C is constant at the full-employment level of aggregate output ($\bar{Y}_1$), irrespective of the price level (P). Thus, in the neoclassical system, aggregate supply will always be perfectly inelastic, equal to the full-employment level of output.

To demonstrate the process of restoring full-employment equilibrium output after a deviation let us assume that real wages rise above equilibrium owing to a temporary market imperfection, such as an incorrect assumption by employers that the supply of labor had decreased as a result of a flu epidemic. The higher wage cost would mean a loss to the firms at the margin, since $MP_L < W/P$, and would consequently force a reduction in employment and output. Some unemployed workers would be willing to work at lower real wages in order to avoid unemployment. The reduction in real wages would lead to an increase in the quantity of labor demanded and consequently to the restoring of full employment.

AGGREGATE DEMAND

Say's Law of Markets

In a barter economy, Say's Law, which holds that supply creates its own demand, will obviously hold true because goods will be produced only for personal use or for trade. If trade should prove unprofitable in a utilitarian sense, the producer will decide to keep the goods for his own use. This version of Say's Law as applied to a barter economy is merely a tautology. However, the neoclassical economists felt that Say's Law had wider applications in a price economy, and that in the final analysis, whether goods were exchanged for other goods directly, or indirectly through a monetary economy, was immaterial. The underlying transaction was goods for goods, facilitated by money as a medium of exchange. Restated in a monetary economy: The money costs of the goods produced are paid out as incomes to the members of the community who in turn would get enough money to buy the goods produced.

Say's Law assumes that over time various kinds of goods will be produced in proportions corresponding to the demands for them. In discussing the business cycle, the neoclassicists and their classical predecessors recognized that temporary gluts could occur and that the economy could momentarily leave full employment. But any such deviation from full-employment equilibrium would automatically set in motion counterforces to restore full employment.

A glut of any commodity or group of commodities would lead to lower prices and increased purchases until the surplus was exhausted, and over time, lower prices would call forth a smaller output of the commodities in oversupply. For example, if too many gloves were produced and too few shoes, the price of gloves would fall to clear the market, and the price of shoes would rise to ration the short available supply. In the next time period, the output of gloves would fall and of shoes increase as resources were bid away from glove manufacturers by shoe makers. Therefore, price and production flexibility will prevent gluts and shortages of particular commodities. And if no shortage or glut can be maintained in the case of any particular commodity, how could it be possible for a general shortage or glut to develop?

In this form—that the income generated by production must be sufficient to clear the market if only the right goods are produced—Say's Law is more than a truism. It is a genuine economic theory, because it proposes a particular response of buyers and sellers to the production of goods.

In addition, proponents of Say's Law assume that any income saved by householders must be spent on investment. Otherwise, if savings should occur without any corresponding investment, unemployment would result. However, the neoclassical system was designed so that planned savings *must* be matched by planned investment, because of free market decisions induced by the level of the interest rate.

In conclusion, Say's Law proposes that supply creates its own demand because the act of producing a supply necessarily creates an exactly equivalent amount of purchasing power. (Remember, in economics, "production" includes everything required to convert raw materials to goods *in the hands of final users.*)

In contrast to Say's Law, Say's Identity merely points out that production will be consumed or not consumed. Whatever is not consumed is saved, and real goods that are saved become investment available for use in later time periods. Say's Identity (Say's Law reduced to a tautology) simply holds that sales and purchases are equal by identity.

A related concept is known as *Walras' Law.*[10] Leon Walras, a founder of the marginalist school, considered money a commodity. But money was the commodity that was used as the *numeraire*, or common denominator for all other commodities. In such a formulation, an excess supply of goods is logically the same thing as an excess demand for money. As long as prices are flexible, an excess demand for money will cause the purchasing power of money to rise as prices fall. The resulting increased value of cash holdings in real terms (the same thing as a reduction in prices) will lead to increased purchases of commodities through the law of demand. Just as Say's Law in

[10]Léon Walras, *Elements of Pure Economics*, trans. William Jaffé (London: Allen & Unwin, 1954), pp. 315–37.

its simplest form is an identity, Walras' Law is also an identity, since money is considered merely another good. Any decision not to purchase some other good is in effect a decision to "buy" or hold the commodity, money.

The Aggregate-Demand Curve

Panel C of Figure 6-1 is an aggregate-supply function (S), showing supply constant at the full-employment level of aggregate output ($\bar{Y}_1$), irrespective of the price level (P). In Figure 6-2, price and quantity have been reversed so

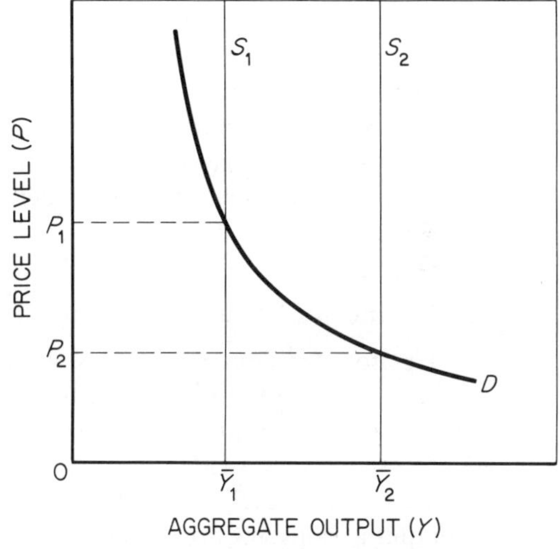

FIG. 6-2 Aggregate Supply and Demand

that they can be represented as they usually appear. Under these conditions, the completely inelastic supply curves S_1 and S_2 appear as vertical straight lines.

The neoclassical system, for reasons explained below, requires that the negatively sloped aggregate-demand curve D shown in Figure 6-2 be a rectangular hyperbola. The characteristic of a demand curve that takes the shape of a rectangular hyperbola is that price times quantity must equal a constant. Therefore, every time the price level decreases, the quantity demanded must increase sufficiently so that the total expenditure ($P \times Q$) remains constant. Since total expenditures remain constant every time the price level changes, such a demand curve must also be of unitary elasticity throughout its length. For example, in Figure 6-2, if the aggregate-supply curve should shift from S_1 to S_2 and the economy is operating on the D aggregate-demand curve, then after the new equilibrium is established, the decrease in the price level from P_1 to P_2 would be exactly proportionate to the increase in aggregate output from $\bar{Y}_1$ to $\bar{Y}_2$, so that total aggregate expenditures remain unchanged.

Geometrically, the area under any point on a rectangular hyperbola equals the area under any other point.

The aggregate-demand curve represents the amount of goods and services the citizens in the economy are willing and able to buy at every possible price. The demand for these goods and services is determined by the stock of money times its average turnover in the purchase of goods and services. This stock of money times its average turnover for goods and services must equal the monetary payments of income to the factors of production. These monetary payments represent the general purchasing power of the households in the economy over a given time period. Therefore, if prices increase, households will be able to purchase less goods and services with their given purchasing power. The monetary payments for the purchases of goods and services must equal the flow of goods and services from business firms to the public. Thus, as discussed in Chapter 4, the circular flow of money payments must be matched by an equal but reverse circular flow of goods and services. In conclusion, because of Say's Law, the money value of aggregate purchasing power equals the constant area under any neoclassical aggregate-demand curve.

The Income Version of the Equation of Exchange

We now introduce the concept of income velocity to represent the average turnover of money in the purchase of final goods and services. Now, if C is a constant representing the general purchasing power of the households in the economy, M is the quantity of money, V is income velocity, P is the general price level of final goods and services, and Y is aggregate income or output at constant prices, then

$$MV = C$$

and since

$$C = PY$$

then

$$MV = PY \tag{6-10}$$

This identity, known as the income version of the equation of exchange,[11]

[11] The most famous version of the equation of exchange, called the transactions version, was popularized by Irving Fisher, in *The Purchasing Power of Money* (New York: Macmillan, 1911), pp. 1–54. The formula for the transactions version of the equation of exchange is

$$MV = PT$$

where M is the quantity of money, V is the transactions velocity, P is an average of all prices, and T is an aggregate of all goods and services that change hands over a given time period. Fisher's formulation of the equation of exchange is more comprehensive than the income version, since T includes not only final goods and services produced during the current time period but also interfirm and financial transactions, as well as the purchase and simply indicates that the stock of money must circulate sufficiently to pay for all final goods and services demanded at market prices at each point on the aggregate-demand curve. Since the aggregate demand curve is a rectangular hyperbola, PY will be constant at every point and will be equal to a constant MV. Therefore, any increase in either M or V will cause an increase in the aggregate demand curve.

Aggregate Supply and Demand Equilibrium

Say's Law requires that a stable, full-employment equilibrium will generally be in existence because aggregate demand must equal aggregate supply, allowing for an adjustment lag. The necessary, long-run tendency in the neoclassical theory is for the economy to automatically move toward a full-employment equilibrium.

Let us consider the process of restoring equilibrium once it has been disturbed. Suppose, for example, prices fall below equilibrium. The quantity demanded of physical goods and services will increase, because lower prices mean increased real purchasing power of money. The excessive quantity demanded for the existing real output will cause prices to increase until equilibrium is restored. For example, in Figure 6-2, assume that the economy is operating on the aggregate-demand curve D and on the S_1 aggregate-supply curve. If the price level falls from the equilibrium price P_1 to P_2, a general shortage of goods will result, caused by excess demand at P_2. Equilibrium will not be restored until the price level is bid back up to P_1, or until aggregate supply increases from S_1 to S_2, because equilibrium requires that the quantities buyers are willing and able to purchase are matched by what producers are willing and able to provide.

On the other hand, if prices should increase above equilibrium, the quantity demanded of physical goods and services would decrease, and the

---

sale of goods that were produced during a previous time period. In addition, all intermediate sales are included at their market prices, so that the value of corn is included once it is sold by the farmer to a distributor, a second time when the distributor sells it to a cereal manufacturer, a third time when the manufacturer sells it to a grocer, and a fourth time when the grocer sells the cereal to the customer. In the income version, only the net value added of goods and services produced during the current period is included, whereas in the transactions version, the general price level would necessarily include an average of all prices involved in general transactions, including the prices of intermediate goods, secondhand goods, and financial transactions.

The transactions velocity includes the number of times the money stock turns over during a given time period. In the transactions version, the elementary event is an exchange of a physical good or a service for money; in the income version, the elementary event is a hypothetical transaction, since it must include, in Friedman's words, "a complete series of transactions involving the exchange of productive services for final goods, via a sequence of money payments, with all the intermediate transactions in this income circuit netted out." Milton Friedman, "A Theoretical framework for Monetary Analysis," *Journal of Political Economy*, 78 (March–April 1970), 199.

The income version is generally preferred over the transactions version, since it avoids double counting by including only those transactions which are included in the gross national product. In addition, there is no satisfactory measure of total transactions at either market or real prices.

result would be a downward pressure on prices until the equilibrium price is restored at the full-employment level of aggregate output.

The equilibrium price level is determined by the volume of spending for the given level of output. The quantity of money in circulation has a significant impact on the price level but not on the volume of output and employment (at least in the strict neoclassical theory), as we shall see in the following discussion of the quantity theory of money.[12]

THE QUANTITY THEORY OF MONEY

According to the quantity theory of money, the general price level is a direct function of the stock of money in circulation.

$$P = f_7(M) \tag{6-11}$$

In order for the quantity theory to hold, income velocity (V) and aggregate income or output (Y) must remain constant. In terms of aggregate demand and supply analysis, if income velocity (V) is held constant and the stock of money is increased, the aggregate-demand curve would shift upward and to the right, but since the aggregate-supply curve remains constant, aggregate income will not change. Only the price level will increase in response to the increase in the money supply. For example, if the economy is operating on the D_1 aggregate-demand curve in Figure 6-3, an increase in the stock of money would cause a shift in the aggregate-demand curve from, say, D_1 to D_2. The new aggregate demand after the shift would form a new equilibrium at a higher price level with the given inelastic aggregate-supply curve.

Because aggregate supply is completely inelastic, the resulting price increase from P_1 to P_2 in Figure 6-3 must be exactly proportional to the increase in the stock of money. The quantity theory of money stresses the use of money as a medium of exchange, implying that the rational person will not choose to hold money for money's sake in normal markets. Money will either be spent on consumption or be saved; if saved, it will flow into investments in preference to nonearning, idle balances.

Individual spending patterns can vary in accordance with personal habits and customs, but once established, will change only slowly over time. Similarly, payment patterns to the factors of production will change very

---

[12]The quantity theory had a long and interesting historical development in economic theory. The quantity theory was implied as early as the 1500's. Jean Bodin, an early mercantilist, observed during the 16th century that the influx of precious metals from Spain into France was the major cause of the price increase observed in that century. Jean Bodin, *Reply to the Paradoxes of M. Malestroit Concerning the Dearness of All Things and the Remedy Therefor* (Paris, 1568). Reprinted in A. E. Monroe, ed., *Early Economic Thought* (Cambridge: Harvard University Press, 1948), pp. 123–41. Early quantity theorists including Bodin are cited and discussed in Eli F. Heckscher, *Mercantilism*, rev. ed. trans. M. Shapiro (New York: Macmillan, 1955), Vol. II, pp. 224–37.

The quantity theory was adopted by the classical school as the basis for their monetary theories although different versions were developed by these economists.

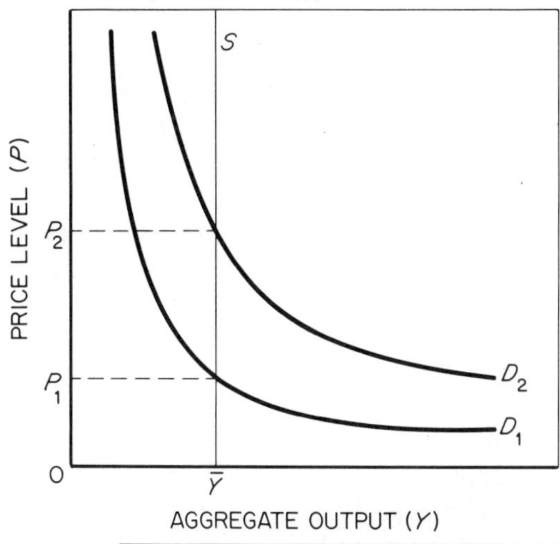

FIG. 6-3 Aggregate Supply and Demand

slowly. Therefore, the neoclassical economists felt that, in the time period under consideration, they could safely assume that the income velocity of money would remain constant and that the price level was a direct function of the stock of money.

The neoclassicists were well aware that income velocity and aggregate output could change and affect the price level. Irving Fisher summarized the neoclassical position with the following statement: (Though the statement was formulated in terms of the transactions version it applies equally well to the income version. For the distinction see Footnote 11.)

> The so-called "quantity theory," i.e., that prices vary proportionately to money, has often been incorrectly formulated, but (overlooking checks) the theory is correct in the sense that the level of prices varies directly with the quantity of money in circulation, provided the velocity of circulation of that money and the volume of trade which it is obliged to perform are not changed.[13]

The reader is left to decide whether changes in the stock of money or changes in aggregate output and income velocity are the more important determinant of the price level. The neoclassicists evidently were persuaded that income velocity and aggregate output were more stable than the stock of money. Their version of the economy was that the underlying forces of change and flux that existed in the very short run would ultimately lead aggregate output and income velocity back to their equilibrium levels more resolutely than changes in the stock of money, and only in the long run would these more stable variables change.

[13]Fisher, *The Purchasing Power of Money*, p. 14.

The Neoclassical System

We have already considered that the economy tends automatically toward achieving full employment under the neoclassical system because of Say's Law. What if savers plan to withdraw more money from the spending stream than investors plan to return to it? Up to now, we have implicitly assumed that planned savings were equal to planned investment. The neoclassical economists realized that planned savings will not by definition equal planned investment, but they were confident that the interest rate would equate the two by relating the preference patterns of savers to the profit opportunities of investors.

As we discussed in Chapter 3, each profit-maximizing firm hires resources up to the point where the marginal return from each resource just equals the marginal cost of the resource, or where the marginal-revenue product (MRP) equals marginal-resource cost (MRC). Assuming capital to be variable and holding all other resources constant, Table 6-1 shows the profit opportunities and the costs facing a theoretical firm operating for the coming year. The decreasing MRP_k from investing in additional units of capital is presented in column 2, under the assumption that each successive unit of capital employed will give rise to a constantly diminishing product. Assuming that the firm can rent as many units of capital as it wants for \$3 a unit, the MRC_k is the constant \$3 shown in column 3, if we do not include the cost of borrowing funds as part of the MRC_k. The rate of return (r) in column 5 may be figured as follows: Subtract the rental cost per unit per time period (MRC_k) in column 3 from the MRP_k in column 2, to calculate the expected return which is presented in column 4. Then divide the expected return in column 4 by the MRC_k in column 3. In formula form, we can express this as

$$r = \frac{MRP_k - MRC_k}{MRC_k} \tag{6-12}$$

The profit-maximizing firm will increase its investment as long as the rate of return (r) is higher than the cost of borrowing funds, which we assume is equal to the going rate of interest. The reason a firm will invest up to this point is that each additional unit of investment adds more to revenue than the cost to the firm of borrowing funds to pay for the investment. Additional investment will cease when the rate of return equals the interest rate.[14] Thus, if the rate of interest is 10 percent, as in column 6 of Table 6-1, investment will be terminated after the firm rents the seventh unit of capital, where the rate of return and the interest rate are both 10 percent.[15]

[14]If the firm had sufficient internal funds accumulated through retained earnings to invest beyond this point, investment will still cease when the rate of return equals the interest rate, as it would pay the firm to lend its funds rather than accumulate more investment at a lower return.

[15]The astute reader will note that the example is simplified because it disregards the

TABLE 6-1 Elements of the Decision to Invest

(1) Units of Capital	(2) Marginal-Revenue Product (MRP_k)	(3) Marginal-Resource Cost (MRC_k)	(4) Expected Return $MRP_k - MRC_k$	(5) Rate of Return of the Marginal Unit (r)	(6) Rate of Interest
1	$5.10	$3.00	$2.10	70%	10%
2	4.80	3.00	1.80	60	10
3	4.50	3.00	1.50	50	10
4	4.20	3.00	1.20	40	10
5	3.90	3.00	.90	30	10
6	3.60	3.00	.60	20	10
7	3.30	3.00	.30	10	10
8	3.00	3.00	.00	0	10
9	2.70	3.00	−.30	−10	10
10	2.40	3.00	−.60	−20	10

The above analysis can be presented in a diagram, with the amount of investment (I) plotted along the x-axis, and the rate of return (r) and the interest rate (i) both measured along the y-axis. The investment-demand curve so derived from Table 6-1 is presented as the negatively sloped demand curve in Figure 6-4.

Since, under perfectly competitive conditions, the individual firm will have little or no effect on the interest rate, the supply of funds that the firm may borrow appears perfectly elastic to the individual firm. The firm will find it profitable to invest up to the point where the rate of return given by the investment-demand curve is equal to the interest rate. In Figure 6-4, the rate of interest is 10 percent, represented by the horizontal straight line i. It would pay the firm in this illustration to rent 7 units of investment. However, if the rate of interest should increase to 40 percent, the firm would profitably employ 4 units.

In addition to their theories explaining why people invest, the neoclassical economists also had to explain why people save. Both the classical and the neoclassical theorists made saving a function of interest, which was considered a reward for thrift. The most widely used of the older classical theories of saving is the abstinence theory, developed by Nassau Senior. In this theory, interest is the reward paid for the real cost of investment, which is simply the investor's abstinence from current consumption. In updating this classical theory, Alfred Marshall pointed out that the term *abstinence*

> . . . has been misunderstood: for the greatest accumulators of wealth are very rich persons, some of whom live in luxury, and certainly do not practice abstinence in that sense of the term in which it is convertible with abstemiousness.

Marshall goes on to point out that

---

effect of time on the value of money, a qualification noted by some neoclassicists such as Irving Fisher, and it also assumes that the interest cost is the only cost of borrowing funds. Fisher, *The Theory of Interest* (1930) (New York: Augustus M. Kelley, 1961), pp. 288–322.

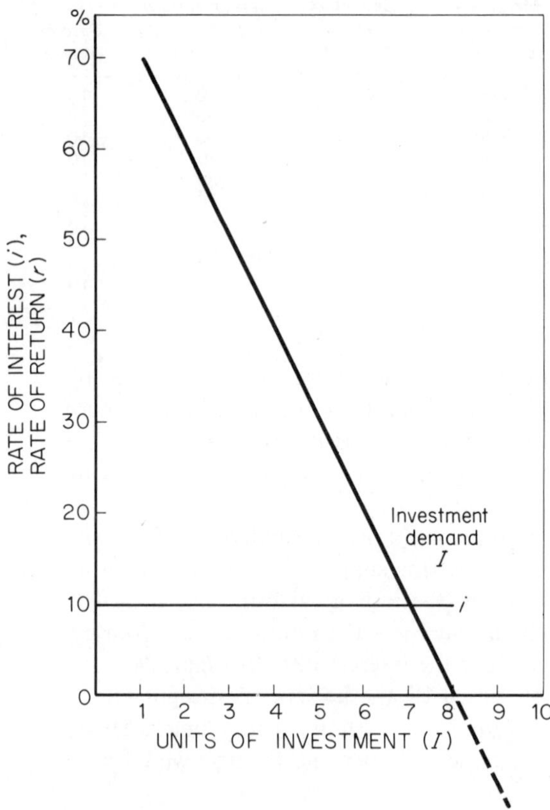

FIG. 6-4 Investment Demand

> . . . what economists meant was that, when a person abstained from consuming anything which he had the power of consuming, with the purpose of increasing his resources in the future, his abstinence from that particular act of consumption increased the accumulation of wealth. Since, however, the term is liable to be misunderstood, we may with advantage avoid its use, and say that the accumulation of wealth is generally the result of a postponement of enjoyment or of a *waiting* for it.[16]

Therefore, considering interest to be a reward for thrift, the neoclassical writers believed that interest was a payment for postponing consumption. They often referred to this postponing of consumption as a "time preference," in the sense that people prefer to consume goods at the present time and must receive a reward in order to be willing to wait or postpone consumption. In the words of Irving Fisher, time preference, or impatience, as he sometimes calls it, is the "marginal preference for present over future goods."[17] The

[16]Marshall, *Principles of Economics*, pp. 232–33.
[17]Fisher, *Theory of Interest*, p. 62.

stronger the time preference, the higher the rate of interest that has to be offered any individual before he will be willing to save a certain amount of his income.

The individual's supply of savings will be positively sloped, indicating that he will be willing to save more at higher rates of interest. In addition, the neoclassicists believed that the elasticity of the individual-savings curve depended on one's level of income. The poor have a very strong preference for present as compared with future income, because their marginal purchases are close to a minimum necessary level of living. Therefore, the supply of savings of the poor is inelastic, whereas it could be quite elastic for the rich, since they are largely indifferent between future and present income in the relevant range.

An aggregate market for savings and investment can be derived by summing the individual savings and investment functions. In Figure 6-5, equilibrium levels of savings, investment, and the rate of interest are determined for

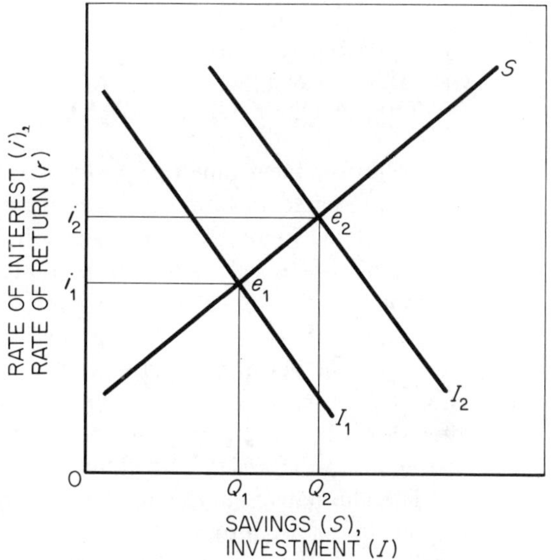

FIG. 6-5 The Supply of Savings and the Demand for Investment

the economy by the intersection of the supply of savings (S) and the demand for investment (I_1) at point e_1, at an interest rate of i_1, and a level of savings and investment of Q_1. This model will automatically seek equilibrium after a change in the demand for investment or in the supply of savings. For example, if the investment-demand curve increased to I_2 because of increased labor productivity, the greater demand for investments compared with an unchanged supply of savings would force the equilibrium interest rate up to i_2 and the equilibrium level of the quantity of savings and investment to Q_2.

This model of the neoclassical theory of interest can be presented algebraically as follows:

$$I = f_8(i) \text{ (investment function)} \tag{6-13}$$

$$S = f_9(i) \text{ (savings function)} \tag{6-14}$$

$$I = S \text{ (where savings and investment are in equilibrium)} \tag{6-15}$$

where

$I =$ aggregate investment demand

$S =$ aggregate supply of savings

$i =$ interest rate

In the neoclassical system, planned savings equals planned investment in equilibrium, Say's Law operates, and the circular flow of aggregate income and expenditure is not disturbed.

INDIFFERENCE-CURVE AND OPPORTUNITY-LINE APPROACH TO THE THEORY OF INTEREST

Following the geometric approach of Irving Fisher,[18] interest-rate theory can be presented in terms of decisions by savers and investors to allocate their available funds between savings and consumption.[19] Assume that the businessman facing the situation presented in Table 6-1 could earn a maximum of $30 if he devotes all his capital resources to present earnings and none to next year's earnings assuming his present machines last only one year.[20] As the per-unit marginal cost of renting capital (MRC_k) is shown in Table 6-1 to be $3, our businessman also has the option of not consuming three-dollar blocks of present income in order to invest and gain income next year equal to the MRP_k of column 2.

The alternative choices open to our hypothetical investor are presented graphically as a continuous curve in Figure 6-6, with this year's potential purchasing power on the *x*-axis and next year's potential purchasing power on the *y*-axis. The curve depicting all the alternative choices is called an investment-opportunity line. The investment-opportunity line is concave to the origin because of diminishing returns to capital.

We have assumed that the possibilities facing our businessman are such

---

[18] *Ibid.*, pp. 231–87.

[19] Fisher uses three distinct approaches in presenting his theory of interest. The first approach is in words, the second is geometric, and the third is algebraic. The third approach is presented in a more sophisticated manner, since Fisher was not limited to two dimensional geometry. However, we shall follow the second approach.

[20] Fisher defines income from these machines in terms of their net cash flow. Thus no deduction is made for depreciation in the example.

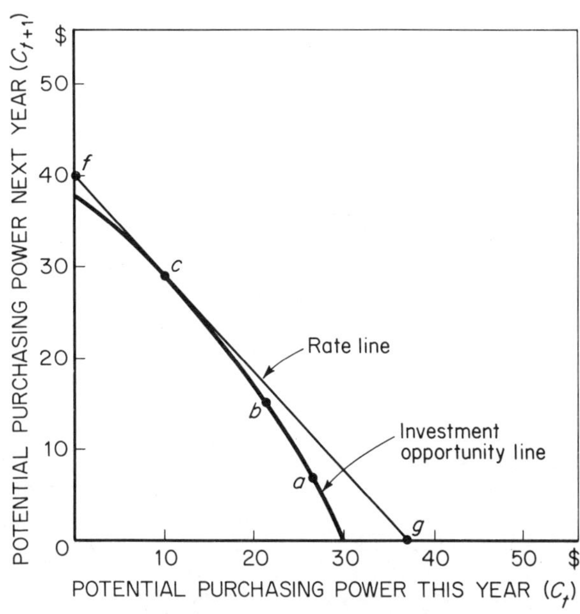

FIG. 6-6 Fisher's Investment Alternatives

that he can earn and spend \$30 of present income if he is willing to be without income next year. However, if he is willing to give up \$3 of present expenditure, he can move to point *a* in Figure 6-6 and thereby gain \$5.10 of future income, the MRP_k of the first unit of capital in Table 6-1. As another alternative, he could sacrifice \$9 of present consumption and gain \$14.40 next year, the sum of the MRP_k of the first three units of capital, by operating at point *b* in Figure 6-6. All his various opportunities for trading off this year's consumption possibilities in order to gain income next year are shown in Table 6-2, which is developed from the data in Table 6-1. In fact, by trading off this year's consumption for next year's purchasing power, he can operate anywhere on the investment-opportunity line shown in Figure 6-6. Therefore, the curve represents all the businessman's investment opportunities. Because the investment opportunity line is drawn on the assumption that next year's investment opportunities can be financed only through this year's savings, the possibility of borrowing or lending up till now has been ignored.

The interest rate (i) is determined by the market and is included on this graph as the slope of the straight line labeled *fg* (hereafter called the rate line) in Figure 6-6. ($1 + i =$ the slope of the *fg* line.) At zero rate of interest, the line would be 45°, indicating a return of capital plus no interest in the next time period. At any positive rate of interest, the line would be steeper than 45°. If the market interest rate is 10 percent, as we have assumed in the slope of line *fg*, the market would permit a lender who is willing to give up \$10 of present purchasing power to gain \$11 next year. Conversely, a borrower would be able to give up $11 of future goods in return for $10 of present purchasing power. The rate line shows that if this year's income were $35.73, an investor could earn $39.30 next year if he were willing to defer all of this year's income.

$$\$35.73 \times 10\% = \$3.57$$

$$\$3.57 + \$35.73 = \$39.30$$

There is a family of 10 percent interest-rate lines that could be drawn on this chart, but only the one that is tangent to the businessman's investment-opportunity line, in the illustration at point *c*, is relevant. An increase in the interest rate above 10 percent would move the relevant rate line to the right along the investment-opportunity line, shifting the point of tangency from point *c* toward point *b*. At the same time, the slope of the rate line would become steeper.

TABLE 6-2 Income Opportunity Schedule

(1) *Units of Capital*	(2) *Next Year's Income*	(3) *Present Consumption*
0	$ 0	$30
1	5.10	27
2	9.90	24
3	14.40	21
4	18.60	18
5	22.50	15
6	26.10	12
7	29.40	9
8	32.40	6
9	35.10	3
10	37.50	0

Assuming that our businessman can borrow or lend at the going rate of interest, he will maximize his next year's return from this year's investment expenditures if he operates at point *c*, where his investment-opportunity line is just tangent to the interest-rate line, and thus the slope of the two lines will be equal. At point *c*, his rate of return on his marginal investment is equal to the rate of interest.[21] At any point below *c*—say *b*, for example—the rate on

[21]The slope of the investment-opportunity line equals 1 plus the rate of return on investment. This follows from the standard-rate-of-return formula.
Since

$$\frac{MRP_k - MRC_k}{MRC_k} = r$$

then

$$\frac{MRP_k}{MRC_k} - \frac{MRC_k}{MRC_k} = r$$

so

$$\frac{MRP_k}{MRC_k} - 1 = r$$

$$\frac{MRP_k}{MRC_k} = 1 + r$$

the marginal unit of investment will be greater than the interest rate, and therefore his incremental return will be greater than his incremental cost. At point *b*, the slope of the investment-opportunity line will be steeper than the slope of the rate line. Therefore, the businessman as investor can earn additional income next year compared with the cost of borrowing funds by investing up to the point where the slope of the investment-opportunity line is equal to the slope of the rate line. Whether or not our businessman will give up present consumption through savings or borrow funds in order to finance next year's investment expenditures depends on the location and shape of his indifference curves between present and future purchasing power.

Because they demonstrate the individual's preference between present and future consumption expenditure, Fisher used indifference curves to present his theory of time preference or impatience. A family of such indifference curves is presented in Figure 6-7, where next year's potential purchasing power is plotted along the *y*-axis and present potential consumption along the *x*-axis. Each indifference curve shows all levels of present and next year's

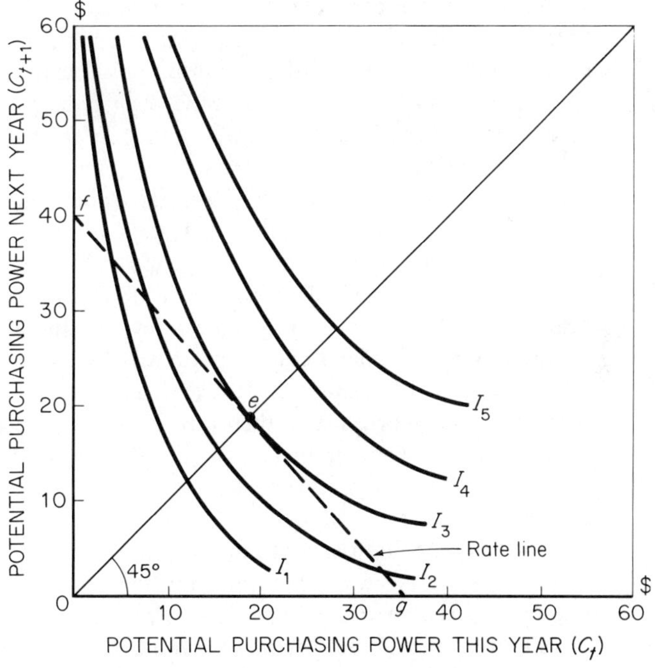

FIG. 6-7 Consumer Preferences for Present and Future Income

The slope of the rate line equals $1 + i$. Therefore, at equilibrium where the two slopes are equal,

$$1 + i = 1 + r$$

Therefore, $i = r$.

consumption expenditure that will yield the same satisfaction to the consumer. A 45° reference line is also drawn, so that the reader can see what is happening along the range where present and next year's consumption expenditures are equal.

Fisher's indifference curves are, like those presented in Chapter 2, convex to the origin, since he assumed that the individual's present and future consumption is subject to diminishing marginal utility. As previously pointed out, Fisher believed that individuals prefer present goods to future goods, or, in other words, have a positive time preference with regard to consumption. Therefore, since people tend to discount the future, savers would finance investment only if thrift were rewarded by additional future income.

The slope of the indifference curve at any point is a measure of the individual's preference for present over next year's consumption. For example, at point *e* on indifference curve I_3, the consumer would be willing to give up only $1 of present consumption to obtain $1.10 next year. His time preference is 10 percent at point *e*. In Figure 6-7, we drew a rate line, *fg*, tangent to *e*, its constant slope reflecting a 10 percent interest rate. This line is analogous to the rate line, *fg*, in Figure 6-6. If the interest rate increased, the rate line would become steeper and could be tangent to I_3, above point *e*. If this occurred, the consumer would prefer to substitute some of this year's consumption expenditure for some additional consumption next year.

As we pointed out in Chapter 2, each higher indifference curve yields greater satisfaction than any lower curve. In addition, each higher indifference curve in Figure 6-7 represents more combined present and future consumption, measured horizontally from any point on the *y*-axis, or vertically from any point on the *x*-axis, than do lower curves. Fisher felt that the indifference curves at the point where next year's consumption expenditure equaled this year's (points that fall along the 45° line drawn out of origin) would be nearly vertical at low present incomes, showing that a consumer would not be willing to give up today's consumption without the expectation of receiving a major increase in consumption next year. The immediate wants of low-income consumers are so urgent that their time horizon is necessarily short. However, as one's present income increases, the preference for today's consumption compared with next year's will gradually decrease. At high levels of income, Fisher believed, the indifference curves approximate a right angle, with the 45° line showing that the consumer was indifferent between a dollar next year and a dollar this year. Therefore, the five indifference curves depicted in Figure 6-7 become increasingly less steep as we move to the right.

Figure 6-8 combines Figures 6-6 and 6-7. It depicts the same opportunity-curve and rate line presented in Figure 6-6 and the same family of indifference curves presented in Figure 6-7. As previously noted, in order to maximize profits next year from this year's investment expenditures, the businessman would invest enough so that the marginal rate of return just equaled the interest rate. That is, he would be operating his firm at point *c*, the point of tangency between the investment-opportunity curve and the rate line. Although point *c* defines the place where the businessman will maximize next

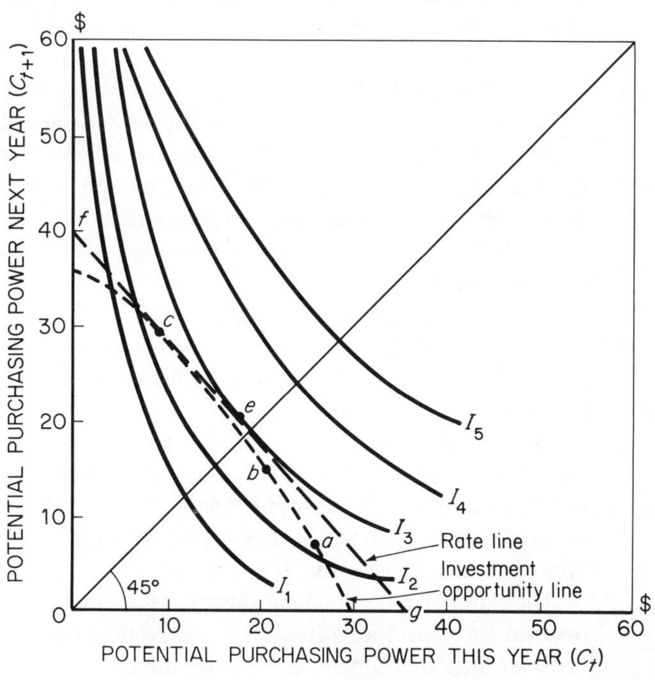

FIG. 6-8 Consumer Equilibrium

year's return, it says nothing about maximizing his satisfaction. In a sense, rate line *fg*, which passes through point *c*, becomes his budget-restraint line, the curve that represents all the possible maximum combinations of present and future goods he can obtain at the going market rate of interest through lending or borrowing.

If his preference patterns so dictate, our businessman will be able to operate at any point on the rate line outside his investment-opportunity curve by becoming either a net borrower or a lender. It is clear in Figure 6-8 that he can improve his satisfaction by moving to the right along his rate line until point *e* is reached, the point of tangency between his rate line and I_3, the highest indifference curve he can reach. Therefore, only at point *e*, the point of tangency between I_3 and the rate line, is the consumer able to achieve his maximum satisfaction.

In order to maximize his return from investments the businessman whose opportunities and preference patterns are shown in Figure 6-8 should invest the amount indicated at point *c*, the point of tangency of the investment-opportunity curve and the rate line *fg*. In order to reach point *c*, he must invest $21 of present income, which could be financed through savings out of his present income of $30. However, his indifference map in Figure 6-8 shows that he can achieve greater satisfaction by moving to the right along his rate line from point *c* to point *e*. In order to move to point *e*, he must borrow $8, thereby reducing his future purchasing power potential earned from $29.40 to $20.60.[22] The businessman of our example reached his final equilibrium point *e* in Figure 6-8 by investing $21, of which $13 was financed through savings out of this year's income and $8 through borrowing.

If the interest rate depicted in Figure 6-8 should increase, the point of tangency would shift to the right along the investment-opportunity line as the rate line became steeper. However, it would be tangent to either a higher or a lower indifference curve, depending on where the point of tangency occurred. The consumer would experience not only a substitution effect but also an income effect.

If I_3 had been tangent to the rate line *fg* to the left of point *c*, then our businessman would be a lender instead of a borrower in order to achieve his equilibrium position, indicating a willingness to add to next year's income at the expense of this year's.

For a savings-investment market to be in equilibrium, the sums loaned must equal those borrowed. Therefore, those individuals who are net borrowers must have a counterpart in others who are net lenders. If the supply and demand for loans do not match, an equilibrium can be obtained through an approximate change in the interest rate.

In summary, neoclassical theory, as expounded by Fisher, requires that investment by an individual be carried out to the point where the return on the marginal investment equals the interest rate. In addition, equilibrium requires that the interest rate be equal to the individual's marginal willingness to substitute future for present consumption expenditures—that is, the slope of the rate line and the slope of the indifference curve must be equal. The equilibrium so established also requires that the amount loaned by creditors equal the amount borrowed by debtors.

WICKSELL'S THEORY OF INTEREST

Knut Wicksell, a Swedish economist of the neoclassical school, developed a sophisticated monetary theory to explain price and interest-rate fluctuations.[23] Wicksell felt that the equilibrium rate of interest between savings and investment might not be achieved because the banks might respond sluggishly to changing market conditions, because (1) they do not know the savings–investment equilibrium level, and (2) they rely on custom more than competition in setting their interest rates. Consequently, he developed a theory of two rates of interest. One he called the "natural" rate of interest and the other the "market" rate of interest. The natural rate equates the

---

[22]He must pay back next year not only the $8 but also an additional $.80 interest.

[23]For a discussion of Wicksell, see: Jacob Oser, *The Evolution of Economic Thought*, 2nd ed. (New York: Harcourt Brace Jovanovich, 1970), pp. 53–59, or Ben B. Seligman, *Main Currents in Modern Economics* (Beverly Hills, Calif: Glencoe Free Press, 1962), pp. 539–61.

demand for investment with the supply of savings; the market rate is that rate charged by the banks. The two rates may differ significantly.[24]

To understand Wicksell's theory, consider the effects of a divergence of the natural rate and the market rate. Assume initially that the two rates are equal at i_1 and the economy is in equilibrium at e_1 in Figure 6-9. Then assume that the investment-demand curve shifts to the right from I_1 to I_2. This increases the natural rate from i_1 to i_2, but the custom-determined market rate will initially remain at i_1. Consequently, the amount of investment funds demanded, Q_3, will exceed by $Q_1 - Q_3$ the amount of savings supplied, Q_1, at the market rate, i_1.

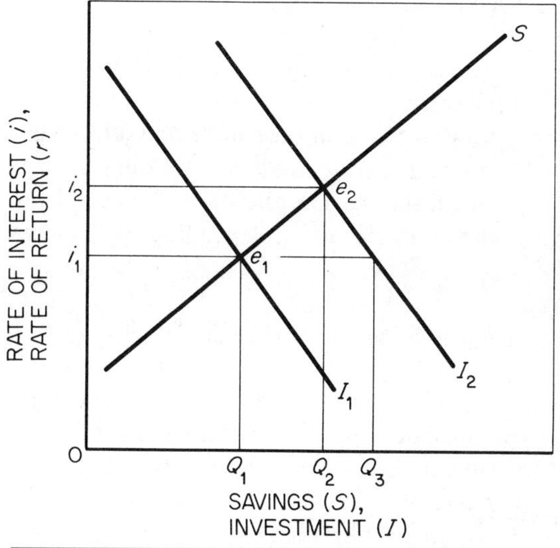

FIG. 6-9 The Supply of Savings and the Demand for Investment

If banks have excess reserves, they will make loans and thereby increase the quantity of money until savings plus the newly created bank credit equal the quantity of investment demanded. Since the economy was at full employment throughout the process, additional investment demand can be satisfied only by bidding up prices. To accomplish the increase in investment, investors must bid resources away from consumers whose money income is fixed. As the additional money is spent by investors bidding resources away from con-

[24]Wicksell sometimes wrote about his market rate as a bank-determined rate, while at other times it seems to be a money rate determined by the supply and demand for money. Compare the following two discussions by Knut Wicksell, *Interest and Prices*, trans. R. F. Kahn (1936) (New York: Augustus M. Kelley, 1962), pp. 102–121 and "The Influence of the Rate of Interest on Commodity Prices," *Selected Papers on Economic Theory*, trans. Sylva Gethin (London: Allen & Unwin, 1958), pp. 77–78.

sumers, prices will increase in proportion to the increase in the quantity of money. This involuntary reduction of real consumption goods to provide the resources to produce investment goods has been called "forced saving." Inflation continues as long as the market rate remains below the natural rate and the banks have excess reserves. Higher prices that would clear the market in one time period must show up as increased money incomes in the next period, unless consumption or investment demand is reduced. The process of bidding resources away from consumers continues until excess reserves are exhausted; the banks will stop expanding their loans and will increase the rate they charge on loans. Equilibrium is restored when the market rate is raised sufficiently to equal the natural rate, and savings and investment are once again in equilibrium. In Figure 6-9, when the market rate rises to i_2, equilibrium is restored at e_2.[25]

Similarly, if the market rate is above the natural rate of interest, savings will exceed investments, and a deflationary process will be initiated as banks increase their reserves and so decrease the stock of money. This deflationary process will continue until pressure of excess reserves forces a reduction in the market rate, and the two rates are again in line. Thus, a divergence between the market rate and the natural rate can be responsible for either inflation or deflation, depending on the direction of the divergence.

ADJUSTMENT PROCESS

The complete neoclassical system is presented in Figure 6-10, which duplicates Figure 6-1 with the addition of an aggregate-demand function (inverted from its usual position as shown in Figure 6-2 to fit the model) in panel A.

Figure 6-10 depicts in panel A an economy operating at full-employment output $\bar{Y}$ and P_1 price level on D_1 aggregate-demand curve, with the related labor market and total-product curves shown in panels C and B. The model allows us to observe how the economy adjusts to real (goods and services and the income derived therefrom) and money changes. When the economy is at full-employment equilibrium, a change in the money stock affects only the price level and cannot affect real output. For example, suppose an increase in the stock of money occurs, shifting aggregate demand from D_1 to D_2 in panel A of Figure 6-10. In consequence, the price level would increase from P_1 to P_2. Aggregate supply cannot increase beyond full employment at $\bar{Y}$, so aggregate output and real wages remain constant despite the increase in the stock of money and in the price level.

In contrast to purely monetary changes, a change on the real side of the economy, such as a shift in the production function or a change in the supply

[25]If we relax the short-run assumption that real output remains constant, then an increase in investment expenditures will increase aggregate income over time, and the increased output will absorb part of the inflationary pressure.

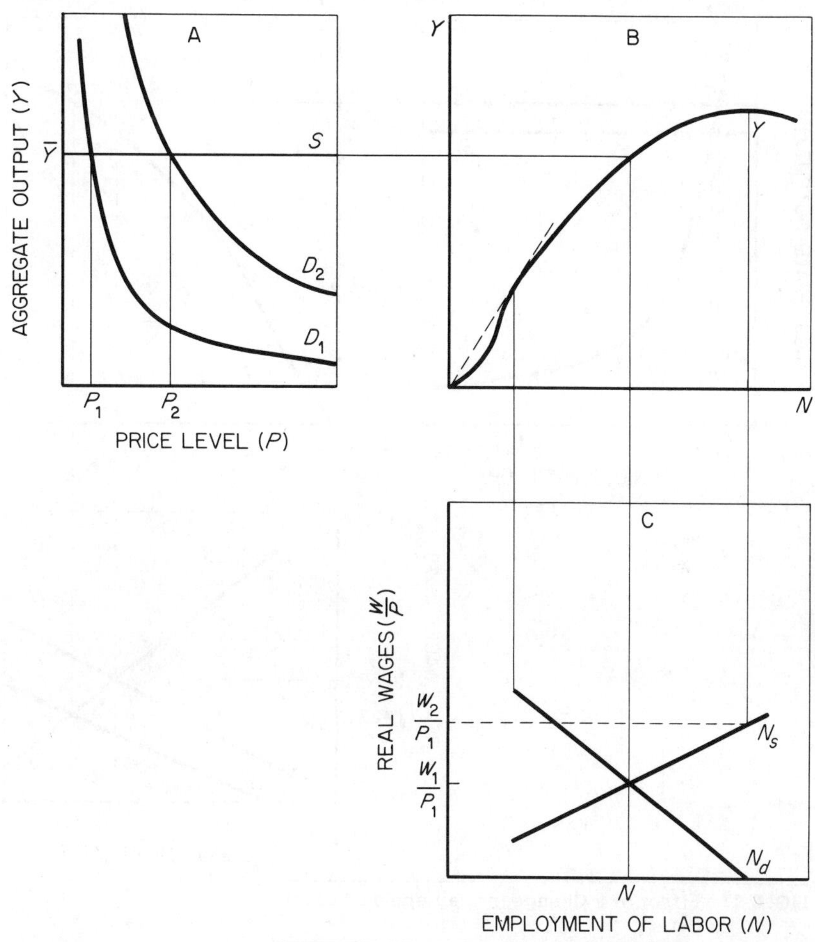

FIG. 6-10 Effects of Changes in Aggregate Demand

of labor, will affect not only the price level but also aggregate output and employment.

Figure 6-11 illustrates the sort of changes just discussed. Suppose the supply of labor increases from N_{s_1} to N_{s_2} in panel C. Employment, after equilibrium has been achieved, will increase from N_1 to N_2, and real wages will fall from $(W/P)_1$ to $(W/P)_2$. As a result of more employment, the economy will move from point *a* to point *b* along the aggregate-production function depicted in panel B. This movement is shown as an increase in aggregate supply from S_1 to S_2 in panel A, which causes the intersection of aggregate supply with the negatively sloped aggregate demand to shift from point *c* to point *d* in panel A. In consequence, prices fall from P_1 to P_2 and the full-employment level of output increases from $\bar{Y}_1$ to $\bar{Y}_2$.

Because of the rectangular-hyperbola shape of the aggregate-demand

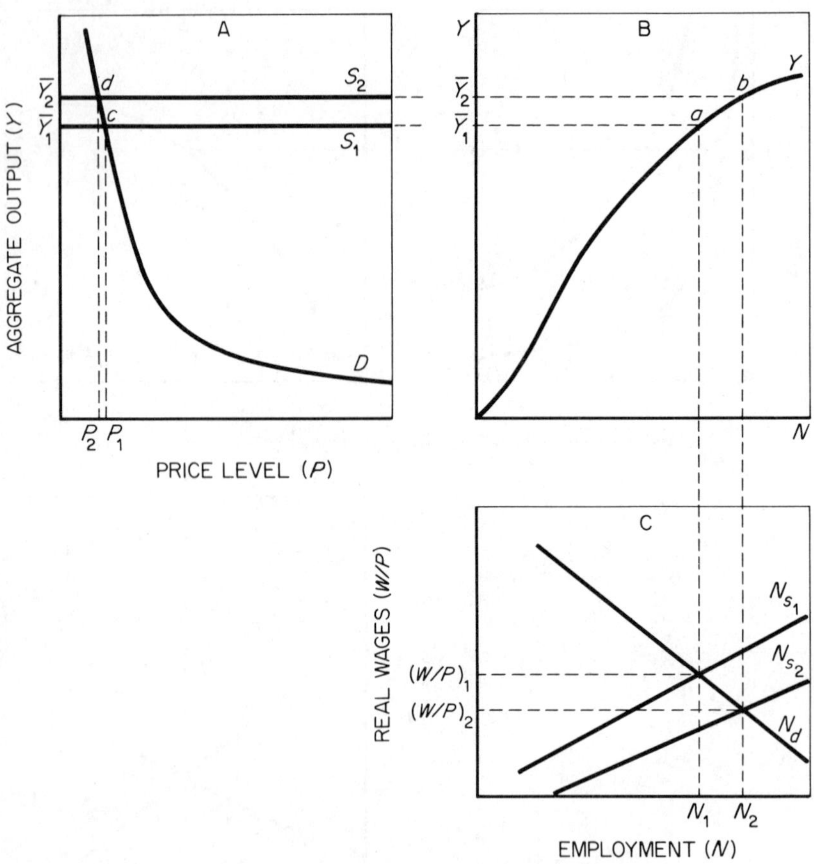

FIG. 6-11 Effect of a Change in the Supply of Labor

curve, the price decrease must be exactly proportional to the increase in aggregate output.

Alternatively, a rightward shift in labor demand (N_d) could occur, occasioned by an increase in the slope and level of the production function. If the demand curve for labor, N_d, increases while the labor-supply curve, N_s, remains unchanged, both real wages and employment increase. As is shown in Figure 6-12, an increase in the demand curve for labor from N_{d_1} to N_{d_2} owing to an increase in the marginal product of labor induces an increase in the aggregate-production function from Y_1 to Y_2. The final result of the increase in the marginal product of labor is that at equilibrium, employment is increased from N_1 to N_2, and real wages are raised from $(W/P)_1$ to $(W/P)_2$. As a result, the full-employment level of output increases from $\bar{Y}_1$ to $\bar{Y}_2$. So the neoclassicists favored increases in the level and slope of the production function—that is, greater worker productivity—as the best available means of increasing both real wages and aggregate output.

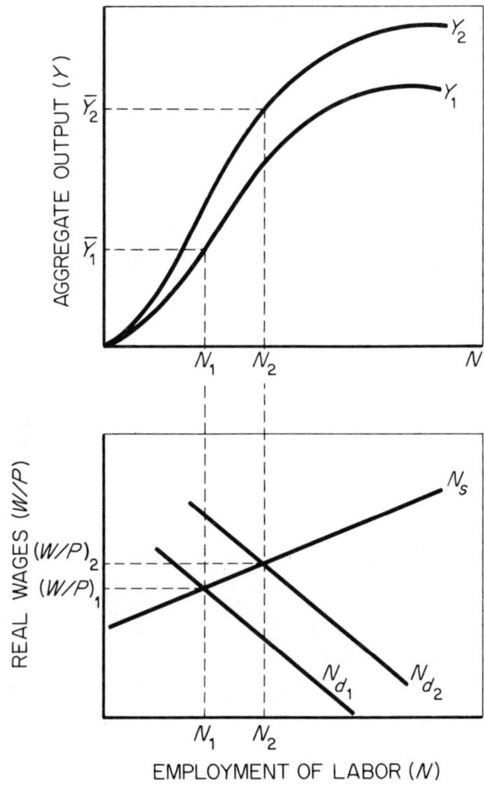

FIG. 6-12 Effect of a Change in Labor Demand

Up to now we have not considered savings and investment in the adjustment process, but any analysis that purports to demonstrate the workings of the neoclassical theory without incorporating savings and investment into the analysis is incomplete. In Figure 6-13, we remedy that shortcoming by specifically introducing investment, savings, and the inverse of savings, consumption (since in a simple model without corporate savings or a government or foreign sector, the income received by households must be either consumed or saved). By combining consumption and investment, we can illustrate in Figure 6-13 how Say's Law can be interpreted to cause a restoration of equilibrium after some initial disturbance.[26]

Figure 6-13 differs from Figures 6-10, 6-11, and 6-12 in that panel A represents consumption and investment expenditures as a function of the interest rate, while panel D presents the demand for investment and the supply of savings. Notice that the axes are reversed in panel D, compared with the

[26]This model is adapted from Barry N. Siegel, *Aggregate Economics and Public Policy* 3rd ed. (Homewood, Ill.: Richard D. Irwin, 1970), pp. 61–65.

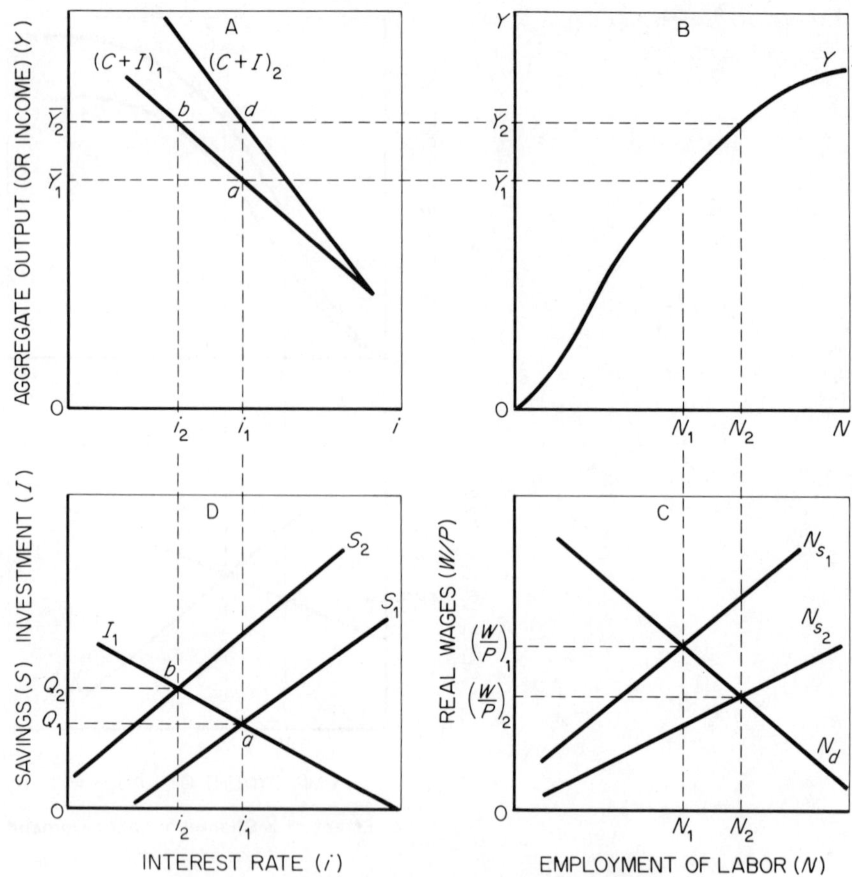

FIG. 6-13 Aggregate Supply and Demand Including Savings and Investment

earlier graphs depicting savings and investment. This is done in order to line up the interest rates in panel D with panel A.

Consumption plus investment equals total spending, which we shall call effective demand, and since, according to Say's Law, supply creates its own demand, effective demand must equal the full-employment level of aggregate output, plotted along the *y*-axis in panel A.

Assume that the economy is operating at N_1 level of employment, determined in panel C by the interaction of the labor demand (N_d) and supply (N_{s_1}) curves. Full-employment output is therefore $\bar{Y}_1$ in panel B. Now assume that the effective-demand curve is $(C + I)_1$ in panel A and that the savings curve (S_1) and investment demand curve (I_1) in panel D are in equilibrium, with a resulting i_1 rate of interest and a level of savings and investment equal to Q_1. Therefore, in panel A the economy must be operating along the $(C + I)_1$ curve at point *a*.

We assume, as we did in Figure 6-11, that the initial disturbance occurs in panel C as an increase in the supply curve of labor, say from N_{s_1} to N_{s_2}. As a result of the increase in the labor supply, equilibrium employment increases from N_1 to N_2, leading to an increase in full-employment output from $\bar{Y}_1$ to $\bar{Y}_2$ in panel B. Because $\bar{Y}_2$ exceeds $\bar{Y}_1$, the old level of effective demand is insufficient, so either consumption or investment, or both, shown in panel A, must increase if full employment is to be maintained, as Say's Law requires.

Let's consider the various possibilities in turn. To begin with, the increased income generated from the increase in full-employment output may all be saved. An increase in the savings function is shown in panel D by a shift in the curve from S_1 to S_2. (Unlike the labor-supply curve in panel C, the increase in the supply of savings causes a leftward shift in panel D, because the axes have been reversed from their usual order.) The increase in the savings function from S_1 to S_2 leads to the demand for a larger quantity of investment (from point *a* to point *b*) at the new equilibrium level of savings and investment, and to the reduction of the interest rate from i_1 to i_2. In fact, the movement from point *a* to point *b* along the investment demand curve I_1 causes investment expenditures to be sufficiently larger than they were before the increase from Q_1 to Q_2, to permit effective demand to equal the full-employment level of income. The effect of the reduction in the interest rate on investment expenditures is also shown in panel A, by a movement from point *a* to point *b* on the original $(C + I)_1$ curve caused by this reduction. Notice that the increase in effective demand is sufficient to purchase the full-employment level of output.

On the other hand, the increase in income owing to the increase in full-employment output may be entirely due to a change in consumption; then the quantity of investment demanded would remain at point *a* on I_1 in panel D, since the entire increase in output from $\bar{Y}_1$ to $\bar{Y}_2$ would be absorbed by the increase in consumption. Therefore, there would be no change in either the supply of savings or the demand for investment, in panel D. However, since consumption expenditures have increased by the amount of increase in full-employment output, the $C + I$ function in panel A would shift from $(C + I)_1$ to $(C + I)_2$, a shift that would retain the original i_1 interest rate. Therefore, equilibrium would occur in panel A at point *d* on the $(C + I)_2$ curve. (Realistically, both investment and consumption are likely to increase, and not one to the exclusion of the other.)

Say's Law is the logic behind the foregoing analysis. Any increase in the full-employment level of output must be either consumed or invested. If the additional income is saved, the supply-of-savings curve increases, causing a reduction in the interest rate and, therefore, an increase in the quantity invested. (An inflexible interest rate would obviously cause unemployment.)

The version of the short-run neoclassical theory presented here ignores the fact that an increase in savings, and thus in the level of investment, would ultimately increase the production function. In a longer-period analysis, such an increase would cause greater output, lower prices, and higher real wages, owing to the increase in investment per worker. The increase in investment, although its effect on output is negligible in the short period, becomes significant over the longer period through its cumulative effect.

NEOCLASSICAL ECONOMIC POLICY

According to the workings of Say's Law, the economy in the long run would operate at the level of full employment. If aggregate unemployment existed, it was generally interpreted to mean that the level of real wages was above the equilibrium wage level, so that the quantity of labor supplied was greater than the quantity demanded, and aggregate unemployment could be overcome by flexible wages and prices, leading to a reduction in the real-wage level until full employment is achieved. A.C. Pigou and Henry C. Simons stated explicitly the neoclassical idea that a flexible wage policy by itself could insure full employment, regardless of general economic conditions. By the 1940's, Pigou had amended his views to allow monetary and fiscal policy to correct the baneful effect of inflexible wages.[27] However, at this point we are interested only in Pigou's earlier theories.

If wages and prices themselves prove inflexible for short adjustment periods or during extraordinary situations such as wartime, both Simons and Pigou felt that changes in the stock of money could substitute for wage–price flexibility.[28] So, if the supply of labor increases and short-run rigidities develop in the average money-wage level, possibly owing to market imperfections (such as labor union monopolies), the resulting unemployment can be overcome by monetary policy designed to increase aggregate demand. For example, if we refer back to Figure 6-10, if real wages rise in panel C above equilibrium (from W_1/P_1 to W_2/P_1), unemployment would result, which could be eliminated by increasing the stock of money sufficiently to increase aggregate demand from D_1 to D_2 in panel A. Such monetary

---

[27]Pigou's acceptance of fiscal policy in the 1940's is more properly a post-Keynesian development and will be reconsidered in Chapter 12, while his acceptance of monetary policy is more clearly within the neoclassical framework.

[28]In 1936, Henry C. Simons wrote, "The problem of booms and depressions is one which must be attacked from both sides, (a) by policies designed to give us a more flexible price structure, and (b) by measures which will minimize the aggregations attributable to the character of the monetary system and financial structure. The former attack, however, must always be regarded as primary. With adequate price flexibility, we could get along under almost any financial system . . . .

"For the present, we obviously must rely on a large measure of discretionary monetary management—on a policy of offsetting and counteracting . . . the effects of monopoly and customs upon prices and wage-rates." Henry C. Simons, "Rules versus Authorities in Monetary Policy," *Journal of Political Economy*, 44 (February 1936), 1–30. Reprinted in *Economic Policy for a Free Society* (Chicago: University of Chicago Press, 1948), p. 170.

In *Lapses from Full Employment* (London: Macmillan, 1945), p. 16, Pigou states, "Experience has shown that in periods of total war, should wage-earners succeed in forcing up money rates of wages, the government, rather than allow man-power to go unused, will cause new money to be created and will force it into the active part of the stock in sufficient amount to absorb nearly everybody into work at the higher wage."

policy would restore full-employment equilibrium at price level P_2, by forcing real wages shown in panel C back to equilibrium, if $W_2/P_2 = W_1/P_1$. The foregoing assumes that the average money-wage level remains rigid at W_2, or if the money-wage level decreases, the price level must not increase as much, so the resulting $W/P = W_1/P_1$. So some of the later neoclassicists felt, even though money could not affect aggregate output when the economy was in equilibrium, monetary policy could be used in the neoclassical system to maintain full-employment equilibrium if real wages were above the equilibrium level. In this way, full-employment equilibrium would result from either flexible wages and prices or from properly implemented monetary policy if money wages are temporarily inflexible.

As we have seen, at least one neoclassical economist, Wicksell, felt that one important link in the economy, the banking system, might not be disciplined sufficiently well by competition and might therefore prevent the market interest rate from performing its role of maintaining savings-investment equilibrium. A divergence between the market and natural rates of interest can be overcome temporarily by flexible wages and prices. For example, if the market rate of interest was above the natural rate, then the quantity of savings would be greater than the quantity of investment goods demanded. Under these circumstances, aggregate quantity supplied would be greater than aggregate quantity demanded. Prices and wages would be forced down in order for aggregate demand and supply to be in equilibrium. Money wages would by necessity go down more than prices, since workers competing for jobs would allow real wages to decrease until full employment was achieved. However, as long as the market rate of interest remains above the natural rate, there will be a persistent tendency during future time periods for aggregate quantity supplied to exceed aggregate quantity demanded. Therefore, the momentary stability brought about by flexible wages and prices in one period will be disrupted by the divergence of the aggregate quantities supplied and demanded, and an inflexible market rate of interest prevents sustained full-employment equilibrium from being achieved.

As a consequence, Wicksell favored state control of the banking system if the banks were continually unable to keep the market rate in line with the natural rate. In Wicksell's words, "If they [the banks] are ultimately unable to fulfill their obligations to society along the lines of private enterprise—which I very much doubt—then they would provide a worthy activity for the state."[29]

A stable equilibrium in the neoclassical concept, therefore, required both flexible wages and prices and flexible interest rates. If either wage–price flexibility or interest-rate flexibility is lacking, then a momentary stability may be achieved in any given time period, but true, lasting equilibrium may be unattainable.

One must remember that the suggestion that all the economists of the neoclassical era favored laissez faire is incorrect and misleading. Those econo-

---

[29]Wicksell, *Interest and Prices*, p. 190.

mists in America who were influenced by the German historical or American institutional schools certainly mistrusted laissez faire,[30] even though they did not develop a generally accepted theory of how the aggregate economy operated.

SUMMARY AND CONCLUSIONS

This chapter was designed to do what few neoclassical economists were inclined to do: build a neoclassical model of the aggregate economy. The key elements may be summarized as follows: aggregate output in the short run is a function of the level of employment (the production function). Assuming perfect competition, the level of employment is determined by the supply and demand of labor, both functions of the real wage. Together these three functions—the production function, the labor-demand curve, and the labor-supply curve—determine the position of the inelastic aggregate supply curve. According to the quantity theory of money, aggregate demand is a function of the money stock. The shape of the aggregate-demand curve must logically be a rectangular hyperbola, with its level depending on the money stock.

The interest rate determines the quantity of both savings and investment, and in turn is uniquely determined by the intersection of the savings and investment curves. Granting the neoclassical assumption of a competitive economy with flexible wages, prices, and interest rates, the only possible equilibrium point would be at full employment. The neoclassical system can be summarized in the following eight equations:

1. $Y = f_4(N, R, K, T)$ (the production function), where R, K, and T are constant in the short-run static model
2. $N_d = f_5(W/P)$ (labor-demand function), where $MP_L = W/P$
3. $N_s = f_6(W/P)$ (labor-supply function)
4. $N_s = N_d$ (labor-market equilibrium)
5. $P = f_7(M)$ (quantity theory of money), where Y is determined by equations 1–4
6. $I = f_8(i)$ (investment function)
7. $S = f_9(i)$ (saving function)
8. $S = I$ (saving-investment equilibrium)

If full employment is not reached, then the competitive system is not doing its job. Government policy should be directed at improving competition, perhaps by breaking up monopolistic firms and labor unions or by controlling the banks, if they cannot keep the market rate equal to the natural rate of interest.

---

[30]For example, Ralph H. Hess pointed out in 1917 that "the old laissez-faire doctrine—that private initiative and unrestrained self-interest always may be depended upon properly to reward individual enterprise and, at the same time, to serve well and adequately the public need—has long been condemned both by logic and by experience." Ralph H. Hess, "Conservation and Economic Evolution," in *The Foundations of National Prosperity*, ed. Richard T. Ely (New York: Macmillan, 1917), p. 144.

Even if the banking system does not keep the interest rate sufficiently flexible and equate the market rate with the natural rate, full employment could still be maintained, if perfect competition prevails, through a second line of defense, flexible wages and prices. However, flexible wages and prices by themselves, without flexible interest rates, cannot bring about equilibrium, only a momentary stability that will be disturbed by further price and wage changes in the next time period.

If a breakdown in wage–price flexibility should occur, some leaders of the neoclassical school, such as Simons and Pigou, felt that conscious monetary policy should be employed to offset a lack of wage–price flexibility.

Although the neoclassical system was internally consistent, logic cannot substitute for realism, as we shall consider in the following chapters. For example, one difficulty with the neoclassical model is that in the real world, income velocity does not remain constant any more than wages, prices, and interest rates fluctuate freely. The neoclassicists were as aware of such realistic difficulties in the application of their theory as any of their critics, but they often tended to persist in their convenient, if unrealistic, assumptions.

QUESTIONS AND PROBLEMS

1. Distinguish the classical from the neoclassical economists.
2. Discuss the assumptions of the neoclassicists.
3. Explain why the economy would tend toward full employment in the neoclassical theory.
4. Distinguish Say's Law, Say's Identity, and Walras' Law.
5. Discuss interest in the neoclassical system.
6. What policy conclusions did the neoclassicists reach?
7. How did Wicksell and Fisher contribute to neoclassical theory?
8. In what way can the demand for labor be related to the production function?
9. Under what conditions would the supply of labor be upsloping
   a. in the case of the individual?
   b. in the aggregate?
10. According to the quantity theory of money, how does a change in the money stock affect the price level? Why?
11. a. Sketch the equilibrium aggregate supply in panel A at the top of page 194.
    b. Aggregate supply equals ——— units of output.
    c. The equilibrium price level will be ——— if the stock of money is $40 and income velocity is 4.

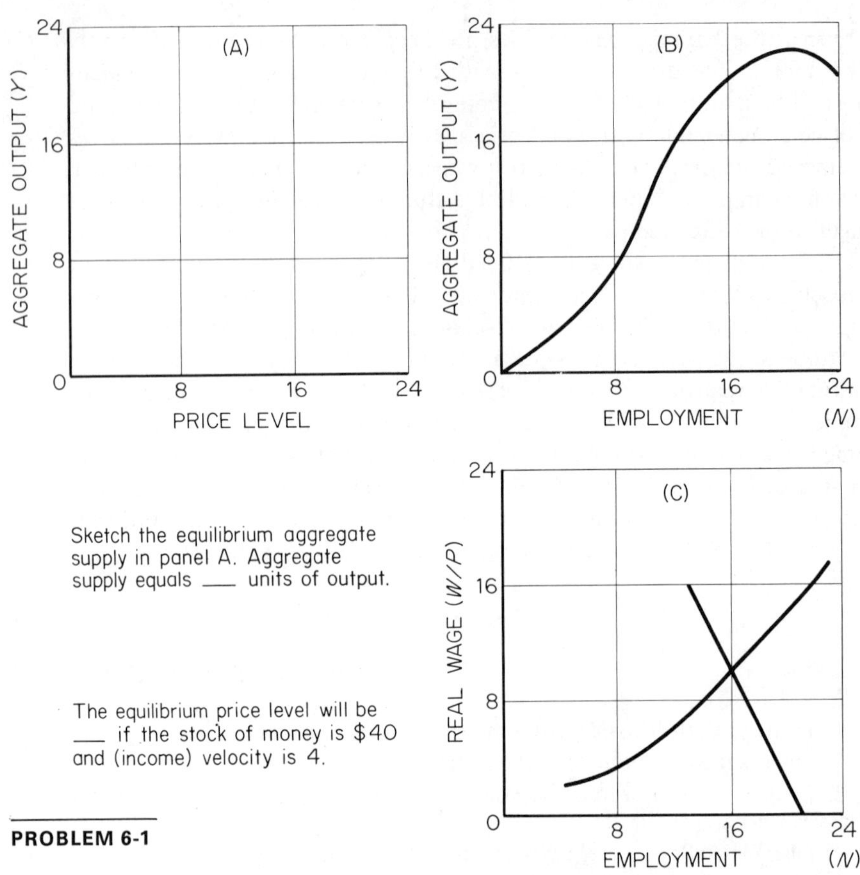

PROBLEM 6-1

12. In the table below, according to neoclassical theory, how would each of the changes indicated in the column on the left affect each of the factors across the top?

	Employment	Price Level	Output	Real Wages	Interest Rates
Increase in the money stock					
Increase in labor productivity					
Increase in investment demand					
Increase in the supply of labor					
Increase in savings					

SECONDARY SOURCES ON FISHER, WICKSELL, AND OTHER NEOCLASSICAL INTEREST AND CAPITAL THEORIES

CONARD, JOSEPH W., *An Introduction to the Theory of Interest*, pp. 25–71. Berkeley: University of California Press, 1959.

LUTZ, FRIEDRICH A., *The Theory of Interest* (English ed.), trans. C. Wittich. Chicago: Aldine, 1968.

SAMUELSON, PAUL A., "Irving Fisher and the Theory of Capital," in William Fellner et al., *Ten Economic Studies in the Tradition of Irving Fisher*, pp. 17–37. New York: John Wiley, 1967.

UHR, CARL G., *Economic Doctrines of Knut Wicksell*. Berkeley: University of California Press, 1960.

THE NEOCLASSICAL THEORY AS DESCRIBED BY KEYNES AND HIS FOLLOWERS

ACKLEY, GARDNER, *Macroeconomic Theory*, pp. 105–67. New York: Macmillan, 1961.

ASCHHEIM, JOSEPH, and CHING-YAO HSIEH, *Macroeconomics: Income and Monetary Theory*, Chaps. 2, 3, 7, and 8. Columbus, Ohio: Charles E. Merrill, 1969.

COCHRANE, JAMES L., *Macroeconomics Before Keynes*, pp. 59–102. Glenview, Ill.: Scott, Foresman, 1970.

KEYNES, JOHN MAYNARD, *The General Theory of Employment, Interest and Money*, pp. 4–22, 175–93, 257–60, 272–79. New York: Harcourt Brace Jovanovich, 1936.

NEOCLASSICAL THEORY OF LABOR

CANNAN, EDWIN, "The Demand for Labor," *Economic Journal*, 42 (September 1932), 357–70.

PIGOU, A. C., *The Theory of Unemployment*, London: Macmillan, 1933.

NEOCLASSICAL THEORIES OF SAVINGS AND INVESTMENT

BÖHM-BAWERK, EUGENE V., *Capital and Interest*, trans. William Smart (1890). New York: Augustus M. Kelley, 1970.

CANNAN, EDWIN, *Wealth*, 2nd ed., pp. 120–38. London: P. S. King and Son, 1916.

HAYEK, FREDERICH A., *The Pure Theory of Capital*. Chicago: University of Chicago Press, 1941.

WICKSELL, KNUT, *Lectures on Political Economy*, Vol. I, trans. E. Classen. London: Routledge & Kegan Paul, 1934.

SAY'S LAW, THE QUANTITY THEORY OF MONEY, AND THE MONETARY THEORY OF INTEREST

BECKER, GARY S., and WILLIAM J. BAUMOL, "The Classical Monetary Theory: The Outcome of the Discussion," *Economica*, 19 (November 1952), 355–76.

DEAN, EDWIN, ed., *The Controversy over the Quantity Theory of Money*. Lexington, Mass.: Raytheon/Heath, 1965.

NEISSER, HANS, "General Overproduction: A Study of Say's Law of Markets," *Journal of Political Economy*, 42 (August 1934), 433–65.

SKINNER, A. S., "Say's Law: Origins and Content," *Economica*, 34 (May 1967), 153–66.

WICKSELL, KNUT, *Lectures on Political Economy*, Vol. II, trans. E. Classen. London: Routledge & Kegan Paul, 1935.

CLASSICAL THEORIES

COCHRANE, JAMES L., *Macroeconomics Before Keynes*, pp. 23–41. Glenview, Ill.: Scott, Foresman, 1970.

CORRY, B. A., *Money, Saving and Investment in English Economics*, 1800–1850. London: Macmillan, 1962.

SAMUELS, WARREN, *The Classical Theory of Economic Policy*. Cleveland: World Publishing, 1966.

Introduction to Keynes's Liquidity Preference and the Stock of Money

7

INTRODUCTION

The neoclassical theory, presented in the last chapter, was constructed with great care for its logical consistency. To quote Keynes, "Our criticism of the accepted classical theory of economics has consisted not so much in finding logical flaws in its analysis as in pointing out that its tacit assumptions are seldom or never satisfied, with the result that it cannot solve the economic problems of the actual world."[1] Keynes attempted to remedy the shortcomings of the classical system (as he interpreted it) by making assumptions that appeared more realistic.

The assumptions and background of the basic Keynesian system, which we shall present in this section, may be summarized as follows:

First, the Keynesian theory is a short-run theory; all factors that tend to change slowly are assumed constant: for example, existing skill levels and quantity of available labor, the level of technology, the quality and quantity of available equipment, the social structure, and the degree of competition. Keynes recognized that his assumed constants change in the long run; however, for select periods, such as the first half of the 1930's when his *General Theory* was in preparation, all these factors could be assumed to be constant. This consideration has led some people to accuse Keynesian economics of being "depression economics"; but Keynes's assumptions are

---

[1]J. M. Keynes, *The General Theory of Employment, Interest and Money* (New York: Harcourt Brace Jovanovich, 1936), p. 378.

useful also during periods of prosperity and inflation in short-run analysis. Then too, the basic neoclassical model, presented in the preceding chapter, is also a short-run theory, even though its time span may be different from Keynes's. At times, confusion has occurred from Keynes's proposals of long-run implications based on his short-run theory without qualifying his original short-run assumptions. But again, the same problem has occurred with the neoclassical model.

Second, Keyness wrote the *General Theory* on more than one level, starting with a set of simplifying assumptions that are relaxed one by one as the theory approaches reality. Much of the criticism concentrates on the first level and its unrealistically rigid assumptions of constant wages and prices. However, since the second level achieves greater realism by relaxing these assumptions and by explicitly introducing the labor market, it is also more complicated. Furthermore, Keynes himself relegated his second level of analysis to only three chapters toward the end of the *General Theory*. Therefore, the basic Keynesian concepts presented in this and the following three chapters represent the ideas of the greater part of his book as modified by sympathetic followers. Those parts of the *General Theory* concerned with prices and money wages were the springboard for much of what we currently consider "post-Keynesian" theorizing. For that reason, the Keynesian theory of flexible prices and wages has been combined with the post-Keynesian analysis and is reserved for Chapter 12. So, a comparison of the completed Keynesian and neoclassical model is delayed until the Appendix to Chapter 12.

Third, Keynes assumed different sets of motives for savers and investors. Saving was considered the residual after consumption, and consumption was a function of income. To the neoclassicists, saving was a function of the interest rate. However, both Keynes and the neoclassical economists proposed that investors were profit maximizers and that investment was therefore a function of the interest rate and the rate of return on investment. The main distinction between the two theories regarding investment was that Keynes stressed uncertainty, risk, and expectations more than the neoclassicists did.

Fourth, the role of money was different in the Keynesian and neoclassical theories, as we shall see in this chapter.

Fifth, Keynes—of all people—understood that in the real world, everything depends on everything else, and that however important it is to isolate the most significant variables, realism requires that strict functional relationships need occasionally to be modified. In addition, because the *General Theory* broke fresh ground and because Keynes's overriding interest was in practical policy recommendations, the book lacks theoretical precision at times. Furthermore, Keynes performed occasional intuitive leaps to conclusions and policy recommendations, and he offered pregnant illustrations, analogies, and digressions, including an implicit theory of macrodynamics from which post-Keynesian economists have spun off a multitude of theories and reinterpretations. As a result, even the basic Keynesian model required a certain amount of rehabilitation to permit a neat textbook presentation. Again, however, the same is true of the leading neoclassical writers.

This section on the basic Keynesian theory begins with the role of money. Chapter 8 covers consumption and saving; Chapter 9 involves investment; and the final chapter of the section is a discussion of the economic policies based on the basic Keynesian model. We have included in this section certain changes suggested by post-Keynesians, which seemed to develop rather than to modify the *General Theory*.

Keynes's major work prior to the *General Theory* was the two-volume *Treatise on Money*.[2] Because of his background as a monetary theorist, it is appropriate to begin any consideration of Keynesian economics with the monetary aspects of his theory.

THE DEMAND FOR MONEY

Neoclassical economists concentrated on the demand for money as a medium of exchange, arguing that maintaining idle balances is irrational when utility could be derived from consumption, or interest could be earned on securities. In contrast, Keynes put greater emphasis on money's function as a store of value, arguing that under most conditions, holding cash balances is rational.

Alfred Marshall, Keynes's eminent teacher, provided a version of the equation of exchange that was a forerunner of Keynes's own ideas on the demand for money balances. Marshall's formulation emphasized not the income velocity of money—the speed with which it changes hands among income recipients—but rather its inverse, the average money balances held by individuals. At any point in time, all money in circulation is part of someone's cash holdings. Focusing on the holding of money balances rather than on the circulation of money (obviously two different aspects of the same question), Marshall led the development of the Cambridge version of the equation of exchange. Using k to designate the proportion of income that people choose to hold in the form of money, the Cambridge group of neoclassical economists rewrote the income version of the equation of exchange, $MV = PY$, to read

$$M = kPY \tag{7-1}$$

where M is the quantity of money, P is the general price level of final goods or services, and Y is aggregate income or output at constant prices.

The value of k represents the proportion of the national product that people will hold in the form of cash balances. The formula may be rewritten to isolate k:

$$k = \frac{M}{PY} \tag{7-2}$$

Notice that relating k to aggregate money income specifically excludes cash

[2]J. M. Keynes, *A Treatise on Money*, Vols. I and II (London: Macmillan, 1930).

balances required to finance intermediate business transactions, financial transactions, or the purchase of secondhand goods. Therefore, k is smaller than the total cash balances actually held at any time.[3]

The Cambridge version is merely a restatement of the income version of the equation of exchange discussed in Chapter 6; k is merely the reciprocal of V, income velocity. If $MV = PY$, then $V = PY/M$. Since $k = M/PY$, then $k = 1/V$. If the price level is held constant, then $k = M/Y$. The commonsense conclusion, to which both the Cambridge and income versions of the equation of exchange lead, is that the more slowly money circulates, the larger will be the cash balances held. But the significance of the Cambridge equation as a forerunner of Keynesian monetary theories was its focus on cash holdings rather than on the turnover of money. In the Cambridge equation, the stress is placed on the usefulness of money as an asset—that is, the role of money in individuals' portfolios. On the other hand, emphasis on the turnover of money leads to stress on such variables as payment practices and the institutional arrangements for effecting transactions whenever a constant income velocity is not assumed.

Keynes, in his emphasis on cash holdings did not neglect money's function as a medium of exchange, since the first motive for holding money in his system was to finance transactions. But in addition, he added two other motives for holding money: the precautionary and speculative motives.[4] Precautionary balances are held to meet unforeseen contingencies, and speculative balances are held as an alternative to securities. Although the division of cash holdings into three compartments is arbitrary and uncertain, as Keynes himself pointed out, it offers analytical advantages. Following Keynes's first level of analysis, we will assume that the price level remains constant; therefore, the relevant demand-for-money equation is $M = kY$. This assumption of constant prices will be eliminated in Chapter 12.

Transactions Demand

Money for day-to-day transactions purposes, commonly called "transactions balances," is held for both individual and business reasons. The individual's demand for transactions balances is based on the need to bridge the time period between income receipt and disbursement; consequently, it depends on the size of his income and the length of his payment period. In general, the larger a person's income and the longer the period between income receipts, the greater will be his absolute demand for money for transactions purposes.[5] This demand for cash is determined by the reciprocal of income velocity, basically Marshall's k in the Cambridge equation of exchange.

For example, if a wage earner who is paid monthly spends his income (Y)

---

[3] Alfred Marshall, *Money, Credit and Commerce* (London: Macmillan, 1923), pp. 1–50.

[4] Keynes, *General Theory*, p. 170.

[5] Poorer people are likely to require a larger proportion of their income for transactions balances than are richer people. However, their total expenditure is less, and so their absolute demand for transactions balances will be smaller.

evenly over a period of a month, his average cash holdings will equal one half his income ($Y/2$) for the month. When his next monthly paycheck arrives at the beginning of month 2, he again disburses it evenly throughout the month. If he followed the same pattern throughout the year, his average cash holdings would equal one half his income receipts per month, or one half of one twelfth of his annual pay. If, on the other hand, he is paid weekly, and he spends his income evenly over each week throughout the year, his average cash holdings equal one half of one fifty-second of his annual pay. A generalized description of the theory above is illustrated in Figure 7-1, where time is

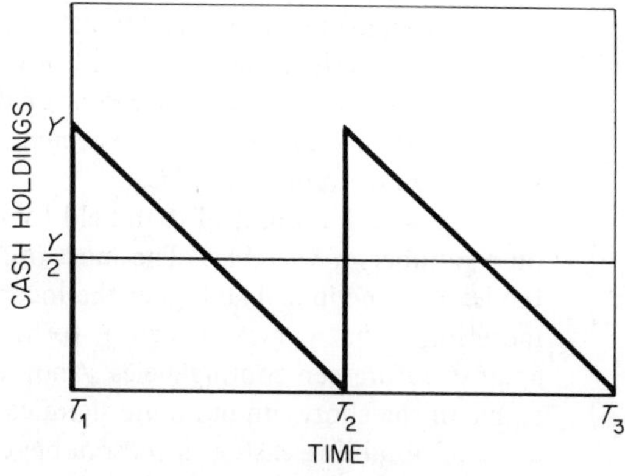

FIG. 7-1 Cash Holdings Over Time

plotted along the x-axis and cash holdings along the y-axis. T_1 and T_2 represent the beginning of each time period when his money income is received, and the negatively sloped straight lines between time periods represent cash holdings, on the assumption that cash expenditures occur evenly between pay periods. The straight line $Y/2$ represents the average cash holdings over the two pay periods.

In practice, many people pay most of their bills shortly after receiving their paycheck, so their average cash balances are less than one half of each period's income receipts, and a graph of their cash receipts and expenditures would show sharper peaks than in Figure 7-1. In addition, the average demand for cash holdings may be drastically reduced in a credit economy such as exists in the United States, where through the use of credit cards, cash payments may be coordinated with income receipts, reducing the need for transactions balances.

Only part of business's demand for transactions money balances—that part spent on the final purchase of investment goods—is related to the income version of the Cambridge equation; the demand for transactions balances by business firms can be computed by dividing their average cash holdings by investment expenditures during a given time period. Business's total needs for money transactions balances are similar to the individual's. Funds are required to bridge the gap between cash receipts and disbursements. Business's requirements for transactions balances depend primarily on the value of firms' cash sales or collections on accounts receivable relative to cash disbursements. In practice large firms employing techniques of financial management may balance out their cash flows better than does the average individual. Theoretically, a diagram such as Figure 7-1 can also be used to illustrate the cash balances of a business.

Precautionary Demand

In addition to holding money for transactions purposes, both business firms and consumers may feel constrained to provide cash balances for the possibility of unforeseen expenses. For example, cash may be required to tide a family over in case of an accident or death. A firm may need cash to pay expenses during a period of unexpected delinquent accounts receivable or an unexpected drop in cash sales.

The actual amount of cash held for precautionary purposes will depend on a number of variables. The most important variable in Keynes's view is the level of income. The higher the income of a person or business firm, the more likely that person or firm is to hold larger money balances to protect against unforeseen contingencies. Another variable, one which is likely to be stable in the short run but quite significant over time, is the ease and convenience of obtaining cash at a reasonable cost when it is needed. If your bank allows overdrafts for a short time, you have less need to hold precautionary money balances, because in effect your bank has guaranteed a short-term loan when needed. On the other hand, if it is not possible to borrow easily or quickly in an emergency at a reasonable cost, or given a high cost of obtaining information where to do so, one may choose to hold larger precautionary balances. Another long-run factor is the availability of reliable low-risk or risk-free money substitutes such as savings bonds. They may lessen the need for precautionary balances.

Finally, the relative cost of holding cash is a consideration affecting the size of these balances. Cash holdings do not earn interest. Consequently, there is always an opportunity cost in the form of a lost return involved in maintaining money balances; the higher this opportunity cost, the less will be the motive for holding them. The precautionary motive represents, in Keynes's words, "the desire for security as to the future cash equivalent of a certain proportion of total resources."[6] The risk of loss if a security has to be sold before maturity is one that precautionary money balances are designed to hedge. The asset holder must decide whether the utility from holding risk-free precautionary balances is greater than the utility from the interest income of an equivalent asset less the disutility of risk of capital loss.

---

[6]Keynes, *General Theory*, p. 170.

A Digression On Capital Loss

When interest rates are high, the risk of capital loss is much smaller than when interest rates are low. Once the risk of loss is determined, the asset holder is in a better position to decide rationally how much money to hold.

Assume a world in which savings may only be held in the form of cash or used to buy perpetual interest-bearing bonds—consols.[7] In such a case, the rational holder of cash balances will need to know the size and likelihood of capital loss.

A consol's present market value is related to the current interest rate. The formula for determining the current market value of a consol is

$$A = \frac{R}{i} \tag{7-3}$$

where A is the present market value, R is the periodic interest payment, and i is the current or market rate of interest. The value of R is usually computed by multiplying the face value of the bond by the nominal rate of interest, the rate stated on the bond. Thus, a bond with a $1,000 face value and a nominal interest rate of 5 percent annually pays a $50 a year interest to its holder. However, the current market value of this bond is determined by dividing the current rate of interest into the $50 annual payment. For example, if the current rate of interest is 5 percent, then the market price would equal the face value of the bond. If the market interest rate increases to 6 percent, then the market value of the bond drops to $833, whereas a decrease to 4 percent would increase the market price to $1,250. Thus, the market value of any bond varies inversely with the market rate of interest.

Table 7-1 illustrates the market value of a $1,000, 5 percent consol at various market rates of interest between 1 and 12 percent. Column 2 shows that the market value of such a bond can vary from $5,000 at a market interest rate of 1 percent to $417 at a market rate of 12 percent. Column 3 shows the change in the market value of the bond due to each 1 percent change in the current interest rate. When the current rate is low, a 1 percent change causes a large change in the market value. For example, if the market interest rate rises from 1 to 2 percent, the price of the bond will fall to half, from $5,000 to $2,500, because the 1 percent change represents a doubling of the market rate. In contrast, if the market rate should rise from 11 to 12 percent, the market value of the bond changes by only $38. Thus, the investor's potential loss of principal owing to a 1 percent change in the market rate of interest is less at higher interest rates. Consequently, the preference for holding precautionary

---

[7]Consols are interest-bearing bonds with no maturity date. They have been issued by the British government, but although some have proposed their use in America, they have so far not been issued. We have employed consols in our example because they are purely the purchase of a stream of income—they have no maturity date, and therefore the principal is never repaid.

TABLE 7-1 Value of a $1,000 Perpetual Bond at Various Rates of Interest

(1)	(2)	(3)
Market Interest Rate	*Market Value of a $1,000 Consol at a Stated 5% Interest Rate*	*Change in Market Value*
1%	$5,000	—
2%	2,500	$2,500
3%	1,667	833
4%	1,250	417
5%	1,000	250
6%	833	167
7%	714	119
8%	625	89
9%	556	69
10%	500	56
11%	455	45
12%	417	38

cash balances increases at lower rates of interest where the potential loss of principal of a bond is greatest, and decreases at higher rates of interest where the potential loss of principal is less.

In order to estimate the risk of loss for purchasing consols, the holder of cash balances must next estimate the probability of a capital loss occurring; that is, what are the chances that interest rates will increase in the foreseeable future. In order to calculate the probability, a host of factors need to be taken into account. Keynes believed that the main variable was the relationship between the current interest rate and the "normal interest rate." (What Keynes called a "safe" rate, a rate offering little chance of capital loss given the current market risks.) The "normal" interest rate is determined by the asset holder on the basis of his past experience and projected market developments; it is likely to be modified as changes occur in the market, but day-to-day fluctuations will not generally influence expectations of a normal interest rate. When the interest rate is above normal, the rational expectation is that it will decrease, and when it is below normal, that it will increase. Therefore, the risk of a capital loss depends on the relationship between the current interest rate and the expected normal interest rate.

The foregoing methods for determining the risk of capital loss are an important consideration to an asset holder deciding the size of his money holdings. Probably even more than transactions or speculative balances, precautionary balances are held for psychological reasons, and the security offered by precautionary balances may be traded off for earnings when the earnings are sufficiently high compared to the risk and size of loss.

If the potential purchaser of bonds can place a subjective probability on the occurrence of capital loss—assuming he has already determined the most likely size of that loss—he then can make a rational comparison between costs and benefits of holding money balances. So, if interest rates are low and expected to rise by enough to make the most probable capital loss exceed the potential interest earnings, money will be more attractive and bonds less so.

In addition to the need for money to finance current transactions and for precautionary purposes, Keynes adds a third demand for money: the speculative demand. Private and business asset holders have the option of maintaining speculative cash balances or of buying securities with funds earmarked for speculation or personal investement.

An expected increase in the price of bonds makes them attractive, because buyers anticipate a capital gain from their purchase. Returning to our previous example of the market value of a consol, if the current market interest rate is 6 percent and the anticipated future rate is 5 percent, then a bond currently selling for $833 will soon be worth $1,000 (as shown in Table 7-1). The purchaser of a consol expects to receive both $50 in interest the first year and a capital gain as the market value appreciates by $167. On the other hand, if the market rate of interest is 4 percent and the normal rate is 5 percent, then a bondholder would anticipate a $250 capital loss, only partly offset by the $50 interest collected, when the interest rate adjusts to normal. But an asset holder maintaining money balances during the same period would lose only $50 potential interest earnings. As long as the interest rate is expected to increase (that is, the rate is below the "normal rate"), a rational asset holder prefers money to bonds. The desire to hold more cash when one expects the interest rate to rise, or, what is the same thing, the price of bonds to fall, is the essence of the speculative demand for money. The unsurprising conclusion of our analysis is that a rational speculator prefers to buy bonds at a low price and sell them at a high price.

One important consideration a speculator faces is that interest earnings are certain, whereas expected capital gains or losses are uncertain. Therefore, risk and uncertainty are as significant in the speculator's decisions as are his calculations of expected gains and losses.

In a world of rational asset holders, when the interest rate is very low, nearly everyone will anticipate future increases in it and will therefore attempt to sell their bonds while the price is high and hold as much money as possible. At very low interest rates, the demand for speculative balances becomes perfectly elastic. On the other hand, if the interest rate is so high that nearly everyone expects it to fall, asset holders will try to reduce their speculative cash balances to the minimum, preferring to hold only bonds. At very high interest rates the demand for speculative balances is perfectly inelastic. In the more usual trading ranges, between the extremely high and extremely low interest rates, speculators will disagree as to the probable future rate. The bulls will anticipate a rise in bond prices and try to buy securities, while the bears expect declining bond prices and try to sell; and the interaction of bulls and bears makes the market.

In the aggregate as in the case of individuals, the speculative demand for money is inversely related to the interest rate, whereas the demand for bonds is directly related to the interest rate; the speculative demand for money balances decreases as the interest rate increases, and the demand to hold bonds increases as the interest rate increases.

The Combined Demand for Liquidity

The distinction among transactions, precautionary, and speculative balances is unimportant except as a help to explicate the individual's total demand for money. The important point is that the individual's demand for money is a function of both the level of his income and the rate of interest. Keynes explained that the subdivision of the total demand for money was a matter of analytical convenience: "Money held for each of the three purposes forms, nevertheless, a single pool, which the holder is under no necessity to segregate into three water-tight compartments; for they need not be sharply divided even in his own mind, and the same sum can be held primarily for one purpose and secondarily for another."[8]

For simplicity, Keynes combined transactions and precautionary balances as functions of the level of income, and left speculative balances a function of the interest rate. He noted, however, that the opportunity cost of holding cash is an additional consideration in determining the size of precautionary balances. A higher interest rate means a greater opportunity cost, whereas a low interest rate means a greater possibility of capital loss for each one percent change. Furthermore, when the market rate is low (below normal), the most likely development would be a rise in interest rates and a loss of capital value. Since the opportunity cost of holding cash and the market risk of capital loss depend on the rate of interest, one may as logically combine the precautionary with the speculative motive as with the transactions motive. Such qualifications, however, do not essentially affect the liquidity-preference analysis, which states that the demand for money is a function of both income and the rate of interest.

Aggregate Demand for Cash Balances

Keynes used the term *money* to refer to the whole range of short-term assets that provide protection against capital loss due to changes in the interest rate.[9] He minimized the importance of interest earnings on such assets (possibly because the absolute amount of interest to be earned is small for the typical small asset holder and short-term rates were very low in the 1930's).[10] Today in the United States, Keynes would probably include as "money" savings accounts,[11] savings bonds, and Treasury bills. Although the latter are subject to capital loss, the risk of a significant amount of capital loss is small in the case of short-term assets such as Treasury bills. The market value of

[8] Keynes, *General Theory*, p. 195.

[9] Axel Leivonhufvud, *On Keynesian Economics and the Economics of Keynes* (New York: Oxford University Press, 1968), p. 355.

[10] Milton Friedman, "A Theoretical Framework for Monetary Analyses," *Journal of Political Economy*, 78 (March-April 1970), 212–13.

[11] The term *savings accounts* is used broadly, to include time and savings deposits at commercial or mutual savings banks, shares, savings certificates, and a variety of special accounts at savings and loan associations.

Treasury bills can change, but it is not likely to change by much. And in any case, the principal will be repaid within 91 days on the shortest-term bills.

Keynes's "bonds," on the other hand, referred to long-term financial assets without capital certainty. For simplicity, he assumed, as we did in the previous section, that all bonds are consols issued by the government, because government bonds are not subject to a default risk and consols are not redeemable. Following Keynes, we will assume a two-way, money-bonds classification of financial assets and assume that the price level remains constant.

In constructing the aggregate-demand function for money, we will follow the usual definition of money as demand deposits and currency (paper money and coins); and use Keynes's simplifying analytical assumption that the transactions and precautionary demands are a function of the level of aggregate income and the speculative demand is a function of the interest rate. Let the demand for transactions and precautionary balances together be M_t—a function of income—and that for speculative liquid balances be M_L—a function of the interest rate.[12] Corresponding to the two types of demand for money balances, M_t and M_L, there are two demand functions for money, L_t and L_L. L_t is a function of the level of aggregate income, and L_L is a function of the interest rate. Therefore, the aggregate demand for money, M_d, can be found by summing the individual's demand for transactions and speculative balances. Restated,

$$M_d = M_t + M_L \tag{7-4}$$

or

$$M_d = L_t(Y) + L_L(i) \tag{7-5}$$

where

$$M_t = L_t(Y)$$
$$M_t = L_t(i)$$

The sum of all individual demands for M_t balances plus the sum of all individual demands for M_L balances together equal the aggregate demand for money, which is usually graphed as the liquidity preference curve. The aggregate demand for M_t balances, as shown in Figure 7-2, is a function of the level of aggregate income. For simplicity, it has been shown as a linear function; however, the relationship may be nonlinear in reality. It is likely that the size of transactions balances may decrease proportionately (not absolutely) as aggregate income increases, because money can be used more efficiently in larger-scale operations.[13] The dotted M_t' curve represents such a propor-

[12]The subscripts, *t* for transactions and *L* for liquidity, refer to the motives for holding money balances. Transactions and precautionary balances are held to be spent under the proper conditions, while the motive for holding speculative balances is specifically to have liquid balances available to profit from changes in the interest rate.

[13]The opposite view, that M_t balances increase more than proportionately as income increases, at least in the long run, is discussed in Chapter 14.

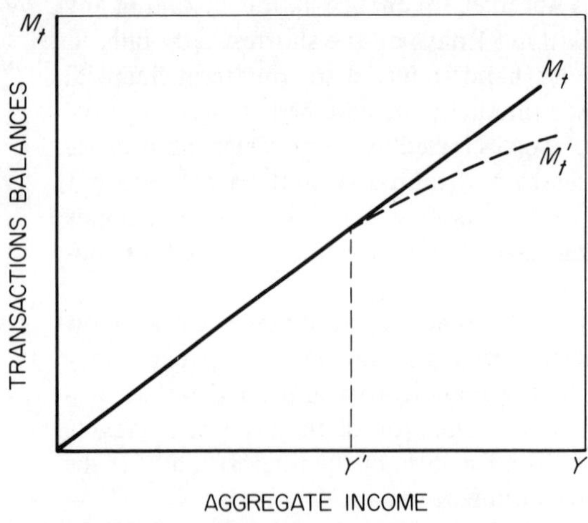

FIG. 7-2 Demand for Transactions Balances

tional decrease in the size of M_t balances assuming economies of scale are achieved beyond Y' level of aggregate income.

The aggregate demand for speculative liquid balances is shown as the M_L curve in Figure 7-3. This aggregate curve is a horizontal summation of the individual demands for speculative balances. As is true for the individual, there is in the aggregate an inverse relationship between the amount of money people wish to hold and the level of the interest rate. Securities lose all attraction at very low interest rates, since speculators anticipate a fall in the price of bonds. Finally, at some point when virtually all speculators anticipate a rise in the interest rate, the demand for speculative cash balances

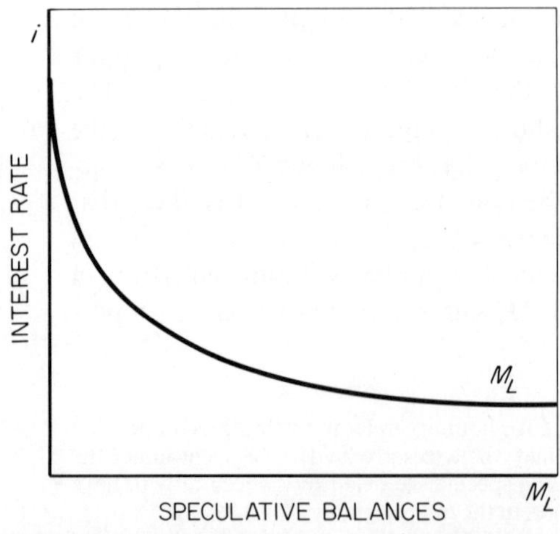

FIG. 7-3 Demand for Speculative Balances

becomes infinitely elastic, represented by the horizontal part of the curve in Figure 7-3. In contrast, at very high rates of interest, the demand for speculative balances becomes completely inelastic when all speculators feel the interest rate has reached its peak.

The total demand for money, Keynes's liquidity-preference function, can be related to the interest rate if we assume a constant level of income. In Figure 7-4, transactions balances of M_t are assumed to be required to finance the current level of income, and the demand for speculative balances has been added to the right of the demand for transactions balances. The liquidity-preference curve $M_t + M_L$ has the same shape as the demand for speculative balances in Figure 7-3, but reflects the total demand for money.

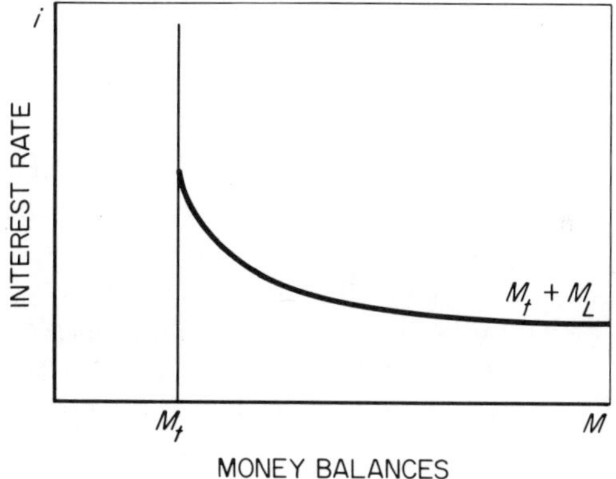

FIG. 7-4 Combined Demand for Transactions and Speculative Balances-Liquidity Preference Curve

The $M_t + M_L$ curve in Figure 7-4 is the liquidity-preference function in the sense that Keynes used the term. It is an aggregate demand for money, but Keynes did not call it that, probably because he realized that certain liquid assets, which were not money by definition, could be included in his liquidity-preference function.

In the next section, we consider some of the modifications to Keynes's liquidity-preference curve that were proposed by Professor James Tobin.

TOBIN'S QUALIFICATIONS TO KEYNES'S DEMAND FOR MONEY

James Tobin has proposed two additional qualifications to the liquidity-preference analysis. It is not clear from the *General Theory* whether Keynes thought that any individual asset-holder would choose to go completely out of money and into bonds at any interest rate that he felt was higher than normal and completely into money and out of securities at interest rates he felt were below normal; or whether he would simply choose to vary the proportion of money to securities according to his idea of the relationship of the going market rate of interest to the normal rate. Certain critics of the liquidity-preference theory have assumed the former interpretation. Tobin has developed a theory of asset holders' portfolio balancing that explicitly involves changing proportions of both money and securities.[14]

The second model developed by Tobin demonstrates that at least part of the transactions demand for money is a function of the rate of interest.

Portfolio Adjustment of Asset Holders

Tobin's theory of asset holders' portfolio adjustment to changes in the interest rate can be demonstrated through the following model. The assumptions are (1) that asset holders must choose between money and consols as the only alternatives, and (2) that the typical asset holder, preferring to avoid risking his capital if possible, will accept additional risk only for a higher return. (In other words, he is a "risk averter.") An asset holder's family of indifference curves is represented in Figure 7-5 by curves I_1, I_2, and I_3. Each shows various combinations of expected rate of return and risk that provide the asset holder the same total utility.

The indifference curves in Figure 7-5 emanate from the *y*-axis, and their positive slope illustrates the principle of risk aversion. The asset holder will accept a higher risk only if it is accompanied by a higher expected rate of return. Curves I_1, I_2, and I_3 are positively sloped, because the return is desir-

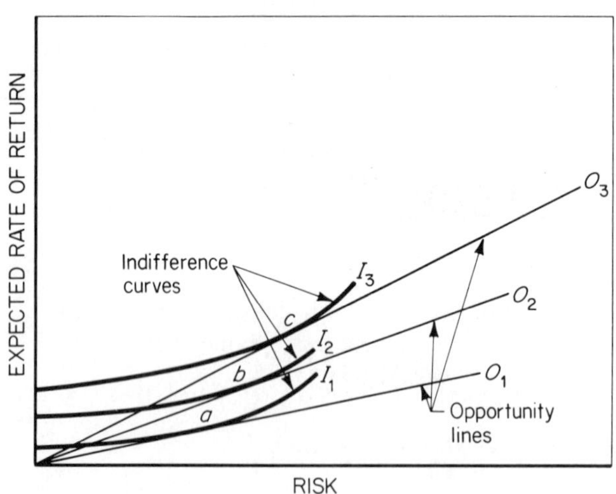

FIG. 7-5 Utility Maximizing—Risk and Return

[14] James Tobin, "Liquidity Preference as Behavior Toward Risk," *Review of Economic Studies*, 25 (February 1958), 65–86.

able, whereas risk is undesirable. The curves are drawn to indicate the additional return required to keep the asset holder's utility constant as the amount of risk is increased.

Curves O_1, O_2, and O_3, radiating from the origin, represent personal financial investment opportunities open to the asset holder positively correlating risk with rate of return (analogous to the investment-opportunity curves of Chapter 6). Opportunity lines O_1, O_2, and O_3 are drawn straight on the assumption of perfect competition—each asset holder is assumed to be too small to influence the market, so he can invest all he is able to at any given risk level without significantly reducing the effective rate of interest on consols. Each additional consol purchased increases both risk and return in the same proportion as any previous bond in the asset holder's portfolio. The opportunity lines rotate to the left as the interest rate increases for a given risk level, or as risk decreases for any given return. The point of tangency between the asset holder's relevent opportunity line and his highest achievable indifference curve determines his optimum combination of rate of return and risk, for a given rate of interest on consols.

Figure 7-5 indicates that as the opportunity line shifts upward from O_1 to O_2 to O_3, the asset holder will increase his utility by accepting more risk as well as a higher rate of return. Since the points of tangency (*a*, *b*, and *c*) between the investment-opportunity line and an indifference curve are increasingly further to the right and higher, the implication is that this asset holder continues to maximize his utility by substituting a degree of security for a higher rate of return. As long as the points of tangency shift to the right as the interest rate increases, the asset holder will continue to convert more of his money into consols.

Consequently, the asset holder's demand for speculative cash balances is inversely related to the rate of interest, so the curve is negatively sloped as in Figure 7-6, when the demand for speculative balances, M_L, is plotted on the

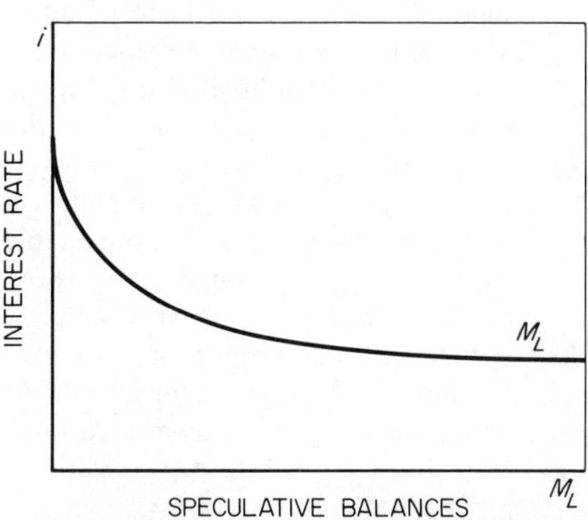

FIG. 7-6 Demand for Speculative Balances

x-axis. At very low rates of interest, the asset holder prefers to hold all his speculative balances in the form of cash, and at very high rates of interest, his entire investment portfolio would be in bonds. Asset holders may all have different utility functions, since each individual may have a different degree of risk aversion. Some may prefer to avoid risk to the extent that as the interest rate increases, they will maximize their utility by accepting a very small increase in yield in exchange for a reduction in risk. Probably most asset holders are willing to accept greater risk, providing they receive an increase in their expected rate of return. Explicitly allowing each asset holder to balance his portfolio of money and bonds does not fundamentally alter the shape of the Keynesian aggregate liquidity-preference curve; it only makes the analysis more realistic, and allows it to match observed behavior.

Relaxing the assumption of a single type of security does not fundamentally alter the analysis above. The main change would be to allow higher rates of return associated with a given risk level, since a diversified portfolio usually reduces risk for each expected return. A lower risk level associated with any given rate of return reduces the demand for money relative to securities at any interest rate. Consequently, the curve in Figure 7-6 would simply be lower if many different types of securities are available than if only one type of security can be purchased.

Transaction Demand as a Function of the Interest Rate

Professor Tobin's second idea relating to liquidity preference is that the demand for transactions balances may be a function of the rate of interest as well as of income.[15] He demonstrates that the higher the rate of interest, the more profitable it is for the asset holder to reduce his transactions balances to a minimum. Suppose the wage earner whose day-to-day transactions balances were shown in Figure 7-1 realizes that interest may be earned on cash held for transactions. If he decides to make three financial transactions with his monthly income, and his consumption expenditures occur at a constant rate throughout the month, he would optimize his monthly income by spending two thirds of it on bonds at the beginning of the month. Then he would earn interest on one half of his bond purchases for ten days, and on the other half for twenty days: When his transactions balances were spent after ten days, he would sell half his bonds to replenish them for the next ten days, after which he would sell his remaining bonds to finance the last ten days' transactions. This process is illustrated in Figure 7-7.

The wage earner in this example could increase his interest earnings by spending a larger proportion of his income on bonds and selling them in more installments throughout the month. As a limit, he could buy bonds with his entire income and sell them each time he required money for a transaction.

---

[15] James Tobin, "The Interest-Elasticity of Trasactions Demand for Cash," *The Review of Economics and Statistics*, 38 (August 1956), 241–47.

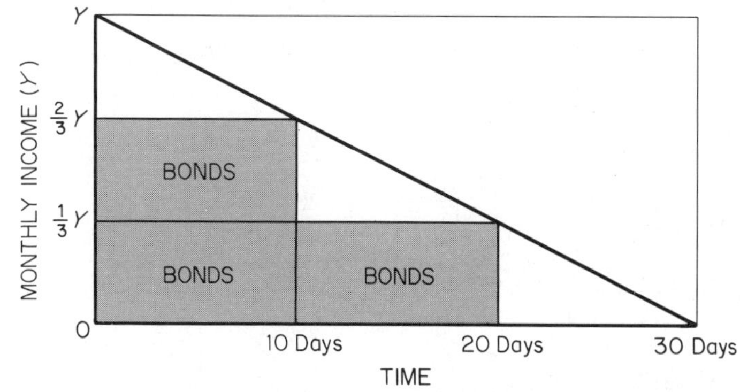

FIG. 7-7 Periodic Bond Purchases and Sales with Transactions Balances

His cash holdings for transactions purposes at any time would then be virtually zero. However, there are limitations to that sort of money management. There is a minimum cost per unit involved in financial transactions, which may vary from market to market. If the wage earner must pay a minimum fee for each sale, he could not profitably make very many small sales, assuming small sales are possible.[16] If we assume that he buys bonds of one denomination and that no minimum transaction is required, his total costs (*TC*) would then increase at a constant rate as transactions increase, as shown by the *TC* curve in Figure 7-8.

The total revenue curve, *TR*, in Figure 7-8 increases at a decreasing rate for the following reason: If the wage earner's cash holdings for transactions were zero, it could mean that he had filled the entire area under the curve in Figure 7-7 with bond purchases. The maximum total income he could achieve would be his monthly money income times the interest rate divided by two (assuming his expenditures occur evenly throughout the month; on the average only half his income will be available to buy bonds). By purchasing a large block of bonds and selling them frequently, an individual reduces his average cash holdings as he increases his average bond holdings. Each additional sale of bonds throughout the month reduces the unshaded area under the curve that, in Figure 7-7, represents cash holdings rather than bond holdings. If the wage earner spends two-thirds his money income on bonds that he then sells during the month, two-thirds of the area under the curve is devoted to bonds rather than cash, as is shown in Figure 7-7. Four transactions, one purchase and three sales of bonds, would increase the proportion

[16]At the time this is written, legal minimum broker's fees for selling or buying listed corporate bonds on the N.Y.S.E. and A.S.E. are as follows: Less than \$100, \$.75 per bond; between \$100 and \$199, \$1.25 per bond; and \$1,000 or over, \$2.50 per bond. And the fees charged are approximately twice the legal minimum on \$1,000 bonds. In addition to being limited by broker's fees on transactions, asset holders are limited by the existence of often sizeable minimum transactions in many markets, including the Federal government bond market.

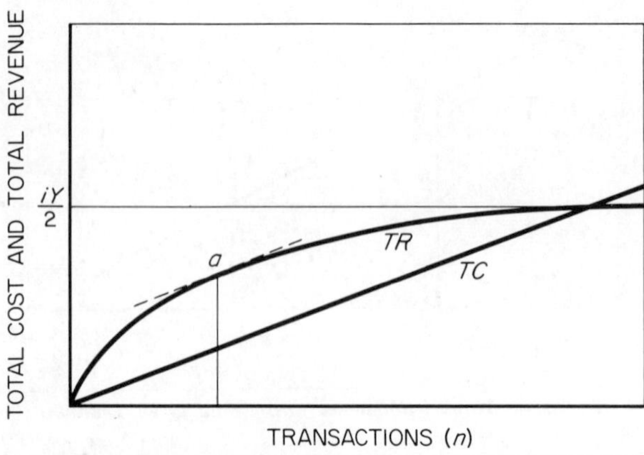

FIG. 7-8 Total Cost and Total Revenue of Securities Purchased with Transactions Balances

of bonds to money to three fourths. As you can see from this progression, each additional sale of bonds adds proportionately less to his holdings of interest-earning assets. This process can be summarized by the following formula:

$$TR = \frac{n-1}{2n} \times iY \tag{7-6}$$

where *TR* equals the total revenue to be earned from bond holdings per time period, *n* equals the number of transactions per time period, (purchases plus sales), *i* equals the interest rate to be earned on the bonds, and *Y* equals the wage earner's money income per time period. Thus, *TR* increases at a decreasing rate, eventually intersecting *TC* and falling below it, as shown in Figure 7-8. The profit-minded wage earner will choose that number of transactions where the difference between total cost and total revenue is the greatest. The profit-maximizing point, *a*, can be found by drawing a line parallel to the total-cost curve and tangent to the total-revenue curve, illustrated by the dotted line in Figure 7-8. The point of tangency occurs where marginal cost equals marginal revenue, since at the point of tangency the rate of change in the two functions is equal.

If the interest rate increases, the total-revenue curve will rotate upward out of the origin, the point of tangency will shift to the right, and the proportion of income that the profit-minded wage earner holds in transactions balances will decrease. A higher cost per transaction will rotate the total-cost function upward out of the origin, and will shift the profit-maximizing point of tangency to the left, reducing the number of transactions and increasing the average size of the wage earner's transactions balances.

The analysis above implies that there is a degree of interest elasticity in aggregate transactions balances, since smaller cash balances will be desired at higher rates of interest.

If this analysis represents rational behavior, why doesn't the average wage earner behave this way? There are several reasons: The first is a lack of knowledge on the part of the average wage earner; the cost in terms of time and trouble of acquiring financial-market information (search or information cost) is relatively high. Most people are unsophisticated about buying bonds and only relatively few are aware of the opportunities. Second, habit may intervene; most people habitually deposit their paychecks in a checking account and do not consider the purchase of securities with their transactions balances. Third, the cost per unit of financial transactions is high enough to prevent most wage earners from earning sufficient interest in the short time they would hold the bonds to warrant the time and trouble of the transactions. The reward for the time spent maintaining a bond portfolio should be high enough to make it worthwhile to give up leisure. A fourth reason is the high minimum purchase or sale of most securities; for example, Treasury bills come only in denominations of from $10,000 to $1,000,000. Finally, there may be a psychological cost (disutility) involved in very small financial transactions; imagine the reaction in a broker's office if you actually followed this program and walked in at noon with instructions to sell a $2 bond if there was such a thing so that you could buy lunch.

In contrast to most wage earners, many corporations and wealthy individuals have discovered that it pays to put transactions balances in short-term securities and to vary their cash holdings with the interest rate. Cash-budgeting techniques permit advance estimates of cash requirements and receipts within a given period of time, eliminating the need for surplus cash.

Tobin's analysis, indicating that transactions balances are related to the interest rate as well as to the level of income, reinforces Keynes's view of the demand for money presented earlier in this chapter. The total demand for money is a function of both income and the interest rate, and the breakdown into transactions, precautionary, and speculative motives is made arbitrarily and only for analytical convenience.

STOCK OF MONEY

Definition

Previously, we defined *money* as demand deposits and currency (paper money and coins). At this point, we will discuss money in more detail. What characteristics distinguish money from other assets? First, money is generally acceptable in exchange for other goods. Second, money is not discounted in exchange for goods—it has no transactions cost. Third, since prices are stated in money terms, money itself has the highest degree of capital certainty; the holder of money is guaranteed the value of his principal. Fourth, under our present monetary system, money per se earns no interest. Fifth, money has the highest degree of marketability of all assets. Capital certainty is present at all times; whereas some other assets, such as bonds, may have only limited marketability, since they offer capital certainty only after a stated time period.

If we use the word "liquidity" to represent the five characteristics of money, assets can be ranged in order of liquidity, or moneyness, from the relatively illiquid—such as equipment or real estate—to the most liquid—currency. Some assets may be sufficiently liquid to serve some of the functions of money. These assets, such as savings accounts, have been called *near-money.* However, the consensus is that near-money assets should not be included in the stock of money, since they do not have general acceptability and they earn interest. In order to purchase a commodity with the monetary value of a savings account, the owner must first convert the financial asset into currency or demand deposits and then pay for the commodity with currency or with a check. Therefore, these assets, while highly liquid, are not literally money. In addition, near-money assets in some cases are not payable on demand, and therefore may not be completely marketable. Near-money assets, however, do provide a store of value and are highly liquid in the sense that they can be readily and conveniently converted into cash, even though they may not be spent directly in the purchase of goods and services.[17]

The stock of money, then, consists of currency and checking accounts (demand deposits), since only they have all the five characteristics of money. In practice, the "stock of money" is defined by the Federal Reserve as money in circulation available for domestic and foreign business transactions. Excluded are (1) demand deposits owed to other commercial banks and the United States government, (2) currency held by the Treasury, Federal Reserve, and commercial banks, and (3) items in the process of collection by commercial banks, including float.[18]

Changes in the Stock of Money

Changes in the stock of money can be considered either from the standpoint of the private market sector of the economy or from that of the public monetary authorities. The commercial banking system can expand or contract the stock of money through multiple expansion of demand deposits. The bulk of the money stock, demand deposits, is provided by bank credit;

---

[17]Keynes himself allowed a loose definition of money—a definition that could vary depending on the situation. For example, an individual might consider a savings account as part of his precautionary and speculative balances. And other highly liquid assets (such as Treasury bills or savings bonds) can also serve the same purpose as cash balances, even though they are not technically cash because they cannot be spent directly and they earn interest. Realistically, we may treat as money any short-term asset that provides high liquidity and some insurance against capital loss, where such assets play the role of money in the individual's portfolio. The important point is that long-term securities such as consols are subject to capital loss and therefore are not well suited to play the role of money in demonstrating why the demand for money is a function of the rate of interest. On the other hand, short-term securities are less responsive to fluctuations in market value, and therefore would be less susceptible to a capital loss. See Keynes, *General Theory*, p. 167, footnote 1. For a more thorough discussion of what Keynes meant by *money*, see Keynes, *Treatise on Money*, Vol. I, pp. 3–49.

[18]*Float* technically refers to credit granted by the Federal Reserve banks to commercial banks for checks in the process of collection by the Federal Reserve after a reasonable time period has expired.

coins and paper money comprise only a small fraction of our total stock of money. Commercial-bank earnings are mainly interest on loans and securities financed with excess reserves—that is, reserves over the legal requirement.

Any individual bank can lend or buy securities with only a certain proportion of the funds that have been deposited in it. For example, if a bank receives additional demand deposits of $100 and the reserve requirement is 15 percent, it may lend $85 but must retain $15 as a required reserve.[19] The recipient of the $85 loan will usually deposit the sum in his own bank, which will then show an $85 increase in its demand deposits. This second bank will retain $13 (15 percent of $85) in required reserves and lend its excess reserves of $72. This process, called the bank credit multiplier, will continue until the original excess reserves of $85 have been expanded to some $570 in new demand deposits. The limit of bank credit expansion is equal to the reciprocal of the reserve ratio times the excess reserves created by the intital deposit.

In practice, the actual amount of new money created by the banking system will be reduced by other leakages in addition to required reserves. Part of the demand deposits may be withdrawn in the form of currency. Some may go into time or savings deposits, hereafter referred to simply as time deposits, at the commercial bank.[20] The banks themselves may choose to hold excess reserves.

Table 7-2 shows how the banking system can create money on the basis of

TABLE 7-2 Hypothetical Balance Sheet of the Commercial Banks ($ in billions)

I	Loans and securities	$360	Demand deposits	$200
	Required reserves: Demand deposits	30	Time deposits	200
	Required reserves: Savings deposits	10		
		$400		$400
II	Loans and securities	$360	Demand deposits	$212
	Required reserves: Demand deposits	32	Time deposits	200
	Required reserves: Savings deposits	10		
	Excess reserves	10		
		$412		$412
III	Loans and securities	$427	Demand deposits	$279
	Required reserves: Demand deposits	42	Time deposits	200
	Required reserves: Savings deposits	10		
		$479		$479
IV	Loans and securities	$412	Demand deposits	234
	Required reserves: Demand deposits	35	Time deposits	224
	Required reserves: Savings deposits	11		
		$458		$458

[19]Fifteen percent is a fair average of reserve requirements, since commercial banks are required to keep 8, 10, 12, 13 or 17½ percent reserves, depending on the aggregate amount of their NET demand deposits, at the time this is written.

[20]Technically, the distinction between time and savings deposits is that savings deposits do not stipulate a maturity date. Although banks can require 30 days' notice of intended withdrawal, they typically pay on request. Time deposits, on the other hand, have stipulated maturity dates.

an increase in demand deposits. Panel I of the table represents a hypothetical consolidated balance sheet of the commercial banking system, based on the assumption of no excess reserves, 15 percent required reserves on demand deposits, and 5 percent required reserves on time deposits. Panel II shows the initial effect on the money stock and on commercial-bank reserves of an increase of \$12 billion in demand deposits. Panel III shows the total amount of money that results after the bank credit multiplier has done its job, assuming the 15 percent reserve requirement and no leakages into currency, time deposits, or excess reserves. Since the reciprocal of the reserve requirement equals 6.66. . . , rounded to 6.7, the \$10 billion excess reserves can, at a maximum, be expanded to \$67 billion of additional demand deposits (\$279 billion minus \$212 billion demand deposits). The fourth panel of Table 7-2 demonstrates a more realistic situation, in which one fourth of the growing demand deposits will be withdrawn by depositors as currency, and time deposits at the commercial bank will increase by \$1.10 for each \$1.00 increase in demand deposits; that is, 110 percent of each increase in demand deposits will go into time deposits.[21] If, as in the previous case, we assume that banks do not desire to retain excess reserves, panel IV shows the results of an increase in \$12 billion in demand deposits. Demand deposits will increase by only \$22 billion and savings deposits will increase by \$24 billion, as compared with the increase in demand deposits of \$67 billion illustrated in Panel III. Leakages into currency and time deposits reduce the bank credit multiplier from 6.7 to 2.2. The \$22 billion change in demand deposits between Panel II and Panel IV of Table 7-2 is derived from the following formula:

$$\Delta D_d = \Delta A \frac{1}{r_d + c + Nr_t + r_e} \tag{7-7}$$

where ΔD_d is change in the dollar volume of demand deposits, ΔA is the amount of excess reserves, r_d is the reserve requirement on demand deposits, c equals the proportion of currency withdrawn per dollar of demand deposits, N equals the proportion of time deposits desired per dollar increase of demand deposits,[22] r_t is the reserve requirement on time deposits, and r_e is the proportion of excess reserves retained by banks.

Applying the formula to the illustration above,

$$\Delta D_d = \$10 \text{ billion} \frac{1}{.15 + .25 + 1.10(.05) + 0} = \$22 \text{ billion}$$

[21]In recent years, time deposits have been growing at a faster rate than demand deposits, indicating a growing general preference at the margin by individuals to put their savings in time deposits, and possibly reflecting a degree of interest elasticity on the part of individuals.

[22]The desired proportion of time deposits to demand deposits is related to the aggregate of individual decisions regarding the allocation of funds among transactions, precautionary, and speculative balances. Particularly when the interest rate is high, people may choose to consign part of their precautionary and speculative balances to time deposits, thus reducing their precautionary and speculative demands for money.

Alternatively, the adjusted bank credit multiplier equals

$$\frac{1}{.15 + .25 + 1.10(.05)} = \frac{1}{.455} = 2.2$$

or may be expressed more generally:

$$\frac{\Delta D_d}{\Delta A} = \frac{1}{r_d + c + Nr_t + r_e} \tag{7-8}$$

If the banks desire to hold excess reserves, the resulting additional leakage would further reduce the value of the adjusted bank credit multiplier.

Although time deposits are excluded from the stock of money, they still affect it, through their effect on the bank credit multiplier. Time deposits reduce the value of the bank credit multiplier. On the other hand, they provide capital certainty and therefore partly fill the demand for precautionary balances, which reduces the liquidity-preference function. Time deposits therefore reduce the supply of money by reducing the size of the bank credit multiplier, but simultaneously reduce the demand for money. (We will return to this topic in Chapter 14.)

The public and the banks both have some control over the money supply. The banks determine the amount of excess reserves; the public determines the amount of cash and time deposits desired. Since banks will probably hold more excess reserves when interest rates are low than when they are high, some economists have suggested that the stock of money has a normal positive slope.[23] Yet the public will want more time deposits when interest rates are high, at least partially offsetting the behavior of banks. In any case, the monetary authorities need only discover the amount of currency and time deposits desired by the public and the level of excess reserves desired by the banks, and adjust for them. Thus, the monetary authorities have the ultimate power to control the size of the stock of money through the use of monetary policy based on a realistically adjusted bank-credit-multiplier formula.

Because the power to regulate the stock of money is ultimately in the hands of the monetary authorities, we will follow common practice and describe the stock of money as a completely inelastic function. However, estimations and projections by the monetary authorities may at times prove inaccurate because of changes in the demand for currency and time deposits by the public and for excess reserves by the banks. Furthermore, these demands change over the business cycle, requiring the monetary authorities to continually adjust the money stock to allow for changes in the bank credit multiplier.[24]

---

[23] M. J. Baily, *National Income and the Price Level: A Study in Macroeconomic Theory*, 2nd ed. (New York: McGraw-Hill, 1971), pp. 127–28.

[24] Because the monetary authorities have complete control over the amount of money in circulation, we have chosen to use "stock of money" rather than "supply of money." However, if monetary policy is assumed constant, then a supply-of-money schedule could be

Iotroduction to Keynes's Liquidity Preference and the Stock of Money

Now that we have built up a theory of the demand for money and considered the sources of the stock of money, the next point to consider is the interaction of supply and demand in the money market, on the assumption that the price level remains constant even when the demand for and stock of money change. In the following analysis, we will for simplicity and convenience ignore Tobin's modifications and follow Keynes's total-demand curve for money, the liquidity-preference curve, in which the transactions and precautionary motives for holding money are a function of income and only the speculative motive is a function of the interest rate. Because the monetary authorities have the ultimate power to determine it, the stock of money ($\bar{M}_s$) is represented in Figure 7-9 as a vertical straight line. The bar is placed over M_s to emphasize the fact that the stock of money is exogeneously determined in this model. If $M_t + M_L$ represents the liquidity-preference curve, equilibrium occurs at the intersection of the two curves.

If the interest rate should be above equilibrium, at i_1, asset holders will be unwilling to hold the entire stock of money, since at that interest-rate level the stock of money supplied is greater than the quantity of money demanded. At this relatively high rate of interest, asset holders would increase the proportion of bonds in their portfolios; so the price of bonds would be bid up and interest rates would fall. As the rates fall, the quantity demanded of

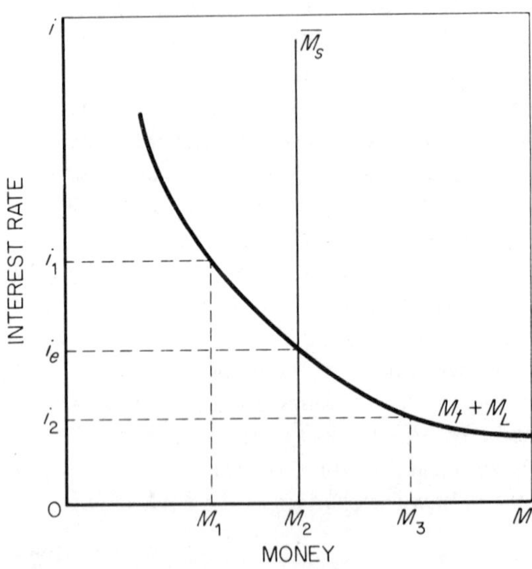

FIG. 7-9 The Demand and Stock of Money

derived to indicate the various quantities of money provided by the banking system under varying circumstances. In reality, the monetary authorities have monopoly power over the output of money, and a monopolist has no supply curve.

speculative money balances increases, and speculators will therefore sell some of their bond holdings. The interaction on the bond market between buyers and sellers of bonds will continue until the equilibrium interest rate is reached. The interest rate must eventually fall to the equilibrium at i_e in order to close the gap between M_1, the demand for money balances, and M_2, the stock of money.

On the other hand, if the interest rate is below equilibrium at i_2, an excess demand for cash balances (M_3 minus M_2) will exist. As asset holders attempt to increase their money holdings by selling securities, interest rates will increase. The lower price of bonds (higher interest rate) will encourage speculators to purchase the bonds, a process that will continue until equilibrium is reached at i_e. Restated, equilibrium requires

$$M_t = L_t(Y) \quad \text{(Transactions demand for money)} \tag{7-9}$$

$$M_L = L_L(i) \quad \text{(Speculative demand for money)} \tag{7-10}$$

$$M_t + M_L = \bar{M}_s \quad \text{(Liquidity preference = money-stock equilibrium)} \tag{7-11}$$

Changes in the Demand for Money

If an increase occurs in aggregate income, then larger transactions and precautionary balances would be required, and the total-demand function for money would shift to the right. Such an increase in the demand for money is shown as the movement from $M_{t_1} + M_L$ to $M_{t_2} + M_L$ in Figure 7-10. If the monetary authorities do not make more money available, but maintain the money stock at $\bar{M}_s$, the equilibrium interest rate would rise from i_1 to i_2. Similarly, a decrease in aggregate income leads to a leftward shift in the demand for money. It is possible that the functional relationship between

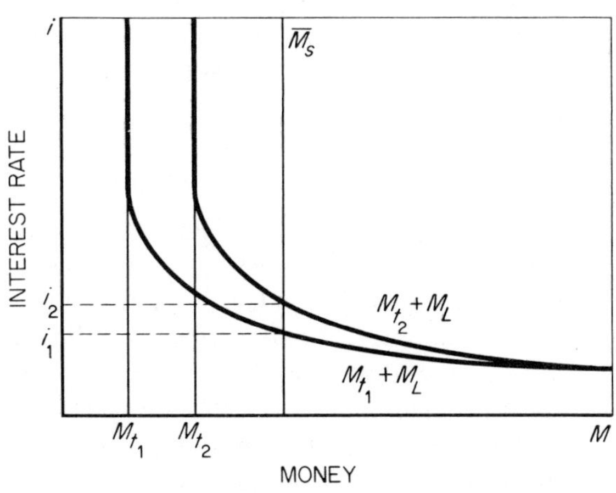

FIG. 7-10 Effect of a Change in Aggregate Income on the Demand for Money

money and income will change, although, like the neoclassical economists, Keynesian economists generally assume this relationship to be stable over the time period under consideration, varying only with such long-run factors as payment practices and consumer spending habits between payment periods, or varying in the very short run in a random manner from a variety of causes. Likewise, the demand for M_L balances could also shift independently of changes in M_t, leading to equilibrium increases or decreases in the interest rate. Although Keynes never made the assumption explicit, much of his theory disregards changes in the demand for money as a function of income (M_t balances) and concentrates on changes in the demand for money as a function of the interest rate (M_L balances).

Since speculation tends to be rather volatile, Keynes felt that changes in the demand for speculative balances would occur frequently. However, if we allow changes in transactions and precautionary balances to affect the rate of interest, the demand for money as a function of the rate of interest should be somewhat less volatile, because the demand for transactions and precautionary balances is apt to be more stable than the volatile speculative demand for money, which changes whenever speculators change their concept of the normal rate.

Speculative Demand for Liquid Balances and Income Velocity

The slope of the demand curve for speculative money balances is related to income velocity and the interest rate. When the interest rate decreases, asset holders desire to increase their money balances. An increased desire to hold money reduces income velocity, since the demand for money is the reciprocal of income velocity. Every increase in the money stock will decrease income velocity (assuming the liquidity-preference curve does not shift), because in equilibrium, a greater quantity of money will be demanded at lower interest rates. Only in the vertical range of the total demand for money would velocity be unaffected by a change in the money stock, because in that range, a lower interest rate could not cause an increase in the quantity of money demanded.

Changes in the Stock of Money

The following example illustrates the effects of a change in the stock of money. If the monetary authority increases the stock of money—say from M_{s_1} to M_{s_2} in Figure 7-11—then the equilibrium interest rate would decrease from i_1 to i_2, since asset holders would be willing to accept the additional stock of money only at an i_2 level of interest. The additional stock of money that the monetary authority injects into the economy would at first be converted into bonds by its recipients. The increase in the demand for bonds would increase their price, thus reducing the rate of interest. Bond prices would continue to rise and interest rates to fall. As interest rates fall, the demand to hold money balances increases, and those desiring to increase their money balances will

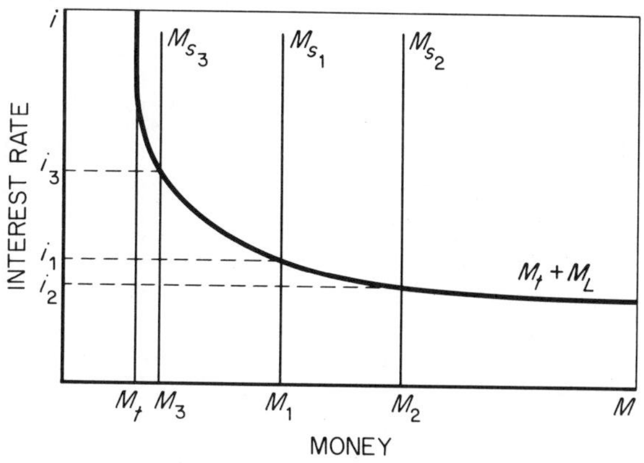

FIG. 7-11 Effect of Changes in the Stock of Money

therefore sell bonds. The interaction in the bond market between the new money-holders buying bonds and those who desire to sell bonds at their increased price will continue until the equilibrium interest rate is reached.

Similarly, if the money stock is decreased from M_{s_1} to M_{s_3}, the reverse process would occur and continue until the new, higher, equilibrium interest rate of i_3 was achieved. (We disregard, for the moment, the question of how the new money is introduced into the economy.)

Liquidity Trap

The one place where changes in the demand for and stock of money may not affect the interest rate is in the liquidity trap. At very low levels of the interest rate, when the consensus among speculators is that interest rates can fall no further but must rise, bond prices will be so high that speculators will prefer to hold only money. Furthermore, at such low levels of the interest rate, there is no incentive for precautionary and transactions balances to be used for the purchase of interest-earning assets, since the rate of return is very low compared with the risk of capital loss. Consequently, if the demand for money shifts, the change cannot be noted in the market, since the demand for money has already become perfectly elastic. For example, in Figure 7-12, a decrease in the speculative demand for liquid balances from M_{L_1} to M_{L_2} or an increase in the stock of money from M_{s_1} to M_{s_2} will not affect the interest rate. One policy conclusion to be drawn from this analysis is that when the economy is in the liquidity trap, it is impossible to lower the interest rate by increasing the stock of money. However, the liquidity trap could develop only in very unusual circumstances. In the *General Theory*, Keynes maintained that he knew of no economy that had ever been in it.[25] Many of his followers

[25]Keynes, *General Theory*, p. 207.

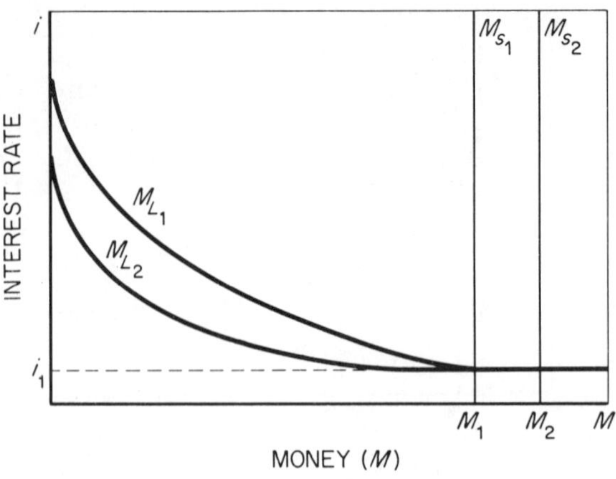

FIG. 7-12 The Effect of the Liquidity Trap

have deemphasized the role money plays in the eonomic system by assuming, often implicitly, that the economy is generally in the liquidity trap.

Leijonhufvud[26] suggests that one must distinguish the case in which near-money assets are included in the money stock from cases in which they are counted as securities. (1) In the first case, when near-money assets are incorporated in the stock of money, the assetholder's only alternatives are highly liquid money or near-money and relatively illiquid long-term bonds. (2) In the second case if near-money assets are counted as securities along with bonds then the alternative to money is a range of long- and short-term securities. This second interpretation abstracts from the realistic observation that usually, interest rates on short-term securities are different from the rates on long-term securities. If the securities market is dominated by risk averters who fear capital loss if they sell their securities before maturity, then the assetholders demand a liquidity premium to compensate them for their added risk of capital loss. Therefore, long-term securities will generally command a higher rate of interest than short-term securities. To assume that one theoretical interest rate could represent the return on a range of long- and short-term securities might result in misleading analysis, because fluctuations in the stock of money may initially affect only the short-term interest rate. Arbitrage between the short and long ends of the securities market may not occur if long-term expectations remain sufficiently inelastic, that is, if expected future rates are not revised because of a change in present short-term rates due to uncertainty about future interest rate movements. The long-term rate (based on expected future rates) will not change so long as speculators believe that the short-term rate will soon revert to its former level. Only after the faith in the normality of previously prevailing rates has been thoroughly undermined

[26]Leijonhufvud, *On Keynesian Economics and the Economics of Keynes*, pp. 198–205, 282–314, 354–66.

will the long-term rate change to equal the short-term rate plus a liquidity premium. Until expected future rates are revised downward, an increase in the stock of money will not decrease the long-term rate of interest, a disequilibrium result analogous to the liquidity trap, because the long-term interest rate is the significant rate in determining the amount of investment.

SUMMARY AND CONCLUSIONS

The strict Keynesian theory puts the individual and aggregate demand for money, the liquidity-preference curve, into three pigeonholes: Two of them, the demands for transactions and precautionary money balances, are a function of the level of income; the third, the demand for speculative money balances, is a function of the interest rate. Keynes felt that, in practice, it would be difficult to separate the three demands, even in the asset holder's own mind, and suggested that the precautionary motive may be partially a function of the interest rate. Professor Tobin stresses that transactions demand for money may also be related to the interest rate. However, making a portion of the demand for transactions and precautionary balances a function of the rate of interest does not essentially change the Keynesian theory. The significant points made by Keynes are (1) that the demand for money is, at least in part, a function of the rate of interest; (2) that if an economy should find itself in the liquidity trap, expansionary monetary policy may be unavailing; and (3) that the equilibrium rate of interest is determined by the demand for and stock of money rather than by the demand for investment expenditures and the supply of savings.

The monetary authorities always have the power to offset the activities of commercial banks and the public, assuming that these authorities forecast correctly how the banks will react to a given situation. So the stock of money is assumed to be a perfectly inelastic function, exogenously determined by the monetary authorities.

A shortcoming suggested by post-Keynesian neoclassical economists is that while Keynes was correct in pointing out the neglect by the earlier neoclassicals of the store-of-value function of money, he failed to consider sufficiently that increases in the stock of money may be used for transactions purposes. In focusing on money as a function of the interest rate, Keynes neglected its significance as a function of aggregate income. This topic will be taken up in Chapter 11, the first chapter on post-Keynesian theory.

QUESTIONS AND PROBLEMS

1. What are Keynes's three demands for money? Describe each.
2. Describe the liquidity trap. How likely is its development?
3. What was Tobin's contribution to Keynes's theory of liquidity preference?

4. How can the banking system increase the stock of money?

5. Describe the process by which equilibrium is restored when the stock of money exceeds the demand.

6. What is the "normal" interest rate? What is its significance with regard to the demand for speculative balances?

7. Suppose the interest rate goes from 5% to 7%? What is the effect on the price of a $100 bond?

8. Define the stock of money. What could cause it to increase or decrease?

9. a. If each $1 million of transactions balances can support $1.5 billion of aggregate income, sketch the transactions demand below.
   b. Assuming that the stock of money is $5 million, what equilibrium levels of income and interest might be established?
   c. Under what conditions would those levels be determinate?

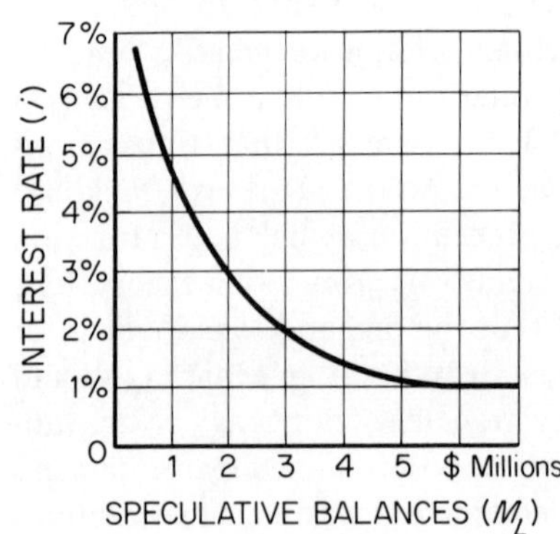

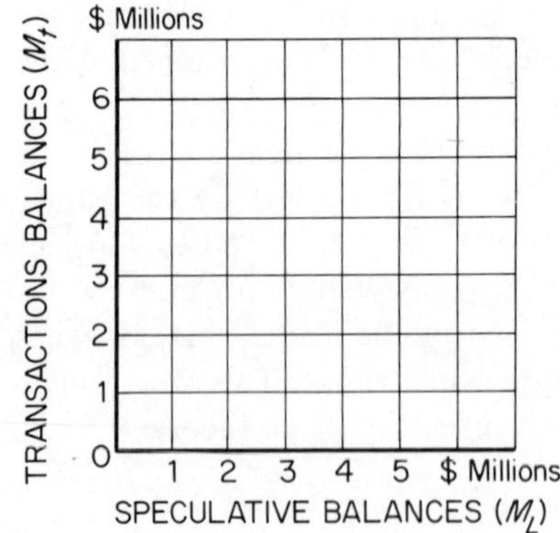

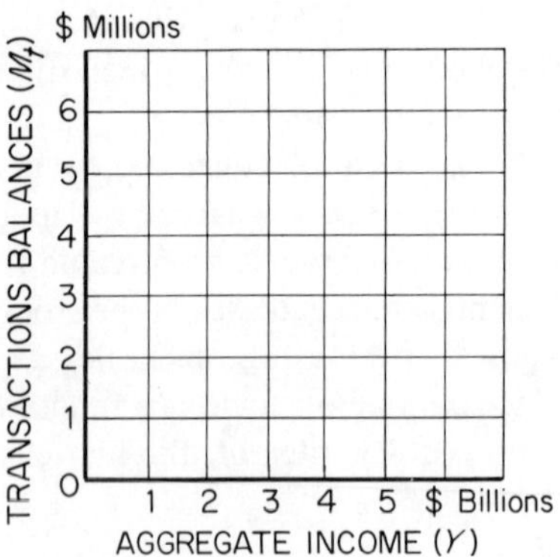

SIMPLIFIED DESCRIPTION OF KEYNES'S LIQUIDITY-PREFERENCE THEORY

DILLARD, DUDLEY, *The Economics of John Maynard Keynes*, pp. 161–88. Englewood Cliffs, N.J.: Prentice-Hall, 1948.

HANSEN, ALVIN H., *A Guide to Keynes*, pp. 126–39. New York: McGraw-Hill, 1953.

THE DEMAND FOR MONEY AND CONTROVERSY OVER INTEREST-RATE THEORY STIMULATED BY THE GENERAL THEORY

ESHAG, EPRIME, *From Marshall to Keynes*. Oxford: Basil Blackwell, 1963.

HAWTREY, R. G., "Alternative Theories of the Rate of Interest," *Economic Journal*, 47 (September 1937), 436–43.

KRAGH, B., "The Meaning and Use of Liquidity Curves in Keynesian Interest Theory," *International Economic Papers*, 5 (1955), 155–69.

LERNER, A. P., "Alternative Formulations of the Theory of Interest," *Economic Journal*, 48 (June 1938), 211–30. Reprinted in *The New Economics*, ed. S. E. Harris, Chap. 45. New York: Knopf, 1947.

———, "Interest Theory—Supply and Demand for Loans, or Supply and Demand for Cash?" *Review of Economics and Statistics*, 26 (May 1944), 88–91. Reprinted in *The New Economics*, ed. S.E. Harris, Chap. 46. New York: Knopf, 1947.

OHLIN, BERTIL, "Alternative Theories of the Rate of Interest," *Economic Journal*, 47 (September 1937), 423–27.

ROBERTSON, D. H., "Alternative Theories of the Rate of Interest," *Economic Journal*, 47 (September 1937), 428–36.

———, "Mr. Keynes and the Rate of Interest," in *Essays in Monetary Theory*, pp. 11–49. London: Staples Press, 1940.

———, "Some Notes on the Theory of Interest," in *Money, Trade, and Economic Growth*, Essays in honor of John Henry Williams, pp. 193–209. New York: Macmillan, 1951.

ROBINSON, JOAN, "The Rate of Interest," in *The Rate of Interest and Other Essays*. London: Macmillan, 1952.

SOMERS, HAROLD, "Monetary Policy and the Theory of Interest," *Quarterly Journal of Economics* 55 (May 1941), 488–507.

WALLICH, H. C., "The Current Significance of Liquidity Preference," *Quarterly Journal of Economics*, 60 (August 1946), 490–512.

POST-KEYNESIAN INTEREST-RATE THEORY

BAUMOL, W. J., "The Transactions Demand for Cash—An Inventory Theoretic Approach," *Quarterly Journal of Economics*, 66 (November 1952), 545–56.

BOULDING, K. E., "A Liquidity Preference Theory of Market Prices," *Economica*, 11 (May 1944), 55–63.

THE THEORY OF MONEY

LAIDLER, D., *The Demand for Money: Theories and Evidence*. Scranton, Pa.: International Textbook Company, 1969.

EMPIRICAL STUDIES: TESTS OF THE LIQUIDITY-PREFERENCE THEORY

BRONFENBRENNER, M., and T. MAYER, "Liquidity Functions in the American Economy," *Econometrica*, 28 (October 1960), 810–34.

CHRIST, CARL F., "Interest Rates and 'Portfolio Selection' among Liquid Assets in the U.S.," in *Measurement in Economics*, pp. 201–18. Stanford, Calif.: Stanford University Press, 1963.

HAMBURGER, M. J., "The Demand for Money by Households, Money Substitutes, and Monetary Policy," *Journal of Political Economy*, 74 (December 1966), 600–623.

HELLER, H. R., "The Demand for Money—The Evidence from Short-Run Data," *Quarterly Journal of Economics*, 79 (May 1965), 291–303.

LAIDLER, D., "The Rate of Interest and the Demand for Money—Some Empirical Evidence," *Journal of Political Economy*, 74 (December 1966), 543–55.

LATANÉ, H. A., "Cash Balances and the Interest Rate—A Pragmatic Approach," *Review of Economics and Statistics*, 36 (November 1954), 456–60.

SELDEN, RICHARD T., "Monetary Velocity in the U.S.," in *Studies in the Quantity Theory of Money*, ed. Milton Friedman, pp. 179–251. Chicago: University of Chicago Press, 1956.

SMITH, LAWRENCE B., and JOHN W. L. WINDER, "Price and Interest Rate Expectations and the Demand for Money in Canada," *Journal of Finance*, 26 (June 1971), 671–82.

TOBIN, J., "Liquidity Preference and Monetary Policy," *Review of Economics and Statistics*, 29 (May 1947), 124–31.

WEINTRAUB, R., and W. HOSEK, "Further Reflections on And Investigations of Money Demand," *Journal of Finance*, 25 (March 1970), 109–25.

Introduction to the Keynesian System—Consumption and Savings

8

Even though Keynes's theories on consumption and savings have become the best known of his contributions to economic theory, perhaps his most important innovation was to recognize explicitly the important economic role of money.

Yet Keynes's theory of the demand for money is peripherally related to his consumption theory. He divided the total demand for money, the liquidity-preference function, into a demand for transactions (M_T) balances (including precautionary balances) that are a function of income, and a demand for liquid or speculative (M_L) balances that are a function of the interest rate. This division is related to the household's decision concerning how much income to devote to consumption and how much to savings. For example, if a household decides to increase its consumption expenditures because of an increase in income, it will typically require more money for transactions purposes (larger M_T balances). So if consumption is a function of income, the demand for M_T balances will also be a function of income.

KEYNES'S PURPOSE

During the depression of the 1930's, when only about half the productive capacity of the western world was in use, Keynes saw that increased effective demand was the key to greater production—not the reverse, as Say's Law would imply. In the neoclassical theory as described in Chapter 6, consumption was deemphasized. Because people generally preferred consumption to saving, the neoclassicists believed that interest was a necessary reward for thrift and that the interest rate would determine the level of savings by offering greater future income for money saved today. Once the level of savings was determined, the residual income would be used for consumption. In the Keynesian formulation, the process is reversed; consumption is determined by a conscious decision, and the amount saved is the residual. In such a scheme, interest is less a reward for thrift than an inducement to surrender liquidity.

A number of Keynes's contemporaries, such as Hobson and Gesell, had considered consumption an important determinant of the level of aggregate economic activity.[1] But their views were unacceptable to the majority of neoclassical economists steeped in Say's Law and the quantity theory of money, even though the unemployment rate remained relatively high during the early years of the Depression. Someone of Keynes's political and academic stature was required to raise the concept of the consumption function from the underworld of economics to the accepted stream of economic thought, even though the younger economists were ready for an analysis that explained the obvious lack of consumption after the Depression started.

THE SAVING–CONSUMPTION RELATIONSHIP

Individual Indifference Functions

We have already discussed the theory of consumer choice in Chapter 2, using indifference curves and budget restraints; and in Chapter 6, we introduced Fisher's investment opportunity curve as a new type of budget restraint relating this year's income to next year's. Fisher employed indifference curves to illustrate his businessman-consumer's preference pattern for present consumption expenditures and future income.

In this section we modify the Fisherian, neoclassical approach in order to set the individual in a Keynesian world as distinct from a neoclassical world. Keynes pictured the individual as a wage earner, not as a businessman with an investment-opportunity curve. The Keynesian consumer was entirely separated from the Keynesian investor; one of Keynes's most useful innovations was to distinguish the wage-earning consumer from the entrepreneur-investor. Keynes's consumers decide whether to spend on consumption or to save, while his investors decide whether or not to undertake investment projects.

The typical Keynesian consumer is someone who apparently anticipates a dependable income this year and next and who has only to decide how much

---

[1] For a good discussion of pre-Keynesian economists who held views now considered "Keynesian," see Harlan L. McCracken, *Keynesian Economics in the Stream of Economic Thought* (Baton Rouge: Louisiana State University Press, 1961)

to borrow to increase this year's consumption at the cost of next year's, or how much to save out of this year's income to increase his consumption next year. On the other hand, Fisher and many neoclassical writers saw the typical individual as an entrepreneur who made consumption, savings, and investment decisions.

In contrast to the neoclassical theory, the Keynesian theory proposed that the level of consumption is determined primarily by the consumer's income. Therefore, the indifference curves presented in Figure 8-1 are drawn almost as right angles, indicating that the substitution effect of an interest-rate change has little influence on an individual's decision to trade off between present and next year's income or purchasing power. If the interest rate had absolutely no effect on the individual's decisions, his indifference curves would all be right angles. They are not quite right angles because Keynes maintained that substantial changes in the interest rate could affect the amount people saved, but that the degree of interest elasticity of savings was slight. For Keynes, income was more important than the interest rate in determining how much will be saved and how much consumed.

In Figure 8-1, the straight lines labeled B_1, B_2, and B_3 are income-or budget-restraint lines drawn to show a 10 percent interest rate. Each income-restraint line represents various possible combinations of purchasing power that might be exercised this year and next by a wage earner from one given expected level of wage income, plus the interest he could receive on his lending,

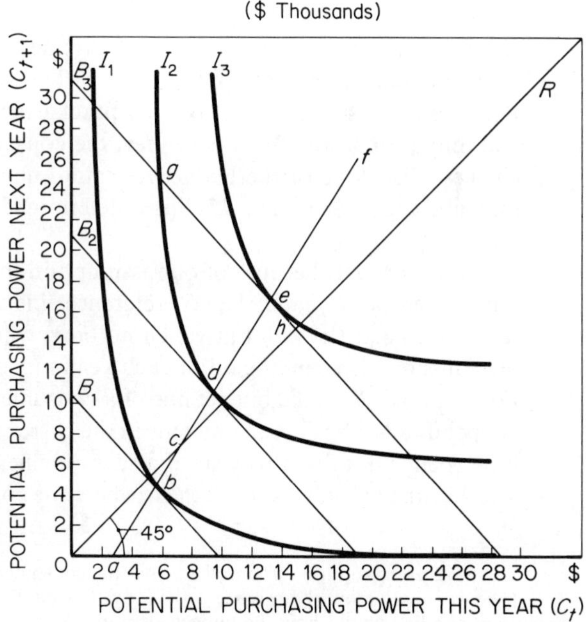

FIG. 8-1 A Consumer's Choice to Anticipate or to Defer Purchasing Power

or minus the interest he must pay on his borrowing at an assumed 10 percent interest rate.

For simplicity, we assume that borrowing and lending occur at the same interest rate. (In practice, the borrowing rate will generally exceed the lending rate to the typical consumer.) And we assume that the shape of the curve will not be modified by expectations of inflation or income changes. In our illustration in Figure 8-1, we assume the same expected income from wages this year and next. The consumer has the choice to borrow against next year's income or to lend this year's. Given the possibility to lend or borrow, this year's potential purchasing power becomes

$$Y_t + Y_{t+1}\left(\frac{1}{1+i}\right)$$

where Y_t is the wage income expected to be received this year, Y_{t+1} is the expected wage income next year, and i is the interest rate the consumer may either earn on savings or pay on loans. The value of $Y_{t+1}[1/(1+i)]$ represents the discounted present value of next year's income if the consumer borrowed using next year's expected income as collateral for the loan.

The maximum potential purchasing power the consumer could exercise next year would be all of next year's expected wage income augmented by all of this year's wage income (which he conceivably could save), plus the interest he could earn on that sum. The formula is

$$Y_{t+1} + Y_t(1+i)$$

We can conclude that the two extremes are $Y_t + Y_{t+1}[1/(1+i)]$, the horizontal-axis intercept, and $Y_{t+1} + Y_t(1+i)$, the vertical-axis intercept.[2] Between those two extremes of only purchasing goods and services this year and only purchasing them next year, the consumer has a variety of possible choices. The slope of the budget-restraint line is determined by the interest rate, and the level along a 45° line is determined by the size of the consumer's income.

In Figure 8-1, because of our assumption that the consumer will earn the same wage both years, the 45° reference line passes through each budget-restraint line at the point at which no borrowing or lending takes place and the consumer is spending all of each year's income in the year it is received. For example, B_1 is the budget line of a consumer earning \$5,000 each year. If he spends all of both years' income in the current year, he could spend \$9,545; if he spends nothing this year and saves for next year, he will have \$10,500. The 45° line OR passes through B_1 where the consumer has \$5,000 each year.

[2]We are assuming for simplicity that the consumer–wage earner is paid once a year. If he were paid monthly or weekly, the formula would have to be adjusted. More frequent compounding would bow the budget restraint somewhat. However, the effect would normally be slight.

The budget lines B_2 and B_3 give the same information if his income grows to $10,000 and $15,000 respectively.

The consumer is in equilibrium where his budget-restraint line is just tangent to the highest indifference curve he can obtain. For example, if the consumer's expected wages were $15,000 a year, he could operate anywhere along his income-restraint line B_3, since any point on line B_3 represents various combinations of present and future purchasing power that this consumer can afford. He could operate at point *g*; however, this would put him on indifference curve I_2, whereas by operating at point *e*, the point of tangency between indifference curve I_3 and the budget-restraint line B_3, he achieves more satisfaction. In our example, I_3 is the highest indifference curve he can achieve with his expected yearly income of $15,000.

As you can see, a positive interest rate or any increase in the interest rate will have an income effect. Savers will experience an increase in income and borrowers a decrease as the curve rotates around the 45° line intercept. Keynes apparently was concerned with the substitution effect (a movement along an indifference curve, which is small or nonexistent if the indifference curve is angular) to the exclusion of the income effect (a shift from one indiffence curve to another that is necessarily always present unless the consumer always spends all his income each year) when he concluded that normal interest-rate changes would have little effect on consumer decisions.

The income-consumption line *af* in Figure 8-1 connects all points of tangency between the indifference curves and the income-restraint lines. From this line we can see that at low income levels, such as point *b* where his yearly wages are $5,000, the consumer would be a borrower; at points to the right of *c*, such as points *d* and *e*, he would accumulate increasing amounts of savings as his income increased. Point *c*, where line *af* crosses the 45° line, represents the breakeven point where the consumer's income would equal his consumption in both years. In the next section we will derive the individual's consumption function from Figure 8-1, using the income-consumption line.

Individual Consumption Functions

Since, in Keynes's system, only substantial changes in the interest rate affect the amount people save, the effect of interest rates on consumption is generally ignored. In addition, primary emphasis in the Keynesian system is placed on present rather than future consumption. Therefore, only the relationship between consumption expenditure and the consumer's present income is included in the individual's consumption function.

The consumption function, like the Engel curve, shows the relationship between the dependent variable, consumption, and the independent variable, present consumer income, assuming that the interest rate and the consumer's tastes remain constant. The individual consumption function constructed in Figure 8-2, based on Figure 8-1, relates present disposable income (short for disposable personal income) on the *x*-axis to consumption on the *y*-axis. In national-income accounting terms, disposable income excludes all taxes paid by consumers and is often the most relevant income concept in the income-consumption relationship; therefore, we have used disposable income to represent present income in our analysis. The income levels of Figure 8-2 are determined by the points where the income-restraint lines in Figure 8-1 cross the 45° reference line. The consumption levels are determined from the income-consumption curve *af*, drawn through the points of tangency between the indifference curves and the income-restraint lines. The method is to relate this year's purchasing power at the point of tangency to the income level associated with the same income restraint line. Then the points of tangency are plotted along the *y*-axis in Figure 8-2 corresponding to the appropriate income level plotted along the *x*-axis. For example, line *af* crosses the income-restraint line B_3 at point *e*, which equals $13,000 of consumption this year. The income level that corresponds to that consumption level occurs at point *h*, where the 45° line crosses B_3 and is equal to $15,000. Consumption of $13,000 corresponding to disposable income of $15,000 enables us to plot one point in Figure 8-2. By plotting several other points an individual consumption curve can be derived.

The 45° line in Figure 8-2 is a convenient reference line connecting all points equidistant from the axes. If the consumption function fell along the 45° line, consumption would always equal disposable income. Therefore, at the breakeven point, where the consumption function crosses the 45° line, saving is equal to 0 and consumption is equal to disposable income; to the left of that point, consumption is greater than disposable income and can be

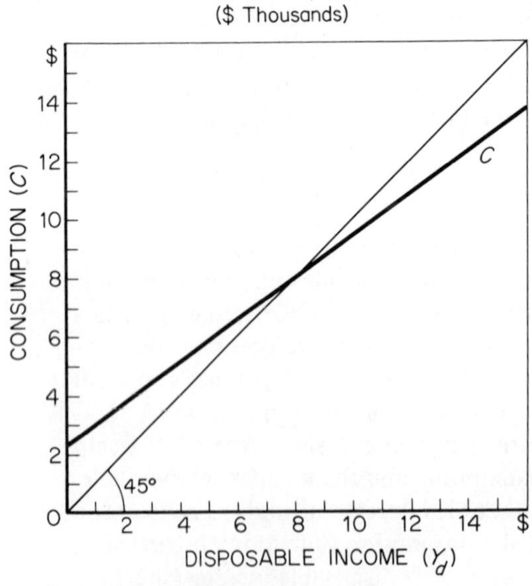

FIG. 8-2 Individual Consumption Function

accomplished only at the cost of dissaving, either by borrowing or using up past savings.

Aggregate Consumption function

An aggregate consumption function can be derived by summing the individual consumption functions to determine the relationship between aggregate consumption and aggregate disposable income.

However, such a simple summation is loaded with problems. It assumes that individuals act independently of each other. That assumption is clearly unfounded.[3] Most consumers are influenced by their peer group and by style leaders. The demand for certain goods and the total amount consumed by any individual may change as he observes the consumption patterns of others—both those he wants to emulate and those he wants to excel. In addition, there may exist a third group made up of persons whose consumption patterns the individual is unwilling to exceed or even match. It can be uncomfortable to appear richer than one's friends or as rich as one's boss. Therefore, a summation of individual consumption functions, made on the assumption that each consumer is independent of all others, is clearly oversimplified. Some possible implications of consumer interdependence are considered in the Appendix to this chapter, in the theory developed by Professor James Duesenberry. Within the chapter, however, we do not specifically allow for the effects of interdependence in constructing aggregate consumption functions.

The consumption function is a useful indicator of the proportion of disposable income that consumers are willing to spend. Consumers' willingness (or propensity) to spend their income on consumption items can be described in two ways: the average propensity to consume, and the marginal propensity to consume. Total consumption divided by the corresponding disposable income has been called the average propensity to consume (APC) and may be stated as a percentage of total income spent on consumption. Alternatively, the ratio of a *change* in consumption to a *change* in disposable income is called the marginal propensity to consume (MPC). Where C equals consumption and Y_d equals disposable income, the average propensity to consume (APC) is C/Y_d, and the marginal propensity to consume (MPC) is $\Delta C/\Delta Y_d$. The significance of the distinction between the MPC and the APC will become clear as we employ the concepts in our analysis; briefly, the APC tells the proportion of total disposable income spent on consumption, and the MPC tells the proportion of additional disposable income spent on consumption. The APC refers to the *level* and the MPC measures the *slope* of the consumption function.

Figure 8-3 illustrates a hypothetical aggregate consumption function, C, in which the marginal propensity to consume, the slope of the consumption line,

---

[3]Harvey Leibenstein, "Bandwagon, Snob, and Veblen Effects in the Theory of Consumer's Demand," *Quarterly Journal of Economics*, 64 (May 1950), 183–207.

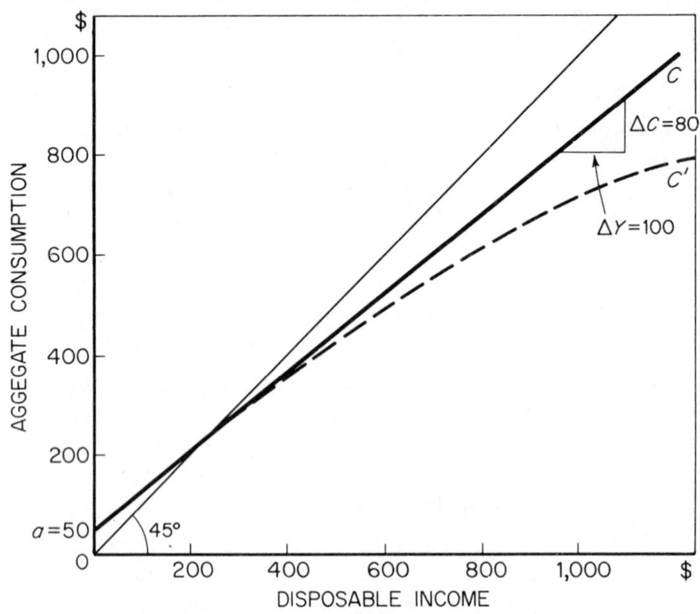

FIG. 8-3 Aggregate Consumption Function

is constant throughout. As the graph shows, any \$100 billion change in disposable income is matched by a \$80 billion change in consumption. Thus, the marginal propensity to consume is 80 percent regardless of the level of income, and the consumption function must be linear. On the other hand, the average propensity to consume varies from over 100 percent at low levels of disposable income (APC = infinity at zero income) and approaches the MPC as a limit at very high levels of income.

The difference between consumption and the 45° line represents savings in Figure 8-3, since any disposable income not spent on consumption is saved by definition. Wherever consumption lies above the 45° line, savings must be negative. The breakeven point occurs where consumption is equal to disposable income and savings are zero. In Figure 8-3, the breakeven point occurs at an aggregate disposable income of \$250 billion. To the right of this breakeven point, savings become positive and continue to increase as income increases.

Table 8-1, a tabular representation of the consumption function of Figure 8-3, presents in columnar form the average propensity to save (APS) and the marginal propensity to save (MPS), as well as the APC and MPC. The APS is total savings divided by disposable income (S/Y_d), and the MPS equals the change in savings divided by the change in disposable income ($\Delta S/\Delta Y_d$), which is the slope of the savings function.[4] Since consumption plus savings equals

[4]Negative savings can occur in the short run through using up previously accumulated savings or increased borrowing by individuals and using up inventories of consumer goods, or using up accumulated capital in the aggregate.

income at all levels of disposable income, the APC plus the APS must equal 1, and the MPC plus the MPS must also equal 1, even though the APC does not equal the MPC nor does the APS equal the MPS.

TABLE 8-1 Disposable Income, Consumption, and Savings ($ in billions)

Disposable Income (Y_d)	Consumption (C)	Savings (S)	Average Propensity to Consume (APC)	Marginal Propensity to Consume (MPC)	Average Propensity to Save (APS)	Marginal Propensity to Save (MPS)
$ 0	$ 50	$−50	–	–	–	–
200	210	−10	1.05	.80	−.05	.20
400	370	30	.925	.80	.075	.20
600	530	70	.88	.80	.12	.20
800	690	110	.86	.80	.14	.20
1,000	850	150	.85	.80	.15	.20

The consumption–disposable income relationship may be stated algebraically as follows:

$$C = a + bY_d$$

where a is the value of consumption at zero income that is where consumption intersects the vertical axis and b is the slope of the consumption function (the MPC). And the savings function can be stated

$$S = -a + (1 - b)Y_d$$

where $-a$ is dissaving at zero income and $(1 - b)$ equals the slope of the savings function (the MPS). Thus, at zero disposable income, dissaving must be equal to consumption.[5]

KEYNES'S PSYCHOLOGICAL LAW

In his *General Theory*, Keynes maintained that

> The fundamental psychological law, upon which we are entitled to depend with great confidence both *a priori* from our knowledge of human nature and from the detailed facts of experience, is that men are disposed, as a rule and on the average, to increase

[5] In the illustration used in Figure 8-3 and Table 8-1 (with savings and consumption in billions of dollars),

$$C = 50 + .8Y_d$$

and

$$S = -50 + .2Y_d$$

Thus when the income level is $250 billion, consumption is also $250 billion and savings is equal to zero. With computation in billions,

$$C = 50 + .8(250) \qquad S = -50 + .2(250)$$
$$C = 250 \qquad S = 0$$

their consumption as their income increases, but not by as much as the increase in their income.[6]

If the "fundamental psychological law" can be depended upon, the numerical value of the MPC must fall between zero and 1. In addition, Keynes felt that the consumption function would be "fairly stable," because the factors that determine its position and slope would either be unimportant or change slowly over time. He observed that a low-income community would probably have a higher MPC than a high-income community, and that in any given community, the MPC decreases as disposable income increases. Decreasing values of the MPC as disposable income increases would require a nonlinear consumption function that will approach a horizontal line at extremely high incomes. Such a consumption function is illustrated by the dotted line labeled C' in Figure 8-3. Fortunately for the *General Theory*, this observation was not a necessary part of the theory, since the short-run MPC appears to be fairly constant, and consequently the short-run consumption function appears to be linear.

Another different but related point, which some have inferred from Keynes, is that the MPC is less than the APC. As we have seen, if the MPC is less than the APC, the APC will decrease as incomes increase and will approach the MPC as a limit. This phenomenon is illustrated in Table 8-1.

The characteristics of the Keynesian consumption function may be summarized as follows: (1) Consumption is a fairly stable function of aggregate disposable income; (2) the marginal propensity to consume is greater than zero but less than 1; (3) the average propensity to consume is greater than the marginal propensity to consume and decreases as disposable income increases; and (4) the marginal propensity to consume will decrease as disposable income increases. The first two points are essential to the *General Theory*; the third, while not essential, seems to be supported by the facts; and the fourth is unessential to the theory and has been rejected in recent years because the facts do not seem to support it. The first three characteristics are illustrated by the consumption function of Figure 8-3 and Table 8-1. As can be seen from the table, the APC declines from 1.05 to .85 while the MPC remains constant at .80. As disposable income continues to increase, the APC will continue to approach the value of the MPC. The dotted line, C', in Figure 8-3 illustrates the fourth characteristic, which, as we have pointed out, has been discarded in recent years.

The Keynesian consumption function, like a Coleridge poem, proceeds on at least three levels simultaneously. On the surface, the distribution of disposable income between consumption and savings depends on the level of disposable income. However, at the same time, the position and the shape of the consumption function depend on certain nonincome factors. Some of these nonincome determinants, which Keynes called the objective factors, are ex-

---

[6]J. M. Keynes, *The General Theory of Employment, Interest, and Money* (New York: Harcourt Brace Jovanovich, 1936), p. 96.

ogenous to Keynes's system, but at times may cause significant shifts in the consumption function. Other factors, which he called the subjective factors, are endogenous to the system and determine the position (APC) and shape (MPC) of the function.

The Objective Factors

Although Keynes lists six objective factors that may cause substantial shifts in the consumption function, Professor Hansen has indicated that only four are significant:[7]

1. *Windfall Profits and Losses.* The consumption function is susceptible to change from sudden, unexpected increases or decreases in wealth. For example, increasing stock prices during the latter part of the 1920's gave stockholders a windfall increase in capital values, which, in turn, apparently increased the aggregate consumption function.

2. *The Interest Rate.* Keynes agreed with the neoclassical theory that changes in the interest rate could affect the level of consumption. A higher interest rate could encourage people to substitute savings for present consumption, because of the promise of greater future consumption. However, he qualified his position by implying that target savers (those saving for a particular level of income) would save less at higher interest rates. Therefore, Keynes felt that the effect of interest-rate change was more complex than did some of the neoclassicists. Keynes pointed out that the effect of an interest-rate change could be indeterminate. He noted that interest changes might significantly affect consumption over a long period; however, in the short run, normal, small changes in the interest rate would have only an insignificant effect. For example, if a man earns $10,000 a year and normally saves $4,000, a change in the interest rate from 5 percent to 4 percent would occasion a loss of only $40 in interest income and consequently would not be likely to change his consumption habits.

On the other hand, *substantial* changes in the interest rate could have a noticeable impact on consumption, even in the short run. For that reason, a slight degree of interest elasticity was built into the individual's indifference curves of Figure 8-1 to illustrate how savings could be affected by an increase in the interest rate.

In this section we have concentrated on the income effect of interest-rate changes. But interest-rate changes also have a windfall effect, by increasing or decreasing the wealth of security holders through capital gains or losses. This concept of a wealth effect operating on consumption decisions will be discussed below, in the section beginning on page 241.

3. *Fiscal Policy.* Changes in fiscal policy also can change consumption patterns. For example, a tax increase with government expenditures held constant will be paid partly with money intended for consumption and partly with intended savings, thus reducing each to some extent.

In addition, Keynes felt that if fiscal policy was used to redistribute income from the richer to the poorer classes by taxes and transfer payments, the effect would be to increase the aggregate consumption function, because he believed the poor had a higher MPC than the rich.

A dramatic example of fiscal policy occurs during wartime, when consumer goods are unavailable owing to government policy, and the purchase of war materials

---

[7] A. H. Hansen, *A Guide to Keynes* (New York: McGraw-Hill, 1953), p. 82.

must be financed through taxes and bond sales, both of which reduce consumption expenditures out of net national product.[8]

4. *Changes in the Expected Relationship between Present and Future Income.* Keynes felt that this factor could be important for an individual but would most likely average out for the community as a whole. However, there have been cases when consumers' expectations of future changes in real income have moved together in the aggregate and have shifted the aggregate consumption function. Professor Hansen cites the start of the Korean War as an example of how a decrease in real-income expectations owing to an expected price increase can lead to an increase in consumption as a ratio of current income.[9] A decrease in anticipated real income because of expected inflation can therefore induce more current consumption. (The reverse happened—people saved more during the inflationary recession of 1969–70.)

Even though Keynes allowed for anticipated inflation, he wrote most of the *General Theory* as though prices were constant (not a bad approximation of reality in the mid-1930's). It was left for post-Keynesian economists to pick up this thread in more recent years. We will reconsider anticipated or ex ante inflation in Chapter 13.

The Subjective Factors

Given the objective factors above, certain subjective or psychological factors then determine the position and shape of the consumption function. Although a list of motives to consume, such as enjoyment and ostentation, are mentioned in the *General Theory*, emphasis is placed on motives to save; that is, on psychological motives to refrain from consuming. This is probably because Keynes, like the neoclassicists, felt that consumption was somehow more normal than saving; therefore, for saving to take place, the urge to consume would be curbed by motives to save. The subjective motives prevent us from consuming all our income and, therefore, require that the value of the MPC must fall between zero and 1. A list of the subjective motives follows:

1. *Precaution*—to build a reserve to protect against unforeseen events.
2. *Foresight*—to provide for future expected needs, such as children's education or income during one's old age.
3. *Calculation*—or, as the neoclassicists would have called it, time preference, to provide for larger future income through earning interest. But unlike the neoclassicists, Keynes felt that normal, small changes in the interest rate would not substantially affect how much was saved for this motive.
4. *Improvement*—to save now to fulfill the common desire for an improved level of living in the future, even though the capacity for enjoyment may be diminishing.
5. *Independence*—to enjoy the freedom not to be subject to control by others.
6. *Enterprise*—to provide a fund for speculation or investment.

---

[8]Until now, the relationship has been between consumption and disposable income. However, in this section we must relate consumption to one of the other national-income accounting aggregates such as NNP in order to allow for changes in taxes. Which income aggregate is most appropriate depends on which tax is considered. NNP includes all taxes.

[9]Hansen, *Guide to Keynes*, p. 83.

7. *Bequest*—a motive that Keynes called *pride;* simply the desire to leave something to future generations.
8. *Avarice*—to satisfy greed or cupidity.

Similarly, Keynes offered a list of analogous motives that would apply to the savings of businesses, governments, or other institutions. Even though they were not emphasized in the *General Theory*, business savings in recent years have grown to about three times the size of household savings and therefor are important.

Keynes pointed out that the strength of both personal and business motives to save are determined by certain underlying factors. Specifically, these are the following:

1. Economic institutions
2. Habits formed by social-group pressures
3. The expectations and experiences of the members of the society
4. Available capital and the state of technology
5. The distribution of wealth
6. The average standard of living

In general, the subjective motives and their underlying factors change only slowly over time and may therefore be ignored in short-period analysis. The objective factors are not apt to be important under ordinary circumstances, according to Keynes, because it is improbable that windfall gains or losses, for example, would occur simultaneously to enough people to cause a noticeable shift in the consumption function; and since they can operate in either direction, they may cancel each other out. Therefore, since the objective factors are apt to be of secondary importance or to cancel out, and the subjective motives and their underlying factors change only over a long period of time, he concluded that the most significant determinant of consumption in the short run is disposable income.

Additional Short-Run Consumption Motives

Post-Keynesian economists have supplemented the list of consumption motives offered by Keynes, especially regarding the relationship between the long- and short-run consumption function (discussed in the Appendix to this chapter). The objective, nonincome short-run determinants of consumption have been reexamined. Certain post-Keynesians have given wealth (the stock of assets as distinct from the flow of income) an increased role in determining consumption levels. For example, immediate post–World War II consumption demonstrated a wealth effect. Potential consumer demand was pent up during the war years of scarcity, while liquid wealth and total wealth from accumulated savings increased far beyond the desired level by years of high earnings and unavailable goods. As a result, the consumption function increased sharply immediately after the war. The demand for consumer durables was particularly affected, since their supply was especially restricted during the war. However, there is no agreement as to whether the shift was due primarily to pent-up demand, increased wealth, or greater liquidity.

Although pent-up demand is a wartime phenomenon, the concept has wider implications. The demand for durable goods depends partly on consumer stocks of durables. Since accumulated stocks of durable goods reduce the current demand, their effect is the obverse of the pent-up-demand theory. However, the effect of regular increases of consumer durables is probably not great, since (1) they wear out at an even rate, (2) the standard of living is continually increasing, and (3) product improvement maintains demand through obsolescence. Only in unusual years following a period of greater-than-usual purchases of consumer durables should "reverse pent-up demand" noticeably reduce the consumption function.

Returning to the wealth effect mentioned on page 239, there is little doubt that a wealthy person may spend more than a person without wealth, if the two have the same income,[10] but whether a change in aggregate wealth has any significant shortrun impact on consumption is not clear from the data. However, in discussing the consumption function, Keynes suggests that "the consumption of the wealth-owning class may be extremely susceptible to unforeseen changes in the money-value of its wealth. This should be classified amongst the major factors capable of causing short-period changes in the propensity to consume."[11]

Based on observations such as that, a second "psychological law," the *windfall effect*, has been inferred from the *General Theory* by Axel Leijonhufvud.[12] As noted above, Keynes specifically allowed for the effect of wealth on consumption, suggesting that wealthy people spend more out of a given income than do those without wealth. Lower interest rates mean higher market values of bonds; the resulting increase in bondholders' wealth causes an upward shift in the consumption function. However, at each point in time the level of the interest rate is fixed, so the consumer's wealth will be determined and the effect of wealth on consumption taken into account, in the shape and position of the consumption function. Therefore, the consumption function is still a function of income as long as the interest rate remains constant. Over time, however, interest rates will fluctuate; lower interest rates will increase the consumption function, the higher interest rates will reduce it. To take a recent example, the decrease in the consumption function during the 1969–71 recession may have been due in part to the record-high interest rates during those years that significantly reduced the current market values of fixed income securities. The high interest rates may also have been responsible for the depressed prices of listed stocks. (Note that an increase in the interest rate, while reducing wealth, increases the return on current savings.)

---

[10]E. g., suppose two households each receive $10,000 income in a given year, but family A has a bank-account balance of $10 and family B has $100,000. Family B will probably spend a larger proportion of its $10,000 income. The point is that income and wealth are two different things, and each affects consumption differently.

[11]Keynes, *General Theory*, p. 92–93.

[12]Axel Leijonhufvud, "Keynes and the Keynesians: A Suggested Interpretation," *American Economic Review*, 57 (May 1967), 406. ———, *On Keynesian Economics and the Economics of Keynes* (New York: Oxford University Press, 1968), pp. 190–95.

Easily available consumer credit probably influences consumption through a perversion of the "second psychological law," as consumers find themselves able to tap the accumulated wealth of lenders. The advertising and promotion of certain credit-card companies and other consumer-credit companies is designed to make the consumer feel that he has large amounts of wealth at his disposal and that he should live as the wealthy live. However, consumer credit must be repaid over time, so this factor should not affect consumption except temporarily, when a change occurs in the size of down payments, the length of the repayment period, the credit standards (ease of obtaining credit), or the cost of consumer credit.

Another postwar nonincome variable affecting consumption patterns is changes in the size or compositon of the population. The larger proportion of young families since World War II may have increased consumption, especially of durables. Any such change in the age distribution of consumers will cause a change in consumption patterns, because both the young and old are typically dissavers, but the middle-aged group normally saves. The recent decline in birth rates during the last couple of years may have been in part responsible, along with the windfall effect and possible anticipation of reduced income or job loss, for the decrease in the consumption function from 1969–71. But, the age distribution or size of the population should change only slowly over time and may generally be disregarded in a typical short-run period.

Despite efforts to relate consumption to nonincome variables, consumption over a ten-year period appears more closely related to disposable income than to any other factor. However, the relevant time period for consumption decisions stretches over more than the immediate present; therefore, in any very short time period, consumption and income may appear unrelated. The objective factors, both Keynesian and post-Keynesian, may be important in any short period but will balance out or be predictable over a longer time. Thus, despite changes in the subjective and objective factors, it is easier to predict consumption for the next ten years than for the coming week.

If we have established that consumption is functionally related to income, can we generalize on the income-elasticity of the aggregate consumption function? Yes; we may use the same technique employed in Chapter 2 to discover the degree of elasticity of Engel curves, as in Figure 2-9. However, the axes for the dependent and independent variables have been reversed in the case of the consumption function; so the typical individual or aggregate consumption function, such as those pictured in Figures 8-2 and 8-3, is relatively inelastic. The inelasticity is indicated by the positive intersection of the function with the y-axis along which the dependent variable—consumption—is measured. The higher the value of the vertical-axis intercept, the less income-elastic the consumption function. And if the consumption function did exhibit a decreasing slope as income increased (as Keynes suggested), one would have to conclude that generally the consumption function would become increasingly inelastic, as one could demonstrate because lines drawn tangent to such a curved consumption function would intersect the consumption axis at constantly higher points.

Assume a simple model involving production and consumption, with no government sector, no foreign trade, and no business savings or transfer payments. Under these simplifying conditions, we can speak simply of aggregate income as net national product, since net national product, national income, personal income, and disposable income will all be equal. Under these conditions, households can either consume or save out of their disposable income. Net national product is equal to consumption plus net investment. If net national product and disposable income are equal, savings equals investment.

The model may be stated algebraically:

$$C + S = Y_d$$
$$C + I = Y$$
$$S = I$$

where

$$Y = Y_d$$
$$Y_d = \text{disposable income}$$
$$Y = \text{net national product}$$

The amounts *actually* saved and *actually* invested (ex post savings and investment) must be equal by definition, but they are not necessarily in equilibrium. Only when *planned* saving equals *planned* investment (or ex ante savings equals ex ante investment) can we say that the economy is in equilibrium, since there will then be no built-in tendency to change either planned or realized savings or investment. A simple model to determine equilibrium levels of employment and income can be constructed on the assumption that investment plans are independent of income; so investment expenditures will remain constant at all levels of income. (Note that when investment is a function of the interest rate we refer to it as investment demand, but when it is a function of income we refer to it as investment expenditures.) In any given brief time period, investment plans will be firm and funds allocated so that existing commitments cannot be avoided. Realistically, considerable time is required to implement much new investment. Therefore, the assumption that investment expenditures remain constant for any given brief time period is not altogether unrealistic.

However, the fact that each firm's investment plans may be frozen at any point in time does not prevent aggregate investment from being more volatile than aggregate consumption. Over just a few months, enough firms normally complete their investment commitments to allow a dramatic fall in aggregate investment expenditures, if economic conditions warrant. Similarly, a few months allows sufficient time for enough firms to develop new investment plans so that aggregate investment can increase sharply, if conditions indicate firms should expand.

The model is described in Table 8-2 and shown graphically in Figures 8-4 and 8-5. Columns 1 and 2 of Table 8-2, and Figure 8-4, relate net national product to employment, embodying the concept of diminishing returns discussed in Chapters 3 and 6.[13] Increasingly large amounts of employment are required to give constant increases in output. Columns 2 and 3 of Table 8-2

TABLE 8-2 Effective Demand and Equilibrium ($ in billions)

(1)	(2)	(3)	(4)	(5)	(6)	(7)
Employment in Millions (N)	*Net National Product (NNP)*	*Consumption (C)*	*Savings (S)*	*Planned Investment (I)*	*Effective Demand (C + I)*	*Tendency of Employment and Income*
0	$ 0	$ 50	$−50	$70	$120	Increase
8	100	130	−30	70	200	Increase
17	200	210	−10	70	280	Increase
27	300	290	10	70	360	Increase
38	400	370	30	70	440	Increase
50	500	450	50	70	520	Increase
63	600	530	70	70	600	Equilibrium
77	700	610	90	70	680	Decrease
92	800	690	110	70	760	Decrease
109	900	770	130	70	840	Decrease
137	1,000	850	150	70	920	Decrease

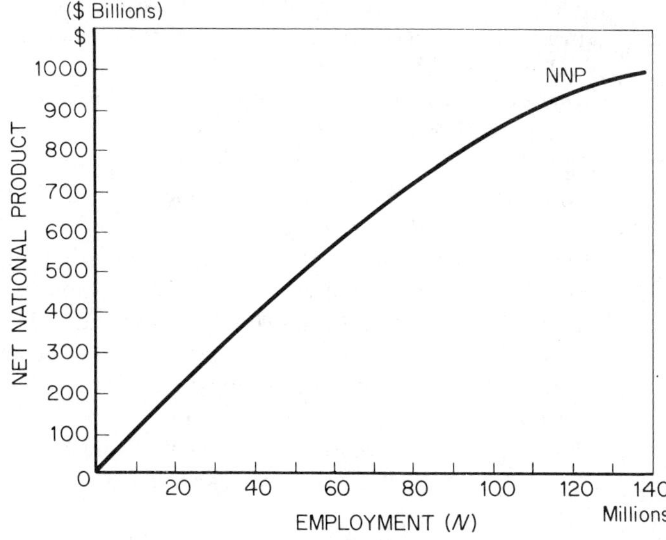

FIG. 8-4 Employment of Labor As a Function of Net National Product

[13]For simplicity, increasing returns in the earliest stages of production have been omitted.

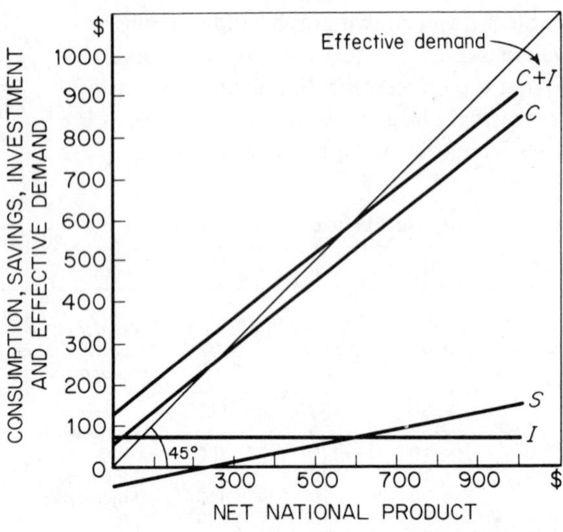

FIG. 8-5 Effective Demand and Equilibrium ($ Billions)

describe the Keynesian short-run consumption function; columns 2 and 4 describe the savings function. Note that savings plus consumption are equal to net national product at all levels. This is the same consumption function already described in Table 8-1 and Figure 8-3. Column 5 shows the constant level of planned investment expenditures, and Column 6 shows effective demand—that is, consumption plus planned investment expenditures.

Some writers use "effective demand" and "aggregate demand" synonymously. We prefer to use "effective demand" to refer to consumption, planned investment expenditures, and government spending (omitted in this chapter) as a function of aggregate income or output at constant prices, and to reserve "aggregate demand" to refer to aggregate expenditure as a function of the price level. Aggregate demand looks like a normal demand curve, while effective demand is more closely related to the Engel curve.

Equilibrium income occurs where effective demand equals net national product; that is, where savings equal planned investment expenditures. The relationships among net national product, consumption, savings, and investment expenditures may also be seen in Figure 8-5, where effective demand $C + I$ crosses the 45° line at the same income level where $S = I$.[14] Only at

[14]The 45° reference line, which some authors designate as an effective-supply function, differs from the effective-supply function envisioned by Keynes in the *General Theory*. However, the line emphasizes the importance of consumption and investment, and is a useful device for determining equilibrium. Keynes's effective-supply function, Z, was defined as the expected cost plus profits that would just cause a certain number of workers to be hired. Such a function might not be linear or might not have a slope of 1. Furthermore, Keynes related effective supply and demand to employment rather than to real income.

that level of aggregate income will effective demand plotted along the y-axis equal net national product plotted along the x-axis. Only at equilibrium will there be no tendency for any of the relevant variables to change.

To illustrate how equilibrium is achieved, assume that the economy finds itself at some other level of net national product, such as \$900 billion. At that level of income, consumption plus planned investment expenditures would equal a level of total effective demand of only \$840 billion. Production exceeds effective demand, causing an unplanned inventory accumulation (or unexpected ex post investment) of \$60 billion. This unplanned increase in inventory investment will lead to a decrease in production in a future time period as firms reduce their purchases for inventory, and net national product will continue to shrink until equilibrium is achieved. To consider this from a different viewpoint, at a net national product of \$900 billion, savings exceeds planned investment expenditures by \$60 billion. Consequently, an unintended investment in inventory of \$60 billion must occur to equate ex post savings and investment. Realized savings and investment will always be equal in an accounting sense, even though they may not be in equilibrium in the sense that the *desired* (ex ante) level of investment expenditure is achieved.[15] This adjustment process will also work in reverse to restore equilibrium when planned investment expenditures exceed actual savings. Only when ex post and ex ante savings and investment are all equal is the economy in equilibrium.

Alternatively, this tendency of the economy to seek equilibrium can be shown algebraically. As previously pointed out,

$$C = a + bY, \text{ and}$$
$$Y = C + I$$

where a is the point where consumption crosses the vertical axis; that is, a equals autonomous consumption spending at zero income, and b is the marginal propensity to consume. Substituting the information in Table 8-2 into the formula, we have

$$C = 50 + .80Y, \text{ and}$$
$$I = 70$$

Substituting these numerical values into the equation $Y = C + I$ gives $50 + .80Y + 70$. Combining all Y terms gives us

$$Y - .80Y = 50 + 70$$

However, since real income and employment are functionally related, the substitution is permissible. Incidentally, the whole graphical presentation of the *General Theory* was devised by post-Keynesian writers.

[15]In our example we have assumed that investment will adjust to match savings, but in reality the plans of both investors and savers may be thwarted by a disequilibrium level of income, so consequently, adjustments may occur either in savings or investment or both when income is in disequilibrium.

Factoring out the Y term gives

$$Y(1 - .80) = 50 + 70$$

Combining terms and dividing both sides of the equation by $(1 - .80)$ shows that $Y = 600$, the equilibrium level of income. This process can be written

$$Y = \frac{a + I}{1 - b}$$

where a and I are exogenous—that is, determined outside the system.

Unfortunately, algebraic illustrations such as this may obscure the fact that while the economy will tend toward equilibrium, it may actually never achieve it. A continuous overcorrection could occur, with inventories continually fluctuating around the desired level. However, the significant fact is that the economy will tend toward equilibrium.

The typical profit-motivated economic man of the neoclassical system could both save and invest, as we have shown in Chapter 6. In contrast, Keynes argued that saving and investing are normally undertaken by different groups of people and for different motives. Savers are for the most part consumers who want security, liquidity, and future income. Investors want output, sales, profits, and growth. In the neoclassical system, the interest rate maintained economic equilibrium by equating savings and investment. In the Keynesian system, however, savers are only weakly motivated by interest-rate changes, so equilibrium is achieved by the attempts to bring planned savings and investment into line. Therefore, the Keynesian system differs from that of the neoclassicists discussed in Chapter 6; for Keynes,

$$S = f_{10}(Y)$$

while for the neoclassicists,

$$S = f_9(i)$$

THE MULTIPLIER

In order to link changes in income with changes in investment, Keynes developed the concept of the investment multiplier, which he denoted k after R. F. Kahn, who first introduced the concept of a multiplier in 1931.[16] (It is

---

[16] R. F. Kahn, "The Relation of Home Investment to Unemployment," *Economic Journal*, 41 (June 1931), 173–98.

Multiplier-like concepts have been bandied about in economic literature since at least 1662, when Sir William Petty wrote, regarding too little money in circulation, "The mischief thereof would be the doing of less work, which is the same as lessening the people, or their art or industry; for a hundred pounds passing a hundred hands for wages, causes a 10,000 pounds worth of commodities to be produced, which hands would have been idle and useless had there not been this continual motive to their employment." Sir William Petty, unfortunate that Keynes used the same symbol for the multiplier that the Cambridge group used to designate cash balances.)

As the term *multiplier* implies, changes in investment are multiplied by the value of k to determine resulting changes in aggregate income. Thus,

$$\Delta Y = k \times \Delta I$$

The multiplier operates on *changes* in investment (or other exogenous sources of spending), because each additional dollar spent will be partly respent according to the individual income-receiver's marginal propensity to consume, and partly leaked out of the spending stream according to his marginal propensity to save.

Since savings and investment depend on different variables, an increase in savings will not, of itself, induce additional investment, so the increments to savings are a leakage out of the stream.[17] Therefore, the greater the proportion of savings out of income, the lower the multiplier. However, consumption expenditures necessarily become part of someone's income, and so the added consumption expenditures increase aggregate income.

To illustrate, assume that an additional $10 billion of investment is introduced into the economy in a given month and that the income received in one time period will be spent in the following period. Table 8-3 shows the effect on aggregate income of this $10 billion increase in investment on the assumption that the MPC is .80. January's consumption increases by $8 billion, out of the increase in investment of $10 billion, which in turn increases income by $8 billion in February with a corresponding $6.4 billion additional consumption. The additional consumption in February in turn leads to $6.4 billion more income in March. Thus the increase in consumption expenditures by those whose income has increased during a given month becomes increased income of those who sell and produce the goods during the succeeding month. Ultimately, the final round of new spending approaches zero, at which point the total incremental income derived from the initial $10 billion investment (including the original $10 billion) approaches $50 billion, with $40 billion going to consumption and $10 billion to savings.[18]

The multiplier, k, is $1/(1 - \text{MPC})$, which is $1/\text{MPS}$ or $1/(1 - b)$. If the MPC is .75, then the multiplier would equal 4, or if the MPC equals .8, the multiplier would be 5. Using the data of Table 8-2 the derivation of the multiplier can be summarized as follows:[19]

"A Treatise of Taxes and Contributions," reprinted in Arthur Eli Monroe, ed., *Early Economic Thought* (Cambridge: Harvard University Press, 1948), p. 205.

Some today might quibble that Petty had confused the stock of money with the flow of spending, but without doubt the germ of a multiplier concept is present.

[17]Realistically, a number of leakages besides savings must be considered, especially the effect of various taxes, in determining the final value of the multiplier.

[18]Since the slope of the consumption function has 1 as its upper limit, the multiplier will work out as an infinite convergent geometric series.

[19]Alternatively, the multiplier (k) can be derived as follows: Let k be the factor by

1. $C = a + bY$	$C = 50 + .80(Y)$
2. $Y = C + I$	$Y = C + 70$
3. $Y = a + bY + I$	$Y = 50 + .80(Y) + 70$
4. $Y - bY = a + I$	$Y - .80Y = 50 + 70$
5. $Y(1 - b) = a + I$	$Y(1 - .80) = 50 + 70$
6. $Y = \frac{1}{1-b}(a + I)$	$Y = \frac{1}{1 - .80}(120)$

where, by definition,

7. $k = \frac{1}{1-b}$	$k = \frac{1}{.20} = 5$

The multiplier times the value of the exogenous spending flows determines the equilibrium level of income. Applied to the illustration above,

$$6(a)\; Y = k(a + I) \qquad Y = 5(120) = 600$$

The larger the MPC, the larger the multiplier. However, a smaller multiplier will require fewer time periods to make most of its impact felt.

Regardless of its size, the multiplier times any given change in investment spending will determine the final effect on equilibrium income. There is a direct relationship between the multiplier and income velocity; money must change hands for a round of income to be generated, and this circulation of money affects income velocity. Thus, when income increases, income velocity must also increase proportionately; otherwise, the equation of exchange would not be satisfied. Therefore, when Y increases, V increases, so that

---

which a change in investment (ΔI) is multiplied to determine the resulting change in income (ΔY).

$$Y = C + S, \text{ and}$$
$$Y = C + I$$

Therefore,

$$\Delta Y = \Delta C + \Delta S, \text{ and}$$
$$\Delta Y = \Delta C + \Delta I$$

By definition,

$$k = \frac{\Delta Y}{\Delta I}$$

and

$$\Delta I = \Delta Y - \Delta C$$

So,

$$k = \frac{\Delta Y}{\Delta Y - \Delta C}$$

and

$$k = \frac{\Delta Y/\Delta Y}{\Delta Y/\Delta Y - \Delta C/\Delta Y}$$

or

$$k = \frac{1}{1 - \Delta C/\Delta Y}$$

However, $\Delta C/\Delta Y$ is the MPC and $[1 - (\Delta C/\Delta Y)]$ is the MPS; therefore,

$$k = \frac{1}{\text{MPS}}$$

$MV = PY$, assuming M and P remain constant. However, the multiplier effect does not depend on income velocity, but on purchasing power actually changing hands.

A formally correct presentation of Keynes's theory would require an instantaneous multiplier, in which a change in exogenous spending circulates immediately and therefore is immediately translated fully into a change in aggregate income. However, Keynes recognized that another sort of multiplier would obtain in a situation where the initial change in investment was not fully foreseen; the multiplier would produce its full effect only over time (as in the example in Table 8-3). To avoid the analytical difficulties inherent in such a consumption-expenditure lag, Keynes generally assumed that producers and consumers plan accurately as a result of good foresight. Under this assumption, the multiplier works so quickly as to be virtually instantaneous.

In another version, the multiplier is presented tautologically as always and instantaneously true. In this version, the values of all the variables affecting the multiplier are revised in each time period. In Table 8-3, for example, in

TABLE 8-3 Investment-Multiplier Illustration ($ in billions)

Month	*Increase in Aggregate Income* (ΔY)	*Increase in Consumption* (ΔC)	*Increase in Savings* (ΔS)
January	$10	$ 8	$ 2
February	8	6.40	1.60
March	6.40	5.12	1.28
April	5.12	4.10	1.02
May	4.10	3.28	.82
June	3.28	2.62	.66
July	2.62	2.10	.52
August	2.10	1.68	.42
September	1.68	1.34	.34
October	1.34	1.07	.27
November	1.07	.86	.21
December	.86	.69	.17
Total	$46.57	$37.26	$ 9.31
Remaining periods	3.43	2.74	.69
Total	$50.00	$40.00	$10.00

January no one but the first income recipient has had time to adjust either his income or his consumption expenditures to the change in investment. In consequence, it could be maintained that the MPC was zero and consequently the value of the multiplier at that point in time was 1, since only the change in investment was added to net national product. In February, when the first round of consumption takes place, the value of the multiplier becomes 1.8, and so on. Clearly, this tautological version of the multiplier is both necessarily true and analytically useless.

An additional way of handling the instantaneous multiplier is to disregard the elapsed time and simply consider the equilibrium situation before and after some change. This is the generally preferred "comparative-statics" approach to multiplier analysis.

This approach is based on the assumption that the multiplier effect works within a short time. Comparing equilibrium levels of income before and after a change in exogenous spending becomes realistic using comparative statics, since the assumption of perfect foresight can be relaxed. This approach is illustrated by Figure 8-6, in which an increase of $50 billion in investment

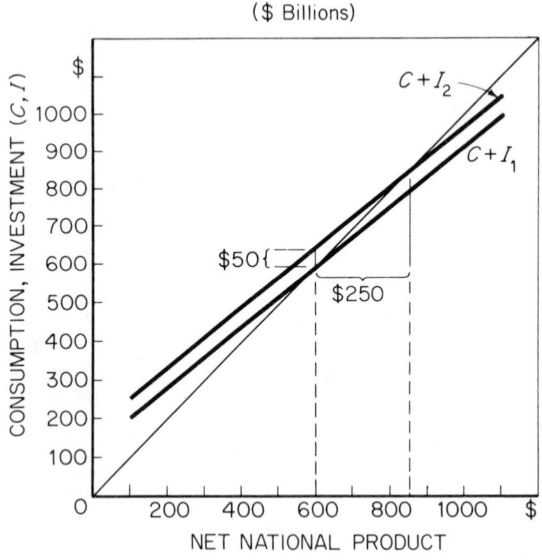

FIG. 8-6 The Multiplier—Comparative Statics ($ Billions)

expenditure results in a $250 billion increase in net national product when investment expenditures shift from I_1 to I_2. Since the value of the marginal propensity to consume is automatically built into the model, some early critics of Keynes claimed that the comparative-statics version of the theory was no better than the tautological instantaneous version.

Despite the confusion caused by the various versions of the multiplier, the consumption function on which the multiplier is based is an *a priori* theory of human behavior and the multiplier is a concept that must be valid over time if the consumption function is valid. As Ackley has pointed out,

> It would have been far better if Keynes had been content to state the multiplier as a relationship which should hold approximately, and over periods of time long enough that consumption and income might be presumed to have adjusted fully to new conditions.[20]

[20]G. Ackley, *Macroeconomic Theory* (New York: Macmillan, 1961), p. 315.

The multiplier effect of a change in investment will be quite different depending on whether the change is permanent or temporary. Figure 8-6 demonstrates the equilibrium positions before and after a permanent increase in the level of investment. Since investment is a flow variable and not a stock, the new, higher equilibrium level can be maintained only if the additional investment is repeated in each time period. Once the new equilibrium level of income is achieved, it will be maintained as long as investment remains constant at the new level.

Based on a multiplier of 5, Table 8-4 shows that a $10 billion additional

TABLE 8-4 The Multiplier Over Time ($ in Billions)

Time Period	T_0	T_1	T_2	T_3	T_4	T_5	. . .	T_n
Δ Investment	$10	$10	$10	$10	$10	$10	. . .	$10
Resulting Δ consumption		8	8	8	8	8	. . .	8
"			6.4	6.4	6.4	6.4	. . .	6.4
"				5.12	5.12	5.12	. . .	5.12
"					4.1	4.1	. . .	4.1
"						3.28	. . .	3.28
"							. . .	2.62
								—
"								0
Resulting Δ income per time period	10	18	24.4	29.52	33.62	36.9	. . .	50.0

investment must be repeated in each time period for the $50 billion increase in net national product to be achieved. In the initial period, T_0, when the $10 billion increase in investment was first experienced, aggregate income increased by only $10 billion, whereas in period T_1, it increased by $18 billion: $10 billion new investment plus $8 billion consumption out of the T_0 investment. By period T_5, over 70 percent of the full multiplier effect will be achieved, and the process will continue until time period T_n, when the full multiplier effect of 5 times the $10 billion change in investment has taken place.

The early New Deal writers suggested that "pump priming"—a one-time injection of government expenditure—would cure the Depression. However, if the increase in investment had been only temporary—if, for example, the investment had been increased only in period T_0 by $10 billion—then aggregate income will be increased by $10 billion in period T_0 but only by $8 billion in T_1, $6.4 billion in T_2, and so on until by period T_n the increases in aggregate income will have returned to zero and the net national product itself will have returned to its previous equilibrium level. The sum of all the increments in aggregate income from the one-shot increase in investment will together total $50 billion. But the effect will be a disappearing multiplier, with the increments in aggregate income becoming continually smaller. Time period by time period, the changes in aggregate income from a one-time investment expenditure will never exceed the initial $10 billion investment and will become smaller and smaller until they eventually become zero and the old equilibrium aggregate-income level is restored.

Qualifications to the Multiplier

Although our discussion has been in terms of increasing levels of equilibrium aggregate income because of increased investment spending, the multiplier will also work in reverse to decrease aggregate income. In our example above, if the $10 billion change in investment had been a reduction rather than an increase, the result would still have been a $50 billion change in aggregate income; however, the change would have been a decrease rather than an increase.

Furthermore, the multiplier will work on any new spending, regardless of its source. A shift upward in the consumption function, holding the marginal propensity to consume constant, will also result in a multiple expansion of equilibrium aggregate income, as will an increase in government spending or an increased export trade balance.

In the *General Theory*, Keynes noted certain qualifications to the multiplier.[21]

1. Clearly anticipating one of the more important post-Keynesian modifications of the *General Theory*, Keynes observed that the value of the multiplier may be affected by changes in the interest rate that are due to changes in investment expenditures or fiscal policy (government spending or taxing). For example, an increase in investment spending would probably raise the interest rate, thus retarding investment.
2. In addition, an increased cost of capital goods could reduce expected rate of return, which would reduce investment and so reduce the effective value of the multiplier.
3. A reduction in the general level of business confidence owing to increasing government expenditures is a third possible source of change in the multiplier, since a decrease in confidence may be associated with increased liquidity preference or a reduction in private investment. The failure of private investment to increase in the wake of increased government spending in the 1930's was probably due to such a failure of confidence.
4. Finally, Keynes assumed for simplicity a closed economy. However, he noted that opening the economy to foreign trade will reduce the value of the multiplier through expenditures on imports, which are another leakage out of the domestic spending stream and have the same effect on the multiplier as savings.

Although all the qualifications above are in the *General Theory*, they are sometimes overlooked by friends and critics alike. However, qualifications of this sort have been incorporated in some of the more recent developments of macro theory.

---

[21] Keynes, *General Theory*, p. 119–22.

FULL EMPLOYMENT AND EQUILIBRIUM INCOME

Unlike that of the neoclassical economists, who felt that there was a natural tendency toward full-employment levels of income, Keynesian theory implies no reason for equilibrium income to occur at full employment. Full employment and equilibrium income could coincide, but it would be accidental. For example, in Table 8-2, equilibrium occurred at a net national product of $600 billion, which coincided with an employment level of 63 million. If there happened to be 63 million people willing and able to work in the economy at that time, then that level of aggregate income would support full employment. However, if there were 77 million people looking for work, then the level of net national product would be too low to support full employment; $700 billion aggregate income would be required.

If 63 million people are willing and able to work, the effective demand function $C + I_2$ in Figure 8-7 would provide the level of net national product necessary for full employment. If effective demand falls below this level—for example, to $C + I_1$—through a $20 billion decrease in investment, the result-

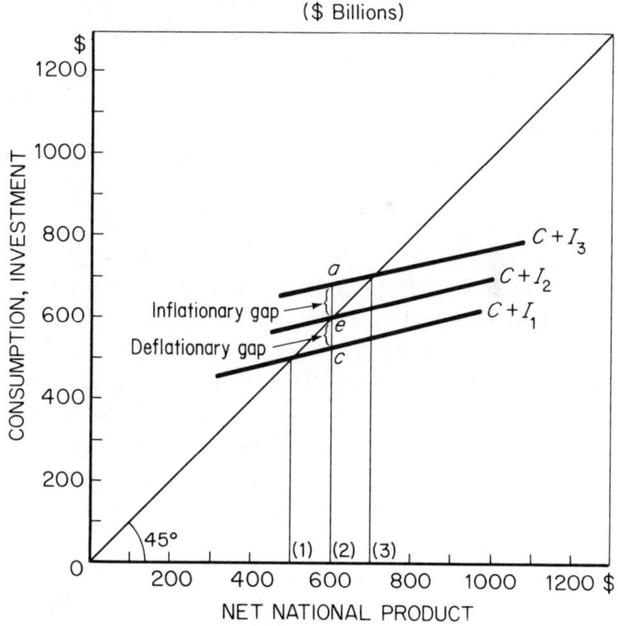

FIG. 8-7 Inflationary and Deflationary Gaps ($ Billions)

ing reverse multipler effect would reduce equilibrium income by $100 billion and cause the unemployment of 13 million workers. In this case, the full-employment level of demand is deficient by $20 billion, represented by the gap from *e* to *c* in Figure 8-7. Such a deficiency of effective demand is commonly called a *deflationary gap*. This deflationary gap of $20 billion, times the multiplier of 5, causes a $100 billion difference between the equilibrium and the full-employment levels of net national product.

Similarly, a $20 billion increase in investment would shift effective demand from $C + I_2$ to $C + I_3$. This initial increase in investment of $20 billion, represented by the gap from *a* to *e* in Figure 8-7, cannot cause increased real output, since the economy was already operating at full employment. Therefore, the equilibrium aggregate income of $700 billion could not be achieved unless an additional 14 million workers enter the work force. The excess demand represented by the difference between *a* and *e* is commonly called the *inflationary gap*, since it causes inflationary pressure in the economy (that is, a level of demand for goods and services in excess of what the economy can supply at full employment). The inflationary gap will not lead to equilibrium but will induce an inflationary spiral. The excess of effective demand over full-employment output will cause higher prices, which in turn will increase the money incomes of suppliers, causing a further upward shift in money demand. Unless restrained by monetary factors, this inflationary spiral will continue until something occurs to reduce real consumption or real investment demand.

The inflationary gap was introduced by Keynes in the *General Theory* and then developed in an article he wrote in 1939.[22] By 1939, he was warning a world approaching another war crisis against repeating the post–World War I experience, when inflation in Austria and Germany was stopped only by complete economic collapse. In marked contrast to the sad post–World War I experience, the concept of the inflationary gap helped governments after World War II to control the rate of inflation through the proper use of monetary and fiscal policies.

To reiterate the major assumption underlying the analysis of all the basic Keynesian chapters (7, 8, 9, and 10) is that the price level is assumed to remain constant. Therefore, we are able to show the effect of the deflationary gap in Figure 8-7 as a decrease in net national product, but we cannot show the effect of the inflationary gap in the figure as an increase in net national product, because there is no way for real NNP to be increased above the full-employment level. In Chapter 12, we will introduce changes in the price level as a variable in the Keynesian and post-Keynesian analysis.

In trying to correct a deflationary gap, an economy with unemployment and a given amount of investment can be in one of the two situations shown in Figure 8-8. Panels A and B both show economies far from full employment equilibrium because of a low level of investment and average propensity to

---

[22] J. M. Keynes, "The Income and Fiscal Potential of Great Britain," *Economic Journal*, 49 (December 1939), 626–39.

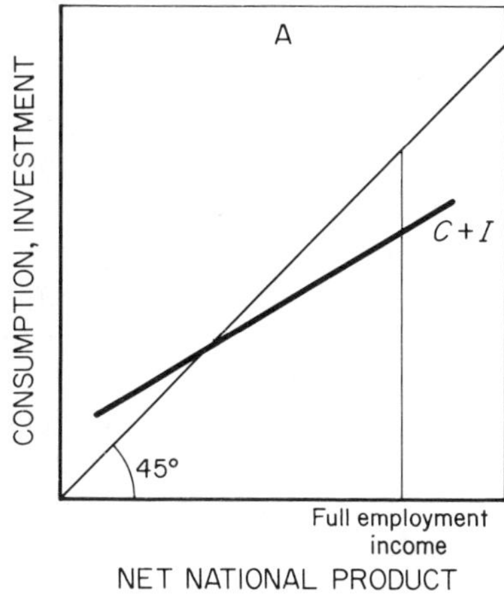

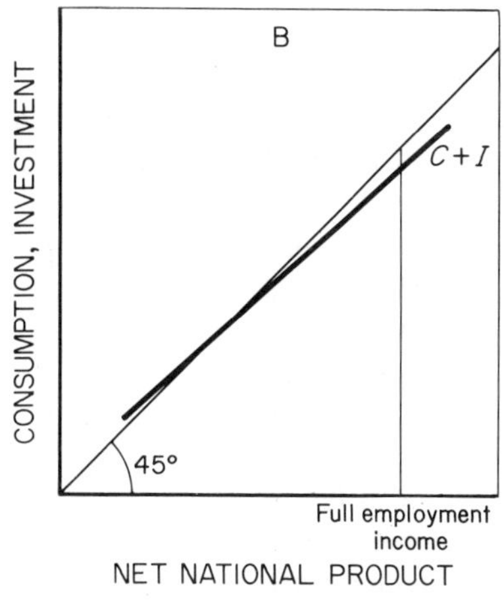

FIG. 8-8 Two Deflationary Gaps

consume (APC). However, because they have different marginal propensities to consume (MPC), the two economies are in quite different situations. Economy A will require a far greater increase than B in either investment or the level of the consumption function to reach full employment, since it has a low MPC and consequently a small multiplier. Because the multiplier is reversible, a small decrease in investment or drop in the APC with the MPC constant will cause a much greater reduction in net national product and consequently a greater reduction in employment in B with its high MPC than in A. Consequently, an economy with a higher MPC is more vulnerable to recession and less stable than an economy with a low MPC, while at the same time it is better able to fill a deflationary gap.

SUMMARY AND CONCLUSIONS

This chapter has continued our discussion of the Keynesian tool chest by developing the concepts of the consumption and savings functions and the multiplier. In turn, these concepts are used to demonstrate equilibrium and disequilibrium levels of aggregate income at various levels of employment.

In the Keynesian system, consumption and savings in the aggregate are essentially functions of aggregate income, rather than of the interest rate as in the neoclassical system. Another distinction between the two systems is that Keynes argued that equilibrium income need not provide full employment. Even though the *General Theory* has been called "depression economics," the possibility of an inflationary gap as well as a deflationary gap indicates that it is more general than some of its critics would allow.

In its simplest form, consumption can be directly related to income. The effect on aggregate income of any incremental spending can be calculated by means of the multiplier, which is derived from the consumption function.

Keynes was careful to qualify his multiplier analysis in various ways that opened up fruitful lines of further inquiry.

Keynes based the consumption function on a number of objective and subjective factors that determine its level and slope. However, the subjective factors change slowly enough to be disregarded in the short run, and the objective factors are generally of secondary importance or tend to cancel each other out. Consequently, the Keynesian consumption function is basically a function of aggregate income in the short run, especially during periods when the nonincome determinants are stable. (Some modifications to the Keynesian consumption function are presented in the Appendix to this chapter.)

Windfall changes in wealth could cause major shifts in the consumption function, especially for the wealth-owning class, and such windfall changes can be induced by changes in the interest rate. Leijonhufvud proposed this windfall effect as a "second psychological law" determining the level of consumption.

The distinction between the APC and the MPC is particularly significant for multiplier analysis, since the value of the multiplier is directly related to the size of the MPC. In turn, the APC determines the *y*-axis intercept of the consumption function, which is one source of autonomous spending. And autonomous spending times the multiplier determines the equilibrium income level. However, a stable, new equilibrium requires a permanent, not temporary or one-time, change in spending.

Consumption and savings are only half the story on the real (nonmonetary) side of the economy. In this chapter, we assumed a constant level of investment. The following chapter will complete the real side of the economy by introducing the variables that affect the market for investment goods.

QUESTIONS AND PROBLEMS

1. In what way is the Keynesian consumption function similar to the Engel curve?
2. What is Keynes's "fundamental psychological law"?
3. Why did Keynes apparently give little weight to the subjective factors behind the consumption function?
4. Explain the fallacy in "pump priming."
5. Describe the multiplier as a tautology and as a behavioral theory.
6. How does the economy respond to an inflationary gap?
7. Distinguish the MPC from the APC.
8. How is the multiplier related to the MPC?
9. What does Leijonhufvud consider Keynes's "second psychological law"?
10. Suppose planned saving exceeds planned investment. How is equilibrium restored?
11. Plot the consumer's comsumption function from the data below, assuming that:

a. The interest rate is 5 percent.
b. His income varies from \$2,500 to \$5,000 a year, but is expected to remain constant for the 2-year time horizon.
c. The function is linear.

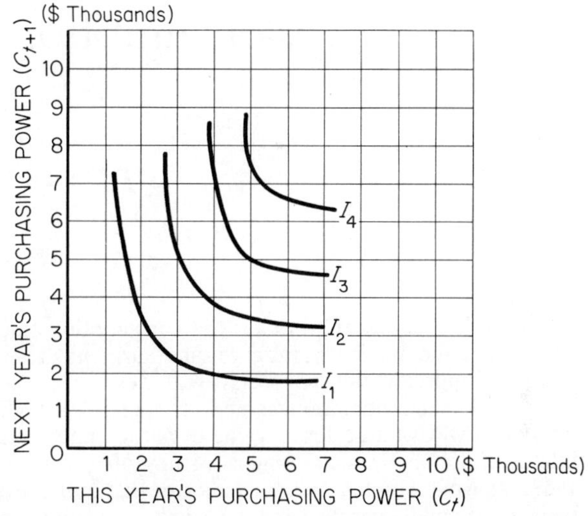

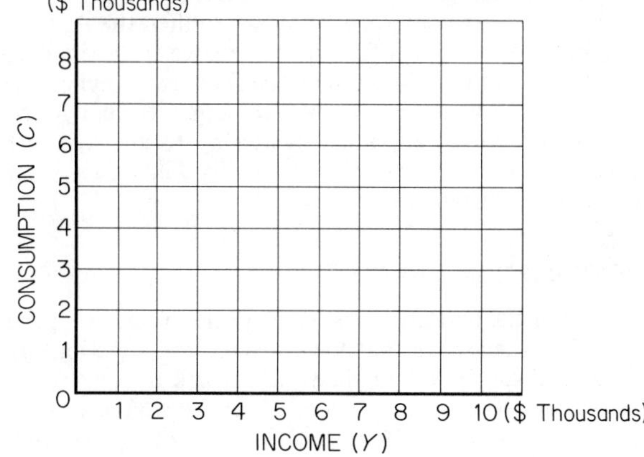

Revising the Keynesian Consumption Function

appendix to chapter 8

Keynes's theoretical work on the consumption function stimulated empirical studies, and the data collected gave some surprising results. One discovery was that periods of approximately ten years revealed consumption patterns like the Keynesian consumption function. Longer periods revealed a higher marginal propensity to consume (MPC) and a lower value of autonomous consumption—*a*, the *Y*—axis intercept. Simon Kuznets' long-run study of consumption patterns from 1869 to 1938, using overlapping decades, indicated that both the MPC and the APC averaged between 84 and 90 percent, and the Y axis intercept equaled zero, if the years of the Great Depression are eliminated.[1] Kuznets' figures are shown in Table 8a-1.

If *a* the Y-axis intercept equals zero then the APC and MPC are equal, and the long-run consumption function emanates from the origin. Therefore the long-run consumption function is unlike the short-run Keynesian consumption function with its positive *a* value for the vertical-axis intercept. Certain ideas were proposed to reconcile the differences discovered by Kuznets, between the long and short-run consumption functions. This Appendix will survey some of the more important of these contributions.

CONSUMPTION DRIFT

One of the first attempts to reconcile the short- and long-run figures was Arthur Smithies' suggestion that the consumption function drifts upward over time even though at any point in time the statistical consumption function resembles the theoretical Keynesian version.[2] Long-run data such as Kuznets' appear to be a single consumption function, whereas the proponents of consumption drift would propose that a whole series of flatter short-run consumption functions lie concealed in the observed long-run data.

Figure 8A-1 demonstrates the consumption drift, with the short-run consumption functions, C_1, C_2, and C_3, cutting through the long-run consumption pattern, C_L. Each short-run consumption function is a theoretical construct showing the relationship of consumption to various levels of disposable income during a time in which the other independent variables remain constant. Each point on the long-run consumption function, C_L, represents an average of all the values included in the

[1]Simon Kuznets, *National Income: A Summary of Findings* (New York: National Bureau of Economic Research, 1946), p. 53.

[2]Arthur Smithies, "Forecasting Post-War Demand: I," *Econometrica*, 13 (January 1945), 1–14.

TABLE 8A-1 Long-Run Income and Consumption

Period	*Aggregate Income* (\$ in billions)	*Consumption* (\$ in billions)	*APC*
1869–78	\$ 9.3	\$ 8.1	.86
1874–83	13.6	11.6	.86
1879–88	17.9	15.3	.85
1884–93	21.0	17.7	.84
1889–98	24.2	20.2	.84
1894–1903	29.8	25.4	.85
1899–1908	37.3	32.3	.86
1903–13	45.0	39.1	.87
1909–18	50.6	44.0	.87
1914–23	57.3	50.7	.89
1919–28	69.0	62.0	.89
1924–33	73.3	68.9	.94
1929–38	72.0	71.0	.99

Sources: Columns 1 and 2: S. Kuznets, *National Product since 1869* (New York: National Bureau of Economic Research, 1946), p. 119. Column 3: Kuznets, *National Income: A Summary of Findings* (New York: National Bureau of Economic Research, 1946), pp. 53 and 32.

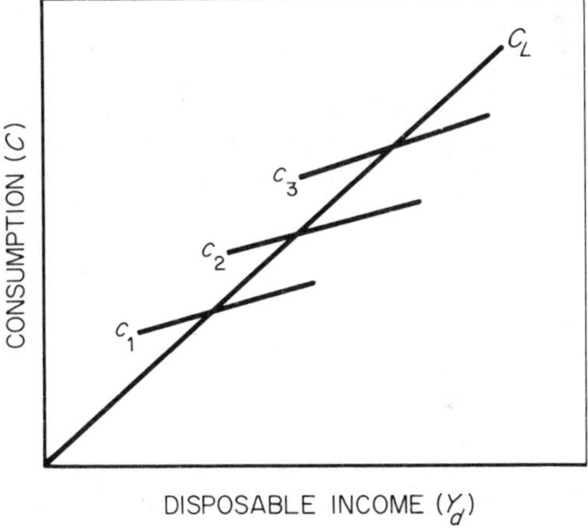

FIG. 8A-1 Consumption Drift

corresponding short-run function, the long-run function itself merely connecting all the average values.

Smithies proposed that the upward drift in the short-run consumption function was just sufficient to match the long-run pattern in the data discovered by Kuznets. Several factors could be responsible for the upward drift in the consumption function: (1) rural-urban migration, (2) redistribution of income in favor of low-income groups, (3) improving the standard of living owing to introduction of new products and product improvement, (4) changing age distribution of the population, (5) a reduction in the motivation to save, (6) availability of credit, and (7) expectations of increasing income.

Regarding the first reason, studies of income and expenditure by occupation and by geographical dispersion reveal that farm and rural families save more of any given income than do urban families. Therefore, one might anticipate that the historical farm-to-city migration would increase the aggregate-consumption function over time.

The second reason suggested for an upward drift in the consumption function is the long-run reduction in income inequality (a tendency existing at the time the theory was proposed, but not since the 1950's). Budget studies have indicated that low-income families tend to consume a much larger proportion of their income than do high-income families. And studies of secular changes in income distribution indicated a tendency toward greater equality of income between the 1920's and 1950's.[3] Consequently, it was inferred that the tendency toward income redistribution in favor of low-income families was another factor in the upward drift of the consumption function.

The standard of living of any society at any given time is partly a function of the consumer's horizon of choice. If there were no development of new commodities or improvements in existing ones, then savings would very likely increase at the margin as incomes increase, because of the diminishing marginal utility from increased consumption of unvarying available goods. However, the introduction of new commodities or product improvements permits current consumption of products that did not previously exist. Therefore, it seems reasonable that this factor will cause the consumption function to shift upward. For example, Shaw related increased consumption of durable goods between 1879 and 1939 to the development of new products such as automotive and electrical goods.[4]

Another important consumption determinant that is independent of income is the average age of the population. Although Smithies himself did not make the point, several proponents of consumption drift maintained in the 1940's that the aggregate-consumption function had increased because of a proportionate decrease in the number of adults in their peak producing years, relative to the number of both younger and older persons. Individuals at both ends of the age distribution consume without producing, since they either have not yet entered the labor force or have retired from it;[5] so they save a smaller proportion of their income than others. Young families also save a smaller proportion of their income because they are raising families, building homes, and acquiring a stock of consumer durables. Such a change in the makeup of the population, then, tends to increase consumption relative to savings, and therefore to cause an upward movement in the consumption function.

In Chapter 8, we dealt with Keynes's list of motives to save and pointed out that in the aggregate those motives would change slowly. One proposed cause of consumption drift is that the psychological motives to save have been weakened over time, causing a proportional increase in consumption relative to saving. One proposed reason for a reduction in the propensity to save would be the decreasing importance of proprietorships and a consequent weakening of Keynes's proposed "enterprise" motive to save. As Kuznets put it, ". . . as the proportion of inde-

---

[3]Simon Kuznets, *Shares of Upper Income Groups in Income and Savings* (New York: National Bureau of Economic Research, 1953), pp. 43–62; and Irving Kravis, *The Structures of Income* (Philadelphia: Wharton School of Finance and Commerce, University of Pennsylvania, 1962), p. 213.

[4]William H. Shaw, *Finished Commodities Since 1879—Occasional Paper No. 3* (New York: National Bureau of Economic Research, 1941), p. 49.

[5]Owing to the lower birthrate during the Depression, the writers in the 1940's felt that the population was aging, whereas at the present time, the World War II baby boom means an increased proportion of young people. However, the data seem to indicate that during the 1940's, the proportion of working-age people actually increased, apparently because of the reduced birthrate of the 1930's and a life expectancy not much beyond retirement age. Because of the baby boom and increased longevity, the data until recently supported the age-distribution thesis—although the current reduction in the birthrate is an ominous sign to those who believe that this factor has been significant in the past.

pendent proprietors of unincorporated businesses declined and that of wage and salary employees rose, there was more exposure to the attractions of a high-level consumption pattern and less drive to save in order to accumulate capital for the expansion of one's own business."[6]

Another suggested reason for a decline in the motive to save out of disposable personal income is the growth of the Social Security system, which makes saving both institutional and automatic, and guarantees income during periods of old age, unemployment, and disability. Such a source of guaranteed income reduces the need to save for Keynes's proposed motives of precaution and foresight; however, for a number of possible reasons, the data do not appear to support this argument. Possibly Social Security stimulated the demand for insurance and pensions by making workers more security-conscious. Longer expected retirement means that more supplementary savings are needed. In addition, the generation of survivors of the Depression seems more security-conscious than either their forebears or their offspring.

The increasing availability and convenience of consumer credit very likely also causes an increase in the consumption function. On the one hand, the availability of short-term credit has skyrocketed in recent years and has simplified the purchase of many consumer goods such as gasoline, lodging, and department-store purchases. The greater ease of buying consumer goods with credit cards and without the need for immediate cash outlay, writing checks, or dealing with credit departments has reduced the disutility or inconvenience of consumer buying. The purchase of expensive consumer durables has been facilitated by the general availability of installment buying. Increasing consumer credit causes an upward drift in the consumption function. But consumer loans must be repaid with interest, so the final effect of any increase in consumer credit remains to be seen.

Finally, referring to item 7 above, average real wages (in constant dollars) of production workers have historically increased about 3.5 percent annually. Consumers who expect to share in future real-income increases may discount their higher future earnings by either reducing their savings or going into debt to increase their present consumption.

The consumption-drift theory represented a major advance in the theory of the consumption function. However, it has one significant shortcoming: The rate of the upward drift appears to be largely a matter of chance. It would be the merest coincidence if the foregoing seven factors (plus an unknown and unnamed number of others) happened to cause the consumption function to increase proportionately as income increases, so that the average of the short-run consumption function would equal a consistent proportion of income. In addition, a former student of Smithies, James Duesenberry, pointed out that all the factors proposed as causes of the upward drift would not have had sufficient force to alter the consumption–savings relationship to a degree that would cause the drift.[7] Furthermore, Duesenberry maintained that many of the proposed causes of the upward drift also had another aspect that would suggest a secular *fall* in the consumption function. For example, increases in contractual saving plans such as life insurance programs tended to increase savings and decrease the consumption function. Duesenberry proposed an alternative to the consumption-drift theory, the consumption ratchet, that he felt remedied its more important defects.[8]

[6]Simon Kuznets, *Uses of National Income in Case of War—Occasional Paper No.* 6 (New York: National Bureau of Economic Research, 1942), p. 11.

[7]James Duesenberry, *Income, Saving, and the Theory of Consumer Behavior* (Cambridge: Harvard University Press, 1952), p. 68.

[8]Ibid., pp. 114–16.

CONSUMPTION RATCHET

One clue to the consumption-ratchet theory may be found in a remark that Keynes made in the *General Theory* regarding consumption patterns over the business cycle:

> [During] . . . the so-called cyclical fluctuations of employment . . . habits, as distinct from more permanent psychological propensities, are not given time enough to adapt themselves to changed objective circumstances. For a man's habitual standard of life usually has the first claim on his income, and he is apt to save the difference which discovers itself between his actual income and the expense of his habitual standard; or, if he does adjust his expenditure to changes in his income, he will over short periods do so imperfectly. Thus a rising income will often be accompanied by increased saving, and a falling income by decreased saving . . . .[9]

In Keynes's view, a family can more easily increase consumption when income is rising than decrease it when income falls. From this observation, we may infer a tendency to protect previously achieved levels of consumption during periods of falling income. Therefore, consumption will increase more rapidly when income rises than it will decrease when income falls.

Duesenberry developed a rigorous theory based on Keynes's quoted observation on the subject of human nature.[10] In Duesenberry's view, the high MPC associated with increasing income applies only to newly achieved high levels of income. The theory is shown graphically in Figure 8A-2, where the C_L curve represents the long-run consumption function and C_1, C_2, and C_3 represent the short-run consumption

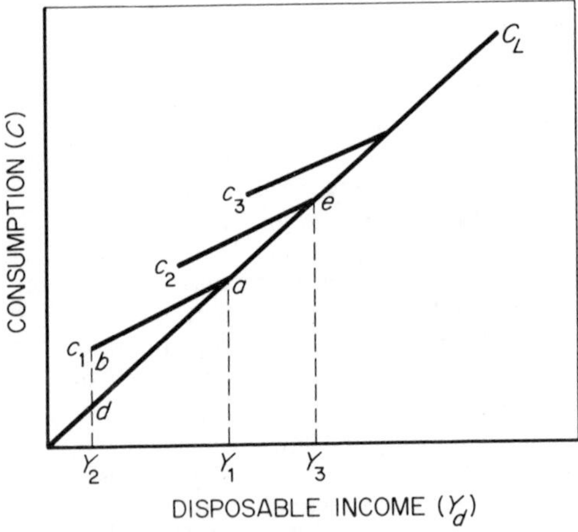

FIG. 8A-2 Consumption Ratchet

functions over three cycles. As is shown in the figure, if disposable income falls from Y_1 to Y_2, with consumption initially at point *a*, consumption will decline along the C_1 function from *a* to *b*, and *not* from *a* to *d*, the path followed during the previous expansion. Recovery will follow the same flatter C_1 path that the decreasing consumption function followed, until the previous high level of income is achieved at

[9] J. M. Keynes, *The General Theory of Employment, Interest and Money* (New York: Harcourt Brace Jovanovich, 1936), p. 97.

[10] Duesenberry, *Income*, pp. 1–46.

point a. Consumption will then advance along the C_L curve until the next income reduction sets in at point e, after an income level of Y_3 has been reached. The appearance of the graph, with the long-run increases in consumption following the steeper C_L path and the short-run decreases and recoveries following the shallower C_1, C_2, and C_3 lines radiating from the long-run function, gives the appearance of a ratchet.

Duesenberry's model may be described algebraically, where b is the long-run MPC, b' is the short-run MPC, Y_d is current disposable income, and $\bar{Y}_d$ is the previous peak disposable income:

$$C = (b - b')\bar{Y}_d + b'Y_d \tag{8A-1}$$

During periods of prosperity, when the current income is also the peak income and the short-run MPC is not relevant, the formula becomes simply

$$C = b\bar{Y}_d \tag{8A-2}$$

During a cyclical decline in disposable income, the first term on the right side of equation (8A-1) becomes constant, because the value of the peak level of disposable income cannot change until the recovery has been accomplished. Substituting a for the constant value $(b - b')\bar{Y}_d$, the consumption function becomes

$$C = a + b'Y_d \tag{8A-3}$$

In summary, the ratchet effect will develop whenever a cyclical decline or recovery in income is experienced. Expansion along the C_L line will occur whenever prosperity beyond the previous peak income level is experienced.[11]

In addition to explaining the short-run ratchet effect, Duesenberry's theory explains the long-run C_L function by use of what has been called the relative-income hypothesis, which holds that long-run consumption patterns are determined in large part by the income group to which a family belongs. A family tends to adopt as its standard of living the consumption patterns of the leaders of its peer group. This form of emulative consumption leads to a linear, positively sloped, long-run consumption function, which indicates that a relatively constant proportion of income will be spent on consumption. As long as the family maintains its relative position in the overall scheme of income distribution, the percentage of income spent on consumption will keep pace with changes in income.

Only when a family leaves its accustomed place in the income distribution will its consumption pattern tend to change. Thus, the families of the second quintile of the population today tend to spend about the same proportion of their income on consumption goods as did the families of the second quintile of the population a generation ago. However, if a poor family moves up to a relatively higher income bracket, after an adjustment lag, it will tend to emulate the consumption patterns of the new group. At that time, while the new standard of living is being adopted, the MPC will be very high, particularly as more costly consumer durables are acquired. But over time, after these goods are acquired and the new style of life has been adopted, the proportion of the incremental income spent on consumption goods will tend to decrease until the family's consumption pattern (APC) is the same as that of its peers.

[11]The sort of ratchet envisioned by Duesenberry differed from Keynes's in that Keynes's was not reversible. Keynes apparently felt that pent-up demand would be released when income recovered, so that the consumption function would increase before income reached its previous peak. Such a formulation would permit a different multiplier to develop during recovery than existed during the downswing. In Duesenberry's formulation, that problem could not develop, since his MPC's are predetermined in both the long and short runs. In addition, Duesenberry's version of the ratchet seems to explain why pent-up demand is not as evident after a recession as after a war.

(The increased proportion of savings to income during the recession of 1969–70 casts some question on the generality of the consumption ratchet.)

PERMANENT-INCOME HYPOTHESIS

Milton Friedman proposes that a major statistical shortcoming of consumption-function theories is that they use an irrelevant time period, usually a year.[12] Suppose a person is paid once a month but spends his income evenly throughout the month; then his daily propensity to consume appears very low on payday and infinitely high on the other days of the month. Clearly, a daily consumption function would be misleading, because consumers do not plan over so short a time period. Similarly, the use of an arbitrary one-year period may not be much more relevant than that of a one-day time period. Most people, Friedman argues, plan their income and consumption expenditures over their life cycles. Someone young just starting his career, will most likely have a high annual propensity to consume, because he expects his income to increase substantially in the future. A middle-aged worker in his peak earning period will most likely have a low annual propensity to consume, since he is also saving for his old age. The older person, who earns little or nothing but still consumes, has a high annual propensity to consume. Therefore, over the period of his lifetime, a consumer can look forward to increasing income during the first years and decreasing income through the later years of his life. According to this theory, measured income typically follows the *MM* line in Figure 8A-3. Knowing this, the consumer makes his consumption a function of his anticipated mean lifetime income —the *LL* line in the figure.

In Friedman's theory, consumption is a constant proportion of permanent income and is represented by the *CC* line in Figure 8A-3.[13] The income recipient

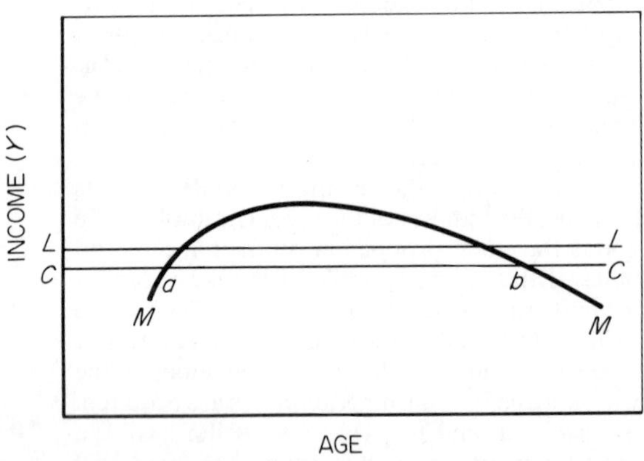

FIG. 8A-3 Income and Consumption over the Consumer's Life

[12] Milton Friedman, *A Theory of the Consumption Function* (Princeton, N.J.: Princeton University Press, 1957), p. 20–37.

[13] Anticipated mean lifetime income (permanent income) will be reevaluated from time to time as the consumer's circumstances and prospects change. Thus, the *LL* line will shift, drawing the consumption function with it, because consumption is a constant proportion of permanent income, so the absolute amount of consumption changes whenever permanent income is reevaluated. However, for simplicity we assume the *LL* function to be constant.

consumes a constant proportion of his permanent income, even though the propensity to consume out of measured income fluctuates from year to year. As the figure shows, the propensity to consume out of measured income is high (probably over 100 percent) in the early and late years and low in the middle years of high earnings.

Assuming that saving is mainly to finance retirement (including a target bequest) and that retired people plan to enjoy approximately the same level of living they enjoyed during their working years, individuals, regardless of their income level, will plan to spend approximately the same proportion of their permanent income on consumption over their lifetime. Therefore, when consumption is assumed to be a function of only the consumer's permanent income, the permanent MPC and APC will be equal for the average family in each income level.

If the average family in each income group has approximately the same MPC as the average family in all other income groups, how can we explain other than by age differences the fact that statistics show high-income people save proportionately more than low-income recipients? The answer proposed by Friedman is that many find themselves in the upper income groups because of some transitory windfall gains. Transitory gains (and losses) are not part of a person's permanent income. Therefore, the tendency on the part of the consumer will be to disregard year-to-year transitory fluctuations in income as a guide to determining his consumption expenditures.[14] Consequently, measured data that correlate consumption with income received during any given year may be misleading, simply because the time period is too short to be relevant to the person's permanent consumption plans. However, in normal years, windfall gains and losses, if they occur randomly, may approximately average out.

Excluding the transitory components of income, Friedman's long-run consumption function follows the same path as Kuznets' statistical long-run consumption function, radiating from the origin and showing a constant proportion of permanent income consumed. However, over the business cycle, recession years will be associated with the predominance of windfall losses, and prosperity with windfall gains. Therefore, consumption patterns plotted against measured income over the business cycle will have the same appearance as C_1, C_2, or C_3 in Figure 8A-1, with only the average year coinciding with line C_L within each business cycle. Owing to the expectation of secularly increasing incomes, each cyclical consumption pattern will be higher than the previous one. While Duesenberry's ratchet effect will only move back from the long-run consumption pattern, Friedman's permanent-income consumption function, like Smithies' drift theory, may move in both directions.

"Permanent" consumption patterns may be described with the help of indifference curves. In Figure 8A-4, potential purchasing power this year, C_t, is plotted along the x-axis, and potential purchasing power next year, C_{t+1}, is plotted along the y-axis. The horizontal-axis intercept of the income- or budget-restraint line labeled B is equal to this year's income plus the present value of next year's income, or $Y_t + Y_{t+1}[1/(1 + i)]$, while the vertical-axis intercept of line B is equal to next year's income plus this year's income, including the interest earned on this year's income, or $Y_{t+1} + Y_t(1 + i)$. Therefore, the income-restraint line B is identical in concept to the B_1, B_2, and B_3 lines in Figure 8-1. The budget restraint line, B, represents all possible combinations of consumption in the two time periods, given

---

[14]Friedman's treatment of windfall gains and losses is diametrically opposed to Keynes's in the *General Theory*, since Keynes felt that windfall gains and losses could be a major reason for shifts in consumption. (Keynes, *General Theory*, pp. 92–93.) Friedman assumes that windfall gains and losses have no effect on consumption. Windfall gains will be entirely saved and windfall losses will be disregarded in consumption decisions. He justifies this extreme assumption by including consumer durables as part of savings and investment. (Friedman, *Consumption Function*, p. 28)

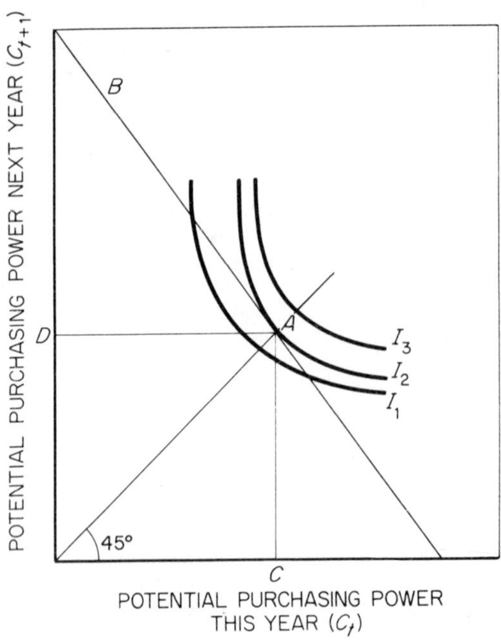

FIG. 8A-4 An Individual's Choice to Consume this Year or Next

the rate of interest, 10 percent in this illustration, and the consumer's expected measured income. Each of the three indifference curves defines all combinations of potential purchasing power in the two time periods to which the consumer is indifferent. Since the consumer maximizes his satisfaction by operating on the highest achievable indifference curve tangent to his budget line, his equilibrium is at point a; on his budget restraint line, that is the point of tangency with indifference curve I_2. Under the permanent-income hypothesis, the consumer's desired purchasing power or consumption this year, the C value on the x-axis, equals his consumption next year, shown at D on the y-axis; consumption will be equal in both time periods if permanent income does not change, regardless of the amount of income actually received. Assuming a two-year period is inconvenient, since consumption in both years can be equal only if the consumer is operating on the 45° line, which precludes the possibility of measured savings as long as the assumption is made that any income saved this year will be spent next year.[15] If his income is changed, the budget line would shift up or down, but in any case his consumption would fall along the 45° line, as shown in Figure 8A-4, in order for his consumption to remain equal in the two time periods. However, if the consumer's lifetime is considered, any particular two-year period might have either positive or negative savings, depending on where in his lifetime earning cycle the two years occurred. Therefore, in any given two years out of a longer time period, a consumer's equilibrium would fall on the budget line only in the years around points a and b in Figure 8A-3, because

[15]Notice that the consumer's decision to consume equally in every year indicates that his time preference for consumption is neutral; that is, he would be equally well satisfied consuming a given amount of goods this year or next.

only at those two points is measured income equal to consumption. If we suppose that next year stands for the consumer's expected income over his work life expectancy, then equilibrium would occur above the 45° line, because consumers are expected to finance their retirement and leave a target bequest to their heirs.

Notice that the indifference curves I_1, I_2, and I_3 in Figure 8A-4 do not show the same degree of complementarity as those presented in Figure 8-1, since Friedman, unlike Keynes, believes that savings, not just significant changes in savings, are a positive function of the rate of interest.

Although income increments or decrements may be considered transitory at first, if they persist, the consumer's concept of permanent income will change. For example, racetrack winnings may be considered transitory income when first received, but if the consumer has a winning record over several years, he may eventually include such winnings in his permanent income. Friedman uses the example of an expected inheritance, which increases consumption before it is received, since it is part of the consumer's expected lifetime income.[16]

One criticism of the permanent-income theory is that no direct measure of permanent income exists; it must be discovered indirectly. Friedman suggests that this be done by extrapolating on the basis of past income, with decreasing weight given to more remote years. In attempting to isolate the "permanent" component of permanent income, Friend and Kravis used a sample of families who had had approximately the same income the previous year, and expected the same income in the subsequent year. They found that the relation between consumption and income was not proportional.[17] Several authors have made empirical studies to discover if there is any relationship between transitory consumption and transitory income. For example, Bodkin found that of the 1950 soldiers' bonus in the United States, the veterans spent a higher proportion and saved less out of the windfall than out of their basic income, empirically supporting the Keynesian view.[18] Margaret Reid, however, using the 1950 *Survey of Consumer Expenditure* published by the Bureau of Labor Statistics, found that a great part of windfall income did go into savings, offering empirical support for the Friedman position.[19] One problem in empirical analysis of this type is the time period used in defining savings. Immediately, any windfall increases savings, simply because no consumption plans are available to absorb the new spending power.

In addition to the problems of isolating and measuring the permanent and transitory components of income, there are some commonsense exceptions that must be made, particularly at the extremes of the income-distribution scale. For example, at very low incomes, the day-to-day, hand-to-mouth nature of life prevents a person from thinking in terms of a longer run or of a permanent income. Some consumers, regardless of their income bracket, discount the future so heavily that the relevant time period for planning consumption becomes so short as to make the concept of permanent income meaningless.[20] At the same time, at higher income levels, savings

---

[16]Friedman, *Consumption Function*, p. 28

[17]Irwin Friend and Irving B. Kravis, "Consumption Patterns and Permanent Income," *American Economic Review*, 47 (May 1957), 536–55.

[18]Ronald Bodkin, "Windfall Income and Consumption," *American Economic Review*, 49 (September 1959), 602–14.

[19]Margaret Reid, "Consumption, Savings and Windfall Gains," *American Economic Review*, 52 (September 1962), 728–37.

[20]One of the major class distinctions cited by sociologists is that lower classes buy impulsively and have short consumption horizons compared with middle classes, who have long-term goals, defer gratification, and practice impulse renunciation. So it appears that the patterns evident in the middle classes may be consistent with the permanent-income hypothesis, but those of the lower classes are not. See Louis Schneider and Sverre Lysgaard, "The Deferred Gratification Pattern: A Preliminary Study," *American Sociological Review*, 18 (April 1953), 142–48; and Murray S. Straus, "Deferred Gratification, Social Class, and

may occur because it is difficult to spend as much as 90 percent of extremely high incomes on consumption. The "super rich" determine the top standard of consumption for society and generally establish themselves as consumption leaders while spending far less than 90 percent of their income. In addition, it seems unlikely that, even in our mobile society, a dominant proportion of people in any income class at a given time would consider themselves transients in that income group.

Although Friedman concludes that the average family in every income class has the same propensity to consume out of permanent income, his consumption function explicitly includes wealth along with other variables such as the interest rate and a portmanteau variable representing the subjective determinants of consumption.

RECENT STATISTICAL EVIDENCE

A considerable amount of statistical evidence has been introduced to substantiate (or disprove) the drift, the ratchet, and the permanent-income hypotheses. The results are inconclusive.[21] However, recent data support Kuznets' concept of a long-run consumption function. Using ten-year overlapping periods, (the last one has only 8) as Kuznets did, starting in 1929 and going through 1971 we see that the mean value of each period, as plotted in Figure 8A-5, falls almost precisely along a straight line out of the origin with a slope of .92. When the annual data for alternating ten-year periods are plotted, short-run consumption patterns may be observed crossing the long-run function at the mean value. Since the long-run function was developed using the mean values of the ten-year overlapping periods, the result appears to support the drift or the permanent-income theory. However, when the data are plotted year to year, relationships more nearly resembling the ratchet emerge. Therefore, the time-series data may be reasonably used to support the drift, ratchet, and permanent-income theories, since there is a reasonable fit in all three cases.

However, historical "proofs" of economic theories are rather meaningless, as the methodological warnings in Chapter 1 indicated. The arbitrary ten-year short-run period selected is clearly long enough for change to occur in those factors assumed constant. Any elapsed time at all may be too much for a true test for even short-run theories. Data always represent what has happened, whereas theory concentrates mainly on what is expected to happen under given circumstances. Consequently, data can only indirectly support any theory. Even if data are consistent with a given theory, the relationship may be coincidental or attributable to other variables not taken into account.

CONCLUSION

This Appendix has considered three of the most prominent amendments to the Keynesian consumption function. The three are representative of a large number of attempts to reconcile the theory of the consumption function with the data that have been collected since publication of the *General Theory*. None of the theories significantly affect the Keynesian type of short-run consumption function. In fact, Yang found that in a study of eighteen countries, "the level of consumption is highly

---

the Achievement Syndrome," *American Sociological Review*, 27 (June 1962), 326–35. In the words of Jack Ossofsky, Executive Director of the National Council of Aging, "The poor never saved for rainy days because it rained every day of their lives." Quoted in Barbara Isenberg, *Wall Street Journal*, Nov. 15, 1972, p. 1.

[21] Ferber has summarized consumption studies through 1962. He found conflicting results and concluded that the budget-study data on which most of the studies were based were undependable. Robert Ferber, "Research on Household Behavior," *American Economic Review*, 52 (March 1962), 19–63.

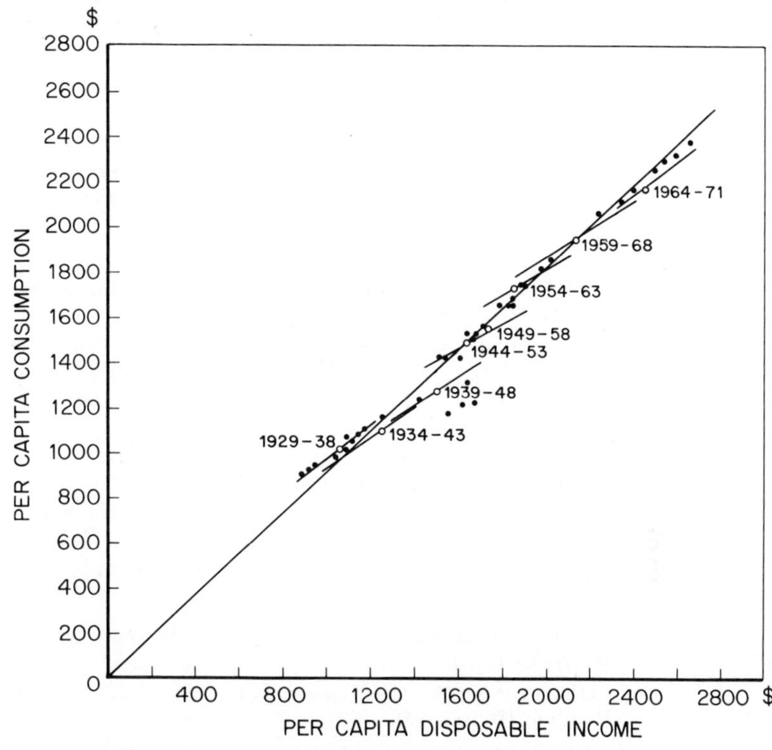

FIG. 8A-5 Empirical Long-run and Short-run Consumption Function

correlated with the level of current income."[22] However, the more recent theories relate changes in consumption to secular and cyclical changes in income more systematically than Keynes's theory did.

ADDITIONAL SELECTED REFERENCES

SIMPLIFIED DESCRIPTIONS OF KEYNES'S CONSUMPTION FUNCTION

MURAD, ANATOL, *What Keynes Means*, pp. 28–42, 59–113. New York: Bookman 1962.

WRIGHT, DAVID M., *The Keynesian System*, pp. 14–24. New York: Fordham University Press, 1962.

THE SAVINGS-INVESTMENT CONTROVERSY

CURTIS, MYRA, "Is Money Savings Equal to Investment?" *Quarterly Journal of Economics*, 15 (August 1937), 604–25.

HANSEN, A. H., "A Note on Savings and Investment," *Review of Economics and Statistics*, 30 (February 1948), 30–33.

[22]Charles Yneu Yang, "An International Comparison of Consumption Functions," *The Review of Economics and Statistics*, 46 (August 1964), 279–86.

Lerner, A. P., "Savings and Investment: Definitions, Assumptions, Objectives," Quarterly Journal of Economics, 53 (August 1939), 611–19.

———, "Savings Equals Investment," *Quarterly Journal of Economics*, 52 (February 1938), 297–309.

Lutz, F. A., "The Outcome of the Savings-Investment Discussion," *Quarterly Journal of Economics*, 52 (August 1938), 588–614.

Ohlin, Bertil, "Some Notes on the Stockholm Theory of Savings and Investment," *Economic Journal*, Parts 1-2, 47 (March 1937 and June 1937), 53–69, 221–40.

MULTIPLIER THEORY

Goodwin, R. M., ,The Multiplier," in *The New Economics*, ed. S. E. Harris, pp. 482–99. New York: Knopf, 1947.

Haberler, Gottfried, "Mr Keynes's Theory of the Multiplier: A Methodological Criticism," *Zeitschrift für Nationalökonomie*, 7 (1936), 299–305. Reprinted in American Economic Association, *Readings in Business Cycle Theory*, Vol. II, Chap. 9. Philadelphia: Blackstone, 1944.

Machlup, Fritz, "Period Analysis and Multiplier Theory," *Quarterly Journal of Economics*, 54 (November 1939), 1–27.

CONSUMPTION ECONOMICS

Ackley, Gardner, *Macroeconomic Theory*, pp. 208–307. New York: Macmillan, 1961.

Burk, M. C., *Consumption Economics: A Multidisciplinary Approach*. New York: Wiley, 1968.

Gilboy, Elizabeth W., *A Primer on the Economics of Consumption*. New York: Random House, 1968.

Mack, Ruth, "Economics of Consumption," in *A Survey of Contemporary Economics*, ed. B. F. Haley, Volume II, pp. 39–82. Homewood, Ill.: Richard D. Irwin, 1952.

POST-KEYNESIAN THEORIES OF CONSUMPTION

Ando, A., and F. Modigliani, "The 'Life Cycle' Hypothesis of Savings: Aggregate Implications and Tests," *American Economic Review*, 53 (March 1963), 55–84.

Farrell, M. J., "The New Theories of the Consumption Function," *Economic Journal*, 69 (December 1959), 678–96.

Modigliani, F., and R. Brumberg, "Utility Analysis and the Consumption Function: An Interpretation of Cross-Section Data," in *Post-Keynesian Economics*, ed. K. K. Kurihara, pp. 388–436. New Brunswick, N.J.: Rutgers University Press, 1954.

Spiro, Alan, "Wealth and the Consumption Function," *Journal of Political Economy*, 70 (August 1962), 339–54.

EMPIRICAL STUDIES—TESTS OF THE CONSUMPTION FUNCTION AND OTHER VARIABLES AFFECTING CONSUMPTION

Ackley, Gardner, "The Wealth-Saving Relationship," *Journal of Political Economy*, 59 (April 1951), 154–61.

Adams, F. G., "Prediction with Consumer Attitudes: The Time Series-Cross Section Paradox," *Review of Economics and Statistics*, 47 (November 1965), 367–78.

BRINEGAR, G. K., "Short-Run Effects of Income Change on Expenditure," *Journal of Farm Economics*, 35 (February 1953), 99–109.

COHEN, MORRIS, "Liquid Assets and the Consumption Function," *Review of Economics and Statistics*, 36 (May 1954), 202–11.

EVANS, MICHAEL K., "The Importance of Wealth in the Consumption Function," *Journal of Political Economy*, Part I, 75 (August 1967), 335–49.

EZEKIEL, MORDECAI, "Statistical Investigations of Saving, Consumption, and Investment," *American Economic Review*, Parts 1–2, 32 (March 1942 and June 1942), 22–49, 272–307.

FERBER, ROBERT A., "Research on Household Behavior," *American Economic Review*, 52 (March, 1962), 19–63. Summarizes the literature up to 1962.

———, *A Study of Aggregate Consumption Functions*. National Bureau of Economic Research Technical Paper 8. New York: N.B.E.R., 1953.

FRIEND, I., and S. SCHOR, "Who Saves?" *Review of Economics and Statistics*, 41, No. 2, Pt. 2 (May 1959), 213–48.

GOLDSMITH, R. W., *A Study of Saving in the United States*, Vol. I, pp. 3–22. Princeton, N.J.: Princeton University Press, 1955.

HOUTHAKKER, H. S., and L. D. TAYLOR, *Consumer Demand in the United States, 1929–1970*. Cambridge: Harvard University Press, 1966.

KATONA, GEORGE, "Effect of Income Changes on the Rate of Saving," *Review of Economics and Statistics*, 31 (May 1949), 95–103.

———, *Psychological Analysis of Economic Behavior*. New York: McGraw-Hill, 1951.

KOSOBUD, R. F., and J. N. MORGAN, eds., *Consumer Behavior of Individual Families over Two and Three Years*, Monograph No. 36. Ann Arbor, Mich.: Survey Research Center, University of Michigan, 1964.

KRAVIS, I., and I. FRIEND, "Entrepreneural Income, Saving and Investment," *American Economic Review*, 47 (June 1957), 269–301.

LUBELL, H., "Effects of Redistribution of Income on Consumer's Expenditures," *American Economic Review*, 37 (March 1947), 157–70.

MCCRACKEN, P. W., J. C. T. MAO, and C. FRICKE, *Consumer Installment Credit and Public Policy*. Ann Arbor, Mich.: Bureau of Business Research, University of Michigan, 1965.

MINCER, JACOB, "Employment and Consumption," *Review of Economics and Statistics*, 42 (February 1960), 20–26.

MODIGLIANI, FRANCO, "Fluctuations in the Savings-Income Ratio: A Problem in Economic Forecasting," in Conference on Research on Income and Wealth, *Studies in Income and Wealth*, Vol. 11, pp. 369ff. New York: N.B.E.R., 1949.

MORGAN, JAMES N., MARTIN H. DAVID, WILBUR J. COHEN, and HARVEY E. BRAZER, *Income and Welfare in the United States*. New York: McGraw-Hill, 1962.

MUELLER, E., "Effects of Consumer Attitudes on Purchases," *American Economic Review*, 47 (December 1957), 946–65.

SUITS, DANIEL, "The Determinants of Consumer Expenditure: A Review of Present Knowledge," in Commission on Money and Credit, *Impacts of Monetary Policy*, pp. 1–57. Englewood Cliffs, N.J.: Prentice-Hall, 1963.

———, and GORDON SPARKS, "Consumption Regressions with Quantity Data," in *The Brookings Quarterly Econometric Model of the United States*, ed. J. S. Duesenberry, et al., pp. 203–23. Chicago: Rand McNally, 1955.

TOBIN, JAMES, "Relative Income, Absolute Income, and Saving," in *Money, Trade, and Economic Growth*. Essays in Honor of John Henry Williams, pp. 135–56. New York: Macmillan, 1951.

ZELLNER, A., D. S. HUANG, and L. C. CHAU, "Further Analyses of the Short-Run Consumption Function with Emphasis on the Role of Liquid Assets," *Econometrica*, 33 (July 1965), 571–81.

TESTING THE PERMANENT-INCOME THEORY

KREININ, M. E., "Windfall Income and Consumption: Additional Evidence" *American Economic Review*, 51 (June 1961), 388–90.

LIVIATAN, NISSAN, "Tests of the Permanent Income Hypothesis Based on a Reinterview Savings Survey," in *Measurement in Economics Studies*, pp. 29–59. Stanford, Calif.: Stanford University Press, 1963.

MAYOR, T., "The Propensity to Consume Permanent Income," *American Economic Review*, 56 (December 1966), 1158–77.

SIMON, JULIAN L., and DENNIS J. AIGNER, "Cross-Section and Time-Series Tests of the Permanent Income Hypothesis," *American Economic Review*, 60 (June 1970), 341–51.

Keynesian Investment Theory

9

INTRODUCTION

The distinction between the investment-goods market and the consumer-goods market is more significant in Keynesian analysis than in the neoclassical theory. In our discussion of the neoclassical system in Chapter 6, we saw that the distribution of total output between consumption and investment goods is largely a function of the interest rate; in contrast, as we saw in Chapter 8, in the Keynesian system, consumption expenditures are basically a function of income. Both Keynes and the neoclassicists proposed that the demand for investment goods, or simply investment, is a function of the rate of interest. Keynes, in addition, offered interesting insights into the demand for investment and the operation of the capital-goods market. As in the case of both the consumption-function and liquidity-preference theories, post-Keynesians have refined the basic model. Remember, in this context, *capital* refers to a stock of producer goods, and *investment* refers to the flow of new producer goods into or out of the stock.

Investment in the Short Run

This treatment of investment in a short-run model is permissible for two reasons, even though capital is usually assumed constant:

1. The short-run assumption of constant capital is not as fundamental in macro as in micro theory; its purpose is simply to permit the passage of a relatively short period of time. The need for a fixed factor to aid the analysis is unimportant here.

Macro models have been developed with both labor and capital inputs variable on the supply side.[1]

2. Even though *investment* is allowed to vary, the *stock of capital* will not be much affected, because the stock of capital is so much larger than one period's investment expenditure. In this way, from the demand side, changes in investment can be a major determinant of changes in aggregate income, while capital inputs are assumed constant on the supply side.

In like manner, technology may be assumed constant over a short period. Realistically, however, technology does change, and later in the chapter we consider the effect of that change on investment and on the employment of capital and labor.

Gross and Net Investment

Gross investment includes both net additions to the stock of capital (net investment) and replacement of depreciated plant and equipment. Accounting practice may not report true wear in depreciation figures; consequently, in practice, the distinction between gross and net investment may be blurred. However, the distinction is analytically useful, because analytically, replacement of worn-out equipment merely maintains a given stock of capital and a given level of aggregate income; whereas net (additional new) investment causes changes in the stock of capital and in the level of aggregate income. In this chapter, unless otherwise noted *investment* shall refer to *net*, not gross, investment.

MARGINAL EFFICIENCY OF CAPITAL

Definition

Keynes's basic concept relating to the demand for investment is the *marginal efficiency of capital* (MEC). This is defined by Keynes as being "equal to the rate of discount which would make the present value of the series of annuities given by the returns expected from the capital-asset during its life just equal to its supply price."[2] Restated, the MEC equals the discount rate or interest rate that equates the present value of an expected net income stream from an investment project with the project's cost. The reader will notice that "the MEC" as the term is used here is an ambiguous concept: it may refer to the demand for investment function or it may refer to the rate of return on the marginal investment.

Keynes maintained that his MEC was identical to Fisher's "rate of return over cost."[3] Fisher states that the rate of return over cost compares the pre-

[1] For example see:
Arthur Benavie, "Prices and Wages in the Complete Keynesian Model," *Southern Economic Journal*, 38 (April 1972), 468–77.

[2] J. M. Keynes, *The General Theory of Employment, Interest and Money* (New York: Harcourt Brace Jovanovich, 1936), p. 135.

[3] *Ibid.*, pp. 140–41.

sent value of the income stream of an investment with its cost.[4] An investor may profit from any investment as long as the rate of return over cost is greater than the cost of capital, assumed to be the market interest rate. If we assume that because of the law of diminishing returns, each successive unit of an investment will yield an increasingly lower rate of return over cost, then the individual investor would stop investing at the point where the marginal rate of return is equal to the rate of interest.

The following discussion will clarify what we really mean by Keynes's marginal efficiency of capital or Fisher's rate of return over cost.[5]

Time Dimension

Two elements are most significant in determining the marginal efficiency of capital. One is the expected net return over the life of the capital asset; the other is the purchase price of the asset. The expected net return is the net flow of expected revenues or receipts in excess of expenses or costs during the anticipated life of the asset; in other words, the expected net income earned from the asset over time.

For example, assume that a business firm is contemplating investing in a soap factory that is expected to have a perpetual life. If net returns of $10,000 per year are expected to extend forever into the future, and the purchase price of the factory is $200,000, then the expected annual rate of return, or the MEC, is 5 percent.

The time dimension is important in a firm's demand for capital assets, because it is unrealistic to assume that any investment lasts forever and because income today is preferred to future income, so the value of each project must be discounted. Discounting is the process of finding the present value of a stream of future returns. The two principal developments that are most apt to reduce the present value of a stream of future returns are these:

1. The income stream will not last forever.
2. Future income is less valuable than present income. One dollar today is worth more than a dollar to be received next year.

As a consequence of point 2, often described as "the time value of money," interest must be paid to an asset holder to encourage him to lend a dollar today in exchange for future money; the future repayment must exceed the present loan, or the asset holder will not save.

To illustrate discounting, assume that the soap factory in our example lasts for only five years. With an annual return of $10,000, the investment earns a total of $50,000. The investor could earn a 5 percent rate of return

---

[4]Irving Fisher, *The Theory of Interest* (1930) (New York: Augustus M. Kelley, 1961), pp. 155–76.

[5]A. A. Alchian has pointed out that if we assume that investment projects are mutually exclusive, a crucial difference emerges between the MEC and the rate of return over costs. However, for our purposes, the two concepts will be treated as identical. See A. A. Alchian, "The Rate of Interest, Fisher's Rate of Return over Costs and Keynes' Internal Rate of Return," *American Economic Review*, 45 (December 1955), 938–42.

only if he could buy the factory for an amount substantially lower than \$50,000—the actual amount in this case would be \$43,294. The mathematical techniques for determining that figure are described below.

The following formula has been developed for determining the present value of an investment with a limited life:

$$A = \frac{R_1}{(1+i)} + \frac{R_2}{(1+i)^2} + \frac{R_3}{(1+i)^3} + \cdots + \frac{R_n}{(1+i)^n} \qquad (9\text{-}1)$$

where A is the present value; R is the dollar value of the expected net return in each year, with the subscript representing the year of each return (the last R includes any expected salvage value); i is the current cost of capital (assumed here to be the market interest rate—an assumption that is qualified later in this chapter); and n represents the number of years that the asset is expected to last.[6]

The formula for the present value of our soap factory, with a five year expected life, assuming the market interest rate is 5 percent, is

$$A = \frac{\$10{,}000}{(1+.05)} + \frac{\$10{,}000}{(1+.05)^2} + \frac{\$10{,}000}{(1+.05)^3} + \frac{\$10{,}000}{(1+.05)^4} + \frac{\$10{,}000}{(1+.05)^5}$$

$$A = \frac{\$10{,}000}{1.05} + \frac{\$10{,}000}{1.102} + \frac{\$10{,}000}{1.158} + \frac{\$10{,}000}{1.216} + \frac{\$10{,}000}{1.276}$$

$$A = \$9{,}524 + \$9{,}070 + \$8{,}638 + \$8{,}227 + \$7{,}835$$

$$A = \$43{,}294$$

Therefore, the present value of the soap factory at a 5 percent market rate of interest is \$43,294.

---

[6]The equation above can be derived as follows:

If P is the principal and i the yearly rate of interest, the interest due at the end of the year is Pi. The amount, S, at the end of the first year is therefore

$$S = P + Pi \quad \text{or} \quad P(1+i)$$

Similarly, the amount at the end of two years is found by multiplying the amount at the end of one year by $(1+i)$:

$$S = P(1+i)(1+i) \quad \text{or} \quad P(1+i)^2$$

In general, the amount at the end of n periods is

$$S = P(1+i)^n \qquad (1)$$

The present value of an amount due in n years at a yearly rate of interest can be found by solving formula 1 for P. Therefore,

$$P = \frac{S}{(1+i)^n} \qquad (2)$$

The formula for the present value, A, of a series of returns can be found as follows: The present value of the first return, expected to be received at the end of the first year, A_1, is $R_1/(1+i)^1$; the present value of the second return, expected to be received at the end of the second year, A_2, is likewise $R_2/(1+i)^2$; and so on. Therefore, the present value of n returns, expected to be received at the end of n years, is

$$A = \frac{R_1}{(1+i)^1} + \frac{R_2}{(1+i)^2} + \frac{R_3}{(1+i)^3} + \cdots + \frac{R_n}{(1+i)^n}$$

Alternatively, the formula can be adapted to determine the marginal efficiency of capital (MEC), Fisher's rate of return over cost, instead of present value. If we use r to represent the MEC and K to represent the purchase price of capital goods, the formula may be restated

$$K = \frac{R_1}{(1+r)} + \frac{R_2}{(1+r)^2} + \frac{R_3}{(1+r)^3} + \cdots + \frac{R_n}{(1+r)^n} \qquad (9\text{-}2)$$

Then, assuming that K is known and that the R's can be determined, the equation can be solved for r. For example, if an investor could purchase the soap factory that earns \$10,000 a year for five years for \$42,124, he would earn a 6 percent return on his investment. This 6 percent is the marginal efficiency of capital, and it is derived from the formula above through a trial-and-error method, utilizing the following information:

$$\$42{,}124 = \frac{\$10{,}000}{(1+r)} + \frac{\$10{,}000}{(1+r)^2} + \frac{\$10{,}000}{(1+r)^3} + \frac{\$10{,}000}{(1+r)^4} + \frac{\$10{,}000}{(1+r)^5}$$

where $r = .06$.

Since the 6 percent return is greater than the market rate of interest of 5 percent, it pays the investor to buy the soap factory. Whenever r exceeds i, the investment project may profitably be undertaken. In addition, when r is greater than i, the present value of the investment will be greater than the purchase price of the capital good (under our simplified assumptions). Therefore, the present value of the soap factory of \$43,294 is greater than its cost—namely, \$42,124.

These two formulas for determining when an investment is profitable, 9-1 (present value) and 9-2 (MEC, or internal rate of return in finance theory), may be compared and contrasted through the use of the figures presented in Table 9-1. To illustrate the use of this table, observe in the 4 percent column that the present value of a dollar to be received after a year would be 96 cents. A dollar received at the end of two years at that interest rate would be worth 92½ cents today. As you can see from the table, the higher the interest rate and the further in the future the payoff is to be received, the lower the present value.

If the firm expects to earn 5 percent on its investments, the 5 percent column in Table 9-1 demonstrates that an investment which earns a dollar a year

TABLE 9-1 Present Value of \$1 Due at the End of *n* Years

Year	Rate		
	4%	*5%*	*6%*
1	.9615	.9524	.9434
2	.9246	.9070	.8900
3	.8890	.8638	.8396
4	.8548	.8227	.7921
5	.8219	.7835	.7473
Total	4.4518	4.3294	4.2124

for each of five years should cost the firm \$4.33. If the firm must pay 4 percent on borrowed credit to finance the investment project, the present value of one dollar received each year for five years is \$4.45. In this example, the present value of the returns would exceed the cost of the asset to be purchased with the borrowed funds, and the firm may profitably make the investment.

In general, whenever present value of the expected returns from an investment exceeds the purchase price of the capital asset, the MEC exceeds the interest rate, indicating that an investment is profitable. In contrast, whenever the asset cost is greater than present value and therefore the interest rate exceeds the MEC, the investment is not profitable. If the market interest rate were 6 percent in the foregoing example, it would exceed the MEC, and the purchase price of \$4.33 would exceed the present value of the capital asset, which would now be \$4.21.

Expected net returns (*R*) may vary from year to year. However, if the yearly returns are equal, present value may be determined with a "present value of an annuity" table. Table 9-2 shows a portion of such a table for the same selected years and interest rates as those in Table 9-1. Using such a table as 9-2, one may multiply the number of dollars received yearly by the factor found in the table. Since \$10,000 will be received each year of the five years that the soap factory lasts, and the interest rate is 5 percent, the factor in the table is 4.3294, which, when multiplied by \$10,000, gives the present value of the investment, \$43,294.

TABLE 9-2 Present Value of \$1 to Be Received at the End of Each Year for *n* Years

Year	Rate		
	4%	5%	6%
1	.9615	.9524	.9434
2	1.8861	1.8594	1.8334
3	2.7751	2.7232	2.6730
4	3.6299	3.5460	3.4651
5	4.4518	4.3294	4.2124

Turning our attention from formula 9-1 to formula 9-2, Table 9-2 permits the MEC to be easily derived without using a trial-and-error method. To compute the MEC from the table, divide the cost of the asset by the expected annual net return to determine the interest factor. Then find in the left column the number of years the asset is expected to earn that return. Read across the rows until you reach the interest factor computed above. The rate at the head of the column in which that interest factor is found is the MEC.

To illustrate this method in our soap-factory example, first divide the purchase price, \$42,124, by the yearly receipt, \$10,000, in order to compute the interest factor:

$$\frac{42{,}124}{10{,}000} = 4.2124$$

Reading across the 5-year row in Table 9-2, we see that 4.2123 appears in the 6 percent column. Therefore, in this case the MEC is 6 percent; so as long as the cost of capital to the firm is equal to or less than 6 percent, the project could be undertaken profitably.

When a firm knows the purchase price of a capital asset, the expected annual net return, the number of years the asset will last, and the market rate of interest, it is in a position to decide on the economic feasibility of any investment project.

The firm can compare the MEC with the interest rate (still employed as a stand-in for the cost of capital) as a technique for making investment decisions. As long as the MEC exceeds the interest rate, the firm could profitably make the investment. Any firm is faced with a range of investment opportunities that may be ranked according to their expected rate of return. The profit-maximizing firm will then take advantage of all oppotunities whose expected rate of return exceeds the interest rate. A ranking of the investment opportunities facing a firm would provide a stair-step MEC or demand function for investment, such as that shown in Figure 9-1. As you can see in the figure, project *a* returns 18 percent and requires a $3,000 outlay; project *b* returns 16 percent and requires an outlay of $2,000; and so forth. If the firm can borrow at a constant rate of interest, 10 percent in Figure 9-1, the supply of investment funds will be horizontal to the individual firm, as represented by i_1 in the figure. Investment equilibrium for this firm occurs where the rate of interest, i_1, crosses the MEC, leading to an $11,000 investment expenditure by the firm. Therefore, the firm would invest in projects *a* through *d* and would reject *e* and *f*.

For simplicity, the MEC can be smoothed out and represented as a continuous straight line, as illustrated in Figure 9-1. The negative slope of the investment-demand curve may be based on diminishing returns and implies that each additional investment project offers a smaller return than the previous one.

Expectations

In the *General Theory*, Keynes points out that all we may be fairly confident of in a stream of returns on an investment is the first year's expected net return. A substantial amount of subjectivity is therefore involved in projecting net returns for more than one year. In practice, projected earnings on any investment must be the most probable expectation, based on the best present knowledge.

Once the estimate of future net returns has been made, the question emerges, How much confidence can be placed in the estimate? It is one thing to project the future based on available data and a different matter to actually invest resources on the basis of the projection. Keynes pointed out that economists generally tend to overlook the importance of confidence; he observed, "If we speak frankly, we have to admit that our basis of knowledge for estimating the yield ten years hence of a railway, a copper mine, a textile factory, the goodwill of a patent medicine, an Atlantic liner, a building in the City

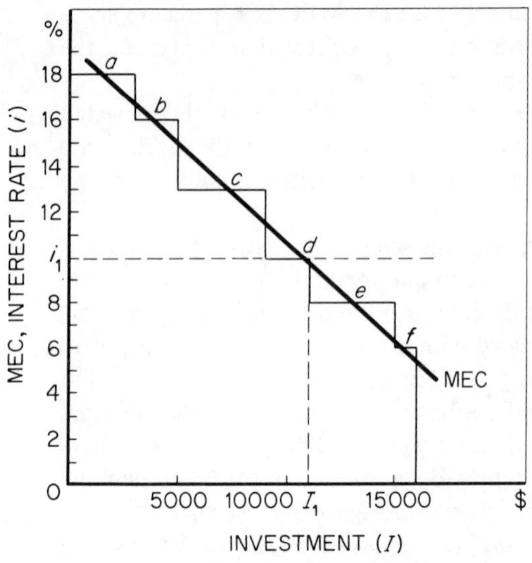

INVESTMENT PROJECTS

a = project 1.	Cost, $3,000; returns 18%
b = project 2.	Cost, $2,000; returns 16%
c = project 3.	Cost, $4,000; returns 13%
d = project 4.	Cost, $2,000; returns 10%
	MEC equal to i_1 at 10%
e = project 5.	Cost, $4,000; returns 8%
f = project 6.	Cost, $1,000; returns 6%

FIG. 9-1 The Firm's Marginal Efficiency of Capital (MEC)

of London, amounts to little, and sometimes to nothing."[7] In another place, he says, "It would be foolish, in forming our expectations, to attach great weight to matters which are very uncertain."[8] Therefore, the decision to invest depends partly on the probable outcome of the investment and partly on the confidence placed in the likelihood that that outcome will be realized. The degree of confidence placed in a projection may depend in part on whether the estimate is based on risk or uncertainty. Risk is involved in a situation where the objective probability of the occurrence can be determined. Uncertainty, in contrast, refers to a unique situation, such as the expected returns from a new product, where objective probabilities cannot be determined.

[7]Keynes, *General Theory*, pp. 149–50.
[8]*Ibid.*, p. 148.

Concrete examples may be drawn from the oil industry. Risk would be involved in drilling a new well, where the proportion of dry holes to producing wells in a given type of terrain can be precisely determined. Uncertainty would be involved in the decision to invest in the production of some newly developed petrochemical.[9]

Where uncertainty rather than risk is involved, Keynes points out, "it can easily be shown that the assumption of arithmetically equal probabilities based on a state of ignorance leads to absurdities."[10] In other words, in many cases, the state of knowledge is insufficient to provide a basis for calculating precisely reliable mathematical expectations under conditions of uncertainty. In the absence of contrary information, the conventional use of recent experience to project the future may be all that is available. Investors often adopt the convention that current trends will continue, and since confidence in such expectations is apt to be low, the convention may lead to alternating waves of optimism and pessimism.

SHIFTS IN INDIVIDUAL MEC FUNCTIONS

Expected Net Returns

The MEC curve for any firm (such as the curve in Figure 9-1) shows the expected rate of return for all possible investment projects. That rate is in part a function of expected net returns (R). The expected net returns from any asset depend on the difference between expected revenues and expected costs. Therefore, any factor that leads to an anticipation of change in either revenues or costs will change the expected net returns, and this in turn will affect the MEC function: Higher expected net returns will increase the MEC curve and lower expected net returns will decrease it.

For example, increasing labor-union militancy might lead a firm to anticipate higher labor costs and, consequently, a lower net return on all its possible investment projects, causing a reduction in the firm's MEC function. Such a reduction is illustrated in Figure 9-2 as a shift in demand from MEC_1 to MEC_2. If the interest rate remains at i_1, then the amount of investment goods demanded will fall from I_1 to I_2. Similarly, an anticipated technological breakthrough that might render a proposed investment obsolete before it has been fully depreciated would reduce the economic life of the capital asset and would therefore reduce the MEC curve. On the other hand, the expectation of a future technological change that would eliminate some production bottleneck would cause an increase in expected net returns from a proposed investment.

---

[9]In light of newly developed simulation techniques, the distinction between risk and uncertainty is becoming blurred. For a concise discussion of risk and uncertainty and a critique of this position, as well as for a list of the major contributors to the theory, see J. David Quirin, *The Capital Expenditure Decision* (Homewood, Ill.: Richard D. Irwin, 1967), pp. 199–200.

[10]Keynes, *General Theory*, p. 152.

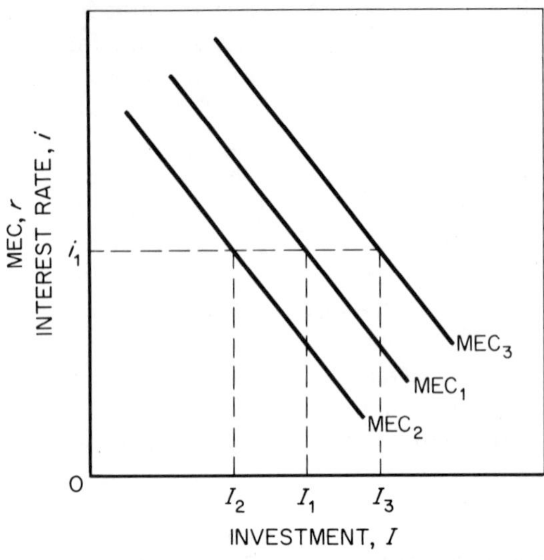

FIG. 9-2 Shifts in the Marginal Efficiency of Capital (MEC)

Expected changes in consumer buying habits affect anticipated sales and, consequently, the expected net returns on an investment. For example, an expected increase in sales owing to a change in consumer taste or income would tend to increase expected net returns, and, as a result, the MEC function would shift to the right, as shown by the shift from MEC_1 to MEC_3 in Figure 9-2. Such a shift would lead to an increase in investment from I_1 to I_3 if the interest rate remained constant at i_1. A similar effect would be obtained if improved waste-recycling techniques increase the salvage value of worn-out equipment, because R_n includes the salvage value as part of the last return.

Resource Interaction

Although increasing labor costs may reduce the net return and consequently reduce the demand for particular investment projects, it does not follow logically that generally increasing labor costs will necessarily reduce the firm's investment demand. To begin with, capital inputs are both a complement and a substitute for labor. A firm faced with higher labor costs may employ more labor-saving capital, but less labor-complementary capital.

The shape of the isoquants in both panels A and B in Figure 9-3 demonstrates that capital is both a complement and a substitute for labor, while the right-angle isoquants of panel C demonstrate a case of perfect complementarity between capital and labor. If labor costs increase for a firm whose isoquants are shaped like those in panels A or B, and the firm desires to produce the same quantity of goods as before the increase in labor costs, then the firm would substitute some capital for labor as may be seen in both panels.

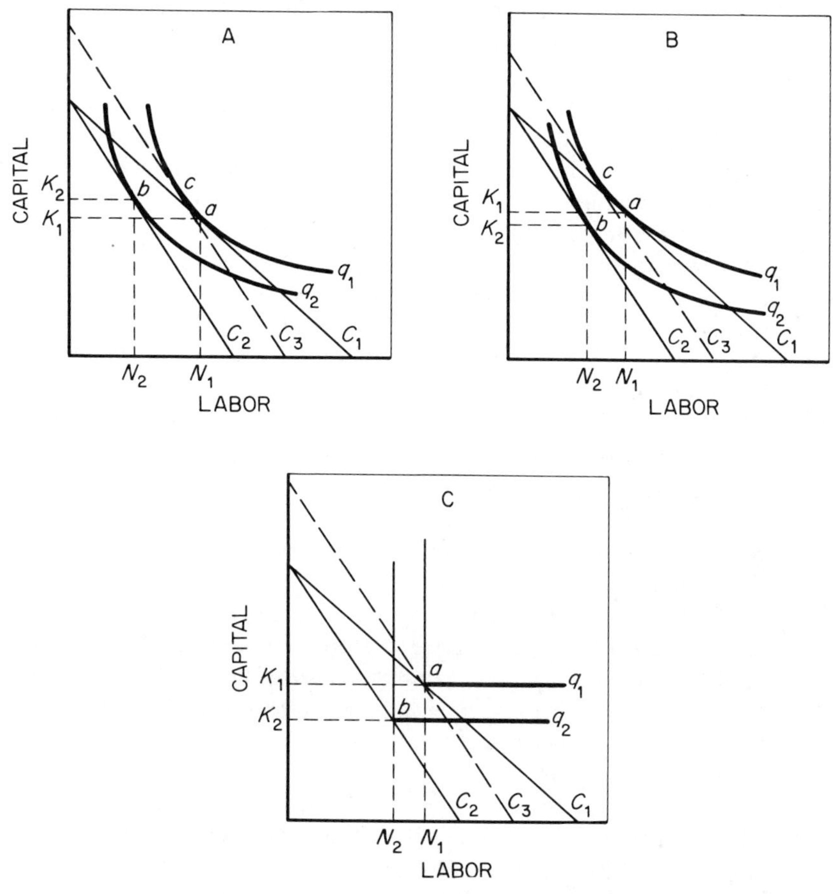

FIG. 9-3 Substitutability and Complementarity of Resources

On the other hand, if the firm's isoquants were shaped like those in panel C, the firm would not substitute capital for labor even though the price of labor increased.

Panels A and B of Figure 9-3 are drawn to illustrate the importance of the position of isoquants as contrasted with their shape. To begin with, assume that higher labor costs shift the isocost curve from C_1 to C_2 in panels A and B. Higher labor costs will lead to a reduction in the employment of labor from N_1 to N_2 in both cases, as is evidenced by the shift of the point of tangency from point *a* to point *b* when labor costs increase. However, in panel A, more capital is employed, K_1 to K_2, after the price of labor increases, whereas in panel B, less of both capital and labor are employed.

The demand for labor is elastic in panel A and inelastic in panel B, since in panel A, the total expenditure on labor decreases as the price of labor increases, and in panel B the total expenditure on labor increases as the price of labor increases. In panel A, the quantity of capital employed increases when the price of labor goes up, but because the price of capital remains constant, the firm must spend relatively more on capital and relatively less on labor after the price change, and because the firm's total expenditures remain constant, the firm must decrease its expenditures on labor. On the other hand, in panel B, the quantity of capital employed decreases as the price of labor increases. Therefore the firm will spend proportionately less on capital and relatively more on labor after the price of labor increases.

In order to determine how much of the reduction in the employment of labor was due to the substitution of capital for labor at the increased price of labor and how much was due to the reduction in output when the total expenditure of the firm is held constant, a technique very similar to that used in Chapter 2 to separate the substitution and income effects for a consumer can be employed. Assume that the business firm will attempt to produce the same amount of output after the increase in the price of labor as they produced before the increase. In order to hold output constant, the firm would have to increase its total expenditure. The output and substitution effects can be separated graphically in panels A, B, and C by drawing a C_3 expenditure curve parallel to C_2 (to maintain the new price ratio) and tangent to q_1 (to restore the original output).

The leftward movement from *a* to *c* represents the substitution of capital for labor, and the distance from *c* to *b* represents the loss of output attributable to the higher wages. As you can see because of the position of the isoquants, the substitution effect is greater in panel B than in panel A, while the output effect is greater in panel A than in B, even though the isoquants are similarly shaped in both cases.

Restoring the original output at the new price ratio between capital and labor results in more capital and less labor being employed (point *c*) in both panels A and B. But in contrast, in panel C, line C_3 is tangent to q_1 at point *a*, indicating that labor and capital are not substitutes in production but are only complements, since the original amounts of both capital and labor will be employed despite the changed price ratio.

Consequently, little can be said *a priori* concerning the effect of higher wages on the total demand for investment goods by a firm. The point here is that increases in the cost of labor may increase or decrease investment in capital equipment, depending on the shape and position of the isoquants, and the resulting elasticity or inelasticity of the demand for labor.

Purchase Price for a Capital Asset

The cost of a capital asset is one important determinant of the rate of return on an investment. An increase in the cost of a capital asset reduces the MEC, and a lower price increases the MEC.

Capital assets, like other products, are traded in a market, and anything that affects either the demand or the supply will affect the price. For example, higher labor costs will reduce the supply and raise the price of capital assets. Similarly, the discovery of a new use for some type of capital equipment would increase the demand for capital and also raise the price of capital assets to the firm.

The marginal efficiency of capital to the firm, then, depends not only on the expected net returns, but also on the initial cost of the asset. And the initial cost or price will vary as supply and demand forces change in the capital-goods market.

Changes in the Level of Technology

Relatively seldom are replacement decisions made to exactly reproduce existing plant and equipment. Generally speaking, new investment embodies improved techniques, since new technology is adopted when the net benefits exceed the cost of implementation. Benefits may take the form of increased revenues owing to product improvement, or of reduction in costs.

Technological improvements can reduce costs, and so affect the MEC function, in several ways. First, investment in improved technology may reduce labor costs by making workers more productive, thereby requiring less labor per unit of output. Such investment is called "labor saving." Second, technological improvements may reduce costs by requiring less capital per unit of output; that is, by reducing the capital–output ratio. Such investment is called "capital saving." But even if the new equipment is capital saving, its purchase represents an increase in the current demand for investment. (However, a capital saving change can reduce the demand for capital, if existing equipment was completely depreciated before an investment in the more efficient capital occurred.)

We can use isocosts and isoquants to distinguish labor-saving from capital-saving investment. If the new technology causes a larger percentage of reduction in labor than in capital inputs, the change is labor saving; if the reverse, the change is capital saving. If labor and capital inputs change in the same proportion, the change is said to be neutral.

Figure 9-4 graphically demonstrates labor-saving, capital-saving, and neutral technological change. In all three cases, the change permits the same output with a lower level of input, as the firm shifts its operations from q_a to q_b, so that q_a and q_b represent the same exact level of output in all three cases. We will choose for analysis the points that fall along ray OR in all three panels.

The labor-saving and capital-saving effects of the change are shown by the slope of the tangents to the isoquants drawn through the intersection with OR. As you can see, in panel A the two tangents indicate that capital has become much more productive than labor as a result of the change. Therefore, a relatively small amount of capital after the technological change can replace (save) a large amount of labor, as indicated by the slope of the tangent to q_b compared with the slope of the tangent to q_a. Panel B demonstrates the opposite case, where after the change, a little labor can substitute for proportionately more capital. Therefore, the case illustrated in panel B is capital saving.

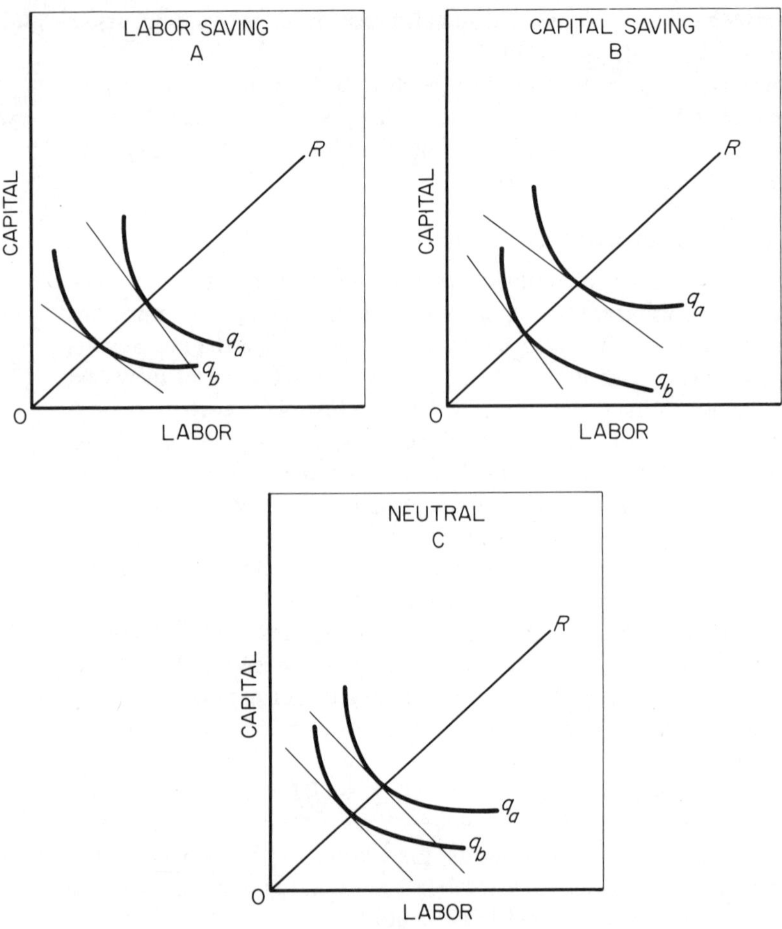

FIG. 9-4 Effects of Technological Change

Panel C shows the third possible case, where a change in technology causes an equal proportionate reduction in both labor and capital. Therefore, the case illustrated in panel C is neither labor- nor capital saving, but neutral, as indicated by the fact that the tangents are parallel.

COST OF CAPITAL

We have assumed up until now that the interest rate is the cost of capital to the firm, either because the firm has to pay the going interest rate to borrow funds or to sell ownership in order to finance an investment, or because the firm faces the opportunity cost of foregone interest earnings if it uses its own funds.

The cost of capital to the business firm represents the opportunity cost of the funds employed in an investment project. In finance theory it represents the rate of return on an investment project that will leave unchanged the market value of an individual's ownership interest or equity in a firm.[11]

In a riskless world of perfectly competitive capital markets, the cost of capital would equal the interest rate.[12] In such a world, the borrowing and lending rate of each firm would be equal, and would equal the interest rate.

In addition, due to the workings of the opportunity cost principal, the expected rate of return on equity would also be equal to the rate of interest. Economists who assume such a world often use "cost of capital" as synonymous with "going interest rate." However, to most business firms, the real world is filled with market imperfections, risk, and uncertainty. As a consequence, the going interest rate often greatly understates the actual cost of capital faced by the individual firm.

We could define a theoretical, pure interest rate as a nonrisk interest rate. However, the holders of securities issued by private firms are subject to several kinds of risk. For instance, corporate bonds are subject to (1) financial risk, or risk of default, (2) market or interest-rate risk, (3) marketability or liquidity risk, and (4) purchasing-power risk. The *risk of default* refers to the possibility that the issuer of the bond will be unable to pay the interest or principal. In the case of government bonds, the risk of default is small enough to be disregarded. The *market* or *interest-rate risk* refers to the likelihood that the interest rate and therefore the price of bonds will fluctuate over the time the bonds are held, so that the bondholder may suffer a capital loss if he sells the bond before maturity. This is closely analogous to the risk of capital loss owing to changes in the level of interest rates, discussed in Chapter 7. The *marketability* or *liquidity risk* refers to the risk inherent in converting an asset into cash. Securities listed on active, organized exchanges can normally be sold quickly for around the last quoted price, without any surprise in the results. This implies small variations in price on successive transactions. In contrast, securities sold in an inactive, poorly organized market cannot always be converted quickly into cash at a price very close to the previous sale. *Purchasing-power risk* refers to the chance that inflation will make the repaid dollars less valuable than the lender had anticipated.

Government bonds must bear a market or interest-rate risk and a purchasing-power risk, because the general level of both prices and interest rates fluctuates over time. So if we take the government-bond rate as our standard, as in Chapter 7, our interest rate includes both a market risk and a purchasing-power risk. The interest rate on private securities, on the other hand, is further removed from a riskless rate than is the rate on government bonds, because lenders to private firms face a risk of default, and lenders to the government do not. The varying securities issued by various firms associated with different industries each bear a different contractual relationship

---

[11] J. Fred Weston and Eugene F. Brigham, *Managerial Finance* 4th ed. (New York: Holt, Rinehart and Winston, 1972) pp. 300 ff.

[12] Such a world could still include the risk of capital loss on a bond because of interest-rate changes.

and a different degree of risk of default. For example, certain liabilities have priority over others, and liabilities have priority over equity financing in case of default. In addition, corporate securities that are not traded on well-organized markets are subject to a marketability or liquidity risk, and they will generally sell at higher rates of interest than those sold in an established market.

Unlike that on bonds, the return on equity is uncertain, since stockholders of corporations receive their dividends out of net income and so have no guarantee of any return whatsoever. Therefore, stockholders face more risk than bondholders. (Likewise, the return to the owners of a proprietorship or partnership is uncertain. However, for simplicity, we will assume during the remainder of this section that all firms are corporations.) Stockholders benefit from both dividends and a higher price for their stock. Higher stock prices are determined by the market, which, in the long run, values stock issues according to potential earnings.

Financial managers theoretically should weigh benefits to stockholders from dividend payments as compared with those from capital gains attributable to profitably reinvested retained earnings. The stockholders' interests are best served by retaining earnings for reinvestment as long as the rate of return to the corporation is greater than that of the stockholders' alternative opportunities. Managers making the decision to pay dividends or to retain earnings must bear in mind the different tax treatments given dividends and capital gains. As this is written, the latter are taxed at a lower rate than dividends, which are generally taxed as ordinary income.[13] The cost of capital to a business firm represents both the explicit costs the firm must pay for borrowed funds and the implicit cost of foregone opportunities on the part of its stockholders. From the viewpoint of the stockholders, the opportunity cost of investing in the firm is the return that could be earned on similar-risk investments elsewhere in the economy. Such a cost represents the minimum rate of return that must be earned on equity-financed investments in order to keep the current market value of the stockholders' interest in the firm unchanged.

As a result, the cost to the firm of common stock equals the stockholders' opportunity cost—in reality, the return that the stockholder expects to earn on his investment in the company.[14] This expected return consists of two items, the stream of dividends and capital appreciation, which together constitute the two types of return available to stockholders. Capital appreciation may reasonably be related to expected future net returns. Both expected future returns and current dividends can be converted into rates of return

---

[13]The first $100 of dividends received by an individual—or $200, if stock is jointly owned by husband and wife—is excluded from taxation on the individual's tax return.

[14]The cost of any new issue of securities must be adjusted for flotation costs, including underwriters' commissions and various other costs such as SEC registration expenses, legal fees, printing costs, accounting fees, and the like. Retained earnings have no flotation costs, but the rate of return on retained earnings should equal the stockholders' opportunity cost, since retained earnings are a form of equity.

in order to arrive at the following formula to determine the rate of return expected by stockholders, which may be defined as the cost of equity capital to the firm; that is,

$$i_e = \frac{\text{Current dividend}}{\text{Price}} + \text{Expected growth rate.}$$

The cost of equity capital, i_e, should at least equal the stockholders' opportunity cost. In order for the stockholder to be satisfied with his capital appreciation, the price of the stock must grow at the same rate as net income earned. Both the absolute amount of the dividends expected to be paid and the amount of the retained earnings must also grow at the same rate. In addition, the retained earnings must earn a return equal to i_e and be a consistent percentage of net returns in order for this growth rate to remain constant.

The cost of debt, i_d, is equal to the interest rate that must be earned on new investments that are financed through the use of debt capital. In the real world, it is necessary to take the effect of the corporate income tax into account when computing the cost of capital of a corporation. The after-tax cost of debt capital such as bonds is a function of the interest rate $\times$ (1 − tax rate), because interest is tax-deductible and dividends on shares of stock are not.

Preferred stock is a hybrid that falls between debt and common stock with regard to risk and return. Like debt, preferred stock generally creates a fixed commitment by the firm to make periodic payments; however, unlike the case with debt, failure to make the payments does not result in bankruptcy. In liquidation, the claims of preferred stockholders take precedence over those of common stockholders but are subordinate to those of bondholders. The cost of preferred stock is the rate of return that must be earned on it in order to keep unchanged the earnings available to common stockholders. The cost of preferred-stock capital is a rate determined by dividing the stated dividends by the proceeds realized from the sale of the stock.

If, for simplicity, preferred stock is omitted, a firm must determine the cost of capital to be borne in financing investment when both debt and equity (common stock and retained earnings) are potential sources of financing. The following illustration is one way of computing the cost of capital to a firm, a way more realistic than simply using the interest rate as a measure of the cost of capital.

Suppose a firm can float a bond issue at 5 percent. A tax rate of 50 percent would effectively cut this rate in half, since interest paid on debt is a tax-deductible expense.[15] Can we infer that the marginal cost of capital to the firm is therefore 2.5 percent? No, because additional debt financing implies that the firm has exhausted part of its potential for floating new bonds. Beyond

---

[15]At the time this is being written, the tax rate on corporate profits is 22 percent on the first \$25,000, and 48 percent on those over \$25,000.

point N in Figure 9-5, the cost of bond financing starts to rise, because bond buyers feel the proportion of bonds to stock is too high for the bonds to be sold at 5 percent.

The average cost of equity increases from the start, because bondholders have a prior claim to assets, and so an increasing proportion of liabilities relative to equity would make stockholders increasingly vulnerable in case of liquidation. Furthermore, and usually more important, interest payments are a fixed cost, and so an increase in interest payments makes the net profits available to stockholders more volatile. The average stockholder would prefer a steady return.

A high bond-to-equity ratio gives bondholders less cushion against losses in case of default, and default itself is more likely, because any significant reduction in earnings before interest expense may deprive the firm of its ability to meet periodic interest payments. However, even though its interest costs rise, the firm in Figure 9-5 will be able to reduce its average cost of capital, *AC capital*, beyond point N by issuing more bonds. The firm can continue to reduce the average cost of capital as long as its ratio of bonds to equity is to the left of point M. Any bonds–equity ratio to the left of point M would permit the firm to reduce its average cost of capital by issuing more bonds, because the marginal cost is still below the average cost of capital up to that point, owing to the increasing proportion of relatively low-cost bond financing.

The marginal cost of capital is made up of the increasing cost of bond financing adjusted for an increase in the average cost of equity financing. Therefore, to the left of point M, the firm can reduce its average cost of capital by exercising leverage, often referred to as "trading on equity." Leverage involves using borrowed funds to earn for the firm a rate of return in excess of the rate paid to the firm's creditors.

To the right of point M in Figure 9-5, the leverage factor becomes unfavorable, because the marginal cost of capital rises further as the effect of increasing proportions of relatively low-cost bond financing is finally more than offset by the two factors already mentioned:

1. The ratio of bonds to equity has risen sufficiently to make bond buyers require a higher rate of return on bonds to compensate for the greater risk inherent in increasing debt.
2. The required rate of return on equity will vary directly with the debt–equity ratio. An increase in the ratio of debt to equity increases the volatility of earnings if output levels vary, because fixed debt operates like fixed costs of a business firm in creating large variations in profits as output levels vary. The average investor prefers a steady return to a changeable one, and requires a higher return on stock as a premium for volatility of earnings available to be paid to stockholders.

The average cost of capital is U-shaped, as in Figure 9-5.[16] Since at the

---

[16]For a good discussion of the traditional view, see Ezra Soloman, *The Theory of Financial Management* (New York: Columbia University Press, 1963), pp. 92–98.

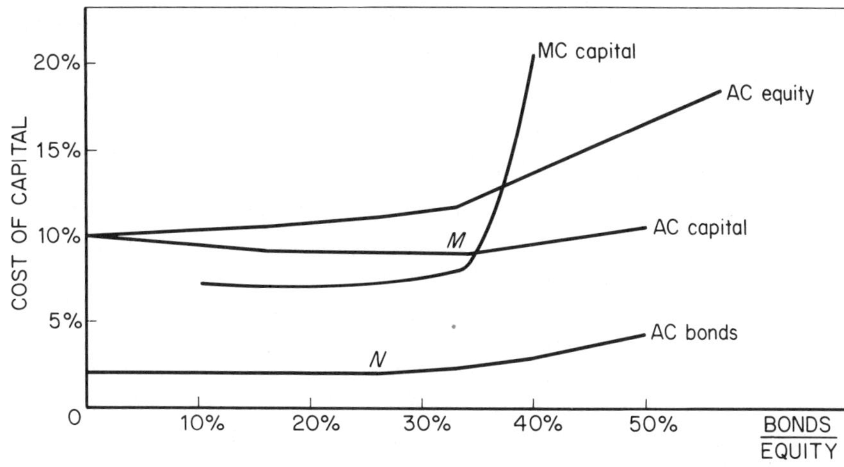

FIG. 9-5 The Cost of Capital and the Leverage Factor

minimum point on the curve average cost is minimized, that point represents an ideal debt-to-equity ratio.

Given this tendency of the average cost of capital to rise if the firm deviates from its ideal debt-equity ratio, how might a well-managed firm expand its capital structure? The answer is that once the minimum average cost is achieved, the firm must expand its debt and equity in equal proportions. Table 9-3 gives an example of how a firm might expand its debt and equity.

In order to maintain the lowest-cost debt-to-equity ratio once it is achieved, the firm will try to increase its debt financing and its equity financing simultaneously and in the same proportion. The firm's debt and equity are listed in column 1 of Table 9-3. Column 2 shows the effective cost after taxes of the components of the firm's capital structure. The cost factor indicated for each component in the table represents the opportunity cost of the current situation, not the historical cost. Assume that the firm has to pay 6 percent

TABLE 9-3

	(1) *Amount of Equity and Long-Term Debt*	*(2)* *Effective Cost*	*(3)* *Proportion of Total*	*(4)* *Weighted Cost*
Debt (i_d):	\$1,000,000	.03	.25	.0075
Equity (i_e):	3,000,000	.08	.75	.0600
Total	\$4,000,000		1.000	.0675

An alternative formulation by Modigliani and Miller, based on the assumption of perfect capital markets, holds that the capital structure of firms is not significant, because arbitrage will equate the value of firms of equal return and risk without regard to capital structure. Thus, cost of capital becomes a function of only the degree of risk associated with any given type of investment. Franco Modigliani and Morton H. Miller, "The Cost of Capital, Corporation Finance and the Theory of Investment," *American Economic Review*, 48 (June 1958), 261–97.

for additional debt financing at its minimum average-cost debt–equity ratio. Then the effective cost of debt is 3 percent, assuming a 50 percent tax rate, regardless of the historical level of costs. The 8 percent indicated as the cost of equity represents the minimum expected returns to common stockholders. Consequently, 8 percent must be imputed to additional retained earnings, which are a part of the common stockholders' interest in the firm.

Column 3 gives the proportion that each component represents in the firm's present (assumed to be ideal) debt–equity mix. Column 4 (column 2 times column 3) indicates the weighted cost of capital of each component, and the summation of column 4 is the weighted average cost of capital for the firm as a whole, in this case $6\frac{3}{4}$ percent.

The function illustrating the cost of capital to the firm will remain a horizontal straight line (as assumed in Keynesian theory) as long as the firm retains its optimum debt–equity structure and the cost of the various components remains unchanged. As the firm expands, to maintain the ideal debt–equity structure debt and equity must both increase in the same proportion.

Considering the absolute amount of financing rather than the debt–equity ratio, two factors exist that may make the average and marginal cost of capital upsloping beyond some point, even if the firm maintains an ideal debt-to-equity ratio.

1. Beyond some safe level of financing, the market will again ascribe a greater risk to both debt and equity as the amount of financing grows within a time period. The market requires a certain amount of time to accustom itself to an unusually large amount of financing by a firm. The average cost of capital will increase by some risk premium until the firm demonstrates an ability to profitably employ the greater amount of financing.
2. As the required amount of financing grows, the firm will use retained earnings rather than new common stock, since there are no flotation costs associated with retained earnings. However, since the quantity of retained earnings is limited, the firm will eventually be forced to issue new common stock to maintain the ideal debt–equity ratio. Since new stock carries a flotation cost, the net proceeds from the sale of the stock will be less than the current market price of the stock. Therefore, the cost of publicly issued common stock must be adjusted upward for flotation costs; and beyond that level where new stock has to be floated, the cost of capital jumps up as the volume of financing increases. (The purchaser of the firm's common stock expects a return on the price he pays, whereas the company receives less than that price, because of flotation costs.)

An upsloping cost-of-capital curve adds a factor to consider in investment decisions by the firm, in that the firm can no longer assume that its cost of capital remains constant. However, the profit-maximizing firm would still increase its financing up to the point where the cost of incremental financing equals the marginal efficiency of capital. An illustration of the behavior of a profit-maximizing firm facing an upsloping marginal cost-of-capital curve is presented in Figure 9-6.

If the marginal cost of capital equals r_1 (point a on the MEC), given an ideal debt–equity ratio and available retained earnings, the firm would operate at point *a* with investment of I_1, if the r_1 rate remained constant. However, the marginal cost of capital jumps when additional retained earnings are

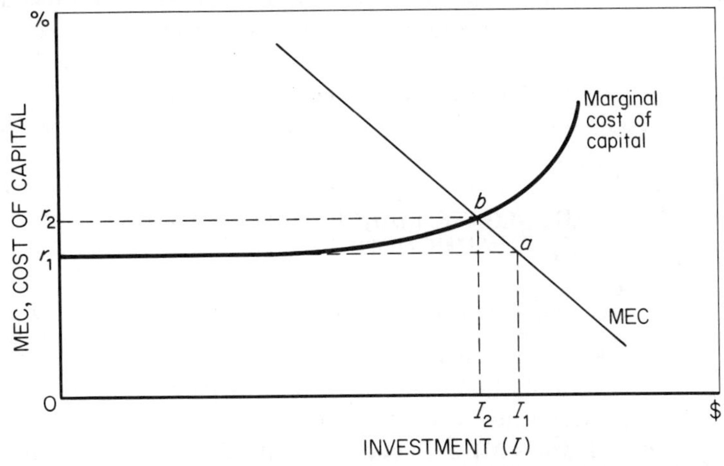

FIG. 9-6 Investment Equilibrium for the Firm

exhausted or when risk begins to increase as a function of the size of financing. At that point, the marginal cost of capital becomes upsloping, so equilibrium occurs not at point *a*, but at point *b*, resulting in a smaller quantity of investment and a higher cost of capital.

One significant conclusion to be drawn from an upsloping cost-of-capital curve is that the firm will invest less than it would if the cost of capital were constant. The firm therefore will be forced to postpone some otherwise profitable investment projects until a future time.

In a riskless world, the cost of capital would simply be the interest rate. But, in a sense, it is illogical to follow the path of conventional macroeconomic theory and imply risklessness on one hand by using the interest rate as a measure of the cost of capital (unless one recognizes the interest rate as a proxy measure for the cost of capital), and at the same time imply risk by using the MEC with business expectations and confidence as major ingredients. In consequence, once the existence of risk is acknowledged, the cost of capital takes on a good deal of significance for macroeconomics, because it, and not the interest rate, determines the level of investment. Each firm is faced with its own cost of capital, a weighted average of several effective rates, which include an imputed rate of return on retained earnings, as well as the flotation costs on new issues of securities; and the riskier the firm, the higher the rates. Changes in a low-risk, relatively pure interest rate (such as that on government bonds) influence the total amount of investment by firms only to the extent that this rate is reflected in their cost of capital. In addition, the average cost of capital faced by a business firm in a risky world will be much higher than a theoretical risk-free interest rate, with a resulting reduction in the number of profitable investment projects over any given time.

However, even though in the real world no firm pays a pure rate of interest, because the cost of capital invariably exceeds "the interest rate" (however defined), it is true that interest rates tend to move together along with stockholders' required rate of return, so investment decisions are linked to changes in "the interest rate." Yet during a recession the risk of default will increase, which may cause an increasing cost of capital even if the pure interest rate is decreasing; therefore, perfect capital markets should not always be assumed.

THE AGGREGATE MARGINAL-EFFICIENCY-OF-CAPITAL FUNCTION

Simple Keynesian Aggregation

Keynes and most later macroeconomists depict the aggregate marginal-efficiency-of-capital function, MEC, as simply the horizontal summation of the investment-demand functions of all the firms in each industry. Therefore, if each firm's MEC function is negatively sloped, the aggregate function will also be negatively sloped and, in a riskless world of perfectly competitive markets (when the cost of capital equals the interest rate), will relate a given quantity of investment to each level of the interest rate. This aggregate investment-demand function, like most other aggregate functions, is based on the assumption that the actions of all the investors in the economy are independent of each other. In the absence of knowing how the individual demand functions will be affected by each other, any other procedure is unreasonable.

Capital Stock and Investment Flows

Keynes's original approach to the question of the MEC was unfortunately marred by confusion between the stock of capital and the flow of investment. His equilibrium concept in the *General Theory* seems to include both. Equilibrium of the stock of capital requires that its value remain constant, that new investment equal depreciation, and that the flow of net investment equal zero. Therefore, when the stock of capital is in equilibrium, only gross investment, in contrast to net investment, will be positive. Positive net investment requires that the stock of capital increase and, therefore, not be in equilibrium.

A continual flow of net investment would occur (1) if the aggregate demand for capital constantly shifted to the right, or (2) if the interest rate continually decreased, so that projects rejected earlier as insufficiently profitable would be undertaken. Positive investment over time increases the stock of capital. More capital, however, is associated with both diminishing returns to capital and the exhaustion of more profitable investment projects.

The original Keynesian theory involved a contradiction. It proposed (1) a stable positive investment-demand function, with (2) a stable equilibrium interest rate. However, it is impossible to maintain both simultaneously over time. Continual net investment required by a stable investment demand would increase the stock of capital. A growing stock of capital reduces the rate of return to capital because of diminishing returns or the exhaustion of profitable investment projects. So a growing stock of capital requires a declining—not a stable—interest rate, as long as the expected rate of return on investment projects remains constant.[17] Therefore, the original version of the Keynesian theory contained a contradiction, because Keynes related the MEC to both the demand for net investment and the demand for the stock of capital. He failed to realize that if the demand for capital and the rate of interest were in equilibrium, the demand for net investment would be zero.

Keynes's failure to distinguish the stock of capital from the flow of investment can be overcome by integrating the two variables in one model. However, before this integration can take place, it is necessary to introduce one more variable, the supply price of capital goods, assumed to be the marginal cost of producing capital goods. Keynes recognized that the production of more capital goods could cause an increase in the marginal cost of producing those goods. However, he did not specify that increasing costs in the capital-goods-producing industry would limit aggregate net investment during any given time period. An increasing aggregate-marginal-cost curve for all the firms in the capital-goods industry may be inferred, assuming short-run diminishing returns. As marginal cost increases, the selling price of capital goods will probably also increase. Therefore, an increasing output of capital goods results in price increases in the capital-goods industry.

Figure 9-7 combines the demand for the stock of capital, the flow of net investment, and the increasing marginal costs in the capital-goods industry. The increasing marginal-cost curve of the capital-goods industry is shown in panel C. For simplicity, we assume perfect competition, so the industry marginal-cost curve becomes the industry short-run supply curve. Keynes's ambiguity regarding stock and flow variables is resolved in Figure 9-7 by presenting the demand for the stock of capital in panel A and the flow of net investment in panel B. As mentioned above, the increasing cost of producing capital goods is presented in panel C. In this section, we have used the marginal efficiency of capital, or MEC, to represent the demand for the stock of capital in panel A and have used a related concept—the marginal efficiency of investment, or MEI—to represent the demand for net investment in panel B. The percentage figure on the vertical axis in panel A represents the rate of return on the total capital plant, and the percentage figure in panel B represents the rate of return on net investment. In panel A, the horizontal axis shows the amount of total capital; in panel B, the amount of net investment. The increasing marginal costs presented in panel C are reflected in the decreasing rate of demand for investment in panel B, in that the rate of decrease in the MEI mirrors the rate of increase in the marginal cost of capital goods.

The example presented in Figure 9-7 starts at an initial equilibrium level at which the stock of capital is $910 billion and the interest rate is 8 percent.

---

[17]If the expected rate of return on investment projects increases, then the demand for capital would increase at a constant rate of interest. However, the demand for capital would have to increase at just the right amount in order to keep the demand for investment stable.

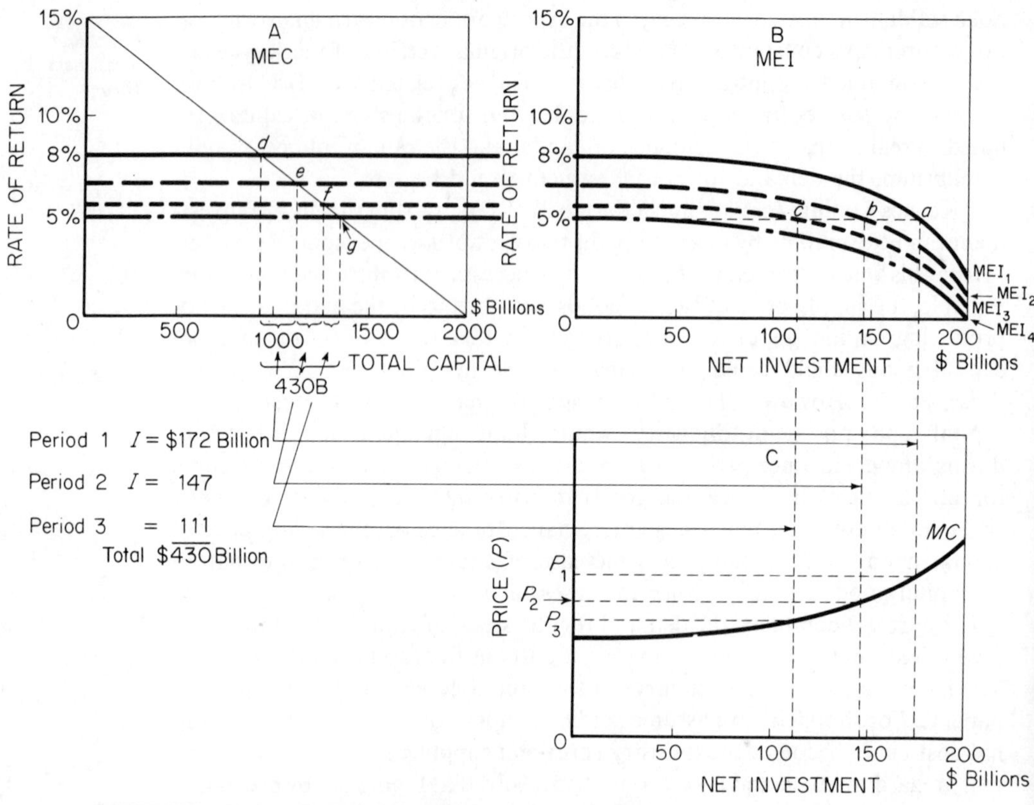

FIG. 9-7 Investment—Long- and Short-run Adjustments

Since the stock of capital is in equilibrium, no net investment occurs unless the MEC schedule shifts to the right or the interest rate falls. Assuming that the interest rate falls from 8 to 5 percent, the new equilibrium stock of capital would be \$1,340 billion, which would require an increase of \$430 billion of investment.

However, the new equilibrium cannot profitably be achieved in one time period, because increasing short-run marginal costs in the capital-goods industry force the price of capital goods above the profitable level of investment long before \$430 billion of investment is undertaken. Our assumption of perfect competition in the capital-goods industry means that the market price of capital goods will not rise above P_1, shown in panel C, because P_1 is the equilibrium price determined by the supply of new capital goods and the demand for net investment at a 5 percent rate of interest. In the initial time period, investment could be profitably expanded to point *a* on the initial investment-demand function (MEI_1) in panel B, permitting a first-period increase of investment of \$172 billion before the cost of capital goods in that time period increases enough to reduce the marginal rate of return on the investment to 5 percent in the short run. As net investment is added to capital stock, a movement occurs from point *d* to point *e* along the demand-for-capital curve in panel A. At the start of period 2, the marginal rate of return on the capital stock, as seen in panel A, will have been reduced from 8 to 6.7 percent. Consequently, a new MEI function (MEI_2) will develop at the new rate of return. The new period-2 MEI function still mirrors the marginal-cost curve in panel C, but at a lower level than MEI_1. MEI_2 intersects the 5 percent interest-rate line at point *b* in panel B, permitting an additional $147 billion of profitable investment. The capital-goods industry can produce $147 billion worth of output in period 2, before the price of capital goods is forced up to P_2 and chokes off any further increase in net investment. This additional investment is shown in panel A as a movement along the demand for capital goods from *e* to *f*. (P_2 is lower than P_1 because the spread between MEI_1 and the interest rate exceeds that between MEI_2 and the interest rate.)

Finally, the new equilibrium stock of capital is reached in period 3, with a movement along the demand-for-capital curve in panel A from *f* to *g*, when $111 billion of net investment occurs as the third MEI function (MEI_3) intersects the 5 percent rate-of-interest line at point *c*, generating just sufficient investment to create the new equilibrium in the capital-goods market. Therefore, because of increasing marginal costs in the capital-goods industry as more capital goods are produced, the marginal rate of return on the total capital stock does not reach 5 percent until the end of period 3, when the new equilibrium stock of capital is achieved.

There is an additional factor limiting investment during any given time period. Firms may face several profitable investment projects simultaneously after a decrease in the interest rate. Realistically, only a limited number of new investment projects can be undertaken in any given period of time. Any new investment project entails difficulties of management, staffing, and integration into the firm's activities, which compound as the number of investment projects increases. Consequently, firms can absorb only a limited amount of new capital within any given time period without experiencing unacceptable increases in their costs. As a result, firms themselves will restrict the number of investment projects undertaken in any given time period, regardless of the availability of profitable investment projects or the cost of capital goods.

However, over time as the new capital can be profitably absorbed, new projects will be undertaken. If we assume sufficient time to allow all profitable new investment to be undertaken, we may, for simplicity, assume away the short-run effect of increasing marginal cost in the capital-goods industry, and we can avoid the need to shift to a new MEI function in each time period because of the cut-off in investment owing to the rising costs in the capital-goods industry.

We employ a linear, negatively sloped investment-demand function that we shall label, following Keynes, the marginal efficiency of capital (MEC), even though the distinction between the MEC and the marginal efficiency of investment (MEI) is analytically more accurate. In much of aggregate analyses, the confusion between the stock and flow concepts in Keynes's analysis is irrelevant; therefore, it is simpler to ignore this distinction in such cases, focusing on the major analytical relationships. However, our simplifying assumption has a shortcoming—it overlooks the problem that an assumed equilibrium between the demand for capital goods and the rate of interest implies no net investment. Therefore, we implicitly assume that net investment occurs as a result of just-sufficient increases in the demand for capital, in order to keep both the demand for net investment and the rate of interest stable.

Now let us consider what would cause such shifts.

Shifts in the Aggregate Demand for Capital Goods

Analytically, a rightward shift in the aggregate demand for capital goods has the same effect as a decrease in the interest rate, because either will encourage firms to employ more capital by increasing the number of profitable investment projects and will require a number of time periods for the equilibrium level of investment to be achieved. The following factors may cause a shift in the aggregate demand for capital goods: (1) changes in expectations; (2) changes in the level of technology; (3) changes in the cost of productive resources; and (4) shifts in the effective demand function [changes in $(C + I + G)$].

As we have seen, Keynes emphasized that widespread expectations of prosperity may induce businessmen to project higher future returns at each possible level of investment. A rightward shift in the demand for capital goods will occur as a consequence of businessmen's optimism. Extended periods of prosperity cause such optimism to be justified, which further increases confidence in profit projections. The reverse is true during recessions, particularly if business is bad for an extended period.

Rightward shifts in the demand for capital goods may also be induced by changes in the level of technology. The discovery and implementation of new business methods or techniques often require additional investment. Net investment increases whether the new investment is required to replace or to supplement existing plant and equipment. Technological change therefore increases the aggregate demand for capital. Even inventions that are capital savings (require less capital per unit of output) still have to be implemented, and so increase the demand for capital in the short run, even though, in the long run, less capital may be required to produce any given output. Therefore, a capital-saving innovation increases the demand for capital goods in the short run but may reduce it in the long run. In contrast, a labor-saving innovation increases the demand for capital goods in both the short and long run.

Any reduction in the prices of complementary noncapital productive resources reduces costs and generally increases the expected net return on investment and, consequently, causes an increase in the demand for capital goods, since expected net income earned may be increased by either increasing total revenue or reducing total cost. A reduction in the price of substitute noncapital resources would be analytically equivalent to a (relative) increase in the price of capital, and so would reduce the MEC. And where resources are both complements and substitutes, the results are indeterminate, depending on the shape and position of the isoquants for all the firms constituting the economy and the relative importance of the various firms in the total production process.

If the reduction in the price of resources occurs in the capital goods industry by reducing the purchase price of capital goods, the demand for capital would shift to the right. (Note that in this case the marginal cost curve of the capital producing industry will also shift to the right.)

Any increase in the effective demand function will generally increase the expected net return on investment by increasing total revenue and will therefore increase the demand for capital goods. The relationship between the demand for capital goods and effective demand or aggregate income has implications beyond merely shifting the demand-for-capital curve, and those implications are the subject of our next section.[18]

INVESTMENT–AGGREGATE INCOME RELATIONSHIP

In the *General Theory*, investment is stated as a function of the marginal effciency of capital and the rate of interest. Although income expectations help to determine the shape of the MEC, Keynes did not specifically make investment a function of either the level of aggregate income or the change in aggregate income. The effects of changes in the level of aggregate income will be reserved for Chapter 16, since such changes involve dynamic analysis outside the framework of the comparative-statics approach of the basic Keynesian model. However, investment expenditure can be related to the level of aggregate income in a static model that fits the Keynesian framework.

Keynes proposed that an increase in the level of business activity raises net income through increased business receipts and that investment decisions are based on the expectation of a continuation of present trends. Thus, Keynes explicitly included income expectations as a determinant of the marginal efficiency of capital. From this, it could be inferred that investment is a function not only of the interest rate but also of the level of aggregate income.

Aggregate income may be considered an independent variable partially determining the level of investment expenditure, because many firms' investment policies are based on it. Increases in profit prospects associated with increasing levels of aggregate income increase demand for investment expendi-

[18]In the real world, when the interest rate changes, the expectations of investors will usually change along with it, causing a shift in the MEC. (E.g., monetary policy used to reduce the interest rate may signal investors that good times are coming.) However, in a formal model, to treat the MEC and the interest rate as independent of each other is permissible.

tures by increasing the expected returns on given investments. In addition, the retained earnings accompanying the increased amounts of net income allow financially well-structured firms to finance investment expenditures without increasing their cost of capital at the margin by the flotation costs of additional common-stock issues.

The investment expenditure function is graphically demonstrated by drawing a positively sloped curve with investment expenditures plotted along the y axis and aggregate income plotted along the x axis. Such an investment-expenditure curve is illustrated in Figure 9-8, which resembles Figure 8-8 except for the positive slope of the investment expenditure function.

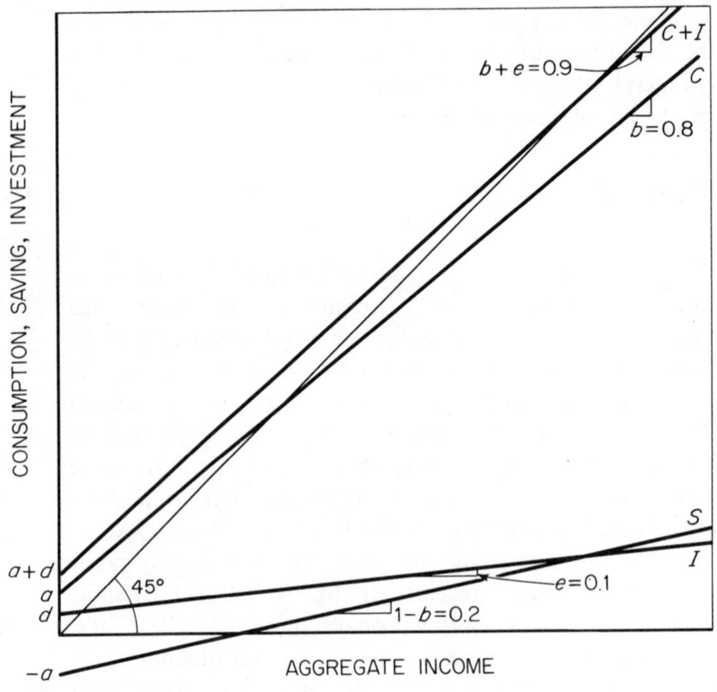

FIG. 9-8 The Super Multiplier

In the *General Theory*, Keynes points out that an attempt to increase savings in the aggregate (an upward shift in the savings function) will result in a reduction in income with no increase in the actual amount saved by the community. A positively sloped investment-expenditure curve, such as in Figure 9-8, makes the analysis even more "Keynesian," or at least more paradoxical, since an attempt to save more causes not only a reduction in aggregate income but also less realized savings. The simple Keynesian multiplier is based solely on the slope of the consumption function. However, the introduction of a degree of income elasticity to the investment-expenditure curve leads to the conclusion that the effective-demand curve ($C + I$) has a steeper slope than the consumption function alone. Consequently, a supermultiplier emerges that incorporates the effects of both incremental consumption and investment.

The positively sloped investment-expenditure curve causes effective demand ($C + I$) to increase at a faster rate than the consumption function by itself. However, as illustrated in the figure, equilibrium still occurs where saving equals planned investment. The effect of the steeper slope of $C + I$, the effective demand curve, compared with C, the consumption function, is to increase the size of the multiplier. Figure 9-8 shows a marginal propensity to consume (MPC) of .8, with the addition of an investment function having a slope of .1. The slope of the investment function may be called the marginal propensity to invest (MPI), since it directly relates investment expenditure to aggregate income. The slope of the effective-demand curve equals the MPC plus the MPI—in this case, .9. If the MPI is designated e and the MPC b, the formula for the supermultiplier, k', becomes

$$k' = \frac{1}{1 - (b + e)}$$

In the illustration above, the effect on the multiplier of including an MPI of .1 is to increase its value from 5 to 10. Thus, even a relatively small amount of income-induced investment can significantly affect the equilibrium level of aggregate income.

Because the supermultiplier has a greater value than the simple Keynesian multiplier, an attempt by the community to save more out of any given level of aggregate income will cause aggregate income to fall more through its use than it would by using only the Keynesian multiplier. The positive slope of the investment expenditure function causes a paradoxical effect from an increase in thrift: An upward movement of the savings function from S to S' in Figure 9-9 causes a reduction in aggregate income from Y_1 to Y_2 and in

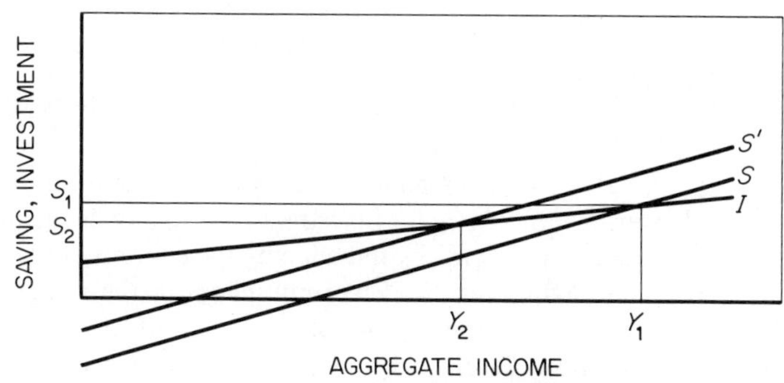

FIG. 9-9 The Paradox of Thrift

savings from S_1 to S_2. Therefore, the attempt to save more actually leads to the economy's saving less. Although individual thrift may still be considered a virtue, the "fallacy of composition" renders aggregate thrift something of an economic vice.

SUMMARY AND CONCLUSIONS

Chapter 9 concludes the discussion of the basic Keynesian model. This chapter has concentrated on the factors behind the demand for investment, in Keynes's view: the marginal efficiency of capital and the rate of interest. One major difference between Keynes's theory and the neoclassical investment theory, as epitomized by Irving Fisher, is that the neoclassicists assumed a degree of certainty regarding the future that Keynes denied. Keynes stressed the importance of expectations in investment theory and argued that the anticipated stream of net income from any investment is based on a very precarious state of knowledge.

We developed Keynes's investment-demand theory by showing the relationship between the MEC and the rate of interest on the one hand, and the present value and the purchase price of a capital asset on the other.

We considered the factors that can shift the firm's MEC function. The major ones are changes in expected net returns, changes in asset cost, and changes in technology.

In this chapter, certain points of confusion in the *General Theory* were considered:

1. Keynes used the interest rate to stand for the cost of capital, a legitimate practice only if a riskless world of perfectly competitive capital markets is assumed. However, the cost of capital is better depicted by a weighted average cost of all components of the firm's optimum debt and equity structure. The cost of capital to the firm, therefore, is higher than the interest rate and includes the opportunity cost of alternative investments available to the firm's stockholders. Using the cost of capital instead of the interest rate adds a new dimension of risk and uncertainty on the cost side, an aspect overlooked by Keynes and by many of his followers.
2. Keynes confused stock and flow concepts in constructing his MEC function. The stock concept, capital, was separated from the related flow variable, investment, by developing an MEC function relating to the stock of capital and an MEI function relating to the flow of investment. The major point that emerged from distinguishing the MEC from the MEI is that increases in aggregate investment require more time to be effected than would appear to be true under the original, unmodified theory.

Finally, we aggregated investment demand and we considered the relationship of aggregate investment to aggregate income—the investment expenditure function—by introducing the concept of the marginal propensity to invest (MPI) and the supermultiplier. In the *General Theory*, it is clear that changes in income expectations would induce shifts in the MEC. However, in more recent writings, the investment expenditure function has been introduced as a separate variable.

In the following chapter, we will present the policy conclusions that Keynes himself derived from his *General Theory*.

QUESTIONS AND PROBLEMS

1. The *Wall Street Journal* reports that investment is expected to increase by 10% next year. What changes in the MEC could account for that forecast?

2. How is the cost of capital related to the interest rate? Which concept is relevant to investment decisions?

3. Demonstrate how it is possible to reconcile the MEC with the MEI.

4. Describe the supermultiplier, and show how it differs from the Keynesian multiplier.

5. What is the paradox of thrift? How likely is it to affect our contemporary economy?

6. Discuss some of the ways in which a change in technology might affect the demand for investment.

7. What variables influence the price elasticity of the demand for investment goods?

8. How important are expectations in the demand for investment?

9. In the graph below, are the resources substitutes or complements? What would be the effect of a decrease in the price of capital?

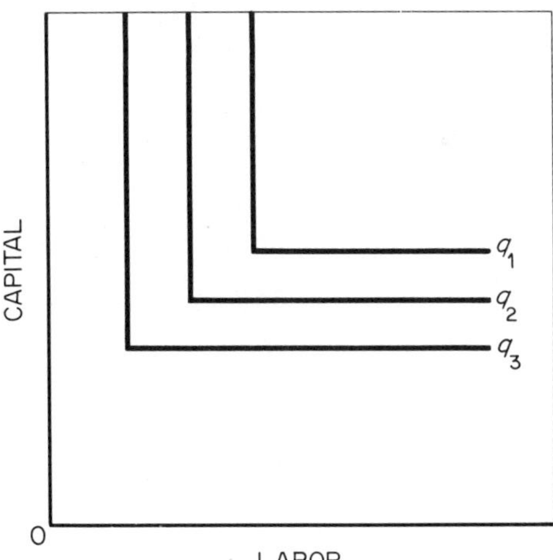

10. Suppose a firm faces the following investment opportunities:

Project A: Costs $5,000; returns 20%
Project B: Costs $3,000; returns 15%
Project C: Costs $2,000; returns 12%

Project D: Costs $4,000; returns 8%
Project E: Costs $4,500; returns 6%
Project F: Costs $3,000; returns 5%
Project G: Costs $5,000; returns 4.5%

a. Sketch the firm's MEC below.
b. If the firm can borrow money for 7.5%, how much will it invest?

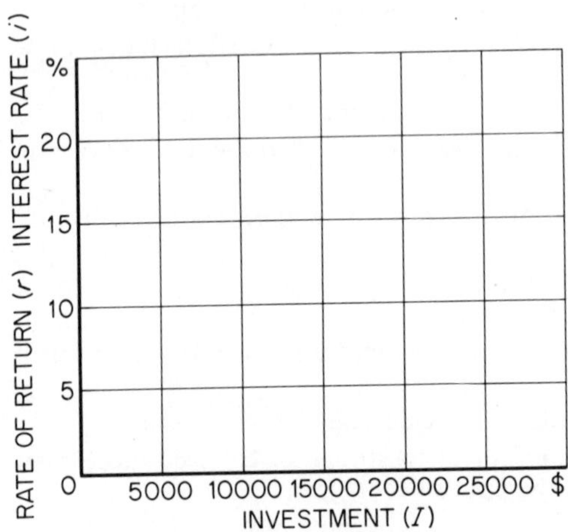

11. In the illustration at the top of page 307, the Keynesian multiplier is ———, the supermultiplier is ———, and equilibrium income is ———. Demonstrate the paradox of thrift.

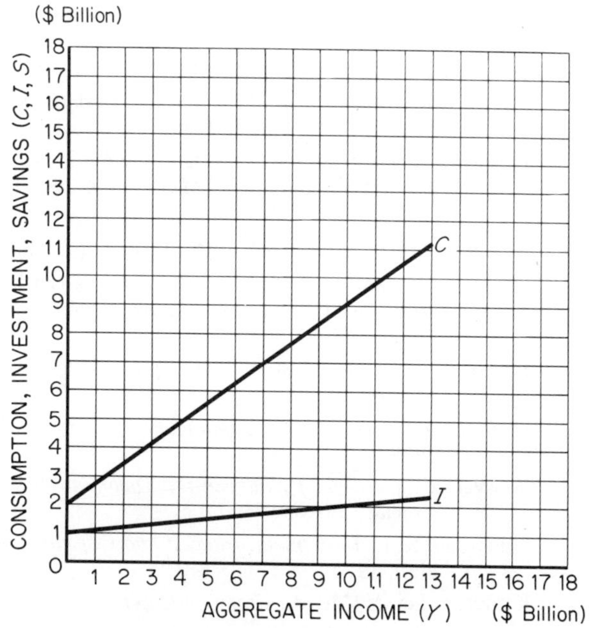

ADDITIONAL SELECTED REFERENCES

KEYNES'S THEORY OF INVESTMENT

DILLARD, DUDLEY, *The Economics of John Maynard Keynes*, pp. 134–60. Englewood Cliffs, N. J.: Prentice Hall, 1948.

HART, A. G., "Keynes' Analysis of Expectations and Uncertainty," in *The New Economics*, ed. S. E. Harris, pp. 415–24. New York: Knopf, 1947.

SHACKLE, G. L. S., "Expectations and Employment," *Economics Journal*, 49 (September 1939), 442–52.

———, "The Nature of the Inducement to Invest," *Review of Economic Studies*, 8 (October 1940), 44–48, 54–57.

WRIGHT, DAVID M., *The Keynesian System*, pp. 25–43. New York: Fordham University Press, 1962.

SEPARATING THE STOCK OF CAPITAL FROM THE FLOW OF INVESTMENT

LERNER, A. P., *Economics of Control*, New York: Macmillan, 1944.

———, "On Some Recent Developments in Capital Theory," *American Economic Review*, 55 (May 1965), 284–95.

———, "On the Marginal Product of Capital and the Marginal Efficiency of Investment," *Journal of Political Economy*, 61 (February 1953), 1–14.

WITTE, J. G., "The Microfoundations of the Social Investment Function," *Journal of Political Economy*, 71 (October 1963), 441–56.

GENERAL SURVEYS OF INVESTMENT AND CAPITAL THEORY

Keynesian Investment Theory

ACKLEY, GARDNER, *Macroeconomic Theory*, pp. 460–504. New York: Macmillan, 1961.

JORGENSON, DALE W., "The Theory of Investment Behavior," in *Determinants of Investment Behavior*, ed. R. Ferber, pp. 129–55. New York: National Bureau of Economic Research, 1967.

KUH, E., "Theory and Institutions in the Study of Investment Behavior," *American Economic Review*, 53 (May 1963), 260–68.

CAPITAL THEORY AND FINANCIAL MANAGEMENT

BAUMOL, W., and B. MALKIEL, "The Firm's Optional Debt–Equity Combination and Cost of Capital," *Quarterly Journal of Economics*, 81 (November 1967), 547–78.

BIERMAN, H., and S. SMIDT, *The Capital Budgeting Decision*, 2nd ed. New York: Macmillan, 1966.

DEWEY, DONALD, *Modern Capital Theory*. New York: Columbia University Press, 1965.

HAAVELMO, TRYGVE, *A Study in the Theory of Investment*. Chicago: University of Chicago Press, 1960.

HIRSHLIEFER, J., *Investment, Interest and Capital*. Englewood Cliffs, N.J.: Prentice-Hall, 1970.

KIRZNER, ISRAEL M., *An Essay on Capital*. New York: Augustus M. Kelley, 1966.

SHACKLE, G. L. S., "The Interest Elasticity of Investment," in *The Theory of Interest Rates*, eds. F. H. Hahn and F. P. R. Brechling, pp. 80–94. London: Macmillan, 1965.

SMITH, V. L., *Investment and Production*. Cambridge: Harvard University Press, 1961.

SOLOW, ROBERT M., *Capital Theory and the Rate of Return*. Skokie, Ill.: Rand McNally, 1965.

EMPIRICAL STUDIES

ALBERTS, W. W., "Capital Investment by Firm in Plant and Equipment," *Journal of Finance*, 21 (May 1966), 178–201.

BARNA, TIBOR, "On Measuring Capital," in *The Theory of Capital*, eds. F. A. Lutz and D. C. Hague, pp. 75–94. London: Macmillan, 1963. Proceedings of a conference held by the International Economics Association.

DEAN, J., "Measuring the Productivity of Capital, *Harvard Business Review*, 32 (January–February 1954), 120–30.

EISNER, ROBERT, "A Distributed-Lag Investment Function," *Econometrica*, 28 (January 1960), 1–29.

———, "Realization of Investment Anticipations," in *The Brookings Quarterly Econometric Model of the United States*, eds. J. S. Duesenberry et al., pp. 95–128. Skokie, Ill.: Rand McNally, 1965.

———, and ROBERT H. STROTZ, "Determinants of Business Investment," in Commission on Money and Credit, *Impacts of Monetary Policy*, pp. 59–337. Englewood Cliffs, N. J.: Prentice Hall, 1963.

FRIEND, I., and JEAN BRONFENBRENNER, "Business Investment Programs and Their Realization," *Survey of Current Business*, 30 (December 1950), 11–22.

GRUNFELD, Y., "The Determinants of Corporate Investment," in *The Demand for Durable Goods*, ed. A. C. Harberger, pp. 209–66. Chicago: The University of Chicago Press, 1960.

JORGENSON, DALE W., "Econometric Studies of Investment Behavior: A Survey," *Journal of Economic Literature*, 9 (December 1971), 1111–43.

INTEREST ELASTICITY OF INVESTMENT DEMAND (SEE CHAPTER 11 FOR DISCUSSION)

ANDREWS, P. W. S., "A Further Inquiry into the Effects of Rates of Interest," *Oxford Economic Papers*, 3 (February 1940), 32–73.

EBERSOLE, J. F., "The Influences of Interest Rates upon Entreprenurial Decisions in Business: A Case Study," *Harvard Business Review*, 17 (November 1938), 35–39.

MEADE, J. E., and P. W. S. ANDREWS, "Summary of Replies to Questions on the Effects of Interest Rates," *Oxford Economic Papers*, 1 (October 1938), 14–31.

SAYERS, R. S., "Businessmen and the Terms of Borrowing," *Oxford Economic Papers*, 3 (February 1940), 23–31.

INVESTMENT DEMAND AND PERMANENT INCOME

EISNER, ROBERT, "A Permanent Income Theory for Investment," *American Economic Review*, 57 (June 1967), 364–90.

Keynesian Monetary and Fiscal Policy

10

This chapter covers policy based on the basic reconstructed Keynesian model, which may be compared with the more complete and more realistic static and dynamic models presented in Chapters 11 through 16. Many of those advances are based on ideas originated by Keynes, such as allowance for price and wage changes. Yet the basic Keynesian model provides the basis for much of our modern monetary and fiscal policy. In addition, Keynesian economics is of historical interest as the basis for much of the economic and social policy of the 1930's and 1940's. Furthermore, built-in stabilizers and certain multiplier concepts, which are implied but not specifically employed by Keynes, have been added to build a model of the theory upon which much of our modern monetary and fiscal policy is based.

It should be remembered that the General Theory involved a technical and rather mechanical theory that is adequately presented by graphic analysis. But at the same time, and perhaps more important, it proceeded on a behavioristic and psychological level that was more flexible and more realistic than the formal theoretical model.

SIMPLIFIED KEYNESIAN MODEL

The basic elements of the *General Theory* have been included in a simple model. One major ingredient—the consumption function—is not explicitly included. However, since

$$\text{MPC} + \text{MPS} = 1$$

and

$$\text{APC} + \text{APS} = 1$$

when the savings function is specified, the consumption function is automatically implied. Therefore, in our illustration, when we specify an MPS of .2, we implicitly specify an MPC of .8. Furthermore, we also imply a multiplier of 5, since the multiplier equals 1/MPS.

Certain concepts that were presented in the last three chapters, but that Keynes did not use in his policy discussions, have been omitted here for simplicity, even though post-Keynesian economists consider them significant, as we shall see in subsequent chapters. The major omission of this chapter is the transactions and precautionary demand for money balances (money as a function of aggregate income). In addition, we continue to assume a hypothetical world with no foreign sector, no business savings, no distinction between the marginal efficiency of capital (MEC) and the marginal efficiency of investment (MEI), and no difference between the cost of capital and the interest rate.

The model, which illustrates Keynesian policy in simplified form, is summarized in Figure 10-1. Panel A shows the aggregate demand for invest-

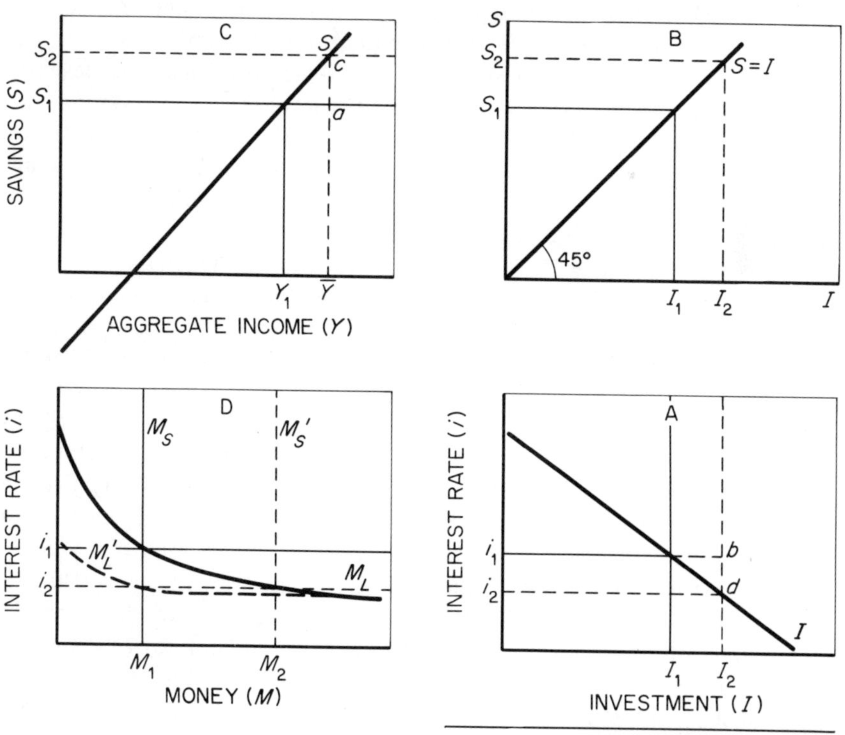

FIG. 10-1 The Basic Keynesian System

ment, I, as a function of the interest rate, i. This function summarizes that part of the basic Keynesian model that was developed in Chapter 9. The 45° line in panel B defines all the possible equilibrium levels of savings and investment, since the two are equal in equilibrium. As was the case in Chapter 8, we will continue to assume that savings adjusts to *ex ante* investment rather than the reverse, although the argument could proceed from either direction. Panel C of Figure 10-1 presents the savings function as shown in Figure 8-5. For simplicity, we hold constant all determinants of savings other than aggregate income or output (using "aggregate income" to refer to some general theoretical measure of real national income). As we already know, the description of a savings function determines at the same time a unique consumption function. Panel D shows the speculative demand for liquid money balance, M_L, and the stock of money, which together determine the equilibrium interest rate. The speculative demand for liquid balances incorporates the demand for money as a function only of the interest rate and not of the level of aggregate income. The speculative demand for liquid balances is also referred to as the liquidity-preference function in this chapter, since the demand for transactions and precautionary money balances is not included here. Therefore, the demand for speculative liquid balances is the total demand for money in the context of this chapter.

Starting in panel A with an interest rate of i_1, which is determined in panel D, investment will equal I_1. We can trace the results through the other three panels. Savings–investment equilibrium is demonstrated in panel B, with an investment level of I_1 on the x-axis requiring a savings level of S_1 on the y-axis. Consequently, in panel C, the level of aggregate income is determined on the x-axis at Y_1. In this example, the equilibrium level of income, Y_1, falls below full employment, represented by the dotted line at income level $\bar{Y}$. The interest rate at which savings was equated with investment is determined at i_1 by the intersection of the stock of money and the liquidity preference curve in panel D. In the basic Keynesian system, changes in the savings and investment functions do not affect the interest rate.

Figure 10-1 indicates that the full-employment level of income, $\bar{Y}$, can be achieved by changing any of the functions in panels A, C, or D. (The $S = I$ equilibrium condition stated in panel B obviously cannot change.) For example, in panel C, the savings function could shift to the right (a decrease in APS and a corresponding increase in APC) and pass through point a. This increase in the average propensity to consume out of any given income level could cause full employment to be achieved with a higher level of consumption (because of the implied shift in the consumption function) and the same level of investment. Alternatively, the investment demand function in panel A could shift to the right at the same rate of interest, intersecting the i_1 interest rate at point b, which would cause full employment by requiring the quantity of savings to increase up to point c on the savings function in panel C, in order that savings and investment be in equilibrium in panel *B*. Full employment could also be restored in this instance through monetary policy, by either an increase in the stock of money (shift to the right), from

M_s to the dotted M_s' line, or a drop in speculative demand for liquid balances to the dotted M_L' curve. Either change would cause a new, lower, equilibrium interest rate of i_2 in panel D. At the lower interest rate, the economy would move down the existing demand-for-investment function to point d in panel A, increasing the quantity of investment from I_1 to I_2, which is sufficient to cause full employment. Figure 10-1 represents a skeleton of the Keynesian system; the rest of this chapter will flesh out the bare bones.

MONETARY POLICY

Liquidity Preference

As previously pointed out, attention in the basic Keynesian model may be focused on only the speculative demand for liquid balances, the liquidity-preference function.

Liquidity preference is based on the expectations of asset holders, whether individual or corporate, and is not under direct control of the monetary authorities. However, these authorities, as Keynes points out, have an indirect influence on liquidity preference; the all-important concept of the "normal" interest rate, on which liquidity preference is largely based, depends in great part on their actions and pronouncements.[1] If the monetary authorities advise asset holders of an impending change in the interest rate, the result may be an induced shift in the liquidity-preference function, which might achieve the desired interest rate without any further action on the part of the authorities. Such reactions by asset holders have been called the "announcement effects";[2] they may be positive and reinforce monetary policy—if the announcements are believed and if asset holders react as the monetary authorities wish.

However, any shift in the liquidity-preference function because of announcement effects depends on changing expectations, as asset holders revise their ideas about the relationship between the "normal" interest rate and the going market rate. The results of the announcement effects may not match the desires of the monetary authorities if people do not react as the monetary authority has anticipated. Keynes stressed the impact of pronouncements by the monetary authorities on asset holders, but he felt that efforts by the authorities to sway popular opinion in the longer run, and thereby shift the liquidity-preference curve, would probably not counterbalance a realistic market appraisal by asset holders.

---

[1]Keynes referred to a "safe" interest rate, one that would be high enough to preclude a strong probability that it would increase and cause a loss of capital value. J. M. Keynes, *The General Theory of Employment, Interest and Money* (New York: Harcourt Brace Jovanovich, 1936), p. 202.

[2]The discussion concerning announcement effects started in the 1950's. A presentation of this idea can be found in Asar Lindbeck, *The "New" Theory of Credit Control in the United States* (Stockholm: Almqvist and Wicksell, 1959), pp. 25–29, 38, and 39; and Warren L. Smith, "The Instruments of General Monetary Control," *National Banking Review*, 1 (September 1963), pp. 47–76.

Since announcement effects operate through changes in asset holders' expectations, they must also affect the demand and supply of securities. For example, if there is an announcement by the monetary authorities that lower interest rates are desired, and if asset holders believe that the authorities have the power to achieve their desired interest-rate reduction, the asset holders will anticipate higher security prices, thus increasing the demand for securities and reducing the liquidity-preference function. The result would be a lower equilibrium rate of interest without further action on the part of the monetary authorities.

The Stock of Money

As we said in Chapter 7, the stock of money in the Keynesian system is best depicted as a vertical straight line, because the monetary authorities have the power to set the stock of money at any desired level. Although the commercial banking system can expand and contract the stock of money through the bank credit multiplier, the system is always ultimately subject to the constraint of the monetary authorities, the Federal Reserve in the U.S., who may correct for any unexpected behavior of commercial banks by policies such as adjusting reserve requirements or by open-market operations.

The bank credit multiplier allows the Federal Reserve to change the stock of money through changes in the reserve requirements. If the Fed reduces the reserve requirement from 15 to 10 percent, the bank credit multiplier would increase from 6.666 . . . to 10 (disregarding the other leakages specified in Chapter 7). Such a change would mean that any given monetary base ("outside money") could be expanded 10 times instead of 6.666 . . . times. The expanded monetary stock (endogenously created money, called "inside money") will reach the potential indicated by the bank credit multiplier, if none of the leakages occur.

In contrast, open-market operations, through which the Fed buys and sells bonds, allows the Fed to directly change the size of the monetary base. For example, if the account manager for the Open Market Committee (a vice-president of the Federal Reserve Bank of New York) buys $1 million of bonds, and if the bank credit multiplier is 6.666 . . . , the final change in the money supply will be $6,666,666.67 ($1 million paid for the bonds, plus $5,666,666.67 of bank loans based on the new $1 million of bank reserves—again assuming that no leakages occur).

Of the two instruments of monetary policy just discussed, reserve-requirement changes are more crude, and open-market operations more subtle. When required reserves are changed, banks and borrowers throughout the country are affected and the impact is strong; open-market operations immediately affect only buyers or sellers who freely choose to come into the market. The secondary effects of selling securities through open-market operations are not as conspicuous as those of raising reserve requirements, since open-market operations work through the banking system by reducing demand deposits, rather than by forcing banks to meet new reserve requirements by calling loans or selling securities—and consequently to convert from an earning asset (loans) to a non-earning asset (reserves).

Furthermore, open-market operations can be employed in any amount and allow instantaneous changes in the direction of monetary policy. Purchases and sales of bonds can be accomplished quickly and without fanfare. Therefore, not only is the size of the stock of money completely under the control of the monetary authorities, but also, adjustments can be made quickly, conveniently, and quietly through open-market operations. In contrast, reserve-requirement changes make Federal Reserve policy obvious to everyone, possibly causing a reaction in the market that could either offset or reinforce the policy—in one case, neutralizing it, and in the other, causing a greater effect than desired.

The third monetary-policy technique employed by the Fed is to change the discount rate, the interest rate at which commercial banks can borrow from the Federal Reserve. Theoretically, a lower discount rate will stimulate bank borrowing from the Fed, and give the banking system more money to operate with; a higher rate would discourage bank borrowing and restrict the amount of credit available. However, in practice, commercial-bank borrowing from the Federal Reserve is normally restricted by tradition, and is used mainly as an "escape valve"—an emergency source of funds needed to meet a deficiency in required reserves. Banks seldom, if ever, borrow from the Fed to expand their business. Therefore, changes in the discount rate generally will not directly affect the availability of credit to bank customers. Of course, borrowing from the Fed is a potential source of bank credit, so it is true that during periods of restrictive monetary policy, more banks will find themselves in need of such borrowing, and raising the discount rate at such times will further restrict credit.

A shortcoming of discount-rate changes is that they leave with the banks, not the monetary authorities,[3] the initiative to change the money stock. Furthermore, like changes in reserve requirements, a change in the discount rate may cause an announcement effect. (In this case, though, it is never quite clear whether the change actually represents a change in Federal Reserve policy, because every time market rates of interest change, the Fed must alter the discount rate; a failure to keep it in line with the other rates would amount to a change in monetary policy.)

In addition to the general devices available to the Federal Reserve, there are also selective weapons. Two such devices are now in use. One is Regulation Q, which limits the interest that commercial banks can pay on time

---

[3]The Fed *can* manipulate the stock of money precisely as desired, but *do* they? Raymond Lambra and Raymond Torto have studied the situation and have concluded that, in reality, a supply function may actually affect the size of the quantity of money in circulation. However, the fact remains incontrovertable that the Fed could at will override any supply-of-money factors, so we will stick by the stock-of-money concept in preference to the supply-of-money concept favered by some.

"Federal Reserve Defensive Behavior and the Reverse Causation Argument," *Federal Reserve Bulletin;* 58 (Nov. 1972), 956–57.

deposits. The other is margin requirements, which limit the amount of credit that can be extended to purchasers of securities such as common stock. Two other selective policies, which have not been used in recent years, involve the size of the down payment and the length of the repayment period for consumer credit and first mortgages on real estate. Although selective controls have little overall impact, they have the advantage of pinpointing particular areas that might need control and are hard to reach through general controls.

Some people think the Federal Reserve has a degree of selective control through "moral suasion"; that is, that it has some ability to influence banks through discussion and advice. However, moral suasion may be ineffective when the Fed's advice conflicts with the bank's profits; commercial banks may not be much swayed by pleading, cajoling, or threats of tighter credit or more strict examinations. It has even been suggested that moral suasion might work in reverse; for example, when the Fed advises commercial banks that tighter money is imminent, the bankers might be tempted to advise favorite customers to "borrow now and avoid the rush."

In conclusion, open-market operations appear to be the most useful monetary-policy technique available to the monetary authorities, and as long as the liquidity-preference function has a normal degree of elasticity expansionary monetary policy can be effective in restoring full employment. For example, to return to the conditions depicted in Figure 10-1, the monetary authorities could cause full employment by increasing the stock of money from M_s to M'_s and thus forcing the interest rate down to i_2.

However, as the stock of money is increased, the demand for speculative balances becomes increasingly elastic, which means an increase in the desire to hold money. Viewed from another angle, a more elastic demand for money implies a slower velocity of money, since velocity is the reciprocal of the desire to hold money. The impact of monetary policy depends in part on its effect on velocity. In the Keynesian system, expansionary monetary policy partially offsets itself by inducing a slowdown in velocity. The more elastic the demand for money, the greater the reduction in velocity and the greater the offset.

In Figure 10-1, a much greater increase in the money stock is required to bring about full employment than would be the case if the demand for money were more inelastic.

Limitations of Monetary Policy

In the Keynesian framework there are significant limitations on the effectiveness of monetary policy. The interest rate cannot, by increasing the stock of money, be reduced below the point at which the liquidity-preference function becomes completely elastic, a segment of the liquidity-preference curve known as the "liquidity trap." Therefore, if an interest rate lower than that encountered in the liquidity trap is required to restore full employment, monetary policy cannot be effective.

A significant point, which has often been neglected by critics of Keynes, is that under usual economic conditions such as have prevailed in the United States since World War II, monetary policy can achieve either expansionary or contractionary effects. Only under extreme conditions, such as severe depressions, when the economy is operating in or near the liquidity trap, will monetary policy become ineffective, and then only as an economic stimulant.

To illustrate how unlikely Keynes himself felt the liquidity trap to be, he points out that "whilst this limiting case might become practically important in the future, I know of no example of it hitherto."[4] These words were written in the depths of the Great Depression, so it is rather clear that, in Keynes's mind at least, no economy has ever fallen into the liquidity trap (even though he applied his theory in places as though the economy were in it).

Keynes did propose that monetary policy in practice had been ineffective largely because it had been misused. He cited two examples of self-imposed limitations on the effectiveness of monetary authorities. One such limitation is what we call today the "bills-only doctrine," under which the monetary authority limits its activities to dealings in very short-term securities. (The Fed imposed such a limitation on open-market operations for almost a decade starting in 1953.) Occasionally, monetary policy applied only to short-term securities does not influence the market for long-term securities enough to alter real investment greatly, because of imperfect arbitrage owing to inelastic expectations.[5] At the time Keynes wrote, the gold standard was a second self-imposed limitation on the effectiveness of monetary policy, a limitation not relevant today. Stocks of monetary gold had no necessary relationship to the quantity of money required to bring about the interest rate that was compatible with full employment. As Keynes put it, regarding gold money, "Unemployment develops, that is to say, because people want the moon;—men cannot be employed when the object of desire (i.e., money) is something which cannot be produced and the demand for which cannot be readily choked off. There is no remedy but to persuade the public that green cheese is practically the same thing and to have a green cheese factory (i.e., a central bank) under public control."[6] So, in Keynes's view, monetary policy makers (such as Congress) and the authority (such as the Fed) had hindered the effectiveness of their own weapons.

In addition, in the real world of risk and uncertainty, depression conditions may further limit the effectiveness of monetary policy, because the risk of default involved in making loans for investment or consumption will most

---

[4]Keynes, *General Theory*, p. 207.

[5]In addition to the theory of Axel Leijonhufvud, starting on page 224 of Chapter 7 and based on inelastic expectations, other writers would explain the same phenomenon with the concept of market segmentation. Certain borrowers and lenders strongly prefer either short- or long-term securities. At times there are enough such borrowers and lenders that a change in the short-term interest rate may not affect the supply-and-demand conditions at the long-term end of the market. J. M. Culbertson, "The Term Structure of Interest Rates," *Quarterly Journal of Economics*, 71 (November, 1957), 489–504; and Charles E. Walker, "Federal Reserve Policy and the Structure of Interest Rates on Government Securities," *Quarterly Journal of Economics*, 68 (February, 1954), 22–23.

[6]Keynes, *General Theory*, p. 235.

likely increase during recessions; consequently, as Keynes noted, the rate of interest that borrowers actually pay would likely decline more slowly than the default-free interest rate. In fact, the risk premium may increase faster than the no-default-risk interest rate can be reduced through monetary policy. Furthermore, the administrative costs of lending are not subject to the control of monetary authorities, but realistically must be met. The monetary authorities can force the government-bond interest rate very low, but interest rates charged by lenders will not go below the administrative costs of lending and a premium for risk.

In the United States at the present time, monetary policy may be less effective than it potentially could be because it is incomplete. Currency held by the public, savings accounts of nonbank financial intermediaries, as well as excess reserves of commercial banks, are beyond the direct control of the monetary authorities and may be used to defeat the desired ends. About half the commercial banks are not members of the Federal Reserve System; these nonmember banks are not subject to the regulations of the Federal Reserve and may, therefore, interfere with Federal Reserve policy. One reason the Fed is disinclined to raise reserve requirements is that it would give nonmember banks not subject to its regulation a competitive advantage. However, the Fed can counteract these limitations, if the reactions of non-regulated components of the monetary system can be predicted.

FISCAL POLICY

Fiscal policy refers to government policy concerning taxation, government spending, and government borrowing. Therefore, fiscal policy affects the real side of the economy rather than the money side. The real side of the Keynesian model is represented by the savings and investment functions in panels A, B, and C of Figure 10-1. The consumption function is included implicitly as the complement of the savings function. Government spending is conveniently introduced into the model through the investment sector, and taxes through the savings function. Since Keynes felt that monetary policy had largely been mismanaged, he concentrated on fiscal policy, a novelty in the 1930's, to restore equilibrium at full employment.

Government Expenditures

Government expenditures can be added to the investment-demand function and therefore may be considered a supplement to private investment, because much government expenditure goes for producer goods such as construction and equipment, which in turn produce services for the rest of the economy. (Alternatively, government expenditures might be considered an addition to consumption; ideally, the total should be distributed between consumption and investment, as was mentioned in Chapter 4.) We have included government spending in our model by adding the total amount to investment demand.

Figure 10-2 abstracts panels A, B, and C from Figure 10-1 in order to depict an economy in unemployment equilibrium at an aggregate-income level of $500 billion without fiscal policy. The initial equilibrium occurs at point *c* on the savings function in panel C, the level at which $S = I$. The figure illustrates how government expenditures can bring about the full-employment level of aggregate income, assumed to be $600 billion, by moving from point *c* to point *d* on the savings curve, without changing the 8 percent interest rate, shown in panel A. Government expenditures of $20 billion are added to investment demand in panel A, forming an $I + G$ curve parallel to the investment-demand function, I. The multiplier of 5 times the government expenditure of $20 billion is sufficient to bring about the full-employment level of income. The shift from point *a* to point *b* in panel A

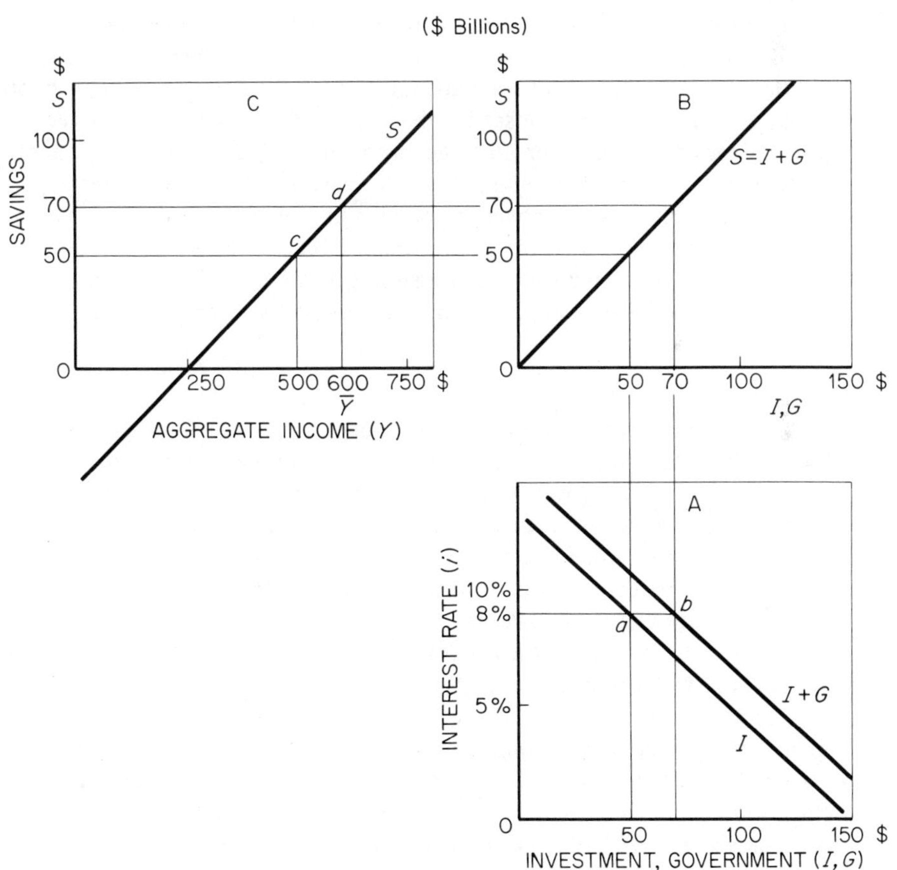

FIG. 10-2 Savings, Investment, and Government Expenditure ($ Billions)

illustrates the addition of \$20 billion of government expenditures to the \$50 billion of investment that occurs at 8 percent interest.

The increase in $I + G$ over I causes the equilibrium point to move upward and to the right on the $S = I + G$ curve in panel B. Consequently, the savings function is intercepted at point d instead of c in panel C, increasing the equilibrium level of savings from \$50 billion to \$70 billion and thus restoring full employment by increasing aggregate income (Y) from \$500 to \$600 billion.

We may conclude that government expenditures have the same multiplier effect on aggregate income as does increased investment in eliminating a deflationary gap. However, a constant level of government expenditures must be maintained in each time period if the full multiplier effect is to be achieved. In this example, government expenditures are assumed to be an addition to existing investment and consumption. This assumption is necessary to achieve the full multiplier effect. If private investment or consumption spending falls by the same amount that government spending increases, added government spending would have no effect on equilibrium income.

Keynes agreed with his critics during the 1930's that the multiplier would not operate fully on government expenditures, since its effect would probably have been at least partly offset by the unfavorable psychological effect on private investors unaccustomed to government involvement in the economy. Particularly, he felt, there might be a decrease in investor confidence as a reaction, and if so, some government spending would be offset, at least in part, by a reduction in private investment.[7] Since the 1930's, any adverse psychological effects of government spending have been reduced or eliminated as everyone has become accustomed to large-scale government expenditures.

Taxes

Taxes can be introduced into the model to demonstrate their role in fiscal policy. Although taxes represent a flow of purchasing power from the private sector to the government sector, their impact is more complicated than that of government expenditures, since only part of them are paid with income that would otherwise have been spent on consumption or investment. The resulting reduction in consumption and investment demand functions tends to reduce aggregate income.

In order to investigate the economic effect of taxes, let us start by assuming only one tax, a lump-sum tax. Such a levy would require that each citizen pay the same amount of tax as everyone else, regardless of his income level. In addition, assume that this tax affects directly only consumption and savings and not investment. The effect of such a tax is illustrated in Figure 10-3, which depicts the same three panels as Figure 10-2. If the government collects \$25 billion from the lump-sum tax, and government expenditures are \$20 billion, a budget surplus of \$5 billion will result.

---

[7]Keynes, *General Theory*, p. 120.

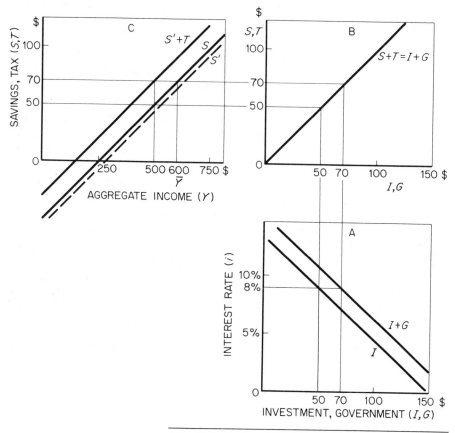

FIG. 10-3 Savings, Investment, Government Expenditure, and a Lump-sum Tax ($ Billions)

The shift from I to $I + G$ in panel A of Figure 10-3 is the same as in panel A of Figure 10-2, and panel B, of course, is the same 45° line in both figures. However, in Figure 10-3, $I + G$ now equals $S + T$. The effect of the tax and the budget surplus on the savings function is presented in panel C, where the addition of taxes makes Figure 10-3 quite different from 10-2. Initially, the savings curve will drop from S to the dotted S' curve, because the tax will not be paid entirely with money earmarked for consumption, assuming that consumers distribute the tax as they would any other marginal-income reduction. In our illustration, the marginal propensity to consume, MPC, is 80 percent and the marginal propensity to save, MPS, is 20 percent; in other words, the slope of the S curve is 0.2. Consequently, the $25 billion reduction in disposable income from the tax will be distributed between savings and consumption on a 2-to-8 ratio. The fall in aggregate income will reduce savings by $5 billion and consumption by $20 billion. The $S' + T$ curve in panel C is constructed by adding the $25 billion total tax collection to S'. As a result equilibrium income is reduced from \$600 to \$500 billion, because taxes have the same economic impact as savings—both are a leakage out of the stream of domestic spending. However, notice that in Figure 10-3, more taxes than government expenditures were required to restore the original equilibrium level of aggregate income of Figure 10-2. The reason is simply that part of the tax is paid out of income that would otherwise have been saved. The savings lost in the shift from S to S' would have been a leakage out of the spending stream in any case.

The effect of government fiscal policy on equilibrium income can be explained through multiplier analysis. However, since taxes do not completely offset government expenditures, the negative multiplier effect as it operates on taxes is somewhat different from the positive multiplier effect applied to government or investment expenditures. The imposition of a lump-sum tax paid out of personal income requires that we distinguish between personal income and disposable income, since personal income includes consumption, savings, and taxes, while disposable income includes only consumption and savings. Let Y represent some measure of real aggregate income such as personal income and Y_d represent disposable income. (Note that in this case personal income would equal national income or net national product.) If we designate taxes as T,

$$Y_d = Y - T$$

The multiplier effect on aggregate income and its components, including taxes can be derived as follows:

1. $C = a + bY_d$
2. $C = a + b(Y - T)$
3. $Y = C + I$
4. $Y = a + b(Y - T) + I$
5. $Y = a + bY - bT + I$
6. $Y - bY = a + I - bT$
7. $Y(1 - b) = a + I - bT$
8. $Y = \frac{1}{1 - b}(a + I - bT)$

where C is consumption, a is the consumption function's vertical-axis intercept, b is the MPC or slope of the consumption function, and I is investment.

Therefore, the multiplier effect of a change in taxes on income may be stated:

$$9.\ \Delta Y = \frac{1}{1 - b}(-b\Delta T)$$

or

$$10.\ \Delta Y = \frac{-b}{1 - b}\Delta T$$

Thus, the multiplier, as it operates on tax changes, equals $-b/(1 - b)$. Since the MPC is less than 1, the multiplier effect on a change in taxes must, necessarily, be smaller than the expenditure multiplier, k, or $1/(1 - b)$. With a tax multiplier, k_t, in an economy with an MPC of .8,

$$k_t = \frac{-b}{1 - b} = \frac{-.8}{1 - .8} = -4$$

whereas

$$k = \frac{1}{1 - b} = \frac{1}{1 - .8} = 5$$

It can be demonstrated that the tax multiplier is one less than the expenditure multiplier. You may wish to experiment with other values of the MPC to test this concept.

Tax reductions provide expansionary fiscal policy to restore full employment. Since the tax multiplier is lower than the expenditure multiplier, taxes must be reduced by a greater amount than any increase in government expenditures to achieve the same effect on aggregate income. However, some economists feel that a tax reduction may stimulate investment more than enough to offset the lower tax multiplier. If so, tax reductions would have a more expansionary effect than that demonstrated here.

Balanced-Budget Multiplier

Simple common sense might suggest that the multiplier effect on government spending would be zero when government expenditures are exactly offset by tax collections. However, as can be inferred from the previous section, simple common sense would be wrong in this case. A balanced government budget would, in itself, have an expansionary impact on the economy, because the value of the tax multiplier is smaller than the expenditure multiplier.[8] The conclusion is that any given level of government expenditures increases aggregate income more than an equal level of taxes would reduce it.

Figure 10-4 uses the same S and I curves of Figures 10-2 and 10-3 to illustrate how the balanced-budget multiplier could achieve full employment. Starting at $500 billion aggregate income, the underemployment equilibrium of Figure 10-2, full employment is reached in Figure 10-4 at an aggregate income of $600 billion through a balanced-budget fiscal policy that equates government expenditures and taxes at $100 billion. Since an increase in aggregate income of $100 billion is required to achieve full employment at $600 billion, the balanced-budget multiplier must equal 1 in this case. To see why, compare the tax multiplier, k_t, with the expenditure multiplier, k,

[8]For two of the early expositors of the balanced budget multiplier, see Trygve Haavelmo, "Multiplier Effects of a Balanced Budget," *Econometrica*, 13 (October 1945), 311–18.; and H. C. Wallich, "Income-Generating Effects of a Balanced Budget," *Quarterly Journal of Economics*, 59 (November 1944), 78–91.

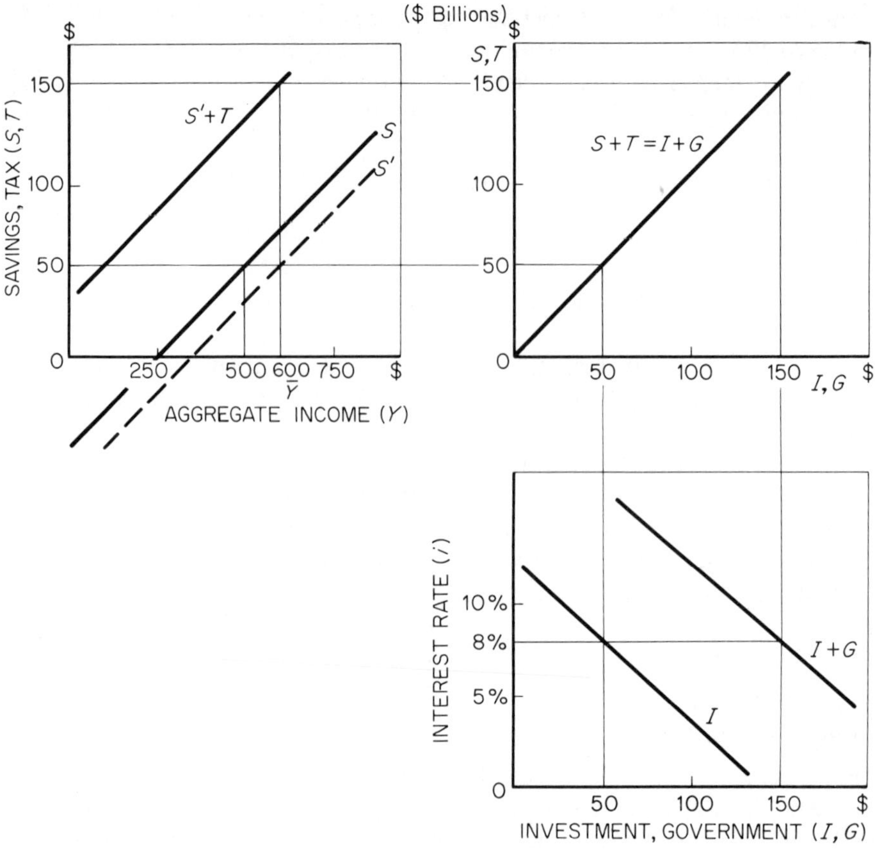

FIG. 10-4 The Balanced Budget Multiplier ($ Billions)

operating on government expenditures. Given an MPC of .8, k equals 5, and k_t is -4.

Therefore, if government expenditures and taxes both equal $100 billion, the Keynesian multiplier, k, operates positively to increase aggregate income by $500 billion, whereas k_t, operating negatively on tax receipts, decreases income by only $400 billion. (Remember, k and k_t operate in opposite directions, since an increase in government expenditures leads to an increase in personal income, whereas an increase in taxes leads to a decrease in personal income.) The net change in aggregate income that results from taxes and government expenditures both equaling $100 billion is, therefore, an increase of $100 billion. The conclusion is that a balanced government budget by itself would tend to expand aggregate income. Algebraically, the balanced-budget multiplier will always equal 1 if taxpayers apportion tax changes according to their MPC and MPS, since the tax multiplier is negative,

$$k + k_t = \frac{1}{1-b} + \frac{-b}{1-b} = \frac{1-b}{1-b} = 1$$

In the real world, taxpayers may not apportion their taxes at the margin as assumed in this theory. Particularly in the short run, taxpayers may choose not to reduce consumption by as much as their normal MPC might indicate, but to use income that would normally be saved to pay the tax. Such an unexpected change in the MPC and MPS is one reason that the effect on aggregate income of the 1968 surcharge was less than anticipated. In conclusion, if the MPC and MPS change as a result of fiscal policy, then the balanced-budget multiplier may not equal 1.

Nondiscretionary Fiscal Policy (Automatic Stabilizers)

Keynes's views on automatic stabilizers must be inferred from remarks scattered throughout the *General Theory* on topics such as taxes, transfer payments, and sinking funds. Since publication of the *General Theory*, automatic stabilizers have achieved enough significance to warrant systematic presentation. At the time the *General Theory* was written, in the midst of the Great Depression, Keynes was more interested in opposing automatic *destabilizers*, such as government sinking funds. Sinking funds are involuntary savings and decrease equilibrium income, since an enormous volume of new investment would be required to absorb the financial resources set aside in them.

However, Keynes did mention that some economic policies are automatically stabilizing. For example, he stated, "Unemployment is likely to be associated with negative saving in certain quarters, private or public, because the unemployed may be living either on the savings of themselves and their friends or on *public relief* which is partly financed out of loans";[9] that is, negative savings are automatically stabilizing during recessions.

Keynes also pointed out that imports are automatically stabilizing. The demand for imports is generally a positive function of income. Therefore, higher incomes lead to more imports, which, in turn, decreases the net foreign balance. The reverse will be true during recessions, making the multiplier smaller in an open economy with imports and exports. Post-Keynesian economists have placed greater emphasis on the automatically stabilizing effect of taxes and transfer payments, especially in the United States, where the foreign sector is proportionately a small part of the total economy.[10]

Imports and taxes, like savings, cause a leakage out of the stream of spending in the domestic economy. Therefore, had we been using a model of an open economy, imports could have been added to the savings-plus-taxes

---

[9] Keynes, *General Theory*, p. 121.

[10] For the view that countercyclical tax policy can rely solely on the built-in stabilizers, see Committee for Economic Development, *Taxes and the Budget* (New York: C.E.D., 1947), pp. 22–28. Also, see Milton Friedman, "A Monetary and Fiscal Framework for Economic Stability," *American Economic Review*, 38 (June 1948), 245–64. For an early rebuttal to Friedman's view, see R. A. Musgrave and M. H. Miller, "Built-in Flexibility," *American Economic Review*, 38 (March 1948), 122–28.

function in Figures 10-3 and 10-4. (Imports are included in the expanded model in the appendix to this chapter.)

Income Taxes The various income taxes collected represent about 70 percent of government revenues, a fact that makes the analysis of the income tax significant in the tax structure as a whole. The American income tax structure is very complex, being partly proportional and partly progressive, and even according to some proponents of tax reform, partly regressive, because of tax loopholes. However, for simplicity, we start by assuming a proportional income tax.

We noted earlier that the effect of the lump-sum per capita tax was to increase the savings-plus-tax function. The substitution of a proportional income tax for the lump-sum tax has the effect of rotating the savings-plus-tax function up and therefore the consumption function down, around their y-axis intercepts. The effect of the tax on the consumption and savings functions is shown in Figure 10-5 by the rotation of the consumption function

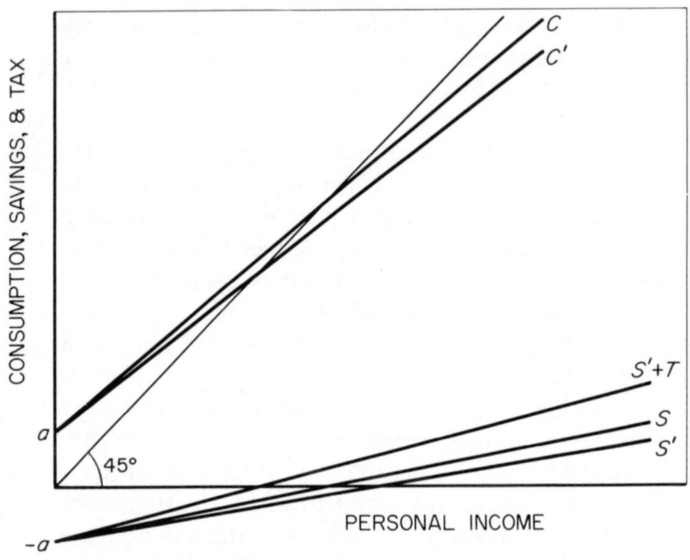

FIG. 10-5 The Effect of a Proportional Income Tax

from C to C' and the savings function from S to S'. Taxes have the same effect as savings in reducing spending on consumption, so it is necessary to add taxes, T, to the S' line (shown as a downward rotation), in order for $C' + (S' + T)$ to equal aggregate income.

The curves are rotated because neither savings nor consumption will be affected by the proportional income tax at zero income, since no income tax will be collected, even though consumption of $+a$ and savings of $-a$ will occur. In Figure 10-5, the $S' + T$ function is higher than the original savings function, S, but (as in Figure 10-3) not by the full amount of the tax, because of the initial downward rotation of S to S' as the tax is divided between savings and consumption in a proportion determined by the MPC and the MPS.

If the lump-sum and a proportional income tax are combined, the result would be both an upward shift and rotation in the $S' + T$ function. The two taxes can be combined by substituting $T_x + t_y Y$ for T in equation 4 on page 322, where T_x is the lump-sum tax, which determines the y-axis intercept of the tax function, and t_y is the proportional component, which determines the slope. The proportional part of the tax structure, $t_y Y$, may be considered the government's marginal propensity to tax out of income, and the equations of pages 322 and 323 become a special case in which the marginal propensity to tax out of income equals zero. Substituting $T_x + t_y Y$ into equation 4, the multiplier effect on aggregate income and its components, including a lump-sum and a proportional income tax, is derived as follows:

$$\text{4a. } Y = a + b(Y - T_x - t_y Y) + I$$

$$\text{5a. } Y = a + bY - bT_x - bt_y Y + I$$

$$\text{6a. } Y - bY + bt_y Y = a - bT_x + I$$

$$\text{7a. } Y(1 - b + bt_y) = a - bT_x + I$$

$$\text{8a. } Y = \frac{1}{1 - b + bt_y}(a - bT_x + I)$$

or

$$Y = \frac{1}{1 - b(1 - t_y)}(a - bT_x + I)$$

Therefore, the multiplier effect of a change in taxes on aggregate income may now be restated as follows:

$$\text{9a. } \Delta Y = \frac{1}{1 - b(1 - t_y)}(-b\Delta T_x)$$

$$\text{10a. } \Delta Y = \frac{-b}{1 - b(1 - t_y)}\Delta T_x$$

In the foregoing illustration, we assumed an MPC of .8 and consequently an expenditure multiplier of 5. Therefore, the lump-sum negative tax multiplier is 4, because the absolute size of the tax multiplier is one less than the expenditure multiplier. When the tax structure includes a proportional component equal to 10 percent of income, the increased leakage into taxes further reduces the negative tax multiplier from 4 to 2.9. To demonstrate the calculation of the tax multiplier (k_t) with an MPC of .80 and a marginal tax rate out of income equal to .10,

$$k_t = \frac{-b}{1 - b(1 - t_y)}$$

$$k_t = \frac{-.80}{1 - .80(1 - .10)} = \frac{-.80}{1 - .80(.90)} = \frac{-.80}{1 - .72} = \frac{-.80}{.28} = -2.9$$

As can be seen from equation 8a, not only is the negative tax multiplier reduced, but the positive multiplier operating on autonomous levels of consumption and investment is also reduced by the introduction of taxes as a function of income. The revised expenditure multiplier (k'') now becomes

$$k'' = \frac{1}{1 - b(1 - t_y)}$$

which would equal 3.6 in the illustration above.

If government expenditures are added to the model, the balanced-budget multiplier would be reduced, in this case to .7, through the effect of the proportional income tax. A balanced budget may still lead to full employment, but additional government expenditures and taxes would be required when a proportional tax is employed than when a lump-sum tax is collected, because the collections from a proportional tax increase as income grows, and those from a lump-sum tax do not.

The introduction of a progressive component in the tax structure would require that the savings-plus-tax function be nonlinear. Thus the $S' + T$ function would increase at an increasing rate. Consequently, the multiplier effect could not be constant but would tend to decrease at higher levels of aggregate income. Therefore, a progressive income tax makes consumption a proportionately decreasing function of personal income, owing to the smaller proportion of personal income going to disposable income at higher income levels.

Transfer Payments Transfer payments are a negative tax and may likewise be divided into two parts—one that is independent of the level of income, and a second that is a function of income. But in practice, any such breakdown is rather arbitrary. Subsidies to any particular industry—for example, to shipbuilders—are difficult to relate to GNP, since the output of any one industry may behave independently of aggregate income. However, under the parity program when prices fall the government buys products from farmers. These payments may vary inversely with income levels.[11]

Social Security payments, a major transfer payment, include survivors and disability benefits, which are largely independent of aggregate income. Other benefits, such as unemployment and old-age payments, are inversely related to the level of income. Cyclical unemployment increases unemployment-compensation payments, and may cause older unemployed who are eligible for old-age benefits to retire sooner than expected. Consequently, aggregate old-age payments should increase during recessions.

Interest on the public debt, often treated as a transfer payment, is partly

---

[11]Subsidies and transfer payments are treated differently in national-income accounting. As we saw in Chapter 4, subsidies are introduced at the level of national income because they represent payments to factors of production, even though they are not included in the market price of the finished product. Transfer payments are introduced at the level of personal income, since they represent payments to households. However, this distinction is irrelevant regarding their function as built-in stabilizers.

a function of the level of income. A full-employment fiscal policy should increase the size of deficits during recessions. However, interest rates tend to fall during recessions and rise during prosperity, so changes in the size of the deficit and changes in the interest rate at least partly offset each other, and the net effect is difficult to assess. Whether interest payments on the public debt are on balance an inverse function of the level of income, and therefore stabilizing, is difficult to determine. (Remember, the interest rate on outstanding securities does not change.)

Transfer payments may be fit into our analysis in much the same way as taxes were handled, and a transfer-payment multiplier, similar to the tax multiplier, may be derived. (The two effects will work in opposite directions; taxes reduce income and transfer payments increase it.) The transfer-payment multiplier is derived from the following formula:

$$T_r = T_a - t_b Y$$

where T_r is total transfer payments, T_a is the maximum transfer payments at zero income, and t_b is the part that is a negative function of income.

The influence of transfer payments on the level of aggregate income (excluding other fiscal policy) may be stated as follows:

$$Y = \frac{1}{1 - b + bt_b}(a + bT_a + I)$$

And the multiplier effect of a change in transfer payments on aggregate income is[12]

$$\Delta Y = \frac{b}{1 - b(1 - t_b)}\Delta T_a$$

---

[12]Substituting $T_r = T_a - t_b Y$ into equation 4 on page 322, the effect of transfer payments on income and its components may be derived as follows:

4b. $Y = a + b(Y + T_a - t_b Y) + I$

5b. $Y = a + bY + bT_a - bt_b Y + I$

6b. $Y - bY + bt_b Y = a + bT_a + I$

7b. $Y(1 - b + bt_b) = a + bT_a + I$

8b. $Y = \dfrac{1}{1 - b + bt_b}(a + bT_a + I)$

or

$$\frac{1}{1 - b(1 - t_b)}(a + bT_a + I)$$

(Remember, T_a is a positive addition to income, and $t_b Y$ varies inversely with income.)

Therefore, the multiplier effect of a change in transfer payments on income may now be restated

9b. $\Delta Y = \dfrac{1}{1 - b(1 - t_b)}(b\Delta T_a)$

10b. $\Delta Y = \dfrac{b}{1 - b(1 - t_b)}\Delta T_a$

and where k_{tn} represents the transfer-payment multiplier,

$$k_{tn} = \frac{b}{1 - b(1 - t_b)}$$

Certain generalizations may be made regarding the transfer-payment multiplier: First, whereas the tax multiplier is negative, the transfer-payment multiplier is positive. Second, only the part of transfer payments that is in-maximum at income, represented by the y-axis intercept, T_a, acts as a negative lump-sum tax. Third, the transfer-payment multiplier, like the tax multiplier, is lower than the expenditure multiplier. Thus, if the marginal propensity to consume is .8 and transfer payments, as a function of income, are .1, then the transfer-payment multiplier, like the tax multiplier in the previous illustration, would be 2.9, while the expenditure multiplier would equal 3.6. Fourth, since the total transfer payments appear to vary inversely with income, the overall multiplier, which incorporates all the different multiplier effects, is reduced.

Income-related transfer payments and taxes are automatically stabilizing and reinforce each other in their effect on employment and aggregate income by lowering the value of the overall multiplier. The difference is that transfer payments introduce more income into the economy during recessions, whereas taxes take less out. Conversely, during prosperity, the transfer-payment multiplier introduces less additional income, whereas the tax multiplier increases the leakage out of spending. Therefore, the tax multiplier and the transfer-payment multiplier reinforce each other in reducing the size of the overall multiplier.

OVERALL MULTIPLIER

The multiplier effect of changes in taxes and transfer payments can be combined with the supermultiplier of Chapter 9 (which included investment as a function of income, where e is the marginal propensity to invest, MPI—that is, the proportion of additional income that will be used to buy additional capital goods). Such an overall multiplier (k^*) can be expressed as follows:

$$k^* = \frac{1}{1 - b + bt_y + bt_b - e} = \frac{1}{1 - b(1 - t_y - t_b) - e}$$

This overall multiplier can be applied to each source of autonomous spending. In a closed economy, the sources of autonomous spending are the vertical-axis intercepts of the consumption function (a), the investment function (I_x), lump-sum tax collections (T_x), and the autonomous component of transfer payments (T_a). Government expenditures (G) are entirely autonomous, on the assumption that there is no income elasticity to the government's demand for goods and services. Therefore, the entire government outlay is subject to the multiplier.

Taxes and transfer payments must be multiplied by the MPC, b, (although the sign of the product will be positive in the case of transfer payments and negative in the case of taxes), because they both directly change disposable income, and only that proportion not paid out of savings is affected by the multiplier.

Aggregate income can be determined by multiplying each source of autonomous spending by the overall multiplier, as follows:

$$Y = k^* (a + I_x - bT_x + bT_a + G)$$

The expanded model can be illustrated using all the variables discussed so far that affect the multiplier: consumption, investment, taxes, and government expenditures. All these variables except government expenditures may be separated into an autonomous component equal to the y-axis intercept, and an income-related component equal to the slope of the line. Since government expenditure is considered to be purely autonomous, it is represented as a constant. Assuming the following values in the formulas, the overall multiplier can be derived in this numerical example:

$$C = a + bY_d$$
$$C = 20 + .90\,Y_d$$
$$I = I_x + eY$$
$$I = 13 + .07\,Y$$
$$T = T_x + t_yY$$
$$T = 20 + .22\,Y$$
$$T_r = T_a + t_bY$$
$$T_r = 8 + .08\,Y$$
$$G = 200$$

$$k^* = \frac{1}{1 - .90(1 - .22 - .08) - .07} = \frac{1}{.30} = 3.33$$

Therefore, given the autonomous levels of consumption, investment, taxes, transfer payments, and government expenditures, equilibrium income may be derived:

$$Y = 3.33(20 + 13 - .90(20) + .90(8) + 200)$$
$$Y = 742.5$$

Even though this model is already rather elaborate, it still grossly oversimplifies reality. However, the model could be extended by such realistic refinements as the use of different tax functions applied to different income aggregates, the introduction of business savings, and the introduction of the foreign sector. Business savings and imports, like taxes, are a negative function of aggregate income, whereas exports are usually assumed to be independent of aggregate income. A multiplier that incorporates business savings and imports is presented in the Appendix to this chapter.

For purposes of exposition, the model above is sufficient to show the main features of the basic Keynesian type of model and to make the multiplier more realistic through the introduction of automatic stabilizers. Even this simple sort of model, if its inherent limitations are kept in mind, can be used successfully in projecting the effects of changes in such things as government expenditures and taxes.

INFLATION

In certain circles, it is fashionable to dismiss the basic Keynesian model as "depression economics." However, as we saw in Chapter 8, the inflationary gap is a part of Keynes's system. In his own words,

> When full employment is reached, any attempt to increase investment still further will set up a tendency in money-prices to rise without limit, irrespective of the marginal propensity to consume; i.e. we shall have reached a state of pure inflation. Up to this point, however, rising prices will be associated with an increasing aggregate real income.[13]

In Chapter 8, we assumed for simplicity that inflation did not start until full employment was reached, although, as we can see from the foregoing quotation, Keynes was aware that the price level as well as output would respond to changes in effective demand before that point. Such inflation prior to full employment is associated with increasing output. In contrast, Keynes defined "pure inflation" as increases in the price level that occur only after full employment has been achieved, and that cannot be associated with any increase in production. Pure inflation with no corresponding increase in real output will induce an inflationary spiral that will continue until a reduction occurs in aggregate demand, possibly through either fiscal or monetary policy. For example, the monetary authorities could reduce the stock of money through monetary policy and so cause higher interest rates, which, in turn, would reduce investment expenditures and thereby close the inflationary gap.

Fiscal policy could also be used to eliminate the inflationary gap, by reversing the expansionary procedures previously discussed. Government expenditures could be reduced, taxes increased, or the balanced-budget multiplier used in reverse, by a simultaneous equal decrease in government expenditures and tax receipts. Any given reduction in aggregate demand would require greater tax increases than reductions in government spending, since part of any tax increase will be paid out of savings. Realistically, a tax increase

---

[13]Keynes, *General Theory*, pp. 118–19.

may discourage investment and so have a greater impact than the simple model might indicate.

Throughout the *General Theory*, Keynes emphasized the problem of unemployment rather than that of inflation. Not until 1939, when wartime made it imminent, did Keynes concentrate on economic policies to subdue inflation.[14] To counteract the inflationary effects of increased government expenditures on war goods, he proposed that private consumption be reduced through the imposition of a compulsory savings plan. Such a proposal could, of course, be applied also to peacetime inflation, although we have never seriously entertained such a plan in the United States, preferring to increase taxes and interest rates or reduce government spending to achieve the same results.

Keynes' ideas on inflation[15] are shown graphically in Figure 10-6 as a

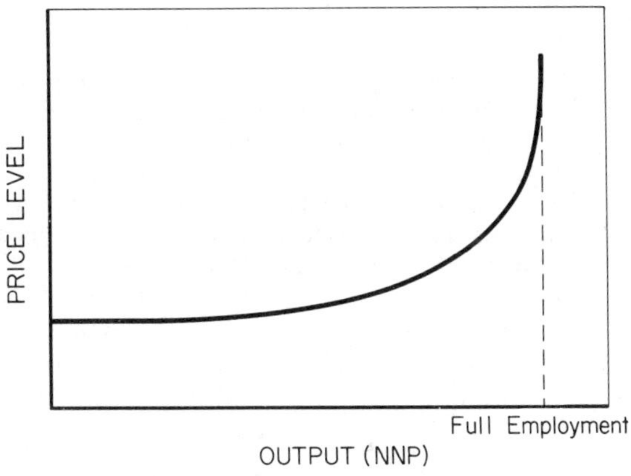

FIG. 10-6 Relationship of Prices to Output

relationship between output (NNP) and the price level, with the price level plotted along the y-axis and output along the x-axis. As the figure illustrates, when output is relatively low, there tends to be less impact on the price level and more on aggregate output from a given increase in output. Price increases become increasingly severe as aggregate output increases, until finally, at the full-employment level of output, pure inflation sets in; the only effect of increases in spending is to raise the price level. An increase in the price level after full employment has been reached is pure inflation, without any further increases in aggregate output.

Keynes disregarded the possibility of higher prices accompanying falling output, a phenomenon that has become important in recent years and that

[14] J. M. Keynes, "The Income and Fiscal Potential of Great Britain," *Economic Journal*, 49 (December 1939), 626–39; and J. M. Keynes, *How to Pay for the War* (London: Macmillan, 1940).

[15] Keynes, *General Theory*, p. 303.

will be considered in Chapter 13, when we take up the post-Keynesian development of inflation theory.

SOCIAL POLICY

Much of the early furor over Keynesian economics concerned his social views rather than his economic theories. Often overlooked in the *General Theory* are Keynes's references to the advantages of the private-enterprise system:

> They are partly advantages of efficiency—the advantages of decentralisation and of the play of self-interest. The advantage to efficiency of the decentralization of decisions and of individual responsibility is even greater, perhaps, than the nineteenth century supposed; and the reaction against the appeal to self-interest may have gone too far. But, above all, individualism, if it can be purged of its defects and abuses, is the best safeguard of personal liberty in the sense that, compared with any other system, it greatly widens the field for the exercise of personal choice. It is also the best safeguard of the variety of life, which emerges precisely from this extended field of personal choice, and the loss of which is the greatest of all the losses of the homogeneous or totalitarian state. For this variety preserves the traditions which embody the most secure and successful choices of former generations; it colours the present with the diversification of its fancy; and, being the handmaid of experiment as well as of tradition and of fancy, it is the most powerful instrument to better the future.[16]

Controversy arose over Keynesian economics because Keynes proposed increased government involvement in the economy. In addition to the monetary policy proposed by the neoclassicists, Keynes added conscious fiscal policy by the government. Furthermore, he advocated that the distribution of income be changed in the direction of greater equality, arguing that the outstanding threat to the economic society he knew was "its failure to provide for full employment and its arbitrary and inequitable distribution of wealth and incomes."[17] Although he felt that significant income inequality is required to reward successful, enterprising workers and businessmen, he believed the existing income disparity was unnecessarily great. Keynes recognized that certain antisocial drives, such as a lust for power, or aggressiveness, can be channeled into relatively harmless economic pursuits. As he put it, "It is better that a man should tyrannise over his bank balance than over his fellow-citizens; and whilst the former is sometimes denounced as being but a means to the latter, sometimes at least it is an alternative."[18] Therefore, because of man's acquisitive tendencies, Keynes felt that correct social policy ought not to eliminate inequalities of wealth and income; but he thought these

---

[16] *Ibid.*, p. 380.
[17] *Ibid.*, p. 372.
[18] *Ibid.*, p. 374.

acquisitive tendencies could be equally well satisfied if the inequalities were substantially reduced.

A third policy advocated by Keynes was the use of monetary policy to effect a generally lower level of interest rates and so stimulate investment sufficiently to achieve full employment. As we have seen, Keynes rejected the neoclassical view that high interest rates stimulate savings. Even though lower interest rates would injure those who live on interest income, he felt the net economic effect would be beneficial to the economy, because the increase in production and consumption encouraged by the lower rates would provide benefits in excess of the injury done to interest recipients (who, in any case, tend to be richer than wage earners).

In Keynes's view, greater income equality was not only ethically justifiable but also quite practical. Besides stimulating investment through lower interest rates, greater income equality would also stimulate the economy by increasing the consumption function, on the assumption that the poor have a higher MPC than the rich.

Keynes himself was no revolutionary, and he argued that his contemporary economy would "need no revolution" but that the economic society he knew could continue to function for the foreseeable future if the proper reforms were instituted.[19]

SUMMARY AND CONCLUSIONS

Keynes believed that certain monetary and fiscal policies were necessary to bring about full employment, since in the 1930's, large-scale unemployment, poverty, and disaffection severely threatened the capitalistic system. The *General Theory* encompasses a model to illustrate the necessary reforms.

In the basic Keynesian model, monetary policy works through the monetary authorities' changing the stock of money and influencing the shape and position of the liquidity-preference function. The interaction of the liquidity-preference function and the stock of money determines the interest rate, which in turn influences the level of investment and hence the level of aggregate income and employment.

However, possibly because of the liquidity trap—or more likely, the conservative nature of the monetary authority, or monetary policymaker—Keynes was skeptical about using monetary policy, through a reduction in the interest rate, to achieve full employment. Consequently, he proposed that government fiscal policy be used to supplement private investment. Additional government expenditure would have the same impact on income and employment as increasing private investment; therefore, fiscal policy could be used to achieve full employment when private investment was insufficient. Lower taxes could also stimulate the economy by increasing consumption,

---

[19] *Ibid.*, pp. 377–83.

although not as effectively as government expenditures (unless lower taxes increased private investment). As Keynesian economists have shown, even a balanced budget will stimulate the economy, although the multiplier effect of a balanced budget would be no more than 1.

The germ of another idea was found in the *General Theory* and developed by post-Keynesians: the concept of automatic or built-in stabilizers. Built-in stabilizers work automatically and immediately in response to an increase in aggregate income, through disproportionately large increases in collections of progressive taxes and reductions in some government transfer payments. The reverse occurs when aggregate income falls. Built-in stabilizers reduce the multiplier, so that changes in autonomous spending have less impact on aggregate income.

Contrary to the opinion voiced by some, Keynes concerned himself with inflation as well as deflation, and proposed policies to cope with expected wartime inflation, although obviously he did not stress problems of inflation in the *General Theory*.[20] Finally, Keynes suggested a more equitable distribution of income, in addition to the main goal of full employment. The achievement of full employment without inflation and of an equitable distribution of income would, according to Keynes, correct the worst abuses of the capitalistic system and therefore enable it to survive and to meet the economic desires of society.

QUESTIONS AND PROBLEMS

1. In what way can monetary policy be effective, in the Keynesian view? Which monetary-policy weapons are most effective?
2. If expansionary policy is required, discuss what approach you would take.
3. As a practical matter, did Keynes prefer fiscal policy or monetary policy? Why?
4. How can fiscal policy be implemented?
5. Compare the tax multiplier with the expenditure multiplier. Which multiplier is larger? Why?
6. Explain the balanced-budget multiplier.
7. Can built-in stabilizers by themselves maintain economic stability? Why, or why not?
8. Which transfer payments are automatically stabilizing and which are not?
9. Even though Keynesian economics has been called "depression economics," it can incorporate inflation. Explain.

---

[20]The monetary authorities did worry about inflation in 1937, however. They tightened the money supply, helping to cut off a mid-1930's recovery.

National-Income Accounting and the Multiplier

appendix to chapter 10

The national-income accounting system described in Chapters 4 and 5 is useful as a source of data for applying Keynesian economic policy. The relationship between national-income accounting and Keynesian theory can be seen if we consider the various items that represent leakages from and additions to the national-income aggregates, in order to relate net national product to disposable income.

The Keynesian system relates the effect of changes in several significant variables on a theoretical "aggregate income." Aggregate income is probably most often best represented by either net national product (NNP) or disposable income (DI). Gross national product (GNP) suffers from the defect that it includes depreciation, and the other two income aggregates, national income (NI) and personal income (PI), have less relevancy to macroeconomic theory. Consequently, our main concern here is to relate NNP and DI.

The overall-multiplier analysis presented on page 330 incorporates personal savings, personal-consumption expenditures, taxes, transfer payments (and net subsidies), government purchases of goods and services, and investment expenditures. Therefore, if we adjust that formula for business transfer payments, interest paid by consumers, personal transfer payments to foreigners, net exports (exports minus imports), and business savings, specifically corporate savings, the relationship between net national product and disposable income will be complete except for the minor adjustments such as wage accruals, inventory-valuation adjustments, and statistical discrepancy. Business transfer payments can be ignored because the account occurs in both net national product and disposable income.

Interest paid by consumers is at least in part a function of consumer income. Consumer interest does not effect net national product, yet it is included in disposable income. Therefore, it can be combined with government transfer payments, since they both vary with income, though in opposite directions, and are included in disposable income but not in net national product.

On the other hand, personal transfer payments to foreigners, another item that varies with consumer income, is part of both net national product and disposable income, and therefore need not be considered separately. However, the account can be calculated by subtracting consumption, personal savings, and interest paid by consumers from disposable income.

Net exports are divided into its two components, exports and imports of goods and services. Exports of goods and services must be computed separately, in light of how efficient our economy is, relative to others. However, the demand for imports is a function of disposable income; therefore, it appears more realistic to include imports as a function of disposable income while treating exports as an exogenously determined variable.

Business savings (limited to corporate savings in GNP accounting) remain to be explicitly incorporated into the overall multiplier. Business savings, like taxes and personal savings, tend to vary directly with the level of net national product, and to grow at a pace related to the growth of aggregate income. In addition, business savings, like taxes and transfer payments, act here as a built-in stabilizer in reducing the size of the mutliplier. As with personal savings, the y-axis intercept of business savings would be negative.

How does the introduction of business savings and net exports revise the overall multiplier? The business-savings function may be represented by $S_b = S_a + s_b Y$, where S_b is total business savings, S_a is the y-axis intercept of the savings function, and s_b is the marginal propensity for corporate firms to save.

In addition, if X represents exports, and the import function is represented by $M = M_a + mY_d$—where M is total imports, M_a is the y-axis intercept and m represents the marginal propensity to import out of disposable income—then m can be added to the marginal propensity to save, since imports are a leakage out of disposable income just like personal savings.

If $1 - b$ represents the marginal propensity to save out of disposable income, then $1 - (b - m)$ represents the total leakage out of disposable income. Now, if b' is used to represent the marginal propensity to consume domestically produced goods $(b - m)$, it can be substituted for b every time b appears in the overall multiplier. Likewise, a' can be used to represent the y-axis intercept of domestically produced consumption $(a - M_a)$.

Incorporating business savings and the marginal propensity to import into the overall multiplier (k^*), we can develop a revised overall multiplier, designated k^{**}:

$$k^{**} = \frac{1}{1 - b' + b't_y + b't_b + b's_b - e} = \frac{1}{1 - b'(1 - t_y - t_b - s_b) - e}$$

Noting the appropriate adjustments, net national product can be calculated by adding exports (X) and the y-axis intercept of business savings (S_a) to the other sources of autonomous spending described on page 330. The evaluation is made by multiplying each source of autonomous spending by the revised overall multiplier. Therefore, if Y_x = net national product,

$$Y_x = k^{**}(a' + I_x - b'T_x + b'T'_a - b'S_a + G + X)$$

where:

1. The appropriate adjustments to transfer payments, T'_a, include interest paid by consumers, since the latter works like transfer payments in increasing disposable income relative to net national product.
2. a' is equal to any domestically produced consumption $(a - M_a)$.
3. b' is the marginal propensity to consume domestically produced goods $(b - m)$.
4. Business savings (S_a), transfer payments (T'_a), and taxes (T_x) must be reduced by the marginal propensity to consume domestically produced goods (b').

The introduction of taxes, transfer payments, and business savings has the effect of separating net national product from disposable income by greater absolute amounts as income levels increase, even if the rate of increase remains constant. The relationship between NNP and disposable income is illustrated in Figure 10A-1. At any level of net national product measured by the 45° line, disposable income measured vertically is equal to net national product minus taxes and business savings, plus transfer payments.

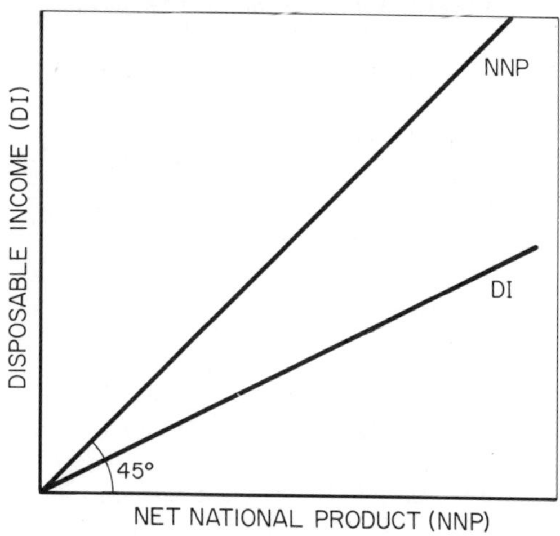

FIG. 10A-1 The Relationship between Net National Product and Disposable Income

The addition of export markets has the effect of increasing the expenditure on domestically produced goods and services, whereas the expenditure on imports reduces spending on domestic production. On balance, the marginal propensity to import reduces the value of the multiplier by introducing another leakage analogous to savings. In effect, business savings and the foreign sector both operate as built-in stabilizers.

ADDITIONAL SELECTED REFERENCES

FISCAL AND MONETARY POLICY

BROWNLEE, O. H., "The Theory of Employment and Stabilization Policy," *Journal of Political Economy*, 58 (October 1950), 412–24.

CLARK, J. N., "An Appraisal of the Workability of Compensatory Devices," *American Economic Review*, 29 (March 1939), 194–208.

COLM, GERHARD, "Fiscal Policy," in *The New Economics*, ed. S. E. Harris, pp. 450–67. New York: Knopf, 1947.

GURLEY, JOHN G., "Fiscal Policies for Full Employment: A Diagramatic Analysis," *Journal of Political Economy*, 60 (December 1952), 525–33.

HALEY, B. F., "The Federal Budget: Economic Consequences of Deficit Financing," *American Economic Review*, 30 (February 1941), 67–87.

HANSEN, ALVIN H., *Business Cycles and National Income*, expanded ed., pp. 195–207, 501–56. New York: Norton, 1964.

———, *Economic Policy and Full Employment*. New York: McGraw-Hill, 1947.

———, *Monetary Theory and Fiscal Policy*. New York: McGraw-Hill, 1949.

HARROD, R. "Reassessment of Keynes's Views on Money," *Journal of Political Economy*, 78: 617–625 (July/August, 1970).

HAYES, H. GORDON, *Spending, Saving, and Employment*. New York: Knopf, 1945.

LERNER, A. P., *Economics of Employment*, pp. 122–38, 270–88. New York: McGraw-Hill, 1951.

MCCRACKEN, H. L., *Keynesian Economics in the Stream of Economic Thought*, pp. 118–50. Baton Rouge: Louisiana State University Press, 1961.

MYRDAL, GUNNAR, "Fiscal Policy in the Business Cycle," *American Economic Review*, 29 (March 1939), 183–93.

POOLE, KENYON E., ed., *Fiscal Policies and the American Economy*. Englewood Cliffs, N.J.: Prentice-Hall, 1951.

SLICHTER, S. H., "The Economics of Public Works," *American Economic Review*, 24 (March 1934), 174–85.

SMITHIES, ARTHUR, "Federal Budgeting and Fiscal Policy," in *A Survey of Contemporary Economics*, ed. H. S. Ellis, Vol. I, pp. 174–209. Homewood, Ill.: Richard D. Irwin, 1948.

TOBIN, JAMES, "Liquidity Preference and Monetary Policy," *Review of Economics and Statistics*, 29 (May 1947) 124–31.

WILLIAMS, J. H., "Deficit Spending," *American Economic Review*, 30 (February 1941), 52–66.

BALANCED-BUDGET MULTIPLIER

BAUMOL, W. J., and M. H. PRESTON, "More on the Multiplier Effects of a Balanced Budget," *American Economic Review* 45 (March 1955), 140–48.

MEASURING THE VALUE OF AUTOMATIC STABLIZERS

CLEMENT, M. O., "The Quantitative Impact of Automatic Stabilizers," *Review of Economics and Statistics* 42 (February 1960), 56–61.

EILBOTT, PETER, "The Effectiveness of Automatic Stabilizers," *American Economic Review*, 56 (June 1966), 450–65.

BIOGRAPHIES OF KEYNES

HARRIS, SEYMOUR E., *John Maynard Keynes*. New York: Scribner, 1955.

HARROD, R. A., *The Life of John Maynard Keynes*. London: Macmillan, 1951.

LEKACHMAN, ROBERT, *The Age of Keynes*. New York: Random House, 1966.

ROBINSON, E. A. G., "J. M. Keynes: Economist, Author, Statesman," *The Economic Journal*, 82: 531–546 (June, 1972).

General Equilibrium

11

INTRODUCTION

As a matter of historical interest, there is no mention of general equilibrium in Keynes's *General Theory*. In our discussion of combined fiscal and monetary effects in the previous chapter, Keynesian equilibrium theory was summarized. However, the fact that the total demand for money—the liquidity-preference curve—will shift to the right or the left with changes in the aggregate-income level was ignored in the discussion.

Certain economists—notably A. H. Hansen,[1] J. R. Hicks,[2] and Franco Modigliani[3]—addressed themselves to the problem of introducing systematically the effect of income changes on the demand for money into the Keynesian model without changing any of the other variables. This refinement modifies certain precepts of the *General Theory*. For example, the so-called "Hicks–Hansen modification" allows changes in the investment or savings function to affect the rate of interest and thereby modify the multiplier, whereas under the fundamental, unreconstructed Keynesian theory, a change in these functions would not affect the interest rate.

In qualifying the simple multiplier, Keynes observed in the *General*

---

[1] A. H. Hansen, *Monetary Theory and Fiscal Policy* (New York: McGraw-Hill, 1949), Chapter 5.

[2] J. R. Hicks, "Mr. Keynes and the 'Classics'; A Suggested Interpretation," *Econometrica*, 5 (April 1937), 147–59.

[3] Franco Modigliani, "Liquidity Preference and the Theory of Interest and Money," *Econometrica*, 12 (January 1944), 45–88.

Theory that an increase in the demand for investment *may* increase the rate of interest and so reduce the multiplier. It is clear that Keynes would not have objected to the analysis presented in this chapter, which maintans that such a change in the demand for investment *does* affect the interest rate, as long as the economy is not in the liquidity trap.[4]

In order to present general-equilibrium analysis, the economy can conveniently be divided into a real or product side and a monetary side. Our discussion will start with the real side of the economy.

In this chapter, as in others, we use the abstract concept, "aggregate income," to stand for "real" national income oı output, which is a national income aggregate divided by the general price level. The general price level is the ratio between dollar expenditures and real output and is computed by dividing current dollar expenditures by national income in real terms. The effects of changes in the general price level are reserved for Chapters 12 and 13.

REAL OR COMMODITY-MARKET EQUILIBRIUM—*IS*

The "real" side, or commodity side, of the economy is classical terminology derived from microeconomics; it refers to the production and sale of goods and services at their respective prices, holding the general price level constant. In other words, the commodity side deals with concepts related to the production and distribution of real income or output, such as the consumer's choice between savings and consumption, as well as the choice made by firms of producing investment or consumer goods.

Derivation of the *IS* Curve

Equilibrium occurs in the commodity market at the point at which savings and investment functions are equal. As we have seen in the simplified Keynesian model with no government sector, savings is a function of aggregate income, and investment is a function of the interest rate. Every savings–investment equality must be associated with a given level of aggregate income and a given rate of interest. The relationship between these is described by the *IS* curve, where each interest rate is associated with a definite level of aggregate income when savings and investment are equal and in equilibrium. It must be remembered from Chapter 8 that realized savings and investment are necessarily equal (assuming no government or foreign sectors); therefore, a meaningful *IS* curve requires that savings and investment be in *ex ante* equilibrium, not simply *ex post* equality.

---

[4]In addition to the clear inferences in J. M. Keynes, *The General Theory of Employment, Interest and Money* (New York: Harcourt Brace Jovanovich, 1936), p. 119, there is also the evidence of a letter from Keynes to David McCord Wright, approving of the idea that the marginal efficiency of capital affects the rate of interest. David McCord Wright, *The Keynesian System* (New York: Fordham University Press, 1962), pp. 35–37.

The *IS* function relating equilibrium savings and investment to aggregate income and the rate of interest is developed in Figure 11-1, from the same data in Table 11-1. Panel A, in the lower right-hand corner of Figure 11-1, shows the demand for investment as a function of the interest rate. As previously developed, the interest rate is measured along the vertical axis, and investment on the horizontal. Panel C presents the standard Keynesian savings function, developed in Chapter 8. The demand for investment, panel A, and the savings function, panel C, are related in panel B, which demonstrates under equilibrium conditions all points of equality of savings and investment. Since they must be equal in equilibrium, this curve is a 45° straight line drawn from the origin. Notice that panels A, B, and C in Figure 11-1 are similar to the same three panels in Figure 10-1.

To describe the relationship among these panels in Figure 11-1, assume

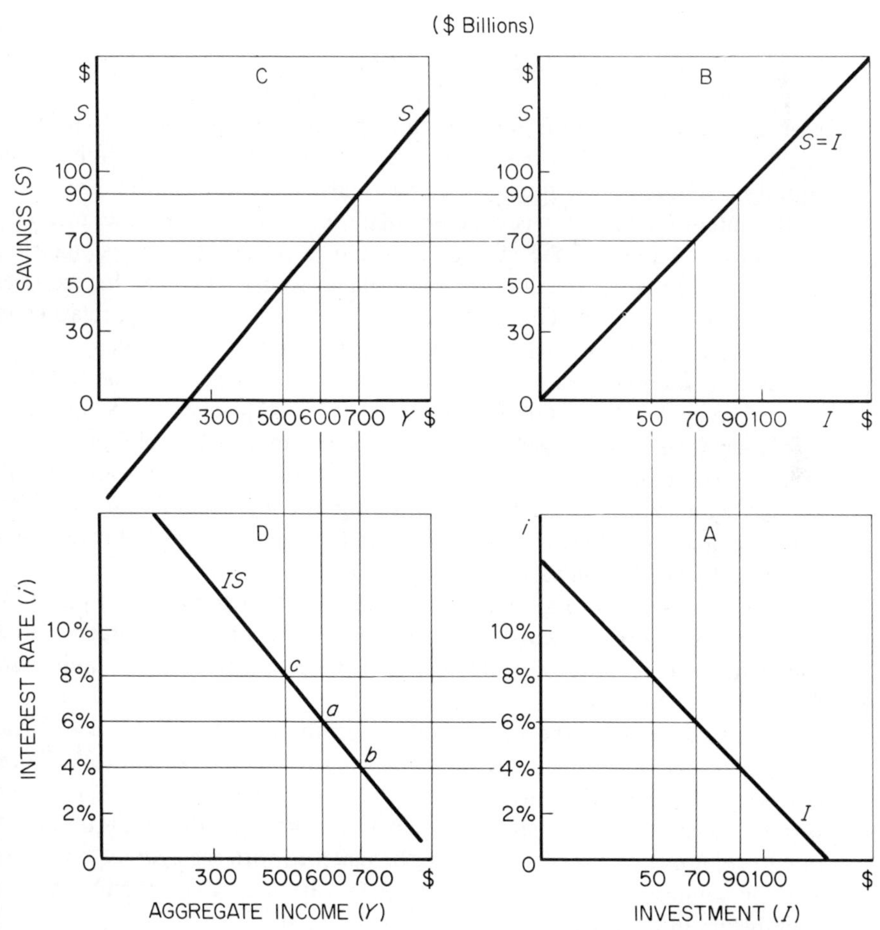

FIG. 11-1 The Real or Commodity Side of the Economy—Derivation of The *IS* Curve ($ Billions)

TABLE 11-1 The Real or Commodity Side of the Economy—Derivation of the *IS* Schedule ($ in billions)

(1)	(2)	(3)	(4)	(5)	(6)	(7)	(8)
Panel A		Panel B		Panel C		Panel D	
Investment-Demand Schedule		*Equilibrium Level of Savings and Investment*		*Savings Schedule*		*Commodity-Market Equilibrium (IS Schedule)*	
i	*I*	*I*	*S*	*Y*	*S*	*i*	*Y*
12%	$10	$10	$10	$300	$10	12%	$300
10	30	30	30	400	30	10	400
8	50	50	50	500	50	8	500
6	70	70	70	600	70	6	600
4	90	90	90	700	90	4	700
2	110	110	110	800	110	2	800
0	130	130	130	900	130	0	900

that the interest rate is given at 6 percent, determining the level of investment at $70 billion in panel A. Since investment and savings must be equal in equilibrium, savings also equals $70 billion, and this amount is associated with aggregate income of $600 billion in panel C. Even though savings is a function of aggregate income, once the level of investment is determined, the equilibrium level of aggregate income is also determined. For each level of the interest rate, there is a determinate level of aggregate income. This relationship, known as the *IS* curve, plotted in panel D, is the geometrical relationship between the interest rate and aggregate income that equates savings and investment. One point, *a*, on the *IS* curve is derived, relating an interest rate of 6 percent with an aggregate income of $600 billion.

To take another example, at an interest rate of 4 percent, the resulting level of investment would be $90 billion, which is consistent with $700 billion of aggregate income in order to achieve the required $90 billion level of savings. Therefore, an interest rate of 4 percent must correspond to an aggregate income level of $700 billion, giving us one more point, *b*, on the *IS* curve in panel D. If the interest rate rises to 8 percent, the level of investment will drop by $40 billion to $50 billion. Savings must also drop to $50 billion, and this corresponds to an equilibrium income of $500 billion. In panel D, another point, *c*, is developed, relating an interest rate of 8 percent to an aggregate income level of $500 billion. Connecting the various points so derived gives the *IS* curve in panel D.

The derivation of the *IS* schedule is demonstrated in Table 11-1. The investment-demand schedule is shown in the two columns of panel A. Panel B describes the savings–investment equilibrium, and panel C shows the savings schedule. When these three panels are properly aligned, the interest rate in column 1 of panel A need only be matched with the aggregate income levels in column 5 of panel C to form the *IS* schedule, or commodity-market equilibrium in panel D.

A normal *IS* curve is negatively sloped, indicating that higher aggregate income levels are associated with lower interest rates. The reason for the negative slope is that aggregate income responds directly to changes in investment, and we assume that the quantity of investment demanded responds to changes in the interest rate as any normal demand curve shows quantity responding to a change in price. We further assume in the Keynesian system that the supply of savings is not interest-elastic, but is related to the level of aggregate income. Since *ex ante* savings and investment must be equal in equilibrium, the savings function only modifies the shape of the *IS* curve, whereas the investment function determines the slope's direction.

Shifts in the *IS* Curve

The stability of the *IS* curve depends on the stability of the savings and investment functions. Any condition that shifts either the savings or the investment curve will also shift the *IS* curve. Suppose, for example, a new invention increases investment demand. Then, at each corresponding level of interest, the *IS* function will also shift to the right by an amount equal to the original shift in the investment demand curve times the investment multiplier. Likewise, the multiplier effect of a decrease in the investment demand will result in a decrease in the *IS* curve (a shift to the left) by the amount of the original decrease in the investment function times the multiplier.

Shifts in the savings function affect the *IS* curve inversely. Since an increase in consumption is shown in this model as a reduction in savings, then if the savings function decreases owing to an increase in the consumption function, shown as a downward shift of the savings function in panel C of Figure 11-1, the *IS* curve will increase by the amount of the shift, times the multiplier. Likewise, an increase in the savings function—that is, a shift upward and to the left—will result in a decrease in the *IS* curve at each level of interest, again equal to the shift in the savings function, times the investment multiplier. Therefore, the *IS* curve will shift upward and to the right whenever the consumption or investment functions are increased.

The government sector can be incorporated into this model by including government expenditures in the investment function in panel A ($I + G$) and including taxes in the savings function in panel C ($S' +$ T)—as we did in Figure 10-3. There is no theoretical reason why savings and taxes cannot be summed or why investment and government expenditures cannot be summed. However, keep in mind that in order to add taxes to savings, the savings function must first be reduced, as explained in Chapter 10. For example, if taxes and government expenditures both increase by the same amount, then the net effect would be to shift the *IS* curve to the right, since part of the taxes would be paid out of a reduction in savings, whereas there is little reason to expect that, with the present level of economic sophistication, an increase in government expenditures would reduce investment through a reduction in business confidence. Once the government sector is incorporated into the *IS* model, a change in taxes will have an effect similar to that of a change in the savings function, and a change in government expenditures will have the same effect as a change in the investment-demand function. Therefore, an increase in government expenditures, like an increase in the consumption or investment function, will increase the *IS* curve, whereas an increase in taxes, like an increase in the savings function, has the effect of reducing the *IS* curve.

MONEY-MARKET EQUILIBRIUM—*LM*

In contrast to the real or commodity-market side of the economy, the money side concerns the stock of money and the liquidity-preference curve. We will not deal with monetary phenomena in the sense of price changes, but rather with the stock of and demand for money, assuming constant prices. In other words, the money side of the economy is stated not in nominal terms, but in real terms. We state the value of money in terms of how much money will buy (its purchasing power) rather than how many dollars are in circulation.

As we have seen, the *IS* curve describes all possible equilibrium points on the commodity-market side of the economy. Similarly, the *LM* function describes all possible equilibrium points on the money side of the economy, which represents money expenditures for commodities.

Derivation of the *LM* Curve

Panel A, the upper left-hand panel of Figure 11-2, is the demand curve for speculative liquid balances, derived from the schedule in panel A of Table 11-2. (The ordering of the panels in Figures 11-1 and 11-2 is different to accommodate the superimposition of the two panels D, to be discussed later.) The demand for speculative balances shows that the desire to hold money as an asset will increase as the interest rate decreases, until at some low level of the interest rate, perhaps 2 percent, the demand for speculative liquid balances becomes completely elastic. On the other hand, as the interest rate rises, the desire to hold speculative balances decreases, until at some high interest rate, in our example at 12 percent, the quantity of speculative liquid balances demanded becomes equal to zero, at which point the vertical segment of the M_L curve coincides with the vertical axis. This segment is sometimes called the "classical range" of the demand curve for speculative balances.

Panel B of Figure 11-2 distributes the stock of money between the two demand functions for money. The stock of money is assumed to be \$180 billion, distributed between speculative liquid balances (M_L) and the combined transactions and precautionary balances (M_t)—referred to for brevity as transactions balances.[5] If the interest rate is 10 percent, the quantity of speculative balances demanded will equal \$20 billion; and consequently, \$160 billion will be available for transactions balances. If the interest rate falls to

[5] For simplicity in this chapter, except where otherwise noted, we are following Keynes in making the demand for both transactions and precautionary money balances a function of aggregate income, and the demand for speculative money balances a function of the interest rate.

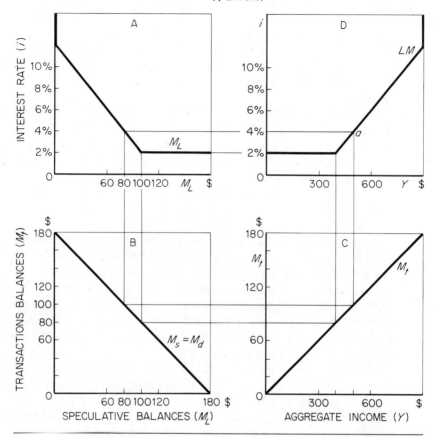

FIG. 11-2 The Money Side of the Economy—Derivation of the *LM* Curve ($ Billions)

TABLE 11-2 The Money Side of the Economy—Derivation of the *LM* Schedule ($ in billions)

(1)	(2)	(3)	(4)	(5)	(6)	(7)	(8)
Panel A		Panel B		Panel C		Panel D	
Demand for Speculative Liquid Balances		*Distribution of Money Stock*		*Demand for Transactions Balances*		*Money-Market Equilibrium*	
i	M_L	M_L	M_t	Y	M_t	i	Y
12%	$ 0	$ 0	$180	$900	$180	12%	$900
10	20	20	160	800	160	10	800
8	40	40	140	700	140	8	700
6	60	60	120	600	120	6	600
4	80	80	100	500	100	4	500
2	100	100	80	400	80	2	400
2	120	120	60	300	60	2	300
		M_s = $180					

4 percent, \$80 billion will be demanded for speculative balances, leaving \$100 billion for transactions balances. The function depicted in panel B will be a 45° negatively sloped straight line connecting the two limits—one with the entire stock of money in transactions balances on the *y*-axis, and the other with the entire stock of money in speculative balances on the *x*-axis. Realistically, the actual equilibrium point must occur somewhere between the two limits, with some money available for both transactions and speculative balances.

The demand function for transactions balances depicted in panel C shows the various quantities of money demanded at various levels of aggregate income. In our example, a linear relationship is assumed in which an additional \$100 of aggregate income leads to the demand for an additional \$20 in transactions balances.

The *LM* curve, or money-market equilibrium curve, in Panel D is derived from the other three panels. For example, if the interest rate is 4 percent, then, as can be seen in panel A, \$80 billion will be demanded for speculative balances, leaving \$100 billion for transactions balances, which, as per panel C, is consistent with an aggregate income of \$500 billion. Therefore, one point of equilibrium in the money market occurs at point *a* in panel D, where a 4 percent rate of interest is associated with aggregate income of \$500 billion. Similarly, selecting other arbitrary interest rates will enable us to determine the level of aggregate income that will yield monetary equilibrium. The *LM* curve is formed by matching these interest rates with their corresponding equilibrium levels of aggregate income.

The *LM* schedule can be derived from Table 11-2. A fixed stock of money, equal to the sum of columns 3 and 4 in panel B, allows us to derive the *LM* schedule by matching the interest rate in column 1 of panel A with the appropriate level of aggregate income in column 5 of panel C. The resulting interest–income relationship is demonstrated in panel D.

The normal *LM* curve has a positive slope, with a horizontal segment to represent the liquidity trap at a low rate of interest, and a vertical segment (the "classical range") that begins at some interest rate universally conceded to be above "normal." The shape of the *LM* curve is a mirror image of the demand for speculative balances, reflecting the influence of the speculative demand in determining the slope of the *LM* curve. The positive slope of the *LM* curve is created by the negative slope of the curve in panel A. The ultimate position of the *LM* curve is further modified by the demand curve for transactions balances shown in Panel C.

Shifts in the *LM* Curve

The demand for speculative balances is a function of the market rate of interest and the expected "normal" rate of interest. In our example, if the interest rate falls to 2 percent, the demand for money to be held in speculative balances becomes perfectly elastic, because there is a widespread feeling, when the interest rate falls that low, that it cannot fall further and will revert toward its normal level, leaving speculators with more to lose from the decreased market value of securities than they might gain from interest earnings.[6]

Suppose a low interest rate persists over a long period of time. Then, inevitably, the typical speculator's concept of the "normal" rate of interest will adjust downward; in other words, the demand curve for speculative balances will shift downward and to the left as a result of changing expectations. However, in our monetary economy, the interest rate must be positive, so a rate of around 2 percent may represent some sort of a practical lower limit below which the demand curve for speculative balances cannot go. So a reduction in the expected "normal" interest rate will cause a leftward shift in the demand for speculative balances, with the lower limit formed by the liquidity trap. A decrease in the demand for speculative balances causes the *LM* curve to increase, that is shift to the right.

Conversely, increases in the expected "normal" interest rate will result in an increase (a shift to the right) in the demand for speculative balances, and such a shift will have the effect of decreasing the *LM* function (a shift to the left). In summary, changes in the demand for speculative balances will induce a change in the opposite direction in the *LM* function.

Changes in monetary policy will also shift the *LM* curve. If the monetary authorities decide to increase the stock of money, the 45° line in panel B of Figure 11-2 would retain the same slope but would shift out to the right, causing an increase (rightward shift) in the *LM* curve without, however, affecting the liquidity trap. Likewise, a reduction in the stock of money will shift the 45° line in panel B to the left, resulting in a decrease (shift to the left) in the *LM* curve.

Changes in the commercial habits of business or consumers will result in a shift in the demand for transactions balances necessary to maintain a given level of aggregate income. For example, if all workers were put on an annual contract and paid once a year, larger transactions balances would be necessary to maintain any given level of aggregate income, since a certain part of transactions balances would have to remain idle for a whole year. Such a decrease in the demand for transactions balances would be shown in panel C of Figure 11-2 as a counterclockwise rotation from the origin in the transactions-balances demand function, the M_t curve. The result of such a change in payment practices would be to decrease the *LM* curve. Or, if wage earners decided to spend their money more quickly after payday and so hold smaller average transactions balances, the effect would be to rotate the transactions-demand function in a clockwise direction, which would in turn increase the *LM* curve, as a smaller amount of money in transactions balances will sustain a higher level of aggregate income.

---

[6]Keynes suggested (*General Theory*, p. 202) that perhaps 2 percent was a practical lower limit to the interest rate, so we have used that figure, even though the liquidity trap could require an even lower rate. No one really knows where the bottom is or if it is unchanging.

If we assume a given *IS* curve, it can be seen that changes in expectations, monetary policy, commercial practices, or spending habits will induce a shift in the *LM* function and affect the interest rate and the level of aggregate income. A rightward shift in the *LM* curve leads to lower interest rates and higher aggregate income, and a leftward shift causes the reverse tendency.

In summary, an increase in the stock of money, a reduction in the demand for speculative balances, or a reduction in the transactions demand for money balances at any given level of income (a rightward rotation in the M_t curve) could each cause an increase in the *LM* curve.

Interest Effects on the Demand for Transactions Balances

Professor James Tobin developed the theory, described in Chapter 7, that the transactions demand for money, M_t, may be responsive to changes in the rate of interest as well as to changes in aggregate income. Adding a degree of interest elasticity to the demand for M_t balances makes the *LM* function more elastic at each level of the interest rate, reducing the range of the liquidity trap (as measured along the horizontal axis) and delaying the onset of the vertical "classical" range. The classical range will be reached only when the demand for transactions balances has reached some irreducible minimum. At that point, the transactions demand is no longer affected by increases in the interest rate; that is to say, further reductions in the demand for transactions balances would cost more implicitly and explicitly than the interest earnings to be derived.

The Tobin effect is demonstrated in Figure 11-3, which is similar to Figure 11-2 except that in panel C, a family of M_t curves is developed. A different M_t curve is associated with each level of the interest rate, and the *LM* curve is formed by relating the speculative and transaction demands at each level of the interest rate. For example, at a 5 percent rate of interest, the appropriate M_t function would be M_{t5}, while M_{t4} applies to a 4 percent interest rate. The *LM* curve with an interest-elastic M_t function is more elastic than the *LM* function associated with an interest-inelastic transactions demand. (Keynes suggested in the *General Theory* that precautionary balances might also be sensitive to interest-rate changes, with results similar to those proposed by Tobin.)

GENERAL EQUILIBRIUM

Combining the real and money markets gives us the general-equilibrium system that was only hinted at in the *General Theory*. Figure 11-1 provided in panel D a locus of equilibrium points, the *IS* curve, in the real or commodity market, and Figure 11-2 provided the locus of equilibrium points, the *LM* curve, in the money market. When we superimpose one panel D on the other, as we have done in Figure 11-4, the *LM* and *IS* functions intersect and determine the one level of the interest rate and aggregate income that will

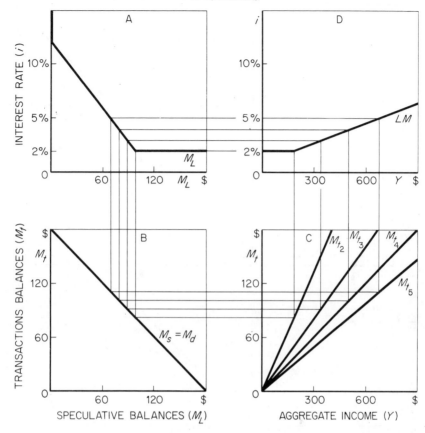

FIG. 11-3 The Interest Effect on Transaction Demand ($ Billions)

permit equilibrium in both the real and money markets. Only by combining the real and money sides of the economy will a determinate system emerge.

All the functions that together determine the *IS* and *LM* curves are shown in Figure 11-4. The three upper-right panels, indentical to panels A, B, and C in Figure 11-1, determine the *IS* curve in panel D; and the three lower-left panels, identical to panels A, B, and C in Figure 11-2, determine the *LM* curve in panel D.

Only at the intersection of the *IS* and *LM* curves can the economy be in both monetary and real equilibrium. For example, suppose the interest rate rises above equilibrium. Certain reactions will occur on both the money and real sides. On the money side, less money will be demanded for speculative balances, leaving more money available for transactions balances. On the real side, the higher interest rate will reduce the quantity of investments demanded and consequently reduce the quantity of savings and, therefore, the equilibrium level of income. The combined pressure of the two factors,

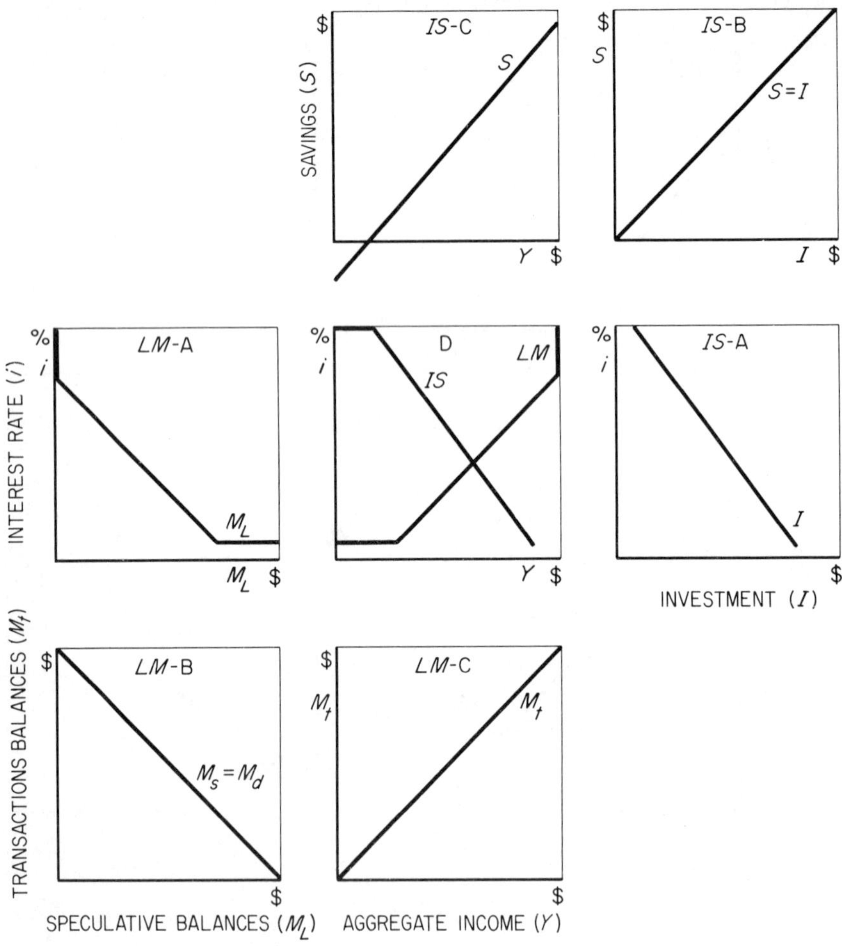

FIG. 11-4 General Equilibrium

increased money balances available for transactions and fewer profitable investment opportunities to absorb the funds, forces interest rates back toward the equilibrium level. Equilibrium will be restored when the interest rate falls sufficiently to shift part of the excess transactions balances back to speculative balances, with the remainder needed to finance the increased number of profitable investment opportunities at the lower interest rate.

Note that when the interest rate rose above equilibrium, there was a tendency for aggregate income to fall on the real side, owing to less investment, and for aggregate income to increase on the money side, owing to increased transactions. Clearly, the economy cannot support these contradictory tendencies. Eventually, the conflict will be resolved by a tendency toward equilibrium.

There is one segment of the *LM* curve where an increase (shift to the right) in the *IS* curve will not result in an increase in the interest rate. If the *IS* curve shifts to the right and still intersects the *LM* curve in the liquidity trap, the full effect of the multiplier will be felt because the interest rate will remain constant. As you will recall, in the liquidity trap the demand for money is perfectly elastic. An increase in real spending will have no effect on the securities market. For example, if a $10 billion increase in investment demand occurs while the economy is in the liquidity trap, assuming a multiplier of 5, a $50 billion increase in aggregate income will result. The income effect from an increase in the *IS* curve is illustrated by the shift from IS_1 to IS_2 in Figure 11-5. Since the multiplier is fully operative when the

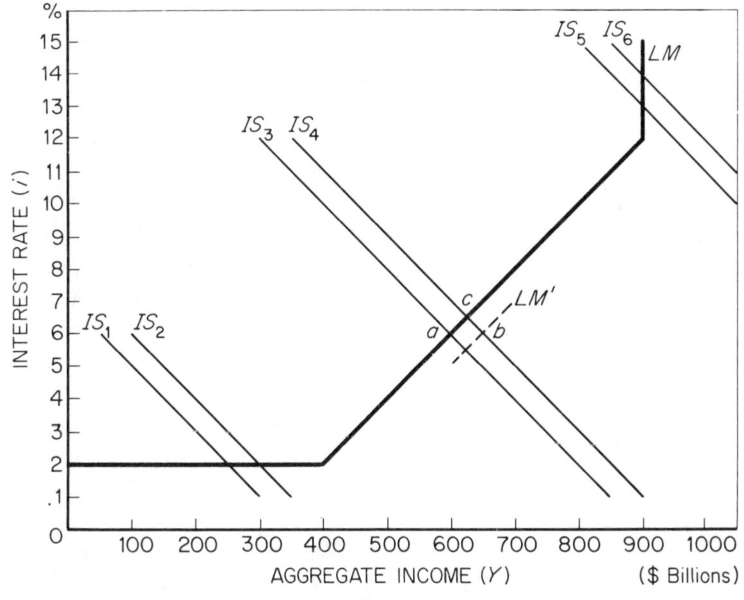

FIG. 11-5 Shifts in the *IS* Curve: The Keynesian Case, the Classical Case, and the Intermediate Range

IS curve intersects the *LM* curve in the liquidity trap, this condition has been called the "Keynesian case" (even though Keynes proposed the liquidity trap only as a limit, not as a normal situation). When the economy is in the liquidity trap, a shift in investment demand has no effect on the rate of interest. Consequently, the simple Keynesian model, in which the interest rate is determined by only the demand for and stock of money, will apply without modification. Since speculative balances are redundant in the liquidity trap, the necessary transfers from speculative balances to transactions balances required by the increase in aggregate income can be accomplished with no increase in the interest rate to compensate asset holders for giving up their money.[7] To call this situation "Keynesian" is not to imply that Keynes felt the economy would normally be in the liquidity trap; it is rather that, in this one situation, the full multiplier effect would be experienced.

In contrast, if the intersection of the *IS* and *LM* curves occurs in the perfectly inelastic, upper segment of the *LM* curve, then aggregate income will be unaffected by any shift in the *IS* curve. An increase in the investment demand curve cannot affect total output, but can only change the rate of interest. In this case there is not even a multiplier effect of 1, since not even the initial increase in investment demand can change aggregate income. In the inelastic segment of the *LM* curve, the interest rate is so high that no one wants to hold money for speculative purposes. In such a situation, all available money will already be in transactions balances, and therefore no further increase in transactions demand for money can be met by shifting money from speculative balances. This situation, generally called the "classical case," to contrast it with the Keynesian case at the other extreme, is illustrated by the shift from IS_5 to IS_6 on the *LM* curve in Figure 11-5. The interest rate increases from 13 to 14 percent in this illustration, with no change in aggregate income.

Our selection of 12 percent for the onset of the classical range is as arbitrary as is 2 percent for the liquidity trap. Determining the actual numbers is an empirical, not a theoretical, question. Two and 12 percent were selected because they have been beyond our post–World War II experience.

An increase in the *IS* curve in the intermediate range affects both aggregate income and the interest rate. In Figure 11-5, a shift from IS_3 to IS_4 leads to an increase in aggregate income from \$600 billion to \$625 billion and leads to an increase in the interest rate from 6 percent to $6\frac{1}{2}$ percent. In our illustration, the multiplier effect on aggregate income has been cut in half by the increase in the interest rate, as the equilibrium point moves not from *a* to *b*, but from *a* to *c*.

As we pointed out earlier in this chapter, fiscal policy can be included in this model by adding government expenditures to the investment function and by adding taxes to the savings function. When the economy is in the classical range, an increase in government expenditures or a reduction in taxes cannot increase aggregate income, but can only increase the interest rate. Private investors and government alike must seek their funds in the money market from lenders who offer their funds to the highest bidder (always allowing an appropriate risk differential). If the government borrows, it must offer an attractively high interest rate to obtain funds which would

---

[7] In the real world, if one group of people holds speculative balances and a second requires more money for transactions balances, the transfer of funds from the first group to the second may require an increase in the interest rate; and so a depressed economy may break out of the liquidity trap sooner than some would expect, unfortunately reducing the multiplier and thereby losing part of the effect of an increase in spending.

otherwise go to private investors. So, government can only spend by reducing private investment spending when the economy is in the classical range.

Suppose the *IS* curve shifts to the right because of an increase in government expenditures that is financed with bonds sold to the general public. The increase in the supply of bonds, in any normal situation, demand remaining constant, tends to force the interest rate up. If the price of bonds falls sufficiently, the interest rate will rise enough to discourage private investment to the point of neutralizing the effect of the government expenditures, preventing output from increasing at all—a situation that will occur when the economy is in the classical range of the *LM* curve. If the interest rate increases only enough to partly offset the multiplier effect due to the increased government expenditures, the economy is in the normal, intermediate range of the *LM* curve.

On the other hand, in the liquidity trap, or Keynesian case, the full multiplier effect of any fiscal policy will be felt on income with no effect on the interest rate, since redundant speculative balances are available to finance the government expenditures.

In the normal, intermediate range of the *LM* curve, the full multiplier effect can be achieved through using monetary policy to hold the interest rate constant by increasing the stock of money. For example, in Figure 11-5, if a shift from IS_3 to IS_4 is accompanied by a shift to the dotted, truncated LM' function, equilibrium will move from point *a* to *b* instead of from *a* to *c*, and the full multiplier effect of $50 billion will occur.

Real vs. Monetary Sources of Change

As we have seen, changes in the real or commodity side of our general-equilibrium system are shown as shifts in the *IS* function. Such shifts can occur because of changes in the savings and consumption functions, changes in the investment function, or changes in fiscal policy. In addition, to summarize the previous section, the *IS* function can intersect the *LM* function in three ranges. If the intersection occurs in the liquidity trap, then a shift in the *IS* function will change aggregate income by an amount equal to the initial change, times the multiplier. If the shift in the *IS* curve occurs in the middle range of the *LM* function, the interest rate and aggregate income will move in the same direction, but the change in income will not be as great as the simple multiplier would lead us to expect, owing to the change in the interest rate. Finally, the *IS* curve can intersect the *LM* curve in the completely inelastic or classical range; here, aggregate income will remain unchanged and the entire effect of the shift in the *IS* function will be felt on the interest rate.

The *LM* function can change because of changes in the stock of money, changes in the demand for transactions balances, or changes in the demand for speculative balances. As in the case of the *IS* curve, the effect of a shift in the *LM* curve may differ, depending on whether the economy is operating in the liquidity trap, intermediate range, or classical range of the *LM* function. In the intermediate and classical ranges, a rightward shift in the *LM* function will increase aggregate income and decrease the interest rate, whereas there will be no effect on either in the liquidity trap. The effects of a shift in the LM curve on aggregate income and the interest rate is illustrated in Figure 11-6. The differing effects of an expansionary monetary change that results in a shift from LM_1 to LM_2 can be seen by comparing the intersection with IS_1 in the liquidity trap, IS_2 in the intermediate range, and IS_3 in the classical range.

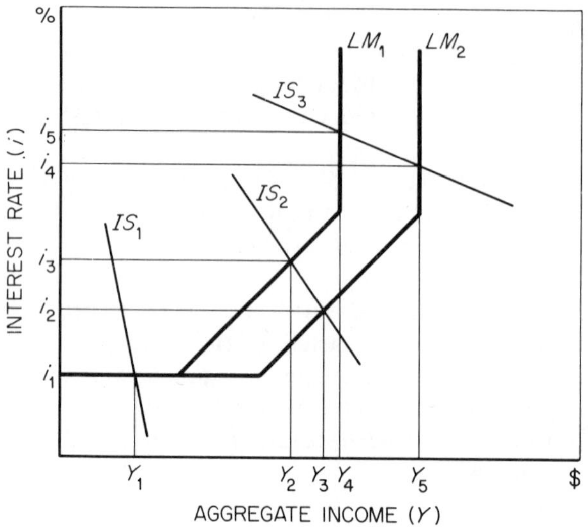

FIG. 11-6 Shifts in the *LM* Curve

In the liquidity trap, an increase in the LM curve has no effect on either aggregate income or the interest rate, which remain unchanged at Y_1 and i_1 respectively. In the intermediate range, both income and interest are affected: Aggregate income increases from Y_2 to Y_3, and the interest rate falls from i_3 to i_2. The greatest effect on income occurs when expansionary monetary policy is applied in the classical range, where expansionary fiscal policy would have no impact whatever. In this case, aggregate income increases from Y_4 to Y_5, and the interest rate falls from i_5 to i_4. The fall from i_5 to i_4 is moderated by the increasing elasticity of the IS function at higher levels.[8]

The increase in the LM curve, as shown in Figure 11-6, might have been due to an increase in the stock of money, a decrease in the demand for transactions balances, or a decrease in the demand for speculative balances. Regardless of the cause, the effect of a given shift in the LM curve on the interest rate and the aggregate-income level will depend on the range of the LM curve in which the IS intersection occurs and on the elasticity of the IS curve. The effect on income velocity will differ according to the *cause* of the

[8] IS_1, IS_2, and IS_3 are increasingly elastic for reasons to be discussed later in this chapter.

shift in the *LM* curve. (You may recall that income velocity is the speed with which money changes hands to buy output included in GNP.)

Monetary Sources of Change

Table 11-3 summarizes the direction of change of aggregate income, income velocity, and the interest rate caused by an increase in the *LM* curve, according to the source of the change and the location of the *IS-LM* intersection. (Remember that income velocity is the reciprocal of the demand for money balances. Thus an increase in the quantity demanded of speculative balances due to a decline in the rate of interest will be the same as a decrease in income velocity.) We break down overall income velocity, V, into its two components, the income velocity of transactions balances, V_t, and the income velocity of speculative liquid balances, V_L.

The analysis begins with the top row of Table 11-3, with an increase in the stock of money, M_s. In the liquidity trap, column 1, the increased stock of money will go into idle speculative balances, reducing V_L enough to completely offset any possible effects on aggregate income of the increased money stock. In the intermediate range, the interest rate will fall as the stock of money increases, increasing the quantity demanded of speculative balances. The resulting decline in V_L, with V_t remaining constant, will partially offset the expansionary effects of the increase in the money stock. At the high interest rates of the classical range, there is no demand for speculative balances. Consequently, the lower interest rate will have no effect on the income velocity of money, and the expansionary effects of an increased stock of money will not be offset.

Row 2 of Table 11-3 summarizes the effects of a rightward shift (clockwise rotation) of the demand for transactions balances, the M_t curve. In the liquidity trap, such a rightward shift would have no effect on income velocity, since the increase in the income velocity of transactions balances V_t would be completely offset by the resulting increases in the quantity of speculative balances (reductions in V_L); therefore, aggregate income will remain constant. In the normal, intermediate range of the *LM* function (column 2), a rightward shift in M_t will increase the quantity demanded for speculative balances through a lower interest rate, but V_L will drop only enough to partially offset the increase in V_t; therefore, aggregate income will increase in response to the net increase in income velocity. In the classical range, an increase in V_t will not be offset by an increase in the quantity demanded of speculative balances, since at such high rates of interest, everyone prefers securities to speculative balances. So speculative balances are maintained at a zero level, and aggregate income will increase by the full amount of the change in V_t, times the stock of money.

The effects of a decrease in the demand curve for speculative balances (a leftward shift in the M_L curve) are summarized in row 3 of Table 11-3. (1) In the liquidity trap, a decrease in the demand for speculative balances will have no effect on income velocity, since the income velocity of speculative

TABLE 11-3 **Aggregate Income, Interest Rates, and Income Velocity in the Liquidity Trap, the Intermediate Range, and the Classical Range**

	Liquidity Trap	*Intermediate Range*	*Classical Range*
(1) Increase in M_S	Income constant V_L Decrease V_t Constant V Decrease (Complete offset) Interest constant	Income increase V_L Decrease V_t Constant V Decrease (Partial offset) Interest decreases	Income increase V_L Constant (zero) V_t Constant V Constant (No offset) Interest decreases
(2) Rightward shift in M_t	Income constant V_L Decrease V_t Increase V Constant (Complete offset) Interest constant	Income increase V_L Decrease V_t Increase V Increase (Partial offset) Interest decreases	Income increase V_L Constant V_t Increase V Increase (No offset) Interest decreases
(3) Leftward shift in M_L	Income constant V_L Constant V_t Constant V Constant (No effect) Interest constant	Income increase V_L Increase* V_t Constant V Increase (Partial offset) Interest decreases	Income constant V_L Constant (zero) V_t Constant V Constant (No effect) Interest constant

**Partly offset by movement along M_L curve after the shift.*

liquid balances, V_L, cannot fall below zero and we have no reason to expect a change in the income velocity of transactions balances, V_t; as a result, aggregate income will remain constant. (2) In the intermediate range, a decrease in the M_L curve will increase V_L. But people will want to hold a larger quantity of speculative balances at the lower rate of interest that results from the decrease in the demand curve for speculative balances, and the larger liquid balances held at the lower rate will partially offset the expansionary effects of the decrease in the demand curve for speculative balances. However, aggregate income will increase in response to the net increase in income velocity. Finally, (3) a leftward shift in the M_L curve while the economy is in the classical range is impossible, since liquid balances for speculative purposes are already zero. So V_L doesn't exist, and money is demanded only for transactions purposes. Thus, when the economy is operating in the classical range, the demand to hold money for speculative purposes is nonexistent, and as a result, there can be no effect on aggregate income.

In summary, in the classical range, only changes in M_s or M_t can affect the level of aggregate income. When the economy is in the liquidity trap, changes in any of these three independent monetary variables (M_s, M_t, or M_L) will be completely offset by the infinitely elastic demand for money and therefore will have no effect on the level of interest rates or on aggregate income. When the economy is in the intermediate range, changes in any of the three variables will be partially offset by the increasing quantities of money demanded for speculative balances at lower rates of interest. The effects of changes in the stock of money due to monetary policy will be strongest when the economy is in the classical range, somewhat weakened in the intermediate range, and nonexistent in the liquidity trap.[9] Much of the controversy over the effectiveness of changes in monetary variables can be reduced to an empirical question of determining which of the three ranges of the *LM* curve most accurately represents the economy at that particular time.

IS–LM Over the Cycle

To trace the *IS–LM* analysis over the business cycle, start with the economy at full-employment equilibrium in Figure 11-7 where IS_1 crosses LM_1, at an aggregate-income level of Y_1 and an interest rate of i_1. If a business crisis occurs under these conditions, the *IS* curve will shift to the left—for example, to IS_2—as a result of the decrease in demand for investment. If, at the same time, a financial crisis occurs, the demand curve for speculative balances will shift upward as speculators sell securities, anticipating lower prices. In addition, the uncertainty associated with a financial crisis usually stimulates an increased desire to hold money at any interest rate. An upward shift will probably occur in the *LM* function; for example, from LM_1 to LM_2. The real-market effects will tend to decrease both aggregate income and the

[9]All the results summarized in Table 11-3 could simply be reversed to determine the effects of a decrease in *LM*.

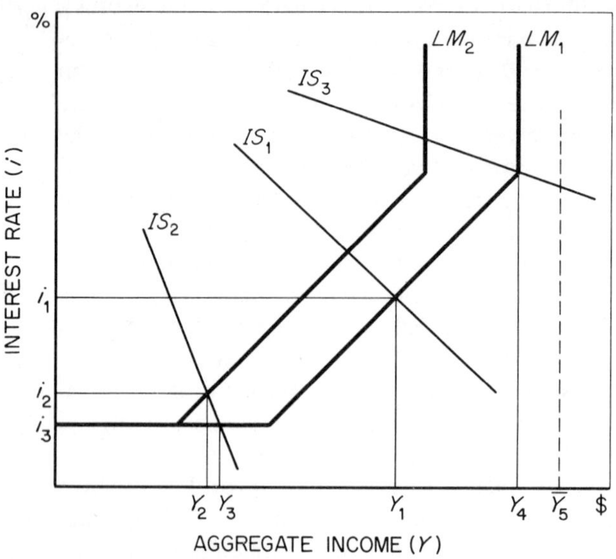

FIG. 11-7 *IS-LM* over the Cycle

interest rate, whereas the money market effects, if they occur, will cause a further decrease in aggregate income but an increase in the interest rate. (Currently, the shift in the *IS* function probably dwarfs the shift in the *LM* curve. Since World War II, few financial crises have been severe enough to cause significant shifts in the demand curve for speculative balances.) The new underemployment equilibrium income at Y_2 is associated in our illustration with a lower rate of interest, i_2. However, i_2 will be higher than the i_3 interest rate that would have occurred if the *LM* curve had not shifted. (In a severe financial crisis, such as that in 1929, the rush to get out of securities and into a strong liquid position would cause a sharp increase in the demand curve for speculative balances, which would cause a sufficient leftward shift in the *LM* curve to raise interest rates despite the decline in the *IS* curve.)

If interest rates rise above "normal" in a severe financial crisis, bond prices will become low enough to make them appear good buys, and a reverse movement from money to bonds should begin when the initial effects of the financial panic wear off. Time will cause the demand for speculative balances to shift back as speculators revert to their previous concept of the normal interest rate. If the demand curve for speculative balances does revert to its original level, the *LM* curve in Figure 11-7 will revert from LM_2 to LM_1, aggregate income will increase to Y_3, and the interest rate will drop to i_3.

However, even if the *LM* curve shifts back to LM_1 from LM_2, the recession will continue as long as the *IS* curve remains depressed. In this illustration, the economy is in the liquidity trap at the intersection of IS_2 and LM_1. Therefore, a change in some real factor, such as an increase in government spending or investment demand would be necessary to initiate a rightward shift in the *IS* curve and to start the recovery phase of the cycle. If unemployment occurs when the *IS* curve intersects the intermediate range of the *LM* function, monetary policy could supplement fiscal policy to restore full employment, or, if the *IS* function is sufficiently elastic, monetary policy might be used exclusively. However, in most cases a combination of monetary and fiscal policy appears preferable, since this would permit full employment at a stable rate of interest.

Suppose that during the recovery phase, the full-employment level of income increases beyond the classical range. Then fiscal policy becomes ineffective, and monetary policy would be required to move the *LM* curve further to the right and restore full employment. For example, in Figure 11-7, if full employment occurs at $\bar{Y}_5$, fiscal policy could not increase income beyond Y_4, because, given LM_1, IS_3 achieves the maximum equilibrium income level attainable through increases in fiscal policy. Any further increase in the *IS* curve could have no effect on aggregate income. If full employment is to be achieved, monetary policy will have to be used to move the *LM* function further to the right.

Minor cycles, such as most of those that have occurred since World War II, will most likely take place entirely within the normal or intermediate range of the *LM* curve, because postwar recessions have not been severe enough to bring us close to the liquidity trap, and interest rates have not gone high enough to carry us into the classical range. However, since World War II, we have relied largely on fiscal policy to stimulate the economy and on monetary policy to slow it down. As a result, interest rates have tended to increase, since both expansionary fiscal policy and contractional monetary policy tend to raise interest rates.

The Effect of an Inelastic *IS* Function

The *IS* curve is apt to be relatively inelastic during a recession, for the following reasons: First, if the *IS–LM* intersection should occur at a low rate of interest, the *IS* curve will be intersected in its lower, less elastic portion.[10] Second, as the *IS* curve shifts to the left during a recession, it will not only decrease but also become less elastic, because (1) during the recession, there will be redundant plant and equipment, and as a result, a small decrease in the rate of interest will probably not encourage much additional investment; and (2) the risk of default will increase which will tend to keep the firm's cost of capital high even if the pure interest rate is decreasing.

In summary, if the money stock increases while the rate of interest is low, the effect on aggregate income will not be as large as when the interest rate is higher, assuming the economy is not in the liquidity trap. (There will be no change at all if the interest rate is so low as to put the economy in the liquidity trap.) Therefore, the decreasing elasticity of the *IS* curve during recessions reduces the effectiveness of monetary policy. The more inelastic the *IS* curve,

---

[10]Remember, the lower portion of a linear demand curve is relatively inelastic compared to upper portions.

the greater the increase in LM that will be required to produce a given increase in aggregate income. In addition, the LM curve itself is less effective at low rates of interest, because it becomes more elastic as it approaches the liquidity trap. Consequently, fiscal policy will probably be more effective than monetary policy as a countermeasure to major depressions.

Some economists have argued that the IS curve is normally inelastic irrespective of the phase of the business cycle, because surveys have apparently demonstrated that businessmen making investment decisions are not much influenced by interest rates.[11] How much weight should the firm place on the going market rate when planning an investment project to be completed in two years? Surveys of the effect of interest-rate changes on investment decisions are not conclusive, because the theory of investment demand involves decisions regarding marginal rather than average investment projects.

Furthermore, even though many firms surveyed reported that interest rates do not affect their investment decisions, we cannot conclude that interest rates are never a factor or that the cost of capital is disregarded. Such surveys merely report incidents in which interest rates were not regarded as significant, and in other investment situations or at other times, the same firms might be sensitive to interest-rate costs.[12] In addition, many of the firms surveyed may have been risky, growing enterprises, and so the lending institutions may have been unwilling to make funds available to them at the going interest rate. Financial markets are organized so that standard financial institutions cannot and will not impose a sufficient risk premium on individual risky borrowers to make lending to them worthwhile. Financial insititutions in general may restrain credit and simply refuse to lend to all their customers rather than raise interest rates when loanable funds are scarce.

In general, one might suggest that the surveys posed the wrong question. As we saw in Chapter 9, management considers not the interest rate, but the cost of capital. The interest rate is only one factor among many in determining the cost of capital.

If it were shown that marginal investment decisions were not influenced by interest-rate changes resulting from monetary policy, then the effectiveness of monetary policy in stimulating aggregate income would be lessened, regardless of the phase of the business cycle. In addition, if a completely inelastic IS curve happened to fall along the completely inelastic classical range of the LM curve, the interest rate (and prices also) could find no resting-place

[11]See J. E. Meade and P. W. S. Andrews, "Summary of Replies to Questions on the Effects of Interest Rates," *Oxford Economic Papers*, 1 (October 1938), 14–31; P. W. S. Andrews, "A Further Inquiry into the Effects of Rates of Interest," *Oxford Economic Papers*, 3 (February 1940), 32–73; R. S. Sayers, "Businessmen and the Terms of Borrowing," *Oxford Economic Papers*, 3 (February 1940), 23–31; and W. H. White, "Interest Inelasticity of Investment Demand—The Case for Business Attitude Surveys Re-examined," *American Economic Review*, 46 (September 1956), 565–87.

For a survey conducted in the United States, see J. F. Ebersole, "The Influences of Interest Rates upon Entrepreneural Decisions in Business: A Case Study," *Harvard Business Review*, 17 (November 1938), 35–39.

[12]White, "Interest Inelasticity," p. 578.

between their level at the onset of the intermediate range and infinity. However, a monetary theory based on credit rationing has been devised that demonstrates the possible effectiveness of monetary policy even if the *IS* function should be somewhat inelastic. We shall develop this theory in Chapter 14.

SUMMARY AND CONCLUSIONS

Keynes's omission of a general-equilibrium solution from his *General Theory* was soon corrected by his followers. In this chapter we have developed such a general-equilibrium model, which balances the equilibrium conditions in the commodity or "real" market with those in the money market. The real-market equilibrium is represented by the *IS* function, and the money-market equilibrium by the *LM* curve. Three basic equations form the *IS* curve: (1) Savings (S) is a function of aggregate income (Y); (2) investment (I) is a function of the rate of interest (i); and (3) savings equals investment in equilibrium. The *LM* curve is also made up of three equations: (1) The transactions demand for money balances (M_t) is a function of income; (2) the speculative demand for money balances (M_L) is a function of the rate of interest; and (3) the sum of the two money demands, the liquidity preference curve, equals the supply of money (M_s) in equilibrium. Combining the *IS* and *LM* curves gives one level of the interest rate and one level of aggregate income consistent with equilibrium.

Our general-equilibrium model can be summarized in the following system of equations:

For the *IS* curve:

1. $S = f_{10}(Y)$ (savings function)
2.[13] $I = f_{8a}(i)$ (investment demand function)
3. $S = I$ (savings–investment equilibrium)

For the *LM* curve:

4.[14] $M_t = f_{11}(Y)$ (transactions demand for money balances)
5. $M_L = f_{12}(i)$ (speculative demand for money balances)
6. $M_t + M_L = \bar{M}_s$ (money demand = money stock equilibrium)

Following the view that the transactions demand for money balances may include a degree of interest elasticity, equation 4 may be rewritten

4a. $M_t = f(Y, i)$

IS–LM analysis provides a convenient way to analyze monetary and fiscal policy. Fiscal policy can be demonstrated by considering government expenditures a form of investment, and taxes a form of savings. The effect of

---

[13]This function is designated f_{8a} to distinguish it from the very similar neoclassical demand for investment, earlier designated f_8.

[14]The functions designated L_t and L_L in Chapter 7 are here redesignated f_{11} and f_{12} for consistency.

monetary policy can be shown as a shift in the stock of money, with the resulting distribution of the change between M_t and M_L balances.

The effect of monetary or fiscal policy, or of any other change in the relevant variables, will differ depending on the stage of the business cycle and the range of the *LM* curve in which the economy is operating. In the intermediate range, monetary and fiscal policy can complement each other. However, in the liquidity trap, monetary policy loses its effectiveness, and in the classical range, fiscal policy becomes impotent. Therefore, granting their assumptions, both the Keynesians and the later neoclassicists were correct in their respective stress on fiscal and monetary solutions to cyclical problems. However, in a sense, both were wrong if they felt that either fiscal or monetary policy alone would be adequate irrespective of the phase of the business cycle, since recession may put the economy in the liquidity trap, and prosperity might put it in the classical range.

Some major shortcomings of this post-Keynesian general-equilibrium model are its omission of the price level, the production function and the labor market. In the following chapters, we will take these omissions into account.

QUESTIONS AND PROBLEMS

1. Show graphically the interaction of the real and monetary sides of the economy.
2. Distinguish the "Keynesian case" from the "classical case." Why is the "Keynesian case" misnamed?
3. Can the full multiplier effect be felt in a general-equilibrium situation?
4. What would be the effect of an inelastic investment demand on general equilibrium?
5. How would the *IS* curve change during the down phase of the business cycle?
6. If the transactions demand for money is a function of the interest rate, show what the effect would be on the *LM* curve.
7. If the *LM* curve increases, what would be the effect on income and on velocity, assuming the economy is in the intermediate range?
8. Which of the variables are independent in the *IS–LM* model?
9. On the graphs (page 365), indicate how monetary policy could be used to increase aggregate income. What would be the effect on the interest rate?

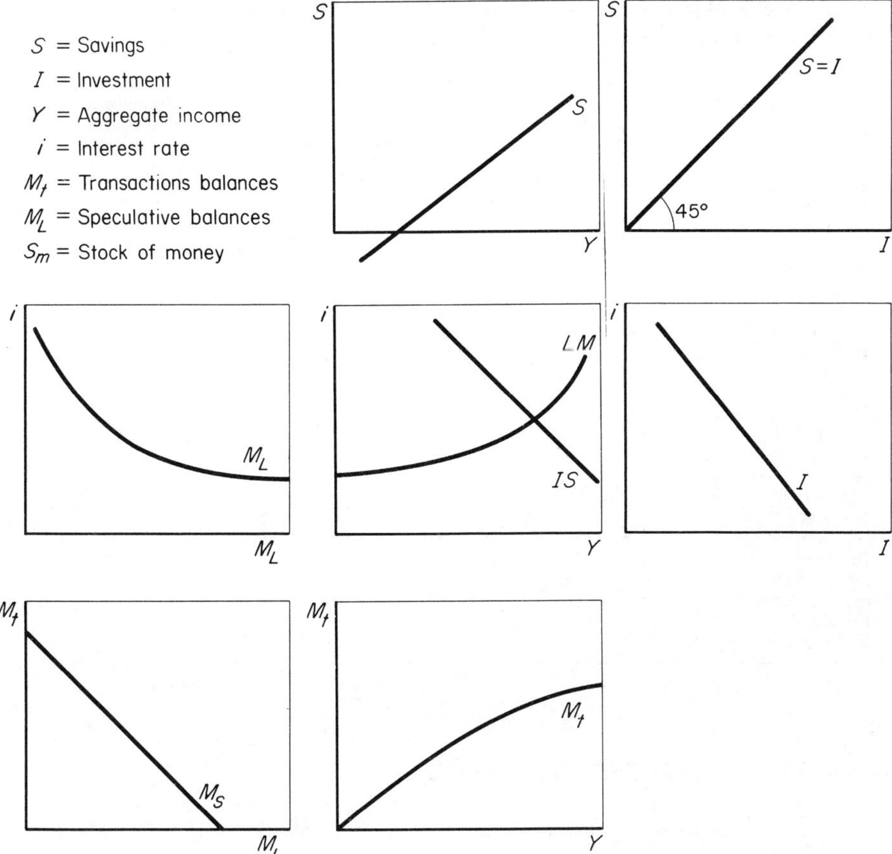

S = Savings
I = Investment
Y = Aggregate income
i = Interest rate
M_t = Transactions balances
M_L = Speculative balances
S_m = Stock of money
S
S
Y
S
S=I
45°
I
i
M_L
M_L
i
LM
IS
Y
i
I
I
M_t
M_S
M_L
M_t
M_t
Y

10. According to the modern theory of *IS* and *LM*, how would the following changes affect each of the items across the top?

	Gross National Product	Interest Rate	Quantity of Savings	Speculative Demand for Money
Increase in the money stock				
Increase in investment demand				
Increase in savings				
Increase in the demand for money				
Increase in net taxes				
Increase in government expenditures for goods and services				

ADDITIONAL SELECTED REFERENCES

ACKLEY, GARDNER, *Macroeconomic Theory*, pp. 359–72. New York: Macmillan, 1961.

CONARD, JOSEPH W., *An Introduction to the Theory of Interest*, pp. 194–202. Berkeley: University of California Press, 1959.

HANSEN, A. H., *A Guide to Keynes*, pp. 140–53. New York: McGraw-Hill, 1953.

LANGE, OSKAR, "The Rate of Interest and the Optimum Propensity to Consume," *Economica*, 5 (February 1938), 12–32.

Demand, Supply, and the Price Level

12

INTRODUCTION

In this chapter, we shall build a Keynesian model relating aggregate output and price levels that parallels the neoclassical model presented in Chapter 6. The curve structure used by J.P. McKenna is followed, employing the traditional approach in dividing the economy into aggregate demand and aggregate supply, and measuring prices on the y-axis and quantity on the x-axis.[1] Aggregate demand and supply relate price and quantity data and must be distinguished from the effective-demand concept, which relates consumption, investment, and government expenditures to real aggregate income or output.[2]

---

[1] J. P. McKenna, *Aggregate Economic Analysis* (New York: Holt, Rinehart & Winston, 1958), pp. 171–97. An earlier, somewhat similar approach was followed by Warren L. Smith, in "A Graphical Exposition of the Complete Keynesian System," *Southern Economic Journal*, 23 (October 1956), 115–25; and O. H. Brownlee, "Money, Price Level, and Employment," in Francis M. Boddy, ed., *Applied Economic Analysis* (New York: Pitman, 1948), pp. 222–48.

[2] Throughout most of the *General Theory*, prices are assumed to be constant; Keynes reserved consideration of the effects of price changes for the latter part of the book. Many economists have mistakenly described the basic Keynesian model of the early chapters as the *General Theory's* last word on the structure of the economy. We will attempt to correct this common misunderstanding and develop a theory of aggregate demand and supply in terms of aggregate price levels, as is suggested in the later chapters of the *General Theory*, incorporating the post-Keynesian *IS–LM* analyses we presented in Chapter 11.

The Keynes Effect

As a background to the Keynes effect, we must consider the effect of price changes on the variables included in the *IS–LM* system. We start with the transactions demand for money balances, because investment and consumption are the fundamental economic activities and are financed with transactions money balances. Then we consider in turn the precautionary and speculative demands for money balances.

Transactions Demand If prices fall, a constant level of real income can be maintained with a smaller stock of money; for instance, if you lived on one candy bar a day and each candy bar cost 10 cents, you could maintain your level of real income with $3.00 per month. Now, if the price of candy bars falls to 5 cents, you only need $1.50 a month to maintain the same level of real income. In real terms, $1.50 becomes the equivalent of $3.00 in purchasing power at the old price level. Therefore, in our example, to maintain the same level of real income, money incomes must fall by half. The transactions demand for *real money balances* (that is, money balances deflated for changes in the price level) remains unchanged for our consumer, if he maintains his old level of real income.

Each spending sector of the economy—businesses, consumers, and government—has a transactions demand for money balances. The size of the money balances required to finance investment and consumption depends on the real purchasing power of money, which is determined by using the price level as a deflator.

Consider the effect of price changes on investment demand. If we assume that a change in the general price level affects the price of capital goods and the expected net return on investment in the same proportion, then the marginal efficiency of capital, MEC, will remain unchanged, since the MEC is the ratio of those two variables. If the interest rate remains constant, the same amount of investment will be as profitable after the price change as before. The demand for capital goods is different from other demands, because it is stated as a function of a rate of return and not as a function of a sum of money. For example, if an investment costing $10,000 returns $1,000 a year, the MEC, or rate of return (assuming the investment lasts forever), is 10 percent.[3] If the price level doubles, and as a result returns increase from $1,000 to $2,000, while the cost increases from $10,000 to $20,000, the rate of return remains 10 percent.

Consumers, like investors, may be assumed to think in terms of the real purchasing power of their money, so that if the price of consumer goods and

---

[3]If, for simplicity, we disregard the fact that investments do not last forever, formula 9-2 may be restated

$$\text{MEC} = \frac{R}{K}$$

where R is the annual expected net return and K is the market price of capital goods.

consumers' money income change proportionately, we may expect the consumption function in real terms to remain unchanged. If the real consumption function remains unchanged, the consumers' demand for real purchasing power for transactions will also remain constant. If prices double, twice as much money income will be required to finance the same real level of consumer demand. We may conclude that the demand for *real* transactions money balances remain constant as the price level changes.

Precautionary Demand In the simple Keynesian theory, the size of precautionary money balances, like transactions money balances, depends on the level of real income. Therefore, if the price level doubles, the desired amount of nominal precautionary balances will also double, in order to keep the demand for real precautionary balances constant. So the demand for real precautionary money balances remains unchanged as the price level changes, as long as nominal precautionary money balances also change proportionately to the change in the price level.

Speculative Demand The demand for money for speculative purposes is similar to the investment demand in that it is a function of a rate of return, which is stated as a percentage. The speculative demand for money is a function of two interest rates: the market rate of interest and the expected or anticipated "normal" rate.[4] Like the demands for real transactions and real precautionary money balances, the demand for real speculative balances is unaffected by price changes. The interest rate is the ratio between the sum of money received annually as income from a financial asset and the sum of money paid for the asset. If money incomes change in the same proportion as prices, it is likely that money savings will also change in the same proportion. For example, if prices double and money savings double, the annual sum of money paid for securities purchased with savings will also double if the interest rate remains constant, and the purchasing power of current savings—not accumulated savings—will remain unchanged.[5] Therefore, the demand for real speculative money balances, like the demands for real transactions and precautionary money balances, is unaffected by changes in the price level.[6]

Stock of Money Turning from the demand for money to the stock of money, you will note that if the nominal stock of money remains unchanged as the price level falls, the purchasing power of the stock of money (that is, the *real stock of money*) would increase. For example, if $100 billion of money

---

[4]"Normal" rate refers to a typical investor's expected average rate in the future. When the market interest rate is sufficiently high that it is equal to or above the normal rate, then the risk of capital loss seems small to a representative investor.

[5]Accumulated savings (wealth) held as money or securities fixed in money terms change in value as inflation or deflation occurs, but the wealth owner can do nothing to offset the resulting windfall loss or gain. So accumulated savings do not influence the interest rate, nor do they influence consumption as a function of income.

[6]Even though a constant interest rate will obviously accommodate any level of current inflation, we will see in the next chapter that *expected* future inflation can affect the current nominal interest rate.

is in circulation and the price level drops to half, the real value of the stock of money would increase to $200 billion.

In order for individuals to hold unchanged real-money balances when the price level increases, the stock of nominal money available for transactions, precautionary, and speculative money balances must also increase in the same proportion. Therefore, whenever the price level changes, real-money balances can be maintained at a constant level only if nominal-money balances change in the same proportion as the price change. For example, if the nominal stock of money remains constant when the price level doubles, the real-money stock, M/P, would be cut in half. Higher prices, therefore, reduce the real-money stock if the nominal stock of money is not increased. A reduction in the real stock of money, whether owing to a smaller nominal stock or to higher prices, in terms of *IS–LM* analysis, has the effect of shifting the *LM* curve to the left, even though the demand for real-money balances remains unchanged.

As we have seen, a change in the price level does affect the real stock of money but does not affect the demand for real-money balances. The transactions component of the demand for real-money balances is derived from the demand for consumer goods and investment goods; price changes will not affect these magnitudes because the demands for consumer and investment goods are functions of real, not money, income. Because the *IS* curve incorporates the demands for real investment and consumption, it will not be affected by price changes.

However, as pointed out above, if the stock of nominal-money balances does not change in proportion to a price increase, the *LM* curve will shift to the left, raising the equilibrium interest rate and reducing aggregate income. (In this chapter as in the previous one, aggregate income or output refers to *real* rather than *nominal* values, unless specified otherwise.) Likewise, if the price level decreases and nominal balances do not change, the *LM* curve will shift to the right, because the increase in the real money stock lowers the equilibrium interest rate and increases aggregate income. This change in real aggregate income resulting from a shift in the *LM* curve because of the change in the real stock of money when prices change is called the *Keynes effect.*[7]

Wage–Price Flexibility Although Keynes devised the Keynes effect, he rejected it as a practical policy to counter a recession.[8] He made it clear that his preferred policy was not to allow prices to fall but to have the monetary authorities increase the nominal stock of money, analytically equivalent

---

[7] Axel Leijonhufvud, *On Keynesian Economics and the Economics of Keynes* (New York: Oxford University Press, 1968), p. 325.

[8] Keynes mentions that falling prices increase the real demand for money and therefore have the same effect on the economy as an increase in the quantity of money, but he does not elaborate on this subject; he is content to point out that "those who believe in the self-adjusting quality of the economic system must rest the weight of their argument" on the effect of price changes on the real quantity of money. J. M. Keynes, *The General Theory of Employment, Interest and Money* (New York: Harcourt Brace Jovanovich, 1936,) p. 266.

to decreasing the price level. Keynes felt that prices and money wages in contemporary society are inflexible downward. In addition, he believed that the effects of wage–price flexibility would be unfortunate, among other reasons because the real burden of accumulated debt increases as prices fall, and so downward price flexibility would threaten investors and dampen their enthusiasm.[9] Therefore, in Keynes's view, general deflation is an impracticable policy for countering recessions.

We may summarize Keynes's criticism of flexible wages as follows:[10]

1. Wage reductions are impracticable because workers resist wage cuts.
2. Wage reductions occur piecemeal, and so the weakest bargainers are most adversely affected. There is no reason to suppose wage cuts on that basis serve either efficiency or equity.
3. Piecemeal wage reductions can lead to the expectation of future wage reductions, which would hurt investment.
4. True wage (and price) flexibility would permit unconstrained changes in wage (and price) levels. Immoderate wage reductions would shatter confidence. And what investor would undertake fixed interest payments if the price of his product was apt to fall without limit?
5. Falling wages and prices would redistribute income from workers with less bargaining power to workers with more, and from investors to rentiers (recipients of a fixed income from accumulated wealth). In Keynes's opinion, such redistribution would reduce the consumption function.
6. Political turmoil accompanying widespread wage decreases could on balance increase the liquidity-preference curve and so lead to less investment and slower income velocity of money.

(On the other side, lower wages could provide an advantage in world trade. If the wage reduction puts domestic wages at a lower level than those overseas, then investment will be stimulated.)

In conclusion, Keynes felt that inflexible wages were preferable to flexible wages, even if wage cuts could be achieved.

It appears that for a number of additional pragmatic reasons besides those presented by Keynes, his basic conclusion about wage-price flexibility was correct. Many prices in our less than perfectly competitive economy are simply not flexible, and any policy that depends on price flexibility could be successful only if the whole structure of the economic society were changed.

1. Even in some fairly competitive industries, certain prices tend to become generally accepted and therefore are seldom changed, such as the price of candy bars, soft drinks, or coffee by the cup. (However, price changes may be effected by varying the quantity sold for the fixed, conventional price.)
2. In addition, widespread market imperfections also cause price rigidities. A large number of our manufactured products are produced by oligopolies, who evidently have relatively rigid administered prices, particularly resistant to price cuts.
3. Some businessmen selling differentiated products may resist price cuts for fear of "cheapening their brands."

---

[9] *Ibid.*, p. 264.

[10] *Ibid.*, pp. 260–71, 303–4.

4. Price rigidities are also built into the system through business contracts with suppliers and customers. Although contractual rigidities are temporary, they retard price adjustments.

5. In regulated industries such as public utilities, transportation, and communications, price changes require approval of regulatory agencies, a process that has been known to drag on for years, delaying price adjustments.

Wages are another example of a price that becomes institutionalized and resists downward pressure. Minimum-wage laws and bargaining between powerful labor unions and big employers tend to reinforce Keynes's view that wages are inflexible downward. In addition workers asked to take a wage cut do not know whether or not they can find another job at their present wage level.

However, even though price deflation may be unworkable, the Keynes effect is still a useful analytical tool for at least two reasons: (1) Lower prices and a greater stock of money are analytically equivalent, and (2) price increases that are observed in the real world are certainly not ruled out by the existence of downward inflexibility.

Keynes Effect Illustration The Keynes effect is illustrated in Table 12-1 and Figures 12-1 and 12-2. Table 12-1 duplicates Table 11-2: Panel A represents the demand schedule for speculative money balances; panel B distributes

TABLE 12-1 Derivation of the *LM* Schedule ($ in billions)

(1)	(2)	(3)	(4)	(5)	(6)	(7)	(8)
Panel A		Panel B		Panel C		Panel D	
Demand for Speculative Balances		*Distribution of Money Stock*		*Demand for Transactions Balances*		*Money-Market Equilibrium*	
i	M_L	M_L	M_t	Y	M_t	i	Y
12%	$ 0	$ 0	$180	$900	$180	12%	$900
10	20	20	160	800	160	10	800
8	40	40	140	700	140	8	700
6	60	60	120	600	120	6	600
4	80	80	100	500	100	4	500
2	100	100	80	400	80	2	400
2	120	120	60	300	60	2	300

$$M_s = \$180$$
$$P = 100$$
$$\frac{M_s}{P} = \frac{180}{100} = 1.80$$

the stock of money between speculative balances and transactions balances; panel C is the demand schedule for transactions money balances; and panel D is the *LM* schedule (money-market equilibrium).

The data in Table 12-1 are plotted in the corresponding panels of Figure 12-1, with the original money stock of $180 billion shown by the M_{s_1} line in panel B and the original LM_1 curve in panel D. The price level is represented by a price index that is assumed to start at 100. Consequently, the real stock

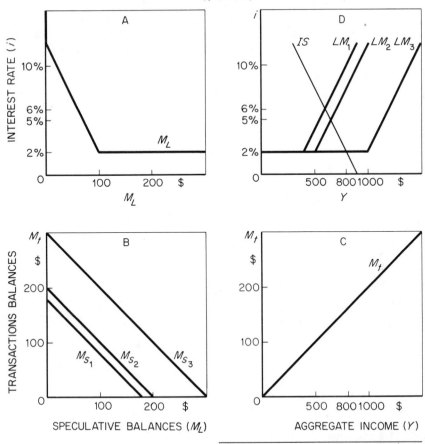

FIG. 12-1 The Keynes Effect ($ Billions)

of money equals the nominal stock. If the nominal stock of money remains constant as the price index drops from 100 to 90 then to 60, the real stock of money in panel B increases from \$180 billion to \$200 billion and then to \$300 billion, as represented by the shift from M_{s_1} to M_{s_2} and then to M_{s_3} in panel B.[11]

Each successive increase in the real stock of money in panel B results in a rightward shift of the *LM* curve in panel D from LM_1 to LM_2 and then to LM_3. The results of the two increases in the real stock of money are shown in panel D of Figure 12–1 as a reduction in the *IS–LM* equilibrium interest rate, first from 6 to 5 percent and then finally to 2 percent in the liquidity trap. The lower interest rate leads to a higher level of aggregate income, reaching a

[11] The original real stock of money (M_{s_1}) is equal to \$180 billion (i.e., \$180 billion/1.00). M_{s_2} is equal to \$200 billion (i.e., \$180 billion/.90). M_{s_3} is equal to \$300 billion (i.e., \$180 billion/.60).

maximum of $800 billion in the liquidity trap. It may be noted that the speculative demand for money balances in panel A, the transactions demand for money balances in panel C, and the *IS* curve in panel D are unaffected by changes in the price level. The only effect of a change in the price index in Figure 12-1 is on the real stock of money in panel B and the *LM* curve in panel D.

Figure 12-2 illustrates the relationship between various price levels,

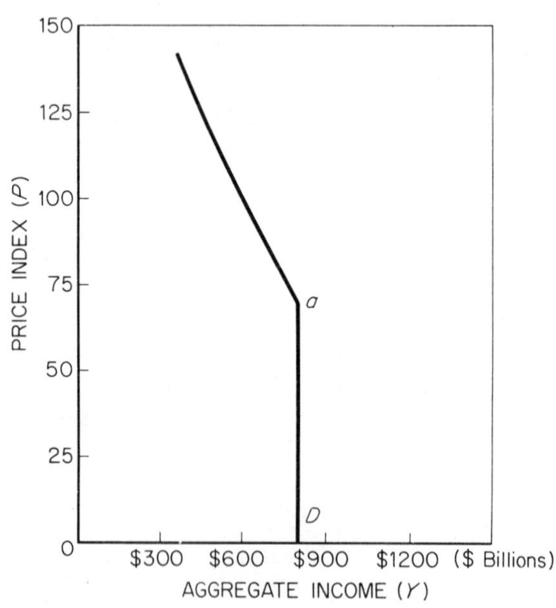

FIG. 12-2 Aggregate Demand Subject to the Keynes Effect

presented in the form of a price index, and the corresponding levels of aggregate income determined from Figure 12-1. The resulting aggregate-demand curve shown in Figure 12-2 becomes completely inelastic at the onset of the liquidity trap. A reduction in the price level increases the level of aggregate income or output except in the liquidity trap, where the aggregate-demand curve becomes completely inelastic below point *a* in the figure. The negative slope of the curve accords with the traditional theory that a reduction in the price level increases the quantity demanded. A lower price index can stimulate the economy as long as the interest rate is free to fall, but once the liquidity trap is reached and the interest rate can fall no farther a lower price index will not call forth greater output. In our illustration, if the maximum level of aggregate income, $800 billion, fell short of the full employment level of income, full employment could not be achieved through a reduction in the price index. If full employment occurs to the right of the point at which the liquidity trap causes the aggregate-demand curve to turn completely inelastic, then full employment could be achieved only through an increase in the *IS* curve, which would shift the aggregate-demand curve to the right.

Keynes Effect Evaluation The Keynes effect—that price changes will affect only the real value of the stock of money—is based on limited assumptions. For instance, the assumption that economic magnitudes, such as the consumption function, would be unaffected by price-level changes may be unrealistic. Price changes affect different groups of consumers differently. For example, the real income of anyone receiving a fixed income, such as a pensioner, would have to increase as the price level fell. Similarly, investors' plans and intentions will be influenced by price changes, because expected net returns may not change in the same proportion as the market price of capital goods.

Therefore, the Keynes effect may not operate in the real world as the theory suggests. The aggregation of consumer and investor plans and decisions, as they respond to price changes, may or may not balance out and leave the Keynes effect to operate. The aggregate impact of any price changes on the economy will depend on the elasticities of supply and demand in each market and on the interaction of all the markets.

The Pigou Effect

Keynes's conclusions were attacked on two grounds: (1) From the standpoint of practical policy, many people were strongly opposed to the implication that government action might be required to lift an economy out of a recession. (2) The members of the neoclassical school, which Keynes was attempting to supplant, believed that flexible wages and prices were always sufficient to restore full employment. The leading representative of this group, A.C. Pigou, proposed a new theory to counter the Keynesian argument that wage–price flexibility might not restore full employment.[12] Pigou acknowledged the possibility that the liquidity trap might choke off investment, but argued that lower prices would induce greater consumption. In Pigou's theory, increased private consumption generated by falling prices would have the same effect as conscious fiscal policy in the Keynesian theory.

The Pigou effect operates basically on some assets that are fixed in money terms, such as money or government bonds. The value of these assets increases proportionately as the prices of all other (nonmonetary) assets fall, because a fixed number of dollars buys more at lower prices. Holders of government bonds or money become wealthier in real terms as prices fall. However, holders of private-debt *assets*, such as corporate bonds, become richer at the expense of debtors who become poorer as the real value of their monetary *liabilities* increases.[13] Therefore, the expansionary impact of the

---

[12]A. C. Pigou, "The Classical Stationary State," *Economic Journal*, 53 (December 1943), 343–51.

[13]There is significant controversy as to whether the Pigou effect operates on the total money supply or just on money created by the government, ("outside money"). It is clear that outside money has private creditors, but only the government as a debtor.

Pigou effect is offset in the case of private debt, but not in the case of public debt, because the government does not and should not react to an increase in the real value of its liabilities as a private debtor does, since the government is not in business to make a profit.

The Pigou effect should not have caught Keynes by surprise. He listed windfall gains or losses in capital values as one objective determinant of consumption. He observed that "The consumption of the wealth-owning classes may be extremely susceptible to unforeseen changes in the money-value of its wealth."[14] But what Keynes missed was that the effect of increasing money value of certain assets during periods of falling prices could call into question the logical validity of his theory of the consumption function. Pigou and his followers observed correctly that, since consumption is positively related to wealth and since falling prices increase the real value of money and government bonds, freely falling prices would always by themselves be sufficient to end a recession.[15]

Pigou Effect Illustration Whereas the Keynes effect works through the *LM* curve, the Pigou effect operates through the *IS* curve, as illustrated in Table 12-2 and Figures 12-3 and 12-4. The figures in Table 12-2 are identical to those in Table 11-1: Panel A depicts the investment demand schedule; panel B, the savings and investment equilibrium; and panel C, the savings

---

On the other hand, demand deposits generated by the commercial banks (commonly called "inside money" in the sense of money endogenously generated by the private economy) are obligations of the commercial banking system. Each dollar created is matched by a dollar of private debt (ignoring the part held as a reserve). Therefore, the creation of bank demand deposits involves both debtors and creditors. Holders of the demand deposits provide credit to borrowers, with the bank acting as middleman. A decrease in the price level would make creditors richer, because the fixed amount of money owed them will buy more goods. At the same time, debtors become poorer in real terms, because the money they repay represents more purchasing power than the money they borrowed. Consequently, at first glance there seems to be no wealth effect associated with bank-created money when the price level changes. The entire inside–outside money controversy stems from the work of Gurley and Shaw, and Don Patinkin. See J. G. Gurley and E. S. Shaw, *Money in a Theory of Finance* (Washington D.C.: Brookings Institution, 1960), pp. 72–75, 132–49, 173–77; and Don Patinkin, *Money, Interest and Prices*, 2nd ed. (New York: Harper & Row, 1965), pp. 295–310.

Pesek and Saving, in contrast, feel that the distinction between inside and outside money is irrelevant. Any money, whatever its source, that is desired by asset holders willing to carry it in their portfolios obviously provides utility to those asset holders. The real value of all money (inside and outside) increases when the price level falls. No seller inquires whether a dollar spent is inside money or outside money. Boris P. Pesek and Thomas R. Saving, *Money, Wealth, and Economic Theory* (New York: Macmillan, 1967), pp. 218–24.

The bank loses its neutral role in the Pesek and Saving theory, because demand deposits are not truly a liability of the banking system from an economic point of view (accounting practice to the contrary notwithstanding). From society's viewpoint, demand deposits *add* to the net worth of the banks. If this is true, then a decrease in the price level makes the bank (or its stockholders) wealthier in real terms. Therefore, the bank is wealthier; the depositor is wealthier; and only the borrower is poorer. The net effect, then, is that a decrease in the price level makes society wealthier in the case of inside money just as in the case of outside money, and a distinction is unnecessary, in their view.

[14]Keynes, *General Theory*, pp. 92–93.

[15]Pigou, "The Classical Stationary State," p. 349.

TABLE 12-2 Derivation of the *IS* Schedule ($ in billions)

(1)	(2)	(3)	(4)	(5)	(6)	(7)	(8)
Panel A		Panel B		Panel C		Panel D	
Investment Demand Schedule		*Equilibrium Level of Savings and Investment*		*Savings Schedule*		*Commodity-Market Equilibrium (IS Schedule)*	
i	*I*	*I*	*S*	*Y*	*S*	*i*	*Y*
12%	$ 10	$ 10	$ 10	$300	$ 10	12%	$300
10	30	30	30	400	30	10	400
8	50	50	50	500	50	8	500
6	70	70	70	600	70	6	600
4	90	90	90	700	90	4	700
2	110	110	110	800	110	2	800
0	130	130	130	900	130	0	900

$W = \$400$
$P = 100$

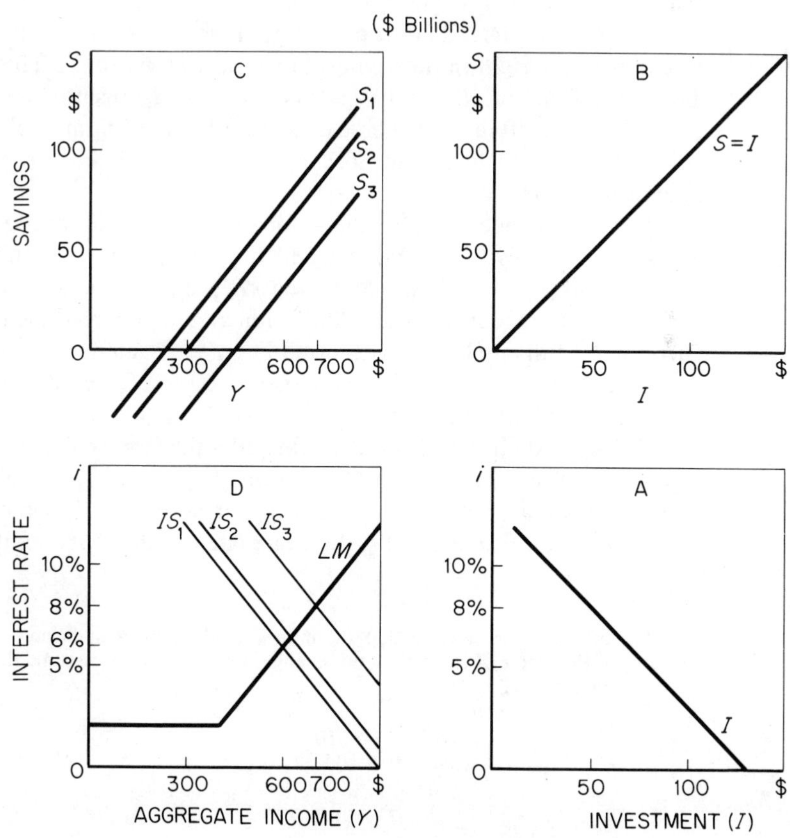

FIG. 12-3 The Pigou Effect ($ Billions)

schedule. Panel D combines panels, A, B, and C to form the *IS* schedule, or commodity-market equilibrium.

To illustrate the Pigou effect, assume that the *LM* curve remains constant[16] and that 10 percent of any increase in wealth owing to lower prices will be spent on consumption. Assume further that the marginal propensity to save is 20 percent and that autonomous savings (savings at zero income) are \$50 billion when the price level is 100, indicating that autonomous consumption must be \$50 billion.[17] The stock of wealth is assumed to be \$400 billion; 10 percent of \$400 billion is \$40 billion; therefore, 80 percent of the autonomous level of consumption must be ascribed to wealth if the marginal and average propensity to consume wealth are equal.

The data of Table 12-2 are plotted in the four corresponding panels of Figure 12-3. The savings function, S_1, taken from Table 12-2, corresponds to an initial price index of 100. The savings function, S_1, shown in panel C, combined with the investment-demand function in panel A and the $S = I$ equilibrium in panel B, results in the IS_1 curve in panel D. If the price index falls from 100 to 80, the 20 percent price decline increases the real value of monetary assets from \$400 billion to \$500 billion. Consequently, autonomous consumption increases from \$50 billion to \$60 billion.[18]

The result of the fall in the price index is shown in panel C of Figure 12-3 as a shift to the right in the savings function from S_1 to S_2. This decrease in the savings function causes the *IS* curve in panel D to shift from IS_1 to IS_2. The rightward shift in the *IS* curve increases the equilibrium level of aggregate income from \$600 billion to \$630 billion, and the interest rate from 6 to $6\frac{1}{2}$ percent.

If the price index falls further—for example, to 50—autonomous consumption increases to \$90 billion, and the savings function shifts to S_3 in panel C, causing a shift in the *IS* curve to IS_3 in panel D, raising the equilibrium aggregate-income level to \$700 billion and the interest rate to 8 percent. Therefore, if full employment occurred at an aggregate-income level of \$700 billion, a decrease in the price index from 100 to 50 would be sufficient to bring about full employment.

The aggretate-demand curve that includes the Pigou effect is illustrated in Figure 12-4. The curve is derived by plotting the various price levels, presented in the form of a price index, with their corresponding levels of aggregate income. As the price level falls, the aggregate-demand curve embodying the

---

[16]In other words, assume that the money stock changes sufficiently to keep M/P constant, so that the *LM* curve does not change; or alternatively, assume that the Keynes effect is nonoperative.

[17]The savings function is $S = -a + (1 - b)Y$
or $S = -50 + .2Y$
when $P = 100$
and $C = a + bY$
$C = 50 + .8Y$

[18]The savings function now becomes $S = -60 + .2Y$; and the consumption, $C = 60 + .8Y$.

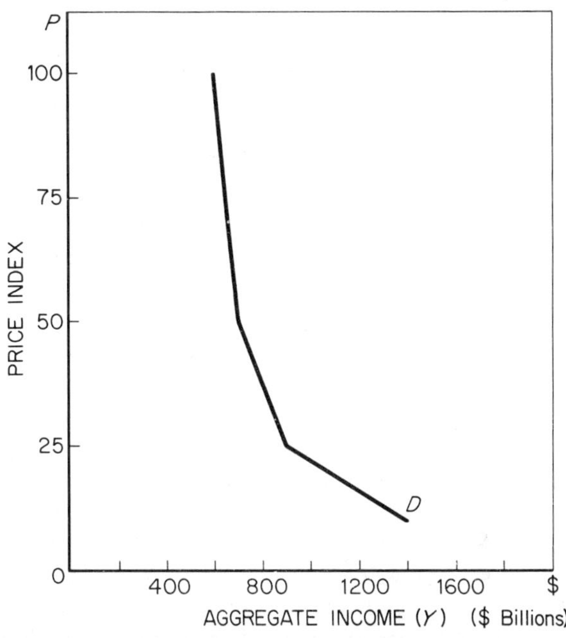

FIG. 12-4 Aggregate Demand Subject to the Pigou Effect

Pigou effect becomes increasingly close to horizontal, because as the price level approaches zero, the real value of monetary assets such as money and government bonds approaches infinity. Since the real value of money and government bonds can expand infinitely as long as the price level falls, and since consumption is positively related to wealth, there is no limit to the possible expansion of consumer demand.

Pigou Effect Evaluation The Pigou effect works because a falling price level causes an increase (upward shift) in the consumption function, which is the same as a reduction in the savings function. The lower savings function leads to a higher *IS* curve, which tends to increase the equilibrium level of both aggregate income and the interest rate. However, part of the effect of higher consumption will be offset by the smaller quantity of investment goods demanded at higher interest rates (unless the increase in consumer demand increases the marginal efficiency of capital, MEC, and offsets the effect of the higher interest rates). Furthermore, if a falling price level should make the *IS* curve intersect the *LM* curve in its inelastic segment, the entire force of the Pigou effect would be dissipated in higher interest rates and could be no more effective than fiscal policy under the same conditions.

Except in the unlikely case of the *IS* curve intersecting the *LM* curve in its vertical (classical) range, the neoclassical prescription of flexible wages and prices would be sufficient to restore full employment, even in an economy threatened by the liquidity trap. On the policy level, however, Pigou was too realistic to recommend flexible wages and prices as a practicable means of restoring full employment. Realizing that such a government policy was politically unacceptable, he concluded, "Thus, the puzzles we have been considering in the last section [of the article describing the Pigou effect] are academic exercises, of some slight use perhaps for clarifying thought, but with very little chance of ever being posed on the chequer board of actual life."[19]

Then, too, all the factors previously discussed that lead one to believe that price deflation is unworkable with regard to the Keynes effect apply with equal force to the Pigou effect. Furthermore, unless the Pigou effect is much stronger than most people believe it to be, unrealistically large price decreases would be required to reduce the level of unemployment substantially. For example, in Figure 12-4, a 50 percent fall in the price level is required to increase aggregate income from $600 to $700 billion.

The decrease in the price level required to bring about full employment depends on the strength of the Pigou effect. It would work best in a world of target savers, who save specifically to achieve some definite real level of purchasing power. In such a world, any excess of purchasing power owing to falling prices would immediately be spent on consumption. However, it is equally possible that the savers' appetite for wealth could increase as they become wealthier. For example, the Keynesian psychological motives to save (see Chapter 8), such as improvement, independence, or enterprise, might be stimulated by windfall increases in wealth owing to falling prices. In addition, during a period of falling prices, potential consumers may expect that prices will continue to fall and that their wealth will continue to grow. Buyers would then decide to postpone consumption as much as possible until they think the bottom has been reached. Since no one knows where the bottom is, the Pigou effect would be delayed.

Also, if a price decrease is considered to be temporary, asset holders would not revalue their portfolios even if they were target savers, provided that they expect prices to revert before the target event occurs. And if a temporary price decrease does not lead asset holders to revalue their portfolios, the Pigou effect will not operate. As a result, a generally recognized, once-and-for-all price decrease that was not expected to be reversed would cause the strongest Pigou effect, but such a price decrease is unlikely especially in an economy dominated by concentrated industries and highly organized labor.

The Combined Effect

The Keynes effect and the Pigou effect operate simultaneously, reinforcing each other in their effects on aggregate real income, but offsetting each other in their effect on the equilibrium interest rate. The combined Pigou and Keynes effects are illustrated in Figure 12-5. In the upper panel, the Pigou

---

[19] A. C. Pigou, "Economic Progress in a Stable Environment," *Economica*, 14 (August 1947), 188.

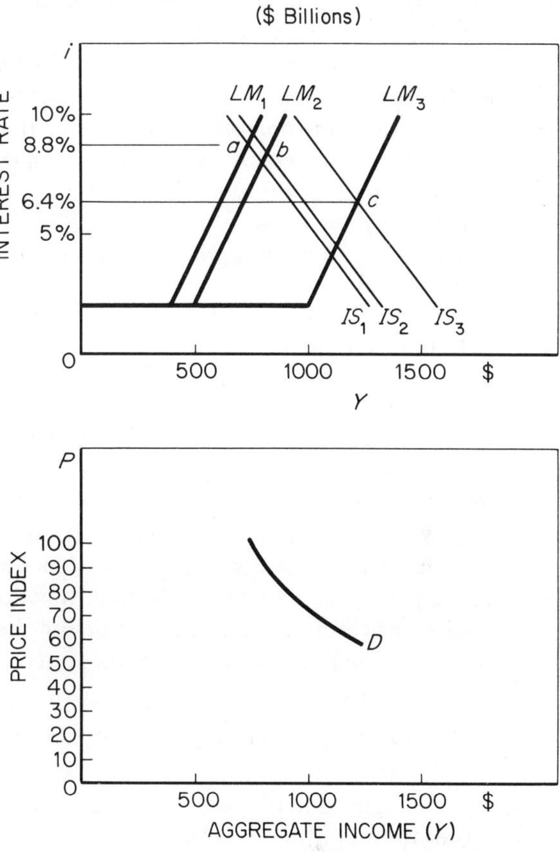

FIG. 12-5 Combined Keynes and Pigou Effects ($ Billions)

effect is shown as successive rightward shifts in the *IS* curve and the Keynes effect as successive rightward shifts in the *LM* curve. (The equilibrium interest rate falls in this example from 8.8 to 6.4 percent; however, the net effect on the interest rate depends entirely on whether the Pigou effect or the Keynes effect predominates, a question that cannot be answered *a priori*.) The intersections of LM_1 with IS_1, LM_2 with IS_2 and LM_3 with IS_3, at points *a*, *b*, and *c* respectively, determine three equilibrium levels of aggregate income, which are plotted in the lower panel of Figure 12-5 against their respective levels of the price index—100, 80, and 60—to form the aggregate-demand curve. The resulting curve is more elastic at any given price level than is the aggregate-demand curve that incorporates only the Keynes effect (Figure 12-2), and becomes more elastic at higher prices than does the aggregate-demand curve that includes only the Pigou effect (Figure 12-4).

One interesting conclusion that can be drawn from the combined effect involves the quantity theory of money. Suppose the stock of money is increased, and the price level increases as a result. If the price change should cause the *IS* and *LM* curves to shift together sufficiently to maintain a constant equilibrium interest rate as equilibrium aggregate income increases, then the increase in nominal income (price level times real income) will just match the growth of the nominal-money stock. In other words, if the interest rate does not vary, income velocity cannot change, because asset holders will have no motive to alter the amount of nominal-money balances in their portfolios and because the transactions demand for money balances is assumed to be proportional to the level of aggregate income.[20]

AGGREGATE SUPPLY

In the aggregate-production function, as described in Chapter 6, aggregate output, or income, is a function of the inputs of labor, natural resources, capital, and technology. Except for a brief discussion of the capital-goods market in Chapter 9, we have neglected until now the market for productive resources in the Keynesian framework. Inputs of productive resources may be used to derive an aggregate-supply function. The aggregate supply may be combined with an aggregate-demand function to determine the equilibrium level of prices and aggregate output for the whole economy, in a manner similar to the neoclassical model presented in Chapter 6.

The Aggregate-Production Function and the Demand for Labor

The aggregate-production function is the starting point in deriving the aggregate-supply curve in the Keynesian system. As a first approximation in the Keynesian as in the neoclassical model for the short run, inputs of capital, natural resources, and technology are assumed to be fixed, and labor is assumed to be the variable factor. The aggregate-production function, relating aggregate output (Y) to employment (N), is plotted in panel A of Figure 12-6 from data in panel A of Table 12-3. The rate of change in output decreases in response to a constant change in labor inputs. (For simplicity, increasing returns in the early stage of production are omitted.)

The demand-for-labor function, N_d, plotted in panel B of Figure 12-6 from data presented in panel B of Table 12-3, represents employment, N, as a function of the real wage, W/P. The curve is negatively sloped, since it embodies decreasing marginal productivity per worker as employment increases. Remember that under the assumption of perfect competition, the real wage per worker, W/P, is equal to the marginal productivity per worker (MP_L), which is the same as the slope of the aggregate-production function,

---

[20]The conclusion that the quantity theory applies in this way is based on an alternative post-Keynesian theory. See Don Patinkin, "Keynesian Economics and the Quantity Theory," in K. K. Kurihara, ed., *Post Keynesian Economics* (New Brunswick, N.J.: Rutgers University Press, 1954), pp. 123–52.

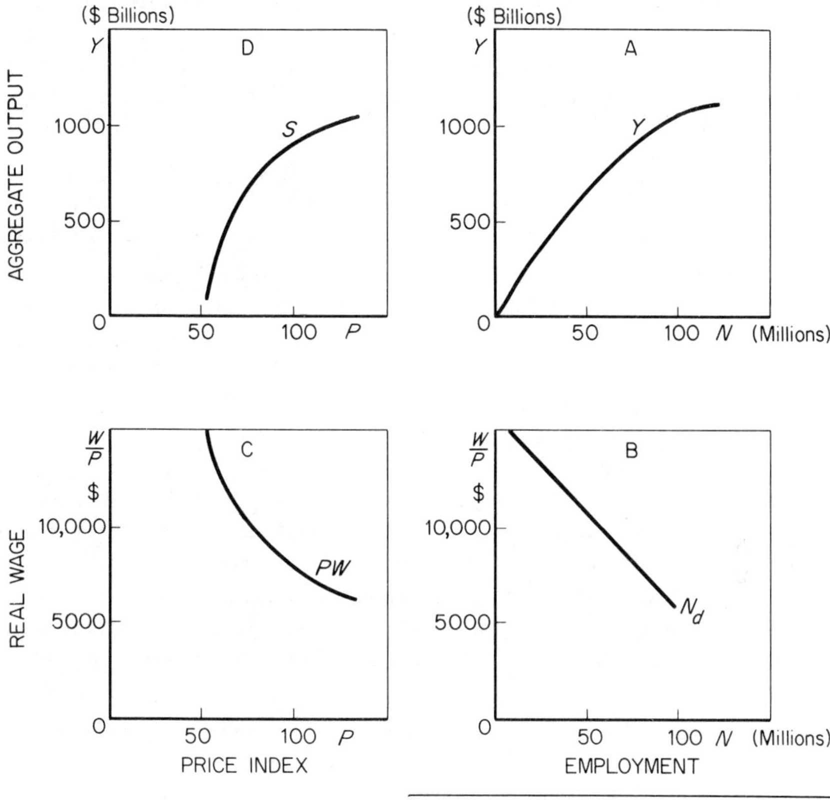

FIG. 12-6 Derivation of Aggregate Supply

TABLE 12-3 Derivation of Aggregate Supply

Panel A		Panel B		Panel C		Panel D	
Aggregate-Output Schedule		Demand-for-Labor Schedule		Real Wage–Price Relationship		Aggregate-Supply Schedule	
Employment N^a	*Output* Y^b	*Employment* N^a	*Real Wage* W/P	*Real Wage* W/P	*Price Index* P	Y^b	P
10	$ 150	10	$15,000	$15,000	53.3	$ 150	53.3
20	290	20	14,000	15,000	57.1	290	57.1
30	420	30	13,000	13,000	61.5	420	61.5
40	540	40	12,000	12,000	66.7	540	66.7
50	650	50	11,000	11,000	72.7	650	72.7
60	750	60	10,000	10,000	80.0	750	80.0
70	840	70	9,000	9,000	88.9	840	88.9
80	920	80	8,000	8,000	100.0	920	100.0
90	990	90	7,000	7,000	114.3	990	114.3
100	1050	100	6,000	6,000	133.3	1050	133.3

Money wage = $8,000

[a] *Millions.*
[b] *Billions.*

Y, presented in panel A of Table 12-3. For example, in panel A of Table 12-3, the difference between \$150 billion and \$290 billion of aggregate output (\$140 billion) is divided by the difference between 10 million and 20 million of aggregate employment (10 million) to obtain the real wage per worker of \$14,000, shown in panel B of the table.

The Supply of Labor

One distinction between the neoclassical model of Chapter 6 and the one developed following Keynes concerns the supply of labor. The Keynesian model, as we saw in Chapter 3, assumes that the money wage rate is fixed. As a result, the supply curve of labor is a horizontal straight line up to full employment of labor. On the assumption that the supply curve turns vertical when full employment is reached, we can omit showing the supply curve explicitly in panel B of Figure 12-6

Any change in the price level would cause a shift in the supply curve, assuming that the money wage level remains constant. Equilibrium in the labor market will therefore take place where a perpendicular from the y-axis intercept crosses the labor-demand curve, given a particular level of real wages.

What causes money wages to remain unchanging, especially in the downward direction, in a Keynesian aggregate-supply model? Several explanations were proposed in Chapter 3, and we will now review them, along with some additional ones.

Money Illusion Keynes proposed that workers are susceptible to money illusion; that is, they pay greater attention to their money wage than to their real wage.[21] They resist cuts in their money wages, but do not have the same resistance to a decrease in real wages resulting from increasing prices.

Money illusion is not necessarily always irrational, particularly where part of the worker's money income goes to pay off accumulated debts. Furthermore, money wages are a concrete piece of information, whereas the cost of living is less obvious, since each individual has a different market basket of goods and since there is a necessary time lag between a rise or drop in prices and an individual's adjustment to the change. Therefore, in the short run, if the price level has been relatively stable in the past, a worker is logical in assuming that his cost of living remains constant. After he becomes aware

---

[21]Keynes, *General Theory*, p. 8–13.

Irving Fisher, before Keynes, developed the concept of money illusion as applied to all segments of the economy, especially business firms. As Fisher put it, "If we ask a merchant whether or not he takes account of appreciation or depreciation of money values, he will say he never heard of it, that 'a dollar is a dollar!' In his mind, other things may change in terms of money, but money itself does not change. Most people are subject to what may be called 'the money illusion,' and think instinctively of money as constant and incapable of appreciation or depreciation." Irving Fisher, *The Theory of Interest* (1930) (New York: Augustus M. Kelley, 1961), pp. 399–400. See also Fisher, *The Money Illusion* (New York: Adelphi, 1928), pp. 3–18.

Yet Fisher believed that people were becoming more sophisticated and therefore more aware of the effect of price changes on their real incomes. Keynes specifically applied money illusion only to labor and not to businessmen.

of an increase or decrease in the cost of living he will readjust his behavior accordingly. Significantly, for some short period of time, money illusion is rational.

Market Imperfections In addition to the money illusion, there have recently been proposed alternative explanations as to why money wages might remain constant when unemployment occurs during recessions. One of them is that market imperfections, such as minimum wage laws, unions' refusal to accept lower money wages, or the establishment of customary wages, prevail throughout the economy, and that such market imperfections prevent workers from taking a wage cut.

For example, a labor leader who permitted a decrease in money wages would probably not have his job for long, irrespective of changes in real wages. Wage cuts are usually resisted even in cases where unemployment is the consequence. Union members with the most seniority often have the most political power in their unions, and these workers are in relatively little danger of being laid off (except during severe recessions).

In addition, a reduction in real wages does not involve a discernible event about which labor leaders could rally support, in contrast to a decrease in the monetary wage, about which specific opposition can be generated. Furthermore, organized labor's resistance to wage cuts is rational if the coefficient of elasticity of the demand for labor is less than unity and if the unions consider the total wage bill. You will recall that any linear demand curve is elastic in the upper portion and inelastic in the lower. Total receipts are maximized at the midpoint, where the coefficient of elasticity is unitary. Since a money wage reduction would decrease the total wage bill, a union concerned with total wages, in an industry whose equilibrium wage rate is at or below the unitary portion of their labor-demand curve, would be wise to resist a decrease in money wages. Such a union would also be wise in resisting any increase in prices, which has the same effect as the reduction in money wages. However, a particular union can exercise little, if any, control over the price level, so it tends to concentrate on money wages, the variable it can influence.

Information Costs An argument that does not rest on market imperfections has been suggested by Professor Alchian, who proposes that labor's refusal to accept a cut in money wages may be based on the idea in the minds of workers that job opportunities exist at about the same level as the uncut wage.[22] A worker who is asked to take a wage cut, therefore, will give up his present job and engage in information hunting if he believes that the expected cost of discovering a job at the current wage level is less than the loss of income from accepting a wage cut. If a substantial segment of the labor force prefers to search for a better opportunity than to accept a wage cut, then money wages will remain constant (the aggregate labor supply will be hori-

---

[22]Armen A. Alchian, "Information Costs, Pricing, and Resource Unemployment," in *Microeconomic Foundations of Employment and Inflation Theory*, E. S. Phelps, ed. (New York: Norton, 1970), pp. 27–52.

zontal) for a time period long enough for workers to assure themselves that they cannot get employment at (or above) the going wage level. If, during a recession, aggregate demand continues to decrease, then higher unemployment rates will continue to exist, since each additional decrease in demand must be discovered by labor. If, on the other hand, the aggregate-demand curve remains constant after having decreased, unemployment will be eventually eliminated, as each worker revises his pattern of expectations based on experience and therefore accepts a wage cut.

Relative Wages Furthermore, as Professor Tobin has pointed out, any worker who is able to maintain his own money wage while prices in general and other wages are falling will be better off in real terms relative to other workers.[23] A successful resistance to lower wages in such circumstances could hardly be considered "money illusion," because successful resistance enhances the position of those workers relative to all other workers.

Expectations of Inflation Expectations of higher future prices may also justify resistance to wage cuts, if workers anticipate resistance from employers when the market would indicate a restoration of former wage levels or a wage increase. Workers may assume that any departure from past experience is temporary and thus will be reversed in a short time. Today it might be rational for a worker to refuse to take a money wage cut even for a short time, in light of the well-recognized trend of price increases over the last few years and the fear of workers that they might become "typed" as low-wage employees.

Conclusion Market imperfections, information hunting, relative wages, and expectations of inflation may be more relevant than money illusion to describe a market made up of sophisticated workers who are well informed about price changes but not about specific job opportunities.

Deriving the Aggregate-Supply Function

The price index associated with the various levels of the average real wage can be combined with aggregate output for the corresponding levels of employment, to derive the aggregate-supply schedule shown in panel D of Table 12-3 and the aggregate-supply curve presented in panel D of Figure 12-6. In order to relate the four panels of Figure 12-6, the usual order is reversed in panel D, with changes in the price index shown on the horizontal axis and aggregate output on the vertical.

To derive the aggregate-supply curve of panel D in Figure 12-6, we relate the aggregate-production function in panel A and the demand for labor curve in panel B with the *PW* curve in panel C. The curve in panel C is derived from the figures in panel C of Table 12-3, and shows the relationship of the average level of real wages, W/P, to the price level, P, represented by a price

---

[23]James Tobin, "Inflation and Unemployment," *The American Economic Review*, 72 (March 1972), 2–3.

index. The average level of money wages are assumed to remain constant at $8,000. The price index is computed by dividing the constant money wage of $8,000 by the real wage for each level of employment.

By the arbitrary selection of a level of employment in panels A and B, the level of aggregate output and the average level of real wages are uniquely determined. Once the average level of real wages is determined, the corresponding price index is found in panel C. The resulting price index and the level of aggregate output enable us to find one point on the aggregate-supply curve in panel D. By repeating the process using several levels of employment, the entire aggregate-supply curve is formed.

The aggregate-supply curve has been redrawn in Figure 12-7 as *SeS* with

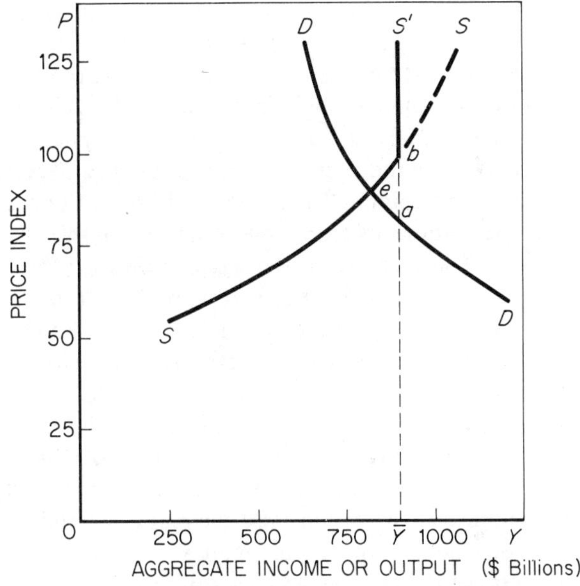

FIG. 12-7 Aggregate Supply and Demand

prices represented by a price index plotted along the *y*-axis and aggregate income or output along the *x*-axis. The resulting curve has the positive slope of a normal supply function of a firm or industry. An aggregate-demand curve is included in Figure 12-7. The equilibrium level of price and aggregate output in this illustration occurs at the intersection of the negatively sloped aggregate-demand curve and the positively sloped aggregate-supply curve, at a price index of 88 and an aggregate-income level of $825 billion.

Given fixed quantities of capital and land, the production function presented in panel A of Figure 12-6 represents a technical relationship between aggregate output and various quantities of labor employed. The technical relationship may have no bearing on the actual number of workers available in the economy. For example, in Figure 12-6, if full employment represents

80 million workers, then any level of aggregate output above $920 billion could not be achieved. The vertical dotted line in Figure 12-7, representing a full-employment level of output of an assumed $920 billion, divides the aggregate supply into an achievable segment to the left and an unattainable segment to the right. Since production cannot be increased beyond the full-employment level of aggregate income, $\bar{Y}$, the intersection of the aggregate supply and aggregate demand curves to the right of $\bar{Y}$ will result in pure inflation. Therefore, the dotted segment of the aggregate-supply curve, labeled *bS*,′ represents levels of output that are unattainable because they occur beyond full employment. As a result, the achievable portion of the aggregate-supply curve, *bS*′, becomes vertical at full employment.[24]

The equilibrium at point *e* in Figure 12-7 is an unemployment equilibrium, since it occurs to the left of $\bar{Y}$. Full employment could be achieved either by increasing (shifting to the right) the aggregate-demand curve to intersect aggregate supply at point *b*, or by increasing the aggregate-supply curve to intersect aggregate demand at point *a*.

If a modern economist with a neoclassical value system were to use this type of analysis, he would recommend that full employment be achieved by increasing the aggregate-supply curve by a sufficient amount so that it passes through point *a*. The result would be not only an increase in output, but also a simultaneous reduction in the price level.

The increase in the aggregate-supply curve could be accomplished by reducing the average money wage. In our model, a lower average money wage level would be shown as a leftward shift in the real-wage–price line (*PW*) in panel C of Figure 12-6. Both the average level of money wages and the price index would fall, but money wages would fall further than prices, since the new equilibrium at point *a* of Figure 12-7 requires a lower price level as well as a lower level of average real wages to achieve a higher level of employment and aggregate output. A lower price level with a constant level of average money wages would raise the real wage and reduce aggregate output. Therefore the level of average money wages must fall more than the price level to reduce the average level of real wages.

An increase in aggregate supply could also be achieved through increasing the marginal product of labor. For example, a technological improvement could cause an improvement in labor productivity that would increase both the slope and the level of the production function in panel A of Figure 12-6, while shifting the labor-demand curve in panel B to the right. Under our assumption of a constant money wage, the result of such a change would be to increase the level of employment and the level of average real wages while lowering the price level.

Most Keynesians, in contrast with the modern neoclassicists, believe

---

[24]As we shall see, a full employment equilibrium where the aggregate demand curve *DD* crosses the vertical portion of the aggregate supply curve *bS*′ is not stable, since the dotted portion of the curve, where a stable equilibrium would be possible, cannot be reached.

that the preferred policy for achieving full employment is to increase the aggregate-demand curve through the use of fiscal and monetary policy by the government. The model developed in this section implies that a policy of increasing aggregate demand is associated with higher prices.

Aggregate Supply under Monopoly in Either the Product or Resource Market

Monopoly in the Product Market In Chapter 3, it was demonstrated that a monopolist hires fewer workers than does a perfectly competitive firm at the same wage, since the marginal-revenue product of labor is lower under monopoly than under perfect competition when the same number of workers is employed.

The effect of this observation for macroeconomics is that if all firms were monopolistic, the demand-for-labor curve, such as the one shown in panel B of Figure 12-6, would no longer be the slope of the production function, but would be less than the slope, thus shifting the aggregate-supply curve in panel D to the right and down, under conditions of monopoly. This is the same thing as a reduction (shift to the left and up) in the aggregate-supply curve when it is presented with the axes reversed, as in Figure 12-7. So under monopoly, employment and output are both lower than under perfect competition, and the average real wage level is lower than it would be for the same level of employment under competition. Therefore, the aggregate-supply curve associates higher prices with lower quantities under monopoly than under perfect competition.[25]

A comparison of the aggregate-supply function under conditions of perfect competition and of monopoly is illustrated in Figure 12-8, where the supply function is represented by S_1 under perfect competition, and by S_2 under monopoly. The effect of monopoly, as compared with perfect competition, is to reduce equilibrium aggregate income from Y_1 to Y_2 and to raise the equilibrium price level from P_1 to P_2. From a social-welfare point of view, other things being equal, monopoly is inefficient, because it leads to higher prices and smaller aggregate output.

In the real world, faced with a range of industries varying from the highly competitive to naturally monopolistic industries such as public utilities, one would expect a degree of social efficiency somewhere between the monopolistic and the competitive cases. If so, the area between S_1 and S_2 in Figure 12-8 might be considered a belt within which the economy operates. An increase in the degree of monopoly would shift the economy more in the direction of S_2 and a decrease, more towards S_1. Empirical studies of the economy since the

---

[25]Although it is possible to derive an aggregate-supply function under monopoly conditions, it is impossible to describe a unique supply function for an individual monopolist. A supply function relates various levels of output that will be sold for different prices. The monopolist may offer quantities according to his marginal-cost function. However, the prices at which the products will be offered is determined by the demand curve. Therefore, under monopoly, no single function relates prices and quantities supplied.

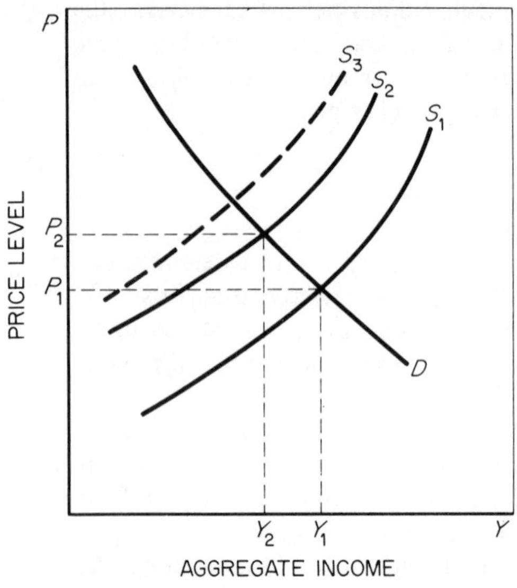

FIG. 12-8 Aggregate Supply Under Perfect Competition and Monopoly

turn of the century differ as to whether the economy is becoming more or less monopolized, although one recent study suggests that a greater degree of monopoly exists now than formerly; nevertheless, all agree that the rate of change is very slow.[26] Therefore, it seems reasonable that once an adjustment is made for the degree of monopoly in the economy, one can disregard any further changes in this variable in the short run.

Most comparisons of perfect competition and monopoly assume that firms in both types of industry maximize profit. Competitive firms are probably forced by the market to maximize profits. Larger monopolistic and oligopolistic firms who are price leaders in their industry may earn a satisfactory return without maximizing profits. Such firms may be motivated by a desire to optimize a combination of profits and some measure of size or growth such as sales volume (output), as we discussed in Chapter 3. If sales volume as well as profits were a goal, the aggregate supply curve would be further to the right in Figure 12-8 than if profits were the only goal. Therefore, equilibrium output would be higher and the price level would be lower

[26]Some of the better-known studies include the following: M. A. Adelman, "The Measurement of Industrial Concentration," *The Review of Economics and Statistics*, 33 (November 1951), 269–96; N. R. Collins and L. E. Preston, "The Size Structure of the Largest Industrial Firms, 1909–1958" *The American Economics Review*, 51 (December 1961), 986–1011; William G. Shepherd, "Trends of Concentration in American Manufacturing Industries, 1947–1958," *The Review of Economics and Statistics*, 46 (May 1964), 200–12; and Joe S. Bain, *Industrial Organization*, 2nd ed. (New York: John Wiley, 1968), pp. 77–111. The recent study which suggests greater concentration is John M. Blair, *Economic Concentration* (New York: Harcourt Brace Jovanovich, 1972), pp. 3–24.

than if firms were simply maximizing profits.[27] As a result, if firms are attempting to achieve some combination of output and profits, even if the economy were completely monopolistic, the resulting price level might not be as high nor the aggregate output as low, at least during prosperity, as is suggested by the S_2 aggregate-supply curve of Figure 12-8.[28]

Monopoly in the Resource Market Just as in the case of the market for finished goods, the market for productive resources may also be imperfectly competitive. For example, labor unions may have a great degree of monopoly power in certain areas and in particular industries. Such unions are often able to force wage increases and may be willing to accept unemployment as the cost. A higher level of average real wages and a decrease in employment reduce the aggregate-supply function, with results similar to those of monopoly in the product market: a higher price level and less aggregate output, with the added result of squeezing profits and raising wages.

The effect of combining monopoly in the product and resource markets might further reduce the aggregate-supply function to the dotted S_3 curve in Figure 12-8.

The Position, Shape, and Elasticity of the Demand for Labor

Under perfect competition, the shape and elasticity of the labor-demand curve depends on labor productivity. The usual presentation of the theory of diminishing productivity of labor, which gives rise to a negatively sloped labor-demand curve, assumes that a constant quantity of capital may be used with varying proportions of labor. To justify this assumption, capital must be adaptable to various quantities of labor. Also, capital must be indivisible, in the sense that all capital may be employed efficiently with varying inputs of labor.

In contrast, much production occurs where capital is divisible, which means that various portions of it can be efficiently used. In addition, under many productive techniques, capital is not adaptable, which means that it must be used with a predetermined quantity of labor.[29] For example, if a small shop has six drill presses, each press must have one operator. If only five operators are hired, then only five drill presses can be used efficiently.

Restated in more traditional terminology, fixed and variable resources are often complete complements, rather than both complements and substitutes for each other. Therefore, during recessions, both capital and labor may be laid off simultaneously and in fixed proportions. Likewise, during

---

[27] Edgar O. Edwards, "An Indifference Approach to the Theory of the Firm," *Southern Economic Journal*, 28 (October 1961), 123–29.

[28] During recessions, such firms may resort to profit maximizing, and raise prices in an attempt to maintain at least a minimum acceptable level of profits. William J. Baumol, *Business Behavior, Value and Growth* (New York: Macmillan, 1959), pp. 45–72.

[29] George Stigler, "Production and Distribution in the Short Run," *Journal of Political Economy*, 47 (June 1939), 305–27.

recovery, both capital and labor will be reemployed simultaneously, up to the point where capital is fully reemployed.

If unemployed capital is divisible and not adaptable (assuming homogeneous capital), the marginal product of labor is constant, and consequently the demand curve for labor would be a horizontal straight line up to full employment of capital. Once capital is fully employed, there will be no motive to increase employment of labor, since additional labor employed with the fixed quantity of machines would add nothing to output. Therefore, if capital is divisible and not adaptable, the demand for labor is completely elastic (a horizontal straight line) up to the point of full employment of capital, after which it would become completely inelastic (a vertical straight line). Keep in mind that such a demand curve for labor no longer assumes that the quantity of other resources, including capital, remains constant. In fact, such a labor-demand curve incorporates the fact that output will be expanded by reemploying additional units of both capital and labor.[30]

Realistically, capital equipment is partially divisible and imperfectly adaptable, and real-world firms are not perfectly competitive. Therefore, although the demand curve for labor has the traditional negative slope, it would be kinked at the point of full employment of capital, being more elastic to the left of the kink and less elastic to the right, compared with the traditional theoretical aggregate demand for labor.[31]

The three panels of Figure 12-9 illustrate through the use of isoquants the three cases discussed above, for a typical firm whose only factors of production are capital and labor. In all three cases, it is assumed that the firm's long-run production function is characterized by long-run constant returns to scale. Therefore, the isoquants q_1, q_2, and q_3 show equal increases in output in all three panels. It is also assumed that in all three cases the same quantity of capital is available to the firm—namely, K^*. Panel A depicts the traditional case, where capital is adaptable and indivisible. Under these conditions, the isoquants are traditionally convex toward the origin, and the entire stock of capital will be used. Diminishing productivity of labor is implied by the fact that as the quantity of output increases from q_1 to q_3, increasing proportions of labor from N_1 to N_3 must be used, given the K stock of capital.

In contrast, panel B illustrates the case where capital is divisible but not adaptable. Under these conditions, the isoquants are right angles, indicating that capital and labor are perfect complements. Panel B shows that equal proportions of labor from N_3 to N_1 and capital from K^* to K_1 would be laid off as output is decreased from q_3 to q_1. Constant productivity of labor is

[30] If we held to the assumption that units of capital employed in the productive process remained constant as additional quantities of labor are added, then the reemployment of capital as labor is added could be shown only as a shift to the right in the demand curve for labor.

[31] G. Brunhild and R. H. Burton, "A Theory of Technical Unemployment: One Aspect of Structural Unemployment," *American Journal of Economics and Sociology*, 26 (July 1967), 265–77.

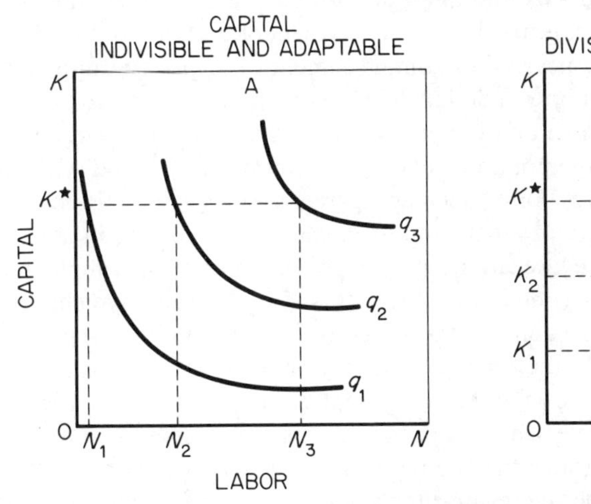

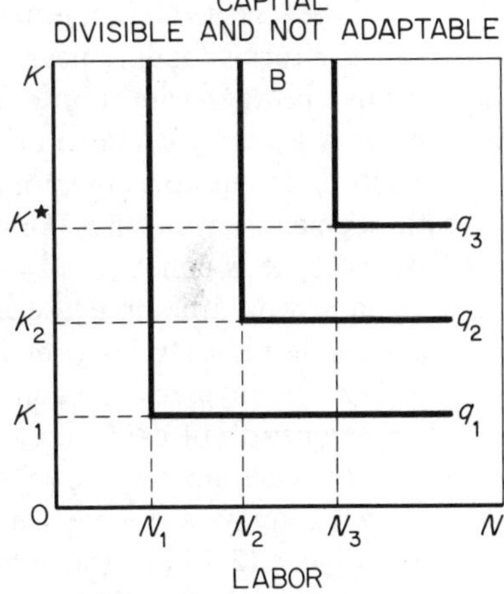

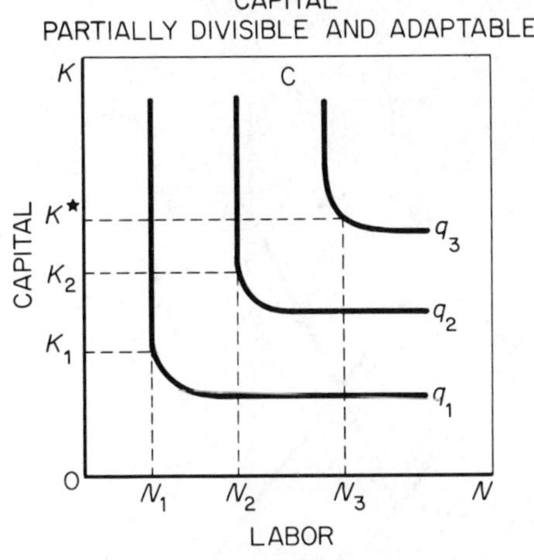

FIG. 12-9 Employment of Labor and Capital

implied by the fact that a constant proportion of labor is laid off as output is decreased.

Finally, panel C of Figure 12-9 demonstrates the case where equipment is partially divisible and imperfectly adaptable. In this third case, a smaller amount of diminishing productivity of labor is illustrated than in panel A, as output is increased from q_1 to q_3. In addition, some capital would be laid off from K^* to K_1 as output is reduced from q_3 to q_1.

What is the significance of the analyses above in determining the shape of the aggregate-supply curve? If the demand for labor is a horizontal straight line up to full employment of capital, then the aggregate-supply curve would likewise be horizontal in the corresponding segment (when the price level is plotted on the vertical axis and aggregate output on the horizontal axis.)[32]

Likewise, an elastic, nearly horizontal segment of the labor demand would cause a corresponding nearly horizontal segment of aggregate supply. As a result, the aggregate-supply function of an economy in which capital equipment is partially divisible and imperfectly adaptable is kinked, with a more elastic segment up to the point of full employment of capital, and a less elastic segment beyond that point. Such an aggregate-supply curve is consistent with Keynes's conclusion that the major impact of an increase in aggregate demand would be on aggregate output up to the point of full employment, and on the price level beyond that point. In this case, "full employment" refers to full employment of capital rather than of labor, but either type of full employment will cause the aggregate supply to kink. Therefore, a model that includes both types of full employment occurring at different levels of output displays a double kink in the aggregate supply curve.

Figure 12-10 illustrates the effect on the economy of a change in aggregate demand when the aggregate-supply curve is kinked, owing to partial divisibility and adaptability of capital. The first kink occurs at full employ-

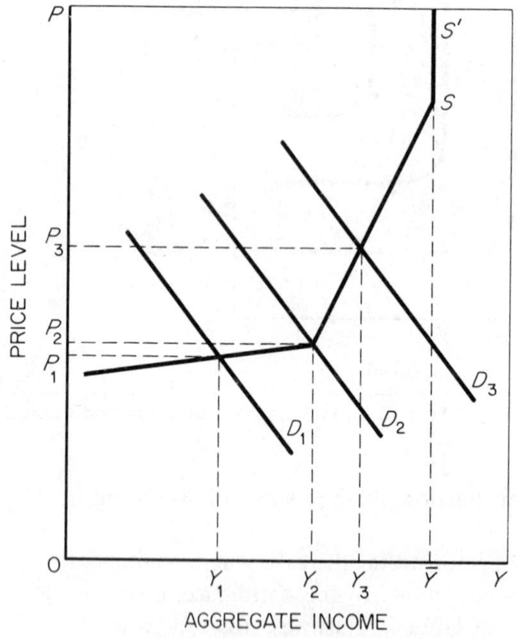

FIG. 12-10 Changes in Aggregate Demand with Kinked Aggregate Supply

[32]In the derivation of the aggregate-supply curve in Figure 12-6, a horizontal labor demand (panel B) would cause a vertical aggregate-supply curve (in panel D), because price is plotted on the horizontal axis and only one price level can exist if the demand for labor is perfectly elastic.

ment of capital and the second at full employment of labor, beyond which point aggregate supply becomes completely inelastic. As aggregate demand increases from D_1 to D_2 in the most elastic segment of the supply curve, aggregate income increases significantly from Y_1 to Y_2, while the price level increases very little, from P_1 to P_2. On the other hand, after full employment of existing capital equipment, further increases in aggregate demand from D_2 to D_3 result in a much smaller increase in aggregate income, from Y_2 to Y_3, and a much larger increase in the price level, from P_2 to P_3. The less-elastic middle portion of the aggregate-supply function will continue up to full employment of labor at $\bar{Y}$, at which point the supply function becomes completely inelastic and further increases in aggregate demand only lead to further increases in the price level. Thus, as full employment of labor is approached, prices respond more than output to further increases in aggregate demand.

An alternative explanation of a kinked aggregate-supply curve may be found in the administered prices of oligopolies. During periods of decreasing demand, price leaders in oligopoly industries tend not to lower prices but to decrease output (and may even increase prices in order to achieve a target return as part of their optimum-goal mix.) During periods of increasing demand, while excess capacity exists, they tend to increase output rather than prices, since growth, as well as profits, is an objective, and their target return can very likely be achieved without increasing prices.[33] (The foregoing assumes that profits and sales volume are both desirable and that the utility of sales volume increases relative to the utility of profits after profits have reached the target level. Goals are not perfect substitutes; their marginal rate of substitution probably varies continuously.)

The theory of a kinked aggregate-supply curve explains how the Kennedy recovery after the Eisenhower recession could occur without significant price changes, and why inflation increases did not start until the Johnson era. However, the theory does not explain the observed tendency for real wages to increase during recovery. Even after the Great Depression of the 1930's, this tendency bewildered economists whose theories indicated that real wages should decrease, or at least remain constant, if employment was to increase. One possible explanation is this: A recession causes increased concern for efficiency and thereby induces the development of cost-saving technology. However, new investment is limited during recessions, so a backlog of technology builds up. When recovery occurs, the new investment expenditures embody the improved technology and thereby increase the slope and level of the production function. Thus, the increase in labor productivity, rather than the increase in aggregate demand, may allow higher real wages during recovery.

The effect of technological change on the economy will be considered in more detail in Chapter 15.

---

[33]John M. Blair, *Economic Concentration* pp. 470–91.

Bottleneck Effects

We have assumed that the supply of any commodity will not become completely inelastic until full employment of labor is reached, on the assumption that productive resources are homogeneous. However, the supplies of some commodities may become inelastic before full employment is reached, because of the development of bottlenecks in the productive process.

One of the most convenient ways to demonstrate the effect of bottlenecks is through the use of input–output analysis. As you recall from Chapter 5, input–output analysis assumes that the productive process requires the use of resources in fixed proportions. If resources were completely homogeneous and mobile, bottlenecks could not develop until the entire supply of some productive factor had been exhausted. But in reality, resources are not homogeneous. For example, labor is a category that includes many individuals with different skills and abilities. Some of the skills required to expand output may not be available in sufficient numbers during a given short period of time. The critical relationship is between the supply of particular subcategories of resources and the quantities demanded to achieve given levels of output. As particular subcategories of resources become fully employed, their prices will be bid up.

Higher resource prices increase production costs, leading in turn to higher prices even in perfectly competitive or monopolistic industries. In the short run, prices will rise in certain industries where bottlenecks develop, long before the point where general full employment is reached. Because prices increase in the bottleneck industries with no corresponding price reduction in other industries, there will be more increase in the general price level before labor is fully employed.

Bottlenecks make aggregate supply generally more steeply sloped than

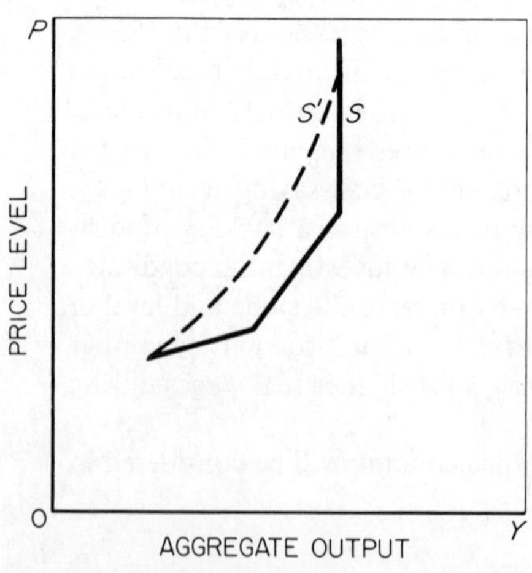

FIG. 12-11 Aggregate Supply with Bottlenecks

it otherwise would be, up to the final, vertical portion. The effect of bottlenecks on the aggregate-supply curve is illustrated in Figure 12-11. The aggregate-supply curve including bottlenecks is shown as the dotted S' curve, whereas S represents the aggregate-supply curve without bottlenecks. S' is similar to S with the kinks smoothed out, and is generally steeper than S. Therefore, prices will increase more and output less up to full employment of labor than if bottlenecks were nonexistent; bottlenecks are only a partial deterrent to full employment.

In contrast, a sort of reverse bottleneck may occur if we drop our assumption of homogeneous resource inputs. Firms may lay off first the least-productive units of capital and labor and thereby cause costs to fall proportionately more than output. This effect will reinforce diminishing returns, and offset to some degree the impact of partial divisibility and imperfect adaptability on the elasticity of the aggregate-supply curve.

THE THEORY OF WAGE–PRICE FLEXIBILITY

The existence of flexible wages and prices would insure full employment through the combined Keynes effect and Pigou effect. To demonstrate how flexible wages and prices must lead to full employment, the following model is illustrated in Figure 12-12. The illustration starts with the system at full-employment equilibrium at point a, the intersection of the aggregate demand curve D_1, and the aggregate supply curve, S_1. Assume that under recession conditions, aggregate demand drops from D_1 to D_2, where the new equilibrium is reached at point c. As a result, the price level falls from P_1 to P_2 and the

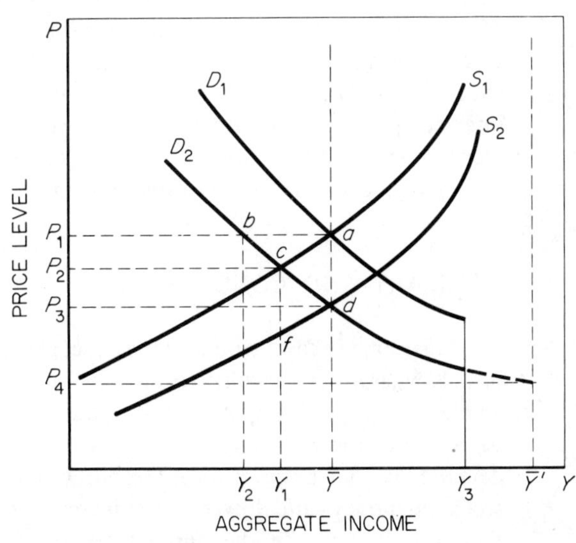

FIG. 12-12 Equilibrium with Wage-Price Flexibility

level of aggregate income from $\bar{Y}$ to Y_1. However, if prices and wages had proved completely inflexible, the price level would have remained at P_1; the economy would have operated at point b on the D_2 aggregate-demand curve, instead of at the D_2S_1 intersection at point c; and the entire effect of the recession would have been felt on aggregate output, with a resulting decrease in income from $\bar{Y}$ to Y_2 instead of from $\bar{Y}$ to Y_1.

Equilibrium at point c implies that prices are flexible but money wages are rigid. Output falls from $\bar{Y}$ to Y_1 rather than to Y_2 when prices fall from P_1 to P_2, and equilibrium shifts from point a to c rather than from a to b. The movement from a to c when aggregate demand decreases occurs because of the higher real wages caused by money-wage rigidity combined with lower prices.

If both prices and money wages are flexible, falling money wages will cause a rightward shift in the aggregate supply function from S_1 toward S_2, eventually restoring full employment at point d at a price level of P_3. Since full employment in this model requires a decrease in real wages, the average level of money wages must fall proportionately more than the price level. The rightward shift in aggregate supply that restores full employment is caused by a rightward movement along the labor-demand curve, a change that is possible only if real wages, W/P, decrease. Therefore, in the Keynesian system, unemployment equilibrium is possible only on the assumption of either rigid money wages or money wages that are more rigid than prices.

The degree of elasticity of the aggregate-demand curve is due to the Keynes effect and the Pigou effect. If the Pigou effect was weak or nonexistent, the aggregate-demand curve would become less elastic, and susceptible to the liquidity trap. If the liquidity trap occurred prior to full employment, then wage–price flexibility alone could not restore full employment. In Figure 12-12, for example, if the dotted line $\bar{Y}'$ represents the full-employment level of aggregate income, and Y_3 represents the liquidity trap, then no amount of wage–price flexibility can restore full employment. However, if the Pigou effect did operate, then the liquidity trap would disappear and D_2 would intersect $\bar{Y}'$ at some positive price level such as P_4, permitting full employment to occur, if the average level of money wages drops low enough to shift the aggregate-supply curve to the appropriate level.

SUMMARY AND CONCLUSIONS

This chapter has introduced the concepts of aggregate supply and demand in a Keynesian framework to demonstrate the causes and effects of price changes. Higher or lower prices are analytically equivalent to increases or decreases in the real stock of money, in the Keynesian theory of aggregate demand. Higher prices reduce the purchasing power of any given nominal stock of money, and lower prices increase it. The effect of lower prices is therefore to increase the purchasing power of the stock of money, and thereby to shift the *LM* curve to the right. The effect on aggregate income (or output) of a shift in the *LM* curve owing to a price change is called the *Keynes effect*. As a result, lower prices are associated with a larger quantity of output demanded. The various equilibrium levels of aggregate income can be related to their respective price levels to form an aggregate-demand function. The aggregate-demand curve formed by shifts in the *LM* curve cannot extend to the right beyond the liquidity trap.

A.C. Pigou proposed that lower prices, and the consequent increase in the value of money and government bonds, would stimulate consumption, causing a rightward shift in the *IS* curve. The aggregate-demand curve that develops through the *Pigou effect* becomes more elastic at lower prices. The combined Keynes and Pigou effects result in a generally more elastic aggregate-demand curve than when only one of the effects operates alone.

The aggregate-supply curve with constant-money wages resembles any normal, positively sloped supply curve, under both perfect competition and monopoly. However, given partial divisibility and imperfect adaptability of capital, the aggregate-supply function may become kinked before full employment of labor, affecting the aggregate price–output relationship.

When the assumption of constant money wages is relaxed and workers are assumed willing to accept lower money wages, then the combined Keynes and Pigou effects will insure the maintenance of full employment, if prices are flexible and the liquidity trap is not encountered. However, both Keynes and Pigou rejected wage–price reductions as a practical policy for restoring full employment.

We considered the effects of bottlenecks on aggregate supply, and found that bottlenecks make the aggregate-supply curve more inelastic.

Through the use of the aggregate-supply-and-demand model, we are able to describe equilibrium levels of price and output, a theoretical advantage not available with other aggregate models. Therefore, through the use of aggregate supply and demand, we can determine the relative changes in output and price as a result of a shift in either aggregate supply or demand. This type of model also permits us to illustrate the effects of either an elastic or an inelastic aggregate-demand or supply curve on the price level and on aggregate income.

Now that the Keynesian model is complete, it can be compared with the neoclassical model. We shall do this in the Appendix to this chapter.

QUESTIONS AND PROBLEMS

1. Distinguish aggregate demand from effective demand.
2. What is the Keynes effect? How is it derived?
3. If prices change while the rate of return remains constant, what is the effect on earnings from new investments?
4. Why did Keynes consider wage and price decreases to be impracticable policy?

5. Describe the Pigou effect.

6. Is the Pigou effect foreign to Keynesian theory?

7. What is money illusion? And what part does it play in the development of the supply of labor?

8. Discuss the actual derivation of aggregate supply and demand.

9. What effect does monopoly have on aggregate-supply-and-demand equilibrium?

10. Why might aggregate supply be kinked? What practical effect would this have?

A Comparison of the Keynesian and Neoclassical Systems

appendix to chapter 12

Now that static models of both the Keynesian and neoclassical systems have been presented, it is time to make a formal comparison of them before considering the basic problems of any dynamic economy: growth, inflation, and fluctuations. Both the Keynesian and the neoclassical models can be described as systems of equations, either graphic or algebraic, and in the following section we compare the two models side by side to discover their differences and similarities.

It should be pointed out at the outset that both the models presented here are highly abstract, rigid, formalized versions, useful for contrast, but not really a fair statement of the position of the theorists.

To consider two examples on the neoclassical side:

1. The level of aggregate output is uniquely determined within the system, so in this Appendix we consider aggregate output to be fixed. However, realistically, the neoclassicists understood perfectly well that aggregate output could vary around the equilibrium level over any very short period and that the level of output increased in the long run.

2. The quantity theory of money leads to the conclusion that prices change in the same direction as the stock of money. Richard Cantillon, for example, states, "Everybody agrees that the abundance of money, or its increase in trade, raises the price of all things." Again realistically, however, the quantity theorists did not picture an instantaneous adjustment process. Cantillon also says this:

> The increase of money will bring about an increase of expenditure, and this increase of expenditure will bring about an increase of market prices in the years of most active trade, *and by degrees in the least active.*[1] [Emphasis added.]

As examples on the Keynesian side:

1. The liquidity trap is an important component of the formal Keynesian model. However, Keynes points out that he knew of no case where the liquidity trap had been of practical importance.

2. In the abstract version of Keynesian theory used here, the transactions and precautionary demand for money balances are made a function of income, and the speculative demand for money balances is a function of the interest rate. But in the *General Theory*, Keynes specifies that realistically, all the motives are inter-

[1]Richard Cantillon, "On The Nature of Commerce in General," in *Early Economic Thought*, ed. Arthur Eli Monroe (Cambridge: Harvard University Press, 1948), p. 263.

mingled and money is held not in separate watertight compartments, but as a single sum available to meet any and all needs.

3. As a final example—although many more could be mentioned—we might cite Keynes's consumption and savings functions. Formally, both are made a function of aggregate income. But more realistically, Keynes cited a long list of objective and subjective factors that underlie savings and consumption decisions—factors that were summarized earlier, in Chapter 8.

One of the values of economic theory is to impute order and process to the never-ending turmoil and flux of real-world markets. Buyers and sellers are perpetually entering and leaving markets, transferring their resources and goods from one market to another, and, in general, responding to the variety of stimuli provided by the economic system. Layoffs, voluntary resignations, and vacancies all occur simultaneously. The astute economist is always well aware of the unending flux and perpetual disequilibrium of the economy, but nevertheless always describes an underlying tendency toward order, process, and eventual equilibrium, even while recognizing that intervening changes may thwart the development of that equilibrium before it is reached.

The real difference among schools of economic thought lies not in the realism of their models—all theories are hopeless oversimplifications—but rather in their disparate visions of those underlying tendencies and the eventual equilibrium. Different groups of economists focus on different variables as crucial. We trust that the following versions of the neoclassical and Keynesian theories explain their essential differences.

AGGREGATE SUPPLY

The first equation, the aggregate-production function, is one area where the Keynesian and the neoclassical systems are in agreement. In both systems, aggregate income or output (Y) is a function of the available supplies of resources—labor (N), land or natural resources (R), capital (K), and technology (T). Furthermore, both schools would agree that land, capital, and technology change only in the long run, so therefore the short-run production function in both cases would make aggregate output or income a function of the level of employment of labor. In addition, both models incorporate diminishing returns in their basic formulation. Formula 1 in both systems is

1. $Y = f_4(N, R, K, T)$ (production function)

where R, K, and T are constant in the short run.

The demand for labor, N_d, represents employment as a function of the real wage, W/P. The curve embodies decreasing marginal productivity per worker and is equal to the slope of the total-output curve. In both the neoclassical and the Keynesian models, the demand for labor may be stated

2. $N_d = f_5\left(\frac{W}{P}\right)$ (Labor-demand function)

where W/P is the real wage, which equals the marginal product of labor.

The first distinction between the two models occurs in the supply-of-labor function. In the neoclassical system, the supply of labor is a normal, positively sloped supply curve, indicating that a larger quantity of labor will be supplied at higher levels of the real wage. In contrast, the Keynesian system incorporates a perfectly elastic labor-supply curve up to full employment, on the theory that workers resist decreases in money wages.

The real wage in the Keynesian system is determined by the ratio of the fixed money wage, W_0, to the variable price level, P, whereas in the neoclassical system, the labor market is simply a matter of supply-and-demand equilibrium with no possibility of involuntary unemployment at the equilibrium wage. Labor-market equilibrium in the two systems in equation form is as follows:

Neoclassical		*Keynesian*	
3. $N_s = f_6\left(\frac{W}{P}\right)$	(labor-supply function)	3. $W = W_0$	(Rigid money wages)
4. $N_s = N_d$	(labor-market equilibrium)	4. $\frac{W_0}{P}(P) = W_0$	(Wage-price relationship)

These first four equations, which determine the aggregate-supply function in both systems, are graphed in Figure 12A-1. Panels A and C show the same production

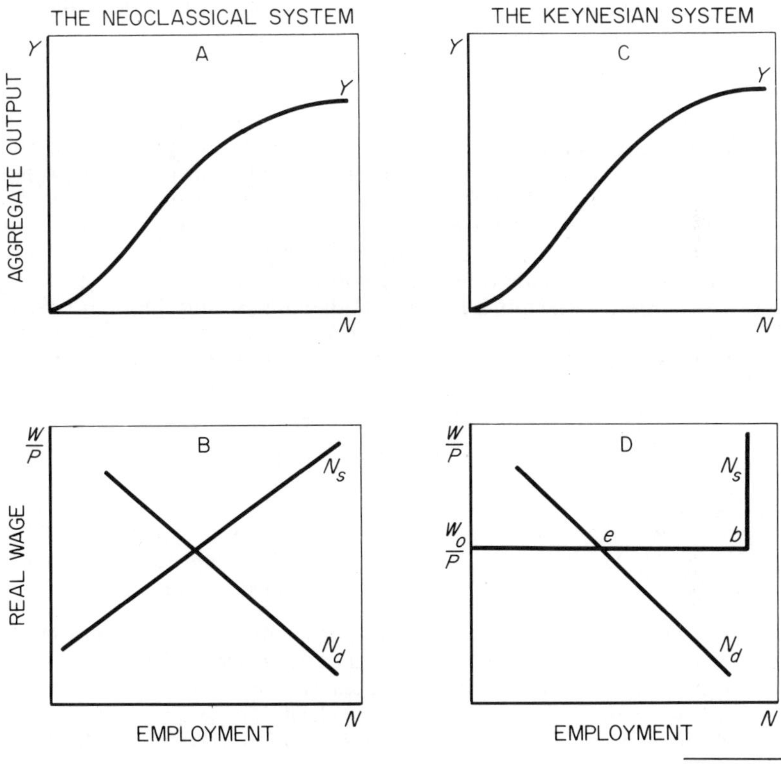

FIG. 12A-1

function in both systems. Panels B and D show the labor market in both systems, with the demand for labor the same in both cases. The only distinction between the two systems is in the different supply-of-labor curves, because of the assumption of money-wage flexibility in the neoclassical system contrasted with money-wage rigidity in the Keynesian. As a consequence, involuntary unemployment is impossible in the neoclassical case, but may occur in the Keynesian. In panel D of Figure 12-1, involuntary unemployment is equal to the distance between point *e* and point *b*.

AGGREGATE DEMAND

Switching our attention now from the supply side to the demand side of the economy, the neoclassicists would have described the aggregate-demand function as a rectangular hyperbola, because any change in prices is exactly offset by a proportional change in quantity. In the neoclassical system, money expenditures always equal the stock of money, M, times income velocity, V; and money expenditure, MV, must equal aggregate output, Y, times the average price level, P, or

5a. $MV = PY$ (The equation of exchange)

As we have already seen, Y becomes constant once equilibrium is established in the labor market, in the neoclassical system. The neoclassical economists assumed that V changes slowly and dependably, and so over a reasonable period of time even though it might fluctuate excessively in the very short run can virtually be assumed a constant. If V and Y are considered fixed, the neoclassicists felt, the price level, P, is a function of the quantity of money, M; the price level will increase or decrease whenever M is increased of decreased. This notion has been called the quantity theory of money, and may be restated

5b. $P = f_7(M)$ (Quantity theory of money)

Let us consider how the Keynesian money market differed from the neoclassical. In the neoclassical system, money is useful only to exchange for real goods and services, but Keynes proposed that money is demanded not only to pay for transactions, but also to hold for speculative and precautionary purposes. If we include the demand for precautionary balances with the demand for transactions balances, then Keynes proposed one demand for money balances for transactions purposes, which is a function of income, and another demand for money balances for speculative purposes, which is a function of the interest rate. In the neoclassical system, money simply mirrors the flow of real goods and services; in the Keynesian system, monetary equilibrium requires that the two separate demands for money together equal the stock of money. Therefore, in the Keynesian system, monetary equilibrium requires the following equations:

5a. $M_t = f_{11}(Y)$ (Transactions demand for money balances)
5b. $M_L = f_{12}(i)$ (Speculative demand for money balances)

where

5c. $M_d = M_t + M_L$ (Total demand for money balances)
5d. $M_d = \bar{M}_s$ (Money-market equilibrium, assuming M_S is given—determined outside the system)

The significance of the speculative demand for money balances is that interest-rate changes cause variations in income velocity. Generally, income velocity decreases as the interest rate falls, because larger money balances are demanded at a lower rate of interest. The income velocity of the speculative component of the demand for money balances could as a limit fall to zero when the interest rate falls sufficiently. At some sufficiently low rate of interest, the demand for speculative balances becomes perfectly elastic. Thus, Keynes recognized that there was a lower limit on the interest rate, called the liquidity trap, caused by an insatiable desire for speculative balances when there is general agreement that the interest rate must rise in the future.

In the neoclassical system, both the supply of savings and the demand for investment are functions of the rate of interest. The savings–investment market in the neoclassical system can be represented by the following three equations:

6. $I = f_8(i)$ (Investment demand function)
7. $S = f_9(i)$ (Savings function)
8. $S = I$ (Savings–investment equilibrium)

In contrast, the savings–investment market in the Keynesian system is somewhat more complicated. Investment demand is a function of the interest rate, but savings is not; therefore, no supply–demand equilibrium insures savings–investment equality at full employment in the Keynesian model.

In this simplified version of the Keynesian system, the primary decision that a household must make is not how much to save but how much to consume, a decision that depends primarily on the level of income rather than the interest rate. Savings in the Keynesian system, therefore, becomes a residual that is indirectly a function of income.

Even though in the Keynesian system, as in the neoclassical, investment is a function of the rate of interest, the Keynesian demand for investment is more sophisticated than the neoclassical. Keynes specified that the actual return on an investment cannot be known in advance, and that investment demand is a function of *expected* net return (anticipated receipts in excess of expected cost). Furthermore, Keynes allowed in his investment theory for a time dimension, which many neoclassicists ignored. The significance of allowing the effect of time and expectations into investment theory is to make investment demand the most volatile element in the economy, because expectations are subject to violent changes over time.

Although the demand for investment is a function of the interest rate in the Keynesian system, the quantity of investment demanded might not vary much as the interest rate changes, particularly if interest rates fall during a depression. Keynes proposed that even if the interest rate were free to fall to zero in a depression, the resulting level of private investment might prove insufficient to bring about the full-employment equilibrium level of income, because a negative interest rate might be required to overcome the prevailing atmosphere of pessimism and observed low returns or losses on business ventures. Furthermore, Keynes felt that alternating waves of optimism and pessimism, because they are contagious in the business community, can cause widespread increases and decreases in the demand for investment.

The savings–investment market in the Keynesian system can be described in the following equations:

6. $I = f_{8a}(i)$ (Investment-demand function)
7a. $S = f_{10}(Y)$ (Savings function)
7b. $C = f_{13}(Y)$ (Consumption function)
8. $S = I$ (Savings–investment equilibrium)

To emphasize the essential differences on the demand side between the neoclassical and Keynesian systems, we present the two systems of equations side by side for comparison.

Neoclassical	*Keynesian*
5a. $MV = PY$	5a. $M_t = f_{11}(Y)$
5b. $P = f_7(M)$	5b. $M_L = f_{12}(i)$
	5c. $M_d = M_t + M_L$
	5d. $M_d = \bar{M}_s$
6. $I = f_8(i)$	6. $I = f_{8a}(i)$
7. $S = f_9(i)$	7a. $S = f_{10}(Y)$
8. $S = I$	8a. $S = I$

Most of the basic distinctions between the two systems can be seen in Figure 12A-2. In the neoclassical system, panels A and B show the four curves that determine the equilibrium interest rate and price level. In panel A, the desire to hold cash balances is the reciprocal of income velocity, $1/V$. The stock of money, $\bar{M}_s$, intersects the $1/V$ curve, and since real income, Y, is constant in the neoclassical system, the point of intersection determines the equilibrium price level. (Remember, $\bar{Y}$ always equals the full-employment level of output.) The equilibrium between the supply-of-savings and the demand-for-investment functions is shown in panel B,

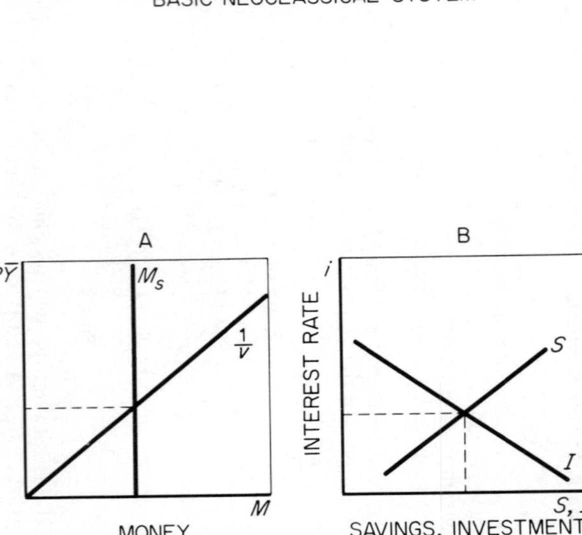
BASIC NEOCLASSICAL SYSTEM
A
$P\bar{Y}$
M_s
$\frac{1}{V}$
MONEY INCOME
M
MONEY
B
i
S
I
INTEREST RATE
S, I
SAVINGS, INVESTMENT

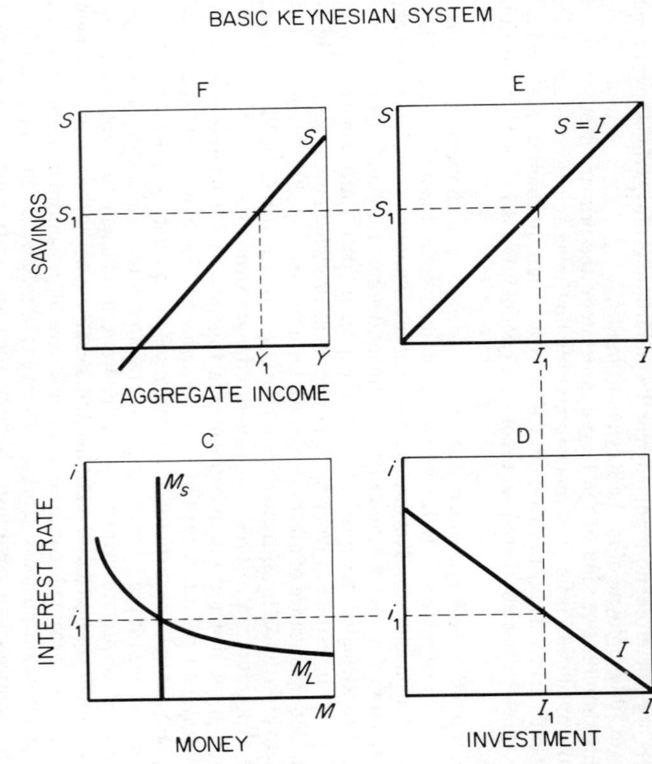
BASIC KEYNESIAN SYSTEM
F
S
S
S_1
SAVINGS
Y_1
Y
AGGREGATE INCOME
E
S
S = I
S_1
I_1
I
C
i
M_s
i_1
M_L
INTEREST RATE
M
MONEY
D
i
i_1
I
I_1
I
INVESTMENT

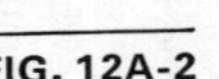
FIG. 12A-2

where the point of intersection determines the equilibrium interest rate and quantity of savings and investment.

The simplified Keynesian system shown in panels C, D, E, and F is the same as in Figure 10-1. The intersection of the stock of money and the demand for speculative balances in panel C determines the equilibrium interest rate (i_1), which in turn determines the quantity of investment, I_1 in panel D. Since the savings and investment functions must be equal in equilibrium, as shown in panel E, the determination of the I_1 quantity of investment in panel D also determines the quantity of savings, S_1 in panel F. But, because savings and aggregate income are uniquely related, S_1 savings must be associated with Y_1 income, which may or may not occur at full employment. If Y_1 is less than full employment, unemployment will result; and if it is greater, inflation will occur. (This simple Keynesian model, which neglects the transactions demand for money balances, differs from the more complete post-Keynesian model of formulas 5 through 8 above and Figure 11-4.)

AGGREGATE DEMAND AND SUPPLY

By deflating the money stock (M) by the price level (P), we can introduce the effect of prices into the demand side of the Keynesian system. The real and the money markets can be combined to get a simultaneous equilibrium, developed in Chapter 11 as the *IS–LM* model, which is a modification of the basic Keynesian system. When the effect of price changes is incorporated into the *IS–LM* model, an aggregate-demand curve relating price and quantity is derived. The price elasticity of aggregate demand in the Keynesian system is due to the reduction in the real value of the stock of money as prices rise (or vice versa), a phenomenon described in the preceding chapter as the Keynes effect.

Now that we have introduced the effect of price changes into the demand side of the economy, we are in a position to compare the relationship of the price level and aggregate output in both the Keynesian and neoclassical systems.

The comparison between the two systems is illustrated graphically, with the neoclassical system shown in Figure 12A-3 and the Keynesian in Figure 12A-4. In Figure 12A-3, the neoclassical aggregate-supply curve, S, is a vertical straight line, and the neoclassical aggregate-demand curve, DD, is a rectangular hyperbola.

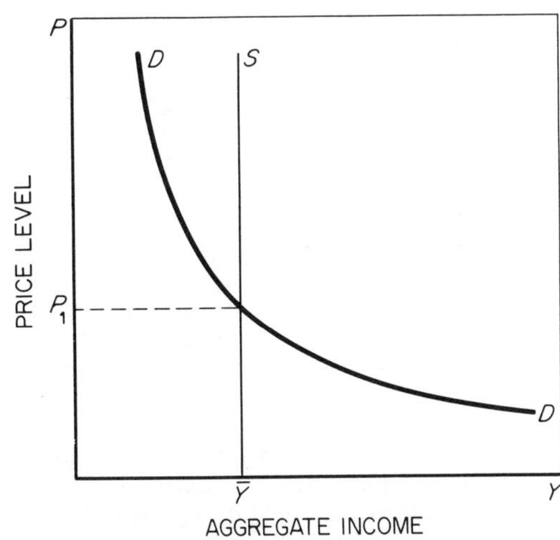

FIG. 12A-3 Neoclassical Aggregate Supply and Demand

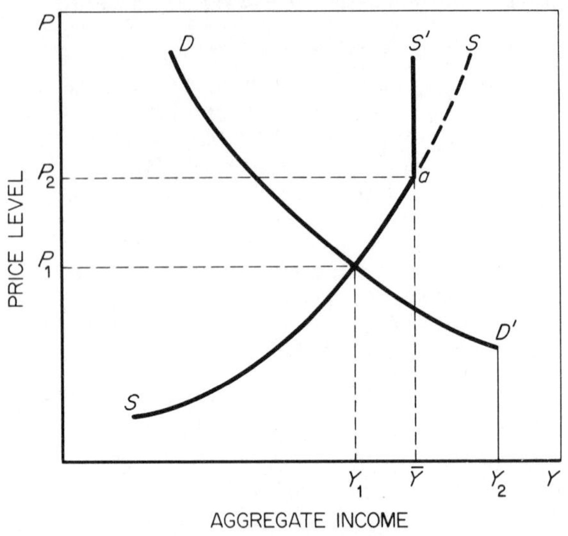

FIG. 12A-4 Keynesian Aggregate Supply and Demand

Since the supply curve is perfectly inelastic, the intersection of the aggregate demand with the aggregate supply curve determines only the equilibrium price level, P_1, and not the equilibrium income, $\bar{Y}$. If the stock of money were increased, the aggregate-demand curve would shift to the right, causing higher prices at the constant level of aggregate income. Aggregate supply would change only if the availability of resources or the level of technology changed, assuming perfectly competitive markets in equilibrium.

In contrast, in the Keynesian system presented in Figure 12A-4, aggregate supply is not vertical until full employment is reached, since in the Keynesian system, involuntary unemployment can exist because money wages are constant. Whenever involuntary unemployment exists, actual output can fall short of potential output. In addition, the aggregate demand, *D*, is no longer a rectangular hyperbola as in the neoclassical system, although it is still negatively sloped. In Figure 12A-4, equilibrium occurs at the intersection of the aggregate supply and demand curves at a price level of P_1, and an aggregate-income level of Y_1. In this example, actual income falls short of potential by the amount of $Y_1 - \bar{Y}$. If demand increased sufficiently by an increase in either the money stock or in the investment or consumption demand curves the aggregate-demand curve would intersect point *a*, the price level would increase from P_1 to P_2, and aggregate income would increase from Y_1 to the full-employment level, $\bar{Y}$.

At point *a*, the aggregate-supply curve kinks and becomes vertical. Any further increase in aggregate demand that causes an intersection above point *a* on the *SaS'* aggregate-supply curve cannot increase aggregate income beyond $\bar{Y}$ and would result only in higher prices. A stable equilibrium could not be achieved above point *a*, however, because the demand for productive resources, labor in our model, would be in excess of the available supplies of those resources at full employment.

The vertical segment of the aggregate-demand curve, represented by $D'Y_2$, represents the part that occurs in the liquidity trap. If full-employment output, $\bar{Y}$, occurs to the right of Y_2, then full employment could not be achieved through an increase in aggregate supply, nor could aggregate demand be increased beyond Y_2 through monetary policy. Full employment could be restored only through an increase in aggregate demand, owing to an increase in consumption or investment. Keynes introduced government expenditures as a type of investment that could be purposely controlled to bring about full employment even in the most severe situations, where an economy found itself in the liquidity trap.

In recent years, there have been modifications of the Keynesian system that have, to some extent, blurred the sharp distinction between it and the neoclassical system. For example, the introduction of the Pigou effect could eliminate the vertical segment of aggregate demand in the Keynesian system, thereby making it impossible for an aggregate economy to be affected by the liquidity trap.

There is a growing feeling on the part of many economists that prices are not determined in a completely competitive way, but rather are administered by businesses, government, or resource suppliers such as labor unions, all of whom may have multiple goals. This idea has, if anything, reinforced the Keynesian position that wage and price reductions are not a feasible method of bringing about full employment.

A final distinction between the neoclassical and Keynesian positions involves the concept or definition of the term *equilibrium*. In the neoclassicists' minds, equilibrium requires a market-clearing mechanism. They cannot accept an equilibrium where markets remain uncleared. Many Keynesians, on the other hand, define equilibrium as a state of rest irrespective of whether markets are cleared. For example, the labor market is in equilibrium in the Keynesian system if there is no tendency for wages or employment to change, even if the quantity of labor demanded at the prevailing real wage is less than the supply.[2]

A REINTERPRETATION OF KEYNESIAN AND NEOCLASSICAL ECONOMICS

One major distinction between Keynes and the neoclassicists has been emphasized by Axel Leijonhufvud[3]—that the neoclassical economists assumed that price adjusted more rapidly than quantity, whereas Keynes assumed the reverse.[4] For example, an increase in demand for the product of a particular industry, produced under perfectly competitive conditions, will, in the very short run, increase prices at the same output. In the long run, new firms will be encouraged to enter the industry and existing firms will expand their plant and equipment, increasing output and decreasing prices until a new long-run equilibrium has been obtained. The long-run equilibrium price that results may be higher or lower than the initial price, depending on whether increasing or decreasing returns to scale exist in the industry. Therefore, a considerable lapse of time is assumed necessary to expand plant and equipment or for new firms to enter the industry, but less time is assumed necessary for the firms of an industry to raise their prices. The neoclassical economists applied this analysis to the aggregate economy. The assumption that it takes longer to increase output than to raise prices has no effect on the final long-run equilibrium, but is vital in discussing the path to equilibrium.

Leijonhufvud suggests that Keynes reversed the reaction time between quantity

---

[2]Conversations with Abba P. Lerner, April 3 and 4, 1972, at the University of South Florida.

[3]Axel Leijonhufvud, *On Keynesian Economics and the Economics of Keynes* (New York: Oxford University Press, 1968), pp. 50–54. More generally, Leijonhufvud's work discussed in this section draws on earlier work of R. F. Clower, "The Keynesian Counter-Revolution: A Theoretical Appraisal," in *The Theory of Interest Rates*, eds. F. H. Hahn and F. P. R. Brechling (London: Macmillan, 1965), pp. 103–25.

[4]Axel Leijonhufvud, "Keynes and the Keynesians: A Suggested Interpretation," *American Economic Review*, 57 (May 1967), 402–4, 409. There is some controversy concerning the accuracy of Leijonhufvud's interpretation of Keynes.

and price, and assumed that for changes in aggregate demand, output adjusted more rapidly than prices, at least in the downward direction, when moving from one equilibrium position to another. At times in the *General Theory*, it seems as if Keynes even assumed that all the adjustment takes place in quantity and none in price, as long as unemployed resources can be reemployed. Therefore, most of the *General Theory* is presented in real terms rather than money terms by assuming a constant price level.

How was Keynes able to assume perfect competition and at the same time propose that prices would adjust slowly to market forces while output adjusted rapidly? Leijonhufvud infers in Keynes an implicit assumption that a lack of good information prevails in real-world markets or that information can be acquired only at a cost. Rational (goal-oriented) behavior based on incorrect or outdated information can result in stickiness of all market prices including wages and interest rates.

If a disturbance occurs where good information is lacking, transactions occur at disequilibrium prices (called false trading), because prices are not perfectly flexible in the sense that they adjust fully to the new equilibrium before any trade takes place.

One of the neoclassical descriptions of the market-clearing mechanism was to propose a Walrasian auctioneer who registers buy and sell offers at various prices until a new equilibrium set of prices has been established before actual trading occurs. But there is no auctioneer, and consumers do not wait until a new equilibrium set of prices have been established before they start trading. Leijonhufvud is concerned with the potential equilibrium transactions not consummated if trading occurs at disequilibrium prices.

Take for example the labor market. Given imperfect market information, a reduction in aggregate demand will cause unemployment. Leijonhufvud uses Alchian's concept of search or information cost to explain why equilibrium does not recur quickly in the labor market. Workers who lack good information on the labor market search for new employment at the old wage level rather than accept work at a lower wage level if they believe that the expected cost of discovering a job at the going wage level is less than the loss of income from accepting a wage cut. The resulting period of unemployment causes a decrease in workers' income, which, in turn, causes a further decrease in aggregate demand. When labor cannot sell all its services for the prevailing wage, workers' demand for commodities will be constrained by their received income rather than by their equilibrium income, and, therefore, demand may, in the aggregate, fall short of a market-clearing equilibrium level.

What about the market for investment goods? As we have seen in Chapter 6 the neoclassical theory envisions a flexible interest rate that leads to an equilibrium between the demand for investment and the supply of savings. Keynes also believed that the quantity demanded of investment goods varies directly with the long-term interest rate, on the assumption that the expected returns and the price on each capital asset are given. Consequently, Keynes used the long-term interest rate to represent the general demand for investment goods. Leijonhufvud points out that a model that assumes that the level of investment is given, such as the one we developed in Chapter 8, misses Keynes's point that the *relative* level of demand for capital goods compared with consumer goods is crucial. If the supply of savings is greater than the demand for investment at the going interest rate, it means that the long-term interest rate is too high relative to the price level for consumer goods, and as a result a recessionary disequilibrium occurs.

As we saw in Chapter 7, so long as speculators believe that the short-term interest rate will soon revert to its former level, the long-term interest rate will not decrease, and the quantity of investment goods demanded will remain below equilibrium.

In addition, even the demand for consumption goods will be retarded by a sticky long-term interest rate due to the wealth effect, "Keynes's second psychological law." A reduction in the long-term interest rate by increasing the price of bonds increases wealth and, in turn, consumption.

Information costs exist in all markets, not only the market for capital goods and the labor market, so all prices will not fall until faith in the normality of previously prevailing prices have been thoroughly undermined. So long as sellers believe that in short order it will again be possible to obtain pre-depression prices, reservation prices will hold up.[5]

However, long-run interest rates will hold up better than other prices because the opportunity cost of switching from short-to-long-term securities does not appear very substantial when conditions are unstable. In fact, once recession emerges, the fall in capital values will convince assetholders who sought greater liquidity that they did the right thing. In contrast, the cost of workers' going unemployed or of sellers' maintaining a sizable inventory of consumer goods is high, compelling a fairly rapid revision in reservation prices.

To demonstrate how Leijonhufvud's version of Keynes's model might work in a dynamic context, assume that firms are unable to sell all their output at prevailing prices following a decrease in the marginal efficiency of capital. The firms would reduce output and employment, if transactions occur at prices above equilibrium, as is likely with a dead auctioneer. The resulting reduction in output will be associated with a lower level of employment by firms at the going wage level. Prices and wages will eventually fall in an attempt to clear markets. But wages and prices must fall below the level that in the initial period would have cleared the markets, because the ensuing false trading and unemployment create a further decline in aggregate demand. Prices and wages may lag behind the necessary reduction required to clear the markets. Each successive increase in unemployment and the consequent decrease in aggregate demand will be less than the last, and will eventually approach an unemployment equilibrium.[6] The whole process is amplified by the stickiness of interest rates owing to the actions of speculators. When households in the aggregate decide to save more and consume less, the interest rate does not decrease fast enough to cause a saving-investment equilibrium, or a sufficiently strong wealth effect, since speculators will be induced to sell long-term and hold short-term securities or money, thereby preventing a sufficient decline in the long-term interest rate. In Wicksellian terms, the market rate of interest does not fall to match the natural rate.

In summary, relative prices of consumer goods, capital, labor, and money must be in balance to prevent an unemployment equilibrium. Leijonhufvud argues that if information were available to obtain the perfect coordination of activities of all people in the market, then the system would work as the neoclassicals envisioned it. Labor would expect prevailing wages, and interest rates would drop to an equilibrium level between savings and investment. Producers would perceive that if the demand for consumer goods has declined, it means that the demand for future consumer goods via current investment expenditures has increased; therefore, resources would be transferred from consumer goods to investment goods.[7] In Leijonhufvud's words,

> The only thing which Keynes "removed" from the foundations of classical theory was the *deus ex machina*—the auctioneer which is assumed to furnish, without charge, all

---

[5]Leijonhufvud, *On Keynesian Economics*, pp. 335–38.

[6]However, Leijonhufvud specifically rejects money illusion on the part of workers as irrational and uses Alchian's search-cost concept instead. There is nothing wrong with substituting the non-Keynesian concept into Keynesian theory. Money illusion and search costs both explain wage stickiness equally well.

[7]Axel Leijonhufvud, *Keynes and the Classics*, pp. 33–40. (Westminster, England: The Institute of Economic Affairs, Occasional Paper Number 30, 1969).

the information needed to obtain the perfect coordination of the activities of all traders in the present and through the future.

Which, then, is the more "general theory" and which the "special case"? Must one not grant Keynes his claim to having tackled the more general problem?[8]

CONCLUSION

Among all the differences discussed between the Keynesian and neoclassical systems, the six most striking are these: (1) Money wages are rigid up to full employment in the Keynesian system, and flexible in the neoclassical. (2) Keynes suggested that output responds more flexibly than price; the neoclassicals proposed the reverse. (3) Keynes concentrated on a speculative demand for money balances, the neoclassicists on only a transaction demand for money balances. (4) Keynes proposed that consumption and savings are primarily functions of income; the neoclassical assumption was that savings are a function of the rate of interest. (5) The neoclassicists pictured a more mechanical, dependable world, in which investment decisions suffer little from the impact of uncertainty or problems of confidence. Keynes, in contrast, stressed the effect of uncertainty and imperfect foresight on investment decisions. (6) To the neoclassicists, equilibrium can take place only when markets are cleared. To Keynes and his followers, equilibrium occurs whenever the economy is in a state of rest, irrespective of whether or not markets are cleared. Leijonhufvud's interpretation attempts to bridge the gap between these two views by attempting to show that Keynes really was developing a disequilibrium model and therefore one can accept Keynesian theory without abandoning the possibility of a potential supply-demand equilibrium. Economists have argued the relative importance of these major distinctions between the Keynesian and neoclassical systems, but any such discussion is futile; all of them are necessary to distinguish the two systems.

Perhaps a more fundamental distinction than the six technical differences mentioned above is that the two systems represent different ways of looking at the world. The neoclassicists, following the classical school, picture the aggregate economy as a deterministic system in which individuals will almost automatically further the best interests of the system by pursuing their own profit or utility, so that any government interference in the economy will generally have bad results. In the Keynesian view, following the mercantilists, the aggregate economy often needs to be directed by government monetary and fiscal policy in order to achieve full employment and a more equitable distribution of income. In the neoclassical framework, any such attempt to direct the aggregate economy would, in any normal situation, give worse results than leaving the economy to operate itself. If artificial restraints and market imperfections exist, the proper role for the government is to eliminate these restrictions so that the competitive system can function efficiently. Keynes and his followers emphasized that market imperfections such as rigid money wages

---

[8]Leijonhufvud, "Keynes and the Keynesians," p. 410.

Grossman has suggested that Leijonhufvud has substituted certain theories proposed by Don Patinkin for those of Keynes. For example, Grossman points out that nowhere in Keynes's works is there a suggestion that firms would be unable to sell their output for the going price, and at certain times producers would be unwilling to absorb excess labor at a wage equivalent to the Walrasian general-equilibrium real-wage rate.

Furthermore, Grossman says, "Interpreted within Leijonhufvud's analytical framework, the *General Theory* deals with the case in which the market for current output is clearing while the market for labor services is in excess supply. The interpretation implies that Keynes' analysis is limited to a very narrowly defined range of wage–price vectors. Had Keynes' thinking tended along these lines, he certainly would not have proclaimed the generality of his discussion." Herschel I. Grossman, "Was Keynes a 'Keynesian'?" *Journal of Economic Literature*, 10 (March 1972), 29.

are the general rule rather than the exception, and that some central direction of the aggregate economy is necessary to offset these imperfections.

ADDITIONAL SELECTED REFERENCES

OTHER GENERAL-EQUILIBRIUM MODELS

ACKLEY, G., *Macroeconomic Theory*, pp. 359–95. New York: Macmillan, 1961.

ALLEN, R. G. D., *Macro-Economic Theory*, Chap. 7. New York: St. Martin's, 1967.

BENAVIE, A., "Prices and Wages in the Complete Keynesian Model," *Southern Economic Journal*, 38 (April 1972), 468–77.

CROUCH, R., *Macroeconomics*, pp. 141–61. New York: Harcourt Brace Jovanovich, 1972.

EVANS, M. K., *Macroeconomic Activity*, Chap. 13. New York: Harper & Row, 1969.

HANSEN, B., *A Survey of General Equilibrium Systems*. New York: McGraw-Hill, 1970.

KOGIKU, K. C., *An Introduction to Macroeconomic Models*, Chap. 5. New York: McGraw-Hill, 1968.

MODIGLIANI, F., "The Monetary Mechanism and Its Interaction with Real Phenomena," *The Review of Economics and Statistics*, 45, No. 1, Pt. 2 (February 1963), 79–107.

PATINKIN, D., *Money Interest and Prices*, 2nd ed., pp. 199–381. New York: Harper & Row, 1965.

PRICE AND WAGE FLEXIBILITY

ECKSTEIN, OTTO, "Money Wage Determination Revisited," *Review of Economic Studies*, 35 (April 1968), 133–43.

HANSEN, A. H., *A Guide to Keynes*, pp. 173–204. New York: McGraw-Hill, 1953.

KALDOR, N., "Professor Pigou on Money Wages in Relation to Unemployment," *Economic Journal*, 47 (December 1937), 745–53.

KUH, E., "Unemployment, Production Functions, and Effective Demand," *Journal of Political Economy*, 74 (June 1966), 238–49.

LEONTIEF, W., "The Fundamental Assumption of Mr. Keynes' Monetary Theory of Unemployment," *Quarterly Journal of Economics*, 51 (November 1936), 192–97.

LONG, CLARENCE, "The Illusion of Wage Rigidity: Long and Short Cycles in Wages and Labor," *Review of Economics and Statistics*, 42 (May 1960), 140–51.

MISHAN, E. J., "The Demand for Labor in a Classical and Keynesian Framework," *Journal of Political Economy*, 72 (December 1964), 610–16.

MURAD, A., *What Keynes Means*, pp. 114–26. New York: Bookman Associates, 1962.

PATINKIN, D., "Price Flexibility and Full Employment," *American Economic Review*, 38 (September 1948), 543–64.

PIGOU, A. C., "Money Wages in Relation to Unemployment," *Economic Journal*, 48 (March 1938), 134–38.

POWER, J. H., "Price Expectation, Money Illusion and the Real-Balance Effect," *Journal of Political Economy*, 67 (April 1959), 131–43.

SMITHIES, A., "Effective Demand and Employment," in *The New Economics*, ed. S. E. Harris, pp. 558–71. New York: Knopf, 1947.

TOBIN, J., "Money Wage Rates and Employment," in *The New Economics*, ed. S. E. Harris, pp. 572–87. New York: Knopf, 1947.

COMPARISON OF KEYNES WITH THE NEOCLASSICAL TRADITIONAL VIEWS

ACKLEY, G., *Macroeconomic Theory*, pp. 399–418. New York: Macmillan, 1961.

JOHNSON, H. G., "The General Theory after Twenty-Five Years," *American Economic Review*, 51 (May 1961), 1–17.

LEONTIEF, W., "Postulates: Keynes' General Theory and the Classicists," in *The New Economics*, ed. S. E. Harris, pp. 232–42. New York: Knopf, 1947.

KEYNES REINTERPRETED

ALCHIAN, A. A., "Information Costs, Pricing, and Resource Unemployment," *Western Economic Journal*, 7 (June 1969), 109–28.

BARRO, R. J., and H. I. Grossman, "A General Disequilibrium Model of Income and Employment," *American Economic Review*, 61 (March 1971), 82–93.

CLOWER, R. W., "Keynes and the Classics: A Dynamical Perspective," *Quarterly Journal of Economics*, 74 (May 1960), 318–23.

PHELPS, E. S., "Money–Wage Dynamics and Labor-Market Equilibrium," *Journal of Political Economy*, 76, No. 4, Pt. 2 (July–August 1968), 678–711.

STIGLER, G. J., "Information in the Labor Market," *Journal of Political Economy*, 70, No. 5, Pt. 2 (October 1962), 94–105.

AN EARLY COMPREHENSIVE CRITIQUE OF KEYNES

MARGET, A. W., *The Theory of Prices*, Vols. I and II. (1942). New York: Augustus M. Kelley, 1966.

Theories of Inflation

13

INTRODUCTION

In the preceding chapter, we saw that price deflation could induce economic expansion through the Keynes and Pigou effects. In addition, we found that full-employment equilibrium could be established, if the economy is in an unemployment equilibrium, by an increase in either aggregate demand or supply. An increase in aggregate demand would be associated with inflation, and an increase in aggregate supply with deflation. There has recently been a reawakening of interest in price deflation as a policy prescription;[1] only time will tell if public policy seriously attempts to deflate prices and if the attempt can succeed. However, we concentrate on inflation rather than deflation in this chapter, because inflation is the problem now facing virtually all nations and because market imperfections seem to make price deflation an anachronism in modern economies.

The concept of inflation refers not simply to an increase in the price level but to the *process* of increasing the price level. To discuss inflation means to discuss *changes* in the price level over time. Consequently, the discussion of inflation in static terms foreshadows dynamic analysis.

---

[1]Milton Friedman, "The Optimum Quantity of Money," in *The Optimum Quantity of Money and Other Essays* (Chicago: Aldine, 1969), pp. 1–50.

Beneficial Effects of Inflation

Inflation prior to full employment is not an unmixed evil. Sumner Slichter, one of the first of the economists in the post–World War II era to anticipate the Phillips-curve relationship discussed in this chapter, suggested that a little inflation does not cause dire consequences but may have a tonic effect.[2] Rising profits encourage producers to increase output. Merchants receive windfall profits as prices increase over the interval between the purchase of inventories and their sale. To the extent that money illusion exists, periodic pay increases associated with inflation will make workers feel wealthier, and may lead to an increase in the consumption function. Furthermore, the anticipation of slowly rising prices may increase the consumption function by causing consumers to buy durable goods sooner than they would otherwise, in order to avoid further price increases.

Another effect of inflation is that it redirects income from fixed-money-income recipients, and possibly from wage earners, to profit recipients.[3] As a consequence, inflation tends to reward innovators and risk takers and to penalize less dynamic economic groups. Furthermore, if prices increase faster than money wages (that is, if W/P decreases), inflation increases employment and real output up to the point of full employment. Therefore, society often faces the choice of inflation or unemployment, and many feel that unemployment is by far the worse evil. At the same time, if higher profits encourage technological improvements, the demand curve for labor would shift to the right because of the higher output per worker. Such a shift would mitigate the lower real wage required to achieve full employment. Thus, a moderate rate of inflation may encourage full employment. And if it is true, as some maintain, that prices are free to rise but not to fall, then optimum resource allocation through the price system can be achieved only through price increases in growing industries, because price decreases in declining industries are difficult or impossible to achieve.

Inflation benefits debtors at the expense of creditors, since debtors pay back cheaper dollars than those they borrow. Many consumers and most investors in capital goods are debtors, whereas creditors are generally savers who are only indirectly involved in production. Inflation could have a beneficial effect on debtors, who have a greater impact on consumption and investment expenditures than do creditors, who are injured by it.

---

[2]Sumner H. Slichter, *Economic Growth in the United States* (Baton Rouge: Louisiana State Univ. Press, 1961), pp. 163–64, 176.

[3]Unionization may protect those workers in highly organized industries against inflation. In fact, at certain times, wages may rise faster than prices. Yet non-union labor may find their wages lagging behind prices. In addition, even in the case of union labor, long-run contracts may keep their wages behind increasing prices.

Harmful Effects of Inflation

The negative aspects of inflation often receive more attention than the positive. The primary disadvantage is that inflation most injures those least able to protect themselves, such as widows, orphans, and retirees living on pensions or insurance. They must stand by, helplessly watching the purchasing power of their fixed incomes dwindle year by year. Compounding the problem, the forms of saving that appeal to lower socioeconomic groups, such as government savings bonds, savings accounts, and insurance policies, are precisely the forms of saving that are the most eroded by inflation, because their payoff is fixed in money terms.

Inflation not only reduces the purchasing power of any given money income, but also reduces the real value of wealth held in forms fixed in money terms, such as money itself or bonds. However, not all people living on fixed incomes are poor. Many savers who live on interest earnings may be rich, so their level of living need not suffer much during inflation even though the purchasing power of their money income is reduced.

When inflation occurs in one country at a faster rate than in others, the prices of that country's exports increase while the prices of imports decrease relatively. The result is that the volume of imports rises and exports fall. Such a change leads to a negative balance of payments, with all its attendant problems: a negative multiplier effect from the net loss of purchasing power flowing out of the country, a resulting loss of jobs, exchange-rate difficulties, key currency shifts, and loss of confidence in the economy and in the stable value of its money.

Hyperinflation

The foregoing discussion implies that moderate rates of inflation have both favorable and unfavorable aspects. However, a high rate of inflation that causes extreme price increases, often called hyperinflation or galloping inflation, has predominantly unfortunate economic consequences.

These unfortunate consequences are due largely to the response of lenders, borrowers, producers of goods and services, and consumers. Lenders suffer tremendous windfall losses and borrowers windfall gains, as once-valuable loans are repaid with nearly worthless money. Speculation and debt become a way of life. Producers of goods and services delay selling their output for the longest possible time in order to achieve the greatest price appreciation. Consumers attempt to spend their money income as fast as they possibly can and to convert their wealth into nonmonetary assets or to consume it, in order to avoid holding depreciating currency.

Worker motivation and performance suffer during hyperinflation, because new pay levels cannot be renegotiated continuously as prices increase, so the real value of money wages depreciates even as money incomes are being earned. In extreme cases, such as the post–World War I inflation in Central Europe, wage rates were sometimes computed on a daily basis, and even that was insufficient to protect workers from price increases. When, finally, it took satchels of money to purchase small parcels of goods, wages began to be set on the basis of *anticipated* price increases.[4]

Orderly conduct of an economy is impossible under severe inflation. The value of savings held as money or bonds is wiped out, and savers who fail to switch into nonmonetary assets or stable foreign exchange may become penniless overnight, while others who hold the right sort of assets become wealthy.[5] Debtors pursue creditors, hoping to pay off loans with worthless currency. In the post–World War I European experience, the money economy ultimately broke down and barter reemerged. A barter economy is less efficient than a functioning money economy, because barter depends on a coincidence of wants, so real income falls. Empirically, hyperinflation appears to have strained to the breaking point those economies that have experienced it.

THE CAUSES OF INFLATION

Since there is a good deal of controversy over the causes of inflation, and since no one theory appears to cover all types of inflation, we will consider several different theories. Five main categories of inflation causes have been proposed: demand pull, cost push, structural, *ex ante*, and a wage-push and markup inflation model.

Demand-Pull Inflation

Demand-pull inflation occurs whenever the aggregate-demand curve shifts to the right. It can be initiated by any increase in the *IS* or *LM* function, most likely due to more consumer, investor, or government expenditures, or to an increase in the stock of money. Demand-pull inflationary pressure causes both an increase in output and a higher price level up to full employment, and only a higher price level thereafter. Such pressure can raise the prices level even when unemployment exists. However, we will illustrate the case in which demand-pull pressure occurs beyond full employment and results in pure inflation.

The three panels of Figure 13-1 incorporate the ingredients of demand-pull inflation. Panel A shows the aggregate supply-and-demand model. Panel B relates effective demand $(C + I)$ and the 45° reference line. Panel C relates demand-pull inflation to the *IS–LM* model. (Notice that, for added realism, the *LM* curves have been rounded off in this chapter, rather than drawn with linear segments.)

Assume that the illustration starts at $\bar{Y}$, the full-employment equilibium level of income, in all three panels, and then that the demand-pull pressure is initiated by an increase in the investment demand function, induced by an

[4] Costantino Bresciani-Turroni, *The Economics of Inflation*, trans. M. E. Sayers (London: Allen & Unwin, 1937), p. 310.

[5] *Ibid.*, p. 292.

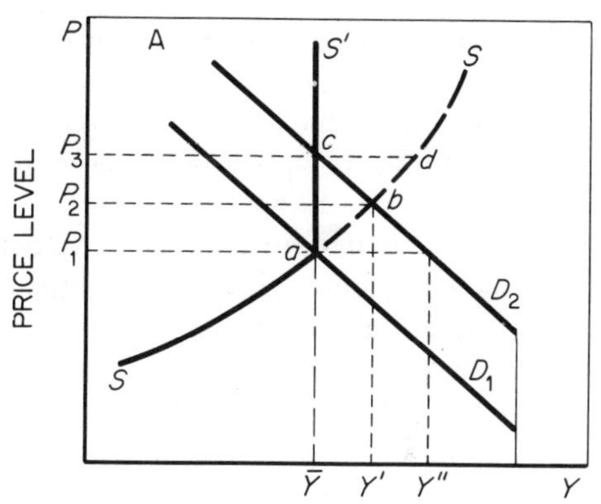

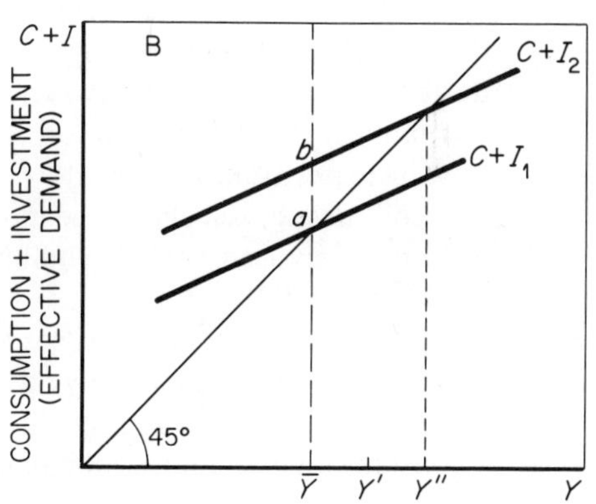

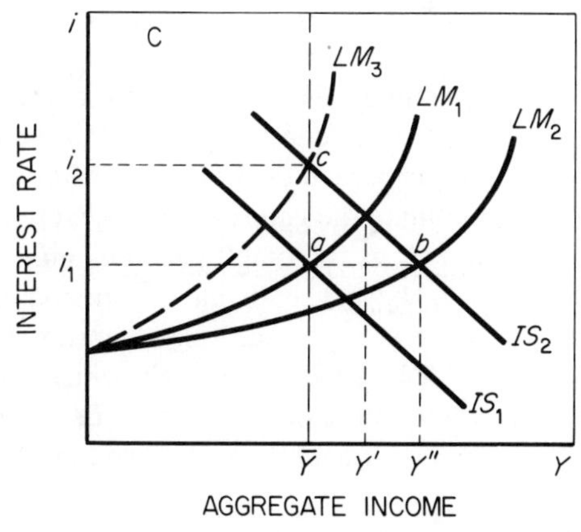

FIG. 13-1 Demand-Pull Inflation

increase in the marginal efficiency of capital.[6] In addition, assume that the monetary authority increases the money stock by just enough to allow the interest rate to at first remain constant. The aggregate demand curve increases from D_1 to D_2 in panel A because of the increase in the investment demand function working through the full multiplier effect. This increase in investment demand increases the effective-demand curve in panel B from $C + I_1$ to $C + I_2$, and leads to a shift in the *IS* curve from IS_1 to IS_2 in panel C. At the same time, the increase in the money stock leads to an increase in the *LM* curve from LM_1 to LM_2 in panel C.

The original intersection of aggregate demand with aggregate supply, point *a* in panel A, occurred at the full employment level, $\bar{Y}$. When aggregate demand shifts from D_1 to D_2, the resulting excess demand, $\bar{Y}$-Y'', leads to a bidding up of prices, which in turn would lead to an increase in the interest rate through the Keynes effect. If output could be expanded beyond $\bar{Y}$, the aggregate supply-and-demand equilibrium would occur at point *b* in panel A, requiring that the price level rise to P_2 and aggregate income increase to Y'. However, the dotted portion of the *SaS* curve is unattainable; therefore, a price level of P_2 is clearly unstable. As the price level increases from P_1 toward P_2, a chain reaction through the Keynes effect is set off, owing to a shrinkage in the real value of the money supply, which will ultimately lead back to equilibrium at full-employment, point *c*, with a price level of P_3.

Moving from panel A to panel B, we see that an inflationary gap from point *a* to point *b* is created by the shift in the effective demand curve from $C + I_1$ to $C + I_2$. This gap, equal to *a-b* assumes a constant price level and a constant interest rate. Full-employment equilibrium can be restored only by closing the gap and reducing the $C + I$ function to its original level. The increase in the interest rate from i_1 to i_2 in panel C, which results from an increase in the price level because of the Keynes effect, eliminates the gap in panel B by reducing back to the original level the quantity of investment goods demanded. Therefore, the increase in the interest rate must be sufficient to drain off the entire amount of the excess quantity of investment and restore the $C + I_1$ effective demand curve at the full-employment level of income. An increase in the price level without an increase in the interest rate could not eliminate the gap for long, because any level of effective demand in excess of $C + I_1$ at full employment cannot be maintained. Higher prices that would clear the market in one time period must show up as increased money incomes in the next period, unless consumption or investment is reduced.

The process through which such a reduction in quantity demanded would affect the economy is demonstrated in panel C. The initial increase in the investment demand function that was the assumed cause of demand-pull

[6] In this illustration capital is variable on the demand side but not on the supply side. The justification for this restricted assumption is that in a short period of time, a change in the demand for capital goods can significantly affect total demand, but any incremental investment is unlikely to be sufficiently large to affect output noticeably.

pressure would increase the IS curve from IS_1 to IS_2 in panel C. Meanwhile, a greater money stock shifts the LM curve from LM_1 to LM_2.[7] The horizontal distance from point *a* to point *b* measures the amount of excess demand created by the shift, equal to $\bar{Y}$-Y''. The excess demand leads to an increase in the price level, with the resulting shrinkage in the real value of the money stock, which in turn will shift the LM curve from LM_2 to LM_3 through the Keynes effect. The decrease in the LM curve causes a new intersection with the IS_2 curve, at point *c* in panel C. Consequently, the higher i_2 interest rate causes a smaller quantity of investment goods to be demanded.

To summarize, when demand-pull inflationary pressure is caused by an increase in the IS curve, the inflationary gap shown in panel B is closed by an increase in the interest rate to a new, higher level, shown in panel C, owing to the Keynes effect, which in turn was activated by the upward movement in the price level. The price level increases until an equilibrium is reestablished between the aggregate supply and demand curves at the full-employment level of output.

A permanent equilibrium, however, cannot be achieved at point *c* in panel *A*, because the aggregate supply-and-demand intersection is on the inelastic aS' segment of the aggregate-supply curve. Producers may attempt vainly to increase output beyond full employment in order to attempt to reach the dotted aS portion of the aggregate-supply curve at point *d*. In this attempt, they will compete for resources and bid up resource prices. Therefore, beyond full employment, stable equilibrium requires that aggregate demand be reduced or that achievable aggregate supply be increased. Otherwise, the demand and supply of labor (and other productive resources) cannot be in balance. A dynamic inflationary spiral would be set in motion in this case. Such a spiral is discussed in the appendix to this chapter.

Not only the LM curve but also the IS curve may be affected by an increase in the price level, because price increases also affect the real value of asset holders' wealth in the form of money and government bonds. Therefore, an increase in the price level may make asset holders poorer by reducing the real value of their wealth (the Pigou effect) and so cause them to decrease their consumption. To the extent that the Pigou effect does operate, the IS curve is reduced by a lower consumption function.[8]

---

[7]The equilibrium of IS_2 and LM_2 at point *b* (panel C of Figure 13-1) is only a theoretical construct designed to keep the interest rate constant at i_1. In reality, point *b* is unattainable, since it is beyond full employment. Possibly, the assumed increase in the money stock could cause the interest rate to fall below i_1 temporarily, perhaps down to the intersection of LM_2 with the vertical line representing full-employment output at $\bar{Y}$. In any case, the unattainability of IS–LM equilibrium will soon cause prices to rise and shift the LM curve to the left through the Keynes effect, raising the interest rate. The practical point is that the interest rate should first drop and then increase, under the conditions assumed here.

[8]Metzler used the Pigou effect in this way to demonstrate that monetary policy affects not only the money side of the economy, but also real markets. Until Metzler's article, the interrelatedness of the money and real sides of the economy had not been widely recognized. L. A. Metzler, "Wealth, Saving, and the Rate of Interest," *Journal of Political Economy*, 59 (April 1951), 93–116.

The interaction of the real (or commodity) and monetary sides of the economy during demand-pull inflation is illustrated in Figure 13-2. In order to demonstrate that price changes affect both sides of the economy, let us suppose that the stock of money is increased. The analysis starts at the full-employment level of income, where the interest rate is equal to i_1, at the intersection of IS_1 and LM_1 in Figure 13-2. We then assume that expansionary

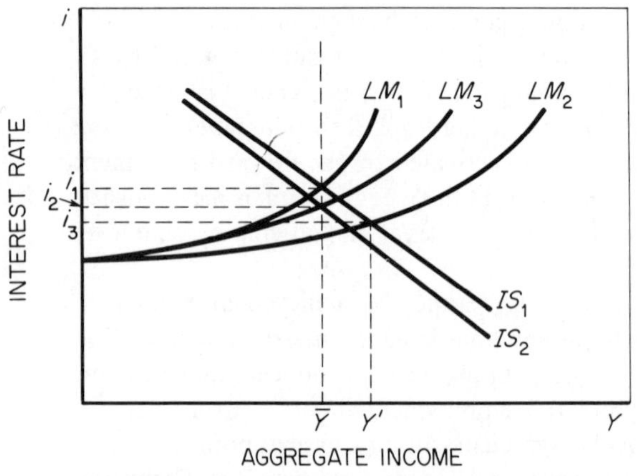

FIG. 13-2 The Pigou and Keynes Effects following an increase in the Stock of Money

monetary policy causes an increase in the *LM* curve from LM_1 to LM_2. The LM_2 function intersects the IS_1 curve at a point that would reduce the interest rate to i_3 and increase aggregate income past full employment to Y'. However, since output cannot be expanded beyond full employment, prices rise as a result of the excess demand created by the decreasing interest rate. Higher prices, in turn, reduce the real value of the stock of money, and the *LM* curve shifts to the left through the Keynes effect. However, increased prices initiate the Pigou effect, shifting the *IS* curve down and to the left, from IS_1 to IS_2. The leftward shift in *IS* offsets the increased quantity of investment demanded because of the lower interest rate. The *LM* curve will not completely revert to LM_1, because the decrease in the *IS* curve causes the full-employment equilibrium level of income to be reached before the *LM* curve reverts completely to its original position. Full employment is reestablished where the IS_2 curve crosses the LM_3 curve with an equilibrium interest rate of i_2, which is lower than the original interest rate of i_1 (assuming that the Pigou effect operates and shifts the *IS* curve down to IS_2 before the *LM* curve decreases —shifts to the left—beyond the LM_3 curve).[9]

[9]A further wealth effect, Keynes's windfall effect or "second psychological law," discussed in Chapter 8, occurs when the interest rate is reduced. As we saw in Chapter 7, a decrease in interest rates increases the price of bonds, causing an increase in the wealth

As a result of the increase in the stock of money, the lower equilibrium interest rate (i_2 as compared with i_1) is consistent with slower income velocity, because money becomes more attractive relative to bonds at lower interest rates. As a result, the increase in the money stock will induce a reduction in income velocity and give rise to a less-than-proportional increase in the price level. Therefore, the quantity theory of money cannot work if the liquidity preference curve is negatively sloped and if the Pigou effect operates to prevent the LM curve from reverting completely to its original level of LM_1.

Irrespective of changes in income velocity, to the extent that the Pigou effect operates, a change in monetary policy has affected the real side of the economy and has somewhat reduced the demand-pull pressure, because prices increase in a smaller proportion than the increase in the stock of money.[10]

Cost-Push Inflation

The pressure for inflation can spring from the supply side as well as the demand side of the economy. If suppliers of productive resources or of goods and services believe that the demand curve they face is relatively inelastic ($\epsilon < 1$), they may attempt to increase their total receipts by raising the price of their resource or product. Often, demands for wage increases or higher prices in imperfectly competitive resource and product markets provide the strongest pressure for cost-push inflation. However, the suppliers of any resource or commodity, even in perfectly competitive markets, can create some inflationary pressure by attempting to increase their prices. In this regard, the cost-push effect of higher interest rates is often overlooked. Businessmen think of higher interest rates as an increase in the cost of doing business; economists think of them simply as a brake on investment. (The high interest-rate level of 1969–70 did not stop inflation, nor did many businessmen expect it to.)

The process of cost-push inflation is depicted in Figure 13-3, which presents the aggregate demand and supply curves in panel A, the effective demand curve in panel B, and the *IS—LM* functions in panel C. A general attempt by suppliers of resources, goods, and services to increase the price level for any given level of output is shown in panel A as a leftward shift in the aggregate-supply function, from S_1 to S_2. As a result, aggregate income falls at equilibrium from the full-employment level $\bar{Y}$ to Y_1, and the price level increases from P_1 to P_2.

---

of bondholders that should work in a fashion similar to the Pigou effect. That is, the lower interest rate can induce bondholders to increase their consumption by making them richer. Therefore, at full employment, an increase in the money stock leads to a lower interest rate and causes an increase in the *IS* curve, to the extent that bondholders are motivated to consume more as a result of the windfall effect. So the windfall effect mitigates the downward shift in the *IS* curve initiated by the price increase.

[10]The student should be wary of economic policies that rely on the Pigou effect for their results, because most of the criticisms of the Pigou effect discussed in the preceding chapter are valid for both increasing and decreasing prices.

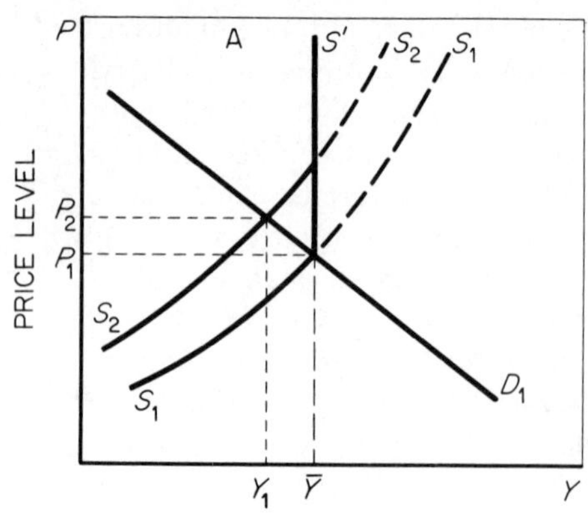

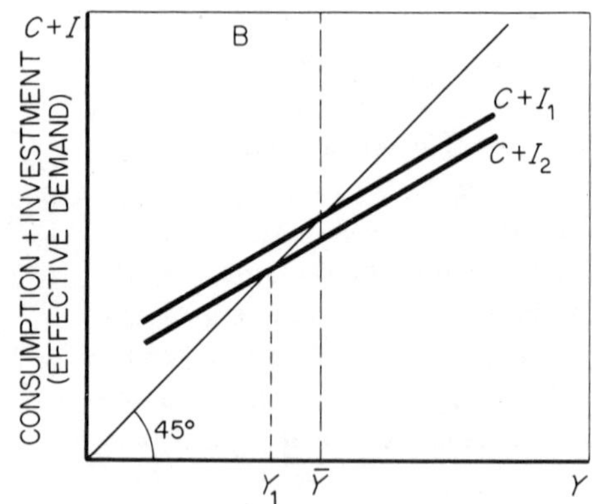

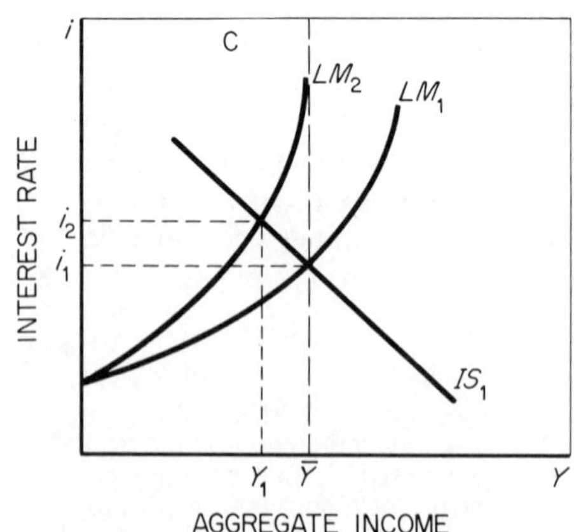

FIG. 13-3 Cost-Push Inflation

The effect of the reduction in the aggregate supply curve in panel A is reflected in panel B as a reduction in the effective demand curve from $C + I_1$ to $C + I_2$ due to a reduction in the quantity of investment demanded.[11] The reduction in the quantity of investment demanded is revealed in panel C to be the result of a decrease (shift to the left) in the *LM* curve from LM_1 to LM_2, which raises the equilibrium interest rate from i_1 to i_2. The shift in the *LM* curve shown in panel C occurs because of the decrease in the real-money stock, which follows from the cost-push-induced increase in the price level. The resulting higher equilibrium interest rate brings forth a smaller amount of investment and causes aggregate income to fall below full employment.

Unless resource prices increase, how is it possible for the aggregate-supply curve to shift to the left? If we lived in a world of profit-maximizing, perfectly competitive firms, equilibrium prices would already have been set at the most profitable level, and suppliers of goods and services would increase prices only in response to an increase in market demand or in resource prices. Therefore, higher prices for goods and services without a corresponding increase in demand could only reduce profits.

However, aggregate supply can shift to the left even if resource prices remain constant, because we do *not* live in a world of perfectly competitive profit maximizers. If enough firms have monopoly power, a perfectly competitive aggregate market equilibrium cannot develop.

For example, the management of firms that are price leaders in oligopoly industries try, not simply to obtain maximum profits but to achieve an optimum mix of different goals, such as sales volume or output and profits. Consequently, such firms may set prices at a level that provides a satisfactory target return on investment but not maximum profits. Whenever their optimum goal-mix changes and profits become more important relative to other goals such firms can increase their profits by raising their prices. Price-leader firms can be reasonably sure that the other firms in their industry will follow.

The "administered price" thesis was introduced by Gardiner Means during the Great Depression as another rationale for a type of cost-push inflation, sometimes called oligopolist inflation.[12] Means developed the administered price thesis after noting oligopolists' prices followed a conspicuously different pattern from competitive prices over the business cycle. Competitive firms have no market power, so their prices behave "normally": generally rising during prosperity and falling during recession. Oligopoly prices, in

[11]This reduction in effective demand could also have been caused by a decline in consumption (perhaps owing to a "consumer strike").

[12]A general assumption is that high levels of concentration indicate the presence of monopoly power. Following on this assumption, recent evidence seems to imply a gradual increase in monopoly power. Blair demonstrates that for the 209 out of the 443 industries (standard 4 digit industrial classification) where comparisons are possible over the period from 1947 to 1967, there has been an increase in concentration in 95 cases while only 75 cases experienced a decrease. John M. Blair, *Economic Concentration* (New York: Harcourt Brace Jovanovich, 1972), p. 470–91.

contrast, were often noted to be rigid—or worse, to increase—during recession and to rise little, if any, during prosperity.

How can oligopolists behave so differently from competitors? And for what motive? The oligopolists' motive is to protect their profits from cyclical fluctuations in demand and to attempt to maximize profits over the cycle. And oligopolists have sufficient market power to pursue their motive by using "full cost pricing," a pricing technique whose existence has been empirically demonstrated. The essence of a "full cost-administered price" is that it will reflect all changes in average variable costs (raw material costs and wages) and ignore short run changes in demand in an attempt to keep the margin between price and average variable costs (or overhead costs and profits) as constant as possible.[13] This pricing model is fully consistent with the achievement of target rates of return, for once margins are determined, it is only one additional step to determine the separate components of margins, overhead costs, and profits.

In the short recessions we have experienced since World War II, raw material costs and particularly wages have continued to rise. The offending oligopolists will boost prices accordingly, and if the recessionary drop in production incurs larger overhead costs per unit of output—a likely event—prices might even be pushed up further in the effort to preserve margins. According to the logic of the full-cost pricing, the reverse occurs during expansions: competitive prices (and margins) rise faster than oligopoly prices. However, during the long expansions since World War II, the slower climb of full cost-administered prices ends when the short run is over, and plant and equipment are replaced or expanded. Then, oligopolists increase prices to take account of higher capital costs and target rates of return. It is further argued that over the cycle and in the long run, prices and profits in oligopoly are higher than they would be if production were competitively organized. Thus, advocates of this theory argue that higher oligopoly profit rates contribute to cost-push inflation both in short run recessions and over the longer term.

In addition, there has been a tendency for oligopolistic industries to grow relative to competitive industries even in cases where the oligopoly industry has become less concentrated. For example, there are more steel companies today than there were in 1901. However, steel has grown relative to many competitive industries, such as agriculture. So the overall result has been to increase the degree of concentration of the aggregate economy, and give a greater role to noncompetitive pricing. For example, over the period 1947–66 Blair points out that the gain of the 200 largest manufacturing firms was from 30 percent to 42 percent of total value added, an increase of 12 percentage points. This increasing prevalence of economic concentration throughout the economy (even though it may be occurring at a slow rate)

---

[13] Howard N. Ross, "Illusions in Testing for Administered Prices," *Journal of Industrial Economics*, 21 (April, 1973), 187–195.

may help explain the upward bias in prices, noted since the time of the Great Depression.

Increases in resource prices would lead to cost-push inflation even in the case of profit-maximizing, perfectly competitive firms. In the short run, when all resources except labor are held constant, decreases in the aggregate-supply curve can be traced back to higher labor costs. In order for labor costs to rise independently of any increase in the demand for labor, it must be assumed that either a substantial proportion of the labor force is organized, or strong unions in key industries set the pattern for wage increases in both other unions and non-union industries. In the United States, the latter assumption is more realistic, since only about 25 percent of the labor force is unionized.

Why would wages increase in highly unionized industries if there is no increase in the demand for labor? Many unions are similar to the firms just discussed, in that they have a degree of monopoly power and multiple goals. Unions that simply wanted the maximum amount of wage income for their total membership would strive for wages at a level where the demand for their particular type of labor was unitarily elastic, and consequently the total wage bill would be maximized.

If unions were so motivated, the potential increase in the price level owing to cost-push inflation would be restricted. However, in reality, unions may attempt to obtain higher wages than are consistent with the maximum wage bill for several reasons:

1. Union members cannot compute the size of the maximum wage bill, so union leaders' success is measured by the level of the wage received by employed workers and by the size of this year's wage increase.
2. During periods of prosperity, economic growth may increase the demand for labor consistently enough to allay workers' fears that higher wages will cause significant unemployment.
3. Older workers with more seniority often have the most political power in unions and have little fear of being laid off themselves. Such workers have the ability and the motive to push for wage increases even though they might cause some unemployment.
4. Some unions whose workers possess scarce skills feel free to demand higher wages because they are confident that any resulting unemployment from the higher wage level will fall on other groups and not on them. Once such groups are successful, the effect can spread, with higher wages and prices spreading through the economy.

The cost-push theory offers a convenient explanation of inflation during the 1957–58 and 1969–70 recessions. But some writers have proposed that this source of inflation does not exist. They argue that apparent cost-push inflation is simply a lagged reaction to previous rounds of demand-pull inflation, and that resource suppliers or business firms are trying to compensate for previous price increases. Further, they argue, true cost-push inflation could be due only to some changes in the degree of monopoly power exercised by firms or resource suppliers, and, as we have seen, the degree of monopoly power changes slowly, if at all. However, this view does not take into consideration the goal of unions to get ever-increasing wages, or of firms to achieve target returns on their investments or change their optimum goal mix especially when the aggregate demand curve has declined.

Certain factors prevent the unlimited continuation of cost-push inflation if public policy does not intervene. Eventually, business firms that are price leaders in oligopoly industries must refuse to increase prices further because of the development of undesired excess capacity. Similarly, labor unions must eventually refuse to push for higher wages because of unacceptably high unemployment. These two factors will at some point call a halt to cost-push inflation; but that point cannot be precisely defined analytically before it is reached. Furthermore, that point may never be reached if both businessmen and union leaders are confident that the government will use monetary and fiscal policy to continually bail them out by increasing aggregate demand in order to avoid unemployment and other negative effects of a long and deep recession. If monetary and fiscal policies are so used, demand-pull pressure from the government sector is thus added to cost-push inflation, with the consequences of further price increases and prevention of the development of the normal deterrents to cost-push inflation, undesired excess capacity and unacceptably high unemployment.[14]

Structural Inflation

The structural-inflation thesis combines elements of demand-pull and cost-push to explain the development of inflation.[15] Suppose that business firms in certain consumer goods industries anticipate an increase in demand for their products. As a result of their expectations, they increase their demand for investment goods, which could lead to an increase in the aggregate demand for the whole economy.

In Figure 13-4 we use the same three panels as in Figures 13-1 and 13–3. The increased demand for investment goods causes the aggregate demand curve to increase from D_1 to D_2 in panel A of Figure 13-4, and the effective demand function to increase from $C + I_1$ to $C + I_2$ in panel B. The IS curve shifts from IS_1 to IS_2 and the LM curve from LM_1 to LM_2, in panel C, since for simplicity, we assume that the money stock is increased just enough to maintain the interest rate at i_1. Because of this excess demand, equal to $\bar{Y}$-Y', shown in all three panels, prices increase leading to a decrease in the real value of the money supply and consequently a shift to the left in the LM curve toward LM_1 in panel C.

---

[14]For three studies concerning different aspects of cost-push inflation, see: F. D. Holzman, "Income Determination in Open Inflation," *Review of Economics and Statistics*, 32 (May 1950), 150–58; and G. Ackley, "Administered Prices and the Inflationary Process," *American Economic Review*, 49 (May 1959), 419–30, and John Hotson, *International Comparisons of Money Velocity and Wage Mark-Ups* (New York: Augustus M. Kelley, 1968).

[15]The idea of structural inflation is generally attributed to Charles Schultze, *Recent Inflation in the United States*, Study Paper No. 1 of the Joint Economic Committee of the Congress of the United States (Washington, D.C.: U.S. Government Printing Office, 1959).

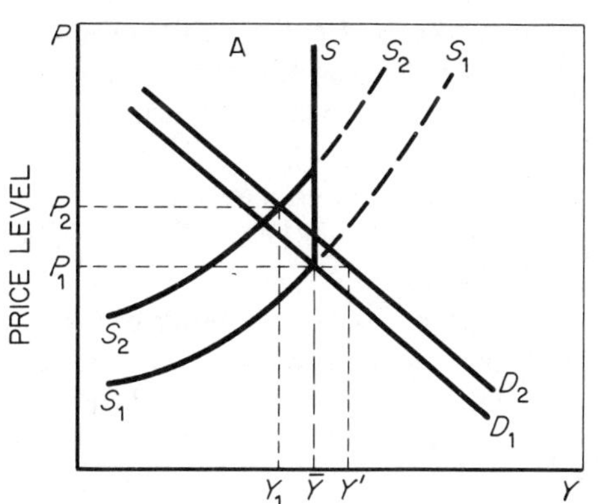

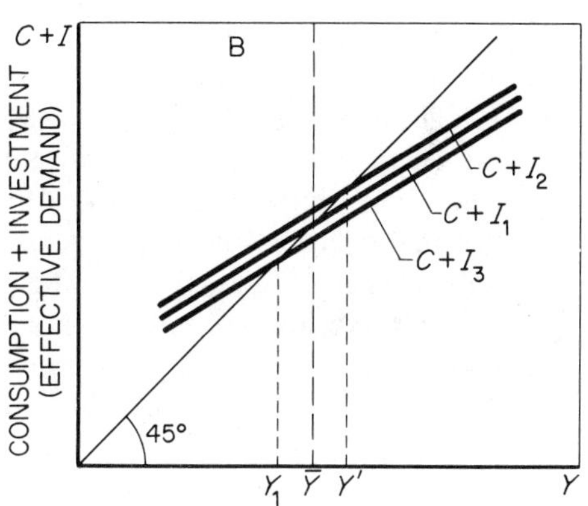

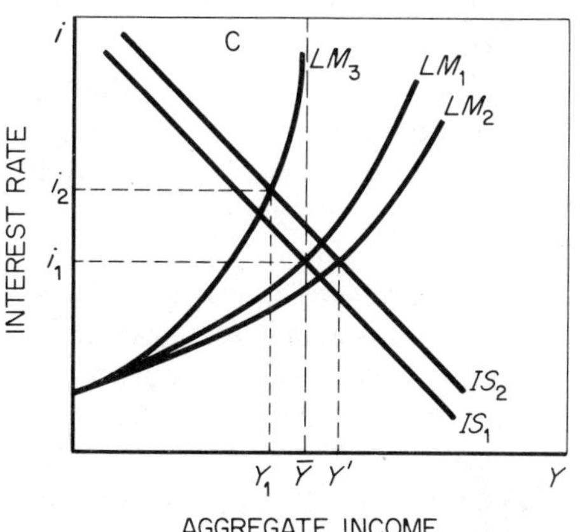

FIG. 13-4 Structural Inflation

However, the structural-inflation hypothesis emphasizes that prices will not increase uniformly. They increase first in industries such as capital goods, which experience the most demand pressure. These will attempt to increase production by bidding resources away from other industries. If labor is imperfectly mobile, wages will be bid up in these industries to attract labor.

Thus, workers in the expanding industries will receive higher wages because of an increase in demand for the output of those industries. Union leaders in other industries, where the demand has *not* increased, will react by pushing for equivalent increases for their own workers, and non-union labor will react in similar fashion. As a result labor costs will go up throughout the economy while demand increases only in certain sectors.

The effect of increased labor costs is demonstrated in panel A of Figure 13-4 as a decrease in the aggregate supply curve from S_1 to S_2, a response to the initial, smaller increase in aggregate demand, from D_1 to D_2. The final net result of the shift in both the aggregate supply and demand curves is to decrease output from $\bar{Y}$ to Y_1, while the price level increases from P_1 to P_2. Just as in the case of cost-push inflation, the Keynes effect induced by higher prices causes the LM curve to decrease from LM_2 to LM_3 in panel C, in turn raising the equilibrium interest rate to i_2 at the intersection of LM_3 and IS_2. The higher interest rate causes a decrease in the effective demand curve in panel B, from $C + I_2$ to $C + I_3$. As a result, the equilibrium level of output falls below full employment at Y_1.

In the example shown in Figure 13-4, structural inflation was initiated by an increase in the aggregate demand curve. However, structural inflation does not require an initial absolute increase in aggregate demand; it could begin with a change in the makeup of aggregate demand. If aggregate demand remains at the same level, but purchasing power is transferred from one industry to another, bottlenecks may occur in the supply of particular types of labor as resources are transferred from declining to the growing industries. As a result, the industries gaining demand will normally charge higher prices, which may even be offset by price decreases in the industries losing demand if their prices are not inflexible downward. The necessity on the part of those industries whose demand has increased to bid scarce or immobile types of labor from other industries will lead to higher wages for those scarce types of labor. Then, pressure for higher wages will spread throughout the economy, as labor unions, and even non-union labor, in other industries try to obtain wage increases equivalent to those obtained in the labor-scarce industries.[16] General demands for higher wages cause a leftward shift in the aggregate-supply function, leading in turn to lower output and higher prices.

Thus, whether structural inflation is initiated by an increase in the aggregate demand curve or by a transfer of demand from one industry to another, it induces the same tendencies as cost-push inflation: a combination

[16]If the labor supply of the growing industries is highly unionized, wages may be bid up even if bottlenecks do not occur, since union leaders in the growing industries can demand wage increases with little fear of unemployment.

of higher prices and reduced employment. However, structural inflation combines elements of demand-pull inflation as the initiating factor and cost-push as the secondary but more powerful reaction.

Ex Ante Inflation

We have treated inflation in a static context as simply an increase in the price level, as the economy moves from one equilibrium position to another. However, inflation is commonly specified as a percentage change in price over a certain time period, usually one year. It is therefore a *rate of change* in the price level, not a one-time increase. That rate of change may be stated

$$\frac{\Delta P}{P}$$

where ΔP is the price change and P is the base price level as measured at the start of the period.

If consumers become accustomed to a 5 or 6 percent general price increase, then goods whose prices increase only 2 or 3 percent will appear cheap, and goods whose prices increase by the 5 or 6 percent average rate will appear to have undergone no price change. In this context, relative prices are significant and absolute prices are not.

After a protracted inflationary period, such as the latter 1960's, people tend to anticipate further average price increases and incorporate inflationary expectations into their everyday economic behavior. Inflation feeds on itself. Inflationary expectations become self-justifying, and equilibrium can be achieved only when the realized rate of inflation becomes equal to the anticipated rate. Most consumers relate their expectations of inflation to their past experience, weighting the recent past more heavily than the more remote past.[17]

During inflation, debtors gain as creditors lose part of the value of their principal or stock of wealth, since debtors repay loans with cheaper dollars than those they have borrowed. Therefore, if both debtors and creditors come to anticipate a certain rate of inflation, creditors will demand an interest premium to compensate for their anticipated loss of capital value, and debtors will be willing to pay such a premium because they pay debts with cheaper dollars. Investors, in particular, will be willing to pay the premium demanded, because they expect the payment to come out of the anticipated inflated net returns on the assets they plan to buy with the proceeds of the loan.

Ex ante inflation, as it involves borrowing and lending, can be demonstrated with a model using two interest rates. One is the interest rate in real

[17]This presentation is based on the concept developed by Irving Fisher, in *The Theory of Interest* (1930) (New York: Augustus M. Kelley, 1961), pp. 399–451; and it uses the model employed by Prof. Martin J. Bailey, in *National Income and the Price Level*, 2nd ed. (New York: McGraw-Hill, 1971), pp. 74–80, and Prof. Milton Friedman, in "Factors Affecting the Level of Interest Rate—Part I," *Proceedings of the 1968 Conference on Savings and Residential Financing* (Chicago: United States Savings and Loan League, 1968), pp. 10–27.

terms, designated r, which does not change as a result of inflation. The other is the nominal rate in money terms, i, which includes a premium for expected inflation. The inflation premium that lenders demand in addition to the real rate may be stated as the expected rate of change in the price level, or $\Delta Pe/P$, where Pe is the anticipated price change and P is the current price level. Therefore, the nominal rate of interest equals the real interest rate plus the inflation premium, or

$$i = r + \frac{\Delta Pe}{P}$$

Borrowers are willing to pay the higher nominal rate, i, rather than r, the lower real rate, because they expect to repay cheaper dollars than those they borrow. In other words, borrowers are concerned, not with the interest rate on money, but with the interest rate on real goods, because the value of money is expected to decrease. The higher nominal rate is required to keep the real rate constant.

The ex ante inflation model is shown in Figure 13-5. Starting from an initial position of equilibrium, where i equals r, the full-employment equilibrium level of income, $\bar{Y}$, occurs at the intersection of the IS_1 and LM_1 curves. Now, if a certain rate of inflation is anticipated, the nominal interest rate will increase by the inflation premium, $\Delta Pe/P$. The anticipated growth in the money value of net returns increases the IS curve with respect to the nominal interest rate, i. Assuming a constant real rate, the IS curve increases from IS_1 to IS_2 by an amount equal to the inflation premium. (Assuming

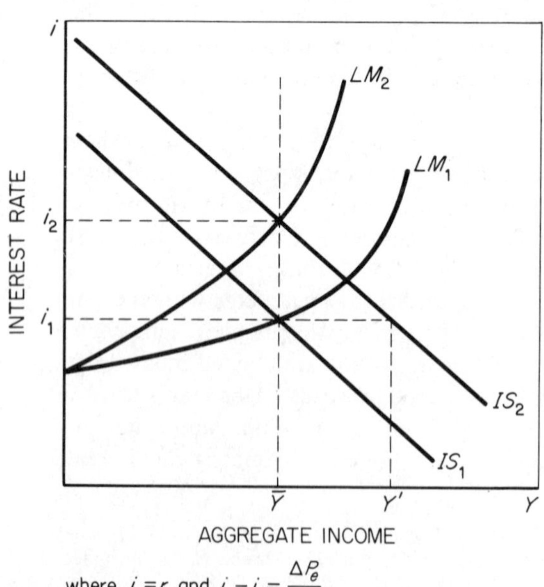

FIG. 13-5 ***Ex Ante*** **Inflation**

that this increase in the *IS* curve is enough to eliminate any incentive on the part of investors to modify their investment spending if it goes up sufficiently.)

The shift in the *IS* curve, at the going nominal rate of interest, sets up an excess in demand of $\bar{Y}$-Y'. This excess demand causes pressure for higher prices and consequently for an increase in the nominal interest rate. Continual inflation reduces the real value of the stock of money, shifting the *LM* curve to the left toward LM_2, a movement that stops when the new, higher, equilibrium nominal rate of interest, i_2, has been reached, restoring full employment, since i_2 rises above i_1 by $\Delta Pe/P$.

Ex ante inflationary pressure results entirely from the expectation of an increase in the price level. Inflation can be realized through the effect on income velocity of increased spending in anticipation of higher prices. The increased spending leads to a proportional increase in the price level without the necessity of an increase in the money stock, and the inflationary tendency is reinforced if the stock of money is increased at the same time. (Ex ante inflation, or any other type of inflation, must be financed somehow. In this model, we assume that the Keynes effect provides a sufficient increase in income velocity to finance inflation. If, for some reason, the Keynes effect does not work—as, for example, when income velocity reaches some realistic upper limit—then inflationary pressures can be realized only if the stock of money is increased at the same rate as expected inflation.)

At most, ex ante inflationary pressures can persist as long as inflation is generally anticipated.[18] The expectation of a once-and-for-all increase in the price level would lead, not to continual inflation, but to a one-time jump to a new equilibrium price and interest rate level.[19]

Milton Friedman makes use of the ex ante inflation concept as part of his solution to the Gibson paradox (that is, the tendency for prices and interest rates to increase together following an increase in the stock of money, whereas the greater stock of money "should" lead to lower interest rates, according to the liquidity-preference theory).[20] According to Friedman, the liquidity-preference effect is ultimately swamped by the combination of ex ante inflation and Friedman's "income and price level effect." This latter effect may be described as a further increase in the *IS* curve owing to a rightward shift in the MEC caused by the anticipation of future prosperity.

---

[18]One difficulty with the ex ante inflation model is that there is no evidence that the lenders' expectations will coincide with those of the borrowers. At least one model of firm behavior has been predicated on the assumption that their expectations may differ. (J. E. Walter, *Planning for Inflation*, unpublished undated manuscript.) For example, an insurance company, faced with a legal requirement to repay only fixed amounts to its policyholders, will regard the prospect of inflation differently from the industrial corporation whose bonds the insurance company buys.

A second difficulty is the loss of capital value and consequent reduction in the consumption function due to higher interest rates.

[19]However, at the new, higher price level, achieveable aggregate supply and demand may not be in balance, and a dynamic inflationary spiral could still be set in motion, a possibility we will consider in the Appendix to this chapter.

[20]Friedman, "Factors Affecting the Level of Interest Rate."

The time sequence of the Gibson paradox is as follows:

1. The money stock increases.
2. The rate of interest declines.
3. The quantity of investment demanded increases.
4. More investment stimulates the economy and causes an increase in the demand function for investment (the income and price-level effect).
5. As a result of the economic stimulation, inflation is anticipated.

Number 2 is eventually swamped by 4 and 5, so ultimately both prices and interest rates rise, even though interest rates first tend to decline.

You may note that the Gibson paradox could also be explained by the Keynes effect, with its induced shift to the left in the *LM* curve as a result of higher prices.

An ex-ante inflation model can be used as an alternative to the cost-push model to explain an inflationary recession. Suppose that aggregate demand is purposely reduced by the government through monetary or fiscal policy following a period when the annual increase in the price level has been substantial for one or more years. An inflationary recession would occur if the rate of change in output, and, in turn, employment decreases while the rate of increase in the price level remains constant or even increases. The inflation rate does not decrease because of lack of information by sellers as to future price trends. So long as sellers believe that prices will continue to advance at the going rate they will continue to raise their prices. Sellers with the power to administer prices must first perceive that demand conditions have changed and will not be reversed before they will stop increasing their prices. Furthermore, businessmen may want to wait and see if the government will bail them out through expansionary fiscal and monetary policy designed to combat unemployment (and to finance the inflation). If the government is resolutely willing to accept unemployment while resisting the bail out, eventually expectations of inflation will decline, followed by an end to inflation. One problem with this theory is that it took over a year of high unemployment before the annual inflation rate started to decline during the recent recession, let alone any drop in the price level. In contrast, prices actually declined during the recessions that occurred prior to World War II, such as those of 1921, 1929, and 1937. If anything, one would think that the availability of information has improved during the last decade, so why did the lag between the onset of the recession and a decline in the price level significantly lengthen?

Wage-Push and Markup Inflation

The inflation of the Johnson era in the United States seemed to result from different types of inflationary pressure. One phenomenon, which has been noted empirically by Sidney Weintraub and built into a formal model, is that the wage share of GNP is relatively constant.[21] Money wages, which are inflexible downward, rise consistently during inflation in order to retain labor's nearly constant share of total output. The following eclectic model is based on Weintraub's theory as developed by John Hotson.[22] This model is based on the assumptions that money wages increase during inflation and that firms use a customary markup by which they multiply their variable cost to determine their selling price. If we assume, for example, that wages are the only short-run variable cost, then if the markup factor is 2, the selling price of any unit of output equals twice the labor cost of producing it.[23]

Weintraub employs the Keynesian supply function, or proceeds supply function, Z, (supply as a function of expected money proceeds or expected total revenue of firms, rather than of price), first developed in the *General Theory*.[24] Weintraub argues that the 45° reference line often used as a stand-in for the Keynesian supply function gives misleading results.

The "proceeds-supply function," Z, is different from the aggregate-supply function of Chapter 12, in that the proceeds-supply function relates the quantities of aggregate output to the anticipated total revenue or proceeds from the sale of output, whereas the aggregate-supply function relates quantities offered for sale to the respective price level.[25]

$$\text{Thus } Z = P \times Y$$

In other words, the proceeds-supply function represents the level of output that businessmen expect to be able to sell and will therefore produce at each level of anticipated total revenue. If businessmen expect sales to rise, they will produce more output.

The model presented in this section assumes constant returns up to a certain level of aggregate output, an assumption that can be justified if labor and capital are laid off together during a recession and then reemployed in fixed proportions. In this model, diminishing returns are assumed to set in after reemployment of previously existing capital, but before full employment of labor. (If capital and labor are not employed in fixed proportions, capital may be reemployed first, if this can be achieved more cheaply than reemployment of labor.)

The model is shown in Figure 13-6. Starting with the upper panel,

---

[21] Sidney Weintraub, *A General Theory of the Price Level, Output, Income Distribution and Economic Growth* (Philadelphia: Chilton, 1959).

[22] John Hotson, "Neo-Orthodox Keynesianism and the 45° Heresy," *Nebraska Journal of Economics and Business*, 6 (Autumn 1967), 34–49.

[23] For evidence that such a markup is actually constant, see John Hotson, *International Comparisons*, 1–65.

[24] Sidney Weintraub, *An Approach to the Theory of Income Distribution* (Philadelphia: Chilton, 1958), especially Chaps. 2 and 3, pp. 24–64.

[25] Hotson, like Keynes and Weintraub, measures employment along the x-axis. However, we have substituted aggregate real income—which is a unique function of the level of employment—for consistency with our previous models.

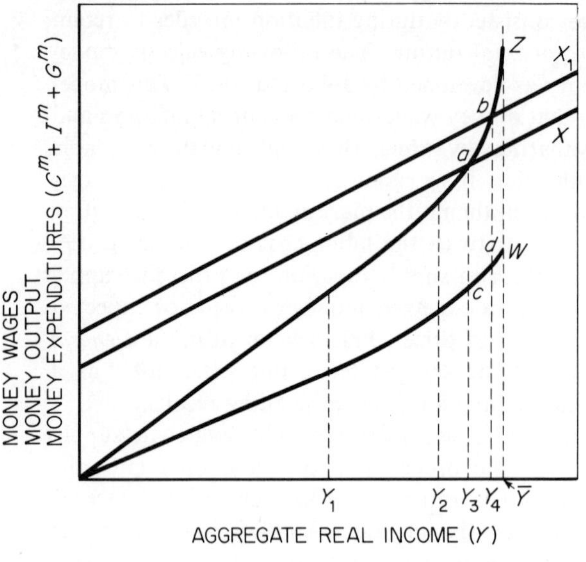

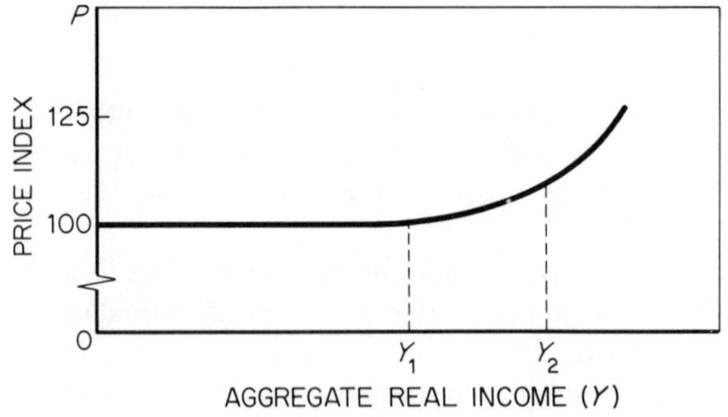

FIG. 13-6 Wage-Push Inflation

aggregate real income is plotted on the *x*-axis and money magnitudes—such as money expenditures or proceeds (real expenditures times a price index)—are measured on the *y*-axis. The aggregate proceeds-supply function, *Z*, relates aggregate output measured in real terms to output in money terms; it is linear and falls along a 45° line up to the Y_1 level of aggregate real income. The *Z* function becomes nonlinear where the price level starts to increase at Y_1. The price level remains unchanged as output increases up to Y_1, because money expenditures change in the same proportion as changes in real expenditures. Average variable cost, marginal cost, and markup are all assumed to remain constant up to that point. However, beyond Y_1 level of aggregate real income, a successful wage push, due to union bargaining strength, bottlenecks, or structural factors, causes inflation to begin, and is shown as an increase in money expenditures by firms, proportionately greater than the increase in aggregate real income. The *Z* function increases even more steeply beyond the point of diminishing returns that set in at Y_2 level of aggregate real income, because the real-wage cost per unit of output (labor input as a proportion of total output) starts to increase beyond that point, and the constant markup is applied to the increasing incremental wage cost.

In this model the price level, represented by a price index shown in the lower panel of the figure, is computed from the ratio of aggregate real income on the x-axis to money expenditures on the y-axis in the upper panel, and equals the slope of Z. As long as the slope is constant and equal to 45°, the price index remains constant and equal to 100. At Y_1 level of aggregate real income, where the wage-push inflation begins, the slope of the Z function increases, and the ratio of money expenditures to real income increases, raising the price level. Inflation continues at an increasing rate beyond Y_1 owing to the increasing slope of Z. Inflation will increase at an even faster rate after diminishing returns set in at Y_2.

The wage function, W, represents the relationship between the total money wage bill, measured on the vertical axis, and real income, on the horizontal axis. The shape of the W function results from the collective-bargaining process and provides the cost basis to which the constant markup is applied. The slope of the W curve continually increases to the right of Y_1 level of aggregate real income, owing to wage-push inflation. The shape of the W curve increases at an even greater rate after diminishing returns set in at Y_2 level of real income, the point where marginal productivity of labor starts to fall since at that point complementary capital becomes fully employed. The assumption that firms use a virtually constant markup above wages to compute their prices is the basis for the relationship between Z and W.

As employment and output increase, wage-push pressures begin to be exerted by workers, assuming that they are not subject to money illusion, and the prices of finished goods are marked up proportionately.

While employers are attempting to increase the price of their output to maintain a constant markup above labor cost, workers are simultaneously attempting to increase their money wages in order to avoid a decline in their real wages. In effect, both employers and workers attempt to use markup pricing, as both groups resist a decrease in their share of total output.

In summary, in Figure 13-6, the wage push starts at Y_1 and the additional impetus of diminishing returns sets in at Y_2, causing the Z function to rise more steeply beyond that point. As long as firms use an unchangeable mark-up over wages, the wage share remains constant. (However, if they shift to marginal-cost pricing after Y_2 level of income is reached, the wage share will fall as a result.) In Figure 13-6, the wage markup is assumed to be 2, so the wage function, W, is always one-half the level of Z, and the wage share remains a constant proportion of aggregate real income up to Y_2. The proceeds-supply function, Z, turns vertical at $\bar{Y}$, the full-employment level of output, and where Z turns vertical, so does the price index, P, in the lower panel.

The ability of employers to raise prices is limited by "proceeds" demand, the X curve in Figure 13-6, which relates total money outlay by consumers, investors, and government to the aggregate real income or output available for purchase. For simplicity, we use a linear function; however, in reality, the curve may have any positive slope, which may vary from point to point as distributive shares change, if the various income-receiving groups have differing propensities to consume. (Labor's share will fall if firms use marginal-cost pricing after Y_2, and the share of fixed-income recipients will definitely fall as inflation develops.)

The proceeds-demand function, X, in Figure 13-6, differs from the aggregate-demand function developed in the preceding chapter, in that total revenue rather than price is plotted along the y-axis. As a result, X has a positive rather than negative slope. It differs from effective demand, the $C + I$ curve of Chapter 8, because X relates money expenditure to aggregate real income, while $C + I$ relates real expenditure to aggregate real income. Thus, $X = (C + I)P$. For simplicity, we assume that government expenditures and investment demand are constant in the short run, and therefore that the rate of change in actual demand depends entirely on consumption.

The equilibrium level of real income and money expenditures occurs in Figure 13-6 at the intersection of proceeds supply curve, Z, and proceeds demand curve, X, at point a. In our illustration, equilibrium occurs before full employment of labor is reached at $\bar{Y}$, the point where Z turns vertical.

If the proceeds demand curve increases in Figure 13-6 from X to X_1, equilibrium between the proceeds demand and supply shifts from point a to point b on the proceeds-supply function, Z. Aggregate money wages increase from point c to point d on the wage function, W, in response to wage-push pressures that are derived from the increase in proceeds demand. Prices of finished goods are marked up in greater proportion than the per worker wage increase, because diminishing returns to labor have already set in and we assume that a constant markup is applied to aggregate wages. Unlike the case with the demand-pull or cost-push models previously presented, it is unimportant whether money wages or prices increase first in response to the increase in the proceeds-demand curve, X. The important point is that firms mark up prices in response to money-wage changes, or that labor "marks up" wages in response to price increases. The interaction of demand and supply finally leads to increases in both prices and wages.

This wage-push–markup inflation model is based on demand-pull pressure. Wages and the price level increase as the result of the increase in expenditures that is due to the increase in proceeds demand. If the Keynes effect or Pigou effect were included, they would limit the increase in aggregate income, because higher interest rates would partially offset the expansionary impact of the increase in proceeds demand.[26] In this model, labor is assumed to have sufficient bargaining power to maintain its relative share of output (at least

[26]To disregard the interest rate may lack a certain theoretical elegance, but if the monetary authorities ultimately have the power to regulate the interest rate, disregard of it might be understood as a tacit assumption that the interest rate is an exogenously determined datum.

up to Y_2), and sellers are assumed to have sufficient market power to employ markup pricing policies.

Markup-inflation models of this type have the advantage of emphasizing, as businessmen and union leaders often do, the relationship of prices and wages and not their absolute levels. Inflation develops because resource suppliers and product sellers attempt to maintain an accustomed relationship between resource prices and output prices. A second broad advantage of this type of model is that it can combine elements of demand-pull, cost-push, and structural inflation in one model.

Price and wage determination based on customary markups builds an inflationary bias into the structure of an economy. The element that initiates a movement out of equilibrium is unimportant; the shift may be due to a demand-pull-induced shift in X, or a cost-push-induced reduction (leftward shift) in Z. More significant than the initiating shift is the process of inflation itself. Once the process is started, the markup over wage costs and wage increases are built into the structure of the economy.

Hotson emphasizes that an increase in the interest rate and in taxes may have an inflationary impact often overlooked.[27] Economists concentrate on the effect of a higher interest rate on reducing demand functions. However, to the extent that businessmen mark up prices over interest cost, the Z function in Figure 13-6 would shift up and to the left as a result of an increase in the interest rate (a view long proposed by Congressman Wright Patman of Texas), leading to a higher price index. Simultaneously, of course, a higher interest rate will reduce the proceeds demand function, X, which would tend to reduce the price level.[28] If businessmen mark up prices over interest costs, the net effect on the price level will depend on whether the demand or supply function is affected most by higher interest rates. Most economists disregard the interest-cost push, but if they were polled, they would probably conclude that the reduction in demand would swamp the supply effect. In the financing of capital assets, interest is a long-run, fixed cost to firms. Only current refinancing is subject to higher interest costs.[29] Therefore, the immediate impact of a higher interest rate on supply would be relatively small. Furthermore, only a very small number of industries, such as public utilities, obviously determine their prices on the basis of a markup over costs, explicitly including interest as a cost.

---

[27]John H. Hotson, "Adverse Effects of Tax and Interest Hikes as Strengthening the Case for Incomes Policies—Or A Part of the Elephant," *Canadian Journal of Economics*, 4 (May 1971), 164–81.

[28]Hotson believes that purchasing power is transferred to rentiers when interest rates are increased, and that the increased consumption by rentiers may offset the decrease in investment expenditures. In such a case, actual demand would remain unchanged (or could even increase). Thus the effect of higher interest rates may not reduce demand. However, higher interest rates reduce the value of previously existing bonds, so bondholders may experience a negative-wealth effect. The higher income on new bonds would have to be sufficiently high to offset the windfall wealth effect on existing bonds.

[29]This point applies especially to firms that finance capital assets with noncallable bonds.

Higher taxes, like higher interest rates, are generally considered counter-inflationary, since taxes are paid partly with money earmarked for consumption. Therefore, higher taxes are assumed to reduce demand and fight inflation. However, the actual result of a tax depends largely on its type. According to standard micro theory, taxes on pure profits (or any other economic surplus) cannot be shifted forward to consumers in the form of higher prices. But that theory assumes profit maximizing in the short run. A non-profit-maximizing firm, such as a markup pricer with monopoly power, may, as a reflex, increase his selling price as a short-run response to an increase in taxes on profits.[30] Other taxes, such as sales taxes, are generally recognized as capable of being passed on to consumers in part, even by profit-maximizing competitive firms. Therefore, the deflationary impact of tax increases is not as clear and unambiguous as many writers have suggested.

The present model, based on empirical evidence of a nearly constant wage share, incorporates a constant markup without explaining its origin. Some feel that markup pricing is more realistic than marginal-cost pricing in a world of imperfect competition, even though it does not necessarily optimize any of the firm's goals (except for the survival value of not rocking the boat). Strict markup pricing implies that firms are probably not maximizing profits in the short run, except coincidentally, and that administered pricing is the norm.

One drawback to the Weintraub–Hotson type of inflation model is that it takes the monetary system as exogenous. Changes in the stock of money or the interest rate cause shifts in proceeds-demand and -supply functions. Monetary effects are central to most standard analyses of inflation and so should, if possible, be included, since inflation is essentially a monetary phenomenon.[31]

THE PHILLIPS CURVE: AN EMPIRICAL ANALYSIS OF INFLATION

The Structure

Without unduly concerning himself with theorizing about the causes of inflation, A.W. Phillips has computed an empirical negative relationship between the rate of inflation and the rate of unemployment, two rates that appear to dominate contemporary economic thinking.[32]

---

[30]Higher taxes on profits could reduce the MEC (reducing investment demand in the short run) and ultimately lead to a smaller plant, a reduced aggregate-supply curve, and higher prices in the long run as a result of less output.

[31]The model can be integrated with the usual *IS–LM* analysis. However, by treating the money stock as the *real* money stock (M/P) and determining P at each real-income level in Figure 13-6, it can be determined how much nominal money is required to increase the real-money stock by a given amount.

[32]A. W. Phillips, "The Relation Between Unemployment and the Rate of Change of Money Wage Rates in the United Kingdom, 1861–1957," *Economica*, 25 (November, 1958), 283–99.

The Phillips curve is shown in Figure 13-7, with the rate of unemployment plotted along the horizontal axis and the rate of inflation along the vertical axes. The left-hand vertical axis shows the rate of price inflation and the right-hand axis that of wage inflation. Wage increases are assumed to run ahead of price increases by about 3 percent, to allow for an observed annual increase of about 3 percent in worker productivity.

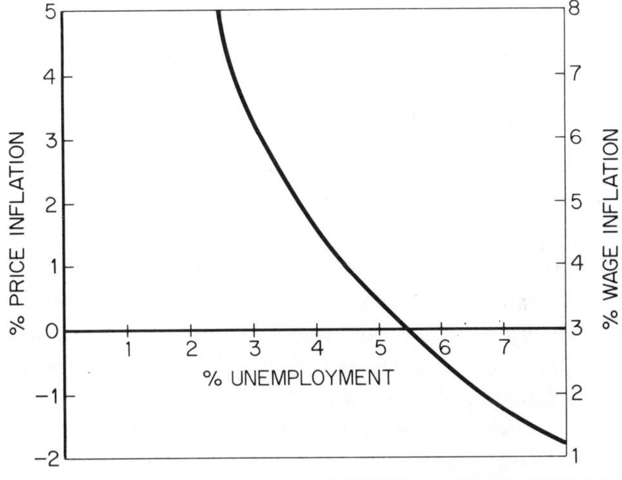

FIG. 13-7 The Phillips Curve

A leftward movement along the curve in the direction of fuller employment also moves the economy in the direction of higher rates of inflation, while a rightward movement along the curve, which could lead toward wage and price stability, leads in the direction of a higher rate of unemployment. For example, on the theoretical Phillips curve drawn in the figure, if we assume that $2\frac{1}{2}$ percent is a practical lower limit to the rate of unemployment, we would face a 5 percent annual rate of price inflation and an 8 percent rate of wage inflation, as long as the curve remains unchanged. On the other hand, price stability could be achieved only if we were willing to accept an unemployment rate of $5\frac{1}{2}$ percent with an annual wage increase averaging 3 percent.

The Cause

As a possible explanation of the shape of the Phillips curve, it has been suggested that each firm attempts to maintain some desired differential between its wage rate and wages paid by other firms.[33] This differential is set at a level that maintains a satisfactory labor turnover in the firm, to mini-

[33] R. G. Lipsey, "The Relation Between Unemployment and the Rate of Change of Money Wage Rates in the United Kingdom, 1861–1957: A Further Analysis," *Economica*, 27 (February 1960), 1–31.

mize search costs incurred in filling vacancies. Therefore, increased labor turnover is a signal for the firm to reevaluate its wage policy. Consequently, if an increase in aggregate demand reduces the unemployment rate, labor turnover will increase.

In order to maintain its turnover at the acceptable level, the firm will raise the wages it pays, to increase the differential between the wages of its workers and those elsewhere. The attempt of all firms to increase the wage differential between themselves and other firms cannot be completely successful, and will cause further increases in per unit labor costs, though higher wages may induce new workers into the labor market. Higher wages cause the cost of production to increase by the amount of the wage increase less any productivity increase.

If the firm, especially one using markup pricing, expects a change in money wages—say, 3 percent a year—and thinks that these higher costs can be passed on to its customers through higher prices, then it will raise wages by 3 percent in excess of productivity increases, to maintain the wage differential at the going level. If the firm is satisfied with the going wage differential and labor turnover, it will merely increase wages every year by the expected change in aggregate average wages, without any effect on unemployment. To reduce its labor turnover, it will have to increase its wages more than the expected change in average wages.

An increase in the rate of price and wage inflation will be associated with a reduction of unemployment if the expected increase in prices and wages was zero, or at least, less than what occurred. To illustrate how this theory could work to form the Phillips curve, suppose we are experiencing a $5\frac{1}{2}$ percent unemployment rate, constant prices, and a 3 percent annual wage increase—shown by the point where the Phillips curve crosses the horizontal axis in Figure 13-7. Now, suppose aggregate demand increases. More workers will be desired to produce the extra output than are available at the going wage. Consequently, labor turnover will increase. Each firm may increase its wages in an attempt to reduce its growing turnover. But the attempt must be at least partially unsuccessful in the aggregate, if firms ultimately bid workers away from each other.

The rate of wage inflation increases, and firms faced with higher labor costs will mark up their prices proportionately. As prices and wages increase, the unemployment rate will fall if the labor supply has a normal, positive slope, and a decreasing unemployment rate accompanying inflation gives the Phillips curve its shape.

If all firms are satisfied with their labor turnover, and therefore with the wage differentials that exist between their own and other firms, any anticipated wage and price increases will not lead to a reduction in unemployment. In fact, two of the authors who have proposed this idea believe that a satisfactory wage differential between firms defines a "natural" rate of unemployment.[34] Lerner has pointed out, however, that the natural rate of

[34] E. S. Phelps, *Microeconomic Foundations of Employment and Inflation Theory* (New York: Norton, 1970), p. 12; and Milton Friedman, "The Role of Monetary Policy,"

unemployment may be unacceptably high from society's standpoint.[35] Those who propose this theory point out that although unemployment can be reduced temporarily through inflation, there is no permanent trade-off between the two. The temporary reduction in unemployment through inflation is a result of unanticipated inflation, which practically means a rising rate of inflation, on the implied assumption that business expects a continuation of the past rate.

Expectations of increases in the rate of inflation would cause an upward shift in the Phillips curve, which would be consistent with an increased rate of inflation at any given rate of unemployment.

Anticipated increases in inflation will most likely breed increased wage demands, which in turn will induce further inflation. This could lead to a continuous upward shift in the Phillips curve. On the other hand, inflationary pressures may be mitigated by increases in labor productivity. Such increases would shift the Phillips curve to the left, allowing price stability at lower rates of unemployment.

DIAGNOSIS AND CONTROL OF INFLATION

Diagnosis

In recent years, a favorite pastime among economists has been for the proponents of each of the different theories of inflation to support their own views with statistical evidence. This discussion over the years has not produced a consensus, and the main conclusion from the debate is that statistical "proofs" of theoretical constructs are generally futile.[36] Even in relatively clear-cut cases, such as the inflation associated with the latter stages of World War II, the Korean War, and the Vietnam War, where most of the inflationary pressure was clearly of the demand-pull variety, the bottlenecks that developed during the war or during the conversion from war to peace caused a certain amount of cost-push, markup, structural, and ex ante pressure on the economy. In contrast, when inflation was accompanied by increases in unemployment, as in 1957–58 or 1969–71, the apparent cost-push basis of the inflation was also accompanied by inflationary expectations, structural problems, and markups induced by the cost push. Even where it appears that either demand pull or cost push has the stronger influence, it is impossible to determine the degree to which each type of pressure is responsible for the

---

American Economic Review, 58 (March 1968), 11. Friedman would include market imperfections such as the costs of gathering information about job vacancies, mobility on the part of workers, and the cost of discovering and enticing labor by employers. If the time span of frictional unemployment is defined as search time, then the "natural" rate of unemployment would be similar to "full employment." However, an extended search time could cause an apparently horizontal labor supply curve with "Keynesian unemployment."

[35]Conversations with Abba P. Lerner, April 3 and 4, 1972, at the University of South Florida.

[36]Alvin H. Hansen, *Economic Issues of the 1960's* (New York: McGraw-Hill, 1960), pp. 9 and 10.

inflation. And in cases less clear-cut than the wartime or recession situations mentioned above, it is virtually impossible to pin down conclusively the main source of inflation.

Why is it so difficult to determine empirically what causes inflation? The first problem involves time lags. Logically, the factor that initiates the inflation should occur at a time prior to the general price increase. However, the lag between the cause and effect may be too short to be observed, since data are generally collected quarterly, or at best monthly, and the effect may be reported within the same time period as the cause. It is also possible that there may be no time lag or that the time lag may be negative. For example, when ex ante inflation occurs, prices are raised on the basis of *predicted* demand-pull or cost-push pressures. In this case, prices may go up even before the basic, measurable, causal element occurs.

On the other hand, even when the original cause of the price increase is eliminated, ex ante inflation may still occur, because the economy expects further increases in prices. For example, in 1969 and 1970, even though counterinflationary monetary and fiscal policies had by that time caused a decrease in aggregate demand, which in turn increased unemployment and decreased production, prices continued to rise because of inflationary pressures built up during the overheated late 1960's, mainly from demand-pull pressures.

In cost-push or markup inflation, it may be particularly difficult to determine the cause, because an administered price increase may occur almost simultaneously with a wage increase. It may be impossible to tell which was the initiating factor, since the firm and the workers will each blame the other. To further complicate the matter, the side that first raised its price may have done so in anticipation of a move by the other.

Another difficulty in assigning the cause of inflation is that economic growth may increase the marginal product of labor and lead to higher wages, which are not inflationary as long as the percentage of wage increase does not exceed the percentage of increase in labor productivity. Therefore, when labor productivity increases, higher wages are not a legitimate source of cost-push inflation. Contrary to the popular view, if wages increase at a faster rate than prices, it is not necessarily evidence that wage-push inflation has occurred, since a gain in labor productivity, by itself, is deflationary without a wage increase. For example, if worker productivity increases by 3 percent and prices rise by 2 percent, wages would have to rise by 5 percent to maintain labor's relative share of aggregate output.[37]

Even during periods of excess demand there is a limit to the number of new workers the labor market can absorb within any given period of time. So, during years when large numbers of new workers are entering the labor force, the data would show an increase in the unemployment rate, when actually the problem is simply one of allowing time for new workers to be absorbed.

---

[37]Thus, a wage freeze automatically increases profits if productivity increases.

How can we isolate "the cause" of a general inflation that results from countless pricing decisions involving thousands of commodities, with some prices determined by rule-of-thumb markup, some determined under competitive supply and demand conditions, while still others result from price leaders attempting to achieve some optimum mix of sales volume and profits while others are attempting to achieve a target return? In addition, the constant change in expectations and economic conditions means that the cause of inflation will vary from time to time. The lack of consensus regarding the cause of inflation is probably healthy, because it leaves us with a number of alternative theories and leaves us free to make use of the theory which seems to apply best in a particular situation.

Controls

The policy to counter inflation should vary depending on the cause of the inflation, and multiple causes require a package of policies. For example, demand-pull inflation can best be handled by reducing aggregate demand through restrictive monetary or fiscal policy. The same restrictive policies directed at cost-push inflation would have the undesirable side effect of increasing unemployment. Cost-push inflation can better be handled through some form of wage and price control. The wage-price guidelines that seemed to work during the early 1960's represented an attempt to prevent the development of cost-push inflation. However, when demand-pull inflationary pressures developed in the course of the Vietnam War, the guidelines broke down, since they were designed to combat a different kind of inflation. In addition, once inflation gets started, expectations of further inflation may become self-justifying and create a situation in which only a recession, or direct controls such as the wage–price freeze in mid-1971, can end these expectations.

Employment, Inflation, and Economic Policy

The Phillips curve indicates that employment may be reduced by an *unanticipated rising rate*, not by a *high rate*, of inflation. The ill effects of inflationary expectations on employment, discussed above, support the idea that recessions perform a positive economic function. If a recession can wring out of the economy all anticipations of inflation (as the 1969–71 recession failed to do), then the short-term unemployment incurred during the recession is the price paid to reposition the Phillips curve and permit fuller employment with less inflation in the subsequent recovery. Recent experience has led many to feel that inflationary expectations are more difficult to exorcise than had previously been thought. The more deeply entrenched that inflationary expectations become, the more severe the recession required to eliminate them. The consensus in the early 1970's was that a severe recession was politically unfeasible because of the high unemployment rate that would result, and therefore that the inflation would continue because the government would be forced to rescue the economy from the recession it had staged to fight inflation in the first place. The subsequent imposition of direct controls represented a second attempt to eliminate inflationary expectations.

Some propose that sufficient increases in labor productivity and economic growth could solve the conflict between full employment and price stability, by relieving the motive for continual inflation—namely, to increase one's share of GNP, if necessary at the expense of others. When increases in output are low (or even negative), each group in the economy can increase its own share of the stagnating total output only by obtaining a higher price for its own output or a higher wage for its labor. Any such attempt for whatever reason will lead to total claims in excess of 100 percent of output, and will cause "seller's inflation," as sellers of resources, goods, and services all attempt to get a bigger share of the economic pie by raising their selling prices. Inflationary pressures of this sort can be relieved by a healthy rate of growth, which permits a satisfactory increase in aggregate real income for all groups in the economy even if they do not receive a greater-than-average increase in money income.

SUMMARY AND CONCLUSIONS

In this chapter, we have considered various theories of inflation, including demand pull, cost push, structural, ex ante, wage push, markup, and a labor-turnover model. Each of these theories identifies different elements as the basic causal factor of inflation. It is a virtual impossibility to determine conclusively "the cause" of any particular inflation; yet, without identifying the cause, effective control of inflation is impossible. Therefore, despite all difficulties, it is imperative that the basic causal element in any inflation be identified as precisely as possible.

The effects of inflation are quite varied. A mild inflation may even have a somewhat beneficial, tonic effect, whereas hyperinflation is always disastrous. The income-distribution effects of inflation are profound. Inflation rewards debtors, speculators, and enterprisers, and it penalizes fixed-income recipients and workers already employed, provided they cannot push their wages up to match price increases.

The Phillips curve describes an observed phenomenon that the rate of both unemployment and inflation are normally inversely related, an observation consistent with the theory of demand-pull inflation. As a possible explanation to the shape of the Phillips curve, it was suggested that an increase in aggregate demand could trigger a requirement for more workers, causing higher labor turnover. Firms raise wages to reduce turnover, and then mark up their selling price on the basis of their increased labor cost. Anticipated inflation can shift the Phillips curve to the right and lead to further realized inflation with no corresponding reduction in unemployment or increase in output. Unanticipated inflation reduces unemployment, but once inflation occurs, further inflation often becomes expected. Therefore, inflation is often only a short-term solution to unemployment. Growth or controls seem to be the only long-term solution to inflation and to the conflict between stable prices and full employment in a world in which cost-push pressures are continually present.

QUESTIONS AND PROBLEMS

1. Can inflation be considered simply increasing prices? If not, what is inflation?
2. Why might prices have an upward bias?
3. Discuss the harmful effects of inflation.
4. Is inflation entirely harmful? If not, why not?
5. What are the effects of hyperinflation?
6. At what point does inflation become hyperinflation?
7. List the main causes of inflation in an industrial economy.
8. Is demand-pull inflation self-limiting?
9. Why are unions often cited as a cause of cost-push inflation? Is the citation justified, in your opinion?
10. Is structural inflation likely to affect a primitive, undeveloped economy? Why, or why not?
11. Does ex ante inflation help explain the experience of the United States in the late 1960's and early 1970's?
12. What does the Phillips curve imply about politicians who promise to stop inflation and end unemployment?

Dynamic Inflation Models

appendix to chapter 13

As we have mentioned, demand-pull inflation does not lead to a stable, static equilibrium. Whenever the aggregate demand and aggregate supply curves intersect to the right of full employment, demand-pull inflation causes a continual inflationary process. In this Appendix, we consider demand-pull inflation from a dynamic viewpoint and demonstrate how a continual inflationary process may develop.

BENT HANSEN'S INFLATION MODEL

Figure 13A-1 illustrates a dynamic inflation model that has been developed by Bent Hansen.[1] The price level (P), deflated by the average-wage level (W), (the reciprocal of the real wage), is plotted along the y-axis to adjust the price level of final output for changes in the labor cost of producing that output; and aggregate real income or output is plotted along the x-axis.

This model uses aggregate supply and demand as developed in Chapter 12, except that here we allow the average money wage level to change. Assume that the aggregate supply and demand curves initially intersect at point e, to the right of the full-employment level of aggregate income, $\bar{Y}$. Since point e cannot be achieved, an initial unstable equilibrium occurs at point d, where the aggregate-demand function, D, crosses the full-employment inelastic segment of the aggregate-supply function, cS', at a price–wage ratio of $(P/W)_1$.

However, at point d, the price level is high enough relative to the average-wage level that suppliers of goods and services try to move out to point a, where the demand for labor exceeds the supply at the going wage, as indicated by the quantity of excess aggregate supply, equal to the distance between point a and point d. Producers would like to supply Y' at $(P/W)_1$ price–wage ratio, but they cannot, because Y' exceeds the full-employment output, $\bar{Y}$. Consequently, because of the labor shortage, wages will be bid up. If the real wage rises sufficiently to drive P/W down to $(P/W)_2$, wages become stable but prices are bid up by excess demand, equal to the distance between points b and c, because aggregate demand exceeds the full-employment output at that price–wage ratio. Then, as prices rise, P/W also rises from $(P/W)_2$ back toward $(P/W)_1$. The model indicates that a stable equilibrium is not achievable as long as aggregate supply-and-demand equilibrium occurs to the right of full employment.

A key determinant of the level of P/W is the flexibility of wages and prices relative

[1]Bent Hansen, *A Study in the Theory of Inflation* (London: Allen & Unwin, 1961), Chap. 7.

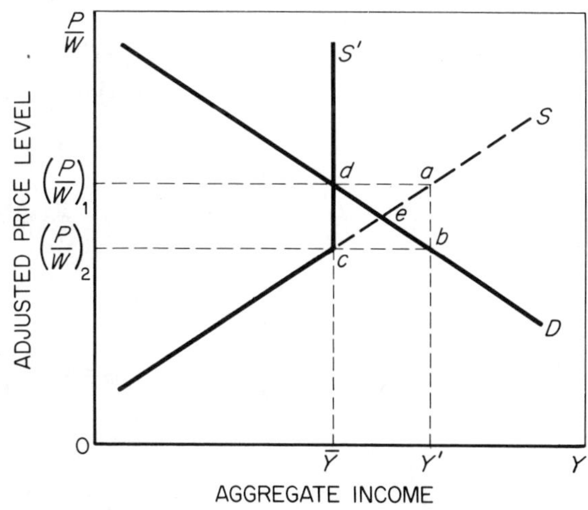

FIG. 13A-1 Bent Hansen Inflation Model

to each other. The more flexible prices are relative to wages, the closer to $(P/W)_1$ the value of P/W becomes; the more rigid prices are relative to wages, the closer to $(P/W)_2$.

This model, based on the work of Bent Hansen, pinpoints the sources of inflationary pressure in the economy and provides some insights into the actual process of inflation. However, as Ackley suggests, the Hansen theory fails to specify the rate at which inflation will occur.[2] In the following section, we will describe a simple model in which the rate of inflation can be determined.

A WICKSELLIAN INFLATIONARY MODEL

In this section, we present a simplified version of a Wicksellian type of inflation model, based on the work of Knut Wicksell.[3] The model is based on the following assumptions: (1) Consumption in each period (C_t) is assumed to be 60 percent of the previous period's money income (Y_{t-1}^M). (2) Real investment plans will be carried out regardless of changes in the price level, if necessary by using credits created by the banking system to finance new investments. (3) Money income in each time period (Y_t^M) equals the nominal value of consumption plus nominal expenditure on investment during that time period. (4) Real income is assumed to remain constant at the full-employment level of output, \$800 billion in this example. (5) Banks are assumed to provide investors with new bank-credit money at the rate of 5 percent in each time period. Such an increase would require the cooperation of the monetary authorities, since additional reserves would be needed each year. (6) Income velocity is assumed to remain constant at 4 throughout the analysis.

The process of inflation is traced through ten time periods in Table 13A-1. Column 2, labeled Y_{t-1}^M, represents money income earned during the previous time period. Column 3, labeled C_t^M, shows the proportion of the previous period's money income spent on consumption. Retaining our assumption of a one-period time lag in nominal consumption, each period's consumption, C_t^M, is spent with

[2]Gardner Ackley, *Macroeconomic Theory* (New York: MacMillan, 1961), pp. 436–39.

[3]Knut Wicksell, *Lectures on Political Economy*, trans. E. Classen (London: Routledge & Kegan Paul, 1935), Vol. II, pp. 190–214.

TABLE 13A-1 Wicksellian Inflation Model (in billions of $)*

(1)	(2) Money Income in Previous Time Period	(3) Current Consumption Expenditure	(4) Current Money Savings	(5) Current Investment Expenditure	(6) Effective Money Demand	(7) Stock of Money	(8) Change in Stock of Money times Velocity	(9) Current Price Index
t	Y_{t-1}^M	C_t^M	S_t^M	I_t^M	D_t^M	M_t	$\Delta M(V)$	P_t
0	$ 800	$480	$320	$320	$ 800	$200	—	100
1	800	480	320	360	840	210	40	105
2	840	504	336	376	880	220	40	110
3	880	528	352	400	928	232	48	116
4	928	557	371	419	976	244	48	122
5	976	586	390	438	1024	256	48	128
6	1024	614	410	458	1072	268	48	134
7	1072	643	429	485	1128	282	56	141
8	1128	677	451	507	1184	296	56	148
9	1184	710	474	530	1240	310	56	155
10	1240	744	496	560	1304	326	64	163

$D_t^M = C_t^M + I_t^M$

$C_t^M = bY_{t-1}^M$

$S_t^M = (1 - b)Y_{t-1}^M$

$I_t^M = S_t^M + \Delta M\ (V)$, assuming $V = 4$

**Any discrepancies are due to rounding.*

money income received by the end of the previous time period, Y_{t-1}^M. Therefore, $C_t^M = bY_{t-1}^M$, where b is the marginal propensity to consume out of the previous period's money income. Assuming that we are dealing with a long-run nominal-consumption function that radiates out of the origin, no positive y-axis intercept is necessary.

Colum 4, S_t^M, represents nominal savings, the residual after subtracting nominal consumption in the present period from money income received by the end of the previous period. Therefore,

$$S_t^M = (1 - b)Y_{t-1}^M$$

Since last year's money income must be either consumed or saved during the current time period,

$$Y_{t-1}^M = C_t^M + S_t^M$$

Current nominal investment plans, I_t^M, shown in column 5, may be greater than money savings, since any excess of nominal investment over money savings will be financed by additional money created by the banking system.

The plans of investors are assumed to be equal to available money savings plus newly created purchasing power (incremental increases in the money stock times income velocity). Therefore, investors are assumed willing to undertake as many projects as they are able to finance, because we assume that during inflation there exists no shortage of apparently profitable nominal-investment opportunities. In Wicksellian terms, the natural rate exceeds the market rate. Investment in nominal terms, I_t^M, may be stated

$$I_t^M = S_t^M + \Delta M(V)$$

where V is assumed constant (thus by assumption eliminating the Keynes effect).

Column 6, D_t^M, is equal to the effective money demand—nominal consumption plus nominal investment—during the current time period.

$$D_t^M = C_t^M + I_t^M$$

The inflationary gap in money terms is equal to the difference between column 6, effective demand stated in money terms, and column 2, the money income available from the previous time period to finance effective demand. Although the money value of the gap between columns 6 and 2 grows continuously, the real inflationary gap—that is, the percentage of excess real demand to be financed in each time period—remains constant.

Column 7, M_t, is the stock of money required to finance effective demand in each time period. Column 8 shows the change in the stock of money, multiplied by a constant income velocity, which is equal to 4 in this illustration. The change in $M(V)$ is equal to the additional financing required to fill the gap between D_t^M and Y_{t-1}^M in each period.

Finally, column 9 shows the price level, P_t, required to clear the market. As long as V and real income remain constant, P_t must increase at the same rate as M_t to maintain supply-and-demand equilibrium.

In each time period, the effective money demand in column 6 equals the amount of purchasing power carried over from the previous time period (column 2), plus the newly created financing made available during the current time period (column 8).

The Wicksellian type of inflation persists as long as excess demand in real terms continues and as long as the banking system can finance it. As you will recall from Chapter 6, the opportunity for inflation exists whenever the market rate of interest is below the natural rate that equates real savings and investment. The device that halts inflation in the Wicksellian model is the realignment of the two rates. This realignment would take place if the real investment or consumption functions were to decrease, or if the banks raised their interest rates to the level where the supply of real savings equaled the demand for real investment.

In our example in Table 13A-1, the effective demand of $800 billion in base period 0 is the income received by the end of period 0, which is available at the start of period 1 to finance nominal expenditures. However, total money expenditures during period 1 are greater than the $800 billion received to start the period, because the nominal demand for investment is greater than the money supply of savings. The excess nominal demand for investment of $40 billion is financed by an increase of $10 billion in the stock of money, which when multiplied by the income velocity is sufficient to finance excess planned nominal investment. As a result of more bank financing, the price level increases from 100 to 105, since the $40 billion increase in financing increases total money spending by 5 percent. But real income is fixed at the full-employment level of $800 billion; therefore, excess demand can be reflected only as a price increase. Since the effective money demand of period 1 becomes the money income available at the start of period 2, the $840 billion effective demand stated in money terms for period 1 becomes the figure out of which nominal consumption and money savings plans are made for period 2. However, in period 2, as in period 1, nominal consumption plus nominal investment is greater than nominal consumption plus money savings, and so the process continues, with prices increasing at a constant rate throughout.

It makes no difference whether or not total real-investment demand is satisfied by the available financing, as long as the rate of growth in the stock of money and income velocity are constant, and as long as the real demand for investment is at least equal to $S^M + \Delta M(V)$. However, if real investment demand exceeds $S_t^M + \Delta M(V)$, then some investors will be unable to satisfy their demands for monetary investments. And part of the demand for real investment will be frustrated by the process of inflation.

In our model, because consumption is lagged and because the new bank credits are assumed to go only to investors, there is, in each time period after the base period, a certain amount of income redistributed from consumers to investors. (This model tacitly assumes that the MPC is unaffected by the redistribution of income.) Other, similar models have been built incorporating, for example, a wage lag that would increase the redistribution effect from consumers to investors. In contrast, a dynamic wage-push inflation model would reverse the redistribution effect, since the wage adjustments would lead the inflationary process rather than lag behind it.

In the Wicksellian model, the redistribution effect is due to inflation and forced saving, which occur because money is created by banks and loaned to investors. Therefore, in each period, investors have a larger proportion of total purchasing power than they would have had without receiving the bank loans. As a result, more resources are devoted to investment and less to consumption in each period than would have occurred in the absence of the bank loans. The difference between the levels of real consumption with and without the bank loans to investors is the amount of forced saving, or more precisely, forced abstinence from consumption.

The Wicksellian type of divergent inflation model described in Table 13A-1 is illustrated in Figure 13A-2, with the components of the effective money demand, C_t^M and I_t^M, plotted along the y-axis, and Y_{t-1}^M plotted along the x-axis. In the short run without inflation, up to the point where $Y_{t-1}^M = \$800$ billion, I_1 and I_2 are shown as constants, on the assumption that all real investment plans will be realized. In order to purchase the planned amount of real investment goods, firms must be willing to raise their nominal investment expenditures as required whenever prices rise. Since every increase in the price level defeats their goal, businesses must further raise their money-investment expenditures in order to achieve their desired proportion of the new higher level of money income. This proportion determines

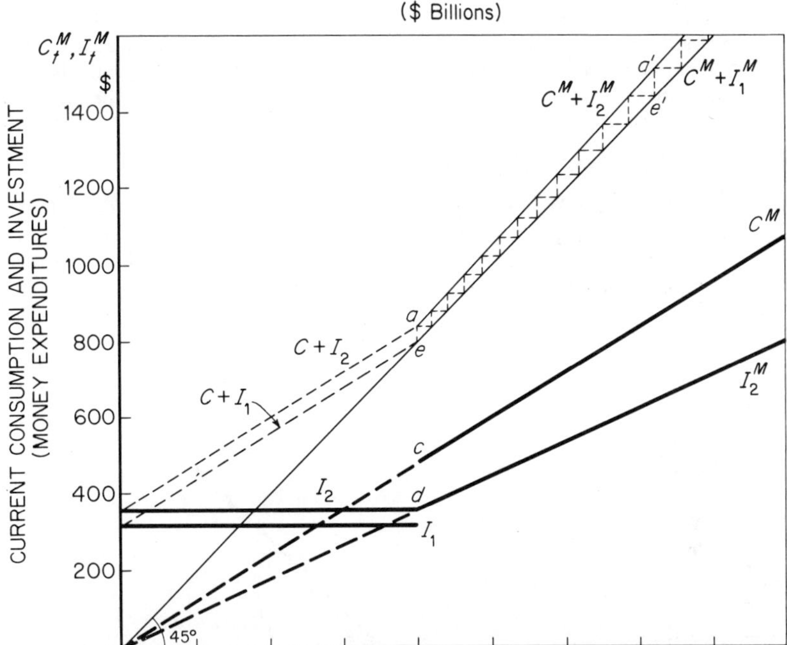

FIG. 13A-2 Wicksellian Inflation Model

the slope of I_2^M beyond point *d*, which is constantly maintained after prices start to increase.

We retain the assumption that consumption is a constant proportion of money income. Therefore, the MPC and APC are equal, so the nominal consumption function must pass through the origin. In base period 0, an increase in real-investment expenditures from I_1 to I_2 at point *d* creates an inflationary gap, starting at an income level, Y_{t-1}, of \$800 billion. Because both consumers and investors are determined to maintain their relative shares in the distribution of income, the inflationary gap, *a-e*, will be perpetuated and maintained proportionately. Therefore, as money income grows beyond \$800 billion, the inflationary gap grows absolutely, because $C^M + I_2^M$ grows at a constant rate, which is in excess of the slope of the 45° reference line. For example, the original inflationary gap, *a-e*, where Y_{t-1} is \$800 billion, is only half the absolute size of the gap at *a′-e′*, where Y_{t-1}^M equals \$1,380 billion, although the relative size of the gap has remained a constant proportion of effective demand.

The steps through which the economy moves in the inflationary process are drawn in between the 45° line and the $C^M + I_2^M$ curve beyond the \$800 billion real-income level where the process of inflation begins. The first ten steps in Figure 13A-2 are graphic representations of the relationship between the data in columns 2 and 6 of Table 13A-1, with the horizontal part of each step representing the change in Y_{t-1}^M that accompanies the movement from one time period to the next, and the vertical distance representing the inflationary gap.

Income velocity is assumed to remain constant. However, it seems reasonable that as prices increase and as the value of money falls in consequence, asset holders might desire a smaller proportion of money in their portfolios, and so income velocity would tend to increase as money is traded for real assets. Therefore, part of the nominal incremental investment may be financed by an increase in income velocity, and only part need be financed by an increase in the stock of money.

A CONVERGENT INFLATION MODEL

Whereas the Wicksellian divergent inflation model presents a situation in which the inflationary gap continually grows absolutely away from equilibrium, it is also possible to propose a situation in which the process of inflation will terminate in a stable equilibrium. Such a situation is depicted in Figure 13A-3, where the same

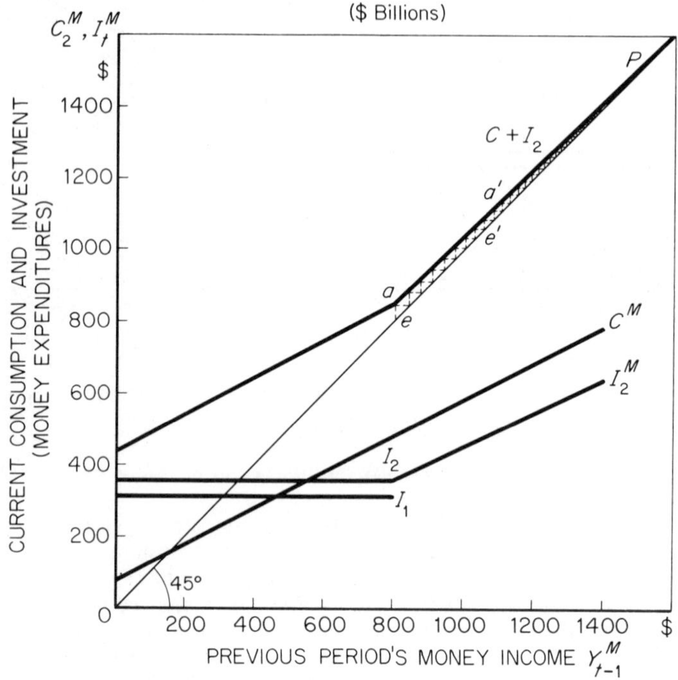

FIG. 13A-3 Convergent Inflation Model

data are plotted on the two axes as in Figure 13A-2. The investment function is also identical to that of 13A-2, and the inflationary process is again started by an increase in effective investment demand from I_1 to I_2, which causes an inflationary gap of *a-e*.

Although consumers increase their nominal consumption expenditures after inflation begins, they fail to maintain their position in the distribution of real income because investment expenditures increase proportionately more than consumption expenditures. In the situation illustrated in Figure 13A-3, the process of inflation terminates in an equilibrium, because the consumption function has a positive *y*-axis intercept, and therefore eventually intersects the 45° reference line. The MPC no longer equals the APC as it does in the previous model, where the consumption function radiates out of the origin. If the consumption function remains unchanged, then a rightward movement along the consumption function means that the MPC remains constant but that the APC decreases.[4] A lower APC brings about a higher average propensity to save, APS, which means that a higher proportion of consumers' incomes go to savings and a smaller proportion to consumption. The increased investment expenditure that initiates the inflation gives investors a larger share of real output and consumers a smaller share.

The decreasing share of real output purchased by consumers in each time period as the APC decreases narrows the inflationary gap proportionately in every round of spending. For example, the inflationary gap *a-e* in Figure 13A-3 is twice the magnitude of the *a′-e′* gap halfway through the inflationary process.

As in the case of Figure 13A-2, each step in 13A-3 represents one time period. However, in this convergent situation, the APC is greater than the MPC but approaches the MPC as a limit every time money income increases. Therefore, the steps become increasingly small and finally converge on an equilibrium at point *P*. A short-run, linear consumption function (one with a positive slope less than 1 and a positive *y*-axis intercept) leads to a convergent model, where inflation will eventually end. The shape of the investment and consumption functions in Figure 13A-3 implies that investors are not subject to money illusion when prices rise, because they attempt to maintain their share of real output in spite of higher prices (even though they may in the short run be forced to settle for a smaller share as real income rises when no inflation occurs). However, consumers may be subject to money illusion, if their falling APC demonstrates that they are willing to let their share of total output fall as money incomes rise. If consumers insisted on maintaining their share of total real output and were able to finance their purchases, then at the point where inflation begins, the short-run consumption function would be kinked upward sufficiently to make the APC equal the MPC, and as a result, a divergent inflationary process would replace the convergent case.

CONCLUSION

We may conclude that, generally, any long-run consumption function that passes through the origin will induce a divergent inflationary process whenever investors (and consumers) attempt to maintain their original share of real output. However, a short-run consumption function with a positive *y*-axis intercept will induce a convergent inflationary process. The convergent model terminates in a stable, static equilibrium, whereas the divergent model produces constant inflation over time. Although they ignore aggregate supply, both these models go a step further than the Bent Hansen theory, which specifies the conditions under which inflation will take place but leaves the rate the inflation and the process of inflation undefined. However, the purpose of the Hansen model is to show that excess demand beyond full employment means that either wages or prices might be in equilibrium, but both cannot be simultaneously in equilibrium.

ADDITIONAL SELECTED REFERENCES

ACKLEY, G., *Macroeconomic Theory*, pp. 421–59. New York: Macmillan, 1961.

BACH, G. L., and A. ANDO, "The Redistribution Effects of Inflation," *Review of Economics and Statistics*, 39 (February 1957), 1–13.

[4]The consumption function in Figure 13A-3 is a straight line, with its slope equaling the MPC. (Remember, the slope of a straight line is constant.) An additional property of a straight-line consumption function is that if the APC is greater than the MPC, the APC will fall and approach the MPC.

BALL, R., *Inflation and the Theory of Money*. Chicago: Aldine, 1964.

BOWEN, W. G., and R. A. BERRY, "Unemployment Conditions and Movements of the Money Wage Level," *Review of Economics and Statistics*, 45 (May 1963), 163–72.

———, and S. H. MASTERS, "Shifts in the Composition of Demand and the Inflation Problem," *American Economic Review*, 54 (December 1964), 975–84.

BRECHLING, F., "The Trade-Off Between Inflation and Unemployment," *Journal of Political Economy*, 76 (July–August 1968), 712–37.

BRIMMER, A. F., "Inflation and Income Distribution in the United States," *Review of Economics and Statistics*, 53 (February 1971), 37–48.

BRONFENBRENNER, M., and F. D. HOLZMAN, "Survey of Inflation Theory," *American Economic Review*, 53 (September 1963), 593–661.

CAGAN, P., "The Monetary Dynamics of Hyperinflation," in *Studies in the Quantity Theory of Money*, ed. M. Friedman, pp. 25–117. Chicago: University of Chicago Press, 1956.

CORRY, B., and D. LAIDLER, "The Phillips Relation: A Theoretical Explanation," *Economica*, 34 (May 1967), 189–97.

DEPODWIN, H. J., and RICHARD T. SELDEN, "Business Pricing Policies and Inflation," *Journal of Political Economy*, 71 (April 1963), 116–27.

DUESENBERRY, J., "The Mechanics of Inflation," *Review of Economics and Statistics*, 32 (May 1950), 144–49.

FELDSTEIN, M., and O. ECKSTEIN, "The Fundamental Determinants of the Interest Rate," *Review of Economics and Statistics*, 52 (November 1970), 363–75.

FELLNER, W. J., "Postscript on War Inflation: A Lesson from World War II," *American Economic Review*, 37 (March 1947), 76–91.

GALLAWAY, L. E., "The Wage-Push Inflation Thesis, 1950–1957," *American Economic Review*, 48 (December 1958), 967–72.

GIBSON, W. E., "Interest Rates and Monetary Policy," *Journal of Political Economy*, 78 (May–June 1970), 431–55.

GRAHAM, F. D., *Exchange Prices and Production in Hyper-Inflation Germany, 1920–1923*. Princeton, N. J.: Princeton University Press, 1930.

HARRIS, S. E., "The Incidence of Inflation: Or Who Gets Hurt?" Study Paper No. 7. Employment, Growth and Price Levels, Joint Economic Committee, Congress of the United States, 1959.

HOLZMAN, F. D. "Inflation: Cost-Push and Demand-Pull," *American Economic Review*, 50 (March 1960), 20–42.

JOHNSON, H., "A Survey of Theories of Inflation," in *Essays in Monetary Economics*, pp. 104–42. Cambridge: Harvard University Press, 1967.

KESSEL, R. A., and A. A. ALCHIAN, "Effects of Inflation," *Journal of Political Economy*, 70 (December 1962), 521–37.

KOOPMANS, T., "The Dynamics of Inflation," *Review of Economics and Statistics*, 24 (May 1942), 53–65.

MACHLUP, F., "Another View of Cost-Push and Demand-Pull Inflation," *Review of Economics and Statistics*, 42 (May 1960), 125–39.

MEANS, G. C., "The Administered-Price Thesis Reconfirmed," *American Economic Review*, 62 (June 1972), 292–306.

MUNDELL, R. A., "Growth, Stability, and Inflationary Finance," *Journal of Political Economy*, 73 (April 1965), 97–109.

PERRY, G. L., "Inflation and Unemployment," in U.S. Savings and Loan League, *Savings and Residential Financing: 1970 Conference Proceedings*, pp. 30–45. Chicago: U.S. Savings and Loan League, 1970.

———, *Unemployment, Money Wage Rates, and Inflation.* Cambridge, Mass.: M.I.T. Press, 1966.

PHELPS, E. S., "The New Microeconomics in Inflation and Employment Theory," *American Economic Review*, 59 (May 1969), 147–60.

———, *Inflation Policy and Unemployment Theory.* New York: W. W. Norton, 1972.

REES, ALBERT, "The Phillips Curve as a Menu for Policy Choice," *Economica*, 37 (August 1970), 227–38.

SAMUELSON, P. A., and R. M. SOLOW, "Analytical Aspects of Anti-Inflation Policy," *American Economic Review*, 50 (May 1960), 177–94.

SARGENT, T. J., "Anticipated Inflation and Nominal Interest," *Quarterly Journal of Economics*, 86 (May 1972), 212–25.

SCHULTZE, C. L., "Has the Phillips Curve Shifted? Some Additional Evidence," *Brookings Papers on Economic Activity*, 2 (1971), 452–67.

SELDEN, R. T., "Cost-Push vs. Demand-Pull Inflation, 1955–1957," *Journal of Political Economy*, 67 (February 1959), 1–20.

SLICHTER, S. H., "Do the Wage-Fixing Arrangements in the American Labor Market Have an Inflationary Bias?" *American Economic Review*, 44 (May 1954), 322–46.

SMITHIES, A., "The Behavior of Money National Income Under Inflationary Conditions," *Quarterly Journal of Economics*, 57 (November 1942), 113–28.

WEINTRAUB, S., and H. HABIBAGAHI, "Money Supplies and Price-Output Indeterminateness: The Friedman Puzzle," *Journal of Economic Issues*, 6 (September 1972), 1–13.

WEISS, L. W., "Business Pricing Policies and Inflation Reconsidered," *Journal of Political Economy*, 74 (April 1966), 177–87.

YORDON, W. J., "Industrial Concentration and Price Flexibility in Inflation: Price Response Rates in Fourteen Industries, 1947–1958," *Review of Economics and Statistics*, 43 (August 1961), 287–94.

Money Matters

14

Is monetary policy effective? If the demand for investment is interest-inelastic, as empirical studies seem to show, then why do changes in monetary policy make headlines? One possible answer is that the data are misleading and that the demand for investment is in fact interest-elastic. A second possibility is that financial intermediaries ration credit and so make monetary policy effective *despite* an interest-inelastic demand for investment. Or perhaps both these possibilities combine to make monetary policy effective.

As we saw in Chapter 10, Keynesian theory gives monetary policy a significant role in combination with fiscal policy. The impact of monetary policy in the Keynesian system occurs through interest-rate changes that, on the assumption of an interest-elastic marginal efficiency of capital (MEC), determines the quantity of investment demanded. In contrast to the Keynesian theory, the first topic of this chapter—the credit-availability thesis—is a disequilibrium model that seeks to explain the impact of monetary policy through credit rationing by commercial banks, even if investment demand is interest-inelastic.

CREDIT AVAILABILITY

Practical financial attention is more often paid to the "looseness" or "tightness" of money than to the level of interest rates, because credit may be rationed not only through high or low interest rates but also through a more stringent screening process by banks and other lenders.

When the interest rate is set at a level that is too low to clear the market, credit rationing takes place because the supply of available credit may temporarily fall short of the quantity demanded *at the going interest rate.* If the banks themselves ration credit, even temporarily, through some means other than interest-rate changes, then for the duration of the rationing, the supply of loanable funds is less than the quantity demanded by borrowers. That is, during the lag, while the interest rate is too low, credit is rationed by administrative decisions of bankers and not by the price system through interest-rate changes.

The Commercial Banking System

The structure of the banking industry suggests one possible explanation of how and why the commercial banks might ration credit rather than change their interest rates. Only a limited number of banks serve any market area. The smaller the community, the smaller the number, and many communities or neighborhoods have only one bank. The reason for the small number of banks in each market area is partly the regulations restricting the entry of new firms into the banking industry. Banks may not cross state lines, and in some states, branch banking is illegal. Furthermore, bank regulations insure uniform behavior in the market by eliminating certain forms of price competition—for example, banks are not allowed to pay interest on demand deposits and are limited regarding the rate they can pay on savings deposits. Regulations and custom lead to bank conformity in commercial practices, such as uniform acounts and minimal, benign advertising. Furthermore, banks cooperate in many activities, such as clearing house arrangements, loan sharing, and correspondent relationships. Therefore, the existence of several thousand banks in the United States does not imply a highly competitive industry.[1]

Since each market area is allocated to only a few banks, they are forced into an awareness of interdependence. Any market structure involving a few interdependent firms fits the oligopolistic model, and the banks in small towns may even be monopolies or duopolies. Leading banks in financial centers are price leaders because of their location, power, and prestige. These price leaders are probably trying to maximize some utility function—perhaps size or prestige—as well as profits. Consequently, the market for the commercial banking system is best represented by a price-leadership oligopoly model in larger communities and possibly even by a monopoly or duopoly model in smaller towns. As one evidence of the oligopolistic nature of the

---

[1] There is a large literature on the noncompetitive nature of the banking industry and the stickiness of bank interest rates. For example, see Franklin R. Edwards, "Concentration in Banking and Its Effect on Business Loan Rates," *Review of Economics and Statistics*, 46 (August 1964), 294–300; Almarin Phillips, "Competition, Confusion, and Commercial Banking," *Journal of Finance*, 19 (March 1964), 32–45; and D. A. Alhadeff, "The Market Structure of Commercial Banking in the U.S.," *Quarterly Journal of Economics*, 65 (February 1951), 62–86.

banking industry, the more competitive Treasury-bill rate changes daily, but the prime bank rate has remained unchanged for as long as five years at a stretch.

Bank Behavior—Portfolio Balancing

How do banks, as financial asset holders, respond to a world of risk and uncertainty? As we saw in Chapter 7, an individual balances his asset portfolio by attempting to achieve certain objectives, such as a high rate of return or low risk. Similarly, banks attempt to balance their portfolios to achieve the highest yield obtainable at an acceptable risk. As in the case of an individual, diversification can be used to reduce risk when the assets held are independent of one another or negatively correlated in terms of their susceptibility to misfortune.

For example, a freeze in Florida could wipe out a bank that had loaned money only to Florida orange growers, since each orange grower is subject to the same risk. But if the bank had loaned half its money to orange growers and half to phosphate producers, who would have been unaffected by the freeze, half the loans would still be good, since the orange and phosphate industries are independent with respect to this type of risk. Or if the bank had loaned half its money to Florida orange growers and half to California orange growers, the loss of Florida oranges would mean higher prices for the California crop, so the risk correlation would be negative. (Note that the negative risk correlation is only with respect to a localized freeze. If some superior substitute for oranges were to appear on the market, *all* orange growers would suffer, and the geographical diversification by the bank would be immaterial.) Therefore, the more ways in which risks are unrelated or negatively correlated, the lower will be the risk undertaken by an asset holder. The recent movement of businesses to get into unrelated lines through conglomerate mergers may be at least partly explained as a technique to minimize risk through unrelated diversification.

The purchase of federal government securities permits the banker to hedge against certain types of risk, because such securities provide, besides risk diversification (assuming, realistically, that the bank buys them in addition to other securities and loans), a high degree of marketability or liquidity. They are traded in active markets and so are highly liquid and offer some protection against unexpected withdrawals, even though they are subject to market risk—the danger of a drop in the market price—a chance that increases when higher interest rates appear likely. In addition, they are free of default risk, and if the securities are purchased at a discount on the open market, part of the return is taxed as a capital gain. Only the interest is fully taxed.

Today, banks buy a significant amount of state and local government bonds. These are tax-free and also provide a high degree of risk diversification, since high-grade bonds of communities located in other parts of the country can be readily purchased, whereas bank loans are generally more geographically restricted. These securities are also traded in an active market, although it is not as active as the federal government bond market. Yet, this type of security is subject to default risk, although high-grade municipal securities are less subject to default than most bank loans.

Even though the return on bank loans is greater than the return on securities, the reduced marketability or liquidity, the greater default risk, the lack of tax advantages, and the greater transactions and handling costs at least partially balance the greater return, not even considering the diversification advantages of adding securities to the asset portfolio of the bank. (Remember, fixed-dollar securities are always subject to purchasing-power risk.)

Significantly, the overall risk of a well-balanced portfolio is less than the sum of the individual risks of the various securities it contains. Although banks always want a diversified portfolio, the degree of diversification will vary according to the goals of the particular bank and the relationship between risk and rate of return of the various alternative assets. Banks will tend to go more heavily into loans when the bank lending rate rises relative to the rate paid on securities and when there is a plentiful supply of borrowers whose credit capacity has not yet been exhausted.[2]

Commercial banks are risk averters, in the sense that they will accept higher risks only if offered a higher, compensatory rate of return. The tradeoff a risk-averting bank makes between risk and rate of return can be optimized by the bank manager only through the use of a probability distribution (which may be unconscious or intuitive) of the risk of gain or loss from various combinations of securities and loans available to him as he attempts to construct an ideal portfolio.

In practice, an ideally balanced portfolio may seldom be attained. During depressions, banks may be forced to carry excessive amounts of securities simply because of the lack of sufficient demand for loans at any positive rate of interest. During periods of tight money, banks may feel constrained to serve old customers (borrowers of long standing or large depositors) at the expense of their ideal portfolio balance, a policy in line with prudent bank management to maximize profits over the business cycle.[3] Banks face a risk apart from the usual business risk—the risk of antagonizing important customers; and banks may be forced grudgingly to depart from some ideal portfolio concept to minimize this risk.

---

[2]Donald R. Hodgman, "Credit Risk and Credit Rationing," *Quarterly Journal of Economics*, 74 (May 1960), 258–78.

[3]Traditional theory, as expounded in most money and banking texts, would explain the increase of loans during tight money not as an attempt by the banks to unload excess securities acquired during recessions, but as an almost reflex response by the banks when demand for loans increases. The traditional theory not only assumes that the banks prefer loans to other earning assets, since the banks are basically lending institutions, but that loans are always preferred by banks because the bank lending rate is normally higher than the rate paid on securities. This theory disregards the risk differential that must be deducted from the bank lending rate before the two rates can be compared, the risk reduction possible through portfolio diversification, and any tax advantages of securities.

The imperfectly competitive market in which banks operate permits credit rationing to occur; and portfolio balancing by the banks, combined with their oligopolistic behavior, can provide them with a motive to ration credit. The following model of the credit-availability thesis is a disequilibrium model, in the sense that it involves a bank interest rate that fails to clear the market.

Credit Availability Model Figure 14-1 illustrates the workings of the credit-availability model. We start with the economy in equilibrium at point a, the intersection of the investment-demand function, I_1, and the savings function, S. At point a, Q_1 quantity of real investment is demanded, and sufficient savings are supplied to finance it at a (Wicksellian) natural interest rate of i_1, the rate at which savings and investment are in equilibrium.

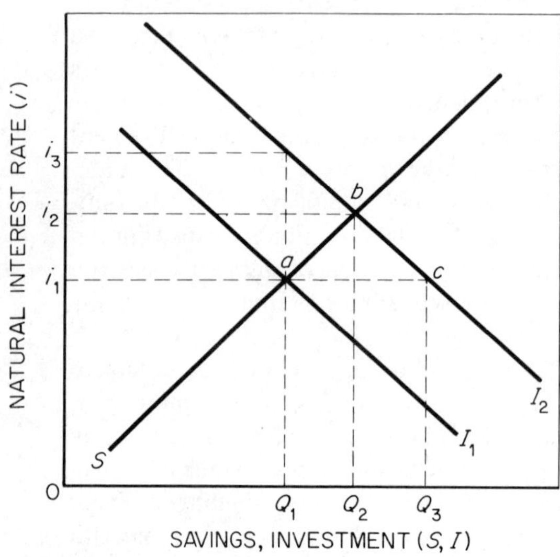

FIG. 14-1 Credit Availability

Assume that the investment demand curve increases from I_1 to I_2. Market equilibrium will move from point a to point b, and the natural rate will increase from i_1 to i_2. The competitively determined interest rate (which could be represented by a federal government-bond rate in this model) may be expected to follow the natural rate toward equilibrium at i_2 (allowing for a risk differential and assuming that monetary policy does not thwart the change in the government-bond rate). However, for reasons to be discussed below, the bank lending rate may remain at i_1, at least temporarily (again, abstracting from any risk differential).

In effect, the credit-availability theory subdivides Wicksell's money (or market) interest rate into two rates—a bank lending rate and a government-bond rate—neither of which is truly a money rate of interest, but both of which are representative market rates. In Wicksellian terms (discussed in Chapter 6), the market rate of interest, our bank lending rate, will be lower than the natural rate that equates savings and investment. In order to restore a savings–investment equilibrium in this type of model, the bank lending rate must increase; in our example in Figure 14-1, equilibrium would be reached when the bank lending rate had increased to i_2. Assuming that the banks possess no excess reserves and therefore cannot increase the money supply as they did in Wicksell's model, credit rationing occurs because the quantity of loanable funds demanded by investors, Q_3, exceeds the quantity of available funds supplied by savers, Q_1, at the i_1 interest rate.

Why might banks choose to ration credit rather than simply charge the equilibrium rate that equates supply and demand? Two possible reasons are proposed:

1. The price leaders in the banking industry might be unwilling to adjust the bank lending rate to match a change in some competitive market interest rate, such as the rate on government bonds, until they determine whether the change in the government bond rate is a temporary adjustment or a more fundamental, lasting change. They would endanger their position and prestige by initiating bank lending rate changes that may have to be immediately rescinded. Changing bank lending rates involves costs in time, effort, and other administrative expenses. And the follower banks will become dissatisfied with any leader that makes too-frequent and unnecessary rate changes.
2. Even if the banks desired to charge the equilibrium rate and had evidence that a bank lending rate change was required (perhaps because the government-bond rate had changed), they would not know the new equilibrium rate. They could at best approach the new bank lending rate through a series of approximations. The cost of such experimentation can be reduced by simply stalling until better market information is available. If financial markets were perfectly competitive and if risk, administrative costs, and tax considerations were equal throughout, then the banks would simply charge the government bond rate. However, banks do not operate in a perfectly competitive market and bank loans are more risky, costly, and possess no tax advantages as do government securities. Therefore, the equilibrium bank rate will not equal the government-bond rate, and the appropriate differential can be learned only over time.

How can this model, which Wicksell used to explain inflation, be used to explain credit rationing? Banks not only lend money to their customers; they also buy securities. When faced with a growing demand for loans, having run out of excess reserves, the banks can sell their securities in an attempt to satisfy the new demand. Bond sales by the banks tend to increase the interest rate on government bonds, while they hold the bank lending rate constant.

However, banks may be unwilling to sell enough securities to finance the entire demand for investment at the going bank lending rate. Why might they withhold funds from investors when the bank lending rate is below the bond rate? The first reason is that the banks may find securities more profitable than new loans as the bond rate increases, relative to the bank rate.[4] The second reason involves the portfolio balancing model. As a diversified-portfolio-balancing institution, the bank has a limit as to how many bonds it wants to sell in order to increase its loans. When price leaders of the oligopolistic banking industry decide to do so, they will bring the bank lending rate into line with the competitive market rate on bonds and the natural rate. Significantly, though, for some period of time the bank lending rate will lag behind the other rates, and the supply of investment financing will fall short of the demand.

In conclusion, any temporary divergence of the bank lending rate from the competitive market rate on bonds and the natural rate can cause credit rationing to occur. The banks, without excess reserves and motivated by a desire to balance their portfolios, do not sell enough bonds to meet the demands of investors. Therefore, the inflationary result envisioned by Wicksell will not develop as long as banks ration credit instead of raising the lending rate.

Credit Availability Policy Implications Concerning the policy implications of credit availability, the time lag of the bank lending rate behind the competitive market rate on securities can cause economic problems. But, the monetary authorities can compensate for the effect of credit rationing with monetary policy, recognizing all the while that the credit-rationing effect is only temporary, and the policy application should similarly be temporary.

One advantage of the credit-availability theory is that it explains the apparent impact of small changes in the government bond rate during the early 1950's. Addressing himself to the question of why small doses of monetary policy appeared to have a disproportionately large impact, Robert V. Roosa emphasized that credit rationing could be more restrictive than the simple price-rationing effect attributable to the interest rate.[5] Because the banks are "locked in" to some of their bonds by their portfolio-balancing behavior, unfilled demand, at most equal to the distance *a-c* at an interest rate of i_1 in Figure 14-1, is as restrictive as an extreme increase in the interest rate to i_3 would have been in the absence of credit rationing.[6] (In reality, credit

---

[4]This analysis assumes equal risk for all loans and securities. In practice, the bank lending rate is normally higher than rates on securities, because bank loans are less liquid, more subject to default, carry a higher transactions cost, and possess no tax advantages. So, in practice, a differential would have to be subtracted from the bank rate to make the two rates comparable.

[5]Robert V. Roosa, "Interest Rates and the Central Bank," *Money, Trade and Economic Growth: Essays in Honor of John Henry Williams* (New York: Macmillan, 1951), pp. 270–95; Roosa, "The Revival of Monetary Policy," *Review of Economics and Statistics*, 33 (February 1951), 29–37; and Roosa, "Monetary Policy Again," *Oxford University Institute of Statistics Bulletin*, 14 (August 1952), 253–61.

[6]An additional reason has been proposed for the "locked-in effect" or "value-of-portfolio effect," a concept proposed by Roosa ("Interest Rates," *loc. cit.*) to explain why bank portfolio managers might be unwilling to sell bonds when bond prices are depressed,

rationing will not be quite so restrictive, because the banks will sell some securities and thereby fill some of the increased demand represented by the shift from I_1 to I_2 in Figure 14-1. If the banks did not sell any bonds and met none of the increased demand for investment, the government bond rate might not approach the natural rate as nearly or as quickly, assuming that the banks play a significant role in the bond market.)

Credit Availability Critique One deficiency of our model above from the standpoint of Keynesian theory is that savings are not specifically made a function of income. Therefore, the savings function has to shift whenever aggregate real income shifts, unless one assumes a neoclassical world.

In addition to the version of credit availability that we have developed above, a number of other models also exist, each stressing different market imperfections.[7] All the formulations of credit availability, including the one presented in this chapter, are subject to certain criticisms. For example, all the models make certain assumptions regarding bank behavior in an uncertain world—in our case, we assumed that banks are both oligopoly firms and portfolio balancers. But there is, in fact, no clear consensus regarding bank behavior or market structure. Further studies are needed to find answers to questions of this sort.

As another criticism of the credit-availability thesis, it has been pointed out that on the surface the theory is not borne out by the data, because banks have been reducing the proportion of securities to loans in their portfolios since World War II. However, this sort of empirical evidence is inconclusive, because the theory allows for some change in the proportion of securities to bank loans. In any case, banks patriotically overloaded their portfolios with federal government bonds during World War II and over the last generation would have wanted to reduce the proportion of these bonds in their portfolios. Furthermore, the data would have to be collected for the exact period of the lag required for the bank to adjust its lending rate to changes in the market rate of interest, and this time lag has never been precisely measured.

A final disadvantage of the credit-availability theory is its incompleteness, not only because of the restricted assumptions already mentioned, but because it includes only one type of financial intermediary, the commercial banks. In the next section, we will consider attempts that have been made to include other types of financial intermediaries in macro analysis.

---

in order to obtain excess reserves to lend. Banks' financial statements report portfolio values at the purchase price of the various issues. Consequently, losses owing to adverse price changes do not become generally evident if the securities remain unsold. Bank executives may be unwilling to report losses on their portfolios for fear of appearing inept managers and losing prestige and business. If this type of locked-in effect works (and some evidence suggests that it does—or did at one time), banks will not expand their loans as much as one might expect when interest rates rise. See Samuel B. Chase, "The Lock-in Effect: Bank Reactions to Security Losses," *Monthly Review*, Federal Reserve Bank of Kansas City, June 1960.

[7]Ira O. Scott, Jr., "The Availability Doctrine: Theoretical Underpinnings," *Review of Economic Studies*, 25 (October 1957), 41–48.

Money Matters

Since 1900, financial intermediaries other than commercial banks have become increasingly important; Gurley and Shaw have expanded economic theory to include their role.[8] These nonbank intermediaries buy primary securities, such as corporation bonds or mortgages, and issue their own, secondary securities, such as savings and loan shares or mutual fund shares. All financial intermediaries, including the commercial banks, serve as middlemen between savers and investors. The secondary securities of nonbank intermediaries offer reduced risk and greater liquidity compared with the primary securities of their borrowers, because (1) secondary securities offer portfolio diversification; (2) nonbank intermediaries employ expert administrators, appraisers, and accountants, who are unavailable to individual investors and who are better able to select primary securities than an individual lender would be; (3) the federal government insures the deposits (liabilities) of some of these intermediaries;[9] and (4) the secondary securities sold by intermediaries are generally short term (highly liquid), whereas primary securities purchased by intermediaries are generally long term (less liquid). The lower risk and greater liquidity that financial intermediaries offer accounts for the demand for secondary securities despite the differential between the interest rates paid to their lenders and those charged to their borrowers.

Nonbank financial intermediaries—such as savings and loan associations, mutual savings banks, credit unions, insurance companies, pension funds, and investment companies—carry on activities similar to those of the commercial banks.[9] Therefore, some economists have proposed that nonbank intermediaries should be regulated in the same way as commercial banks. If it could be shown that all financial intermediaries have the same effect on the economy, then regulation of the commercial banks alone would be arbitrary, capricious, and unfair, as well as being inefficient monetary policy, because much of the monetary system would not be subject to regulation. If nonbank intermediaries perform the same functions as commercial banks, the intermediaries may, as a reaction to monetary policy applied only to banks, offset the effects of that policy.[10]

One significant distinction between commercial banks and nonbank intermediaries is that only the commercial banking system can create money. Nonbank intermediaries create and issue their own secondary securities,

---

[8] John Gurley and Edward Shaw, "Financial Aspects of Economic Development," *American Economic Review*, 45 (September 1955), 515–38; and Gurley and Shaw, "Financial Intermediaries and the Saving–Investment Process," *Journal of Finance*, 11 (March 1956), 257–76. John Gurley and Edward Shaw, *Money in the Theory of Finance* (Washington, D.C.: Brookings Institution, 1960), pp. 191–298.

[9] James Tobin and William C. Brainard, "Financial Intermediaries and the Effectiveness of Monetary Controls," *American Economic Review*, 53 (May 1963), 383–400.

[10] General monetary policy in the form of increases and decreases in the stock of money does have some impact on nonbank intermediaries. However, the impact is diffuse and will differ from one intermediary to the next.

which substitute for money in many respects, but only coins and paper money (claims on the Treasury or Federal Reserve) and checks (claims on the commercial banks) are literally money—that is, can be spent directly on the purchase of goods and services. A few economists would broaden the usual definition of money to include time deposits of commercial banks and certain other near-money assets. However, the standard definition of money is currency and demand deposits in the hands of the public—immediately spendable financial assets.

Nonbank intermediaries such as savings and loan associations and mutual savings banks are capable of multiple expansion of credit much the same as commercial banks. For example, assume that $1,000 is deposited in a savings and loan association; the stock of money is unchanged, since now the association rather than an individual has claim to a $1,000 demand deposit. The individual obtains $1,000 worth of shares in the savings and loan association. The association will in turn lend much of that amount to a home buyer, who may pay the money to a contractor. The contractor could redeposit the money in a savings and loan association, which would in turn issue more shares, so more than $1,000 worth of shares could be issued on the basis of the original deposit.

Thus, savings and loan deposits (shares, CD's or any other form) can undergo a multiple expansion much like the bank credit multiplier. The leakages in this instance would probably be greater than in the case of the bank credit multiplier, because most of the funds will probably be redeposited in commercial banks rather than in other savings and loan associations. Furthermore, the savings and loan associations must maintain cash reserves and must also pay out interest to shareholders and other depositors.

The secondary securities of nonbank financial intermediaries perform some of the functions of money; for example, savings and loan shares or the cash value of insurance policies may perform the same function as precautionary money balances. The existence of these secondary securities, therefore, reduces the need for the public to hold money, which in turn reduces the liquidity-preference curve, and so leads to a lower equilibrium rate of interest. Intermediaries increase income velocity to the extent that they reduce the total demand for money balances, since asset holders desire to hold less money than they otherwise would at any interest rate. (Furthermore, that part of the stock of money held by the nonbank intermediaries may move at a different income velocity than the same funds would in the hands of others.)

To illustrate, suppose that an economy without any financial intermediaries is in equilibrium at the intersection of the liquidity preference curve $(M_t + M_L)_1$, and stock of money, M_{s_1}, in Figure 14-2. After the nonbank intermediaries are introduced, their securities substitute for part of the demand for money balances.[11] As a result, the liquidity-perference curve falls to $(M_t + M_L)_2$, and the equilibrium interest rate falls to i_2. If the monetary

[11]Remember that commercial banks themselves provide near-money, in the form of time deposits.

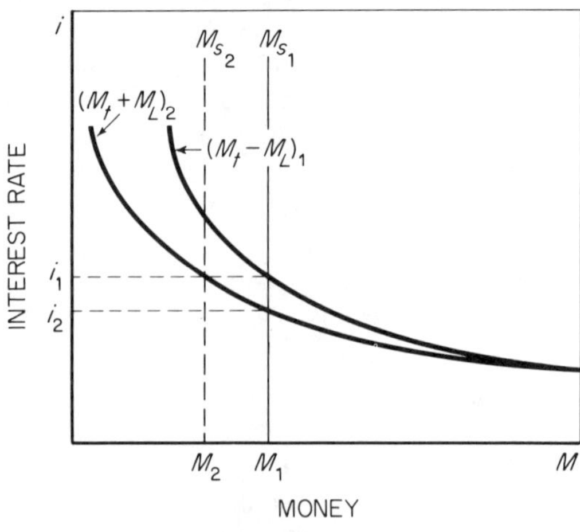

FIG. 14-2 The Impact of Financial Intermediaries

authorities wish to maintain an interest rate of i_1 without regulating the nonbank intermediaries, the stock of money would have to be reduced from M_{s_1} to M_{s_2}. Generally, to overcome the activities of unregulated financial intermediaries, the monetary authorities must apply monetary policy more forcefully than they would in their absence.[12]

Up to this point, we have assumed that the creation of money substitutes is independent of the stock of money. However, if the change in the stock of money induces a flood of money substitutes from the nonbank intermediaries to the public, restrictive monetary policy will induce its own offsetting reaction. The degree of offset (if any) will depend on the responsiveness of the supply of money substitutes to changes in the interest rate. In other words, the degree to which monetary policy will be offset by money substitutes depends on the elasticities of demand and supply of those money substitutes.[13] This situation would be shown graphically by accompanying any decreases in the stock of money with a simultaneous decrease in the liquidity-preference function as a response to the increased supply of money substitutes offered by nonbank intermediaries. The reverse would also be true: An increase in the stock of money would be associated with an increase in the liquidity-preference function as asset holders reduce their demand for money substitutes.

Since the secondary securities of nonbank intermediaries are imperfect

---

[12]The money-substitute function and the ability to multiply secondary securities vary from one financial intermediary to another. One would expect less ability to offset monetary policy on the part of pension funds and insurance companies than on the part of mutual savings banks and savings and loan associations.

[13]Abba P. Lerner, "Discussion of Papers on Financial Institutions and Monetary Policy: A Re-examination of Their Inter-relationship," *American Economic Review*, 53 (May 1963), 401–7.

substitutes for money, their availability does not completely offset monetary policy. The greater the number and variety of these money substitutes, the greater will be their acceptability, so the effect of nonbank intermediaries on monetary policy will depend on the supply and demand conditions in the market for their secondary securities. The demand for them will depend on the demand for liquidity generally and the degree to which society is willing to accept secondary securities of financial intermediaries as a substitute for money.[14] The supply of secondary securities depends on the differential between the lower borrowing rate paid on deposits and the higher lending rate of the nonbank intermediaries. Because of government restrictions on the maximum rates some nonbank intermediaries may pay depositors, the spread between the two rates normally increases as interest rates go up, thereby encouraging the intermediaries to offer premiums and gifts as well as more and more varied securities in order to entice more depositors.[15]

Addressing themselves to the role of financial intermediaries in the economy, Gurley and Shaw argued that "the parallelism between banks and other intermediaries . . . imposes on the central bank responsibility for supervision over indirect finance generally rather than over indirect finance through the banks alone."[16] However, even if the liquidity-preference function does decrease as a response to reductions in the stock of money, and as a result more securities are offered by the nonbank intermediaries, monetary policy will still be effective, although more will be required to achieve a given result; and the more perfectly secondary securities can substitute for money, the larger will be the change in the stock of money required. If nonbank intermediaries were subject to the same regulations as commercial banks regarding reserves and interest rates, then monetary policy would be that much more effective, and smaller doses of it would be required to achieve the same objective.[17]

THE BASIC THEORIES OF THE MONETARISTS

Many of Keynes's theoretical leads were developed by those of his followers who concentrated on short-run phenomena in real (or commodity) markets. However, one center of economics, the University of Chicago, maintained throughout a strong interest in longer-run monetary phenomena.

---

[14]The secondary securities offered by nonbank financial intermediaries may provide a safe haven for even speculative balances, since in may cases the principal is guaranteed and the funds are actually available on demand, even though technically they may be withheld for a certain period, at the option of the intermediaries.

[15]Furthermore, at such times the spread between the borrowing and lending rates applies to only new loans, but to all deposits. Therefore, higher interest rates may actually hurt savings and loan associations and mutual savings banks.

[16]Gurley and Shaw, "Financial Aspects of Economic Development," p. 538.

[17]There have been many critiques of the regulation of nonbank intermediaries. For one example, see Ezra Solomon, "The Issue of Financial Intermediaries," *Proceedings of the 1959 Conference on Savings and Residential Financing* (Chicago: United States Savings & Loan League, 1959), pp. 31–41.

This section is a systematic presentation of some of the ideas on monetary theory associated with the monetarists. Where members of the school disagree, we have followed Professor Milton Friedman's ideas, since he is generally acknowledged the leader of the group. The economic stabilization model employed in this section was developed by economists at the Federal Reserve Bank of St. Louis.[18]

The Demand for Money

Some commentators on the monetarists have suggested that their major contribution lies in their concept of the demand for money. One simplistic interpretation of this monetarist theory proposes that the economy generally behaves as though the *LM* curve (always constructed in real terms) were vertical in the short run; that is, as though the economy is always operating in the classical range. In effect, a vertical *LM* curve assumes that there is only a transactions and precautionary demand for real money balances.

This oversimplified version, which we use to introduce monetarist theory, has one advantage for our purposes: It follows the post-Keynesian model with which we are already familiar, so it is a convenient bridge from the theories already developed to those of the monetarists. A completely inelastic segment of the *LM* curve where it intersects the *IS* curve leads to the conclusion that a change in the *IS* function does not change aggregate income, but could affect only the interest rate.

Another way of looking at the effect of a vertical *LM* curve is to say that income velocity will remain constant. An increase in government expenditures would not lead to an increase in the level of aggregate income, but only to the substitution of government expenditures for private investment expenditures. For example, in Figure 14-3, if the *IS* curve shifts from IS_1 to IS_2, aggregate income would remain constant at Y_1, and the equilibrium interest rate would increase from i_1 to i_2. If Y_1 level of aggregate income falls short of full employment ($\bar{Y}$), expansionary monetary policy would be required in order to shift the *LM* curve to the right and bring about full employment. Under those conditions, fiscal policy can affect only the interest rate, not aggregate income.

The major flaws in this simple interpretation of the monetarist model are (1) the implicit assumption of constant prices; (2) the failure to distinguish between the short run and the long run; and (3) the failure to make the demand for real money balances a function of the rate of interest.[19] (In contrast to the Keynesian economists, the monetarists, like the neoclassical economists, believe that real aggregate income is determined outside the monetary system and depends on the growth of resources and technology.)

The modern monetarists' views on the relationship between interest rates and the demand for money are much more subtle than one might infer from

---

[18] L. C. Andersen and K. M. Carlson, "A Monetarist Model for Economic Stabilization," *Review*, Federal Reserve Bank of St. Louis, 52 (April 1970), 7–25.

[19] M. Friedman, "A Theoretical Framework for Monetary Analysis," *Journal of Political Economy*, 78 (March–April 1970), 216.

FIG. 14-3 A Simple Interpretation of Monetarist Theory

the foregoing model. The intellectual forebears of the monetarists, the neoclassicists, whose theory was presented in Chapter 6, unabashedly assumed that the demand for real money balances was not a function of the interest rate. Making use of the ex ante inflation model, the monetarists propose, as we have seen in Chapter 13, a sequential process in which the effect of the speculative demand for money balances is eventually swamped by changes in the demand for investment and by expected inflation even in the short run. Therefore, Friedman has maintained, an increase in the money stock may at first lead to a reduction in the interest rate, partly absorbing a portion of the increase in the money stock through a reduction in income velocity. Then after a time, interest rates increase, thereby speeding up income velocity.[20]

Furthermore, the monetarists maintain that the demand for real-money balances is a stable long-run function of the increase in per capita wealth or in per capita permanent income. Permanent income is the present value of expected lifetime-average real income and can be used as an index of wealth. Holders of money are assumed, in this view, to be ultimately interested in the real quantity of money they hold rather than in the nominal quantity, and there is some definite quantity of real money that people wish to hold at any given time. However, the monetarists do not suggest that the demand for real money balances is constant; it does change over time, as habits, attitudes, and customs change.

On the empirical level, the monetarists have found a relationship

[20]M. Friedman, "Factors Affecting the Level of Interest Rates—Part I," *Proceedings of the 1968 Conference on Savings and Residential Financing*, (Chicago: United States Savings & Loan League, 1968), pp. 10–27.

between the long-run demand for money and secular changes in real income. The data indicate that between 1870 and 1945, there was a continual increase in the demand for money, or, restated, a secular decrease in velocity. Over the same period, there was a long-run increase in per capita real income, which Friedman proposes caused an increased desire to hold cash balances. According to this theory, people desire to increase holdings of assets such as money at a rate faster than the increase in per capita real income. Thus, money is a superior good, along with such items as consumer durables and houses. The demand for money as a function of the level of per capita real income would follow an increasingly steep path. Therefore, as income increases over the long run, cash holdings will increase at an even faster rate.[21]

The complete monetarist version of the demand for real-money balances, as developed by Professor Friedman, is summarized in the following equation:[22]

$$\frac{M_d}{P} = f\left(i_m, i_b, i_s, \frac{\Delta P^e}{P}, w, Y_p, u\right)$$

where M_d/P is the demand for real-money balances; i_m is the expected rate of return on money; i_b is the expected interest rate on bonds (debt); i_s is the expected yield on stock (equity);[23] $\Delta P^e/P$ is the expected rate of change in prices; w is the ratio of nonhuman to human wealth;[24] Y_p is permanent real income, which could be defined as the present value of expected lifetime-average real income (permanent income is actually an index of wealth in Friedman's equation); and u is a portmanteau variable used to summarize the tastes, preferences, habits, and attitudes of business and consumers.

The monetarist demand for real-money balances is a formulation that includes many subtle interrelationships. For example, it converts the demand for transactions balances to a long-run concept by using permanent income as an index of wealth. In addition, as in the Keynesian system, the interest rate is included in the demand function for money. Yet this formulation of the demand for money is more general than that of Keynes, since Friedman's demand function takes into account the interest rate on money and equities as well as on bonds.[25] Two variables of special interest, (1) the expected change in prices and (2) the ratio of nonhuman to human wealth, are not

---

[21] M. Friedman, "The Demand For Money: Some Theoretical And Empirical Results," *Journal of Political Economy*, 67 (August 1959), 327–51.

[22] Adapted from M. Friedman, "The Quantity Theory of Money—A Restatement," ed., *Studies in the Quantity Theory of Money* ed. Friedman (Chicago: University of Chicago Press, 1956), Chap. 1.

[23] Friedman includes, in the case of both debt and equity, expected changes in their prices as part of the return.

[24] Nonhuman wealth could be considered the present value of capital, including consumer durables; human wealth, the present value of potential income anticipated over a worker's life.

[25] The nominal rate of return on money is zero in the case of currency, and negative in the case of demand deposits subject to a service charge. However, Friedman includes time deposits in which interest is paid as part of the money stock.

incorporated in the Keynesian system. The demand for real-money balances is negatively affected by the rate of expected price changes. However, Friedman does not explain how *w* affects the demand for money. Perhaps a larger proportion of nonhuman wealth (which leads to more income received from stocks and bonds relative to wages) could influence individuals to hold less money, if they feel that nonwage income is more secure than wages—less subject to loss because of sickness, unemployment, or age. The opposite effect on the demand for money is also possible, since wage earners are generally paid more often and more dependably than non–wage earners.[26]

The factors included in *u* incorporate a wide variety of motives involving the habits, tastes, and preferences of consumers and businessmen. However, these factors are expected to remain constant in the short run and to change only slowly over time.

What are the major distinctions between the Keynesian and the monetarist demand function for money? In a sense, the two formulations are similar, since both make the demand for money a function of income and of the interest rate. However, there are significant differences. Friedman does not subdivide the demand for money into two components as Keynes does. There are certain subtleties in the monetarist version—such as distinguishing the yield on money, stocks, and bonds—that are lacking in the Keynesian formulation.[27]

A major distinction between the two is that Friedman's demand function is proposed as a stable, long-run function, whereas Keynes's is a short-run function; therefore, the portmanteau variable and the ratio of nonhuman to human wealth, which are long-run variables, are disregarded by Keynes. Perhaps the main difference between the two theories is that in the monetarist version, expected price changes are explicitly included; but Keynes, for the most part, assumed that prices would remain constant.

In conclusion, the monetarists' interest in money and their neoclassical bias has led them to include more variables in their demand for real-money balances than other groups of economists do and to concentrate especially on long-run factors. The monetarists conclude that the long-run demand for real-money balances is relatively stable and is increasing gradually over time.

The Stock of Money

As in any of the theories considered so far, the stock of money is determined through the interaction of the monetary authorities' provision of the monetary base (outside money) and the banking system's provision of the endogenously created bank credit money (inside money). The total quantity

---

[26] J. N. McKinney, "The Monetary Theories of Milton Friedman," paper presented at the Western Economic Association meeting, 1970, p. 4.

[27] The inclusion of three interest rates is more or less significant, depending on how perfect arbitrage is. In the real world, yields often differ among different types of assets, even when arbitrage works, because of all the various risk premiums and expectations.

of nominal-money balances supplied at any time is simply the sum of the exogenously determined monetary base and the bank credit money created from the base through the bank credit multiplier.

The stock of nominal balances is ultimately controlled by the monetary authorities, and therefore, the monetarists concentrate on the stock of nominal balances as the key datum in monetary policy. The stock of real money is the quantity of nominal balances in circulation, deflated by the price level. However, the monetarists propose that real balances, not nominal balances, are desired, and that ultimately any given stock of nominal balances can and will be converted to the desired level of real balances by price changes and possibly output changes brought about by changes in the level of expenditures.

Measured and Permanent Magnitudes

The monetarists maintain that the demand function for money is more stable than are other significant economic variables such as the consumption function or the investment-demand function, and therefore income velocity can be considered more nearly constant than other variables in the economy.[28] In contrast to the stable long-run function, the short-run demand for money is quite variable, and velocity related to aggregate real income over the business cycle appears to behave in a manner opposite to that in the long run. During periods of cyclically high aggregate income, income velocity increases, and it appears to decrease in periods of cyclically low income. In other words, cyclical income velocity increases during prosperity and decreases during depression.

This paradoxical behavior of income velocity is explained by Professor Friedman, who distinguishes between permanent and measured magnitudes of income and income velocity.[29] During a cyclical peak, real measured income exceeds expected permanent income; consumers adjust their consumption patterns to match their own concept of expected or permanent income over their lifetime.[30] Measured income is recorded for a period no longer than one year, which in Friedman's view is too short to be analytically relevant. He feels that a more valid theory would relate consumption to the consumer's expected lifetime-average income. For example, a medical intern earning $500 a month will probably spend more than his measured income, since he is confident that his future income will increase; but the same doctor in his peak income years will spend less than his measured income, as he pays off debts incurred in his student days and saves for retirement.

Periodically, income recipients reevaluate their permanent income in the light of past experience and new prospects. Since permanent income is

---

[28]M. Friedman, *Studies In The Quantity Theory of Money*, p. 16.

[29]The following discussion is based on M. Friedman, "The Demand For Money," *op. cit.*

[30]Students who covered the discussion of the permanent-income hypothesis in the Appendix to Chapter 8 will notice that the hypothesis would lead one to expect that savings would be increased during cyclical peaks when the transitory-income component is higher, and reduced during cyclical troughs when transitory losses predominate.

defined and redefined by each individual in his own mind, it cannot be measured directly. In the following illustration, we have assumed for simplicity that the level of permanent income is determined by using the current and previous year's measured incomes (Y_m and Y_{m-1}) equally weighted. Permanent income (Y_p) may be stated

$$Y_p = \frac{Y_m + Y_{m-1}}{2}$$

where Y_m is the current and Y_{m-1} the previous year's income.

In terms of the income version of the equation of exchange—$MV = PY$—the stock of money, M, can be stated in real terms by deflating it by the price level, P. Thus, the real stock of money, M_r, equals M/P. The entire equation of exchange can be restated in real terms as

$$M_r V = Y$$

Solving for measured income velocity,

$$V = \frac{Y}{M_r}$$

Permanent income velocity, V_p, can be computed by dividing permanent income by the real stock of money:

$$V_p = \frac{Y_p}{M_r}$$

and transposing to determine permanent income indicates that

$$Y_p = V_p M_r$$

In Friedman's view, permanent velocity is more stable than measured velocity, which deviates from it over the cycle. Permanent velocity is assumed constant for simplicity in the following illustration, although, as we have seen, according to the monetarists, money is a superior good, and as a consequence, permanent velocity may be expected to decrease slowly as incomes increase secularly.

Table 14-1 illustrates how the constant permanent velocity, in column 4, and measured velocity, in column 6, will deviate over one phase of the business cycle. The real stock of money, M_r in column 3, is the independent variable. The nominal stock of money (as distinct from the real stock) can be manipulated arbitrarily by the monetary authorities; and we assume that they decide to change it. This change, when deflated by the price index, gives a 10 percent increase in the real stock of money in the second year, a 27.3 percent increase in the third year, no change in the fourth, a 21.4 percent decrease in the fifth year, and a 9.09 percent decrease in the sixth year to reestablish the conditions of the base year.

Year 1 in Table 14-1 begins in equilibrium, with permanent and mea-

TABLE 14-1 A Monetarist Model of Aggregate Economic Activity ($ in billions)

(1)	(2)	(3)	(4)	(5)	(6)
Year	Permanent Income	Real-Money Stock	Permanent Velocity	Measured Income	Measured Velocity
	Y_p	M_r	V_p	Y_m	V_m
1	$100	$10	10	$100	10
2	110	11	10	120	10.9
3	140	14	10	160	11.4
4	140	14	10	120	8.6
5	110	11	10	100	9.0
6	100	10	10	100	10

sured velocity both equal to 10, permanent and measured income both $100 billion, and the stock of money at $10 billion. The $1 billion increase in the stock of money in year 2 sets off the following reaction. Permanent income, Y_p in column 2, becomes $110 billion, since $Y_p = V_pM_r$, or $10 \times 11 = 110$. Measured income, Y_m in column 5, must be $120 billion, since

$$Y_p = \frac{Y_m + Y_{m-1}}{2}$$

therefore,

$$Y_m = 2Y_p - Y_{m-1}$$

or

$$2(110) - 100 = 120$$

Measured velocity is 10.9, since $V_m = Y_m/M_r = 120/11 = 10.9$. The values for measured velocity in years 3 through 6 in Table 14-1 can be derived in the same way, given the figures in columns 3 and 4. It appears from the table that when measured income is increasing at a faster rate than the real money stock, measured velocity is greater than permanent velocity. Conversely, when measured income is decreasing at a faster rate than the money stock, measured velocity is less than permanent velocity.[31]

One problem the monetarists need to cope with is the persistence over the last twenty years of the cyclically high post–World War II income velocity. The almost continual prosperity of the 1950's and 1960's was apparently responsible for reversing the secular decline in velocity usually associated with increasing aggregate real income.

[31] In this illustration, we concentrate on the effect of changes in the stock of money on income velocity. A similar example could be constructed to demonstrate their effect on prices, and price changes are a key policy consideration, especially in the monetarists' view. Friedman incorporates the difference between measured prices and permanent or expected prices. The recognition of this effect reinforces the distinction between permanent and measured velocity. The model could be expanded to incorporate such effects, but for simplicity, they have been omitted.

Realistically, we should repeat that in addition to the effects of prosperity on income velocity, consumers' cash requirements for transactions balances are reduced by the availability of ready credit, particularly for consumer durables, an increasing part of consumer expenditures, and by the growing use of credit cards, as convenient as cash, for consumer purchases. Furthermore, improved business techniques in communications, transportation, and warehousing mean that less money is needed to finance a given level of business operations. And new financial techniques having improved the efficiency with which money is used, proportionately less money is needed to handle larger volumes of transactions. Consequently, income velocity *should* have increased since World War II.

In contrast, the precautionary motive for holding money may have increased, because asset holders can afford greater security at higher levels of permanent income. However, the actual situation suggests that the potential reduction in income velocity from increases in precautionary money balances (other things being equal) must have been swamped by something besides the reduction in transactions balances, since the latter probably would not be sufficient by itself to account for the overall increase in permanent velocity—that is, if we assume that money is a superior good—because of the increases in real aggregate income during these years.

Friedman suggests, quite plausibly, that the increase in income velocity in the postwar era has been caused by changing expectations regarding economic stability, since we have not had a serious depression in that time. Confidence in our ability to avoid such depression, whether or not it is justified, has increased through the years and, as a result, the demand for precautionary balances has been significantly reduced and in turn has led to the decrease in the demand for total money balances as a proportion of income.[32]

If Friedman's theory is correct, the demand curve for precautionary money balances should eventually stop falling, as the anticipation of prosperity spreads throughout the economy. When that occurs, further increases in real income should be associated with a greater quantity of precautionary money balances demanded. Unfortunately, inflation in the later 1960's bred the expectation of further inflation, which increased measured velocity by making it more expensive to hold money. This concept of ex ante or expected inflation, adapted by Friedman from Irving Fisher, was considered in Chapter 13.

There are two popular alternative explanations of the recent increase in income velocity. The Keynesian interpretation would be that higher interest rates have led to a smaller quantity of speculative money balances demanded as a response to a leftward movement along the liquidity-preference function; some empirical evidence has been offered to support this explanation.[33] The

---

[32]M. Friedman, "The Demand for Money," *Proceedings of the American Philosophical Society*, 105 (June 1961), 259–64.

[33]H. R. Heller, "The Demand for Money: The Evidence from Short-Run Data," *Quarterly Journal of Economics*, 79 (May 1965), 291–303.

second alternative explanation is, in terms of the Gurley–Shaw thesis, that the increased number and variety of financial intermediaries and secondary securities have brought about the increase in velocity by reducing the demand for money balances. Financial intermediaries not only provide good money substitutes in their secondary securities; they also offer a convenient source of credit that reduces the need for precautionary money balances.

A MONETARIST MODEL OF THE AGGREGATE ECONOMY

One innovative branch of the monetarist school is the group of economists at the Federal Reserve Bank of St. Louis. That group has developed a model to illustrate the workings of the aggregate economy, specifically relating changes in economic activity to changes in the quantity of money.[34]

In the monetarist view, the rate of change in the nominal stock of money is the primary determinant of the change in spending for GNP. Changes in spending, in turn, influence production, employment, and prices. Basic to the monetarist position is the assumption that the aggregate economy is basically stable and that instability is introduced mainly through mismanagement of monetary policy. (Keynes, in his day, would have had no argument with this second point.)

The St. Louis model is illustrated in Figure 14-4. Panel A shows the direct relationship between changes in the stock of money, ΔM, the independent variable on the x-axis, and change in money expenditure (or money income), ΔY^M on the y-axis, which we shall call the total-spending function. Panel A, therefore, simply illustrates the working, at the margin, of a sophisticated quantity theory of money—that is, a change in the money stock can influence real aggregate output as well as prices—assuming that V is constant, implied by the linearity of the total-spending function. Any increase in government expenditures would have to be shown as a shift upward and to the left in the total-spending function. However, the St. Louis Fed group believes it can be empirically demonstrated that an increase in the money stock has much more impact on total spending than does an equal dose of fiscal policy.[35] They estimate that monetary actions generally affect total spending with a six- to nine-month lag.

Unlike the case with the standard *IS–LM* and aggregate demand-and-supply models, changes in interest rates do not affect aggregate output and prices in the St. Louis Fed's model. Interest-rate changes are an effect and not a cause in this model.

Panel B of Figure 14-4 demonstrates the relationship between changes in

---

[34]Andersen and Carlson, "A Monetarist Model."

[35]L. C. Andersen and J. L. Jordan, "Monetary and Fiscal Actions: A Test of Their Relative Importance in Economic Stabilization," *Review*, Federal Researve Bank of St. Louis, 50 (November 1968), 11–24.

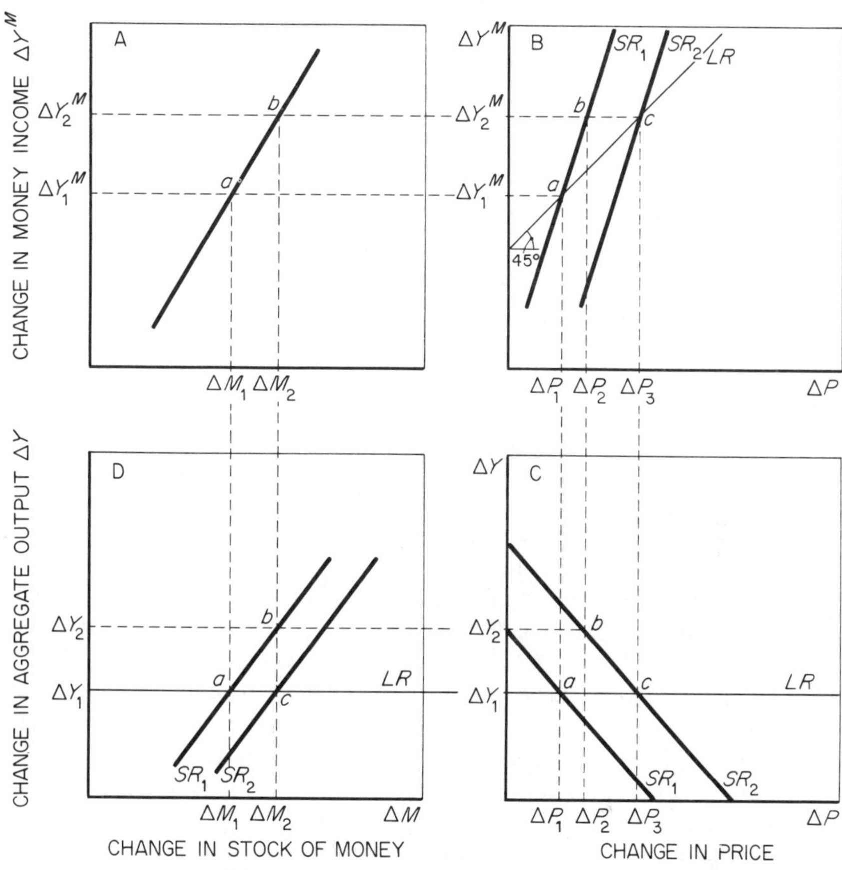

FIG. 14-4 Monetarist Model of Aggregate Economic Activity

total spending and prices.[36] The steeper, short-run price curves indicate that price changes are relatively inelastic with respect to changes in total spending. The shallower, 45° long-run price curve indicates that in the long run, a change in total spending will have an exactly proportionate effect on prices. The model assumes that the natural rate of unemployment will exist in the long run but not necessarily in the short run. Therefore, in the short run, output may exceed its natural incremental level of growth. This could occur if job seekers reduce their time spent in search or employers step up their search for employees in response to an increase in the stock of money. For example, higher wages could at first be interpreted as a lucky employment opportunity.

[36]The effects of ex ante inflation could be incorporated in this relationship, but they have been omitted in the presentation for simplicity. The original formulators of this theory incorporated the effects of anticipated price changes on prices and output. However, they did not explicitly include these effects in their formal diagrammatic model, which we follow in this section.

But when the incremental price changes that workers expect catch up to the actual change in prices, the normal search time would be resumed. The tendency toward the natural rate of unemployment that emerges in the long run means that increases in aggregate output will tend around the natural unemployment rate—so in the long run, the full effect of additional spending is felt on prices, because output will not increase by more than its long-run increment.

Panel *C*, the total spending identity, consists simply of a negatively sloped 45° line that divides incremental changes in spending between changes in price on the horizontal axis and changes in aggregate real output on the vertical. There is a family of 45° lines, one for each possible ΔY^M. The horizontal line in panel *C* shows the natural incremental growth level of aggregate real output, to which the economy will tend in the long run. (Over time, the incremental level of output could increase, as new or better quality resources and techniques are developed.)

Panel *D*, the output-money relationship derived from panels *A*, *B*, and *C*, shows the relationship between changes in the stock of money (which initiated the change in spending) and resulting changes in aggregate real output. In the short run, a change in the increase in the stock of money can increase aggregate output by more than its long run incremental level. But in the long run, aggregate output reverts to its natural, incremental growth level.

To illustrate the workings of this monetarist model, we start in panel A with the assumed shift from ΔM_1 to ΔM_2, causing a movement along the total spending curve from point *a* to point *b* and an increase in ΔY^M from ΔY_1^M to ΔY_2^M. As a result, the economy moves along the short-run price function, SR_1, from point *a* to *b* in panel B, leading to a new level of price change, an increase in ΔP from ΔP_1 to ΔP_2. In panel C, the negatively sloped 45° line shifts up and the economy moves from point *a* on the original SR_1 to point *b* on the new, SR_2 curve. Given the incremental price change ΔP_2 determined in panel B, incremental real output must increase from ΔY_1 to ΔY_2. The resulting relationship between change in the stock of money and change in aggregate real output is plotted in panel D as the movement from point *a* to point *b* along the SR_1 curve.

In this illustration, the increase in ΔM initially causes incremental output to increase above the long-run equilibrium, because prices do not immediately adjust completely to increased spending. However, in the long run, prices do adjust from ΔP_2 to ΔP_3, as the short-run curve in panel B shifts to allow the new equilibrium at point *c* on the long-run price curve. In panel C, the economy reverts to its long-run equilibrium, from point *b* to point *c*, where the new short-run function intersects the long-run curve. And finally, in panel D, the short-run curve shifts to intersect the long-run curve at point *c*, again allowing long-run equilibrium to occur at the natural-increment growth of output and at the new, higher ΔP_3 change in prices.

In conclusion, this model would lead one to expect that short-term variations in total spending that are due to ΔM have little impact on real output, given sufficient time to adjust, and therefore the quantity theory of money holds in the long run. Any increase in the money stock in excess of the natural increase in output will lead to an increase in the rate of inflation. This model allows an incremental increase in prices, even in the long run, equal to the expected rate of inflation. Unanticipated price increases can temporarily reduce unemployment below the natural rate, but, over time, anticipated price increases will re-establish the natural rate, so the Phillips curve and ex ante inflation are built into this model.

MONETARIST POLICY RECOMMENDATIONS

One point consistently made by the monetarists is that attempts to fine-tune the economy usually do more harm than good. In the late 1960's, everyone was agreed that a tax increase was the correct economic prescription, yet political squabbling between the president and Congress prevented constructive action for nearly two years. On the basis of this and other, similar examples, it is argued that our political institutions and our economic knowledge are at too primitive a level to permit economic fine-tuning.

One of the major proposals of the monetarists is the use of monetary policy in the short run to avoid monetary crises that cause inflation and recession.[37] They would avoid monetary mismanagement (such as the downswing starting in year 4 of Table 14-1, triggered by failure to maintain a rate of increase in the money stock) by avoiding premature shifts in monetary policy. If the economy tends toward its long-run equilibrium level of aggregate output in any case, then fiscal policy can only replace private spending with government spending and cannot affect aggregate employment and output. Also, short-run fiscal policy is ineffective unless it is financed by new money—in which case, it is a sort of disguised monetary policy.

Government expenditures financed by taxes would, in Keynesian terms, have a balanced-budget multiplier of 1. To some monetarists, the balanced-budget multiplier would be zero; if households count government expenditures as income and government services as consumption in kind, then an increase in taxes would be paid out of consumption, and households would simply replace their own consumption with government services.

Even fiscal policy financed by borrowing from the general public will not be expansionary, in the view of some monetarists, if the public feels that deficit financing is equivalent to increased taxes—that is, if the households reduce their consumption expenditures by as much as the government spends. Under the permanent-income hypothesis, a householder expecting future taxes to cause a reduction in his permanent income will increase his savings out of his present income to pay those taxes; in the same spirit, he will plan to save enough to pay the interest and possibly the principal on the government bonds.

---

[37]M. Friedman, "The Role of Monetary Policy," *American Economic Review*, 58 (March 1968), 13–14.

Therefore, fiscal policy is ineffective in both the long run and the short run, according to the monetarists holding this view.[38]

Although the monetarists generally favor a free market with minimum official intervention, they would use monetary policy to make the free market work more efficiently. However, they have a tendency to favor nondiscretionary monetary policy over both discretionary fiscal and monetary policy. Discretionary policy, they believe, is likely to be applied too late and too enthusiastically; and a too-slow overreaction will cause more harm than good.

One difficulty is the economy's reaction time. If six months are required for a decrease in the stock of money to have a major impact on aggregate income, then a decision made today that aggregate income should be reduced is already six months overdue.[39] For example, suppose that during January, inflation occurred to an annual rate of 6 percent, and the decision was made in February, when the January figures became available, to retard the rate of inflation by reducing the stock of money. The stock of money could be changed almost immediately in February, but the main impact of the policy change would not be felt for six months, or until after July. The effect of the reduced stock of money during the early months would be small. Therefore, unless the monetary authorities were content to live with inflation for the next several months, they would be tempted to overreact and cut the money stock drastically in order to achieve immediately a significant reduction in the rate of inflation. As a result, when the six-month time period had elapsed, the economy would be forced to operate with too small a stock of money for its needs. Such discretionary monetary policy would lead to unemployment after the six-month reaction time had elapsed. Likewise, during periods of unemployment, the temptation would be to apply expansionary monetary policy too vigorously, thereby creating the conditions for inflation.

The monetarists argue that as long as the monetary authorities are not gifted with the power to predict economic conditions accurately months in advance, the best policy is a nondiscretionary one, permitting a consistent rate of growth in the stock of money, in line with the natural growth rate of output. As Milton Friedman expressed it in his presidential address to the American Economic Association,

> . . . By setting itself a steady course and keeping to it, the monetary authorities could make a major contribution to promoting economic stability . . . steady monetary growth would provide a monetary climate favorable to the effective operation of those basic forces of enterprise, ingenuity, invention, hard work, and thrift that are the true springs of economic growth. That is the most that we can ask from

---

[38]In terms of *IS–LM* analysis, fiscal policy does not work because it cannot shift the *IS* curve. Any increase in *G* will be offset by decreases in *C* or *I*. This would be true even without an inelastic *LM* curve, granting the monetarists' assumptions about consumer behavior.

[39]The six-month time lag is suggested by Philip Cagan and Arthur Gandolfi, in "The Lag in Monetary Policy as Implied by the Time Pattern of Monetary Effects on Interest Rates," *American Economic Review*, 59 (May 1969), 277–84.

monetary policy at our present stage of knowledge. But that much—and it is a great deal—is clearly within our reach.[40]

CRITIQUE OF THE MONETARIST THEORIES

The monetarists' theories, like any others, are subject to certain criticisms:

1. The basic theory assumes a natural growth in long-run output and fails to specify the process of growth.
2. From the Keynesian viewpoint, the theory disregards the impact of managed interest rates. The monetarists regard interest rates as the result, not the cause, of market activities.
3. The monetarists use a rather unconvincing argument for the general ineffectiveness of fiscal policy. It has not been demonstrated that consumers save more in anticipation of higher taxes. They might equally well spend, in anticipation of future inflation as a result of deficit spending. In addition, many government goods are complements to private goods. Better roads induce the purchase of more cars, not fewer. An increase in the public debt need not lead to higher taxes if refinancing is used, so even sophisticated consumers may not reduce their consumption in anticipation of higher taxes.
4. Although only the simplistic interpretation of the theory specifically calls for a constant V, the more sophisticated version seems to imply the same characteristic. There is no theory of measured velocity in the short run.
5. The analysis tends to disregard short-run unemployment equilibrium and to assume perfect markets.

However, despite any criticism, the monetarists have been responsible for most of the fresh insights in macroeconomics in recent years, especially in restoring to the roles of money and wealth their proper importance.

SUMMARY AND CONCLUSIONS

This chapter has reviewed three of the more important post-Keynesian monetary theories. The first of these, credit availability, proposes that banks tend to ration credit during the initial phase of a tight money policy rather than to immediately raise the bank lending rate. Nonprice rationing of credit occurs because of the oligopolistic nature of the banking industry and because banks avoid risk through portfolio balancing, seeking an optimum balance between loans and securities to provide the highest possible rate of return consistent with an acceptable level of risk. The crucial consideration in the portfolio-balancing model is the relationship between three interest rates: the natural rate, the bank lending rate, and the bond rate; nonprice credit rationing occurs for as long as the bank lending rate lags behind the natural rate and the bond rate. In this model, the lag is due to oligopoly and portfolio balancing. Credit rationing, therefore, is only a short-run phenomenon, lasting for the duration of the adjustment lag.

---

[40]M. Friedman, "The Role of Monetary Policy," p. 17.

The second theory considered was that proposed by Gurley and Shaw regarding the role of financial intermediaries. According to this thesis, nonbank financial intermediaries have assumed an increasingly important role in the economy but have escaped most of the regulations imposed on commercial banks. Gurley and Shaw propose that this situation is both unfair and inefficient, since monetary policy has unnecessarily been restricted to only a small segment of the financial intermediaries. Just as banks are capable of a multiple expansion of money, some nonbank financial intermediaries are capable of a multiple expansion of their own secondary securities. Since secondary securities perform some of the functions of money, their increased supply induces a reduction in the liquidity-preference function. Tight money can lead to a larger supply of secondary securities by these intermediaries. Therefore, monetary policy is partially self-defeating, because it fails to regulate nonbank financial intermediaries.

Finally, we reviewed the theories of the monetarists, including one simplistic interpretation of their thinking, based on the notion that the vertical or "classical" range of the *LM* curve predominates under most conditions, and therefore, fiscal policy is unable to affect the level of aggregate income, except in unusual circumstances.

A more sophisticated version of their theory emphasizes the demand for money, which includes in one function the Keynesian variables, as well as several additional ones.

One of the key distinctions made by the Chicago group of monetarists is between measured and permanent magnitudes. The most important variables in their system are permanent velocity and permanent income.

A monetarist model developed by economists at the Federal Reserve Bank of St. Louis illustrates the interaction of changes in significant variables —money, spending, prices, and aggregate output.

The conclusion of the monetarists is that the quantity theory of money has relevance in the long run, and from this they draw two conclusions: (1) fiscal policy can have little impact in the long run; and (2) monetary policy should be geared to the economy's long-term growth potential.

All the theories considered in this chapter represent attempts to restore an important role to money in economic analysis. And, as we shall see in the next chapter, even growth theory, long a province of the "real" theorists, has incorporated the effects of money into certain formulations.

QUESTIONS AND PROBLEMS

1. Define monetary policy.
2. How can the Fed introduce new money into circulation?
3. Is there any guarantee that money put into circulation will actually be used?
4. Suppose the demand for investment is interest-inelastic. Can monetary policy be effective?

5. What effect on monetary policy were the banks likely to have, in Wicksell's view?

6. Discuss Roosa's concept of credit rationing.

7. Which aspects of "locking in" are rational, and which are irrational?

8. What effect do secondary securities issued by nonbank financial intermediaries have on liquidity preference?

9. How does measured velocity differ from permanent velocity, in Friedman's view?

10. Using the St. Louis Fed model, discuss the initial impact of an increase in the stock of money. What is the ultimate effect?

ADDITIONAL SELECTED REFERENCES

GENERAL DECISIONS ON MONETARY THEORY

ARCHIBALD, G. C., and R. G. LIPSEY, "Monetary and Value Theory: Further Comment," *Review of Economic Studies*, 28 (October 1960), 50–56.

CHRIST, C. F., "Patinkin on Money, Interest, and Prices," *Journal of Political Economy*, 65 (August 1957), 347–54.

CROOME, D. R., and H. G. JOHNSON, eds., *Money in Britain, 1959–69*. London: Oxford University Press, 1970.

FEIGE, E., *The Demand for Liquid Assets: A Temporal Cross-Section Analysis*. Englewood Cliffs, N.J.: Prentice-Hall, 1964.

JOHNSON, H. G., *Essays in Monetary Economics*. London: Allen & Unwin, 1967.

———, "Monetary Theory and Policy," *American Economic Review*, 52 (June 1962), 335–84.

LAIDLER, D., *The Demand for Money*. Scranton, Pa.: International Textbook, 1969.

LINDBECK, A., *A Study in Monetary Analysis*. Stockholm: Almqvist and Wiksell, 1963.

MUNDELL, R. A., *Monetary Theory*. Pacific Palisades, Calif.: Goodyear, 1971.

PATINKIN, D., *Money, Interest, and Prices*, 2nd ed. New York: Harper & Row, 1965.

———, *Studies in Monetary Economics*. New York: Harper & Row, 1972.

THORN, R., ed., *Monetary Theory and Policy*. New York: Random House, 1966.

TOBIN, J., "A General Equilibrium Approach to Monetary Theory," *Journal of Money, Credit, and Banking*, 1 (February 1969), 15–29.

CREDIT AVAILABILITY

BEAZER, WILLIAM F., "Tax Law, Lock-ins, and Bank Portfolio Choice," *Journal of Finance*, 20 (December 1965), 665–77.

BRECHLING, F., and G. CLAYTON, "Commercial Banks' Portfolio Behavior," *Economic Journal*, 75 (June 1965), 290–316.

CATT, A. J. L., "Credit Risk and Credit Rationing: Comment," *Quarterly Journal of Economics*, 77 (August 1963), 505–10.

LINDBECK, A., *The New Theory of Credit Control in the U.S.* Stockholm: Almqvist and Wicksell, 1959.

MODIGLIANI, F., "The Monetary Mechanism and Its Interaction with Real Phenomena," *Review of Economics and Statistics*, 45 No. 1, Pt. 2 (February 1963), 79–107.

TOBIN, J., "Monetary Policy and the Management of the Public Debt: The Patman Inquiry," *Review of Economics and Statistics*, 35 (May 1953), 118–27.

NONBANK FINANCIAL INTERMEDIARIES

BRUNNER, K., and A. H. MELTZER, "The Place of Financial Intermediaries in the Transmission of Monetary Policy," *American Economic Review*, 53 (May 1962), 372–82.

MARTY, A. L., "Gurley and Shaw on Money in a Theory of Finance," *Journal of Political Economy*, 69 (February 1961), 56–62.

THE MONETARISTS AND THEIR CRITICS

ALLAIS, M., "A Restatement of the Quantity Theory of Money," *American Economic Review*, 56 (December 1966), 1123–57.

ANDO, A., and F. MODIGLIANI, "The Relative Stability of Monetary Velocity and the Investment Multiplier," *American Economic Review*, 55 (September 1965), 693–790.

BRUNNER, K., "A Schema for the Supply Theory of Money," *International Economic Review*, 2 (January 1961), 79–109.

BRUNNER, K., ed., *Targets and Indicators of Monetary Policy*. San Francisco: Chandler, 1969.

BRUNNER K., A. H. MELTZER, J. TOBIN, P. DAVIDSON, D. PATINKIN, and M. FRIEDMAN, "Symposium on Friedman's Theoretical Framework," *Journal of Political Economy*, 80 (September/October, 1972), 837–950.

BRUNNER, K., and A. H. MELTZER, "Predicting Velocity: Implications for Theory and Policy," *Journal of Finance*, 18 (May 1963), 319–54.

———, "Some Further Investigations of Demand and Supply Functions for Money," *Journal of Finance*, 19 (May 1964), 240–83.

DE PRONTO, M., and T. MAYER, "Tests of the Relative Importance of Autonomous Expenditures and Money," *American Economic Review*, 55 (September 1965), 729–52.

ENTHOVEN, A. C., "Monetary Disequilibrium and the Dynamics of Inflation," *Economic Journal*, 66 (June 1956), 256–70.

FAND, D. F., "Keynesian Monetary Theories, Stabilization Policy, and the Recent Inflation," *Journal of Money, Credit, and Banking*, 1 (August 1969), 556–87.

———, "Some Issues in Monetary Economics," *Review*, Federal Reserve Bank of St. Louis, 52 (January 1970), 10–27.

FISHER, I., *The Purchasing Power of Money*. New York: Macmillan, 1911.

FRIEDMAN, M., and D. MEISELMAN, "Reply to Ando and Modigliani and to De Pranto and Mayer," *American Economic Review*, 55 (September 1965), 753–85.

FRIEDMAN, M., and A. J. SCHWARTZ, *A Monetary History of the United States, 1867–1960*. Princeton, N.J.: Princeton University Press, 1963.

GIBSON, W., "Interest Rates and Monetary Policy," *Journal of Political Economy*, 78 (May–June 1970), 431–55.

HICKS, J. R., "A Suggestion for Simplifying the Theory of Money," *Economica*, 2 (February 1935), 1–19.

JOHNSON, H., "The Keynesian Revolution and the Monetarist Counter-Revolution," *American Economic Review*, 61 (May 1971), 1–14.

MEIGS, A. J., *Money Matters*. New York: Harper & Row, 1972.

MEISELMAN, D., ed., *Varieties of Monetary Experience*. Chicago: University of Chicago Press, 1971.

MINTS, L. W., *Monetary Policy for a Competitive Society*. New York: McGraw-Hill, 1950.

PIGOU, A. C., "The Value of Money," *Quarterly Journal of Economics*, 32 (November 1917), 38–65.

ROUSSEAS, S. W., *Monetary Theory*. New York: Knopf, 1972.

WARBURTON, C., *Depression, Inflation, and Monetary Policies: Selected Papers, 1945–53*. Baltimore: Johns Hopkins Press, 1966.

YOHE, W. P., and D. S. KARNOSKY, "Interest Rates and Price Level Changes," *Review*, Federal Reserve Bank of St. Louis, 51 (December 1969), 18–36.

The Theory of Economic Growth

15

Economic growth is defined simply as an increase over time in output per capita. According to standard growth theory, in a dynamic, changing economy, the alternatives to economic growth are inflation or unemployment, although the presence of economic growth does not completely exclude the other alternatives.

Economic growth should be distinguished from economic development, even though some writers have used the terms interchangeably. By economic development, we mean not simply an increase in output per capita, but also a change in the structure of an economy—for example, from an economy that produces mainly primary agricultural products to one in which agricultural processing, manufacturing, or trade predominates. Also characteristic of economic development is a substantial increase in savings to finance the investments required for advanced productive techniques. Economic growth, in contrast, refers to increases in real income or output per capita without necessarily any simultaneous change in the structure of the economy.

Structural change, in the sense in which it is used here, refers to massive economic change, such as the commercial revolution of the sixteenth century, or the Industrial Revolution of the eighteenth or nineteenth century. Identifying structural change is a matter of opinion and of degree. The Industrial Revolution clearly qualifies, but was the introduction of the automobile or of television sufficiently important? For purposes of explaining the theory of economic growth, we may say that economic development has occurred whenever there has been a sufficient change in the structure of the economy to cause a change in the assumptions, constants, or functional relationships upon which growth theory is based.

Disregarding development and turning specifically to economic growth, growth models can be either equilibrium or disequilibrium models. For example, an economy may be described as growing along some equilibrium growth path, or may be shown to deviate from that path. The concept of a moving equilibrium in dynamic analysis has not been introduced before, although the ex ante inflation theory in Chapter 13 and the demand-pull models presented in the Appendix of that Chapter are examples of dynamic models. A moving equilibrium requires continuous change in one or more variables, whereas static equilibrium describes an economy at rest. To be truly complete, an economic model should explain the process of change. And such change in dynamic models may move the economy explosively away from equilibrium as well as toward it.

In this chapter, we not only substitute dynamic for static analysis; we also move out of the short run and into the long run, although it is possible for economic growth to occur in the short run by reducing unemployment. An increase in output per capita brought about by reducing unemployment has already been covered as a basic feature of Keynesian economics and will be taken up again in our consideration of business cycles. However, economic growth in the context of this chapter excludes increases in output as a result of decreases in unemployment, specifying, rather, increases in full-employment-equilibrium output.

Our main concern is economic growth resulting from a change in the quality or quantity of a productive resource. An improvement in technology in this context could be interpreted as a change in the quality of one of the productive resources, most generally as an increase in the quality of labor or capital.[1] Technological change can also be looked upon as another resource.

The early classical economists pictured a process of economic growth as tending to move the economy toward a "stationary state"—that is, toward a condition of long-run static equilibrium. For Ricardo and his followers, the stationary state was a gloomy prospect, with no net saving or investment, although in the view of others, such as J.S. Mill, the stationary state was more attractive. The Victorian and neoclassical writers on economic growth, in contrast, felt that through population control, increased investment, technological change, and further division of labor (especially world-wide geographical specialization), advances in economic well-being could be achieved. Then the Great Depression restored an attitude of pessimism.

Three things happened simultaneously around the time of World War II to stimulate interest in economic growth. (1) A worldwide communication explosion occurred, creating universal interest in economic growth and

[1]Some new techniques may even increase the *quantity* of a productive resource. For example, learning to produce iron from low-grade ores or to extract oil from previously inaccessible pools can effectively increase the supply of economic productive resources.

development, and showing the have-not nations that the economic aspects of their lives could be improved. (2) At the same time, new economic-growth theories were developed, based on the Keynesian model. In the post-Keynesian era, growth models have been developed that use both a Keynesian and a neoclassical base. (3) Finally, the conflict between Russia and the United States often focused on comparative growth rates.

One aid to the development of theories of economic growth in the post–World War II era has been the collection and reporting of national-income statistics. In some cases, historical data have been reconstructed. In the United States, reconstructed figures go back to the early days of the Republic, and although their accuracy can be questioned, such statistics have proved useful. The statistical patterns developed on the basis of these reconstructed figures have enabled economists to build and test theories of economic growth.

KEYNESIAN GROWTH THEORY

The pessimistic concept of economic growth held by the classical economists was supplanted by the optimism of the Victorian neoclassicists. The persistence of the Great Depression soon dissipated confidence in the neoclassical theories, however, and replaced that optimistic concept of economic growth with the Keynesian theory of long-run stagnation, as pessimistic in its own way as the early classical theory.[2]

Keynes's theory, as elaborated by Alvin H. Hansen, suggested that certain factors present in the nineteenth century made economic progress virtually automatic by requiring large amounts of investment.[3] According to the theory, these factors—an expanding population, undeveloped frontier lands, and significant capital-using innovations—appeared exhausted by the time of the Great Depression. Let us explore each of these three factors in turn.

The rate of change in the population fell off during the 1920's and even more during the 1930's. Demographers at that time proposed that the populations of western Europe and of North America were becoming stable, and would remain so. Hansen's studies indicated that 60 percent of America's investment demand was motivated by population growth; therefore, the stable population envisioned by the "stagnation theorists" would severely reduce the investment component of effective demand. Similarly, the passing of the American frontier around the turn of the century appeared to mean that by the 1920's another major source of investment demand had dried up in this country.

Faced with population stability and the exhaustion of the frontier, only

---

[2] J. M. Keynes, *The General Theory of Employment, Interest and Money* (New York: Harcourt Brace Jovanovich, 1936), pp. 217–22, 306–309.

[3] Alvin H. Hansen, "Economic Progress and Declining Population Growth," *American Economic Review*, 29 (March 1939), 1–15.

technology remained as a major exogenous stimulus to investment demand. In the 1930's, none of the stagnation theorists foresaw any dramatic capital-using technological developments, as the railroads or the automobile of earlier decades had been. And new techology often appeared to be capital-saving. In the absence of any reason to anticipate growth in the demand for new investment, it was proposed that effective demand would languish, and the economy along with it. The result would be a long-run unemployment equilibrium.

At the time of the Great Depression, it appeared that the stock of capital had ceased to grow, so additional investment would equal zero unless there were a reduction in the rate of interest.[4] But the liquidity-preference curve tended not to fall, because the speculative demand for money balances was postulated on previously existing expectations of a normal rate of interest, and the transactions demand for money balances was a function of a stagnating level of income. Keynes concluded that if the liquidity preference curve would not shift downward, only an increase in the stock of money could lower the interest rate sufficiently to reach a high-enough level of investment to maintain long-run full employment. But sooner or later, even monetary policy would lose its effectiveness, when the interest rate approached its lower limit determined by the liquidity trap (without any growth in the demand for capital goods).[5] Positive savings would cause a decrease in aggregate income until income fell low enough to make the equilibrium level of savings equal the zero level of net new investment.

The probability that zero savings and investment and the full-employment level of income will coincide is extremely remote. It is more likely that a level of effective demand supported only by consumption expenditures would equal effective supply well below full employment. Therefore, a long-run unemployment equilibrium appeared likely to develop if the economy were left to the forces of laissez-faire. Keynes envisioned cycles occurring around the long-run unemployment equilibrium. Imperfect foreknowledge would occasionally increase the demand for capital for brief periods, leading to flurries of positive investment and a short boom, followed by a recession that would temporarily force the economy below its unemployment equilibrium.

Keynes felt that a well-developed economy organized along laissez-faire lines could work itself into a long-run unemployment equilibrium within a generation. ". . . I should guess that a properly run community equipped with modern technical resources, of which the population is not increasing rapidly, ought to be able to bring down the marginal efficiency of capital in equilibrium approximately to zero within a single generation . . ."[6]

---

[4]Once the stock of capital grows to the point where the rate of return on capital is equal to the interest rate, the demand for net investment would drop to zero, and only replacement expenditures would be made. (See Chapter 9, pages 269–300.)

[5]This analysis relies on the assumption that monetary policy could not force a negative interest rate.

[6]Keynes, *General Theory*, p. 220.

Neither Keynes nor Hansen felt that stagnation was inevitable. They both maintained that expansionary fiscal policy could offset the long-run unemployment equilibrium.[7]

Recent history has proved the stagnation theorists wrong in their assumptions. The population growth since World War II, investment opportunities in underdeveloped areas in the United States and in the rest of the world, and technological innovations, such as space travel, computers, air-conditioners, and television, have combined to permit rapid economic growth.[8] However, perhaps the stagnationists would have been right if the Keynesian prescription to increase effective demand had not been followed by each administration since Franklin D. Roosevelt's, and if the various hot and cold wars had not occurred.[9] After our post-Depression experiences, a return to a 1920's-type budget, designed only to finance the government's expenditures and not to stabilize the economy, is unthinkable.

THE HARROD–DOMAR GROWTH MODEL

A growth model related to "Keynesian economics," rather than to the theories of Keynes, was devised by Roy Harrod, one of Keynes's most illustrious followers, and modified by Evsey Domar.[10] The following is a combined version of the Harrod–Domar growth model.[11]

The Harrod–Domar model is based on very restricted assumptions. It is assumed that the average and marginal propensities to consume are equal, and therefore that the consumption function is linear and passes through the origin. As a result, the average and marginal propensity to save are also equal. A simple version also assumes no government expenditures or taxes, so aggregate income can be only consumed or saved.

Three further assumptions are these: (1) The average output–capital ratio is constant, and consequently equals the marginal output–capital ratio.[12] (2) The economy is perpetually in an investment–savings equilibrium, so ex ante savings and investment are always equal and equal to ex post savings and investment. (3) Finally, it is assumed that there is no adjustment lag in any of the variables.

---

[7] Alvin H. Hansen, *Economic Policy and Full Employment* (New York: McGraw-Hill, 1947), p. 306.

[8] For an early criticism of the stagnation theory, see George Terborgh, *The Bogey of Economic Maturity* (Chicago: Machinery & Allied Products Institute, 1945).

[9] For those readers with a monetarist bent, we note that the money stock has been increased at a healthy rate at various times over the last thirty years.

[10] Roy F. Harrod, *Towards a Dynamic Economics* (London: Macmillan, 1948); and Evsey Domar, *Essays in the Theory of Economic Growth* (New York: Oxford University Press, 1957).

[11] This section has been adapted in part from Kenneth K. Kurihara, *National Income and Economic Growth* (Skokie, Ill.: Rand McNally, 1961).

[12] The output–capital ratio is the reciprocal of the more familiar capital–output ratio. The significance of this concept in growth theory will be considered in detail in the following section on the warranted growth rate.

This version of the Harrod–Domar model proposes the existence of a warranted growth rate (G_w) and a natural growth rate (G_n). For the economy to remain in equilibrium, both these growth rates must equal a third, the actual rate of growth (G) permitted by effective demand. The warranted growth rate is the rate the economy can afford with its given flow of savings to finance investment. The natural growth rate, on the other hand, is determined by the rate of change in the labor force or in the total number of hours of labor worked (N), and the rate of increase in worker productivity, tied to improvements in technology. These two factors, the change in the labor force and the change in worker productivity, together determine the rate of change in labor efficiency. The actual growth rate the economy can achieve depends on the rate of change in effective demand, D_y, or $(C + I + G)$.[13] The economy is in dynamic equilibrium only when the three rates of growth are equal.

The Warranted Growth Rate

The warranted-growth concept employed here follows the Domar model, since it specifically introduces excess capacity resulting from investment expenditures. Up to now we have considered investment mainly from the demand side, without considering that investment creates additional productive capacity in future time periods. The warranted growth rate is simply the rate that keeps capital fully employed, and is determined by the level of investment, which in turn must equal the level of savings that the economy will sustain in equilibrium.

Whether the warranted rate of growth will actually be achieved depends on whether effective demand, D_y, grows fast enough to absorb the growing capacity created by the additional net investment of each time period. Therefore, the warranted growth rate G_w equals the growth rate of productive capacity, or potential supply $\Delta Y_s / Y_s$. This relationship may be restated by the following formula:

$$G_w = \frac{\Delta Y_s}{Y_s}$$

What determines the warranted rate of growth? In part, it depends on the period-by-period change in the capital stock (ΔK), which is the same as net investment (I). It depends also on the productivity of capital, called the output–capital ratio, which indicates the relationship of capacity output to capital stock. (Domar uses lower-case sigma, σ, to represent the output–capital ratio.) To illustrate how the output–capital ratio is determined, suppose that $1 of final output is produced through the use of $3 of capital. Then, a GNP of $800 billion would be produced with the employment of $2,400 billion worth of capital, and the output–capital ratio is 1:3. The relationship between the output–capital ratio, σ, the change in the capital

[13] Note that "effective demand" is the concept developed in Chapter 8 and is distinct from the "aggregate demand" concept developed in Chapter 12.

stock, ΔK, and the change in productive capacity, ΔY_s is as follows:

$$\sigma = \frac{\Delta Y_s}{\Delta K}$$

Since I is identical to ΔK, if we multiply both sides by I,

$$\sigma I = \Delta Y_s$$

The absolute period-by-period increase in the economy's capacity to produce, ΔY_s, equals σI, which means that the total amount of net investment (I) multiplied by its productivity (σ) determines the absolute increase in the economy's capacity to produce.[14] This absolute increase can be converted into the warranted growth rate, G_w, by dividing the change in productive capacity by achievable capacity, Y_s.

To summarize the discussion up to this point,

1. $\sigma = \frac{\Delta Y_s}{\Delta K} = \frac{\Delta Y_s}{I}$
2. $\Delta Y_s = \sigma I$
3. $G_w = \frac{\Delta Y_s}{Y_s}$

where

σ = output–capital ratio
Y_s = productive capacity of the economy
ΔY_s = change in productive capacity
ΔK or I = change in capital stock, which is the same as net investment

Since a change in productive capacity is equal to the output–capital ratio multiplied by net investment, the warranted growth rate must equal the output–capital ratio multiplied by the ratio of net investment to productive capacity:

Since

$$\Delta Y_s = \sigma I$$

Then

$$\frac{\Delta Y_s}{Y_s} = \frac{\sigma I}{Y_s} = G_w$$

If a lower-case delta, δ, is used to represent the ratio of net investment to

---

[14]Alternatively, starting with $\frac{\Delta Y_s}{\Delta K} = \frac{Y_s}{K}$ (equality of marginal and average output–capital ratios)

Since $\sigma = \frac{Y_s}{K}$ by definition

then $\frac{\Delta Y_s}{\Delta K} = \sigma$ (by substitution)

so $\Delta Y_s = \sigma \Delta K$ (multiplying both sides by ΔK)

Since $\Delta K = I$ by definition

$\Delta Y_s = \sigma I$

productive capacity, I/Y_s, then

$$\frac{\Delta Y_s}{Y_s} = \sigma\delta \quad \text{or} \quad G_w = \sigma\delta$$

Therefore, if the output–capital ratio is 1:3, net investment is \$20 billion, and productive capacity is \$100 billion, then the warranted rate of growth equals

$$\frac{1}{3} \times \frac{20}{100} = .067$$

The Actual Growth Rate

Turning our attention to the actual growth rate, G, which is equal to the growth in effective demand $\Delta D_y/D_y$

$$G = \frac{\Delta D_y}{D_y}$$

We have noted that the warranted rate of growth will not be achieved unless effective demand keeps pace with it. In the simplified economy that we have assumed, there is no government or foreign sector; so effective demand D_y equals consumption (C) plus investment (I), or

$$D_y = C + I$$

As we noted in Chapter 8,

$$C = a + bY$$

where a equals the y-axis intercept, and b equals the marginal propensity to consume. By assumption in the Harrod–Domar model, a equals zero, because the consumption function passes through the origin. Therefore, $C = bY$, and substituting for C in the second equation above,

$$D_y = bY + I$$

which may be rearranged as

$$D_y - bY = I$$

Factoring,

$$D_y(1 - b) = I$$

and solving for D_y,

$$D_y = \left(\frac{1}{1 - b}\right)I$$

As you may remember from Chapter 8, the multiplier, k, equals $1/(1 - b)$. Therefore, effective demand equals the multiplier times investment, kI, and a change in net investment, ΔI, will induce a change in effective demand by an amount equal to $k\Delta I$. Restated,

$$D_y = \left(\frac{1}{1 - b}\right)I$$

$$D_y = kI$$

$$\Delta D_y = k\Delta I$$

Let us consider the influence of a change in effective demand on the actual growth rate, G. Since

$$G = \frac{\Delta D_y}{D_y}$$

and since

$$\Delta D_y = k\Delta I$$

then by substitution,

$$G = k\left(\frac{\Delta I}{D_y}\right)$$

If a lower-case alpha, α, is used to represent the ratio of an incremental change in investment to effective demand, $\Delta I/D_y$, then

$$G = k\alpha$$

Since $G = k\alpha$, the actual rate of growth can be computed by multiplying k by the ratio of an incremental change in net investment to effective demand. If the MPC is .80, the multiplier, k, equals 5. Now, if ΔI is \$1 billion and effective demand is \$100 billion, then the actual rate of growth equals

$$5 \times \frac{1}{100} = .05$$

The Interaction of the Warranted and Actual Growth Rates

Assuming no change in the long-run consumption function, effective demand at any given level of aggregate income will not increase unless net investment increases. But a constant level of net investment will increase the economy's capacity to produce, without causing a corresponding increase in effective demand. Equilibrium implies that total productive capacity, Y_s, equals total effective demand, D_y. Once excess capacity develops, future investments will be reduced if effective demand remains unchanged. Consequently, a constant level of investment demand cannot be maintained over the long run without creating disequilibrium. Net investment must continuously increase, or it will eventually decrease because of excess capacity. Therefore, static equilibrium, which implies a constant level of net investment, cannot be maintained in a dynamic economy.[15] Only in the classical stationary state with zero net investment (and zero savings) can a static equilibrium be maintained in a dynamic framework.

If equilibrium is to be achieved, the warranted growth rate (G_w) and the actual growth rate (G) must be equal. When they are equal, the required rate of growth in investment ($\Delta I/I$) must equal the productivity of capital (output–capital ratio), σ, times the marginal propensity to save $(1 - b)$.

The proof of the equality between $\Delta I/I$ and $\sigma\,(1 - b)$ when G_w and G are equal is as follows:

1. $G = \alpha k$
2. $G_w = \sigma\delta$
3. $\alpha k = \sigma\delta$ in equilibrium

Since

$$\alpha = \frac{\Delta I}{D_y},\ k = \frac{1}{1-b},\ \delta = \frac{I}{Y_s}$$

Substituting for α, k, and δ,

4. $\dfrac{\Delta I}{D_y}\dfrac{1}{(1-b)} = \sigma\dfrac{I}{Y_s}$

Multiplying both sides by $D_y\,(1 - b)$ and dividing by I gives

5. $\dfrac{\Delta I}{I} = \sigma\dfrac{D_y}{Y_s}(1-b)$

Since $D_y = Y_s$ in equilibrium, then

6. $\dfrac{\Delta I}{I} = \sigma(1-b)$

The significance of equation 6 is that the required rate of growth in investment, $\Delta I/I$, is equal to $\sigma(1 - b)$, which, in turn, is equal to the warranted growth rate, G_w, when the economy is in equilibrium. Therefore, when G_w and G are in equilibrium, the warranted growth rate is equal to the output–capital ratio times the marginal propensity to save.

The proof that $G_w = \sigma(1 - b)$ when $G_w = G$ is as follows: As we have seen from equation 6 above,

1. $\dfrac{\Delta I}{I} = \sigma(1-b)$
2. $G_w = \sigma\delta$ where $\delta = \dfrac{I}{Y_s}$. Where equilibrium occurs, Y_s must equal D_y, and by one of the original assumptions of the model, $S = I$. Therefore,

---

[15] Like Alice's having to run faster to stay in the same place in *Through the Looking Glass.*

3. $\frac{I}{Y_s} = \frac{S}{D_y}$. Since one of the original assumptions of the models is that the APS, S/D_y, is equal to the MPS, $\Delta S/\Delta D_y$, and since the MPS is also $(1 - b)$,

4. $\frac{I}{Y_s} = (1 - b)$

Substituting in equation 2,

5. $G_w = \sigma(1 - b)$

when G_w equals C in equilibrium.

The process by which the warranted growth rate is established and maintained is shown in Table 15-1. The illustration is based on a marginal propensity to consume, MPC, of 80 percent, and an output–capital ratio of 1:4, or 25 percent. The marginal propensity to save, MPS, is 20 percent. Multiplying σ by the MPS determines the warranted growth rate, 5 percent.

TABLE 15-1 Harrod–Domar Illustration

	(1)	(2)	(3)	(4)	(5)
Time	Productive Capacity	Consumption	Investment–Savings	Effective Demand	Absolute Growth in Productive Capacity
	Y_s	C	I	D_y	σI
1	100	80	20	100	5
2	105	84	21	105	5.25
3	110.25	88.20	22.05	110.25	5.51
4	115.76	92.61	23.15	115.76	5.79
5	121.55	97.24	24.31	121.55	6.08
6	127.63	102.10	25.53	127.63	6.38
7	134.01	107.21	26.80	134.01	6.70
8	140.71	112.57	28.14	140.71	7.04
9	147.75	118.20	29.55	147.75	7.39
10	155.14	124.11	31.03	155.14	—

Given: MPC or b = 80%
(1 − b) or MPS = 20%
σ = .25
$(1 - b)\sigma$ = .05

The economy starts in equilibrium in period 1, with productive capacity, Y_s in column 1, and effective demand, D_y in column 4, both equal to \$100. Savings and investment are equal in equilibrium, and column 3 illustrates their level in any given period of time. In period 1, savings and investment are \$20 (20 percent of \$100), and consumption, shown in column 2, equals \$80 (80 percent of \$100). (Remember, $C = bY$ and $S = (1 - b)Y$, since the consumption function passes through the origin.) Column 5 shows the amount of additional capacity created by the net investment of each time period, equal to σI, by which amount effective demand must grow in the subsequent time period to maintain full employment of capital.

The amount of additional capacity created at the end of period 1, when the new investment projects are completed, is 25% × \$20, or \$5. Therefore, at the start of period 2, effective demand must increase by \$5 in order to maintain full employment of capital. Similarly, the value of σI at the end of period 2 indicates that a growth of \$5.25 must occur in time period 3 in order to utilize the excess capacity created during period 2. Since effective demand equals kI, net investment must increase from \$20 to \$21 between periods 1 and 2 in order to raise effective demand to \$105. As long as the output–capital ratio (σ) and the ratio of net investment to productive capacity (I/Y_s) remain unchanged, the warranted growth rate will remain 5 percent, and as long as investment and consumption both increase by 5 percent annually, effective demand will increase by 5 percent a year.[16] The excess capacity created in one time period will consistently be absorbed in the following period, and the savings of each period will equal the investment of that same period.

The particular version of the Harrod–Domar growth model that we have been describing is shown graphically in Figure 15-1. The savings function,

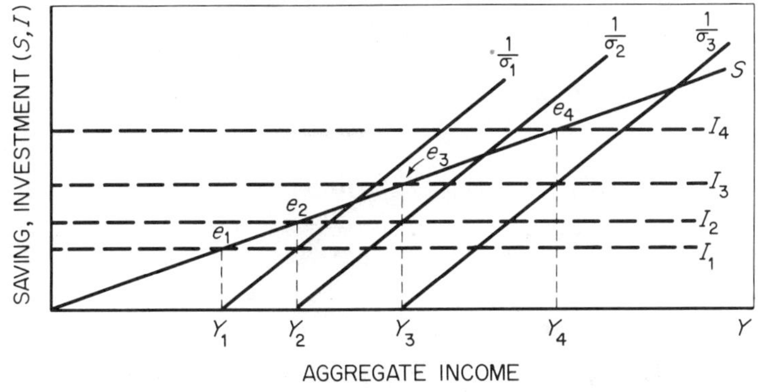

FIG. 15-1 Harrod-Domar Growth Model

S, passes through the origin because the MPS and APS are equal. Net investment is assumed constant in each time period; therefore, each investment function is drawn as a horizontal line. The initial equilibrium occurs at point e_1, where the savings function crosses the I_1 line. Therefore, Y_1 is the initial equilibrium level of aggregate income at which capital is fully employed. In a static model, the economy would settle down in a stable equilibrium at that level; however, in a dynamic model, the economy cannot stay at I_1 because of the existence of excess capacity. The exact amount of added capacity depends on the output–capital ratio, represented in Figure 15-1 by its reciprocal, the capital–output ratio, or $1/\sigma$. The higher the capital–output ratio,

[16]Remember, $G_w = G$ in equilibrium; therefore, the ratio of net investment to productive capacity must also equal the marginal propensity to save. Since effective demand increases by 5 percent a year, the actual growth rate, G, must also equal 5 percent. Since $G = k\alpha$, then $G = 5(1/100) = 5\%$.

the steeper the slope of the $1/\sigma$ function, since a steeper $1/\sigma$ curve implies that a greater quantity of investment is required for a given increase in output to occur.

The x-axis intercept of $1/\sigma_1$ is the equilibrium level of aggregate income for period 1. The point at which $1/\sigma_1$ crosses the I_1 line indicates the amount of excess capacity added during period 1, and therefore indicates how much aggregate income will have to grow during period 2 to maintain full employment of capital. At the Y_2 aggregate-income level, equilibrium savings exceed I_1 level of investment. Therefore, an investment level equal to I_2 is required in period 2 to maintain equilibrium. So equilibrium in period 2 occurs at point e_2, where the savings function crosses the I_2 level of investment. The added excess capacity caused by the excess of I_2 over I_1 in period 2 requires aggregate income increase even further in period 3 than it would have by the original, built-in increase in capacity. The equilibrium level of aggregate income for period 3, Y_3, is determined by the intersection of the $1/\sigma_2$ line with the I_2 level of investment. This indicates how much Y will have to grow in period 3 to absorb the excess capacity created in period 2. Again, at Y_3 level of aggregate income, the quantity of income saved has risen above the I_2 level of investment, and therefore net investment must increase to I_3 in period 3 to achieve a savings–investment equilibrium at e_3. The I_3 investment, in turn, adds still more capacity, and so the process continues. In Figure 15-1, the process is arbitrarily terminated at Y_4 level of aggregate income, where savings is equal to the I_4 level of investment; however, as long as effective demand continues to grow sufficiently, and as long as the marginal propensity to save and the output–capital ratio are unchanged, the growth process would continue unchecked.

What happens if the warranted and actual growth rates diverge? Deviations between the two rates will induce either inflation or recession. Therefore, some writers have referred to the Harrod–Domar theory as a "razor's-edge" theory of economic growth. For example, suppose that in our illustration in Table 15-1, net investment in period 3 falls short of the required level of \$22.05. As a result, effective demand would fall short of potential output. Insufficient investment would then lead to excess capacity and would halt the growth process, causing still further reductions in investment in period 4, when the existence of excess capacity is recognized. No firm with excess capacity will be apt to increase its capital expenditure, and a shortage of net investment can have the paradoxical effect of creating excess capacity and giving the appearance of too much investment, which would lead to a state of chronic unemployment, with an output level that falls below the potential.

Similarly, if investment had been in excess of \$22.05 in period 3, effective demand would exceed productive capacity, causing demand-pull inflation and giving the misleading appearance of too little investment. The effect of excessive effective demand can be cumulative; it can induce businessmen to increase investment during the next period in an attempt to increase output to the level of effective demand. But the added investment may itself increase the divergence between the economy's output potential and effective demand, thereby stimulating a further round of demand-pull inflation.

Let us summarize what happens to the economy if the warranted and actual growth rates diverge. If the warranted exceeds the actual growth rate, excess capacity leading to chronic unemployment results; if the actual exceeds the warranted growth rate, chronic inflation of the demand-pull type results.

Policies for Growth Without Inflation or Recession

The growth rate can be influenced by very diverse policies, which must be tailored to fit a particular situation. The determination of the proper growth policy is difficult, since the same policy may give opposite results under different conditions. And as the Harrod–Domar model shows, the penalties for allowing the warranted and actual growth rates to deviate are severe. Mistakes in public policy can set off self-sustaining waves of unemployment or inflation.

Technically, the warranted growth rate can be increased either by increasing the output–capital ratio or by increasing the ratio of net investment to productive capacity. As we have previously seen, when G_w and G are in equilibrium, the ratio of net investment to productive capacity is equal to the marginal propensity to save. Therefore, to increase the equilibrium growth rate (that is, where $G_w = G$) would require an increase in either the output–capital ratio or in the marginal propensity to save.

For example, in the illustration in Table 15-1, where $G_w = G$, if a technological change increased the output–capital ratio from 1:4 to 1:3, the equilibrium growth rate (MPS $\times\ \sigma$) would increase from .05 to .067. The same growth rate could also be achieved if σ were unchanged at .25 and the MPS rose from 20 to $26\frac{1}{2}$ percent.[17]

Although the warranted growth rate can be increased by increasing the propensity to save, all added savings must go into investment for the policy to be effective. Any economy attempting to speed up economic growth should attempt to increase savings at the expense of consumption only as long as there are sufficient investment opportunities to absorb all savings. (The difficulties that may be encountered in undertaking new investment projects—the capital absorption problem—was considered in Chapter 9).

Once the warranted and actual growth rates get out of line, public policy should be directed to restoring an equilibrium between the two. Whether it is more desirable to increase the lower growth rate or reduce the higher one depends upon the economic goals of society and the difficulty and uncertainty involved in implementing the necessary policy to achieve those goals.

---

[17]Remember that the increase in the marginal propensity to save reduces the multiplier (k), which would in turn slow down the actual rate of growth. Therefore, the ratio of an incremental change in investment to effective demand, α, must increase enough not only to compensate for the reduction in k, but also to equal the higher warranted growth rate, if the economy is to reach a higher equilibrium.

For example, assume that the actual rate exceeds the warranted rate, threatening the economy with chronic inflation. In order to eliminate inflation, it may be desirable to reduce the rate of increase in actual demand by reducing the multiplier. The multiplier could be reduced by decreasing the marginal propensity to consume—possibly by introducing a compulsory savings plan under which an individual's after-tax income would be temporarily turned over to the government. Unfortunately, any attempt to decrease α will surely decrease the ratio of investment to productive capacity (δ), which may prevent the gap between the two growth rates from closing. If, on the other hand, we try to increase the warranted growth rate by increasing δ through accelerated depreciation or an investment tax credit, then α will also tend to increase, worsening the inflationary pressure. A convenient solution to the problem is either to introduce into the model a type of government expenditure and tax that will not affect the private economy, or to attempt to influence the propensity to consume, and thereby the multiplier. Another possibility is to change the output–capital ratio. An increase in the output–capital ratio would increase the warranted growth rate, but it is not clear what government policy could be used to accomplish this.[18]

However, it is likely that the simplified assumptions of this model make the balance appear somewhat more precarious than it is. As we shall see in the next chapter, on business cycles, forces may develop that will choke off cumulative inflation or recession. However, the lesson is clear that the actual and warranted rates of growth must be in reasonably close balance to maintain orderly economy growth. Furthermore, the Harrod–Domar type of growth model suggests that economic growth is directly related to the rate of growth in net investment, because a failure of investment to increase each year at the proper rate either causes excess- or under-capacity, with resulting unemployment, or causes demand-pull inflation.

The equilibrium growth rate under the Harrod–Domar model need not be a socially optimum rate. Clearly, in poor countries, the equilibrium growth rate may fall below the level required to provide a satisfactory level of living for the people. In contrast, some argue that the Harrod–Domar equilibrium may exceed the socially desirable level of economic growth in certain cases. But regardless of what the socially desirable growth rate may be, economic growth requires that both productive capacity and effective demand grow together.

The Natural Growth Rate

In addition to the warranted and the actual rates, Harrod describes a third rate of growth—the natural rate. The natural rate of growth is derived

---

[18]However, if the productivity of old capital equipment suddenly improved, excess capacity would be further increased, thus damping the stimulating effect on new investment. In practice, the output–capital ratio might also be increased if the additional investment was more productive than the average-investment level, although this possibility is eliminated by one of our earlier assumptions.

by combining the rate of change in the labor force with the rate of change in labor productivity that is tied to labor-augmenting technology.[19] For example, if the labor force grows at 1 percent a year and new investment implements labor-augmenting technology to increase by 2 percent annually, the natural rate of growth would be 3 percent a year. The significance of the natural growth rate is that it is the rate of growth required to maintain full employment of labor rather than full employment of capital.

Growth-Rate Equilibrium

Although in a well-balanced, growing economy, all three growth rates will tend to be equal, the introduction of a third rate makes economic balance even more difficult to achieve. Suppose the warranted rate, G_w, tends to be larger than the natural rate, G_n.[20] The result will be excess capacity, because it is impossible for an economy to produce at a rate greater than the full employment of labor for an extended time. As we saw in our discussion of the warranted growth rate, the existence of excess capacity leads to a reduction in investment, which in turn causes a decrease in effective demand in the next time period, and causes unemployment when G falls below G_w, resulting in a dynamic deflationary gap.[21]

On the other hand, if G_n is greater than G_w, the result will be structural unemployment, because capacity is insufficient to employ all available workers productively. Relaxing the assumption of a homogeneous labor force in industrial economies, workers with low marginal productivity may be least able to find a job. Such non-Keynesian unemployment can be counteracted

---

[19] The effective labor supply realistically depends on more than the number of workers and amount of labor-augmenting technology. The Scandinavian experience has shown that a nation's productivity can be increased without an increase in new plant and equipment. When the government of Norway, for a while quite collectivist in ideology, placed so low a ceiling on profits of enterprise that there was relatively little new investment in plant and equipment during the 1950's, the national real income still grew. This anomaly has been attributed to a sizable increase in expenditures on education and training of the populace. Allan G. Gruchy, *Comparative Economic Systems* (Boston: Houghton Mifflin, 1966), pp. 294–446.

The point is that "investment," as it is usually construed, may be zero and still we may have growth, at least for a limited period of time. The French experience, when worker productivity increased after general wage increases, seems to indicate that the natural growth rate may change as the result of morale changes, unaccompanied by any objectively measurable investment in human capital, such as increased education.

[20] It may be possible to operate at more than 100 percent of the labor force for a short period of time, by having people work overtime, reemploying retirees, or inducing those not normally part of the labor force to come into it, as happened in the United States during World War II; however, such conditions would probably not persist for very long and would probably require that some exceptional inducement such as patriotism be added to the usual economic rewards of work.

[21] In this section, full employment is assumed, but if the economy is below full employment and the warranted rate of growth is greater than the natural rate (if $G_w > G_n$), the economy will move toward full employment of labor. However, once full employment is achieved, if the economy tries to maintain the same rate of growth, a labor shortage will result and force a decrease in investment expenditures. Therefore, the natural growth rate acts as a full-employment ceiling beyond which the economy cannot expand.

by either increasing the warranted rate of growth or decreasing the labor force. Inflation may occur in the midst of such unemployment if the actual growth rate is higher than the warranted rate. Whichever way the warranted and the natural growth rates diverge, the result will be unemployment, in one case because of excess capacity and in the other because of a lack of capacity to profitably employ less skilled workers.

The possibility of G_n and G_w failing to adjust automatically to each other is based on either the assumption of fixed proportions of capital to labor in the production function, or the assumption that the payments to labor and capital remain constant in real terms; otherwise, substitution of one factor for another should bring the two into line.

To illustrate the case of fixed proportions, where G_n exceeds G_w, a decrease in the real wage will not bring about increased employment, because the marginal product of the added workers would be zero. Under the assumption of fixed proportions, no matter how low in price one resource becomes relative to another, only a constant amount of it will be employed with any given amount of the other resource. From another vantage point, fixed factor proportions, which could be shown as right-angle isoquants, imply that to maintain a given quantity of output, a certain amount of both capital and labor must be employed. If the quantity of either factor decreases, the volume of output will likewise decrease, even if the other factor should remain constant or even increase. For an economy with a given capital stock, aggregate output and labor inputs are both fixed, or conversely, for an economy with a given level of employment of labor, capital inputs and aggregate output are both fixed. Therefore, if the proportion of workers exceeds the availability of capital, unemployment will result.

To illustrate the situation where payments to labor are fixed but where varying proportions of inputs are possible, suppose again that G_n exceeds G_w. Labor will not be substituted for capital if workers in an economy are not subject to money illusion and if union and government action are designed to maintain the real wage. This concept of maintaining the real wage, reflected in formulas tying wage rates to the cost of living in some labor contracts, will perpetuate unemployment, because greater employment of labor would reduce the marginal product of labor and therefore require a reduction in the real wage.

The moral of the Harrod–Domar model is that policy recommendations must be based on an accurate, realistic appraisal of underlying conditions, or the policy may produce unexpected and undesirable results.[22]

---

[22]In the 1940's, some economists in low-income countries used a simplistic interpretation of Keynes's *General Theory*, and argued in favor of increasing effective demand to encourage economic growth, expecting productive capacity to follow along. Such a policy may work where the productive capacity already exists, but in many of the poorer countries, to increase effective demand without a simultaneous increase in capacity led only to inflation, while structural unemployment remained.

The so-called modern neoclassical growth theory, usually associated with R.M. Solow and others, represents a logical development from the Harrod–Domar model.[23] The neoclassical model allows us to relax the rigid assumption of fixed proportions of capital and labor and also permits the output–capital ratio (σ) to vary. The basic version of the neoclassical model assumes that savings and investment plans are always fulfilled and that the quantities demanded equal the quantities supplied in all markets. As a result full employment will always prevail. Yet the Keynesian MPC and MPS are retained in this otherwise neoclassical model.

One way in which the modern neoclassical growth theory returns to the classical concepts is through the assumption of diminishing returns. As capital is increased per unit of labor, capital becomes less productive, so the output–capital ratio decreases. Likewise, σ will increase if more labor is employed with a given capital stock. Assuming that capital and labor can be substituted for each other as cost and productivity dictate, equilibrium can be achieved even where one resource is scarce.

The introduction of decreasing returns to capital—that is, dropping the assumption of a constant value for σ—signifies that increasing the proportion of savings relative to consumption does not necessarily increase the equilibrium rate of growth. In terms of the equilibrium-growth formula, $\sigma(1 - b)$, when the $1 - b$ factor increases, σ will simultaneously decrease. Assuming that the decrease in σ just offsets the increase in $1 - b$, growth in the neoclassical model requires an increase either in the labor supply or in the level of technology. (If we specify per capita rather than total growth, the only source of economic growth is technological advance.) If the growth rate of capital exceeds that of the labor force, the output-capital ratio will decline, thereby leading to a decrease in G_w. Solow[24] proposes that, of the economic growth we have experienced, about one eighth can be attributed to increased capital per worker, and about seven eighths to higher levels of technology.[25]

---

[23]A large body of literature has grown up on the subject of neoclassical growth theory. Some of the most important contributions are Robert M. Solow, "A Contribution to the Theory of Economic Growth," *Quarterly Journal of Economics*, 70 (February 1956), 65–94; Solow, "Technical Change and the Aggregate Production Function," *Review of Economics and Statistics*, 39 (August 1957), 312–320; Edmund S. Phelps, "The Golden Rule of Accumulation: A Fable for Growthmen," *American Economic Review*, 51 (September 1961), 638–43; Phelps, "The New View of Investment: A Neoclassical Analysis," *Quarterly Journal of Economics*, 76 (November 1962), 548–67; and J. E. Meade, *A Neoclassical Theory of Economic Growth* (New York: Oxford University Press, 1961).

[24]Solow, "Technical Change," p. 316.

[25]The empirical application of modern neoclassical growth theory generally employs a Cobb–Douglas production function, which is linear and homogeneous in the first degree, so that if capital and labor inputs both change in the same proportion, output also changes by that proportion. For example, if capital and labor are both doubled, output will also double; if both are increased by 1 percent, output will increase by 1 percent. In addition,

For technological change to have an impact on sustained growth, the new technology must increase labor productivity and so increase G_n. *Disembodied technology* (that is, technological change not incorporated in new capital equipment) is almost certain to increase labor productivity and so increase G_n. *Embodied technology* (technological change embodied in new capital equipment) will almost surely increase G_w, but will most likely also cause a simultaneous increase in labor productivity and in G_n.[26]

Solow's attribution of seven eighths of economic growth to technology is due to an assumption of disembodied technology. If embodied technology is assumed, then capital must grow if new technology is to be adopted, and the proportion of growth attributed to technology itself will decrease.[27]

It may be observed empirically that societies with high rates of savings and investment are also the societies that have high rates of technological change. Therefore, it has been proposed that technological change is itself a function of the level of investment and that higher levels of technology embodied in new investment offset the tendency toward diminishing returns to capital. If this is indeed the case, then σ is, in effect, a constant, and the Harrod–Domar model is fortuitously applicable without modification.

An advantage of the neoclassical over the Harrod–Domar model is that by allowing for factor substitutability, the modern neoclassical theory leads to an eventual balance between the warranted growth rate and the natural growth rate.[28] Suppose, for example, the warranted rate exceeds the natural rate, and the effective labor force grows at a slower rate than capital. Profit-maximizing producers will invest more, but each increase in capital will add

---

each factor's marginal product, multiplied by the number of units of input and summed, is equal to the total product. Paul H. Douglas, *The Theory of Wages* (New York: Kelley and Millman, 1957), pp. 113–58.

The specific Cobb–Douglas production function generally used is

$$Y = AK^{a}N^{1-a}$$

where K is the quantity of capital; N is the quantity of labor; a is the change in output resulting from a change in capital inputs, holding labor constant; and A is a scale factor representing technological change. The supply of land is assumed constant, so land is omitted from the formula.

The values that Douglas and colleague, C. W. Cobb, found empirically from production data for the early 1900's were

$$P = 1.01N^{3/4}K^{1/4}$$

However, it should be noted that the use of data from different years will give different values for A and for the coefficients of N and K.

[26]Technological change may be capital saving, labor saving, or neutral. The difference between capital-saving and labor-saving technological change was discussed in Chapter 9. Neutral technological change, as its name implies, increases both worker and capital productivity in the same proportion. The technological change generally assumed in neoclassical growth theory is of the neutral variety.

[27]R. M. Solow, "Technical Progress, Capital Formation, and Economic Growth," *American Economic Review*, 52 (May 1962), 76–78.

[28]The assumption of factor substitutability not only automatically tends to bring the natural and warranted rates into balance, but also allows the two rates to diverge temporarily without necessarily causing a recession or structural unemployment. If the supply of one factor is growing at an excessive rate, excess capacity need not result, since the more abundant factor can be substituted for the scarcer.

less to output than did the preceding one. Any decrease in the productivity of capital will reduce the value of σ, and any decrease in σ reduces the warranted growth rate. The decrease in the warranted rate would continue until it equaled the natural rate. Therefore, in the long run no difficulties can develop because of deviations of the warranted from the natural growth rate in the neoclassical system.

Figure 15-2 shows a graphical presentation of the neoclassical growth

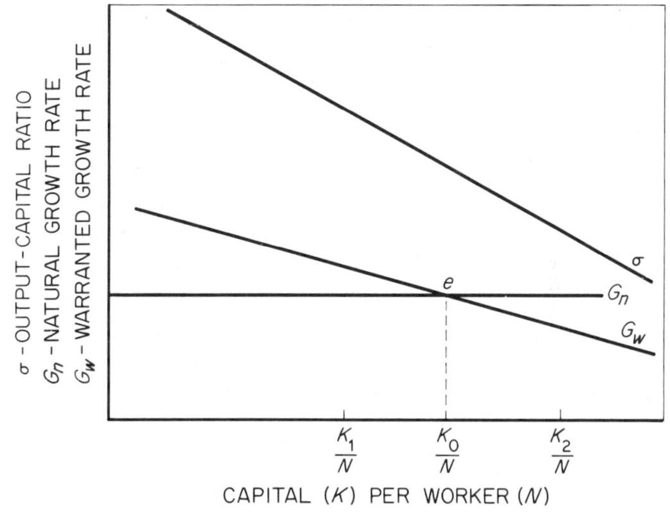

FIG. 15-2 Neoclassical Growth Model

model, devised by James Tobin.[29] It presents all the components of the neoclassical model as linear functions. Capital per worker, the reciprocal of the N/K relationship, is plotted on the x-axis. A movement to the right along the x-axis shows more capital being used per unit of labor; that is, capital deepening occurs. The y-axis measures the output–capital ratio, σ; the natural growth rate, G_n; and the warranted growth rate, G_w. Because of diminishing returns to capital, σ decreases as more capital is used per worker. Therefore, the σ curve in the figure is negatively sloped. However, unlike the case in the Harrod-Domar model, σ represents here only the *average* output–capital ratio, and not the marginal output–capital ratio. Because the average ratio is negatively sloped, the marginal will no longer equal the average.

The equilibrium warranted growth rate, where $G_w = G$, is equal to the MPS multiplied by the output–capital ratio, or

$$G_w = (1 - b)\sigma$$

[29]James Tobin, "Money and Economic Growth," *Econometrica*, 33 (October 1965), 671–84.

As long as the MPS is unchanged, the G_w function will remain a constant proportion of σ. Therefore, the G_w curve in Figure 15-2 is also negatively sloped, but not as steeply as the σ curve, since the proportion determined by $(1 - b)$ is less than 1. The σ curve and the G_w curve would both intersect the x-axis at the same point. The natural growth rate, G_n, defined as the rate of increase in the labor force plus the rate of change in labor productivity, is assumed to be independent of capital per worker, and is shown as a horizontal line.

Equilibrium occurs at point e, where the warranted and natural growth rates are equal. If the economy was at K_1/N in Figure 15-2, where the warranted rate is above the natural rate, there would be a tendency for capital deepening to occur. As a result, the warranted rate would fall until it equaled the natural rate. Similarly, if the economy finds itself at K_2/N, where the warranted rate is below the natural rate, the slower pace of investment relative to the rate of change in the labor force would automatically cause capital shallowing to occur and force an adjustment back toward equilibrium at point e. A technological change that increases σ for any given level of K/N will also raise the G_w growth path. However, an increase in the G_w growth path alone does not affect the equilibrium growth rate; in order to increase the equilibrium rate, the G_n growth path must increase. Assuming a constant labor supply, the equilibrium economic growth rate could be increased only if technology raises the G_n growth path by increasing the productivity of labor.

Putty–Clay Models

As a natural development from the Harrod–Domar and neoclassical growth models, the "putty–clay" models offer certain insights into the nature of capital.[30] Ex ante, capital may be compared to putty. Both are malleable; they can assume any desired shape. Ex post, capital may better be compared to clay. Its shape, once determined, may be difficult or impossible to change.

The significance of the putty–clay analogy to questions of economic growth lies in the relationship of capital to labor. Ex ante, virtually any degree of capital or labor intensity is possible. Ex post, the proportion of capital to labor is uniquely determined. Therefore, capital deepening or shallowing can occur only in the planning stage, or ex ante. Since the natural growth rate, G_n, is assumed to be independent of the amount of capital per worker, changes in the planning stage cannot affect G_n but can affect only the

---

[30] Putty-clay models were originated and extended by the following: Leif Johansen, "Substitution vs. Fixed Production Coefficients in the Theory of Economic Growth: A Synthesis," *Econometrica*, 27 (April 1959), 157–75; W. E. G. Salter, *Productivity and Technical Change* (Cambridge: Cambridge University Press, 1960); R. M. Solow, "Substitution and Fixed Proportions in the Theory of Capital," *Review of Economic Studies*, 29 (June 1962), 207–18; and E. S. Phelps, "Substitution, Fixed Proportions, Growth and Distribution," *International Economic Review*, 4 (September 1963), 265–88.

warranted growth rate, G_w. Consequently, the putty-clay concept does not affect the final equilibrium growth rate, but may affect the path to equilibrium.

Many versions of this putty–clay concept have been developed, depending on the underlying assumptions.[31] For example, a change in the assumptions regarding wage rates or depreciation will influence investment decisions; or different assumptions regarding the malleability of capital give rise to putty–putty or clay–clay models. The possible variations on this theme appear to be many, but as long as the putty-clay models do not affect the natural growth rate and as long as the warranted and natural rates intersect, the models do not appear to change the equilibrium growth rate.

Money and Economic Growth

Up to this point, we have considered growth theory mainly in real terms. The introduction of money means that members of the economy can now choose to hold wealth either in the form of real assets, as they could previously, or in the form of money.[32] Therefore, as long as a demand for money exists, the community's total wealth exceeds the value of its real assets. The individual holding money sees himself as wealthier (and in fact he does have a proportionately greater claim to the economy's real wealth), even though the real wealth of the economy is unchanged. Although the existence of money does not change the amount of real assets, its existence as an alternative means of holding wealth does affect the economy's equilibrium, by adding a demand for money in addition to and as an alternative to a demand for real assets. Money facilitates exchange and so permits increased output. Holding money carries a zero opportunity cost for the economy, because the society can produce money for virtually no cost. In contrast, holding real assets implies a real, positive opportunity cost for society.

In addition to its zero opportunity cost, money also carries virtually no market, default, or liquidity risk for the asset holder. So money is the least risky asset in an investor's portfolio. (Of course, it is subject to a purchasing power risk.)

The decision of the individual wealth holder regarding the proportion of real and monetary assets he desires to hold in his portfolio will depend on his own optimum portfolio mix. That optimum mix is based on the risk and yield of the available assets. All investors in the economy will be faced with the same decision—about the amount and proportion of money to hold relative to other assets—which they will make according to their utility functions and on their information.

---

[31]For a generalized model, see C. Bliss, "On Putty–Clay," *Review of Economic Studies*, 35 (April 1968), 105–32.

[32]Tobin, "Money and Economic Growth," *op. cit.*; and James Tobin, "Notes on Optimal Monetary Growth," *Journal of Political Economy*, 76 (August 1968), 833–59.

What effect does the introduction of money have on the warranted and natural growth rates? Money itself probably could not change the size of the effective labor force; therefore, money may have little effect on the natural growth rate. It does, however, affect the warranted rate of growth.[33]

Although there is no reason to expect that money could shift the output–capital ratio, σ, its introduction may induce a change in savings decisions (remember, MPS and APS are equal in this long-run model). Assume that savings is a function of the level of *money* income not *real* income and that savers are subject to money illusion, that is, they look upon money and real wealth as interchangeable. Under these conditions the introduction of money will not change the MPS out of money income but will reduce the MPS out of real income. For example suppose the MPS is 20% and real output is $100 billion and money income increased from $100 billion to $110 billion through the introduction of money, then money savings will increase from $20 billion to $22 billion. The public now feels that they are 110% as rich as their true output reflects and spend 80% of the increase in their money income or $88 billion on real goods or services. As a result the propensity to save out of *real* income will have been reduced to 12%. Any such induced reduction in the propensity to save will reduce the warranted growth rate, G_w; if a monetary economy has a lower equilibrium capital–labor ratio than a barter economy, it also has a lower per capita output.[34]

In Figure 15-3, the effect of the introduction of money is shown by a leftward shift in the warranted rates growth path, G_w, to G_w'. The result is a shift in the equilibrium from point e to point e' and a decrease in the amount of capital per worker—that is, a capital shallowing—as the economy shifts from K_1/N to K_2/N. In summary, the introduction of money leads to the reduction in the amount of capital per worker, caused by the reduction in the growth path of the warranted rate for any given level of capital per worker. The reduction in the warranted growth path was in turn caused by the reduction in the MPS.

To the extent that output per worker depends on capital per worker, capital shallowing, as a result of the introduction of money, will reduce worker productivity. This result is illustrated in Figure 15-4, where output per worker, Y/N, is plotted on the y-axis, and capital per worker, K/N, on the x-axis. The introduction of money induces a reduction in output per worker

---

[33] This version arrives at Tobin's conclusions by a considerably simplified route. The interested student should compare this with Tobin's original article.

[34] This paradoxical conclusion is based on the assumption that the barter economy has capital as productive as that of the monetary economy. The conclusion was challenged by Levhari and Patinkin on the grounds that money performs a productive function not usually attributed to it: Its existence provides a service to both consumers and business firms. If money is considered either a consumer or a producer good, then its introduction may increase the output–capital ratio for any given level of K/N and more than offset the decline in the MPS. See Don Patinkin and David Levhari, "The Role of Money in a Simple Growth Model," *American Economic Review*, 58 (Sept., 1968), 713–53.

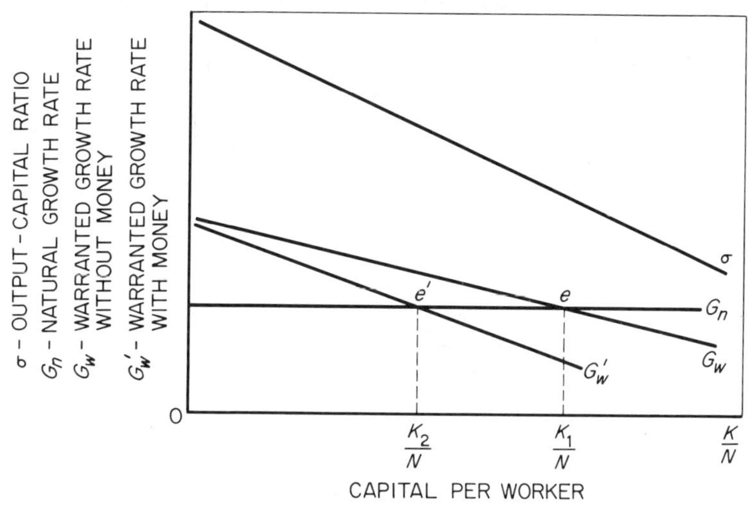

FIG. 15-3 Money in the Neoclassical Model

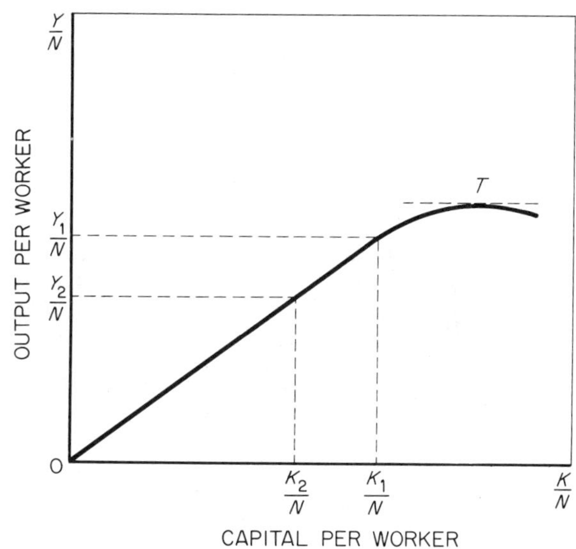

FIG. 15-4 Variable Proportions and Economic Growth

from Y_1/N to Y_2/N when capital shallowing occurs from K_1/N to K_2/N.[35] However, it does not change the equilibrium growth rate if the natural growth rate remains unchanged.

[35]Note that if equilibrium occurred to the right of point T, the capital intensity per worker would be so great that output per worker could be increased by the introduction of more money with the given stock of real capital, because such a change would shift the warranted growth rate to the left, moving equilibrium toward point T.

In the neoclassical theory, aggregate demand will equal aggregate supply at full employment. Therefore, the aggregate actual growth rate, G, which we have related to effective demand, will equal the equilibrium growth rate where G_w equals G_n. However, the Keynesian problem of deficient demand can be incorporated into the neoclassical growth model. This is done in Figure 15-5,

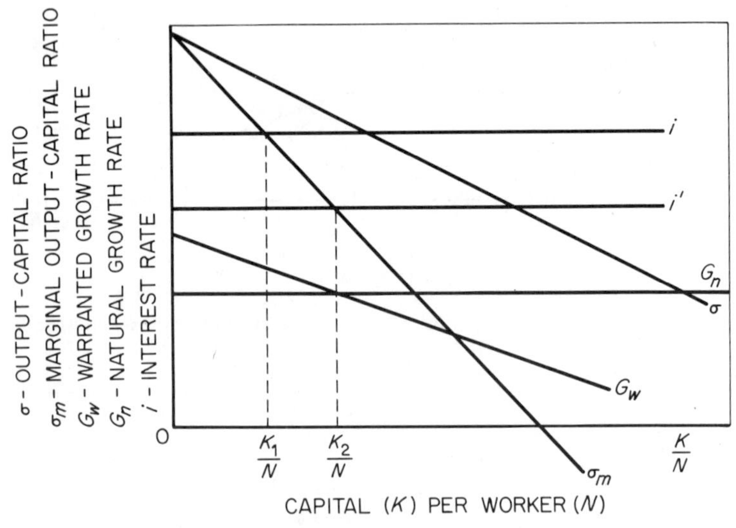

FIG. 15-5 The Neoclassical Growth Model with Deficient Demand

by assuming that investors require a higher rate of return than they would achieve at the normal equilibrium, the intersection of G_w and G_n. Assume that investors desire a return equal to i level of the interest rate in Figure 15-5. Then profit-maximizing investment per worker will be pushed only to the point where i crosses the marginal output–capital curve (σ_M),[36] which is left of the equilibrium level determined by the intersection of G_w and G_n.

Investors' insistence on a higher return per unit of investment reduces the capital available per worker below equilibrium and consequently reduces output per worker. The deficient demand for investment goods that results from this insistence reduces effective demand and forces the actual growth rate, G (for simplicity, omitted from Figure 15-5), below the natural rate, G_n. The result is a Keynesian type of unemployment—a lack of jobs for people who are willing and able to work for the going wage. The introduction of money, by lowering the required return on real investment, would reduce the i function, and equilibrium would be achieved when i fell to i' and sufficient capital deepening occurred (as the economy moved to the right along the

[36]Note that the capital intensity per worker will occur at K_1/N, which falls short of K_2/N. Since the average output–capital ratio, σ, is negatively sloped, its marginal function, σ_M, must fall below it.

warranted-growth-rate curve by enough to increase the investment per worker from K_1/N to K_2/N). Therefore, under certain conditions, monetary policy may be used to induce capital deepening and increase the actual rate of growth, and so to bring about equilibrium among the three growth rates.[37]

The Effect of Inflation on Growth

The introduction of money into the theory of growth not only influences economic growth by affecting capital intensity per worker; it may also affect economic growth through changes in the price level.

There is a possible transfer of purchasing power from consumers to investors as a result of demand-pull inflation.[38] Such a transfer means that a larger proportion of aggregate income goes to investment and a smaller proportion to consumption, a process that has been called "forced saving." In contrast, wage-push inflation transfers purchasing power from investors to consumers. Such a process would be a form of "forced consumption."

Demand-pull inflation has the effect of increasing the ratio of net investment to productive capacity.[39] The warranted-rate growth path is thereby increased, and the effect is illustrated as a shift from G_{w_1} to G_{w_2} in Figure 15-6. A shift to the right in the G_w curve means that capital deepening must occur where G_w and G_n are equal, as evidenced by a shift to the right in the equilibrium between the two growth rates, from e_1 to e_2. The more resources shifted from consumption to investment by inflation, the further the G_{w_2} curve will shift to the right. Capital deepening can increase labor productivity and thereby increase output per man-hour and the real wage. We may conclude, therefore, that any type of inflation that affects the proportion of spending between investment and consumption affects the growth path of the warranted rate.

Notice that a rightward shift in the warranted-growth-rate curve, although it causes capital deepening, does not change the equilibrium growth rate between the warranted and natural growth rates. In contrast, a movement along a G_w curve, induced by a shift in the natural growth rate, does change the equilibrium growth rate. Therefore, inflation, like the introduction of money, does not affect the equilibrium (achieved) growth rate if the natural growth rate remains constant. If we assume that the supply of labor is completely inelastic because the economy is at full employment, and that labor-augmenting technology is not a function of capital deepening, then the

---

[37]Any attempt to achieve capital deepening will increase the ratio of additional investment to effective demand (α) and will tend to increase the ratio of investment to productive capacity (δ), which in turn would tend to shift the warranted growth rate to the right and therefore require even more of a reduction in the required return on investment to fill the gap.

[38]The conditions under which purchasing power is thus transferred are described in the Appendix to Chapter 13.

[39]In a sense, society's marginal propensity to save out of current income is increased, even though the "forced savers" never have the alternative option to consume, because they never have access to the funds loaned to investors.

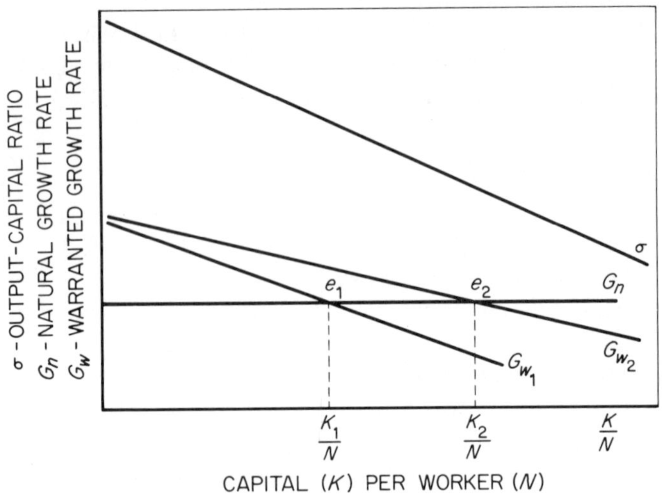

FIG. 15-6 Inflation in the Neoclassical Model

natural-growth-rate function could not be affected by the same factors that influence the warranted rate.

In conclusion, demand-pull inflation can cause capital deepening, but is not likely to influence the natural-growth-rate function and therefore the equilibrium rate, where $G_n = G_w$. However, if our rigid assumptions are relaxed and capital deepening is accompanied by labor-augmenting technological change, then capital deepening would increase the natural growth path and so the equilibrium growth rate, where $G_n = G_w$.

THE COST OF ECONOMIC GROWTH

The benefits of economic growth are obvious. Up to this point we have considered it to be a desirable social goal, with the implication that more economic growth is equivalent to increased welfare. However, it is possible that economic growth could conflict with other goals, such as price stability. For example, the warranted-growth path can be increased through demand-pull inflation.

Conflicting social goals may be involved in the costs of economic growth itself. While we are considering the advantages of a growing per capita GNP, it may be easy to overlook the degree to which growing output is accompanied by growing social costs. Many of these may not be immediately apparent because they are difficult to measure. For example, the pollution of air and water by firms producing output counted in GNP has been noted for over a century, but not until fairly recently has there been much concern over its dangers, nor have techniques for measuring pollution been developed. And even now, the standard method of computing GNP does not make a deduction for air and water pollution caused by industrial production.

The rank-size rule developed by demographers indicates that economic growth goes hand in hand with increasing numbers of large urban centers. But greater urbanization is accompanied by social problems such as increasing crime rates, traffic congestion, and urban blight. In addition, the need for social services such as schools, hospitals, and police seems to be an increasing function of population density.

A problem inherent in our system of social accounting is our failure to account for externalities in GNP; that is, all additional goods produced are simply included as part of GNP, whereas much of our increased output is, in fact, required to remedy conditions created by economic growth itself. For example, devices to clean industrial wastes, which are included as part of GNP, would never have been required if the industry producing the waste had not been built. Large numbers of police cruisers, which are added to GNP, are required to service urban areas that are themselves the products of economic growth. Strip-mining operations leave thousands of acres of blighted land, which on rare occasions is reclaimed, and the value of such reclamation is counted as a contribution to our aggregate income. Lumber and agricultural enterprises have destroyed the natural usefulness and beauty of large areas. Restoration of such blighted areas is not only expensive but often incomplete, since many resources once used can never be restored to the earth. When land in the north of the Florida Everglades was drained for agriculture, the value of the resulting agricultural output was included in GNP, but the decimation of wildlife that resulted from the ecological change in the Everglades was never deducted.

One of the problems of growth—slums—occurs because we erroneously act as though there is free disposal of the buildings. That is, the ability to abandon one's property without penalties can often cause dislocations in local economies. In our haste to induce growth and construction, we often reject policies that might force developers and owners of both commercial and residential dwellings to provide necessary guarantees that discarded property will be properly disposed of. We might also take the view, similar to that of the Japanese, that dwellings should be built for limited periods of time; then we should not view the disposal of a dwelling to be inappropriate.

Furthermore, many of the costs of economic growth are still not clear. The very economic success of the human species seems to be causing long-run ecological imbalances that could conceivably endanger our existence. America's economic success could ultimately involve the irony of the Midas story; our golden touch could, through its long-run subversion of nature, lead to our own destruction in the midst of food unfit to eat, water unfit to drink, and air unfit to breathe, without the possibility of the eleventh-hour reprieve available to Midas.

The trade-off between the benefits of economic growth and its costs can be described through indifference-curve analysis. This process is shown in Figure 15-7, where economic growth is plotted along the x-axis and the costs of overcoming its diseconomies along the y-axis. Line AB represents the various possibilities available to society, with point A on the y-axis representing the maximum achievable benefits of clean water, unpolluted air, uncrowded

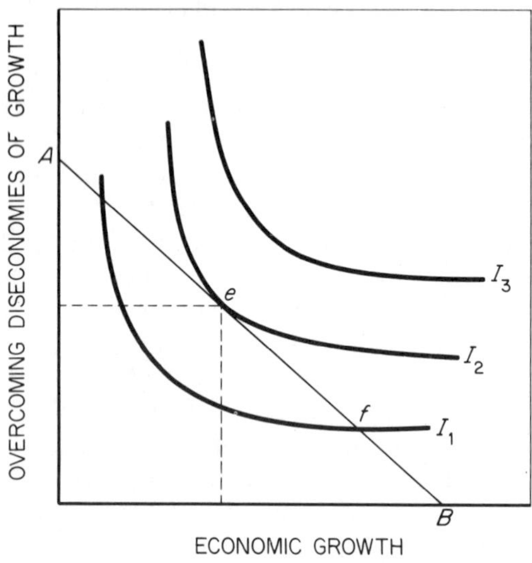

FIG. 15-7 Cost-Benefit Analysis of Economic Growth

cities, and the like. In contrast, point B on the x-axis represents the maximum achievable level of economic growth we could obtain if we completely disregarded its costs. Indifference curves I_1, I_2, and I_3 represent society's marginal rate of substitution of the benefits of economic growth for the natural benefits obtainable in its absence. Equilibrium is achieved at point e, where society's willingness to trade off the advantages of economic growth for its disutilities is tangent to line AB. The possible, achievable part of the graph consists of all points on line AB and to its left and below it; the unachievable part is all points to the right and above AB. The point of tangency with the highest achievable indifference curve, I_2 at point e, represents society's optimum achievable solution.

The indifference curves represented by I_1, I_2, and I_3 are drawn on the assumption that society has complete knowledge of both the costs and the benefits of economic growth. However, widespread ignorance of the costs has been systematically cultivated. The world's largest teaching machine, the advertising industry, continually stresses the advantages of economic growth, because its sponsors, almost without exception, are producers of output included in GNP. Automobile advertising, for instance, commonly stresses the high rates of acceleration that many cars can achieve, without mentioning that traffic congestion in large cities has reduced the average speed of automobiles to something under the level formerly achieved on horseback.

Widespread lack of knowledge and systematic manipulation of public opinion in favor of economic growth may mean that the apparent point of tangency occurs to the right of point *e* on a lower indifference curve; for example, at point *f* on indifference curve I_1.

A further difficulty is that, even among the most well-informed members of society, the actual costs of economic growth can never be completely known. Some of them defy any objective measurement; others that are identified may not actually materialize as growth occurs. For example, some 25 years ago, conservationists estimated that a ten-year supply of oil remained in the ground, whereas the current estimate is that a 40-year supply is available. Within the next 40 years, new petroleum discoveries could increase the supply; or new sources of energy may become available that could make petroleum obsolete as a major source of power.

Therefore, the typical American attitude of discounting future costs in order to achieve greater economic growth may not be completely irrational. Only the future will tell.

SUMMARY AND CONCLUSIONS

The major accepted theories of economic growth from the classicists up to the present have followed a manic-depressive pattern: Expectations of furture growth were high in the Adam Smith era, low in the later classical period, high again in the Victorian neoclassical time, back down during the Depression days of the Keynesian stagnationists, and currently somewhat ambivalent.

Victorian optimism was cut short by World War I and its aftermath, especially the Great Depression. Economists responded by producing theories to explain the stagnation. Keynesian stagnation theorists suggested several different causes: population stability, exhaustion of the frontier, and of significant capital-using innovations, among others.

In the post-Keynesian era, growth theory has perhaps achieved a better balance. Most economists no longer look forward to inevitable prosperity or stagnation. The Harrod–Domar model implies that the economy is poised on a "razor's edge." Correct policies can create the climate for growth, and incorrect policies can cause an economy to stagnate. The razor's-edge concept emphasizes that growth equilibrium can be achieved only when the natural, warranted, and actual growth rates are in balance.

Of the three growth rates, the warranted rate, the contribution of the Harrod–Domar model, is unique because it is the first theoretical construct encountered so far that specifically introduces the concept of excess capacity. The growth equation developed under the warranted rate was a step away from the Keynesian emphasis on consumption and a step back toward the neoclassical emphasis on investment and savings.

The modern neoclassical growth theory follows from the Harrod–Domar model and gives the theory a classical twist by introducing market flexibility, diminishing returns and factor substitutability, so that the output–capital ratio is no longer constant, but declines as capital deepening occurs. Once the output–capital ratio is no longer constant, capital deepening will reduce the warranted growth rate until it becomes equal to the natural rate, and so the razor's edge is blunted.

More recently, a monetary dimension has been added to the neoclassical theory of economic growth. The first introduction of money into a barter system paradoxically reduces the warranted growth rate, even though a monetary economy is assumed to be more efficient than a barter economy. In addition, demand-pull inflation can increase the warranted growth rate. But in any case, the equilibrium rate will not increase unless the natural rate can be pushed up, a process that most likely requires technological change.

The equilibrium growth rate, however determined, provides a long-run trend around which the economy may fluctuate. In the next chapter, we will explore the nature and causes of business fluctuations.

QUESTIONS AND PROBLEMS

1. What is economic growth? How do population and quality considerations become involved?
2. Do you feel that there is a preoccupation with quantitative measures? Why?
3. Distinguish between growth and development.
4. What factors determine the warranted growth rate in the Harrod–Domar theory?
5. What factors determine the actual growth rate?
6. How are the two rates brought into balance?
7. What is the natural growth rate, and how does it affect the analysis?
8. In what way does the neoclassical growth theory blunt the "razor's edge"?
9. How does money influence growth?
10. What are some of the costs of economic growth?
11. Using the figure below, explain why an economy must either grow or suffer severe consequences.

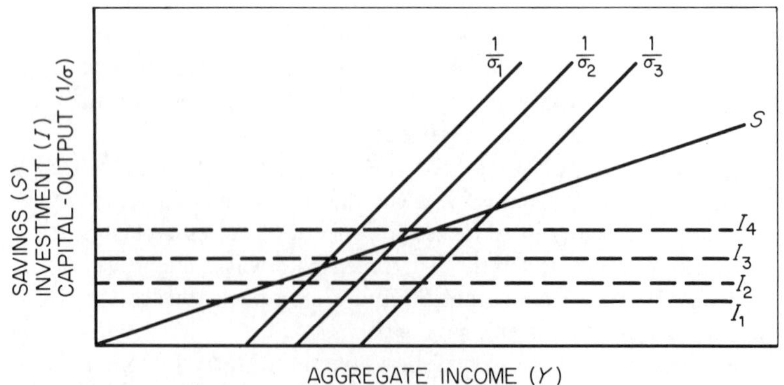

PROBLEM 11 The Harrod-Domar Model

12. In reference to the figure below:
    a. What is the equilibrium growth rate?
    b. Would a change in σ affect the equilibrium rate?
    c. Would capital deepening affect the equilibrium rate? the warranted rate?
    d. How could the equilibrium rate be increased?

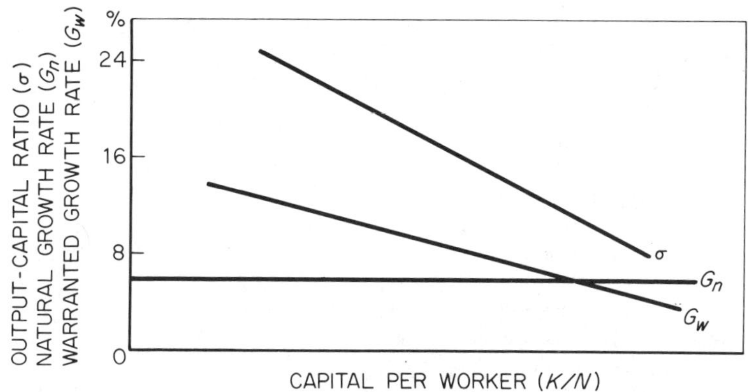

PROBLEM 12 The Neoclassical Model

ADDITIONAL SELECTED REFERENCES

A VARIETY OF GROWTH AND DEVELOPMENT THEORIES

BAUMOL, W. J., *Business Behavior, Value and Growth*, pp. 131–59. New York: Macmillan, 1959.

———, *Economic Dynamics*, 2nd ed. New York: Macmillan, 1959.

BREMS, H., *Output, Employment, Capital and Growth*, pp. 231–338. New York: Harper & Row, 1959.

BRENNER, Y. S., *Theories of Economic Development and Growth*. London: Allen & Unwin, 1966.

HAHN, F. H., and R. C. O. MATTHEWS, "The Theory of Economic Growth: A Survey," *Economic Journal*, 74 (December 1964), 779–902.

HICKS, J. R., *Capital and Growth* (Oxford: Clarendon Press, 1965).

HIGGINS, B., *Economic Development*, rev. ed., especially pp. 55–360. New York: Norton, 1968.

KALDOR, N., "A Model of Economic Growth," *Economic Journal*, 67 (December 1957), 591–624.

———, and J. A. MIRRLEES, "A New Model of Economic Growth," *Review of Economics Studies*, 29 (June 1962), 174–92.

KOGIKU, K. C., *An Introduction to Macroeconomic Models*, pp. 145–84. New York: McGraw-Hill, 1968.

KUZNETS, S., *Economic Change*. New York: Norton, 1953.

LEIBENSTEIN, H., *Economic Backwardness and Economic Growth*. New York: John Wiley, 1957.

ROBINSON, J., "Equilibrium Growth Models." *American Economic Review*, 51 (June 1961), 360–69.

———, *Essays in the Theory of Economic Growth.* London: Macmillan, 1962.

———, "Mr. Harrod's Dynamics," in *Collected Economic Papers*, Vol. I, pp. 155–74. Oxford: Basil Blackwell, 1960.

ROSTOW, W. W., *The Process of Economic Growth*, 2nd ed. Oxford: Clarendon Press, 1960.

STEIN, J., "Neoclassical and Keynes–Wicksell Monetary Growth Models," *Journal of Money, Credit, and Banking*, 1 (May 1969), 153–71.

WAN, H. Y., *Economic Growth.* New York: Harcourt Brace Jovanovich, 1971.

ADDITIONAL ADVANCED ARTICLES INVOLVING NEOCLASSICAL GROWTH MODELS

CASS, D., and J. E. STIGLITZ, "The Implications of Alternative Savings and Expectations Hypotheses for Choices of Technique and Patterns of Growth," *Journal of Political Economy*, Part II 77 (Jul-Aug 1969). 586–627.

CASS, D., and M. E. YAARI, "Individual Saving, Aggregate Capital Accumulation and Efficient Growth," in *Essays in the Theory of Optimal Economic Growth*, ed. K. Shell. Cambridge, Mass.: M.I.T. Press, 1967.

EISNER, R., "On Growth Models and the Neoclassical Resurgence," *Economic Journal*, 68 (December 1958), 707–21.

JOHNSON, H. G., "The Neo-classical One-Sector Growth Model," *Economica*, 33 (August 1966), 265–87.

JORGENSON, D. W., "The Embodiment Hypothesis," *Journal of Political Economy*, 74 (February 1966), 1–17.

KOOPMANS, T., "Objectives, Constraints and Outcomes in Optimal Growth Models," *Econometrica*, 35 (January 1967), 1–15.

LIVIATAN, N., and DAVID LEVHARI, "The Concept of the Golden Rule in the Case of More Than One Consumption Good," *American Economic Review*, 58 (March 1968), 100–119.

MARTY, A. L., "The Neoclassical Theorem," *American Economic Review*, 54 (December 1964), 1026–29.

———, "Notes on Money and Economic Growth," *Journal of Money, Credit, and Banking*. 1 (May 1969), 252–65.

MORONEY, JOHN R., "The Current State of Money and Production Theory," *American Economic Review*, 62 (May 1972), 335–43.

PHELPS, E. S., "Second Essay on the Golden Rule of Accumulation," *American Economic Review*, 55 (September 1965), 793–814.

SAMUELSON, P. A., "Parable and Realism in Capital Theory," *Review of Economic Studies*, 29 (June 1962), 193–206.

———, "A Theory of Induced Innovation Along Kennedy-Weizsächer Lines," *Review of Economics and Statistics*. 47 (November, 1965), 343–44.

HU, SHENG CHENG, "Putty-Putty vs. Putty-Clay: A Synthesis," *International Economic Review*, 13: 324–341, June, 1972.

SIDRAUSKI, M., "Inflation and Economic Growth," *Journal of Political Economy*, 75 (December 1967), 796–810.

———, "Rational Choice and Patterns of Growth in a Monetary Economy," *American Economic Review*, 57 (May 1967), 534–44.

SOLOW, R. M., J. TOBIN, C. C. VON WEIZSÄCHER, and M. E. YAARI, "Neoclassical Growth with Fixed Factor Proportions," *Review of Economic Studies*, 33 (April 1966), 79–116.

TOBIN, J., "Notes on Optimal Monetary Growth," *Journal of Political Economy*, 76 (July–August 1968), 833–59.

UZAWA, H., "Neutral Inventions and the Stability of Growth Equilibrium," *Review of Economic Studies*, 28 (February 1961), 117–24.

———, "On a Two-Sector Model of Economic Growth" (three parts), *Review of Economic Studies*, 29 (October 1961), 40–47; 30 (June 1963), 105–18; 31 (January 1964), 1–24.

EMPIRICAL INVESTIGATIONS

ABRAMOVITZ, M., "Economic Growth in the United States," *American Economic Review*, 52 (September 1962), 762–82.

———, "Resources and Output Trends in the United States since 1870," *American Economic Review*, 46 (May 1956), 5–23.

DENISON, E., *The Sources of Economic Growth in the U.S.* New York: Committee for Economic Development, 1962.

KENDRICK, J. W., "Productivity Trends in the United States." Princeton, N.J.: Princeton University Press, 1961.

SCHMOOKER, J., "The Changing Efficiency of the American Economy, 1869–1938," *Review of Economics and Statistics*, 34 (August 1952), 214–31.

SOLOW, R. M., "Technical Change and the Aggregate Production Function," *Review of Economics and Statistics*, 39 (August 1957), 312–20.

Economic Fluctuations

16

INTRODUCTION

Orthodox classical economists, with the exception of Malthus, felt that the business cycle would not and, in fact, could not be a serious economic problem because of the operation of Say's Law, which would always keep aggregate supply and demand in balance. As we noted in Chapter 6, temporary imbalances could occur; however, they could not persist, because the economy itself would automatically set corrective forces in motion. Thus, while the economic underworld, including the Marxians, seized upon business fluctuations like those of 1815, 1825, 1836–39, 1847–48, and 1857 as evidence of the impending breakup of capitalism, the classical economists saw them as merely temporary deviations from normal full employment.

In time, however, economists accepted the position that gluts and crises were parts of a larger process, which came to be identified as the business cycle. The modern concept of the business cycle starts with Clement Juglar. In the mid-1800's, Juglar described a business cycle of nine or ten years, in which one phase would automatically lead to the next.[1] His was the well-known statement, "The only cause of depression is prosperity." In Juglar's system, prosperity—overactive business activity—would lead to depression, as bank credit dried up and increases in effective demand slowed. However, he was less clear as to why depression would lead back to prosperity.

---

[1] C. Juglar, *Des Crises commercials et des leur retour périodique en France, en Angleterre et aux Etats Unis*, 2nd ed. (1889). Reprinted, New York: A. M. Kelley, 1967.

Later economists, following Juglar's lead, discovered other cycles of different lengths. For example, in the 1920's, Kitchin discovered a cycle of approximately three years, and Kondratieff identified a longer cycle of approximately 40 to 50 years.[2] Under the influence of Juglar, Kitchin, and Kondratieff, economists came to regard business cycles as automatically repeating phenomena of regular length and of possibly predictable magnitude and the cycles of various lengths were given the name of the three economists who first described them.

Joseph Schumpeter, in his theory, makes use of the three types of cycles, the Kitchin, Juglar, and Kondratieff, to explain the severity of certain depressions and the relative mildness of others.[3] The most severe depressions occur when the three types of cyclical downturns coincide. For example, the Juglar downturn would be partially offset if it occurred during the upward phase of the Kondratieff cycle. According to Schumpeter's data, the depressions in 1825–30, 1873–78, and 1929–34 all occurred when the three types coincided, thus explaining the severity of those three depressions.

Schumpeter's prototype cycle consisted of four phases, as shown in Figure 16-1, with prosperity leading into recession, followed by depression

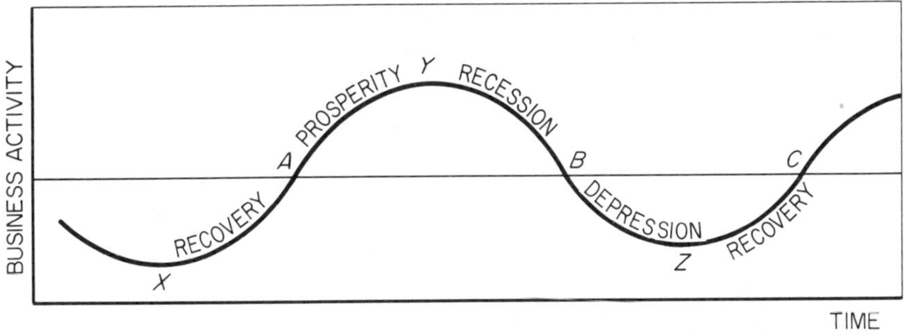

FIG. 16-1 Schumpeter's Prototype Cycle

and recovery. The crucial point in this cycle theory is the point of inflection, where the rate of change itself changes. In Figure 16-1, *A*, *B*, and *C* represent points of inflection, where the business cycle forms itself around a normal level of business activity. Starting at point *X*, at the bottom of the depression, the rate of recovery of economic activity increases until it (the rate, not the level) hits a maximum at point *A*, the point of inflection. Afterwards, economic activity continues to increase during prosperity, but at a decreasing rate, up to point *Y*, the peak of the cycle, where a new recession begins, with economic activity decreasing at an increasing rate. Once the rate of change starts

[2]N. D. Kondratieff, "The Long Waves in Economic Life," (trans. W. F. Stolper), *Review of Economics and Statistics*, 17, Part 2 (November 1935), 105–15; J. Kitchin, "Cycles and Trends in Economic Factors," *Review of Economics and Statistics*, 5 (January, 1923), 10–16.

[3]J. A. Schumpeter, *Business Cycles* (New York: McGraw-Hill, 1939), Vol. 1, 193–219.

to slow down at point B, the economy enters the final stage of the business cycle, called the depression, which ends at point Z, where the economy bottoms out and begins its new recovery.

(We shall consider the Schumpeter cycle theory later in this chapter.)

For certain other cycle theorists, such as Arthur Burns and Wesley Mitchell, the peaks and troughs of the cycle are more significant than the points of inflection.[4] The National Bureau of Economic Research, which Mitchell founded, measures the cycle from peak to peak and trough to trough, determining the reference date for each peak or trough by a number of different indexes. Since the indexes do not all move together, the National Bureau has separated them into three groups—leading, lagging, and coinciding series—and the reference dates for cyclical turning points are pinpointed by an average of the coinciding indexes.[5] The six coinciding indexes of business activity change approximately in step with changes in overall business activity; the 18 leading indicators anticipate these changes, and the six lagging indicators follow them.

More recently, there appears to be a consensus that the term "business cycle" implies too much automaticity. Current thinking is more in terms of "business fluctuations." Although this term is a synonym for "business cycles," it implies less inexorability and regularity, and perhaps at the same time leaves more room for corrective monetary and fiscal action. Also, modern thinking, in contrast to the Schumpeter model, does not consider recession and depression two segments of the same cycle, but more simply defines a recession as a mild business decline and a depression as a severe one.

The Statistical Pattern

The lack of cyclical regularity in measured business activity can be seen in Figure 16-2, where the measured business cycles lack both the regularity and periodicity of the ideal cycle in Figure 16-1.

---

[4]A. F. Burns and W. C. Mitchell, *Measuring Business Cycles* (New York: National Bureau of Economic Research, 1946).

[5]The 18 leading indicators used as of this writing are these: the average workweek of manufacturing production workers; nonagricultural placements in all industries; initial unemployment insurance claims; net business formations; new durable-goods orders (two indexes); new plant and equipment orders; new housing permits; changes in inventory book value (two indexes); industrial-materials prices; stock prices; after-tax corporate taxes; the ratio of price to unit labor cost in manufacturing; changes in the stock of money and time deposits; changes in mortgage debt; changes in consumer installment debt; and changes in bank loans to business.

The six roughly coinciding indicators currently used are nonagricultural employment, total unemployment, GNP, industrial production, personal income, and sales in manufacturing and trade.

The six lagging indicators currently used are the unemployment rate of persons unemployed for 15 weeks or longer, expenditures on new plant and equipment, manufacturing and trade inventories, labor cost per unit of manufacturing output, business loans outstanding, and bank rates on short-term business loans.

Julius Shiskin and Geoffrey H. Moore, *Composite Indexes of Leading, Coinciding and Lagging Indicators, 1948–67.* A supplement to National Bureau of Economic Research, Inc., *Report #1*, 1968.

In both Figures 16-1 and 16-2, the trend is represented by the center horizontal line, representing a "normal" level of economic activity. In this sense, the business cycle represents fluctuations around a trend line, which could incorporate a normal growth rate. If such a growth rate were incorporated in Figure 16-2, the horizontal trend line and the adjacent business-fluctuations would have to be tilted up. A regular cyclical pattern around a trend implies the operation of constant processes generating fluctuating levels of economic activity.

Exogenous and Endogenous Factors

Current cycle theorists separate the causes of business fluctuations into two categories: endogenous and exogenous. The endogenous factors are those forces built into the economy itself. In theoretical models, they usually provide a regular cyclical pattern, and the resulting waves may be of increasing, constant, or decreasing amplitude. The other approach to the business cycle depends on exogenous forces, those generated outside the economic model, which often cause less regular fluctuations than those endogenously caused. Proponents of exogenous theories often suggest that random fluctuations rather than cyclical patterns represent the real nature of business activity.

In the past, many different factors have been identified by different economists as basic exogenous causes of the business cycle. Some important exogenous variables that have at times been fashionable are of a political, innovative, psychological, demographic, or monetary nature. These have been termed sources of *stochastic shock*, and can be combined with endogenous variables such as the multiplier and the accelerator to form a modern theory to explain economic fluctuations.

ENDOGENOUS THEORIES OF THE CYCLE

The real and monetary cycle theories presented in this section are basically endogenous cycle models that depend on some stochastic shock to inaugurate the cyclical action. This presentation begins with real theories, based on changes in investment in plant and equipment, which make use of the acceleator and multiplier.

The Accelerator

One of the hardiest of the endogenous factors in business cycle theory is the accelerator, whose roots have been traced back to the 1800's. The first full exposition of the acceleration principle was probably T.N. Carver's in 1903, and the best-known early presentation was proposed by J.M. Clark in 1917.[6]

---

[6]T. N. Carver, "A Suggestion for a Theory of Industrial Depressions," *Quarterly Journal of Economics*, 17 (May 1903), 497–500; and J. M. Clark, "Business Acceleration and the Law of Demand," *Journal of Political Economy*, 25 (March 1917), 217–35.

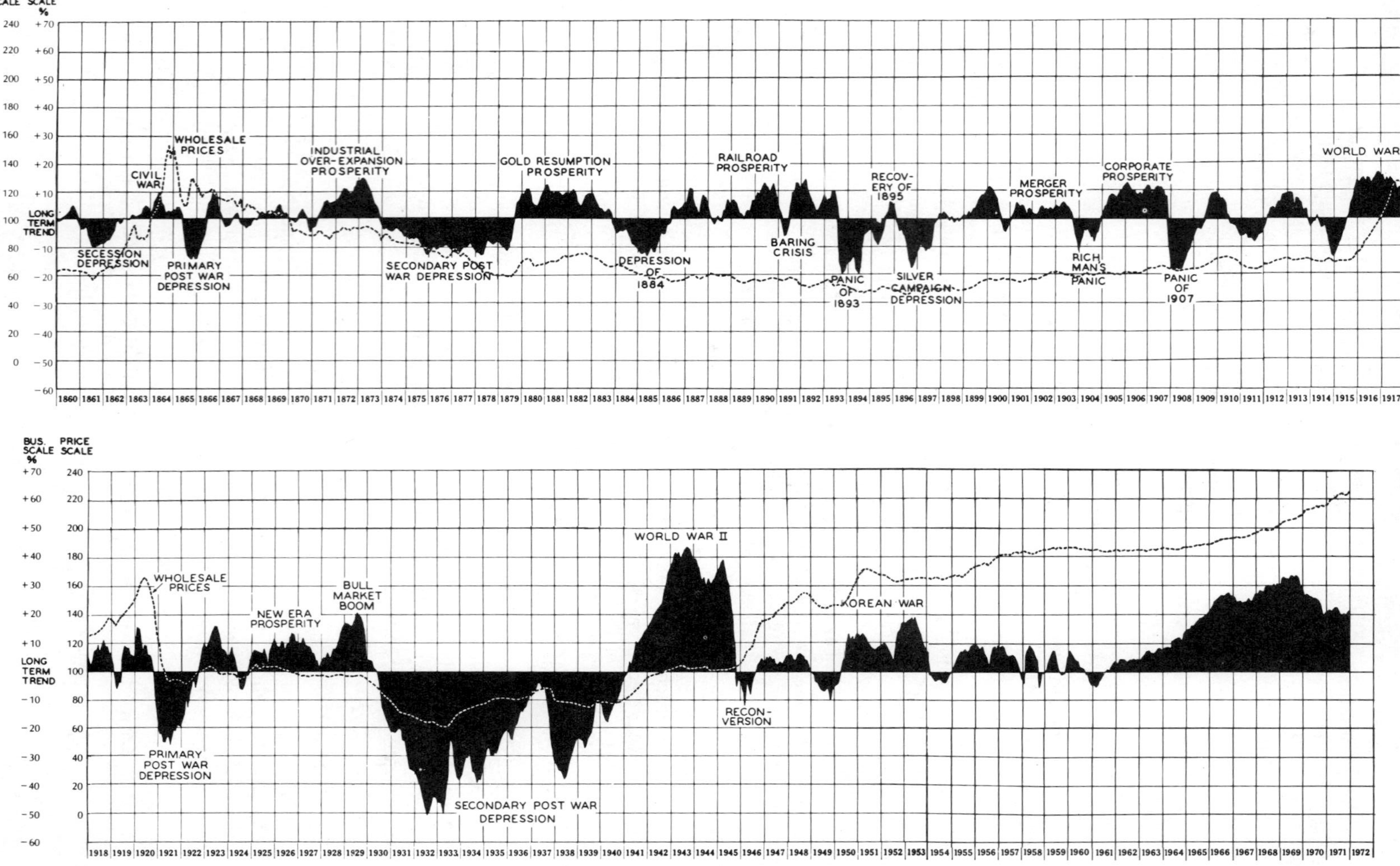

FIG. 16-2 Historical Business Fluctuations (Source: The Cleveland Trust Company, Cleveland, Ohio, 44101. Reprinted by permission from the 1971 edition.)

The acceleration principle, or more simply, the accelerator, refers to the tendency under certain conditions for increased aggregate spending of households to cause a greater-than-proportional increase in investment. Under these conditions, investment becomes a function of the change in consumer demand, or

$$I = f(\Delta C)$$

The acceleration principle should be distinguished from the concept of induced investment expenditures, which was discussed in Chapter 9. There are two distinct differences between them: First, according to the accelerator, investment expenditures are a function of changes in consumption, whereas induced investment makes investment expenditures a function of aggregate income. Second, the accelerator operates on *changes* in consumption, and induced investment is a function of the *level* of real income.

Table 16-1 is a representation of how the acceleration principle works with respect to some typical commodity, X. The production of commodity X requires investment in machines, and each machine is capable of turning out 1,000 units per year. Assume that the industry starts with a consumer demand of 100,000 units per year, shown in column 2. Then 100 machines (column 4) would be required to produce the total output. Further, assume that each machine lasts ten years and that the purchase of the original 100 machines was spread evenly over a ten-year period. Ten machines will wear out per year, and the new machines that were purchased as a result of the increased demand for X in year 3 begin to wear out starting in year 13. For simplicity in this illustration, we are dealing with the actual replacement of machines rather than the accrual of depreciation reserves as exemplified by the capital consumption allowance in GNP accounting.

Since ten machines wear out per year for the first three years of the period under analysis, only 90 machines are available at the beginning of those years (column 5), and ten machines (column 6) must be purchased to have 100 machines available. In year 3, estimated consumer demand (exogenously determined) increases by 1,000 units, requiring the addition of one machine. (Assume that all the changes in column 2 are exogenously determined.) Therefore, in year 4, the machines on hand at the start of the period have increased to 91. The machines available at the start of the period (column 5) are subtracted from the required machines (column 4) to arrive at the investment expenditures required to meet consumer demand for the year in question (column 6). Net investment expenditures (column 8) are determined by the required investment expenditures (column 6) minus the machines worn out during the period (column 7).

The term "accelerator" derives from the fact that a small initial change in estimated consumer demand, C, may give rise to a proportionately greater change in investment expenditures, I. A 1 percent increase in consumer demand in year 3 (column 3 of Table 16-1) leads to an infinitely large percentage change in net investment expenditure (column 9), and a 4 percent increase in C in year 4 leads to a 300 percent increase in I. As capacity in the industry

TABLE 16-1 Accelerator Example

(1)	(2)	(3)	(4)	(5)	(6)	(7)	(8)	(9)
Time Period	*Estimated Consumer Demand* (C)	*% Change in* C	*Required Machines*	*Machines Available at Start of Period*	*Required Investment Expenditures*	*Machines Worn Out During Period*	*Net Investment* (I) *Expenditures*	*% Change in* I
1	100,000	—	100	90	10	10	0	—
2	100,000	0	100	90	10	10	0	0
3	101,000	1	101	90	11	10	1	Inf.
4	105,000	4.0	105	91	14	10	4	300.0
5	113,000	7.6	113	95	18	10	8	100.0
6	123,000	8.8	123	103	20	10	10	25.0
7	133,000	8.1	133	113	20	10	10	0
8	141,000	6.0	141	123	18	10	8	−20.0
9	145,000	2.8	145	131	14	10	4	−50.0
10	146,000	.7	146	135	11	10	1	−75.0
11	146,000	0	146	136	10	10	0	−100.0
12	146,000	0	146	136	10	10	0	—
13	146,000	0	146	136	10	11	−1	—
14	146,000	0	146	135	11	14	−3	—
15	150,000	2.7	150	132	18	18	0	—

increases, the acceleration effect becomes diluted, until by year 7, an 8 percent increase in C causes no further increase in I. Smaller increases in consumer demand, C, in years 8 through 10 result in successive decreases in the rate of net investment expenditures. When C levels off at 146,000 units in years 10 through 14, I continues to decrease, as the worn-out machines purchased in years 3 and 4 are not replaced. Finally, in year 15, the negative net investment expenditure is ended by a 2.7 percent increase in consumer demand.

This example demonstrates that the durability of investment goods, coupled with changes in consumer demand, can cause great economic instability by inducing severe changes in the rate of net investment expenditures. The accelerator effect is magnified in proportion to the durability of the investment.

Another effect of the accelerator is that a substantial increase in effective demand may be required to offset recessions. Since recessions are generally accompanied by excess capacity, the long life of capital goods restricts net investment expenditures until consumer demand increases enough to reemploy laid-off machines or until the machines have to be replaced.

The durability of capital goods may also lead to replacement waves. In our example, the additional machines purchased in years 3, 4, and 5 wear out in years 13, 14, and 15. If there was no excess capacity in the industry, additional investment expenditure would be required after a ten-year lag just to maintain a stable level of capacity.

Although replacement waves may be serious and significant in particular industries, in the aggregate they probably tend to become diffused, so statisticai evidence for these waves in the aggregate economy is difficult to discover. Even a single industry employs many different types of equipment with different life spans, and therefore the investment waves may not be very pronounced. However, in an undiversified economy where the major industries have equipment with a similar life span, replacement waves may cause severe economic shocks for the whole economy.

The Accelerator-Multiplier Model

The first important post-Keynesian cycle model was developed by Paul A. Samuelson, based on earlier work done by A.H. Hansen.[7] In this dynamic model, the accelerator is combined with the Keynestian multiplier in order to generate cyclical activity in aggregate income over a period of time. Samuelson's model adds three new dimensions to the traditional multiplier analysis: In the Keynesian investment multiplier model (Chapter 8), some given level of exogenous investment must be sustained for the multiplier to operate fully, whereas in the multiplier-accelerator model, a portion of the total investment is generated endogenously. A second distinction of the multiplier-accelerator model is that the introduction of the accelerator provides additional leverage

---

[7]P. A. Samuelson, "Interactions Between the Multiplier Analysis and the Principle of Acceleration," *Review of Economics and Statistics*, 21 (May 1939), 75–78.

to alter real income through investment expenditure changes that result from an initial change in consumption or aggregate income. The third difference is that the multiplier-accelerator model leads to fluctuating levels of aggregate income, whereas the simple Keynesian model leads to a constant equilibrium level. Depending on the values assigned to the multiplier and the accelerator, aggregate income will either oscillate around some trend line, or move explosively away from the trend either by increasing or decreasing. The amplitude of the oscillations in real income can be either damped, regular, or increasing, depending on the particular numerical values assigned to the multiplier and to the accelerator.

Table 16-2 demonstrates a numerical example of how the interaction

TABLE 16-2 Multiplier-Accelerator Cycle Model (in billions of dollars)

(1) Period	(2) *Aggregate Income**	(3) *Consumption**	(4) *Autonomous Investment*	(5) *Accelerator Investment**	(6) *Total Investment**
1	$700	$490	$210	—	$210
2	710	490	220	—	220
3	725	496	220	$ 9	229
4	738	505	220	14	234
5	745	513	220	12	232
6	743	517	220	6	226
7	734	516	220	−2	218
8	722	510	220	−8	212
9	713	503	220	−11	209
10	709	498	220	−9	211
11	712	495	220	−3	217
12	720	497	220	3	223
13	729	502	220	7	227
14	736	507	220	8	228
15	737	511	220	6	226
16	734	512	220	1	221
17	727	510	220	−3	217
18	720	506	220	−6	214
19	716	502	220	−6	214
20	716	500	220	−4	216

**Any discrepancies are due to rounding. In this illustration we assume MPC = .60 and accelerator, X = 1.5.*

of the multiplier and accelerator can generate cyclical waves in aggregate real income. The example shown approximates a Juglar cycle with damped oscillations (oscillations of decreasing amplitude). As the accelerator works itself out, aggregate income will approach a constant-trend value equal to the multiplier times autonomous consumption plus autonomous investment. In equation form, the equilibrium value of aggregate real income to which the cycle will lead is

$$Y = k(a + A)$$

where A is autonomous investment, a is autonomous consumption, k is the multiplier, and Y is aggregate income. In the example in Table 16-2, $a =$

\$70 billion, A = \$220 billion, and $k = 2.5$.[8] Therefore, the constant-trend value of aggregate real income is \$725 billion, the multiplier times exogenous spending. The cycle will oscillate around, and eventually approach, this value.

The illustration in Table 16-2 starts with an assumed level of aggregate income of \$700 billion (column 2) and an average propensity to consume (APC) of 70 percent, giving consumption of \$490 billion (column 3) and savings of \$210 billion. Since savings equals investment in equilibrium, investment is also equal to \$210 billion (column 4). The business cycle is initiated by a \$10 billion increase in investment introduced in period 2. Assume that the new level of autonomous investment of \$220 billion (column 4) remains constant throughout the illustration. The marginal propensity to consume (MPC) is assumed to be a constant 60 percent, and the accelerator (X) a constant 1.5.

These values of the MPC and the accelerator cause cycles of decreasing amplitude. New investment expenditures in column 5 occur as a result of the accelerator, assumed to be 1.5 times the change in consumption between the current period and the previous period. The additional consumption in any time period is equal to the MPC times the difference in income between the two previous time periods. Consumption therefore is no longer exogenously determined as in the previous example, but is a function of a change in aggregate income between the two previous time periods. For example, the increase in consumption in period 3 is 60 percent of the change in aggregate income between periods 1 and 2. The increase in investment expenditures in period 3 is the change in consumption between periods 2 and 3, times the accelerator, or $6 \times 1.5 = 9$.

To restate this process algebraically, the part of the change in investment, ΔI_{A_t}, induced by the accelerator in the current year, period t, equals

$$\Delta I_{A_t} = X(C_t - C_{t-1})$$

where X is the accelerator, C_t equals consumption in the present year, and C_{t-1} equals consumption in the previous year.

The change in consumption in period t, ΔC_t, equals

$$\Delta C_t = b(Y_{t-1} - Y_{t-2})$$

where b is the marginal propersity to consume (MPC), Y_{t-1} is aggregate income in the previous year, and Y_{t-2} is aggregate income two years ago. In order to solve for the level of aggregate income in period t, the following formulas can be used: Aggregate real income in period t equals consumption in period t plus investment in period t, or

[8]Remember, $k = 1/(1 - \text{MPC})$; if the MPC is .60, then $k = 2.5$.

1. $Y_t = C_t + I_t$

Consumption in period t equals autonomous consumption, a, plus the MPC, b, times the income in period $t - 1$, or

2. $C_t = a + bY_{t-1}$

Total investment in period t, shown in column 6 of Table 16-2, is equal to autonomous investment, A (column 4), plus the accelerator investment (column 5). The latter is computed by multiplying the accelerator, X, by the change in consumption from one time period to the next, or

3. $I_t = A + X(C_t - C_{t-1})$

Substituting equations 2 and 3 into equation 1 gives

4. $Y_t = (a + bY_{t-1}) + [A + X(C_t - C_{t-1})]$

In conclusion, given the values of the multiplier and the accelerator used in Table 16-2, a departure from equilibrium sets off alternating and self-generating waves of prosperity and recession. The table illustrates two such waves.

In accelerator-multiplier cycle models, the nature of the cyclical departure from equilibrium is determined by the values of the MPC and the accelerator. In his original article, Samuelson considered possible values for them, and arrived at the four regions illustrated in Figure 16-3. Each region initiates one of four different types of departures from equilibrium.

The four regions are calculated using second-order difference equations. The cyclical pattern so computed is the time path of aggregate income as it changes in response to an exogenous change. Solving equation 4 for the various possible combinations of values for b and X will allow the student to determine the various possible time paths for Y, without going through the

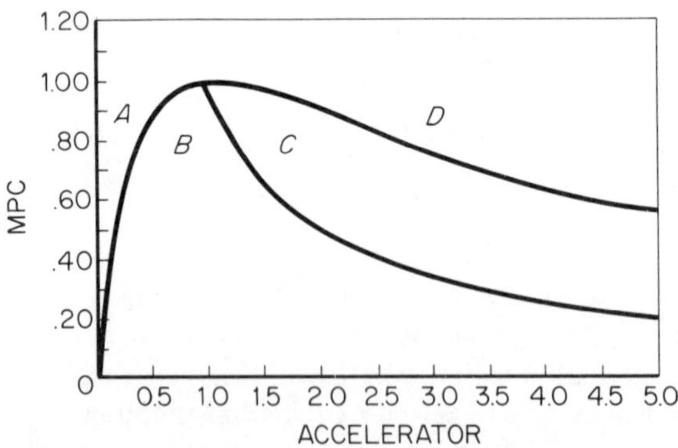

FIG. 16-3 Samuelson's Accelerator-Multiplier Cycle Regions (Source: P.A. Samuelson, "Interaction Between the Multiplier Analysis and the Principle of Acceleration," *Reviews of Economics and Statistics,* 21 : 75, May 1939.)

laborious process of working out an example such as that presented in Table 16-2. Alternatively, a trial-and-error method could be used to determine the sort of cyclical pattern that would develop for all possible combinations of values of b and X, by working through changes in aggregate income for several time periods for each possible set of values.

In region A of Figure 16-3, the value of the accelerator is very small, so the major effect on aggregate real income is due to the multiplier. If exogenous expenditures are constant, aggregate income will approach a stable equilibrium equal to the multiplier times the value of exogenous expenditure, and the solution is similar to the simple multiplier model. However, in region A, fluctuations can still be induced in aggregate income by periodic changes in the level of autonomous investment.

In region B, the values of the MPC and the accelerator will result in damped cycles of the type represented in Table 16-2, resembling the top panel of Figure 16-4. As the oscillations diminish over time, aggregate real income will asymptotically approach the equilibrium trend. Values of the MPC and the accelerator that lie on the dividing line between regions B and C would generate regular cycles, such as in the center panel of Figure 16-4.

The values within region C would generate explosive cycles, such as those in the bottom panel of Figure 16-4. If equilibrium were disturbed, increasingly severe fluctuations would commence, with each succeeding cycle moving further and further away from the equilibrium level of aggregate income.

Region D denotes values of the MPC and the accelerator that would cause any departure from equilibrium to be monotonically explosive. Any initial increase or decrease will move the economy directly away from equilibrium, and the resulting increase or decrease in aggregate income will never reverse itself to form a "normal" cyclical pattern. Assuming that the MPC is less than 1, high levels of the accelerator are required for a single injection of autonomous spending to cause an economic explosion. Perhaps the economists of the early New Deal who advocated massive, temporary government expenditures felt intuitively that the U.S. economy was characterized by a high acceleration effect. However, as we pointed out in Chapter 10, expansionary fiscal policy depending on a one-time expenditure was fallacious if based only on the multiplier, because of the continual leakage of potential spending into savings.[9]

Many economists feel that the values of the accelerator and the MPC would place the U.S. economy within region B. If so, values such as those in Table 16-2 would be fairly realistic. Within region B, combining the multiplier-accelerator model with exogenously generated stochastic (random) shocks would produce fluctuations approximating a regular business cycle. Others have estimated that the marginal propensity to consume in the United States is about .5 and the accelerator about 2.0. These values would place the

---

[9]In an open economy with a government sector, expenditures on imports and taxes are additional leakages from the stream of domestic income.

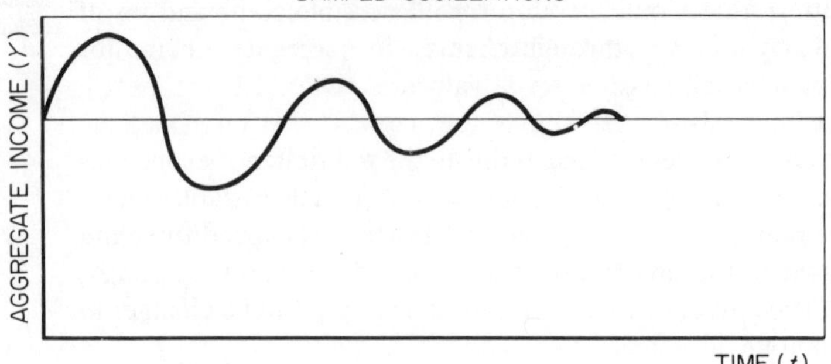

BORDER BETWEEN REGIONS B AND C
REGULAR OSCILLATIONS

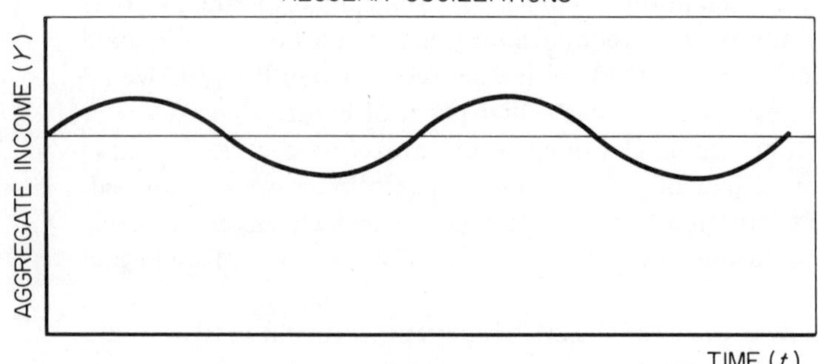

REGION C
EXPLOSIVE OSCILLATIONS

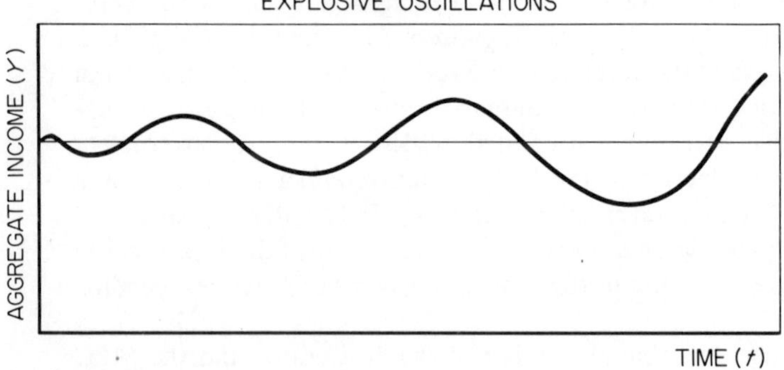

FIG. 16-4

economy right on the border between regions B and C, thus generating a regular business cycle.

One difficulty in applying the multiplier-accelerator theory is that the analysis does not work conveniently if the relevant multiplier and accelerator time periods do not coincide. For example, if the accelerator time period is three months, then the effective accelerator would be 4 times the annual-basis accelerator; the accelerator of 1.5 in Table 16-2 would become 6. Such an accelerator would move our model from region B into region D and would result in an explosive increase in aggregate real income. On the other hand, the accelerator would be effectively reduced if a lead time for investment is assumed to lengthen the investment time period.

Furthermore, the assumption of a fixed accelerator coefficient may not be realistic, since the value of the accelerator itself may change from period to period. To begin with, as technology improves over time, the accelerator should change, since the amount of capital equipment required to produce a given quantity of consumer goods would change in response to a change in technology. Whether the amount of capital required per unit of output increases or decreases depends on the nature of the technological change. In addition, changes in consumer demand can be met by selling off inventories or by working existing productive facilities overtime, so there is no rigid relationship between a given level of consumer demand and investment expenditures. Also, investment is a function of *expected* consumer demand, so an accelerator based on *realized* changes (such as that in Table 16-2) may often be wrong. In addition, there are short-run supply limitations on the possibilities of producing additional investment goods, but the accelerator theory assumes that buyers of investment goods will be able to adjust their purchases promptly at a fixed price to changes in the consumer demand for their output.

The negative net investment caused by the accelerator during a recession is of a different nature from the positive investment during prosperity. In most cases, true disinvestment can occur only through gradual wearing out of plant and equipment. Therefore, the positive rate of change in investment during prosperity will probably be greater than the negative rate during recessions. Consequently, the accelerator is not truly reversible, and to get the same effect on aggregate real income in recession as in prosperity, a greater increase in consumer demand is required, because of excess capacity that develops during recessions. The long life of some capital goods means that investment will be restricted until consumer demand increases enough to re-employ existing machines or until the machines wear out.

There is an additional reason that the accelerator is not reversible, even in the long run when all equipment can wear out. The previous achievement of a level of living attributable to investment implies that society can never return to some earlier condition. Technically, this process has been called *hysteresis*, and refers to a change in a variable that over time is not reversible. To take an extreme example, if an atomic bomb destroyed all capital goods and men went back to live in caves, the way of life and attitudes of the survivors would probably be significantly different from those of the original inhabitants of the caves. Even the physical destruction of investment will not destroy knowledge once it has been acquired.

Therefore, because of a number of inherent difficulties, theories that employ the accelerator must be used with care.

Hicks's Contribution to the Theory of the Business Cycle

Professor J. R. Hicks developed a theory of constrained cycles, with a ceiling limiting the expansion phase and a floor limiting contractions.[10] The values of the MPC and the accelerator could then fall within the explosive range, and cyclical activity would still appear to be either regular or damped, because the cycle could not break through the ceiling or the floor.

The Hicksian ceiling is imposed by the full-employment level of aggregate output, which is proportional to the growth rate of both the labor force and worker productivity (similar to the natural growth rate of the Harrod model). When shown on semilog paper (as in Figure 16-5), the ceiling has the same slope as the equilibrium growth rate of capital, represented by the growth rate of autonomous investment in Hicks's model.

The accelerator is asymmetrical because disinvestment can occur only through wearing out existing investment or reducing autonomous investment. Thus, lower values of the accelerator occur during the down phase of the business cycle, and this eventually builds in a floor. The accelerator works only on investment initiated by changes in consumer demand, not on auto-

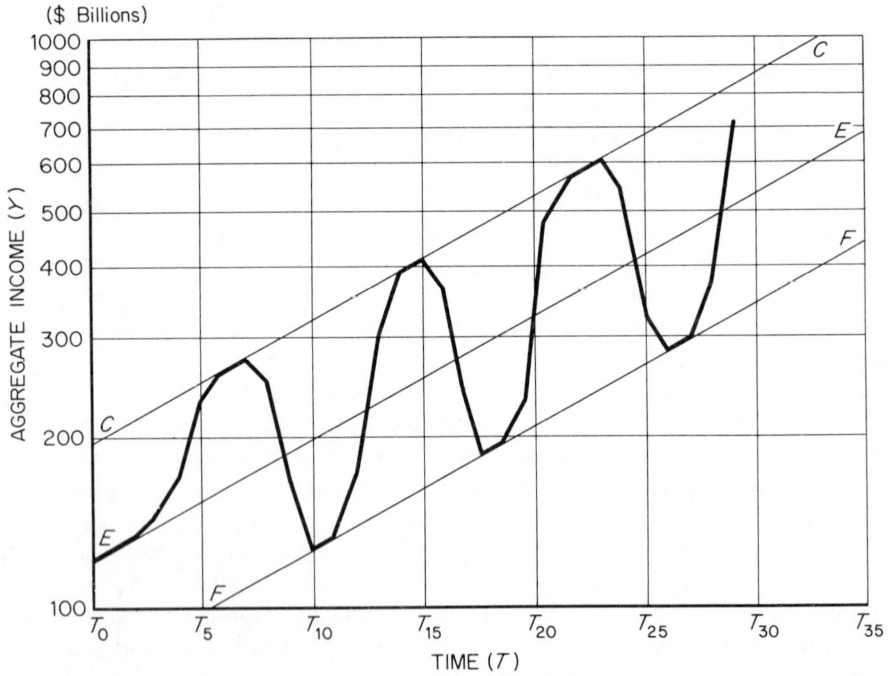

FIG. 16-5 Hicks's Constrained Cycle

[10] J. R. Hicks, *A Contribution to the Theory of the Trade Cycle* (London: Oxford Clarendon Press, 1950).

nomous investment that may decrease during a slump; so the accelerator could appear to reverse itself in a symmetrical fashion for a short time, since less autonomous investment has the same effect as less accelerator investment. However, soon the accelerator effect will probably slow down as autonomous investment stops falling. Consequently, accelerator-initiated disinvestment must stop, and the simple multiplier (with no accelerator to reinforce it) emerges before a slump equilibrium is established.

Once stability is reestablished in the slump, a positive accelerator effect will again be felt. The multiplier will operate on the accelerator-initiated investment and the recovery will begin. The floor is established by the fact that autonomous investment will eventually reassert itself when slump equilibrium is reached.

The floor is not as firm as the ceiling, since it depends on a technical support level created by the accelerator's lack of symmetry. If business firms proved continually unwilling to invest during a slump, then no floor would be established, and the society could continue its depression unhampered until autonomous investment reached zero. But as long as autonomous investment grows in step with the equilibrium growth rate of the economy, then the floor, once it is established, grows at the same rate as the equilibrium trend, and the two would graph as parallel lines on a semilog scale.

Hicks begins his analysis at an underemployment equilibrium level. The equilibrium level grows over time as the capacity of the economy increases. In our illustration of the Hicksian-type cycle, illustrated in Figure 16-5 and Table 16-3, the cycle oscillates around an equilibrium path, which we assume will grow at 5 percent annually. The MPC of .6 and the acceleration coefficient of 6 used in constructing Figure 16-4 would cause explosive oscillations without the floor and ceiling to constrain the cycle. Assume that the economy is well structured and that the combined growth of the labor force and its productivity is 5 percent, which will be matched by a 5 percent annual increase in autonomous investment. Consequently, the ceiling and floor both grow at a 5 percent rate. Because of the 5 percent increase in autonomous investment and the resulting increase in equilibrium output, the acceleration effect will be felt only when changes in consumption exceed 5 percent.

In Table 16-3, the column heads are the same as in Table 16-2; however, the calculations are different. Each level of consumption in Table 16-3 is a function of only the previous period's income, or

$$C_t = bY_{t-1}$$

Therefore, the consumption function in this model, if it is graphed, passes through the origin, whereas in Table 16-2, the consumption function included an autonomous factor, *a*.

Accelerator investment (I_A) in column 5 is defined as

a. $I_{A_t} = X[C_t - (1 + g)(C_{t-1})]$

when consumer spending is increasing; and

TABLE 16-3 Hicks's Constrained Cycle Model (in billions of dollars)[b]

(1) Period	(2) *Aggregate Income*	(3) *Consumption*	(4) *Autonomous Investment*	(5) *Accelerator Investment*	(6) *Total Investment*
0	$125				
1	131	$ 75	$ 56		$ 56
2	138	79	59		59
3	150	83	67[a]		67
4	173	90	65	$ 18	83
5	232	104	68	60	128
Ceiling 6	268	139	71	58	129
Ceiling 7	281	161	75	45	120
8	248	169	79	0	79
9	160	149	83	−72	11
floor 10	128	96	87	−55	32
floor 11	134	77	91	−34	57
12	170	80	96	−6	90
13	311	102	101	108	209
Ceiling 14	396	187	106	103	209
Ceiling 15	416	238	111	67	178
16	367	250	117	0	117
17	235	220	123	−108	15
floor 18	189	141	129	−81	48
floor 19	198	113	135	−50	85
20	261	119	142	0	142
21	498	157	149	192	341
Ceiling 22	586	299	156	131	287
Ceiling 23	615	352	164	99	263
24	542	370	172	0	172
25	344	325	181	−162	19
floor 26	279	206	190	−117	73
floor 27	293	167	200	−74	126
28	392	176	210	6	216
29	755	235	220	300	520

[a]*Exogenous change in investment demand.*
[b]*Computations performed with rounded figures.*

b. $I_{A_t} = X[C_t - (1 - g)(C_{t-1})]$

when consumer spending is decreasing, except when the value of the accelerator investment is constrained by the floor or the ceiling.

The formulas above are the same as the formula for determining accelerator initiated investment used earlier in this chapter, $\Delta I_{A_t} = X(C_t - C_{t-1})$, with the addition of the $(1 + g)$ and $(1 - g)$ terms to reflect the growth trend of the economy. As in Table 16-2, the accelerator investment (I_A) in column 5 of Table 16-3 must be added to autonomous investment in column 4 to obtain total investment in column 6. Autonomous investment is simply some initial level of investment (assumed to be $56 billion in this example) that grows at 5 percent in subsequent time periods; the only exception occurs in period 3, when an exogenous increase in investment is assumed in order to initiate the cyclical activity.

As in Table 16-2, total investment in column 6 must be added to consumption in column 3 to obtain aggregate income in column 2.

(In formula b, designed for use when consumption is decreasing, the asymmetrical nature of the accelerator could be allowed for by arbitrarily reducing the value of the accelerator during a cyclical downturn. If such an adjustment had been made, the cycle in Figure 16-5 would not appear to be so regular.)

To illustrate the working of this model, we start from an equilibrium level of aggregate real income in Table 16-3 and Figure 16-5. The economy remains on the equilibrium growth path for two time periods, as increases in autonomous investment are matched by increases in consumption. Then, in period 3, an exogenous investment of $5 billion occurs for only one time period, whereafter autonomous investment reverts to its equilibrium 5 percent growth path. However, this one spurt is enough to generate a never-ending cycle. Given this one departure from the equilibrium level of investment, the rate of change in investment thereafter will never permit more than a momentary return to the equilibrium growth trend, line E in Figure 16-5.

By period 6, the rate of increase in output is slowed by an encounter with the ceiling. Since the path to the ceiling necessarily occurred at a growth rate faster than the equilibrium rate, the economy will be unable to crawl along the ceiling for any length of time (no more than one time period, in our illustration). Consequently, the slowdown in the rate of change in aggregate income at the ceiling reduces the level of accelerator-initiated investment. Less investment eventually causes a reduction in aggregate real income. The inability of an economy to successfully crawl along the ceiling after an initial upward displacement from the equilibrium growth trend, E, starts a downturn or recession phase of the cycle. The accelerator causes a precipitous drop in income that is stopped only by the floor in the tenth period.

When the economy settles in its slump equilibrium, line F, in Figure 16-5, it will follow that path for at least one time period. At the floor, the negative accelerator effect is reversed by the positive autonomous investment that occurs in the slump equilibrium. The positive accelerator will push the economy away from the floor quickly if there is no excess capacity. The economy then starts on an upward path toward equilibrium, which will again be overshot if the MPC and the accelerator remain unchanged.

In Figure 16-5 and Table 16-3, we have carried our example of the Hicksian type of constrained cycle model through three complete cycles. In practice, the accelerator may not work quickly at the bottom of the cycle. Redundant capital equipment may have to be reemployed before new capital equipment will be bought, so the downturn may last long enough to wear out old equipment.

A Monetary Endogenous Model

Although his basic theory is stated in real terms, Hicks supplements his real theory of the business cycle with a monetary endogenous model.[11] He uses his own *IS–LM* model, presented in Chapter 11, to isolate monetary sources of income instability. In Hicks's real theory, the accelerator, operating with the multiplier, is the main factor causing cyclical fluctuations; but

[11]Hicks, *A Contribution to the Theory of the Trade Cycle*, pp. 137–68.

in his monetary theory, adjustment lags are responsible for the fluctuations. The most important lag in this model, as in Wicksell's, is the adjustment of the bank rate of interest as it lags behind changes in the equilibrium rate of interest, determined by the *IS–LM* intersection.

The second lag in the Hicksian monetary theory is in the adjustment of the stock of money to changes in demand. Hicks allows the *LM* curve to remain stationary by relating it to a "given monetary system" rather than to a "given stock of money." Relaxing the assumption that banks are continually loaned up allows a degree of play in bank credit (bank-created money) and a degree of freedom to move off the *IS* and *LM* curves.

Assume that the economy is in equilibrium at point *a* in Figure 16-6 and

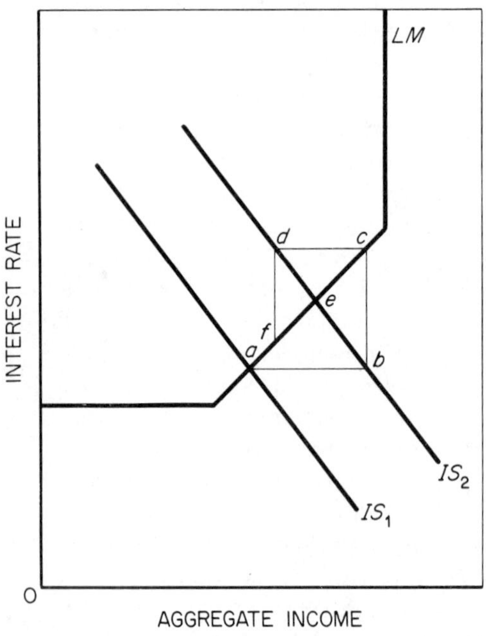

FIG. 16-6 Hicks's Monetary Cycle

that the *IS* function shifts from IS_1 to IS_2. The new equilibrium level of the interest rate would occur at point *e*; however, the economy does not move directly to point *e*, because of the lags in the response of the bank rate of interest and the adjustment in the stock of bank-created money. If banks are not loaned up, the initial demand for increased loans owing to the shift from IS_1 to IS_2 will be met by an expansion of bank-created money, at the going interest rate. The banks will not immediately raise their going interest rate for two related reasons we discussed in Chapter 14 in connection with the credit availability theory: First, they have no immediate way of knowing whether the increased demand for loans is due to a permanent shift in the *IS* curve, requiring an interest-rate adjustment, or merely to a momentary departure, requiring no adjustment. Second, the oligopoly structure of the bank industry means that the bank rate will most likely be at least temporarily inflexible even if the *IS* shift is permanent, because banks will not change their rates until they have a good idea what the new equilibrium rate is.

Money and credit become increasingly tight as the economy moves from point *a* to point *b* in Figure 16-6, and the amount of money demanded for transactions balances increases in response to the higher level of aggregate income. Under pressure of tighter money and credit, excess reserves become depleted, and the banks will eventually be forced to adjust their interest rate in the direction of point *c*. The economy will not be in equilibrium at point *c*, since the bank interest rate has now risen above equilibrium. The quantity of investments demanded will be too small at the new, higher bank rate of interest, and consequently, if that higher-than-equilibrium interest level is maintained, a contraction in aggregate income from point *c* toward point *d* will begin. The small amount of money demanded (relative to the supply) at the interest rate encountered at point *d* will ultimately result in a decrease in the bank rate, as the banks try to lend their excess reserves. The economy will move toward point *f*. As bank interest rates fall, the cycle will begin again at point *f*. With each additional cycle, the economy moves ever closer to *IS–LM* equilibrium at point *e*.

The inevitable lags on the real side of the economy in the adjustment of investment and savings have been overlooked for the sake of simplicity. Since the cyclical activity in this model depends on lagged monetary adjustments, a change in the duration of the lags would probably alter the amplitude and certainly the duration of the cyclical swings.

Hicks's monetary theory of the cycle could be combined with his constrained real cycle model. For example, as the real cycle approaches a peak, monetary factors such as the shortage of money could by themselves cause the downturn, although Hicks feels that this is unlikely, since money substitutes are fairly easily available. However, once the downturn does occur, whether caused by monetary mismanagement or by the real factors involved in bouncing off the ceiling, monetary factors will speed the downturn and aggravate the cycle. Not only does the cobweb accelerate the downturn, but at such times responses by asset holders and the monetary authorities may be reflected as an increase in the liquidity preference curve or a decrease in the stock of money, thus shifting the *LM* curve to the left. Hicks would agree that monetary factors are important, but he would not agree with those writers who have claimed that monetary disturbances are the major cause of the business cycle.

Cost of Capital

Including monetary factors makes the basic multiplier-accelerator model more realistic, but it is still a very abstract theory. Additional realism can be obtained by bringing in other variables, such as the cost of capital.[12]

---

[12] James S. Duesenberry, *Business Cycles and Economic Growth* (New York: McGraw-Hill, 1958), Chaps. 5 and 9.

A firm will undertake a new investment project if the marginal efficiency of capital of that project is greater than the marginal cost of capital, including both debt and equity. In Chapter 9, we considered the cost of capital to a firm, and found that the average and marginal cost of capital are upsloping, even if the firm maintains an ideal debt-to-equity ratio. A larger volume of financing by itself causes lenders and stock purchasers to ascribe a greater risk to the firm's operations. Therefore, the return paid to those supplying funds must be increased to include a risk premium as the volume of financing grows.

In addition, new stock issues are subject to flotation costs, which further increase the cost of capital as the firm expands beyond the point where retained earnings comprise sufficient equity to maintain the ideal debt–equity ratio.

During prosperity, the firm's total demand for investment will increase, but the cost of capital will also go up. The rising cost of capital will, in part, offset the increasing total demand for investment, and will reduce the accelerator. Any reduction in the accelerator during a cyclical upswing will tend to choke off the boom before Hick's ceiling is reached.

Cost-Push Inflation

In a theory developed before the multiplier-accelerator model, W. C. Mitchell stressed the importance of what we would today call "cost-push" inflationary pressures in ending the boom, for he felt that the purchase price of resources would rise at the peak of a business cycle.[13] In addition, the quality of marginal units of capital and labor resources hired at the cyclical peak will deteriorate, because the most productive units are hired first and the least efficient are employed only when the demand is stimulated by high cyclical activity. The combination of increasing resource costs and decreasing resource productivity at the margin squeezes profits at the end of the boom and, in current terminology, reduces the accelerator effect by increasing operating costs. Furthermore, since investment depends on *expected* net returns to capital, price expectations will have a strong effect on investment, and management will anticipate resistance to higher prices near the peak of the cycle.[14] As in the case of the upsloping cost-of-capital curve, the effect is to damp down the boom before Hick's ceiling is reached.

Inventory Fluctuations

Given the existence of a relationship between expected sales and desired levels of inventory, a cycle model can be developed that is independent of both investment in capital equipment and monetary factors. Inventory cycles

---

[13] W. C. Mitchell, *Business Cycles* (1913) (New York: Burt Franklin, 1970), pp. 475–511.

[14] Buyer resistance also implies a reduction in the multiplier, an effect that could reinforce the declining accelerator.

can be related to the short-term cycles of the type which were developed by Kitchin and are often conceived of as small fluctuations occurring within larger business cycles. Modern inventory cycle models are largely based on early work by L. A. Metzler.[15]

To the individual business, inventories are simply another asset, and their optimum level depends on a number of variables relating inventories to other possible alternative assets. For example, the interest rate as a component of the cost of capital is significant whether the firm borrows to finance its inventory or uses its own funds. A low interest rate reduces the cost of borrowing to finance inventory, and it also reduces the alternative return the firm could earn by lending the money. Therefore, a low interest rate tends to increase the desired ratio of inventory to sales volume, since merchants can have more inventory for less cost, whereas a high interest rate encourages merchants to operate with a smaller inventory–sales volume ratio.

Anticipated changes in prices are another example of a factor influencing the desired inventory level. Expectations of fluctuations in the price level introduce the possibility of speculative gains or losses from inventory holdings. Anticipated inflation will encourage firms to hold larger inventories in order to make a speculative profit, and expectations of a decline in the price level will have the opposite effect.

To build an inventory model, we assume for simplicity a constant interest rate and price level. The significant relationship is the ratio of the desired inventory level to estimated consumer demand. A model of an in-

TABLE 16-4 Inventory Cycle Model (figures in units)

				Purchases for Inventory		
(1)	(2)	(3)	(4)	(5)	(6)	(7)
Period	*Consumer Demand*[a]	*Desired Inventory*[a]	*Beginning Inventory*[a]	*Replacement of Sales*[a]	*Adjustment Purchases*[a]	*Total Inventory Investment*[a]
1	100	150	150	100	0	100
2	120[b]	180	150	120	30	150
3	150	225	180	150	45	195
4	177	265	225	177	40	217
5	190	285	265	190	20	210
6	186	279	285	186	−6	180
7	168	252	279	168	−27	141
8	145	218	252	145	−34	111
9	127	190	218	127	−28	99
10	120	180	190	120	−10	110
11	127	190	180	127	10	137
12	143	214	190	143	24	167

[a]*Discrepancies are due to rounding.*
[b]*Exogenous change in consumer demand.*

[15]L. A. Metzler, "The Nature and Stability of Inventory Cycles," *Review of Economic Statistics*, 23 (August 1941), 113–29; and Metzler "Business Cycles and the Modern Theory of Employment," *American Economic Review*, 36 (June 1946), 278–91.

ventory cycle with such a constant relationship is presented in Table 16-4.

The desired inventory (column 3) is a function of consumer demand (column 2). If the desired inventory is achieved and maintained, it becomes the beginning inventory for the succeeding time period (column 4). Inventory purchases are made for two motives: One is to replace sales (column 5); the other is to adjust the total inventory to the desired relationship with consumer demand (column 6). Column 6 equals column 3 minus column 4. The adjustment may be positive or negative. Replacement of sales (column 5) plus adjustment purchases (column 6) equals total inventory investment (column 7). The MPC applied to the *change* in inventory investment between the two previous time periods determines the increment (or decrement) in consumer demand in the ensuing time period, or

$$\Delta C_T = b(I_{i_{t-1}} - I_{i_{t-2}})$$

where I_i equals total inventory investment.

In the example in Table 16-4, consumption is assumed to be a function of the change in inventory investment through its impact on aggregate income, and the change in consumption induced by the inventory investment is assumed to be 60 percent of the change in inventory investment between the two previous time periods. The desired change in inventory level is assumed to be 150 percent of the change in consumption. We assume that the desired inventory is achieved by the end of each time period and becomes the beginning inventory of the following period. To concentrate on inventory change, all other investment is assumed to be constant. Furthermore, since inventory investment can be accomplished more quickly than other types of investment, the time periods may be shorter.

Table 16-4 illustrates a cycle that works itself out in ten or eleven periods. A cycle is generated in this model by the ratio of desired inventory to consumer demand (a relationship analogous to the accelerator) and by inventory purchases for replacement of sales. Assume an exogenous increase in consumer demand from 100 units in period 1 to 120 units in period 2. The increase leads to a desired inventory level of 180; that is, 150 percent of estimated consumer demand. The firm will make replacement purchases of 120 units plus an inventory adjustment of +30 units by the end of period two in order to bring inventory up to the desired level. So the increase in total inventory investment between periods 1 and 2 is 50 units. Given an MPC of 60 percent, this increased investment in period 2 will increase consumer demand by 30 in period 3, as the income generated in period 2 is spent on consumption. As a result, in period 3, the desired inventory level is 225—that is, 150 percent of 150—and thus the cycle is generated.

The inventory cycle model is a variation on the accelerator-multiplier model, and the turning points occur for the same reasons. To make a more realistic accelerator-multiplier model, the effects of changes in inventory investment could be built in, allowing for change in total investment.

Any economic model can have only a relatively small number of endogenous variables and still remain comprehensible. A virtually infinite number of sources of economic change can occur, and they cannot all be incorporated in any single model. In addition, many random variables affecting the economy do not occur in any systematic fashion and therefore cannot be included as endogenous variables in a cycle model. Any significant change in our society, including political and social change, is apt to have an effect on the economic system. The economic system, in this sense, is rather like a ship that has been set on a certain heading but is inevitably affected by waves, currents, winds, and storms. If these outside influences become too severe, they may change the course significantly, or even sink the ship. Although it is clearly impossible to catalog each of the possible exogenous changes or stochastic shocks that can set off cyclical waves in the economy, it is possible to identify some of the major sources of change.

Monetary Shocks

Some monetary shocks can originate in ways that are exogenous to the monetary model previously discussed. For example, the gold discoveries in California and Alaska helped cause the booms of 1849 and 1900, by increasing the stock of money, shifting the *LM* curve to the right. Again, the specie circular initiated by Andrew Jackson in an attempt to end the era of wildcat banking reduced the stock of money and caused the panic of 1837.

Those occurrences were fortuitous, with results forced by the existing situation and personalities. But exogenous pressures can also be brought about by conscious design; for example, in 1862 the creation of the National Bank System was designed to increase the stock of money so that the federal government could finance the Civil War.

Exogenous changes can occur in the demand for money as well as in the stock of money. For example, the wave of pessimism accompanying the collapse of the stock market in 1929 created an excessive demand for speculative liquid balances that reduced the *LM* curve, and this reduction was partly responsible for the financial crisis and subsequent depression.

Psychological Shocks

Psychological factors affect the demand for investment as well as for money. The marginal efficiency of capital (MEC) depends on the expected net income stream and the cost of a project.

Therefore, calculations of project costs and expected net returns play a large part in the investment process. However, as we noted in Chapter 9, the significant problem is how much confidence to place in one's expectations of expected net returns under conditions of uncertainty. As Keynes put it, "If human nature felt no temptation to take a chance, no satisfaction (profit apart) in constructing a factory, a railway, a mine or a farm, there might not be much investment merely as a result of cold calculation."[16] The psychological factors make investment a sort of game, once the precarious nature of our expectations is taken into account. As in any game, optimism and enthusiasm can be generated by the confidence developed during long periods of winning play.

If long periods of prosperity stimulate investment and possibly overinvestment, the converse is also true. Once pessimism sets in, it has a tendency to become cumulative. Near the peak of the cycle, expectations of future net returns may become so optimistic that they overcome the diminishing returns to capital accompanying a growing stock of capital goods. Glowing expectations concerning future net returns also tend to overcome the increasing costs of production of capital goods and the increasing interest rate. In the latter stages of prosperity, optimism may cause investors to lose sight of realistic future-profit projections, and may leave the investment market in a very precarious position. In Keynes's words, "when disillusion falls upon an over-optimistic and over-bought market, it should fall with sudden and even catastrophic force."[17] After the collapse, a wave of pessimism follows, which persists until it is reversed by real factors, such as wearing out of capital equipment in relationship to the normal growth rate (Hicks's floor), and the eventual reduction in the carrying costs of inventory. The collapse of the MEC owing to unfavorable expectations may induce a sudden increase in the demand for speculative money balances, since both the MEC and the liquidity preference are based on psychological factors. Disillusionment will affect both the real and monetary sides of the economy, further intensifying the downturn of the cycle. Thus, in Keynes's view, the boom and the crisis are caused by exogenous psychological factors operating on both the demand for investment and the demand for money.

In addition, any sudden change in any of Keynes's subjective factors underlying the consumption function (discussed in Chapter 8) would cause a psychological effect capable of inducing cyclical consequences. Keynes proposed that those motives—precaution, foresight, calculation, improvement, independence, enterprise, bequest and avarice—would generally change only slowly over time. However, a sudden change in any of them is conceivable.

Innovations

J. A. Schumpeter related his cycle theory to his growth theory in proposing innovation as a major exogenous source of shock to inaugurate the business cycle.[18] Innovation is not invention, but rather the successful commercial

---

[16] J. M. Keynes, *The General Theory of Employment, Interest and Money* (New York: Harcourt Brace Jovanovich, 1936), p. 150.

[17] *Ibid.*, p. 316.

[18] J. A. Schumpeter, *The Theory of Economic Development* trans. R. Opie (1934) (New York: Oxford University Press, 1961), pp. 212–55.

application of a new process or product. Since most people are essentially conservative, innovation will not occur until some bold individual takes the lead in the process. Then, if the innovation is successful, market pressures will force rivals to follow suit, and a wave of investment spending based on the original innovation will follow. If this occurs during periods of unemployment, it will push the economy toward prosperity. After all rival firms involved in the change have adopted the innovation, exogenous investment will run out, and the economy will be forced to operate with only endogenous investment expenditures.

Innovations will hit one industry first, or perhaps a group of industries. The strength and speed of impact on the aggregate economy will vary, depending on the degree of interaction of the input–output relationships between the industry or industrial group immediately affected and the other sectors of the economy. At the end of the gestation period of the innovation, when the added capacity is completed and in production, the economy may find itself with excess capacity that could reduce the accelerator coefficient, in turn reducing endogenously generated investment. Not only will the exogenous wave of innovation investment run out; a reduction in the accleration coefficient would tend also to reduce endogenous investment and hasten the end of prosperity.

If innovations are hampered by other existing exogenous conditions, such as wars, a backlog of potential innovations may build up that may then be introduced in larger-than-expected numbers when conditions are ripe. For example, after the immediate postwar chaos has been resolved, investment booms have often occurred, stimulated by the backlog of innovations, some of them due to wartime discoveries. Consequently, innovation-induced cyclical activity has often followed war.

Political Shocks

A change in political climate may affect the economy in many ways other then by inducing monetary shocks. Historically in America, increased investment expenditure for military use during wars stimulated the economy, creating a wartime boom. On the other hand, in future wars, any stimulating economic effect of government expenditures may be more than offset by the destruction of people and property.

During peacetime, increased political pressure for roads, schools, or public parks may similarly increase government expenditures and exogenous investment. A reduction in corporate taxes may encourage investment by increasing corporate savings. These are all examples of government fiscal policy that may be unplanned and uncoordinated, but which achieve an economic effect incidentally to some other objective.

In contrast, political shocks may also be caused by planned and coordinated programs, specifically designed to achieve some economic end. For example, the imposition of wage–price controls caused a severe stochastic shock in many areas of the economy during 1971.

The intent of consciously applied monetary and fiscal policies will normally be contracyclical (even though their effect might be different from what was intended) and will therefore be an exogenous shock designed to damp down the cycle. However, they may be designed to achieve various goals and may even appear to conflict. For example, government policy designed to achieve full employment may create inflationary tendencies, calling for some form of wage and price controls to be maintained. So, an expansionary (inflationary) policy and a counter-inflationary policy can reasonably be employed simultaneously.

Population Changes

Demographic factors, the size and composition of the population, may also provide stochastic shocks. Generally, these shocks will be felt through shifts in the consumption function, the investment demand function, or the supply of labor.

The size of the population will depend on the net reproduction rate and net migration. Through its effect on consumption, the low birthrate of the thirties helped to prolong the Great Depression; the higher rate since the end of World War II has helped to maintain a long period of prosperity. As this is being written the birth rate in the U.S. has declined to a level of about 2.1 children per family or just about the level to achieve zero population growth. The maintenance of this figure would lead to a stable population of 280 million by the year 2037.

Normally, migration is a slow, orderly process; however, any sudden change can be a source of stochastic shock to an economy through the effect on both effective demand and the labor supply. For example, immigration into the United States during the end of the 1800's, or into Israel since World War II, has been partly responsible for economic booms, whereas the migration out of Ireland after the potato famine had the reverse effect.

Not only the size but also the composition of the population can be a source of stochastic shock. In the United States, the coming of age of the post–World War II baby crop has increased the supply of labor, thereby increasing the country's potential productive capacity and raising the aggregate-consumption function. However, as young adults mature and begin to think of their old age, their propensity to save may increase, a tendency that would reduce the aggregate-consumption function without a corresponding effect on potential productive capacity.

Other demographic factors, such as the ratio of urban to rural, the ratio of black to white, and the average family size, can affect the level of economic activity. But these factors tend to change slowly. Only when some sudden shift occurs, can population change become a source of stochastic shock.

Keynes's "Objective Factors"

Keynes's list of objective factors may also be sources of stochastic shock, if they cause a sudden shift in consumption. The list includes windfall gains or losses, substantial changes in the interest rate, changes in consumer expectations, and changes in fiscal policy. This sort of change, which could radically affect consumption patterns, was discussed in Chapter 8.

Other Sources of Shock

Any number of other sources of stochastic shock might be noted—for example, the discovery, development, and exploitation of new lands and resources; the discovery and exploitation of the New World helped to stimulate the European economy during the 1500's. Or sudden changes in consumer demand can cause cyclical effects; the pent-up consumer demand during World War II caused a postwar upsurge in the consumption function.

Simulated Stochastic Shock

In experiments using random numbers to simulate stochastic shocks, Fisher and Kalecki found that random shocks would keep a damped cycle from dying out, and they inferred that random shocks would actually improve the regularity of a damped-cycles model.[19] So if the values of the multiplier and accelerator place the economy in the region of damped cycles, the occurrence of randomly timed shocks could cause business fluctuations to assume a regular pattern. There is no guarantee that shocks in the real world will occur randomly, but once we make an assumption about the occurrence of stochastic shocks, we can devise a public policy to counteract the resulting fluctuations.

THE INTERRELATIONSHIP OF ECONOMIC GROWTH AND FLUCTUATIONS

The ceiling in Hicks's cycle model could be achieved and maintained through ideal monetary and fiscal management of the economy. Under such conditions, operating along the Hicksian ceiling would represent a conjunction of the natural and warranted growth rates in the Harrod–Domar growth model. As we previously pointed out, the ceiling in Hicks's theory represents the maximam rate of growth in aggregate output at full employment of labor, allowing for changes in the labor supply and in labor productivity. The natural growth rate described in Chapter 15 represents an upper limit to the rate of growth in aggregate output and the cycle models presented in this chapter indicate that any departure from the natural growth rate will lead to a downward spiral.

In contrast, the *equilibrium* level in Hicks's accelerator-multiplier model involves a certain amount of unemployment. Hicks's equilibrium growth path does not contradict the Harrod–Domar growth theory, if one allows for the

---

[19] G. H. Fisher, "Some Comments on Stochastic Macroeconomic Models," *American Economic Review*, 42 (September 1952), 528–39; and M. Kalecki, *Theory of Economic Dynamics*, 2nd ed. (London: Allen & Unwin, 1965), pp. 137–42.

possibility of an unemployment equilibrium as the norm around which the economy fluctuates. To put the cycle in terms of a full-employment norm, it might be convenient to picture the cycle as dropping down from the natural-growth-rate ceiling and eventually returning to it, rather than fluctuating around Hicks's equilibrium trend line.

As we saw, the ceiling in Hicks's cycle model could be interpreted as the natural-growth path of economic activity in the Harrod–Domar model. And the actual path could be interpreted as a combination of the warranted and actual growth rates, where those two rates are equal. If the warranted and actual rates are higher than the natural rate, economic activity could run up against the ceiling, and inevitably bounce off as excess capacity develops. The actual rate could fall from the ceiling (imposed by the natural rate) until it was constrained by the floor (imposed by autonomous investment). (The warranted rate could continue to grow past the natural rate—but could not be achieved.)

As the foregoing example implies, there is no necessary conflict between cycle theory and growth theory, and in fact, one can be used to illuminate the other.

SUMMARY AND CONCLUSIONS

After languishing in the underworld of economics, cycle theory became academically acceptable around the turn of the century, owing largely to the work of economists such as T. N. Carver, J. A. Schumpeter, and W. C. Mitchell.

The endogenous multiplier-accelerator models presented in this chapter can produce regular cycles if the multiplier-accelerator coefficients happen to be of the proper values. Hicks's "ceiling" and "floor" answer the problem of deriving a constrained or regular cycle when the values of the multiplier and accelerator put the economy in the explosive range.

The basic cycle model presented here depends on real factors. However, most theorists agree that the cycle is at least partly a monetary phenomenon, at the very least in the sense that "business cycles" in the current usage could not occur in a premonetary economy because a pure barter economy would not possess a monetary sector. Furthermore, monetary factors will affect any business cycle, whether its original cause was monetary or real, and a purely monetary-cycle model was suggested by Hicks.

Modifications to the basic multiplier-accelerator model employing inventory adjustments, cost-push factors, and the cost of capital, are offered as examples of the sort of adjustments that can be included for added realism.

Some writers have tried to explain the cycle as an exogenous phenomenon. However, it seems preferable to use a more comprehensive cycle theory in which exogenously generated stochastic shocks provide the initial impetus and an endogenously generated cycle ensues. Further shocks occurring randomly can maintain a regular cycle, as Fisher and Kalecki demonstrated.

But apparently, stochastic shocks do not occur randomly, since business-cycle data show a marked lack of regularity. Furthermore, the level of business activity depends in part on countercyclical monetary and fiscal policy designed to make the economy operate near the full-employment ceiling. Therefore, "business fluctuations" might be a better term than "business cycles," since the latter implies a degree of regularity not found in observed data.

Fluctuations in business activity and economic growth are two phenomena that are closely related, and the two theories can be used to help explain each other. Business fluctuations are a main concern of economic policy—the topic of the next, and final, chapter.

QUESTIONS AND PROBLEMS

1. Why did cycle theory not become respectable until fairly recently?
2. Who were the developers of the three prototype cycles?
3. In Juglar's opinion, what was the cause of recession? Explain.
4. Describe the nature and phases of Schumpeter's cycle.
5. What was the crucial point in Schumpeter's cycle? In Mitchell's?
6. How did Samuelson contribute to business-cycle theory?
7. After Samuelson, what were the major theoretical problems facing students of the cycle?
8. How did Hicks solve the problem of explosive cycles?
9. What are the most important sources of stochastic shock?
10. Explain the ceiling and the floor in Hicks's cycle model.
11. In the figure below, assuming a 5% equilibrium growth rate, indicate the ceiling, trend, and floor, if the floor in period 1 is $1, the ceiling $5, and the equilibrium trend is midway between.

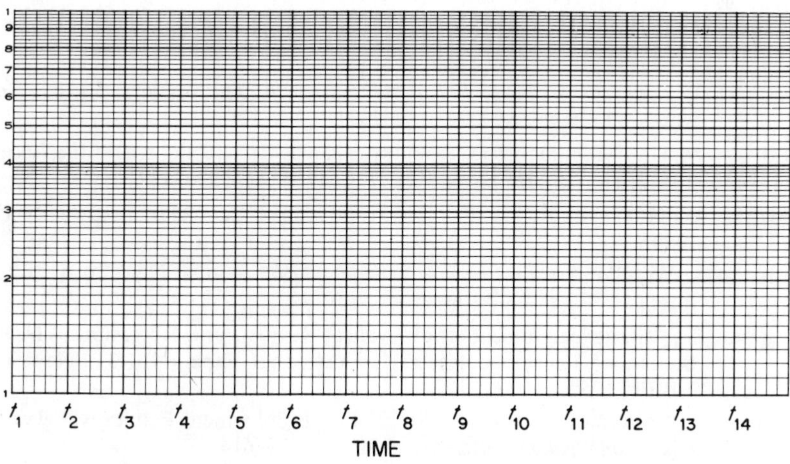

12. How does Hicks's monetary cycle operate?

ADDITIONAL SELECTED REFERENCES

ADELMAN, I., "Business Cycles—Endogenous or Stochastic?" *Economic Journal*, 70 (December 1960), 783–96.

BAUMOL, W. J., *Economic Dynamics*, 2nd ed., Chaps. 9, 10, 11. New York: Macmillan, 1959.

BURNS, A. F., "Hicks and the Real Cycle," *Journal of Political Economy*, 60 (February 1952), 1–24.

CHOW, G. C., "Multiplier, Accelerator, and Liquidity Preference in the Determination of National Income in the United States," *Review of Economics and Statistics*, 49 (February 1967), 1–15.

CLARK, J. J., and M. COHEN, eds., *Business Fluctuations, Growth and Economic Stabilization*. New York: Random House, 1963.

DUESENBERRY, J. S., O. ECKSTEIN, and G. FROMM, "A Simulation of the United States Economy in Recession," *Econometrica*, 28 (October 1960), 749–809.

ESTEY, J. A., *Business Cycles*, 3rd ed. Englewood Cliffs, N.J.: Prentice-Hall, 1956.

FELNER, W., *Trends and Cycles in Economic Activity*. New York: Holt, Rinehart & Winston, 1955.

FOSTER, E., "Sales Forecasts and the Inventory Cycle," *Econometrica*. 31 (July 1963), 400–421.

FRIEDMAN, M., and A. SCHWARTZ, "Money and Business Cycles," *Review of Economics and Statistics*, 45, No. 1, Part 2 (February 1963), 32–64.

GOODWIN, R. M., "The Nonlinear Accelerator and the Persistence of Business Cycles," *Econometrica*, 19 (January 1951), 1–17.

HABERLER, G., *Prosperity and Depression*, 4th ed. London: Allen & Unwin, 1958.

———, ed., for the American Economic Association, *Readings in Business Cycle Theory* Vol. II. Philadelphia: Blakiston, 1944.

HANSEN, A. H., *Business Cycles and National Income*, expanded ed. New York: Norton, 1951.

KALDOR, N., "A Model of the Trade Cycle," *Economic Journal*, 50 (March 1940), 78–92. Reprinted in *Essays on Economic Stability and Growth*, Chap. 8. New York: Free Press, 1960.

KALECKI, M., "A Macrodynamic Theory of Business Cycles," *Econometrica*, 3 (July 1935), 327–44.

LEE, M. W., *Macroeconomics: Fluctuations, Growth, and Stability*, 5th ed. Homewood, Ill.: Richard D. Irwin, 1971.

LOVELL, M. C., "Manufacturers' Inventories, Sales Expectations, and the Acceleration Principle," *Econometrica*, 29 (July 1961), 293–314.

MATTHEWS, R. C. O., *The Trade Cycle*. Cambridge: Cambridge University Press, 1959.

MITCHELL, W., *Business Cycles: The Problem and Its Setting*. New York: National Bureau of Economic Research, 1927.

MOORE, G., "Statistical Indicators of Cyclical Revivals and Recessions," National Bureau of Economic Research Occasional Paper No. 31. New York: NBER, 1950.

POOLE, W., "Alternative Paths to a Stable Full Employment Economy," *Brookings Papers on Economic Activity*, 3 (1971), 579–614.

SMYTH, D. J., "Empirical Evidence on the Acceleration Principle," *Review of Economic Studies*, 31 (June 1964), 185–202.

TOBIN, J., "A Dynamic Aggregative Model," *Journal of Political Economy*, 63 (April 1955), 103–15.

WARBURTON, C., "The Misplaced Emphasis in Contemporary Business-Fluctuation Theory," *Journal of Business*, 19 (October 1946), 199–220.

Goals and Policies

17

INTRODUCTION

Until now, we have concentrated mainly on the various theories of macroeconomics and paid little attention to the use of those theories to further the economic aims of society. The principal exceptions were in Chapter 6, which focused on neoclassical policy; Chapter 10, on Keynesian policy; Chapter 14, which presented some policy implications of the monetary theories considered in that chapter; and Chapter 15, which discussed some of the policy implications of various growth theories.

Current conditions are quite different from those at the turn of the century, or those of the severe depression of the 1930's that motivated the writing and publication of Keynes's *General Theory*. In practice, monetary policy must be integrated with fiscal policy. One complicating development of the post-Keynesian world is that there is now no single agreed-upon economic goal, such as eliminating the unemployment created by the Great Depression, much less agreement on *the* cause or cure for the various economic problems facing society.

Goals

Economic goals are a reflection of society's values and therefore are not subject to logical challenge. Goals are usually accepted by economic practitioners, who try to discover efficient means of pursuing and achieving them.

There are any number of possible goals that a society might consider desirable, all of them involving a larger number of factors and interrelationships than we could detail in one book. But in our society, the basic economic goals, as we saw in Chapter 1, are growth, stability, justice, and freedom. Let us briefly review each goal in turn.

Economic growth generally refers to increases in output per capita over time. As generally defined, it has two aspects. One concerns shorter-period growth, which occurs during periods of unemployment and which may be required during the business cycle to reach full employment; the second concerns the longer-term question of increasing output per capita at a full-employment level of output. Such an increase in output requires increasing the quality and quantity of resources by implementing technological innovations, discovering raw materials, or producing capital goods. Although we will discuss policies for achieving full employment, we pay relatively little attention to long-run growth in this chapter, because the policies to achieve economic growth over the long-term period have been covered in Chapter 15.

Stability, the second major goal, refers to several different concepts. Price stability may mean either constant prices or some acceptable rate of inflation or deflation. Employment stability means keeping the economy at or near full employment. In addition, the goal of stability may also refer to providing a stable level of living for members of the society through programs such as Social Security or Medicare. However, macroeconomic policy is concerned mainly with price and employment stability.

The third goal, justice or equity, as it applies to macroeconomics, generally involves the question of a fair distribution of income among the various sectors of the economy, such as wage earners, rentiers, and profit recipients. Economic justice is often taken to mean rewarding income recipients on the basis of their productivity or distributing income according to need. Redistribution of income by inflation follows neither social fairness nor productivity, and is usually considered unjust, but it is a politically practical means of redistributing income without fanfare, and so might be continued even if the results are less than optimal, assuming the groups being rewarded are those society wishes to reward.

The fourth goal, freedom, as it pertains to macroeconomics, is generally used to refer to two concepts—the existence of neutrality and the lack of coercion. Neutrality means the designing of government policies so that they do not materially improve the position of one member of society at the expense of any other. The second concept, lack of coercion, means government policies designed in such a way that the individual members of society are left as free as possible to manage their own resources, set their own prices, and enter or leave markets as they see fit.

Of all the economic goals pursued by our society, the one to which most of the government's efforts are devoted is the achievement of stable prices and stable high employment. Stability of prices and employment are matters of public interest, and therefore, of political concern. Price and employment data are readily available and easy to interpret, whereas the other goals are difficult to quantify and interpret. Even with regard to increasing output per capita, our quantification is subject to criticism: Does more output per capita as we measure it really contribute to marginal utility, or simply to social clutter? Does the ecological and environmental damage caused by increased output outweigh the value of that output?

We have considered in Chapters 1, 4, and 5 some of the shortcomings of our measures of economic growth—failure to include nonmarket activities, failure to allow for the depletion of raw materials, and failure to deduct for such costs of economic growth as pollution and urban blight. In addition, our measures of economic growth concentrate on quantity rather than quality. Generally acceptable quality measures are difficult to devise, a fact that accounts in part for the emphasis on quantity. One criticism often leveled at industrial societies is that they regard the quantity of output more highly than the quality of life.

If economic growth is difficult to measure and interpret, economic justice and freedom are much more so. Not only are these nebulous and relative concepts—no program is unqualifiedly just or can leave all members of society completely free—but there is strong disagreement among members of society regarding their very definition. Angela Davis and Barry Goldwater could probably agree on a definition of stability or growth, but never on a definition of freedom or justice.

As a practical matter, therefore, stability of prices and employment receives more government attention than the other goals. And the economic policies we employ, especially fiscal and monetary policies, have been designed, for the most part, to help in achieving economic stability, the focus of attention in this chapter.

Policies

We have retained for study only those policies that are specifically monetary or fiscal in nature (including direct controls), because these specifically fit the theoretical structures of this book. Direct controls—which include wage and price controls administered by federally appointed boards, such as those imposed in 1971 to 1973 by the Nixon administration—are an attempt to alter the parameters of the economy to supplement monetary and fiscal policy. Interestingly, a Republican administration was first to tacitly acknowledge that market imperfections—cost-push, ex ante, and markup inflation—are capable of rendering both monetary and fiscal policy weak or ineffective in achieving both full employment and a stable price level.

The employment of monetary and fiscal policy over the last generation represents a victory for the Keynesian viewpoint that one appropriate function of government is maintaining reasonably full employment without excessive inflation. The imposition of direct wage–price controls, in this context, is a sort of "super-Keynesianism." Evidently, there now exists no area of the economy that the government is not free to enter.

The traditional devices to regulate the economy are three: fiscal policy, debt management, and monetary policy. The main instruments of *fiscal policy*, which may be either discretionary or automatic, include government expenditures and taxes. The existence of a public debt incurred to finance deficit spending gives rise to *debt management* as a potential means of helping to control the economy. *Monetary policy* generally involves changing the stock of money. Although the banking system can expand or contract the stock of money, the expansion or contraction takes place under the indirect control of the monetary authorities, who have the power to correct for unanticipated changes in bank-created money. Changing the money stock is for the most part accomplished through Federal Reserve open-market operations.

CURRENT FISCAL POLICY

Discretionary Fiscal Policy

As we saw in Chapter 10, fiscal policy can be incorporated into the simplest Keynesian model by adding government expenditures to the consumption plus investment ($C + I$) function and by adding taxes to the savings function. Taxes have a negative multiplier effect, since they represent a leakage out of the spending stream, whereas government expenditures have a positive multiplier effect, since they represent an autonomous injection of spending into the system. The multiplier effect of taxes is mitigated by the fact that taxes are paid at least in part from income that would otherwise have been saved. Therefore, the value of the tax multiplier, as we derived it in Chapter 10, is always one less than the government-expenditure multiplier.[1]

Consequently, the expansionary effect of a tax reduction is less than the effect of an equal-sized increase in government expenditures, but in either case, some appropriate multiplier can be derived and applied to determine the expansionary effect on aggregate income of either an increase in govern-

---

[1]The economic impact of taxes goes far beyond the effects usually depicted. At the simplest level presented above, taxes are analogous to savings; they both represent spending power diverted from the income stream. In reality, specific taxes have other, additional effects. For example, the corporate income tax not only removes purchasing power from the economy but also affects (normally reduces) the MEC. The periodic after-tax returns from any investment are reduced by the imposition of the tax.

The average cost of capital will be increased, although not proportionately since the typical firm will employ both equity and debt financing. Interest payments are tax-deductible expenses to the corporation, while dividends and retained earnings are not; dividends are subject to personal income taxes—excluding the first $100 of dividends. Stockholders demand a higher before-tax return from the firm's investments than bondholders do, because stockholders have the option to buy other, equal-risk securities not subject to the tax.

Consequently, the imposition of a corporate income tax (1) shifts the MEC to the left by reducing the periodic returns, and (2) causes an upward movement along the MEC by raising the cost of capital. In addition, the price of capital goods may increase if the producers shift the corporate income tax forward to their consumers—the purchasers of the capital asset.

Similar ramifications could be discovered in the case of any tax—and any realistic appraisal of a particular tax needs to incorporate all side effects.

ment expenditures or a decrease in taxes. Likewise, the contractional effect of a decrease in government expenditures or a tax increase could be determined by deriving the appropriate multiplier for such a policy. And we can also find the appropriate multiplier if government expenditures and taxes are both increased or decreased by the same amount.

However, the simple analysis presented in Chapter 10 can lead to incorrect conclusions if it is not qualified with what we have learned in subsequent chapters.

The IS–LM Model The first qualification is indicated by applying fiscal policy to the *IS–LM* model as presented in Chapter 11. If government expenditures and taxes are incorporated into the *IS–LM* model, as may be seen in Figure 17-1, the value of the multiplier could change. The multiplier effect

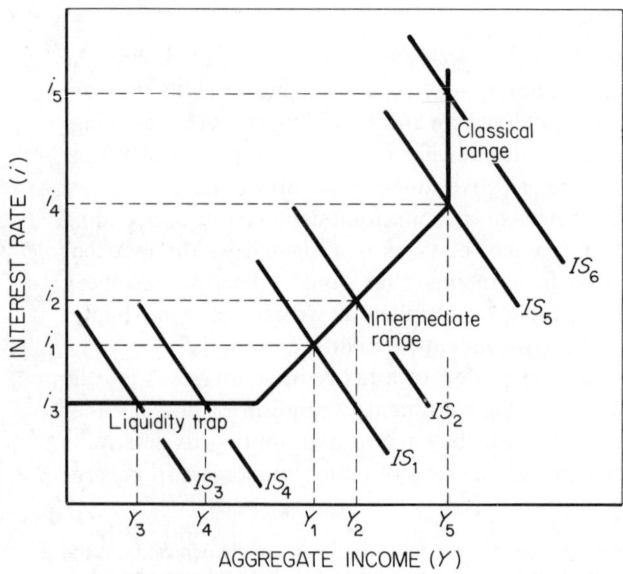

FIG. 17-1 ***IS-LM*** **Model**

of any increase in government spending or tax reduction that would cause a rightward shift in the *IS* curve will be partly dissipated by higher interest rates, as shown by the shift from IS_1 to IS_2, which causes an increase in aggregate income from Y_1 to Y_2 and also an increase in the interest rate from i_1 to i_2. The full multiplier effect of fiscal policy would be felt only in the liquidity trap, where the *LM* curve is horizontal, as shown by the shift from IS_3 to IS_4, which causes an increase in aggregate income from Y_3 to Y_4 with no effect on the interest rate, which remains at i_3. On the other hand, in the equally extreme and unlikely case of an economy that found itself in the vertical, classical range of the *LM* curve, an increase in government expenditures or reduction in taxes would not change equilibrium income, as shown by the shift from IS_5 to IS_6, which leaves aggregate income unchanged at Y_5. The entire multiplier would be dissipated in higher interest rates, which increase from i_4 to i_5. The significant point is that in the normal, intermediate range of the *LM* curve, expansionary fiscal policy would be partly offset by a higher interest rate, and contractional fiscal policy partially offset by a reduction in the interest rate. Monetary policy could be used simultaneously to stabilize the interest rate and guarantee a full multiplier effect from fiscal policy by increasing the money stock when expansionary fiscal policy is introduced and reducing the money stock when contractional fiscal policy is used.

The Price Level The second qualification to the effectiveness of fiscal policy involves its impact on an economy with a flexible price level.

The effect of price changes on fiscal policy is similar to the effect of interest-rate changes. As we have seen, expansionary fiscal policies lose part of their effect in higher interest rates in the *IS–LM* model. Likewise, the multiplier effect of expansionary fiscal policy on aggregate real income will be reduced by any increase in the price level.

The effect of fiscal policy on aggregate income when the price level is allowed to vary is demonstrated in Figure 17-2, which essentially duplicates

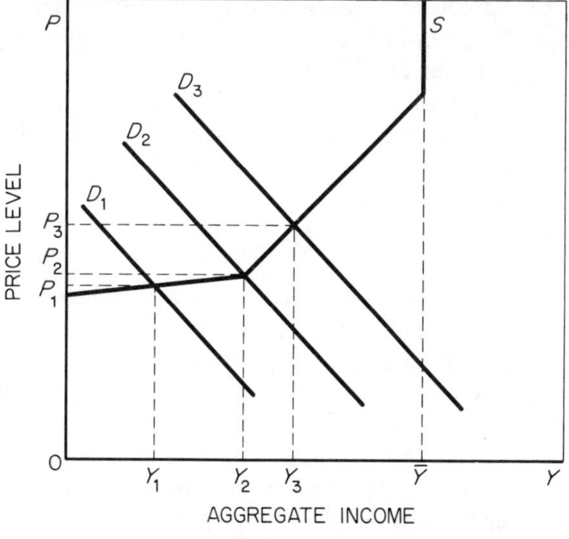

FIG. 17-2 Aggregate Supply and Demand

Figure 12-10. In the figure, the price level is plotted on the vertical axis and aggregate income on the horizontal axis. As in Figure 12-10, it is assumed that aggregate supply is highly elastic for low levels of aggregate income and becomes steeper at Y_2, after capital becomes fully employed. Finally, aggregate supply turns completely inelastic when labor becomes fully employed at $\bar{Y}$.

To illustrate how fiscal policy influences not only aggregate income but also the price level, assume that in Figure 17-2, the economy is at equilibrium where the D_1 aggregate-demand curve intersects the aggregate-supply curve. Now, if the aggregate demand curve shifts up to D_2 through an increase in government expenditures or a reduction in taxes, aggregate income will increase from Y_1 to Y_2, with only a relatively small accompanying increase in the price level, from P_1 to P_2. However, if additional fiscal policy is employed to cause an identical rightward shift in the aggregate demand curve from D_2 to D_3, where the aggregate-supply curve is less elastic, the result is a relatively smaller increase in aggregate income, from Y_2 to Y_3, and a relatively larger increase in the price level, from P_2 to P_3.

Obviously, if expansionary fiscal policy were employed to shift the aggregate demand curve beyond $\bar{Y}$, the result would be pure inflation, higher prices with no accompanying increase in aggregate output. This concept of the kinked aggregate-supply function helps to explain how the Kennedy recovery could occur in the early 1960's without significant price increases, and why the price level rose substantially during the Johnson administration, when military expenditures were increased after business firms had exhausted their excess capacity.

In earlier days, inflation was considered symptomatic of an overheated economy in need of fiscal restraint. However, recessions since the 1950's have been characterized by price increases, in part owing to higher prices in concentrated industries and to higher wages in unionized sectors (see Chapter 13). Fiscal restraint in an economy subject to administered-price, cost-push, or ex ante inflation is an ineffective means of fighting higher prices, because tight fiscal (or monetary) policy can induce a recession without ending inflation.

Automatic Stabilizers

The main automatic stabilizers are changes in taxes, particularly personal and corporate income taxes, and changes in government transfer payments such as old age and survivors insurance, unemployment compensation, and interest payments. As we saw in Chapter 10, income tax collections and transfer payments are structured to automatically reduce the amplitude of business fluctuations. For example, as aggregate income increases, during prosperity tax receipts automatically increase, thereby reducing potential effective demand. At the same time, transfer payments decrease as welfare payments and unemployment compensation fall. (In addition, farm subsidy payment may be automatically stabilizing if the government buys less surplus farm commodities during prosperity, when farm prices tend to be high, than during recession. But if farmers overproduce because of prosperity-induced optimism, the subsidy would be destabilizing by increasing incomes during prosperity.)

Automatic stabilizers also work in the opposite direction during recessions. When aggregate income falls, income tax receipts fall and government transfer payments increase, reducing the amplitude of the recession. Therefore, there is a tendency for aggregate income to fall less during a recession than it would in the absence of these automatic stabilizers. The impact of automatic stabilizers is felt on the economy through their effect on the multiplier. The reduction in potential effective demand during prosperity as tax receipts increase and government transfer payments decrease reduces the multiplier. Similarly, the negative multiplier that would be experienced during recession is reduced by an increase in transfer payments and a decrease in income tax collections.[2] Consequently, economic fluctuations will be of smaller amplitude. (Over the cycle the magnitude of the multiplier does change because of automatic stabilizers. Once a given structure of automatic stabilizers is established, the multiplier will not change—it will simply be smaller than the "unstabilized" multiplier.)

Households, like the government, may act in a countercyclical way if consumers attempt to maintain their level of consumption when incomes fall, and fail to increase their consumption proportionately when incomes rise.

Paradoxically, consumers reacted to the recession in 1970 by cutting expenditures as a proportion of income and saving more. Evidently many people anticipated worse times coming and chose to save to meet the augured economic contretemps (an attitude reinforced by some security analysts' references to 1929), or conceivably, consumers were resisting existing inflation in a sort of widespread, uncoordinated consumer strike. Perhaps both motives worked together: If consumers had anticipated either a rapid resumption of prosperity or continued future inflation, the consumption function should not have fallen.

However, a more conventional explanation is possible. The higher interest rates of 1970 could have induced consumers to save more and spend less. In addition, higher interest rates have a negative wealth effect by reducing the market value of bonds. To the extent that consumption is a function of interest or wealth, the shift in the consumption function could be ascribed to higher interest rates at that time. In addition, the fact that prices continued to rise during this recession may have triggered a reverse Pigou effect. That is, holders of money and government bonds surely felt poorer every time they went shopping.

In any case, to the extent that they work, built-in stabilizers have the effect that their name implies.

The Full-Employment Budget Surplus

Even though tax rates and government-expenditure programs can be planned in advance, the actual size of the deficit or surplus cannot be accurately predicted. The precise level of future aggregate income is unknown, and actual tax collections and transfer payments are related to the level of aggregate income. Any planned program of taxes and expenditures might

---

[2] In addition, certain other tax collections, such as collections of sales and excise taxes, may increase during prosperity and fall during recessions.

cause a whole range of possible deficits or surpluses, depending on the actual level of aggregate income achieved. Figure 17-3 relates the deficit or surplus that would result from a given tax and expenditure program at levels of aggregate income between 94 and 100 percent of potential full-employment GNP.

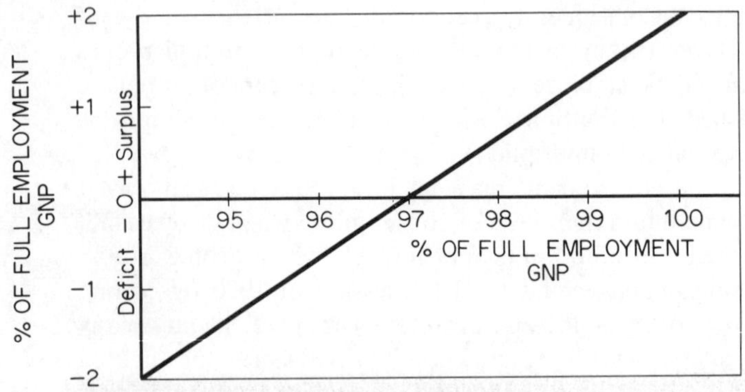

FIG. 17-3 Full-employment Budget-surplus Curve

In our hypothetical illustration, if GNP is only 94 percent of the potential, the estimated deficit will equal 2 percent of full-employment GNP. If GNP is 97 percent of the full-employment level, then the government budget will be just balanced. If we achieve 100 percent of our GNP potential, the result will be a budget surplus of 2 percent. Such a surplus is sometimes called a full-employment budget surplus, and the line relating the possible deficits and surpluses that would result at different levels of GNP, given the structure of the fiscal-policy mix, may be called a full-employment budget-surplus line. (The implicit assumption is that, under most conditions, any given fiscal-policy mix will lead to a budget surplus, if the economy is at full employment.)

Any change in fiscal policy will cause a shift in the curve. More expansionary fiscal policy will shift it to the right; more contractional, to the left. In effect, automatic stabilizers are endogenous fiscal policy and so can cause a movement along a given curve. In contrast, changes in discretionary fiscal policy are exogenous, and must be shown as a shift in the curve.

To take the example shown in Figure 17-3, suppose that in preparing the budget estimates, it had been projected that GNP would equal 98.5 percent of full employment and that a budgetary surplus of 1 percent had therefore been anticipated. Now, suppose the actual level of GNP turned out to be only 94 percent of full employment. Then, if the hypothetical data of Figure 17-3 accurately represented the economy, the result would be a deficit equal to 2 percent of the full-employment level of GNP. The measured deficit that occurs instead of the anticipated surplus is due to the lower-than expected level of GNP. Such a deficit is not related to government spending and taxing plans, but to the automatically stabilizing effects of higher transfer payments and lower tax receipts.

The full-employment budget surplus became significant in the early 1960's and again in the early 1970's, when there were government deficits that were entirely due to low tax receipts and high transfer payments, which occurred because the economy was operating below its potential. However, the deficits of those two periods were not truly expansionary, if allowance is made for the fact that the economy was operating below its full-employment potential. The government budget of both periods actually showed a large full-employment surplus, and therefore, fiscal policy during those periods was not sufficiently expansionary, even though the government ran measured deficits.

In reality, expansionary fiscal policy was required to close the gap between actual and potential GNP, as was evidenced by widespread unemployment in both periods. President Nixon made conscious use of the full-employment budget-surplus concept in designing his economic policies of the early 1970's.

The major weakness in this analysis is that it is difficult to determine from available data the exact nature of the fiscal drag resulting from the reduction in the multiplier that is due to automatic stabilizers. The points on the full-employment budget-surplus curve are mutually exclusive. Therefore, the precise relationship between various deficits or surpluses and various employment levels must remain speculative.

Formula Flexibility

Formula flexibility has been proposed by some as a device for making fiscal policy more responsive; it can reduce the length of the administrative lag in the application of fiscal policy. For example, in 1963, President Kennedy proposed a tax cut to offset recession conditions that had been lingering since 1958, but it was not until 1964 that Congress actually passed a law to reduce taxes. Similarly, after President Nixon proposed a tax cut in August 1971, Congress debated for several months before giving approval. When fiscal policy is imposed after such a lengthy administrative lag, there is a temptation to apply it more vigorously than would have been necessary if it had been imposed more promptly; and it is even possible that the policy has become inappropriate because of the time lapse.

The fiscal-policy time lag can be broken down into three main components:

1. The *recognition lag*, which exists between the time the need arises for the fiscal policy and the recognition of that need, when the data are finally collected and made available.

2. The *administrative lag*, which includes the time that elapses between the recognition of the need for fiscal policy and the actual implementation of that policy. The administrative lag has three subparts: (a) the administration devises the

policies; (b) Congress votes approval; and (c) the administration puts the policy into effect.

3. The *economic lag* which is the time that passes between the implementation of the fiscal policy and its effect on the economy.

The concept of formula flexibility suggests that tax rates should automatically be adjusted downward when actual GNP falls below its potential by a certain percentage or when some other significant economic indicator such as an index of industrial production or the employment rate falls below some specified value. Other suggestions for formula flexibility involve government expenditure programs or transfer payments. For example, standby public works could be available for implementation immediately, or unemployment compensation could be increased when the unemployment rate reaches a certain level.

Despite its advantage of reducing the length of the administrative lag, however, formula flexibility is subject to certain criticisms. First, it would react blindly to changes in certain economic indicators. Suppose, for example, that formula-flexibility policies were keyed to a 4.5 percent unemployment rate, that is, certain tax cuts or government expenditures would be implemented when unemployment had remained at 4.5 percent for, say, three months. It is possible that that one economic indicator might lag behind the others, remaining at that level after other indicators had turned upward in response to a recovery. In such a situation, formula flexibility would require that expansionary fiscal policy be added to the recovery phase of the business cycle; this could lead to a too-rapid rate of recovery, cause the economy to collide with the ceiling of the Hicksian cycle model, and so force a subsequent recession.

Another defect of formula flexibility is that any given formula may prove to be too rigid if the structure of the economy changes. For example, at one given time, a 4.5 percent rate of unemployment might signal a severe recession; but at another time, given different economic conditions, such as large structural unemployment, the same rate might be acceptable, and an unemployment rate of 5 or 5.5 percent might be required to signal the need for fiscal policy.

So far, however, the whole question of formula flexibility is academic, since Congress has been unwilling or unable to give the required power to the executive branch of the government.

Fiscal Policy in a Dynamic Framework

A convenient device for putting fiscal policy into a dynamic framework is the concept of the difference between potential and actual GNP. This difference can be illustrated in a time series, such as Figure 17-4, with the difference between actual and potential GNP shown as the shaded area.[3]

---

[3]The annual figure used by the Council of Economic Advisers (CEA) to represent potential full-employment output incorporates a 4 percent rate of unemployment to represent a practical, noninflationary, full-employment level.

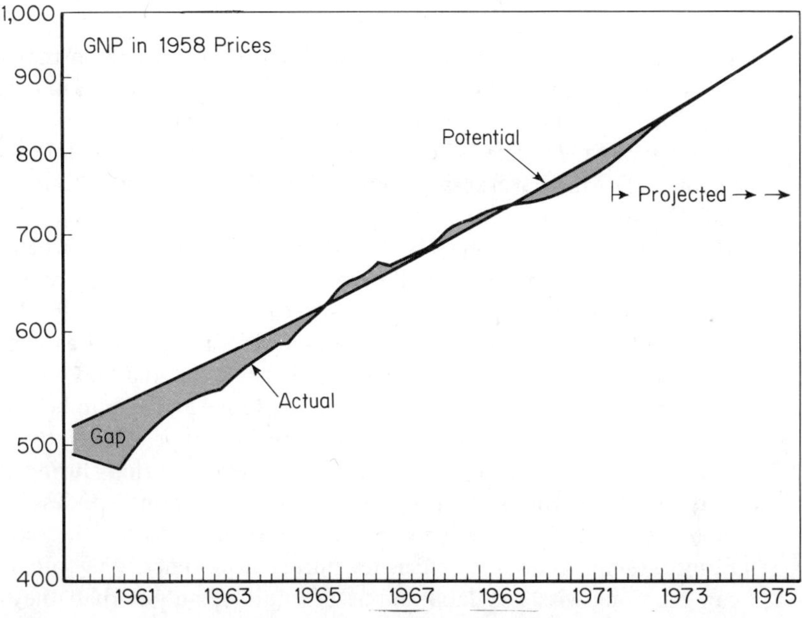

FIG. 17-4 Gross National Product, Actual and Potential (Sources: *Economic Report of the President*—1970; *Survey of Current Business*).

In measuring potential output, the Council of Economic Advisers has used a growth-rate concept similar to the natural growth rate in the Harrod model presented in Chapter 15. Potential output is determined by the number of available man-hours, multiplied by productivity per man-hour and adjusted for 4 percent unemployment. The annual percentage increase in the labor force has accelerated from around 1.25 percent in the early 1960's to about 1.75 percent by the end of the decade, reflecting the arrival of the wartime baby boom into the labor force. At the same time, the number of hours worked per person has decreased by about .25 percent a year, leaving a current net growth rate in the effective labor force of about 1.5 percent per year. Meanwhile, worker productivity has been increasing annually at about 3 percent, a figure the CEA has adjusted downward to 2.5 percent on the assumption that government workers' productivity does not increase (a convenient assumption because of the difficulty of measuring the productivity of government workers). Combining the growth rate of the effective labor force of 1.5 percent with the growth rate in productivity of 2.5 percent gives a potential or natural growth rate of 4 percent.

Because output fell below potential from 1958 through 1963, a total of $188 billion of real output was lost, an annual average of $31 billion for the period. So the recovery that started in 1963 required that the economy grow at a faster rate than 4 percent in order to close the gap between potential and actual output. Similarly, the gap between actual and potential output that opened in 1969–70 was designed to slow down the inflation that stemmed from the negative-gap years 1966–68.

Arthur M. Okun, while working on the CEA, estimated that it takes a 3.2 percent increase in GNP to achieve a 1 percent drop in the unemployment rate. The necessity of having to increase GNP substantially in order to reduce the unemployment rate by 1 percent is primarily due to the following seven factors: (1) Many workers, retained by their firms because they would be difficult to replace, are actually underemployed during slack times. (2) The plants themselves may be less than optimally efficient when operated below their designed capacity during slack times. (3) During prosperity, the availability of jobs and high pay adds to the labor force people who had not previously been looking for work and so were not counted as unemployed. (4) Increased economic activity leads to overtime and moonlighting, and temporarily slows the secular increase in leisure. (5) The number of involuntary part-time workers is reduced during periods of prosperity. (6) A backlog of unimplemented labor saving technology may develop during recessions which enable a firm to produce a given quantity of goods with less labor input than formerly. This new equipment is purchased during the recovery. (7) Firms attempt to improve efficiency during slack times. They often find they can get along with less labor input per unit of output than they formerly thought possible. Therefore they do not hire back as many workers as they laid off when prosperity returns.

Viewed from another angle, if GNP grows at a faster rate than unemployment falls, then a disproportionately large increase in output is required to reduce the unemployment rate. The Nixon administration discovered this paradox anew. A mild recovery during 1971 and 1972 was not sufficient to reduce the unemployment rate to a reasonable level. In fact, the level of unemployment actually grew for a time while the recovery was in progress. The labor force was growing faster than workers could be reemployed.

In a process similar to that described in the upward phase of the Hicksian cycle model, an economy leaving the floor and approaching the ceiling must grow at a faster rate than the equilibrium growth rate. The growth in potential GNP is not the Hicksian equilibrium growth path, but is more closely akin to Hicks's ceiling. And, as we saw in Chapter 16, it is very difficult to design a fiscal policy that would keep an economy crawling along the ceiling, because the growth process feeds on itself, and the growth rate that carried the economy to the ceiling cannot be continued once the ceiling is reached. In addition, there is the problem, raised by the neoclassical growth model, of how to maintain the productivity of capital as the stock of capital grows. Fiscal policy cannot directly control this variable, but technological advances may retard the onset of diminishing returns to capital.[4] However, an advantage of the neoclassical growth model is that policy makers are spared the

---

[4]In the Harrod–Domar type of model, constant returns are assumed, so there is no need for technology to bail the economy out.

difficult job of trying to match the warranted growth rate with the natural rate, because in this model the two rates naturally tend to coincide. On the other hand, if the Harrod–Domar model is more realistic, then those in charge of fiscal policy have a significantly more difficult job because of the problems involved in equilibrating the two rates of growth, probably by manipulating savings, taxes, and government expenditures.

In any case, an ideal fiscal policy in a dynamic framework would attempt to keep the actual GNP as close to the potential as possible, assuming that no major conflict arises between full employment and price stability, a topic to be reconsidered later.

CURRENT MONETARY POLICY

In addition to fiscal policy, the other major device used to achieve stability is monetary policy.[5] This section is organized by schools of thought rather than functionally. The major schools included are the neo-Keynesians, the monetarists, the credit-availability theorists, and the financial-intermediary theorists.

Neo-Keynesians' Monetary Policy

In general, the neo-Keynesian position would require discretionary monetary policy. Neo-Keynesians would prescribe specific monetary and fiscal policies to remedy particular types of cyclical disturbances, with the appropriate monetary policy determined through the use of *IS–LM* type of analysis. For example, during a recession, expansionary monetary policy would result in a rightward shift in the *LM* curve, leading to a higher level of aggregate income and a lower interest rate. The effect of monetary policy on aggregate income will depend on the elasticity of the *IS* function. The group of economists who feel that the *IS* curve is fairly interest-elastic believe that monetary policy can effectively change aggregate income, as long as the economy is not operating in the liquidity trap, where the interest rate is already at its lowest possible level.

Since expansionary fiscal policy results in a shift in the *IS* curve, part of its effect is lost in higher interest rates, and only through the use of supplementary monetary policy can the equilibrium interest rate be maintained at a given level and the full multiplier effect of expansionary fiscal policy be realized. Therefore, fiscal policy is less effective when not supplemented by monetary policy.

The neo-Keynesian analysis, like the Keynesian, implies the possibility that a larger stock of money will induce people to hold larger money balances

[5] An immediate problem arises in defining the monetary authority in the United States, because it has two heads, the Federal Reserve and the Treasury, and occasionally the two are in conflict. However, in general, when we speak about "the monetary authority," we mean the Board of Governors of the Federal Reserve System.

and so reduce income velocity, thus partially offsetting the effect of any expansionary increase in the stock of money. Conversely, restrictive monetary policy will lead to increased velocity, which will partially offset the contractional effect of monetary policy.

Perhaps the most glaring shortcoming of neo-Keynesian monetary policy is the scant attention paid to prices. The incorporation of some device such as the ex ante inflation model would be a step forward, and would represent an improvement if combined with the demand-pull, cost-push inflation models currently employed by neo-Keynesians.

At present, about all that can be said about the impact of monetary policy on the price level is that a change in aggregate demand can influence the price level (depending on the elasticity of aggregate supply), whether the initiating cause was fiscal or monetary.

The main impact of monetary policy on real markets in the Keynesian system occurs through its effect on the interest rate: Expansionary monetary policy is consistent with lower interest rates, which reduce the costs of capital and stimulate investment. Therefore, in this system, increases in the stock of money stimulate spending indirectly, through their effect on the interest rate (an effect that disappears in the liquidity trap).

Most neo-Keynesian economists generally recognize (as do the monetarists) that monetary policy is more flexible than fiscal policy. Monetary policy can be applied quickly without the need for congressional action; it can be applied unobtrusively without announcement effects, through open-market operations; and the direction can be reversed instantaneously, if necessary. In addition, monetary policy can be applied in as large or as small doses as might be required in any set of circumstances. It is recognized, even by the relatively small group of neo-Keynesian economists who propose that the *IS* curve is generally inelastic because of a lack of interest elasticity in the investment-demand function, that certain types of investment, particularly residential housing, may respond to changes in the interest rate.

The Monetarist View of Public Policy

The monetarists' view of monetary policy is related to their concept of monetary theory, presented in Chapter 14. In general, the members of that group feel that any expansionary impact of a budget deficit comes not from the increase in government spending itself, as is generally assumed, but from the monetary effects of the additional spending. In the monetarist view, price instability or unemployment follows from improper Federal Reserve policy that has provided too little or too much money.

The monetarists suggest that in the short run changes in the stock of *nominal* money balances are perhaps the most important single determinant of short-run changes in real output and prices, and that in the long run the quantity theory of money is valid.[6] The practical monetary policy that Milton

---

[6] L. C. Andersen and K. M. Carlson, "A Monetarist Model for Economic Stabilization," *Review*, Federal Reserve Bank of St. Louis, 52 (April 1970), 7–25.

Friedman recommended involves increasing the stock of money at a constant rate sufficiently high to finance increases in the real GNP. In addition, the rate of increase in the stock of money should provide enough funds to bring money balances up to the desired level. Since money is a superior good, higher GNP calls for larger money balances. The correct rate of increase in the stock of money has been calculated to be somewhere around 4 percent, to allow for about a 3 percent increase in GNP and an approximate 1 percent annual decrease in long-run velocity, which accompanies the growth in average money holdings.[7]

Discretionary monetary policy, which involves changing the stock of money as the Federal Reserve interprets the needs of the moment, will, in the view of the monetarists, invariably be wrong except through coincidence, because of the lagged response of the economy to such changes. In the view of the monetarists, the Board of Governors of the Federal Reserve cannot accurately predict economic conditions far enough in advance to compensate for the lag in the effect of monetary policy, so they will tend to overreact and bring about excessive increases or decreases in the stock of money. They should instead restrict themselves simply to increasing the stock of money at a rate that is in line with increases in the natural growth rate of GNP.

The basic differences between the monetarists' and most other economists' monetary-policy views are that (1) monetarists expect the monetary authorities to do the wrong thing if left to their own discretion, whereas most economists are more confident that discretionary policy would be correctly applied; (2) the monetarists' view is that the stock of money is the single most important economic variable, whereas other economists feel that money is only one of several variables; (3) the monetarists believe interest-rate changes are generally an effect of economic policy, whereas other economists feel that the interest rate is the means by which monetary policy affects the real side of the economy. (4) Contrary to the standard Keynesian position that changes in income velocity will somewhat offset changes in the stock of money, the monetarists propose that changes in income velocity often reinforce the effect of changes in the money stock. Their basic thinking with regard to the 3rd and 4th points raised above is that ex ante inflation and expectation of profitable opportunities will swamp the liquidity-preference effect that Keynes concentrated on. (5) In the long run, the monetarists suggest, changes in the stock of money will have little impact on real income, but will mostly affect prices so long as the money stock is sufficient to finance the economic natural growth rate. The Keynesians aren't so sure.

---

[7]Recently, Friedman has suggested that from a purely theoretical standpoint, welfare maximizing would require a slow rate of price deflation, and that that could be accomplished by holding the rate of increase in the stock of money down to 1 or 2 percent. The result should be factor price stability, and then increases in real income would be distributed through lower prices on consumer goods. Milton Friedman, *The Optimum Quantity of Money and Other Essays* (Chicago: Aldine, 1969), Chap. 1, pp. 1–50.

Monetary Policy of the Credit-Availability Theorists

The credit-availability model discussed in Chapter 14 has implications for the effectiveness of monetary policy. In most economic theory, the lender is simply a middleman who transfers loanable funds from saver to investor. However, according to the credit-availability thesis, the lender may play a more active role in determining the level of economic activity, and because of his role, monetary policy may be more effective in the short run than is commonly imagined. If, in addition to the normal market rationing performed by interest-rate changes, the lender also rations credit at his own discretion—portioning out the available loanable funds among the various demanders, granting loans to some and withholding loans from others—then a given reduction in the money stock becomes even more effective than it otherwise would in restricting aggregate income. According to credit-availability theory, lenders normally react to reinforce monetary policy, increasingly restricting loans during tight money and adopting a more liberal lending policy during periods of loose money. However, these theorists will concede that credit rationing operates only as long as the lenders fail to adjust their interest rate to the equilibrium market level.

Monetary Policy of Financial-Intermediary Theorists

Another question raised about monetary policy concerns the role of nonbank financial intermediaries. Some types of intermediaries other than commercial banks apparently perform some of the functions of commercial banks, including multiple expansion, if not of money, at least of their own credit instruments that serve some of the functions of money. As we have already mentioned, monetary policy can generate its own partially offsetting change in income velocity through the liquidity-preference function. It has been suggested that financial intermediaries may cause still further increases in income velocity during periods of tight money by offering their own secondary securities as a substitute for money in the portfolios of asset holders, since this substitution reduces the liquidity-preference function and thereby reduces the effectiveness of restrictive monetary policy.

Furthermore, it has been suggested that it is inequitable to regulate commercial banks and not to regulate other financial intermediaries that perform similar functions. Therefore, it has been proposed that regulation should include all financial intermediaries and not merely commercial banks, and that monetary policy would become more effective as a result of such extended regulation.

COORDINATING FISCAL AND MONETARY POLICY

From time to time it may appear that monetary and fiscal policies are heading in different directions, a divergence that gives the appearance of economic mismanagement. However, the appearance may be deceiving, because monetary and fiscal policies have different side effects. For example, suppose an economy is faced with demand-pull inflation and languishing growth, owing to a deficient warranted growth rate. The most appropriate economic policy might be to use expansionary monetary policy to encourage investment by reducing the interest rate, and thereby increase the warranted growth rate. At the same time, restrictive fiscal policy could be employed on consumers to cut down their effective demand and reduce the demand-pull inflationary pressure.

Appropriate combinations of monetary and fiscal policy may therefore require a subtle balance, and the best prescription may at times—on the surface—even appear to be illogical.

DEBT MANAGEMENT

Some writers have maintained that the goal of debt management should be to eliminate the public debt. However, paying off the debt could work against the stability of the economy: Such a policy would require continual budget surpluses over an extended period; the budget surplus would be destabilizing during recession, and the repayments to bondholders could be destabilizing during prosperity. In addition, the complete elimination of the public debt would also eliminate the possibility of open-market operations—the most effective technique of monetary policy.

A second, more serious proposal for debt management is to influence the level of economic activity by changing the maturity structure (average term) of the public debt. This theory proposes that a public debt with an average maturity far in the future is less liquid than short-term debt, because of the greater market risk if the securities are converted into money.

Because they minimize market risk, the shortest-term Treasury bills (such as 91-day Treasury notes) are a closer money substitute than are long-term bonds. Consequently, asset holders may substitute bills for money. The substitution of Treasury bills for long-term bonds will reduce the liquidity-preference curve to the extent that asset holders are willing to hold Treasury bills in place of part of their monetary balances. (This excludes any interest-earning assets from the stock of money.) As a result of the reduction in the liquidity-preference curve, the *LM* curve will shift to the right—say, from LM_1 to LM_2 in Figure 17-5—with an effect similar to that already discussed under financial intermediaries—a lower equilibrium interest rate, i_2, and a higher level of aggregate income, Y_2. In contrast, lengthening the maturity structure of the debt by converting it into longer-term bonds, which are not good substitutes for money, increases the liquidity-preference function and shifts the *LM* curve to the left, from LM_1 to LM_3. In this illustration, the longer-term debt tends to reduce equilibrium income to Y_3 and raise the equilibrium interest rate to i_3.

To generalize on the illustration above, it is proposed that proper debt management would lengthen the term structure of the debt by the sale of

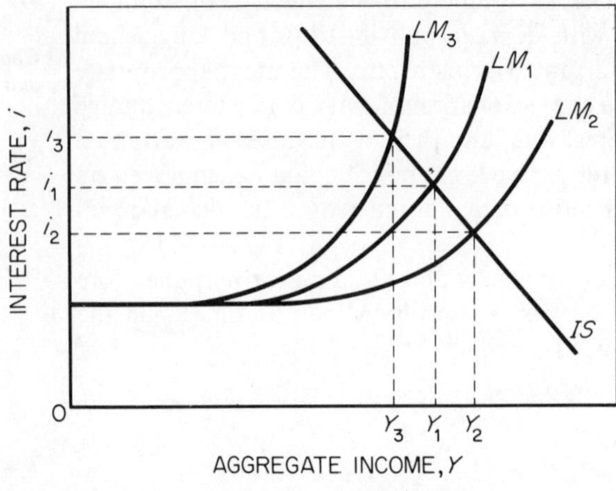

FIG. 17-5 The Effect of Debt Management

Treasury bonds to replace bills during prosperity, and shorten the average term of the debt by the sale of bills to replace bonds during recession. Thus, manipulating the term structure of the debt could foster economic stability.[8]

A third proposal is that proper debt management should strive to reduce the interest cost of the public debt, on the theory that interest payments cause an economic burden, owing to the transfer effect as taxes are collected from the population at large and used to pay interest to the smaller and generally wealthier group of bondholders. This proposal, however, ignores the fact that the real burden of the debt (as opposed to the money burden) results from the transfer of resources out of the private sector into the public sector of the economy. The real burden is proportionate to the amount of private consumption and investment that have been given up in exchange for public goods. If the government program is carried on with resources that would otherwise have been unemployed, then there is little or no real burden.

Abba P. Lerner has suggested that an increase in the public debt (to finance a deficit) makes holders of the new bonds feel wealthier and increases their propensity to consume.[9] If bond holders are so motivated, then deficit financing not only increases effective demand directly through government expenditures and through the multiplier, but also through a third route, an increase in consumption based on the wealth represented by the new bonds.

Consequently, we may conclude that attempting to minimize the size

[8]The more-frequent refinancing required in the case of Treasury bills could, however, induce instability and pose the possibility of conflict with other monetary and fiscal policies. Refinancing may require substantial interest changes, and Treasury bills must be refinanced more often than bonds. Furthermore, asset holders are denied a type of security they might wish to hold when bonds are substituted for bills, and vice versa.

[9]Abba P. Lerner, Economics of Employment. New York: McGrow-Hill, 1951, pp. 274–75.

of the public debt is a questionable debt-management policy, when the debt is incurred to achieve some definite worthwhile economic goal, such as full employment. Even though debt management probably has only a slight overall impact, it seems unwise to forego even a small chance of stabilizing the economy through its use.

THE POSITIVE ASPECTS OF RECESSIONS

Throughout this book we have concentrated on the maintenance or restoration of full employment. But it has been suggested that under certain conditions, recessions and unemployment might have beneficial side effects, and that there are some unfortunate aspects to prosperity and full employment.

Recessions serve to render the fat out of the economy. Unproductive work habits will often be eliminated. Cost-saving innovations may be instituted. Excessive expense accounts and other executive prerogatives that short-circuit profits from corporate stockholders to management will be trimmed or eliminated. In general, the operations of firms will be gone over carefully with an eye to making them more streamlined and efficient. Recessions may also encourage firms to introduce newly developed products or to develop new products in an attempt to stimulate consumer interest. Hard times will challenge successful firms to innovate in order to survive. Once it becomes clear, through a government-induced recession, that government monetary and fiscal policies will not bail out the economy, there will be less tendency for workers to push for higher wages as unemployment is growing, and for firms to demand higher prices while inventories are increasing. So, although most of this book has been concerned with the ill effects of unemployment and recession, they are not an entirely unmixed curse.

THE CONFLICT BETWEEN FULL EMPLOYMENT AND PRICE STABILITY

The Phillips curve, discussed in Chapter 13, shows that a trade-off may be required between price stability and unemployment. Society is often unwilling to accept a recession as a device of fiscal or monetary policy, but would prefer price stability without high unemployment.

Unfortunately, the tradeoff may not occur and both unemployment and inflation can exist simultaneously, as occurred during the recessions of 1958 and 1970. One possible explanation for this unfortunate conjunction, already discussed in Chapter 13, is cost-push pressure exerted by firms in concentrated industries or by unions with monopoly power. Such pressure could cause the Phillip's curve to shift in the direction of both higher rates of inflation and unemployment. Whatever the source of the pressure, whether due to cost-push pressure by unions or striving for target returns by oligopolistic firms, Blair has found that the likelihood of a price decrease during recessions is far smaller in concentrated than in more competitive industries. And two-thirds of the product classes in one sample of mostly concentrated firms showed price *increases* during the 1970 recession.[10] Evidently, policies which rely on downward price flexibility are likely to give disappointing results. The ex ante model gives the same results if the information time lag is as long as it recently has appeared to be.

Wage–Price Guidelines

One proposed device for resolving the conflict between full employment and price stability is wage–price guidelines. These guidelines, which appeared to work briefly in the early 1960's, amounted to a sort of fiscal moral suasion by which the U.S. government suggested that in the aggregate, wage increases should be related to productivity increases. Industry in general was encouraged to grant wage increases no greater than the average productivity increases, but exceptions were allowed. Certain industries could reasonably argue that greater-than-average wage increases were required to overcome bottlenecks, while other, declining industries might grant smaller-than-average increases to encourage workers to leave the industry.

Wage increases of the same percentage as the increase in worker productivity do not, as some people have suggested, give the entire increase to workers. They merely maintain the workers' proportion of the total product. Profits and payments to other, nonlabor resources can also rise by the same proportion, and, on the average, would have to, in order to create claims on the entire increase in output.

Guidelines worked during the early 1960's for a particular reason: The economy was growing at a satisfactory rate and inflationary expectations were low. Workers were willing to accept a percentage increase in wages equal to their productivity increases, because they knew the result would be a satisfactory increase in their level of living.

However, by the latter part of the 1960's, economic growth had slowed, because we were close to full employment and were no longer able to achieve the increases in output that accompany a reduction in unemployment. So the customary satisfactory increase in wages required that wages increase faster than productivity. At the same time, inflation was becoming more severe because of the demand-pull pressures created by the Vietnam War. Therefore, the guidelines broke down; the inflation that followed was apparently of the demand-pull type, and, as we have seen, such inflationary pressure, once set in motion, leads to further anticipated increases in inflation, besides cost-push and structural pressures.

One difficulty in applying guidelines is that higher wages and other factor payments may be demanded across the board, even though productivity increases are localized in certain industries and often in particular firms. The

---

[10] John M. Blair, *Economic Concentration*, (New York: Harcourt Brace Jovanovich, 1972), pp. 544–45.)

danger is that structural inflation will develop—notably from strong unions in industries with low or negative growth.

Direct Wage–Price Controls

As an alternative to the guidelines that eventually failed, some have proposed that when inflationary pressures become too strong, direct wage–price controls be instituted, such as those inaugurated in mid-1971. Whereas wage–price guidelines did not have the force of law, direct wage–price controls can be enforced and can work in situations where guidelines break down. Any such direct regulation of the economy is an extremely difficult job, because of the innumerable interindustry relationships that must be considered by the wage and price administrators. One lesson implicit in models such as input–output analysis is that flexible wages and prices permit the most efficient structure of interindustry relationships to develop. However, in the opinion of the economists who favored direct wage–price controls in mid-1971, the only workable alternative was for the economy to undergo a sharp recession or depression in order to wring out the inflationary thinking of businessmen and workers.

By mid-1971, the recession had eliminated neither inflation nor the anticipation of inflation. So the president inaugurated a system of direct controls, starting with a 90-day price freeze, imposed without warning. The freeze, which was obviously too inflexible to be more than a temporary expedient, was followed by a system of wage and price administration, under a pay board and a price commission.

The phases following the initial freeze were increasingly flexible, to allow for needed adjustments and perhaps in tacit recognition of the difficulty of enforcing wage and price controls, especially when they can be evaded simply by quality decreases. An additional difficulty is that of measuring productivity (the basis of wage increases), especially in service industries.

The pay board and the price commission recognized that a zero rate of inflation might not be the best policy. Ideas on the optimum rate of inflation have been offered by several authors. For example, one study, by Prakash Lohani and Earl A. Thompson, concludes that various optimum rates of inflation prevail in different countries, and that 4.2 percent would be the optimum rate in the United States.[11]

In its operations, the price commission decided to concentrate on large firms and to prohibit price increases that increased their ratio of earnings to sales. Thus the commission had, in effect, institutionalized inflation by giving advance approval to large firms to allow them to meet their target rate of profit in recession. The smaller, more competitive firms are then free to raise their prices unhindered by the price commission during prosperity. The result is to build the price ratchet into the economy by official decree. A saving

---

[11]Prakash Lohani and Earl A. Thompson, "The Optimal Rate of Secular Inflation," *Journal of Political Economy*, 79 (Sept./Oct., 1971), 962–82.

grace of the system (if it works) is that the rate of price inflation would be held down to around $2\frac{1}{2}$ or 3 percent. (Wage inflation could proceed at a faster pace—around $5\frac{1}{2}$ percent—to allow for productivity increases.)

The experience of the Nixon Administration with regard to controls is illustrative in many ways, two of which deserve mention here:

1. The recession induced by policy makers to cool down the inflationary pressure inherited from the Johnson era failed to reduce prices. A possible reason was widespread power to set prices in concentrated industries that experienced cost increases during the recession (intensified by labor union demands) coupled with strong general inflationary expectations. As a result, the recession, which was the standard macroeconomic policy to counter inflation, failed to work, partly because it overlooked changed microeconomic considerations—the effect of the inflation on the production costs of concentrated industries and the continual effect of inflationary expectations on the micro-units of the economy.

2. Because the recession did not stop inflation, the administration was forced to use wage-price controls, an abandonment of standard Republican principles. The result was the 1971–72 partial recovery initiated by expansionary monetary and fiscal policy, a standard Keynesian prescription. Under controls, wages could rise by a maximum of only 5.5 percent a year. However, in a number of cases, corporate income rose by considerably more. The design of price controls approximated full-cost pricing, the rule-of-thumb pricing adopted by many oligopolists when free of controls. Certainly one of the reasons that price controls succeeded was that business could comfortably live with them, as was reflected in a survey of businessmen who said they preferred controls to no control.

The wage-price regulations as they developed in the early 1970's focused on concentrated, oligopolistic industries, and labor unions, and largely disregarded the less concentrated, more competitive sectors of the economy. As a result, during recovery, inflation was insured because the price-controlled industries had little motive to raise prices; and the uncontrolled industries, such as agriculture, are likely to experience strong inflationary pressures. So, the regulations that were logically devised to fit the recessionary conditions of 1969 and 1970 hardly affected the inflationary pressures during the subsequent recovery when firms in concentrated industries had little motive to raise prices.

Phase III in early 1973 was an attempt to partially decontrol and to reestablish guidelines similar to those that seemed to work during the early 1960's. Even though the price commission and pay board were abolished, the "voluntary" guidelines started in 1973 had the force of a government threat that companies that deviated would be "clobbered" with an official jawbone. Controls were left on processed food and medical services, two areas where price increases had proceeded at the fastest pace. Inevitably, compliance became poor and inflation soared. A second freeze was established for 60 days on June 13th, followed by Phase IV, which was a return to wage and price controls. The intent is to eventually remove controls.

Whether the free market will be left to operate in the future or whether more controls will be initiated cannot be predicted. Even though Republicans and Democrats alike are talking about "fiscal restraint," probably neither will forget the lesson of the futile, induced recession of 1969.

Perhaps, in the final analysis, the hardest problem facing the designers and administrators of direct economic controls in the United States, particularly under a Republican administration, is a genuine disinclination to depart from a free-market economy, combined with a genuine desire to thwart inflation. Such ambivalence is bound to take its toll in doubt and reduced efficiency.

POLICIES INVOLVING ECONOMIC GROWTH

Except for occasional flurries of interest when the rate of economic growth in this country falls behind that of other industrialized countries, economic growth receives relatively little attention. Even during the early 1960's, when it was a major concern, that concern involved national pride as much as economic considerations. Most of the outrage voiced at that time was over the fact that countries such as Germany, Japan, and the USSR had growth rates far in excess of ours.

On a technical level, growth theories themselves have been relatively underdeveloped until recently and conflict has existed among the theories. For example, consider the conflict between the Harrod–Domar and the modern neoclassical growth theories. According to the Harrod–Domar model, any public policy designed to achieve a sustained level of growth requires a precarious balance of the warranted, actual, and natural growth rates; a policy that increased one rate without keeping the other two in perfect step could precipitate disaster. In contrast, the modern neoclassical theory in effect merely assumes a balanced long-run equilibrium among its growth rates, and economic growth requires only that the natural growth rate be stimulated.

In addition, many of the significant variables involved in economic growth are inaccessible to public policy as it is practiced in our country. For example, the government can do little to influence the output–capital ratio. However, it could do more to stimulate growth than has been done until now: use taxes and subsidies to develop human and nonhuman capital, or provide more government development of technology and further encouragement of investment. Many countries have successfully used public policies to encourage growth. France, Russia, Germany, and Japan have encouraged investment at the expense of consumption, with beneficial results for the long-term warranted growth rate.

A FINAL NOTE

Throughout much of this chapter, we have concentrated on the difficulties inherent in applying macroeconomic theories to the real world. The difficulties are great, but it would be unfortunate if we decided they were too great. It would be better to use a theory as rationally as possible in an attempt to develop a coherent, effective set of monetary and fiscal policies. An effective set of policies should not be subject to the conflict of interests that now occasionally surfaces among the various heads responsible for different parts of our current policies. Squabbles among the agencies responsible for monetary and fiscal policy are unproductive, as are squabbles among economists regarding whether fiscal or monetary policies are more effective. Rather, productive efforts are those designed to better coordinate our current monetary and fiscal policy so as to overcome the difficulties in the pursuit of our economic goals.

The theories themselves often appear contradictory, but there may be a germ of truth in all of them. The art of economics lies in selecting the most useful theory in any situation. And one major goal of economists should be to produce a truly eclectic theory of macroeconomics. Coordination among theory makers is as desirable as among policy makers.

Unfortunately, there is a tendency in the academic world to scoff at any ideas that are original or different, especially if presented by someone not in authority. As John Kenneth Galbraith put it, there has developed "a new despotism that consists in defining scientific excellence as whatever is closest in belief and method to the scholarly tendency of the people who are already there. This is a pervasive and oppressive thing not the less dangerous for being, in the frequent case, both self-righteous and unconscious."[12]

With the exception of the section on Keynes' social policy in Chapter 10, policies to achieve the goal of social justice have been generally ignored in this book; as we pointed out at the beginning of this chapter, not much government effort has been devoted to this subject. Part of the neglect has been due to the inability to quantify the goal and disagreement as to the definition of the concept. Then, too, orthodox economic theorists have largely neglected the subject of social justice, leaving it to the radical economists and economic cranks. Yet a sizable section of the general public has recently become interested in the quality of life and the elimination of poverty. According to Joan Robinson, this neglect by the profession has created a second crisis of economic theory, no less important than the mass level of unemployment during the 1930's that originally gave rise to Keynes's *General Theory*.[13]

This may indicate the direction of the next development in economic theory.

---

[12]J. K. Galbraith, "Power and the Useful Economist," *American Economic Review*, 63 (March 1973), 2.

[13]Joan Robinson, "The Second Crisis of Economic Theory," *American Economic Review*, 62 (May 1972), 1–10.

QUESTIONS AND PROBLEMS

1. Distinguish between discretionary and nondiscretionary fiscal policy.

2. In what ways can a lack of coordination between the executive and legislative branches thwart fiscal policy?

3. Would a more formal relationship between monetary and fiscal policy makers be advantageous?

4. Do you feel the Keynesian or the monetarist view more adequately describes the modern economy? Is there necessarily a conflict between the two?

5. Discuss debt management and its relationship to monetary and fiscal policy.

6. Consider how economic growth might help solve the unemployment-inflation dilemma.

7. What do you think is the likliest future direction of development for economic theory?

ADDITIONAL SELECTED REFERENCES

MONETARY AND FISCAL POLICY

ANDO, A., E. C. BROWN, and A. F. FRIEDLAENDER, *Studies in Economic Stabilization.* Washington, D.C.: Brookings Institution, 1968.

———, E. C. BROWN, J. KAREKEN, and R. M. SOLOW, "Lags in Fiscal and Monetary Policy," *Commission on Money and Credit, Stabilization Policies,* pp. 1–163. Englewood Cliffs, N.J.: Prentice-Hall, 1963.

———, and F. MODIGLIANI, "Econometric Analysis of Stabilization Policies," *American Economic Review,* 59 (May 1969), 296–314.

BACH, G. L., *Making Monetary and Fiscal Policy.* Washington, D.C.: Brookings Institution, 1971.

BAILEY, M. J., R. EISNER, A. P. LERNER, and J. L. STEIN, "The 1971 Report of the President's Council of Economic Advisers," *American Economic Review,* 61, (September 1971), 517–37. (Separate articles by each of the authors.)

BARRETT, N. S., *The Theory of Macroeconomic Policy.* Englewood Cliffs, N.J.: Prentice-Hall, 1972.

BLACKABY, F., "Economic Policy: A Review Article," *Scottish Journal of Political Economy,* 19 (June 1972), 189–206.

BRIMMER, A. F., "The Political Economy of Money: Evolution and Impact of Monetarism in the Federal Reserve System," *American Economic Review,* 62 (May 1972), 344–52.

BROWNE, ROBERT S., "The Twilight of Capitalism," *Business and Society Review,* Spring 1972 p. 29–35.

BRUNNER, K., "The Ambiguous Rationality of Economic Policy," *Journal of Money, Credit, and Banking,* 4 (February 1972), 3–12.

BURNS, A. F., and P. A. SAMUELSON, *Full Employment, Guideposts and Economic Stability.* Washington, D.C.: American Enterprise Institute for Public Policy Research, 1967.

CULBERTSON, J. M., "Friedman on the Lag Effect of Monetary Policy," *Journal of Political Economy,* 68 (December 1960), 617–21. Critique by Friedman and Culbertson reply, *Journal of Political Economy,* 69 (October 1961), 447–77.

———, *Macroeconomic Theory and Stabilization Policy*, pp. 381–539. New York: McGraw-Hill, 1968.

EVANS, M., *Macroeconomic Activity*, Part III. New York: Harper & Row, 1969.

FEIGE, E. L., P. B. KENNEN, R. A. KESSEL, E. S. PHELPS "The 1972 Report of the Presidents' Council of Economic Advisors" *American Economic Review* 62 (September 1972), 509–39 (separate articles by each of the authors.)

FRIEDMAN, M., *A Program for Monetary Stability*. New York: Fordham University Press, 1960.

———, "The Role of Monetary Policy," *American Economic Review*, 38 (June 1948), 245–64.

———, "The Role of Monetary Policy," *American Economic Review*, 58 (March 1968), 17.

———, J. B. GURLEY, and A. M. OKUN, "Have Fiscal and/or Monetary Policies Failed?" *American Economic Review*, 62 (May 1972), 10–30. (Separate articles by each of the authors.)

———, and A. J. SCHWARTZ, *A Monetary History of the United States, 1867–1960*. Princeton, N.J.: National Bureau of Economic Research, 1963.

GORDON, R. J. "Inflation in Recession and Recovery" (with comments) *Brookings Papers on Economic Activity*, 1 1971 105–166.

GRAMLEY, L. E., "Guidelines for Monetary Policy—the Case Against Simple Rules," in *Money, National Income, and Stabilization Policy*, rev. ed., eds. W. L. Smith and R. L. Teigen, pp. 488–495. Homewood, Ill.: Richard D. Irwin, 1970.

GRAMLICH, E., "The Usefulness of Monetary and Fiscal Policy as Discretionary Stabilization Tools," *Journal of Money, Banking, and Credit*, 3 (May 1971), 506–32.

HANSEN, A. H., *The Economic Issues of the 1960's*. New York: McGraw-Hill, 1960.

HANSEN, B., *The Economic Theory of Fiscal Policy*, trans. D. E. Burke. London: Allen and Unwin, 1958. Cambridge: Harvard University Press, 1958.

HARDY, C. O., "Fiscal Operations as Instruments of Economic Stabilization," *American Economic Review*, 38 (May 1948), 395–403.

HARRIS, S. et al., "The Controversy over Monetary Policy," *Review of Economics and Statistics*, 33 (August 1951), 179–200.

HARRIS, S. et al., "Controversial Issues in Recent Monetary Policy: A Symposium," *Review of Economics and Statistics*, 42 (August 1960), 245–82.

HELLER, W. W., *New Dimensions of Political Economy*. Cambridge: Harvard Univ. Press, 1966.

HOLT, C. C., "Linear Decision Rules for Economic Stabilization and Growth," *Quarterly Journal of Economics*, 76 (February 1962), 20–45.

KAUFMAN, G. B., "Current Issues in Monetary Economics and Policy," *The Bulletin*, No. 57. New York: New York University Graduate School of Business Administration, Institute of Finance, May 1969.

DE LEEUW, F., and E. Gramlich, "The Channels of Monetary Policy," *Journal of Finance*, 24 (May 1969), 265–90.

MAYER, T., *Monetary Policy in the United States*. New York: Random House, 1968.

MILLER, H. L., JR., "The New and the Old in Public Debt Theory," *Quarterly Review of Economics and Business*, 6, 4 (Winter 1966), 65–74.

MODIGLIANI, F., "Some Empirical Tests of Monetary Management and of Rules vs. Discretion," *Journal of Political Economy*, 72 (June 1964), 211–45.

MUNDELL, R. A., "The Appropriate Use of Monetary and Fiscal Policy for Internal and External Stability," in *Money, National Income, and Stabilization Policy*, rev. ed , eds. W. L. Smith and R. L. Teigen, pp. 611–16. Homewood, Ill.: Richard D. Irwin, 1970.

———, "Growth, Stability, and Inflationary Finance," *Journal of Political Economy*, 73 (April 1965), 97–109.

MUSGRAVE, R. A., *The Theory of Public Finance*. New York: McGraw-Hill, 1959.

OKUN, A. M., *The Political Economy of Prosperity*. Washington: Brookings Institute, 1970.

PERRY, G. L., "Wages and the Guideposts," *American Economic Review*, 57 (September 1967), 897–904.

RASCHE, R. H., and H. T. SHAPIRO, "The F.R.B.—M.I.T. Econometric Model: Its Special Features," *American Economic Review*, 58 (May 1968), 123–49.

SAMUELSON, P., "Wage–Price Guideposts and the Need for Informal Controls in a Mixed Economy," *Full Employment, Guideposts, and Economic Stability: Rational Debate Seminars*. Washington, D.C.: U.S. Government Printing Office, 1967.

SCHLESINGER, J. R., "Monetary Policy and Its Critics," *Journal of Political Economy*, 68 (December 1960), 601–16.

SIMONS, H. C., "Rules vs. Authority in Monetary Policy," *Journal of Political Economy*, 44 (1936), 1–30.

SMITHIES, A., and J. K. BUTTERS, eds., for the American Economic Association, *Readings in Fiscal Policy*, Vol. VII. Homewood, Ill.: Richard D. Irwin, 1955.

STEIN, H., *The Fiscal Revolution in America*. Chicago: University of Chicago Press, 1969.

TINBERGEN, J., *Economic Policy: Principles and Design*. Amsterdam: North Holland Publishing Co., 1956.

TOBIN, J., *National Economic Policy*. New Haven: Yale University Press, 1966.

WALLICH, H. C., "Quantity Theory and Quantity Policy," in *Ten Economic Studies in the Tradition of Irving Fisher*, pp. 257–80. New York: John Wiley, 1967.

WEIDENBAUM, M. L., G. ACKLEY, C. H. MADDEN, H. S. HOUTHAKKER, "Symposium: The Future of U.S. Wage-Price Policy," *Review of Economics and Statistics*, 54 (August 1972), 213–234.

WICKER, E. R., *Federal Reserve Monetary Policy, 1917–1933*. New York: Random House, 1966.

WRIGHTSMAN, D., *Introduction to Monetary Theory and Policy*. New York: Free Press, 1971.

ZWEIG, MICHAEL, "New Left Critique of Economics," *Review of Radical Political Economics*, 3 (July 1971), 67–74.

DEBT MANAGEMENT

CHANDLER, L. V., "Federal Reserve Policy and Federal Debt," *American Economic Review*, 39: (March 1949), 405–29.

DOMAR, E. D., "The Burden of the Debt and National Income," *American Economic Review*, 34 (December 1944), 798–827.

SHOUP, C. S., "Debt Financing and Future Generations," *Economic Journal*, 72 (December 1962), 887–98.

TOBIN, J., "Monetary Policy and the Management of the Public Debt," *Review of Economics and Statistics*, 35 (May 1953), 118–27.

Index

Q

R

S